D0214554

SCHOENBERG, BERG, AND WEBERN

Arnold Schoenberg (1874–1951). Courtesy of the Arnold Schoenberg Institute.

SCHOENBERG, BERG, AND WEBERN

A Companion to the Second Viennese School

Edited by
BRYAN R. SIMMS

GREENWOOD PRESS
Westport, Connecticut • London

Library of Congress Cataloging-in-Publication Data

Schoenberg, Berg, and Webern : a companion to the second Viennese school / edited by Bryan R. Simms.
p. cm.
Includes bibliographical references and index.
ISBN 0–313–29604–9 (alk. paper)
1. Schoenberg, Arnold, 1874–1951—Criticism and interpretation. 2. Berg, Alban, 1885–1935—Criticism and interpretation. 3. Webern, Anton, 1883–1945—Criticism and interpretation. 4. Composers—Austria—Vienna. 5. Music—Austria—Vienna—20th century—History and criticism. I. Simms, Bryan R.
ML390.S389 1999
780'.9436'130904—dc21 98–28960

British Library Cataloguing in Publication Data is available.

Library of Congress Catalog Card Number: 98–28960
ISBN: 0–313–29604-9

First published in 1999

Greenwood Press, 88 Post Road West, Westport, CT 06881
An imprint of Greenwood Publishing Group, Inc.
www.greenwood.com

Printed in the United States of America

The paper used in this book complies with the Permanent Paper Standard issued by the National Information Standards Organization (Z39.48–1984).

10 9 8 7 6 5 4 3 2 1

Copyright Acknowledgments

The editor and publisher gratefully acknowledge permission to reprint the following material:

Excerpt from a letter of June 1, 1938 from Arnold Schoenberg to Professor Spencer Welch, from the Schoenberg Collection, Library of Congress. Cited with permission of Lawrence Schoenberg.

Example 4.3 from Schoenberg, *Das Buch der haengenden Gaerten* for voice and piano, Op. 15 (© Universal Edition 1914), song no. 10 (''Das schöne Beet''), measures 1–2; Example 4.4 from Schoenberg, *Vier Lieder*, Op. 22 (© Universal Edition 1917), song no. 1 (''Seraphita''), mm. 14–15; Example 4.5 from Schoenberg, *Pierrot lunaire*, Op. 21 (© Universal Edition 1914), piece no. 8 (''Nacht''), mm. 1–5. Used by permission of Belmont Music Publishers, Pacific Palisades, California.

Example 4.6 from Piano Piece, Op. 23, No. 3 by Arnold Schoenberg. Copyright © 1923 (Renewed) by Edition Wilhelm Hansen. International Copyright Secured. All Rights Reserved. Reprinted by permission of G. Schirmer, Inc.

Example 4.7 from String Quartet No. 4, Op. 37 by Arnold Schoenberg. Copyright © 1939 Renewed by G. Schirmer, Inc. (ASCAP). International Copyright Secured. All Rights Reserved. Reprinted by permission.

Example 7.1 from Walter Piston, Partita for Violin, Viola, and Organ, in Elliott Carter and Jonathan W. Bernard, *Elliott Carter: Collected Essays and Lectures, 1937–1995* (Rochester, N.Y.: University of Rochester Press, 1997), III, mm. 85–90.

Example 7.2 from Ernst Krenek, *Lamentatio Jeremiae Prophetae*, published by Bärenreiter-Verlag, 1942.

Example 7.8 from Henri Pousseur, *Quintette à la mémoire d'Anton Webern*; Example 7.13 from Luciano Berio, *Nones* (for orchestra). Reprinted by permission of Edizioni Suvini Zerboni, Milan, Italy.

Example 7.9 from Milton Babbitt, *Three Compositions for Piano* (1947). © Copyright 1957 by Boelke-Bomart, Inc.; used by permission.

Example 7.10 from Igor Stravinsky, *Canticum sacrum* © Copyright 1956 by Boosey & Hawkes, Inc. Copyright Renewed. Reprinted by permission.

Excerpts from *The Berg-Schoenberg Correspondence: Selected Letters*, edited by Juliane Brand, Christopher Hailey, and Donald Harris (New York and London: W. W. Norton & Company, 1987). Reprinted by permission of W. W. Norton & Company, Inc.

Excerpts from *Anton von Webern: A Chronicle of His Life and Work* by Hans Moldenhauer, in collaboration with R. Moldenhauer. Copyright © 1978 by Hans Moldenhauer. Reprinted by permission of Alfred A. Knopf Inc.

Excerpts from Arnold Schoenberg, *Style and Idea*, Leonard Stein, ed., Leo Black, trans. (Berkeley: University of California Press, 1984). Reprinted by permission of University of California Press.

CONTENTS

PREFACE

The first decade of the twentieth century saw the formation of the Second Viennese School; in the century's last decade, the appearance of the present volume is witness to the continuing vitality of its music and philosophy of art. Arnold Schoenberg, Alban Berg, and Anton Webern, the principal composers of the Second Viennese School, engaged in a great experiment that would shape serious music for almost the entire century, directing the course of modern musical history along paths that only now can begin to be accurately mapped. Schoenberg and his two brilliant students attempted nothing less than to bring the future of music into their own present time. They succeeded in changing the principal inherited idea of what music was—an enlightened form of entertainment—making it instead a profound mode of communication that was engaging to both the heart and mind in a manner deeper than ever before. They turned away from consonant intervals, diatonic scales, and keynotes, the basic tonal materials that had been used in music since at least the Middle Ages, and replaced them with more universal concepts and expressive tools perhaps more suited to the future than to their own day. Equally remarkable was their insistence upon a synthesis of their own revolutionary outlook—on its surface so futuristic and iconoclastic—with the traditional forms derived from the past, especially from the musical oeuvre of the ''First'' Viennese School of Haydn, Mozart, and Beethoven. Unlike many other musical experimentalists of their day, they insisted upon preserving the past at the same time that they leapt toward the future.

This remarkable artistic legacy is the subject of this volume. The seven chapters that follow contain a broad and coherent study of the works of Schoenberg,

Berg, and Webern, the artistic milieu that produced them, and the influence that they exerted upon musical culture. This handbook provides reliable and up-to-date information about their lives and music, an examination of their relation to the fine arts in Vienna near the turn of the century, and an assessment of their enduring importance to serious music to the present day. The reader will find here a summary and critique of recent thinking about their musical oeuvre and its most distinctive technical features, atonality and the twelve-tone method, presented in a manner equally accessible to the inquisitive amateur, the serious student, and the specialist.

In Chapter 1, Joseph Auner studies the historical concept of the Second Viennese School from its emergence as a critical term early in the century to the present. He examines the teaching of Arnold Schoenberg as the chief unifying element in the school, the stylistic similarities that inevitably arose among its three principal figures, and the potential for misunderstanding that the concept has produced. Margaret Notley explores Vienna's vibrant but highly polarized musical culture in Chapter 2. Her study reveals an intricate interlacing of music criticism and political ideology as it explores the important but now-little-known institutions that left their mark on Vienna's musical life around 1900. The non-musical arts in Vienna are the subjects addressed by Dagmar Barnouw in Chapter 3. By looking closely at aspects of the work of Adolf Loos, Karl Kraus, Ludwig Wittgenstein, Sigmund Freud, Ernst Mach, and Robert Musil, the author finds a strongly diversified interaction of forces and objectives characterizing *Wiener Moderne*, or Viennese modernism.

Chapters 4 through 6, by Bryan R. Simms, David Schroeder, and Anne C. Shreffler, deal with the three central figures of the Second Viennese School. Each of these chapters contains a survey of the life and works of its subject, to which additional specialized discussions are appended. Chapter 4, on Schoenberg, contains a musical and historical analysis of atonality and the twelve-tone method—the hallmarks of style that help to identify the Second Viennese School. Alban Berg's reliance upon modern literature is underscored in Chapter 5, and a new portrait of Webern's career (especially its early phases) is sketched in Chapter 6.

Jonathan W. Bernard tells precisely in Chapter 7 how composers from the 1950s to the present have adapted Schoenberg's twelve-tone method, and he speculates about the apparent decline of interest in the method in recent decades at the same time that it has continued to exert its influence from a higher level of musical consciousness. A selective, up-to-date Bibliography concludes the volume.

INTRODUCTION

Bryan R. Simms

"All good things . . ." is the cryptic motto that Alban Berg placed at the head of the score of his Chamber Concerto. Just beneath it, three instruments are instructed to play short phrases, one after the other without conductor, each made from the musical letters of three names. The first and longest is Arnold Schoenberg, next the brief Anton Webern, and finally Alban Berg. For the astute listener, the motto becomes clear: "All good things come in threes," Schoenberg, Webern, and Berg in particular. With this conceit so typical of the composer, Berg affirms publicly the mutual admiration and artistic affinity among himself, his teacher, Schoenberg, and his friend and fellow student, Webern. Indeed, so intense was the perceived closeness shared by the three composers that by 1925, when the Chamber Concerto was written, they were widely regarded as members of a single group, a "school," as it were, today commonly termed the Second Viennese School. It was "second" only to the eighteenth-century Viennese School, populated by no lesser figures than Haydn, Mozart, and Beethoven.

Berg was plainly intent upon displaying the unity of the school to the public eye. In an "open letter" to Schoenberg published in the journal *Pult und Taktstock*, also in 1925, he reasserted the connection of the three composers and the leadership of his teacher, Schoenberg, for whom he declared his boundless affection. Berg also explained that the allusion to the three personages in the motto of the new concerto was only the beginning of a multidimensional use of the number three throughout the entire work, reaching to every corner of its conception and structure. Although the trinity is a firmly bonded unit, it is clearly not made from equals, as Schoenberg is central and supreme. The work is dedicated to him alone, and Berg defers to his master, as he would always do in public, with fulsome declarations of praise and fealty.

Berg's Chamber Concerto thus stands as a musical symbol of the Second Viennese School, embodying on its surface a triad of musicians steadfastly linked together by personal friendship and common artistic objectives. The origins of the school hark back to 1904, when Schoenberg, having just returned to Vienna from a sojourn in Berlin and eager to develop his credentials and considerable skill as a pedagogue, advertised for private students in composition. Among several talented musicians who came to him at this time were Alban Berg, nineteen years old and lacking any formal training in music, and Anton Webern, then a university student in musicology. The details of their training at his hands and their subsequent emergence as internationally renowned composers are sketched in Chapters 4, 5, and 6 of this book. In a broad sense, the Second Viennese School extends to Schoenberg and all of his students, including Edward Steuermann, Rudolf Kolisch, Erwin Stein, Egon Wellesz, and many other leading musicians of the twentieth century. But, as Berg intimated in the motto of his Chamber Concerto, only Schoenberg, Berg, and Webern from this group were composers of the first rank. In a precise sense, these three are synonymous with the school.

An intense and complex relationship that went far beyond musical matters arose between Schoenberg and his students. Although he was quick to observe that he did not force his own musical style upon them in the way that other famous teachers such as Paul Hindemith did, Schoenberg was exceedingly dictatorial and paternal, in effect demanding a conformity in his students' outlook on artistic issues and a readiness to be his personal assistants. These expectations continued even after his students had ceased to receive musical tuition. He was the general and they were the foot soldiers in the great war of art. Berg and Webern thrived, to an extent, under this regime. Webern's almost fanatical respect for authority is vividly described by Anne C. Shreffler in Chapter 6, and in David Schroeder's Chapter 5 we learn poignantly of Berg's debt to his teacher but also the humiliations that he continually suffered, which he accepted, at least outwardly.

On a personal level, the warmth and unity among the three figures of the Second Viennese School, so fastidiously maintained by Berg in his dedication and motto to the Chamber Concerto, were often strained to the breaking point. An especially astute and well-positioned observer of their personal dynamic was Theodor Adorno, who was a student of Berg's from 1925 and a lifelong apologist for music of the entire school. In his article "Im Gedächtnis an Alban Berg" (1955) he reflected upon Berg's relationship to Schoenberg and Webern:

> Their relationship was ambivalent, and Berg knew enough about psychoanalysis to be aware of it. . . . Schoenberg envied Berg's successes; Berg, Schoenberg's lack of them. The night after the premiere of *Wozzeck* and without the slightest disingenuousness, he seemed to be quite upset by its success. He thought that any music that could immediately

appeal to the public had to have something wrong with it. He was very conscious of a definite jealousy that Schoenberg had toward him. He never quite got over a son's fear of Schoenberg. . . .

He loved Webern very much, but not without an undertone of ridicule for his brevity. . . . In all innocence we once made up a parody of a Webern piece; it consisted solely of a quarter rest decked out with all conceivable expression signs and performance instructions.[1]

Despite the potential for personal conflict among the three composers, their aesthetic outlook was cut entirely from the same cloth and based directly on the ideas of Schoenberg. A central precept was the supremacy of German classical music—the art, that is, of the First Viennese School, extended backward in time to Bach and forward to Brahms and Wagner. True to this legacy, they persistently argued that their own music, seemingly revolutionary in style and aesthetic, was, in fact, firmly based on the classical style, from which it deviated in only a few areas as demanded by the processes of an orderly historical evolution. Berg's often-stated emphasis upon the presence of classical instrumental forms in his opera *Wozzeck* is one well-known manifestation of this tendency to find tradition and regularity within the apparently innovative.

Again taking their cue from Schoenberg, all members of the Second Viennese School forcefully rejected neoclassicism, the main rival to their own brand of modernism and by the 1920s the dominant international movement in modern music. But as with many aspects of their aesthetic program, their words do not entirely conform to musical realities. Berg and Schoenberg plainly made concessions to the objectivist style of neoclassicism in their own works of the 1920s and 1930s at the same time that they were railing against it in their essays and lectures. In his often-reprinted article ''The Problem of Opera'' (1928), for example, Berg dismissed the use of cinema and jazz in contemporary opera virtually at the same moment that he was installing precisely these fashionable trappings in his own opera *Lulu*.

The music of Schoenberg, Berg, and Webern, on the other hand, is not especially similar, other than at a superficial level. Both Berg and Webern followed their teacher in writing atonal music in the years before World War I and twelve-tone music following the war, but, like all great composers, they developed their own essentially distinctive styles. Berg's remained closest to the German romantic school of the late nineteenth century; Webern's departed the most radically from this model. Each of the three had his own stylistic fingerprints—Schoenberg's predilection for the speaking voice, for example, or Berg's use of quotation and Webern's radical brevity and concentration.

The phenomenon of Schoenberg's school was distinctly Viennese. Like other modern arts in Vienna at the turn of the century, it stemmed from an intellectual *Gesamtkunstwerk*, closely related to new ideas then overflowing from science, literature, and painting that quickly intermingled with those emanating from music per se. In fact, Schoenberg's decision around 1908 to forgo the use of key and henceforth to write atonal music might not have occurred without the inspiration that he received from modern literature, especially the works of German symbolist writers such as Stefan George, and new directions in the visual arts by his Viennese contemporaries Oskar Kokoschka and Adolf Loos.

The Second Viennese School existed also in a fascinatingly complex relationship with the great tradition of music in Vienna, a topic discussed by Margaret Notley in Chapter 2. As much as anywhere in the world, Viennese audiences took their music seriously and were ready to invest it with a near-religious importance going far beyond mere pleasure and entertainment. This was the conception of music to which Schoenberg, Berg, and Webern subscribed; theirs was not a music for easy listening but for an intellectual and artistic enlightenment of the highest and most recondite order. They were not partisans in the quarrel between Brahms and Wagner that characterized German musical criticism at the end of the nineteenth century; they looked instead for ways in which the legacies of both of these eminent forerunners could point them toward the future.

Following World War II, the music of the three composers quickly rose to an importance that it had never experienced before that time. In the 1950s major performances took place worldwide: *Wozzeck* at the Metropolitan Opera and Covent Garden, *Moses und Aron* in Hamburg, and a recording of Webern's complete known works issued by Columbia Records. Their works were studied and pondered by young composers in Europe and America and painstakingly analyzed. Indeed, their oeuvre seemed to coincide with the artistic spirit of the postwar period—highly controlled by the twelve-tone method, filled with a certain angst in its pervasive dissonance, and, especially in the case of Webern, characterized in the minds of most listeners by more than a touch of abstraction and depersonalization.

By the 1970s, as postwar anxieties began to wane, a younger generation of classical composers, especially in America, became increasingly uncomfortable with the modernism of the Second Viennese School, preferring instead to advance a more relaxed and eclectic idiom and to return to known values rather than to continue the relentless exploration that was so much a part of the art of Schoenberg and his students. Now, at the dawn of the twenty-first century, the stage is at last set for the music of the Second Viennese School to detach itself from the limited perspectives created by fashions and passing tastes and to take a more permanent position among the greatest phenomena in the art of music.

NOTE

1. Theodor W. Adorno, "Im Gedächtnis an Alban Berg" (1955), in Adorno, *Gesammelte Schriften*, vol. 18, edited by Rolf Tiedemann and Klaus Schultz (Frankfurt: Suhrkamp Verlag, 1984): 491–93. Translated by the author.

1 THE SECOND VIENNESE SCHOOL AS A HISTORICAL CONCEPT

Joseph Auner

> Center of gravity of its own solar system, encircled by shining satellites, thus appears your life to an admirer.
>
> —Arnold Schoenberg, text for a canon in C major (1949)

The cover for *The New Grove Second Viennese School*, a reprint of the articles on Arnold Schoenberg, Alban Berg, and Anton Webern from *The New Grove Dictionary of Music and Musicians*, presents a group portrait of the three composers.[1] A middle-aged Schoenberg occupies the center foreground, his photograph in sharp focus. Pictured in grainy images with deep shadows on their youthful faces, Webern and Berg stand close behind him. Because nowhere on the front jacket or spine of the book is the title further clarified, this artwork serves to identify which composers are included in the Second Viennese School and to define their respective roles as the mature leader and his younger followers. Even the relative orientation of the figures is significant, with Webern on the right side of the page, as if to point toward the future, and Berg on the left, pointing toward the past, while Schoenberg is positioned as mediator between them.

Such a conventional representation of the Second Viennese School would scarcely appear to warrant comment were it not so readily apparent that the group portrait has been assembled from two photographs dating many years apart, as is evident in the quality of the images and in the contrast between Schoenberg's modern suit and the turn-of-the-century clothing worn by Berg and Webern. Determining just when and where the photographs originated is made difficult by the close cropping of the figures; the heads and shoulders of the three composers stand out against a stark white background from which all traces of historical or geographical location have been removed.

While it may not have been the publisher's intent, the graphic design of the book cover can in fact reveal a great deal about the current ambiguous status of the concept of the Second Viennese School. The conventionality and familiarity of the portrait and the fact that it was not felt necessary to identify the composers by name except for the small print on the back indicate the degree to which the Second Viennese School has entered the discourse of twentieth-century music. Conversely, the artificiality of the image strikingly symbolizes how the idea of a school consisting of Schoenberg, Berg, and Webern has been actively manufactured in the course of the century. At the same time the collage attempts to pull the three figures into the closest relationship, the obvious discrepancies between the component photographs underscore their significant differences in background, character, and artistic temperament. More specifically, this constructed image calls attention to many problematic aspects of thinking about the composers in terms of a school. The anachronistic juxtaposition of the photographs significantly exaggerates the difference in age, and thus by implication in artistic stature, between Schoenberg and his pupils. Through the contrasts in lighting and focus and the careful arrangement of the figures, Berg and Webern remain blurry and indistinct, partially obscured by the clearly defined and dominating presence of their teacher. A comparison between the portrait and the original photographs, which are printed elsewhere in the book, shows further that the relationship between Berg and Webern has been altered to bring the two pupils more closely together and to adjust their heights to be approximately equal. Even the nature of the school's difficult relationship with the broader public is made manifest in the book's design. The assumption that anyone likely to purchase the book would recognize the photographs suggests that it was targeted primarily at the limited circle of readers already well acquainted with the school.

DEFINING THE SECOND VIENNESE SCHOOL

Only an extraordinarily prescient observer in 1904, the year Berg and Webern began their studies with Schoenberg, would have picked the three of them to become the avatars of modern music. The differences between Berg and Webern can perhaps be best symbolized through a comparison of the paths by which they first came to Schoenberg. Webern began his composition lessons on the advice of the esteemed scholar Guido Adler from the University of Vienna, where he conducted research on the Renaissance composer Heinrich Isaac. Berg, on the other hand, had little formal musical training and was accepted as a pupil on the basis of some songs his brother submitted in response to a newspaper advertisement. Schoenberg at this time was a little-known and largely self-taught composer with no significant institutional affiliations and few publications. Although he was already earning a reputation through such significant works as *Verklärte Nacht*, Op. 4 (1899, premiered in 1902), and *Pelleas und Melisande*, Op. 5 (1902–3, premiered in Vienna in 1905), his most important innovations were still ahead of him. At thirty years of age, Schoenberg was not substantially older than his pupils; all three traveled the "path to the new music" together.

Given these rather inauspicious beginnings, it is remarkable that only eight years later an article by Egon Wellesz, who was himself a student and later a biographer of Schoenberg, identified him as the head of the "Young Viennese School," with Berg and Webern figuring prominently among his circle.[2] Already in this article Wellesz offered the hope that the works of this group of young composers brought together in the country of Haydn and Johann Strauss would lead to a revival of the musical glories of Beethoven's time. During the 1920s and 1930s the identities of Schoenberg, Berg, and Webern became still more closely entwined. Although there were periods of less contact resulting from geographical separation and personal differences, the three composers remained closely linked artistically and intellectually throughout their lives.

The Second Viennese School is one of a long list of movements and schools that have figured in music history, such as the New German School, the Mighty Five, and Les Six, along with more general categories like neoclassicism and impressionism. But to a far greater extent than these other movements, and even more than the "First" Viennese School of Haydn, Mozart, and Beethoven to which the name refers, the linkage of Schoenberg, Berg, and Webern has become almost axiomatic.[3] It is particularly striking that no other comparable schools or movements are reinscribed so palpably in the companion volumes to *The New Grove Second Viennese School*. Rather than being joined in collections organized around terms like impressionism, neoclassicism, or serialism, the other major twentieth-century composers are dealt with in books with much more generic titles, including *Turn of the Century Masters* (Janáček, Mahler, Strauss, and Sibelius) and *Modern Masters* (Bartók, Stravinsky, and Hindemith). The concept of national origin is preserved in volumes dedicated to French and Russian composers, but without any attempt to impose a specific stylistic or chronological homogeneity. The range of labels, each with its own connotations, that have been assigned to Schoenberg, Berg, and Webern over the century, such as the Young Viennese School, the Atonal School, the Twelve-Tone School, the Schoenberg School, and the Central European Group, only emphasizes the durability of their attachment. This linkage has been created and maintained through their own efforts, as I shall discuss later, and through writings by generations of historians, theorists, composers, and critics. Even where little emphasis is placed explicitly on the idea of a "school," the three composers are invariably discussed together, and the story of their compositional innovations has left deep imprints on virtually all historical narratives of twentieth-century music.

Notwithstanding the frequency of its usage, many have treated the Second Viennese School and the other related labels with caution. There are no separate entries for the term in the *New Harvard Dictionary of Music* or *Die Musik in Geschichte und Gegenwart.* Surprisingly, it is also lacking in *The New Grove Dictionary of Music and Musicians* itself; and the articles on Schoenberg, Berg, and Webern say little about a "school," stressing instead the individual qualities of each composer. In lexica where the term does appear, the definitions for the Second Viennese School are noticeably diffident. The *Oxford Dictionary of Music*, for example, defines the school as a "somewhat imprecise generalization, usually understood to mean the group of composers who worked in Vienna (and Berlin) between 1910 and 1930 under the moral leadership of Schoenberg (e.g., Berg, Webern, Skalkottas); their common ground being adoption of the 12-note method of comp[osition]."[4] Noteworthy here is the emphasis on twelve-tone composition and the historical restriction to the second and third decades of the century. The mention of the Greek composer Nikos Skalkottas (1904–1949), who studied with Schoenberg in Berlin from 1927 to 1931, along with the parenthetical reference to Berlin, suggests a more inclusive idea of the school while at the same time indicating that the "Viennese" aspect is largely symbolic. A quite different definition appears in *The Companion to 20th-Century Music*:

> The collective name given to Schoenberg and his pupils Berg and Webern, the trinity that overturned tonality. The grouping was in some sense misleading, for each wrote music that reflected personal traits. Schoenberg's was lofty, unyielding yet humane; Berg's was ingratiating and erotic; Webern's was precise, neurotic, authoritarian. They were united only by a technique, a time, and a place which wholly rejected them.
>
> There was never a First Vienna School. That name was assigned retroactively to Mozart, Haydn and Beethoven. A Third Vienna School arose in the 1970s around Schwertsik and Gruber, who ridiculed the established aristocracy of modernism.[5]

Here the break with tonality is stressed; twelve-tone composition is only indirectly implied by the term "technique." Although the definition evokes many of the elements of the conventional portrait of the school noted earlier, it does so only to call them into question. According to this account, the Second Viennese School was neither a school nor actually Viennese; even the notion that it was the "second" in line is disputed. Judging from the intentional omission of the term in important musicological texts and the diversity of the definitions where it is included, it would be easy to conclude that the concept of the Second Viennese School had outlived its usefulness. Even Schoenberg challenged the idea of a school in an essay about his students, "The Blessing of the Dressing" (1948): "All my pupils differ from one another extremely and though perhaps the majority compose twelve-tone music, one could not speak of a school. They all had to find their way alone, for themselves."[6]

As the chapters in this book will demonstrate, the idea of a Second Viennese School that defines some degree of commonality of compositional and aesthetic purpose among the three composers has considerable historical justification. At the same time, it is important to call attention to ways in which the label can control and in some cases limit or distort our understanding of the individual qualities of Schoenberg, Berg, and Webern.[7] Since the early years of the century the notion of a school around Schoenberg has been enmeshed in larger debates and polemics about the past, present, and future of music. To use the label of the Second Viennese School or any of the other terms by which the school has been known is by no means a neutral act, but has significant ramifications for how we think about each of the composers individually, how we conceive of their relationship to each other, and how we understand them historically, whether in the context of contemporary artistic movements or in reference to broader social and political developments. The concept of a ''school'' can create a false sense of understanding when it is used by such diverse communities as the composers themselves, theorists, musicologists, journalists, publishers, and concertgoers. This is especially the case for such an ideologically loaded concept as the Second Viennese School, which, at least in part, owes its persistence to the controversies that have surrounded it. While it might be possible to find significant common ground between what each of these groups understands by the term ''Second Viennese School,'' it is also clear that there are important differences both in the details and the connotations of the term. Such distinctions are only magnified when we turn our attention to how the conceptions of what the three composers represent have changed throughout the century.

Subsequent chapters in this volume will lay the groundwork for a reappraisal of the idea of the Second Viennese School through focused studies of each of the composers, the Viennese context, and the legacy of the school. My concern here is to define the most basic identifying characteristics of the Second Viennese School and to explore their implications for our understanding of the music of Schoenberg Berg, and Webern.[8] The first of the following sections discusses Schoenberg's role as teacher and his relationship to his students. The second section traces the emergence of Berg and Webern as the most important pupils and some of the broader ramifications that have ensued from the idea of a ''trinity'' of composers. The third section considers the impact on the school's reception of the emphasis on compositional techniques, namely, the emancipation of the dissonance and twelve-tone composition. To contribute to the process of putting the concept of the Second Viennese School back into history, I will conclude by charting the shifting relationship of the school to Vienna and its traditions.

A crucial characteristic of the concept of the Second Viennese School is that it originated with the composers themselves through their compositions, writings, and other activities. This is in marked contrast to notions such as the ''First'' Viennese School, which were retrospective constructs, to groups like the New German School or Les Six that were formulated by critics and that had little inner cohesion, and to movements like the Italian Futurists that were known primarily for their polemics rather than through a body of works. All three composers were involved in the promotion of their status as a group and their identification with the Viennese musical heritage. Berg, for example, in his *Wozzeck* lecture of 1929, spoke of a ''Viennese school under the leadership of Arnold Schoenberg.''[9] Schoenberg wrote, ''Let us, for the moment at least, forget everything that could separate us and so preserve for the future what can only begin to take effect posthumously: one will have to name the three of us together—Berg, Webern, Schoenberg—as a unity.''[10] While the many writings from within the school are a valuable part of the historical record, we must be aware of the danger that in adopting their formulations, our understanding of their relationship and their historical position will merely reproduce their own self-image. Recognizing that their writings to some degree served purposes of self-promotion or self-justification, however, does not mean that we must discount them. Rather, as Carl Dahlhaus has suggested, we will consider their writings as a part of the ''objects of enquiry, and not its precondition''; ''that the theories are thus dependent on or partly determined by practical considerations does not mean that they are without foundation, for something that is true does not stop being true by serving an interest.''[11] In addition to writings by Schoenberg, Berg, Webern, and others closely associated with the school such as Wellesz, René Leibowitz, and Theodor Adorno, my study will draw upon a range of both well-known and forgotten critics and historians.

SCHOENBERG AS TEACHER

A fundamental unifying factor among all the many meanings and labels that have accrued to the Second Viennese School is the importance of Schoenberg as a teacher. Indeed, in contrast to most other examples from music history, what is implied by the word ''school'' in the case of Schoenberg and his pupils comes very close to the customary usage of the term. Schoenberg's sense of himself was tied up with proselytizing and teaching to a far greater extent than was the case for either his younger contemporaries like Stravinsky or composers of the older generation such as Gustav Mahler and Richard Strauss. In addition to his direct involvement with a large number of students, Schoenberg also published many articles and books concerning the theory and practice of teaching, and still more of his teaching materials have been published posthumously. He clearly expressed the relationship between his role as a teacher and his Viennese identity in a 1938 letter of recommendation for the Viennese composer Karl Weigl to Professor Spencer Welch at Princeton University, referring to ''the uninterrupted succession of the great teachers of composition: Porpora, Fux, Albrechtsberger, Sechter, Mandiczewsky, etc. . . . which for almost two centuries was the pride of Vienna.''[12]

From the early years of the century both Schoenberg and his pupils emphasized his role as a teacher as an integral part of the public identity of the group. The special Schoenberg issue of the biweekly Viennese theater and music journal *Der Merker* from June 1911 highlighted his teaching concerns by printing the final chapter of the *Harmonielehre*, along with other aspects of his creative activities, including two songs (Op. 2, No. 4, and Op. 15, No. 13), the libretto of *Die glückliche Hand*, facsimiles of several paintings by Schoenberg, and articles by Karl Linke, Richard Specht, and Rudolf Réti.[13] The 1912 book, *Arnold Schönberg in höchster Verehrung von Schülern und Freunden* (Arnold Schoenberg in highest admiration from students and friends) makes this manifestly clear in its title and through a large section devoted to accounts of Schoenberg's teachings, including statements by Berg, Webern, Linke, Wellesz, Karl Horwitz, and others.[14] In the special issue of *Musikblätter des Anbruch* from 1924 on the occasion of Schoenberg's fiftieth birthday, Webern's very short contribution consists exclusively of a testimony of devotion to their relationship: "It is now twenty years that I have been a pupil of Arnold Schoenberg. But as much as I try, I cannot take in the difference between now and then. Friend and student: one was always the other."[15] Schoenberg's lecture "How One Becomes Lonely" (1937) describes standing alone "against a world of enemies," with his only support "that small group of faithful friends, my pupils":

> among them my dear friend Anton von Webern, the spiritual leader of the group, a very Hotspur in his principles, a real fighter, a friend whose faithfulness can never be surpassed, a real genius as a composer. He is today recognized the world over among musicians, although his works at the present time have not yet become as familiar to the great audience as his genius deserves. Among them also was Alban Berg, one of the dearest to me, whose death we deplored in 1935. He gained worldwide fame through his opera, *Wozzeck*, which was played in every important musical center; he, too, was a most faithful friend to me. There were and still are many others of reputation among them. It was a fact which has always made me proud, and for many years beyond these thirteen they were my only moral support in the struggle for my work.[16]

When asked about Schoenberg's friends in fields other than music, his student and son-in-law Felix Greissle replied: "Not friends! He had Loos, not too frequently; Kraus also, but not too frequently. . . . Schoenberg was wholly with his pupils. He did not want to see too many other people."[17]

As with so many aspects of Schoenberg and the Second Viennese School, the centrality of his teaching also proved to be a liability. In "How One Becomes Lonely" Schoenberg wrote, "While today one inclines perhaps to count in my favour the fact that I was surrounded by pupils of talent and genius, in 1910 I was merely blamed for that. I was called a 'seducer of young people.' "[18] Throughout the century Schoenberg has been attacked for his teaching and his association with, as it was referred to in an article published shortly after the 1912 book appeared, a "small circle of admirers [*kleiner Verehrerkreise*] that raises him up to the heavens."[19] Adolf Weissmann, in his *Problems of Modern Music* (1925), described the "crippling influence" of his teaching in Vienna, where he had become "almost a secret cult."[20] As I will discuss further later, his interpretation of the damaging effects of Schoenberg's teaching is closely related to the image of the Second Viennese School as overly intellectual and scientific: "While he undoubtedly awakens the consciences of his followers and discourages dabblers in modernism, he is inclined to damp their creative ardor. When every step has to be deeply thought out, few steps are taken. This is illustrated in Anton von Webern, a highly gifted composer whose caution is increasing to the point of immobility."[21] Hugo Leichtentritt wrote in 1958 of the "unique and abnormal peculiarity of Schoenberg's position in contemporary music," that his fame had nothing to do with the musical public or with his music, but resulted from "the extensive propaganda of a little party intensely interested in the cause of modernistic music: a little coterie of enthusiastic pupils, radical young composers, a few conductors, his publishers who specialize in modernistic music (the Vienna Universal Edition), and a few progressive critics in various countries, intent on discussing sensational matters."[22] Schoenberg's teaching has also been held against him as evidence of creative weakness in that he was not able to survive on his compositions alone, a charge that has been made as recently as 1984 by Martin Vogel in *Schönberg und die Folgen: Die Irrwege der Neuen Musik.*[23]

Built into the concept of the Second Viennese School is an emphasis on Schoenberg as the teacher of Berg and Webern, and accordingly on the earliest phase of his teaching in Vienna before the First World War. Many factors contributed to the deserved reputation of Berg and Webern as the most important students, including their compositional achievements and their writings. Moreover, it is no coincidence that limiting the circle to three and stressing the connection to Vienna strengthens the analogy to the three great composers of the First Viennese School. Leibowitz, for example, argues that the three composers are "the only musical geniuses of our time," adding with an implicit reference to Haydn, Mozart, and Beethoven, "I personally do not find it depressing that our century has produced *only* three musical geniuses. . . . There have never been more at any one time in any period of musical history."[24] Yet this formulation of the Second Viennese School distorts the reality of Schoenberg's long teaching career, which included Vienna, Berlin, and California and a roster of pupils that numbers, in a list compiled by R. Wayne Shoaf at the Arnold Schoenberg Institute, over 250 names, among them many figures who have had a significant impact on the composition, criticism, and performance of music in the twentieth century. Similarly, the emphasis on Schoenberg as a teacher has overshadowed the fact that Berg and Webern also had students of accomplishment, including Theodor Adorno, Humphrey Searle, and others.

In addition to many private pupils throughout his life, Schoenberg's teaching affiliations included the Schwarzwald School and the Academy of Arts in Vienna, where he taught as a *Privatdozent*. In Berlin he was affiliated with the Stern Conservatory before the First World War and then most importantly with the Prussian Academy of the Arts, where he directed a master class in composition between 1926 and his emigration in the spring of 1933. After a year on the East Coast, where he taught at the Malkin Conservatory in Boston and in

New York, he moved to California in 1934, where he taught one year at the University of Southern California and then at the University of California at Los Angeles until his retirement in 1944. Something of the range of Schoenberg's pupils in Europe and America is evident in "The Task of the Teacher" (1950), in which Schoenberg reflects on a half-century of teaching. He still gives Berg and Webern pride of place as the students who studied with him the longest, but he also lists "[Karl] Horwitz, [Victor] Krüger, [Heinrich] Jalowetz, Erwin Stein, [Eduard] Steuermann, [Josef] Polnauer, Cort van der Linden, [Josef] Rufer, [Olga] Novakovic, [?] Toldi, [Karl] Rankl, [Max] Deutsch, [Erwin] Ratz, [Walter] Herbert, [Hanns] Eisler, [Josef] Trauneck, [Rudolf] Kolisch, [Winfried] Zillig, [Peter] Schacht, [Norbert von] Hannenheim, [Adolph] Weiss, [Roberto] Gerhard, Erich Schmidt, [Gerald] Strang, Leonard Stein, [Dika] Newlin, [Richard] Hoffman, [Donald] Estep and others, [who] studied more than two, even three or four years with me."[25] Without displacing Berg and Webern from their rightful positions next to Schoenberg, allowing more of these figures—such as Hanns Eisler, whom Schoenberg numbered among his most important students into the 1940s despite their political and compositional differences, and still other students not yet mentioned such as John Cage and Marc Blitzstein—into our conceptions of the school could only enrich and clarify our understanding of the contributions of the Second Viennese School.

Such a broader conception of the school would also reflect the fact that neither Schoenberg nor his pupils connected his teaching to specific techniques, but rather to a way of thinking. In "The Task of the Teacher" Schoenberg differentiated himself from those who "teach their students nothing but the peculiarities of a certain style," arguing that along with the "tools of our art," he provided the students with "the technical, aesthetic and moral basis of true artistry."[26] Heinrich Jalowetz stressed the importance of both the technical and moral dimensions of what it meant to be a student of Schoenberg: "For anyone who has been his pupil, his name is no mere reminder of student days: it is one's artistic and human conscience."[27]

Closely bound up with the image of the Second Viennese School depicted on the *New Grove* cover is the relationship of the single master and his subservient pupils. Given the range of Schoenberg's teaching activities and the many near-idolatrous testimonies of his pupils, it is easy to see how the idea of the dominant teacher became established. But Schoenberg's actual relationship to his students was far more complex and ambivalent, as might be expected from someone who himself was largely self-taught.[28] Schoenberg's attitude toward the conventional master-pupil relationship is evident in the ironic tone of the canon text from near the end of his life that serves as the epigraph to this chapter; he summons up the image of the solar system and satellites, but then implies that this is only an appearance.[29] Opposed to this conception of the teacher and dependent students is the very different model that can be defined by Schoenberg's famous opening to the Preface of the *Harmonielehre*: ("Dieses Buch habe ich von meinen Schülern gelernt'' (This book I have learned from my pupils).[30] Here teaching is characterized as a communal process of discovery, where the goal is less important than the journey and the product is held in common.

Throughout Schoenberg's life these two models of the teacher's role—defining the center and leaving the disciples to explore subsidiary areas, or permitting the pupils to have their own trajectory—often came into conflict. Adorno adroitly characterized the difficult position in which these competing claims placed his pupils: ''Therefore it is not surprising that in the face of this double requirement of the most loyal discipleship and most resolute independence, there are very few who can hold their ground.''[31] Fundamental to Schoenberg's sense of history was the conviction that his ideas were the product of historical necessity and would therefore be continued beyond the point that he had taken them. Implicit in this is the notion, so important to accounts of the Second Viennese School by Adorno and Leibowitz, that it is only through his students that Schoenberg's innovations were developed to their full extent. But at the same time, Schoenberg jealously defended his historical role as the first to break with tonality and as the discoverer of the twelve-tone system. He viewed Webern in particular as a threat to his rightful position, as is evident in a short essay from the last year of his life in which he challenged the claim that *Klangfarbenmelodie* originated with Webern:

> Anyone who knows me at all knows that this is not true. It is known that I should not have hesitated to name Webern, had his music stimulated me to invent this expression. One thing is certain: even had it been Webern's idea, he would not have told it to me. He kept secret everything ''new'' he had tried in his compositions. I, on the other hand, immediately and exhaustively explained to him each of my new ideas (with the exception of the method of composition with twelve tones—that I long kept secret, because, as I said to Erwin Stein, Webern immediately uses everything I do, plan or say, so that—I remember my words—''By now I haven't the slightest idea who I am.'').[32]

This echoes a similar complaint about the pressure he felt from his students in his diary from 12 March 1912, in which among the reasons he cites for his difficulty in composing is

> the persistence with which my students nip at my heels, intending to surpass what I offer, [this] puts me in danger of becoming their imitator, and keeps me from calmly building on [the stage] that I have just reached. They always bring [in] everything raised to the tenth power. And it makes sense! It is really good. But I do not know whether it is necessary. At least not whether it is necessary to me. That is why I am forced to distinguish even more carefully whether I must write than [I was forced to do] earlier. Since I do not care all that much about my originality; however, sometimes it does give me pleasure, and in any case I like [it] better than un-originality.[33]

Schoenberg's role as teacher must be understood in the context of this continual struggle with what he described as the ''Problems in Teaching Art''

(1911). In this essay he argued that traditional artistic education based on the principle "you must be able to walk before you learn to dance" teaches the pupil only the easily mastered fundamentals of a craft. When it comes to the important aspects of aesthetics, however, the pupil is left to his own resources.

For a teacher can show how to dance, but not how to be inspired or how to invent an exceptional method for an exceptional case. And the exceptional case, calling for the exceptional method, at every moment confronts the man who produces art. The man who has to dance, on the other hand, is confronted by the everyday case; the effect he is to produce is of a purely formal nature and has relatively little to do with his personal leanings and needs. Art, though, answers only to these, and everything merely formal is contingent—regular contingencies, perhaps, but hardly the main thing. So what is the point of teaching how to master everyday cases? The pupil learns how to use something he must not use if he wants to be an artist.[34]

Schoenberg characteristically experienced this ambivalence about his teaching on a very personal level. The tribute paid to him by the book *Arnold Schönberg in höchster Verehrung von Schülern und Freunden* was especially troubling. In his diary he wrote: "I feel I am being talked about in really much too effusive a way. I am too young for this kind of praise, have accomplished too little that is perfect. My present accomplishment, I can still only regard as a hope for the future, as a promise that I may keep; but not as anything more. And I have to say, were I not spoiling the joy of my students by doing so, I might possibly have rejected the book."[35]

"BERG AND WEBERN: SCHOENBERG'S HEIRS"

Viewed in the context of Schoenberg's many influential students from throughout his life, the extent to which the idea of the trinity of Schoenberg, Berg, and Webern has become so much a part of our historical thinking is all the more striking. Although in retrospect it is easy to see the important role played by Berg and Webern from the second decade of the century on, the notion that they occupied the dominant positions on the right and left hand of their teacher was not self-evident, but was produced through their own actions and writings and even more through subsequent accounts of the school. Equating the Second Viennese School with the closed circle of the three composers has had many implications for how we conceive of the works and the historical roles of Schoenberg, Berg, and Webern. Indeed, the usage of the term "trinity" for Schoenberg and his pupils, even where it is with an ironic intent, as in the definition from *The Companion to 20th-Century Music* cited earlier, indicates the almost metaphysical connotations that have become attached to their relationship.

In the period before the First World War, the special status of Berg and Webern among Schoenberg's pupils only gradually emerged. Schoenberg's Preface to the *Harmonielehre* from July 1911, for example, includes them among a list of eight names: "Alban Berg (who prepared the topical index), Dr. Karl Horwitz, Dr. Heinrich Jalowetz, Karl Linke, Dr. Robert Neumann, Josef Polnauer, Erwin Stein, and Dr. Anton von Webern."[36] Similarly, in *Arnold Schönberg in höchster Verehrung*, none of the seven students represented is singled out, though Webern's essay on Schoenberg's music is the longest contribution. Wellesz's 1912 article on "Schoenberg and the Young Viennese School" cites four students, with Webern identified as "l'élève préféré," while Berg appears third after Karl Horwitz and Heinrich Jalowetz.[37] In Hugo Fleischmann's discussion of "Die Jung Wiener Schule" from the same year, Berg is left out entirely, with Schoenberg's circle defined as Webern, Jalowetz, Wellesz, Réti, and Fritz Zweig.[38]

Yet a number of factors contributed to the fulfillment for Berg and Webern of the prophecy Schoenberg made at the end of the *Harmonielehre* Preface about his students: "Some of them will soon be heard from in better circumstances."[39] In the main body of the book Schoenberg already favored Berg and Webern by including excerpts from their compositions to illustrate characteristics of the new harmonic practice, thus placing them in the very select company of contemporary composers cited: Bartók, Debussy, Mahler, and Franz Schreker. Similarly, in the discussion of the construction of "seven, eight, nine, ten, eleven, and twelve-part chords," he wrote, "Besides myself, my pupils Dr. Anton von Webern and Alban Berg have written such harmonies." Strikingly, he already differentiated his and his pupils' approach from that of Bartók and Schreker, who, while "probably not far" from using similar harmonies, were "following a path more similar to that of Debussy, Dukas, and perhaps also Puccini."[40] It was also through Schoenberg's influence that Vasili Kandinsky included works from Berg and Webern in the almanac *Der blaue Reiter*, along with the facsimile of Schoenberg's *Herzgewächse*, Op. 20. Still more important than these written testaments to his faith in Berg and Webern were concerts that brought their works together in the public eye. A defining event was undoubtedly the so-called *Skandalkonzert* of 31 March 1913 in the Vienna Musikverein, which included Schoenberg's First Chamber Symphony, Op. 9, movements from Berg's *Altenberg Lieder*, Op. 4, and Webern's Six Pieces for Orchestra, Op. 6. Newspaper coverage of the altercations and disturbances along with the resulting lawsuits brought the group notoriety well beyond Vienna.[41] The concert served the function not only of tightly linking Schoenberg and his pupils, but also of differentiating them from their close contemporaries Mahler and Alexander Zemlinsky, whose works were also included.

It was not until the 1920s and 1930s that the trinity of composers was firmly established as Berg's and Webern's compositional achievements became better known as a result of their prominent roles in the Society for Private Musical Performances, through their writings, and by their adoption of the twelve-tone technique.[42] Schoenberg specifically narrowed the circle to three in his tribute to Alban Berg published in connection with a 1930 performance of *Wozzeck*:

"I gladly take the chance of paying my tribute to the work and creation of my pupil and friend Alban Berg. For he and our mutual friend, his fellow-pupil Anton von Webern, were after all the most powerful confirmation of my effect as a teacher, and these are after all the two who in times of the severest artistic distress gave me support so firm, so reliable, so full of affection, that nothing better is to be found in this world."[43] Webern helped to define the group in the lectures published as *The Path to the New Music*. He mentions many influences throughout, in particular Goethe and Karl Kraus, but Schoenberg is always at the center of his thoughts explicitly or implicitly. Of the students, he mentions only Berg and himself: "All the works that Schoenberg, Berg and I wrote before 1908 belong to this stage of tonality."[44] Writing on the breakdown of tonality, he stresses that he and Berg were there from the beginning: "We—Berg and I—went through all that personally. I say this, not so that it will get into my biography, but because I want to show that it was a development wrested out of feverish struggles and decisively necessary."[45] Berg similarly helped to create the link with Schoenberg in his guides to *Gurrelieder* (1913) and *Pelleas und Melisande* (1920) and the essay "Warum ist Schönbergs Musik so schwer verständlich?" published in the *Musikblätter des Anbruch* (1924). Berg is also responsible for one of the most remarkable monuments to the idea of the trinity of composers in his Chamber Concerto (1925). As he explained in an open letter of dedication to Schoenberg published in *Pult und Taktstock* shortly after the work's completion, the piece is based on three themes that "contain the letters of your name as well as Anton Webern's and mine, so far as musical notation permits."[46] He went on to show how the concept of the trinity is reflected in the formal organization, the trinity of available instrumental genres (keyboard, string, and wind instruments), three rhythmic forms, and many other aspects of the work.

The broader historical and compositional implications of the idea of the trinity were further developed by Berg's student Theodor Adorno.[47] Moreover, Adorno's essay "Berg and Webern: Schönberg's Heirs" demonstrates the extent to which the central importance of Berg and Webern still had to be forcibly argued at the time of its publication in 1931.[48] Adorno expressed directly what remains implicit in the remarks of those within the school cited earlier, namely, that only Berg and Webern were composers of the first rank. He did acknowledge that some of the other pupils, including Horwitz, Alexander Jemnitz, Eisler, Zillig, and Skalkottas, managed to live up to Schoenberg's "double requirement" of discipleship and independence, but claimed that beyond this circle the number of the disciples "seriously to be considered as composers" was exhausted. "Though the pedagogue Schönberg has influenced musical creation today to a degree difficult to estimate, though he has trained a whole generation of conductors, few of his pupils have survived as composers. Only Berg and Webern remain, both but a decade younger than himself, both associated with him throughout their lives. They are in the strictest sense his pupils, and yet at the same time autonomous composers."[49]

Beyond their individual importance, Adorno argued that Berg and Webern serve as the unfolding and fulfillment of different aspects of Schoenberg's creative personality. In a formulation closely linked to Schoenberg's concept of developing variation, in which a musical idea only takes shape in the course of the development that proceeds from it, Adorno wrote, "With Schönberg the creations of his followers [are] necessarily the stage on which his own are linked to the broad stretch of musical history."[50] More specifically, he argued that Berg and Webern each had a unique role developing out of "the extreme poles of Schönberg's domain": "Berg unites him with Mahler on one hand and on the other with the great music drama and legitimizes him from this point. Webern pursues to its furthest extreme the subjectivism which Schönberg first released in ironic play in *Pierrot*."[51] To support this claim, Adorno provided brief accounts of selected works by Berg and Webern showing their relationship to different aspects of Schoenberg's output. Webern was linked to the vocal compositions, while Berg's works were traced to the Chamber Symphony and the "organic essence . . . which unites him with the nineteenth century and Romanticism," a claim further reinforced by comparisons with Mahler and Wagner's *Tristan und Isolde*.[52] Also, in a passage of great significance for later accounts of the Second Viennese School, Adorno argued that even when the two students appeared to be on intersecting paths—as with Berg's aphoristic Four Pieces for Clarinet, Op. 5, and Webern's miniatures written in the years before the First World War—their compositions were based on fundamentally different principles. The prophetic tone of his conclusion vividly demonstrates the importance the notion of the trinity had assumed: "In the strict execution of the composer's problems, Schönberg's pupils have become heirs who have inherited what they possess, and thereby carry that inheritance toward the obscure yet nevertheless certain goal of all music. The making of music history could not be in better hands."[53]

Adorno's account of the relationship between the three composers is carried still further in the book *Schoenberg and His School* by the composer and conductor René Leibowitz, who moved from Paris to Berlin in 1930 to study with Schoenberg. Leibowitz also exemplifies the degree to which the reception of the school has been influenced by their own writings. Throughout the study he adopts their conceptual formulations and even their language. He begins his preface, for example, with a paraphrase of Schoenberg's statement "Dieses Buch habe ich von meinen Schülern gelernt." Similarly, in his discussion of Schoenberg's First String Quartet, Op. 7, he quotes large passages from Berg's "Why Is Schoenberg's Music So Hard to Understand?"[54] Adorno's writings are also an important source, as is acknowledged at several points throughout the text.

Leibowitz extends Adorno's notion that Berg and Webern present "commentaries" on Schoenberg to argue that there is an essential interdependence among the three: "It does not seem to me an exaggeration to say that, without the addition of the two others, no one personality of this group would have a complete meaning.'' He writes that without ''the teaching and example of Arnold Schoenberg,'' the very existence of Berg and Webern as composers would be ''inconceivable.''

> Appearing as prolongations of the activity of the Master, and forming contrasts among themselves, the activities of the two disciples, while shedding a new light on the problems posed by Schoenberg, acquire their own distinct and clearly individualized directions. In the same way, the powerful and integral personality of Arnold Schoenberg takes on a higher meaning and more universal significance through the contributions of those whose genius he was able to discover and to guide.[55]

It is also in Leibowitz's presentation that the idea of Berg as the link to the past and Webern as the bridge to the future, a concept that we have seen embodied in the photographic collage on *The New Grove Second Viennese School*, takes its most concrete form.[56] With striking similarity to Schoenberg's anxious comments from 1912 about the pressure he felt from his students, Leibowitz writes, ''Step by step, Berg and Webern follow the evolution of their master; as soon as he penetrates into a new realm the two disciples follow him there immediately. But, while the genius of Berg always strove to establish a connection between the discoveries of Schoenberg and the past—thus profiting by the 'retroactive' elements in Schoenberg's work—the genius of Webern is concerned with the *possibilities* for *the future* inherent in this work, and thus succeeds in *projecting* its particularly novel and radical elements.''[57]

This idea of a trinity of composers, each with his own complementary qualities and compositional concerns, fixed in the historical configuration of Berg looking back to the past and Webern pushing ahead to the future, with Schoenberg as the generating force linking them all together, has been extremely influential in the reception of the school by both sympathetic and hostile critics. In his history of twentieth-century music, to cite only one example, Eric Salzman calls attention to the ''convenient historical niches'' in which the composers are often placed: Berg is the ''instinctual lyricist'' linked with tradition, while Webern is ''the intellectual, numerical abstractionist and the prophet of the avant garde.''[58] One benefit of this way of conceiving of their relationship to the past, present, and future has been to make the status of the school somewhat resilient in the face of changing fashions since the Second World War. Several generations of composers with shifting compositional concerns have been able to find continuing sustenance in the school by turning their attention to different composers or different stages in their development. This is most obvious in the transition from the strong interest in Webern by avant-garde composers in the 1950s and 1960s to the Berg revival in the 1970s and 1980s paralleling the resurgence of neoromantic and eclectic elements in many new works.

But as should be evident, this historical formulation of the school carries with it a range of connotations that can interfere with how we conceive of the composers individually and as a group. Some examples have already been cited that make this explicit, such as the highly charged language about their music quoted earlier from *The Companion to 20th-Century Music*: ''Schoenberg's was lofty, unyielding yet humane; Berg's was ingratiating and erotic; Webern's was precise, neurotic, authoritarian.'' Hans Mersmann in the 1928 *Moderne Musik seit der Romantik* demonstrates how very early on Webern and Berg came to stand for negative and positive paths of development leading out of Schoenberg. Berg is described as more active and healthy, while Webern demonstrates with ''frightening clarity'' what happens to a student who subscribes to all of Schoenberg's restrictions.[59] The ever-stronger linkage of the three composers traced here represents in many ways the inverse of the actual situation in regard to their compositional development and their biographies. Indeed, only shortly after Adorno's article appeared, the reality of the Second Viennese School was ended with Schoenberg's emigration in 1933 and Berg's death in 1935.[60] At various stages in the preceding years significant personal and aesthetic differences led to major rifts between Schoenberg and his pupils. A central and still-unresolved issue between Schoenberg and Webern, for example, was the nature of Webern's relationship to the Nazi party.[61] The many difficulties between Berg and Schoenberg are documented in their correspondence, such as the letter from November 1915 in which Berg describes the anguish of ''these last four years when forced to see your affection slowly and inexorably ebb, *even though* I tried and tried to please you; when—while trying to correct one mistake—I always unwittingly committed another; when I finally had to recognize that you hated, or at least were annoyed by, everything I did or anything at all to do with me.''[62]

More specifically, the notion of the trinity has colored the interpretation of their works. Thus in keeping with his role as the ''retroactive'' member of the group, Berg's twelve-tone works have been viewed as representing an imperfect understanding of the twelve-tone system corrupted by links to the past and romanticism. Yet recent scholarship has demonstrated that much of Berg's music depends on abstract, ''intellectual'' constructive schemes to a far greater extent than that of either Webern or Schoenberg. Similarly, the view of Webern's music as cerebral and disembodied obscures his strong links to the past his mystical leanings, and the important inspiration poetic texts provided. A more general problem resulting from these categories is that each composer has been granted a certain turf from which the others are excluded. Accordingly, brevity has been the province of Webern, so that the miniatures by Schoenberg or Berg have been regarded as exceptional or provisional. Incorporating tonal references, quotations, and folk songs into twelve-tone compositions is Berg's territory, so that Schoenberg's very similar practices in works such as the Suite, Op. 29, are little discussed.

Various aspects of all these problems are evident in Leibowitz's discussion, as is the still more general danger of the tight formation of the school enveloping Berg and Webern in Schoenberg's shadow. Indeed, Leibowitz's use of the term ''Schoenberg School,'' rather than Viennese School or the other possibilities, reflects the extent to which he defines the roles of Berg and Webern as primarily bringing to fruition facets of their teacher's thought. Thus like Adorno, he stresses that the students' major works are all prefigured in specific compositions by Schoenberg.[63] Perhaps compensating for Schoenberg's suspicions that Webern sought to take credit for his innovations, Leibowitz writes that through the time of the Symphony, Op. 21, composed in 1928, when Webern was forty-five years old, "he had not written a page which—exaggerating a little—might not have been written by his master."[64] Just as Webern and Berg are reduced to satellites of their teacher, Leibowitz's historical model of the trinity leads him to the conclusion that rather than striving after originality, it was the task of the later generations of Schoenbergians to explore the territory opened up by the master and his pupils. Thus of Schoenberg's "other direct or indirect disciples" he writes: "What especially characterizes their activity is that, instead of trying to make new discoveries at all costs (as is often the case today), they try to assimilate the discoveries of their masters, and thus to consolidate these discoveries. Here, I think, we see the initial effort and conscious will to construct a truly contemporary musical speech."[65]

THE EMANCIPATION OF THE DISSONANCE AND TWELVE-TONE COMPOSITION

Fundamental to almost all accounts of the Second Viennese School is an emphasis on compositional techniques, most importantly the "emancipation of the dissonance" and the "method of composing with twelve tones which are related only with one another." To these two terms have been joined a whole range of ideas associated with the music and thought of Schoenberg, Berg, and Webern, including—as will be discussed in the subsequent chapters—musical prose, *Grundgestalt*, developing variation, and *Klangfarbenmelodie*, along with more general notions such as organicism, the musical idea, and comprehensibility. On a still deeper level Dahlhaus has identified a network of concepts underlying Schoenberg's thought that have clear resonance for that of his pupils as well: "Nature as the origin of music, history as unfolding, the genius as the executor of what nature has prefigured, and the masterpiece as the end result."[66] But it is the two epoch-making ideas of the break with tonality and twelve-tone composition that have received the most attention, both for their individual significance and for their close interdependence in a historical developmental process. Indeed, in the case of no other twentieth-century composers or movements from the first half of the century is their reception so dominated by specific technical features. The definition of the Second Viennese School in the *Brockhaus Riemann Musiklexikon* can serve as a particularly concise example of this trend, describing "the historical achievement of the school as having brought late-Romantic harmony to its conclusions and at the same time establishing new starting points, first compositionally with free atonality around 1907, and then theoretically with twelve-tone composition around 1920."[67] Though without making the historical narrative so explicit, the descriptive blurb on the back of the *New Grove* volume lays out the same terrain, identifying the Second Viennese School through "their early 20th-century atonal and 12-note compositions [that] marked the abolition of the traditional tonal functions and an entirely new treatment of dissonance."

As with so many aspects of the Second Viennese School, Schoenberg, Berg, and Webern all contributed to this emphasis on compositional technique through their own historical, analytical, and theoretical writings. The overall concern with technique is foreshadowed in the *Harmonielehre*, where Schoenberg attacks aestheticians and theorists who would pronounce eternal laws for art, proposing instead to teach "the pupil the handicraft of our art as completely as a carpenter can teach his."[68] The notion of clearly defined stages of development is perpetuated in many of their writings, both directly and indirectly, as in Berg's description of the composition of *Wozzeck* in terms of a transition between two periods: the "Viennese school, under the leadership of Arnold Schoenberg, had just developed beyond the beginnings of the movement that people quite wrongly called atonality."[69] The story of the break with tonality and the discovery of twelve-tone composition dominates many of Schoenberg's later writings, such as "Composition with Twelve Tones" (1941) and "My Evolution" (1949). Both of these essays explicitly link Berg and Webern to these stages of his development, though always giving clear priority to Schoenberg: "The first compositions in this new style were written by me around 1908 and, soon afterwards, by my pupils, Anton von Webern and Alban Berg."[70] His insistence on receiving the credit for the discovery of these compositional techniques and the resulting private and public quarrels with Webern, Josef Hauer, Thomas Mann, and others further focused attention on the techniques themselves. In *Structural Functions of Harmony*, first published in 1954 and his last completed theoretical work, Schoenberg brought all of the elements of the historical narrative together explicitly to define his "school": "My school, including such men as Alban Berg, Anton Webern and others, does not aim at the establishment of a tonality, yet does not exclude it entirely. The procedure is based upon my theory of 'the emancipation of dissonances'. . . . For the sake of a more profound logic, the Method of Composing with Twelve Tones derives all configurations [elements of a work] from a basic set (*Grundgestalt*) [tone-row or note series]."[71] Webern virtually identified himself with the path to twelve-note composition: "What I'm telling you here is really my life-story. This whole upheaval started just when I began to compose. The matter became really relevant during the time when I was Schoenberg's pupil. Since then a quarter of a century has already gone by, though."[72] He equated undertaking twelve-tone composition with entering into a marriage or the revelation of divine truth, writing that in 1921, "Schoenberg expressed the law with absolute clarity. . . . Since that time he's practiced this technique of composition himself (with one small exception), and we younger composers have been his disciples."[73]

The attention to compositional issues in the writings of the school has had many positive results. Most important, the substantial literature on the theory and analysis of atonal and twelve-tone composition by subsequent generations of composers and scholars has contributed to an appreciation of the music of the Second Viennese School, both on its own terms and as a resource for subsequent compositional developments. Yet just as in the case of Schoenberg's reputation as a teacher or the construction of the trinity, while there are sound reasons for the concentration on technical features in the formulation of the Second Viennese School, there have been significant costs as well for the understanding of the composers' works and for their historical legacy. A major problem that still continues today has been that Schoenberg, Berg, and Webern have been known more through their writings and reputation than through their music. To cite only one example, Leichtentritt pointed out in 1958 that "even as late as 1937," *Verklärte Nacht* was the only one of Schoenberg's works at all well known in America.[74] The small number of performances, coupled with the relatively easy availability of publications like *Harmonielehre* and still more significantly the volume of journalistic commentary about the school, has placed a disproportionate emphasis on the written word. A short essay by Otto Besch that appeared in the *Allgemeine Musik-Zeitung* in 1912 demonstrated the extent to which Schoenberg was from very early on evaluated in terms of his own writings and those of his pupils. Not surprisingly, Besch shows an awareness of the *Harmonielehre*, published the previous year, but he also refers to the 1910 program note from a performance of *Das Buch der hängenden Gärten*, Op. 15, about "having broken off the bonds of a bygone aesthetic," and essays by Webern from the *Rheinischen Musikzeitung* and *Arnold Schönberg in höchster Verehrung*. In an extreme recent example of this tendency, *Schoenberg's Error* by William Thomson, the author focuses almost exclusively on Schoenberg's writings to argue that "the rationale he devised for his music was derived from untenable hypotheses." While he leaves it to posterity to determine "the merit of his innovations as a composer," the strong implication is that by disproving his "theoretical claims—many of them formulated as apologia for his compositional actions," he will undercut the validity of the works themselves.[75]

The most obvious impact of the proliferation of theoretical and analytical writings about the Second Viennese School has been the notion that it is only through the detailed understanding of compositional techniques that one can appreciate the music of Schoenberg, Berg, and Webern. The resulting verdict that their works are purely intellectual and best reserved for experts is probably more widespread today than it was a half-century ago when Schoenberg attempted to refute it in his essay "Heart and Brain in Music." His challenge to the "misconception . . . that the constituent qualities of music belong to two categories as regards their origin: to the heart or to the brain"[76] is a reaction to attacks such as that by Adolf Weissmann in *The Problems of Modern Music* (1925): "Arnold Schönberg is a master of atonality, an analyst of the elements of music and a transvaluer of the values of tune. . . . The evidence suggests that his art springs from an imagination injured and finally crippled by too much theory.''[77] As in many such criticisms of Schoenberg as a brain musician, Weissmann's account is explicitly informed by anti-Semitic stereotypes:

> Schönberg shows his Jewish blood by a passionate exclusion of the palpable and the representational, combined with a sophistication which would leave nothing unproved. These qualities would appear mutually exclusive, but they contrive to exist side by side in Schönberg and must finally cramp his creative imagination. . . . Dialecticism, excess of cleverness constantly seeking expression, fetter the creative artist in Schönberg. Other artists let their works speak for them, but in him the spirit of controversy is almost as strong as the spirit of creative work. The result is that since 1913 Schönberg has given the world little music of value, but has nevertheless exercised a vast influence, increasing as his productivity lessens, through the fanatic devotion of his disciples.[78]

As this passage makes clear, frequent connections were made between Schoenberg's ''intellectual'' compositional techniques and his reputation as a teacher. That both activities were regarded as impaired by the overabundance of brain is evident in Leichtentritt's conclusion that ''it is probable that he is a greater theorist than creative artist. Like Moses, he has led musicians to the frontiers of the new land, but it has been reserved to others to exploit the new fields profitably. That immature youthful enthusiasts may be led thoroughly astray by Schoenberg's difficult speculations needs no proof.''[79] Yet it is important to point out that Schoenberg and his pupils rarely connected his actual teaching to specific techniques, particularly to atonality and twelve-tone composition, but rather related it to more general ways of thinking about music as well as larger philosophical issues. Indeed, it should be stressed that all three composers actually wrote very little about the specifics of either the compositional techniques of their posttonal works or twelve-tone composition. It was, in fact, far more common for Schoenberg to dissuade pupils from using the new means, as, for example, in the final chapter of the *Harmonielehre*, where he writes, ''I do not recommend that the pupil use the harmonies presented here in his attempts to compose, so far as they do not also appear in other, older texts.''[80] In ''The Blessing of the Dressing'' (1948) Schoenberg differentiates his approach from those of other teachers who teach a style ''in the manner in which a cook would deliver recipes.''[81]

Beyond these more general consequences, the focus on the break with tonality and twelve-tone composition in the formation of the idea of the Second Viennese School has had important implications for the evaluation of individual works by Schoenberg, Berg, and Webern and for the understanding of their historical development. The relationship between theory and practice is particularly complex for the Second Viennese School. Although all three composers strongly resisted the tendency to reduce their compositional approaches to any system, this has not stopped commentators from formulating abstract conceptions of atonality or twelve-tone composition that are then used as a measure to judge individual works. In his *Problems of Modern Music*, for example, Weissmann simultaneously criticizes Schoenberg for presenting theories and for not living up to these theories in his works: "There is a degree of compliance beyond which the ear refuses to go; moreover, Schönberg has not found it possible to be quite consistent to his own conception of a new form."[82] Leichtentritt demonstrates another version of this approach by first presenting caricatures of the techniques, then on the basis of these inaccurate definitions showing their shortcomings: "Two labels have been attached to Schönberg's music: atonality and the twelve-tone technique. These terms seem to become more mysterious the more one ponders over them."[83] A major problem with such an approach is, of course, that the techniques themselves are often not well understood, as is evident in this discussion of Schoenberg's music from the *Standard History of Music* by James Francis Cooke from 1936: "The later music of Schoenberg . . . sometimes called 'impressionism,' is based upon a very much more involved system, in which he recognizes over two thousand chords. The present effect upon most hearers is that of great confusion, discord, and unrest."[84] Yet that Schoenberg himself was by no means immune to the blurring of theory and practice is clear in his need to defend his later twelve-tone works for the "impurities" of their style due to the inclusion of tonal elements.[85] Similarly, he anticipated later critics who found fault with Berg's twelve-tone works for similar impurities. In the 1946 Addendum to "Composition with Twelve Tones," Schoenberg writes, "I have to admit that Alban Berg, who was perhaps the least orthodox of us three—Webern, Berg and I—in his operas mixed pieces or parts of pieces of a distinct tonality with those which were distinctly non-tonal."[86]

Implicit in the neat progression of compositional problems and solutions in the story of the Second Viennese School—developing from late-romantic chromatic harmony through the emancipation of the dissonance to twelve-tone composition—is the language of periodization, transitional works, breakthroughs, and mainstream and margin.[87] While scholars have challenged the teleological historical model underlying this conception of the school, it has had many consequences. Defining twelve-tone composition as the central evolutionary path has meant relegating works such as Schoenberg's late tonal pieces and the arrangements of works by Bach, Handel, Matthias Georg Monn, and Brahms to the peripheries of historical interest. Schoenberg himself implicitly signaled their secondary status by withholding opus numbers from the arrangements, while apologetically describing the late tonal works, such as the Suite for String Orchestra in G major from 1934, as the product of a nostalgic "longing to return to the older style," comparable to the pleasure one obtains from occasionally riding in a carriage rather than a fast automobile.[88] Together with the definition of an ideal type for either atonality or the twelve-tone method comes the idea of the transitional—as opposed to the truly representative—work. The early emergence of this way of thinking can be seen in a 1912 discussion of *Pelleas und Melisande* and the Second String Quartet, Op. 10, which already refers to the tone poem as "merely a transitional work."[89] This approach affected both friendly and hostile critics. In ''The Musical Messiah or Satan'' from 1915, Harry T. Finck described earlier works like the First String Quartet, Op. 7, and *Pelleas* as not representing the ''later tendencies fully,'' while the Chamber Symphony, Op. 9, ''sounds already like Schönberg's most 'mature' works; that is, as if all the players were improvising, regardless of the others, and each one trying to play the wrongest notes he could think of.''[90] From such a perspective nearly every work of a composer like Schoenberg, who changed so much from piece to piece, or Berg, with his small and heterogeneous output, can be viewed as transitional in some sense.

Finally, built into the history of twelve-tone composition as the product of historical necessity is the implication that the preceding stages were in some sense deficient.[91] This is particularly evident in the treatment of the issue of the extraordinary brevity of many works by Schoenberg, Berg, and Webern from before the First World War. Webern, as with the others, attributes this to the abandonment of tonality and the loss of the ''most important means of building up longer pieces.'' In this interpretation the use of a text to provide a framework for longer compositions was a temporary measure until the formulation of the ''new twelve tone law'' rendered such a dependence on the ''extra-musical'' unnecessary.[92] The return to the genres and forms of the classical masters in the twelve-tone works underscores the sense of an end to the state of emergency often associated with the atonal works. The risks inherent in such a historical narrative are apparent not only in the ambivalent status of works from the earlier periods, but in the inevitable subsequent development that twelve-tone composition as formulated by Schoenberg was itself only an intermediate stage. This became clear in the writings and works of younger composers after the Second World War, such as Ligeti, who in his ''Metamorphosis of Musical Form'' extrapolated beyond twelve-tone composition through serialism to group composition.[93]

THE SECOND VIENNESE SCHOOL AND VIENNA

Perhaps the most controversial aspect of the Second Viennese School is the nature of its relationship to Vienna itself. The dialectic between tradition and revolution that so characterizes this relationship is already built into the name of the school, with its claims to the mantle of the city's great musical legacy balanced by the inevitable anxiety of belatedness that comes with being the second in line. This ambivalence of Schoenberg, Berg, and Webern toward their Viennese heritage as both the ultimate legitimation of their activities and as an obstacle to be overcome played an important role in their development and has had significant ramifications for how we understand them individually and in the context of a school. Throughout the history of the school different sides of this tension with their ''loved and hated'' Vienna—between the conservative and the revolutionary impulses—came to the fore in response to their evolving compositional concerns and to the changing cultural and social situation in which they lived and worked. The complexity of this relationship reflects the fact that the concept of Vienna itself represented no single thing, but in different contexts and at different times could refer to an empire, and after the First World War, a empire that was no more; distinguished artistic and intellectual traditions alongside modernist innovation; a history of powerful critics; and a range of different audiences for music. Thus the undeniably profound importance of the Viennese context for Schoenberg, Berg, and Webern has been construed variously in terms of their links to the city's musical traditions from the ''First Viennese School'' through Brahms and Mahler, their connections to contemporaneous artistic and cultural trends (i.e., the Vienna of Sigmund Freud, Karl Kraus, Adolf, Loos, Gustav Klimt, and Oskar Kokoschka), or still-deeper manifestations of something inherently Viennese. In regards to the latter, Hartmut Krones has defined a lexicon of Viennese elements in the music of Schoenberg, Berg, and Webern, including an inclination toward theatricality, the idea of music as rhetoric, program music, number symbolism, and the use of musical ciphers.[94]

Vienna occupied a special place in Schoenberg's thought throughout his lifetime. His application for the position of *Privatdozent* at the Akademie für Musik und Darstellende Kunst in Vienna in March 1910 stressed ''the special nature of my artistic development, which, taking the classical masters as its point of departure, has led me—as I must suppose: logically—into the forefront of the modern movement in music.''[95] In a letter to Josef Hauer in 1923 he emphasized the national identity of the new music: ''Let us show the world that *music*, if nothing else, would not have advanced if it had not been for the Austrians, and that *we* know what the next step must be.''[96] Near the end of his life Schoenberg responded to the honors bestowed upon him by the city of Vienna, writing, ''It is with pride and joy that I received the news that I had been given the freedom of the city of Vienna. This is a new, or rather, a renewed, bond bringing me closer again to the place, its natural scenery and its essential character, where that music was created which I have always so much loved and which it was always my greatest ambition to continue according to the measure of my talents.''[97]

But the relationship to Vienna for all three composers was always profoundly problematic, as can be symbolized by Schoenberg's indecision in the last-cited letter about whether to characterize his bond to the city as ''new'' or ''renewed,'' both words that imply various degrees of discontinuity and rupture. In practical terms, only Berg was a lifelong resident of the city, while both Schoenberg and Webern were away for long periods, Schoenberg for the last two decades of his life. In addition to its role as cradle of the new, Vienna was also marked by the extreme conservatism and hostility of many of its critics and portions of the public toward innovation. Hermann Bahr's comments in 1899 about the Secession painters could be extended to many of the prominent figures in fin-de-siècle Vienna: ''One must know how to make oneself hated. The Viennese respects only those people whom he despises. . . . The Viennese painters will have to show whether or not they know how to be agitators. This is the meaning of our Secession.''[98] As has been amply documented in the case of all the arts, the weight of tradition was often used as a cudgel to strike down those who sought to deviate from the past. Schoenberg's justified feelings of persecution and martyrdom as a result of the hostile reception of his music in Vienna became an important factor in his psychological makeup for the rest of his life. When, in the year after his move to Berlin in 1911, a position at the Academy of Music and Graphic Arts in Vienna was finally offered to him in 1912, he refused, writing: ''I could not live in Vienna. I have not yet got over the things done to me there.''[99] In reaction to the *Skandalkonzert* Berg wrote: ''Yes, that's Vienna! You are so right, dear Herr Schönberg! Your revulsion against Vienna has always been justified and I see—unfortunately too late—how wrong I was to have tried to reconcile you to Vienna, dear Herr Schönberg. It's true! One can't hate this 'city of song' enough!!''[100]

During much of the first quarter of the century, Schoenberg and his school were often associated with the most extreme radicalism and hypermodernity as a result of their works, writings, concert activities, and journalistic accounts. Indeed, the label of the ''Young Viennese School,'' used by Wellesz in 1912, stresses the aspect of generational conflict and youthful revolution associated with other modern movements in Vienna, such as the group of writers known as Die Jungen, the Secession in the visual arts, and still more radical figures like Kokoschka, Loos, and Egon Schiele, as well as Kandinsky and the Blauer Reiter circle in Munich.[101] Writing a decade later in his 1925 biography, Wellesz describes Schoenberg's growing reputation among the younger generation around 1904 who ''were interested in all that was new and out of the ordinary,'' and all ''had a strong dislike of the cut and dried instruction given us at the Conservatories at that time.''[102] Throughout the biography he stresses the revolutionary aspects of Schoenberg's development, describing the period beginning in 1907 as a ''break away from bad tradition'' so that he could ''speak in his own language.''[103] While Wellesz is careful to distinguish Schoenberg from the urge ''*pour épater le bourgeois*'' or from the ''the joy in upheaval and revolutionary activity with which so many young artists seek to intoxicate themselves,'' he claims that from the period of the First Chamber Symphony onward ''he followed the dictates of the voice within and severed all connection with the traditions of the past. This represented the real liberation of his nature from ties that were only an impediment to his development.''[104] A striking sign of this revolutionary image of Schoenberg, and in strong contrast to later accounts of his historical heritage, is the absence of any mention of Brahms as a major influence. When Wellesz looks to history to name a historical precursor for Schoenberg, it is the composer of eccentric madrigals Gesualdo.[105]

The revolutionary reputation of Schoenberg, Berg, and Webern was reinforced in the period after the First World War as their ''expressionistic'' works became better known through such important premieres as *Erwartung, Die glückliche Hand*, and *Wozzeck*. At the same time, it is important to stress that the twelve-tone works only gradually came to the public's attention. *A History of Music* by Charles Villiers Stanford, published in 1925, associates Schoenberg with "what seems to be almost a new type of music—a music which is founded, not on the direct harmonic forms that have come down to us, but on extensions and adaptations of those forms. . . . Among his published works are the *Five Pieces* (for orchestra), the *Kammersymphonie*, the *Sextet* (for strings), and the two *String Quartets* (one with vocal accompaniment)."[106] Weissmann's *Problems of Modern Music* reaches the same verdict: "Schönberg, however, questions all the elements of music with ruthless logic and seeks a new *melos* after ridding himself, as he believes, of every scrap of tradition."[107] In the 1928 historical survey *Die Moderne Musik seit der Romantik*, Hans Mersmann writes similarly, "Arnold Schoenberg is the single greatest revolutionary in music of our time. . . . He breaks all boundaries, destroys all that music previously affirmed."[108]

But the idea of Schoenberg, Berg, and Webern as radicals waging a futile battle against a Vienna "that wholly rejected them" exaggerates their isolation from the public and simplifies the position of the new art movements in Vienna. In his study "Music and Its Public: Habits of Listening and the Crisis of Musical Modernism in Vienna, 1870–1914," Leon Botstein argues that, contrary to the image of Vienna's ingrained conservatism, there was considerable official and popular support for modern art:

> In Vienna before 1907, the "modern" in music, both in new repertoire and interpretation, therefore meant primarily Mahler, Zemlinsky, Schoenberg, and Richard Strauss and a group of less well-known enthusiasts who followed them. The irony was that these musical "moderns" were, like the Secessionists, not on the margin, but in the limelight. Not that there was not a vocal anti-modern sentiment in the press, in the audience, in the conservatory, and at the Ministry of Education and Culture. But as the repeated and ultimately successful attempts by Schoenberg to get appointed to the conservatory between 1909–1912 indicate (and Schoenberg by 1908 was widely considered the most radical innovator), the struggle between progressive and conservative forces in Vienna was an equally matched one, with the moderns enjoying their share of success and recognition.[109]

In the case of Schoenberg, support for this claim could be cited in the considerable attention he received in the press, such as the special edition of *Der Merker* devoted to his works, opportunities for major performances, conducting engagements throughout Europe, and his ability to publish his music and writings, including *Harmonielehre*. Indeed, the *Skandalkonzert* takes on its full significance only when it is viewed in the context of the triumphant premiere of Schoenberg's *Gurrelieder*, which took place a few weeks earlier. Christopher Hailey has discussed the importance of the Vienna opera house as the gathering place of the young radicals in Vienna as a symbol of how, in contrast to modern movements in Italy or Germany, the stability of Viennese musical life provided a foundation for avant-garde experimentation that remained, nevertheless, firmly grounded in the past.[110]

The emphasis on scandal, rejection, and controversy that has shaped accounts of the school's early relationship with Vienna has often proven to be a burden for its subsequent history. Ernst Krenek in 1937 predicted a "thorny path" in the wilderness for the school, writing that the "ear of the masses . . . will naturally revolt for some time to come against the lack of harmony, against the seeming ugliness of modern music . . . and neither Arnold Schoenberg nor his immediate followers will be destined to set foot in the promised land."[111] Yet such statements have often served as a self-fulfilling prophecy, so that today critics still write about Schoenberg, Berg, and Webern against the background of anticipated rejection. To be sure, members of the school to some extent embraced this notion of isolation from the public, which was to be so much a part of the ideology of modernism, and even thematized it in their works with figures such as Moses from *Moses und Aron* or the Man in *Die glückliche Hand.*[112] In a letter from 1911 Berg referred to Schoenberg as a "holy person," divorced from the world: "What meaning can time or things temporal have for you, dearest Herr Schönberg—even sublime moments of suffering—since you have been granted the 'deep deep eternity of all joy'?!"[113] This alienation of the Second Viennese School from life becomes in the writings of Adorno a sign of the ultimate authenticity of their music: the relentless purification of their compositional language results in a music into which "no social function falls—indeed, which even severs the last communication with the listener."[114]

But the tendency to view the three composers as standing apart from the world and isolated from the merely "temporal" has obscured their complex relationships to contemporaneous cultural and social trends. This is nowhere more apparent than in their gradual reorientation to the Viennese musical tradition in the period after the First World War. The revolutionary reputation so bound up with the idea of the Young Viennese School became problematic for the three composers in the 1920s and 1930s as they sought to forge renewed links to the past. Numerous examples could be cited from the writings of all three composers in the interwar years challenging the radical label and arguing for their connections to tradition. This strategy took many forms, such as Berg's guide to *Pelleas und Melisande*, which demonstrated how Schoenberg preserved a classical approach to form, or his "Credo," published in 1930, which compares Schoenberg's historical position to Bach's.[115] Analogies with the First Viennese School became increasingly common in writings about Schoenberg, Berg, and Webern, such as Adolph Weiss's essay on "The Twelve-Tone Series" from the 1937 collection *Schoenberg*, edited by Merle Armitage:

> Members of the Schoenberg school differ widely in their individual application of this technic. Such individuality is ensured by the plasticity of the system. There are those who cannot yet discern the great differences in the works of the Schoenbergians, to whom "in the dark all cats are black." But let them observe the rhythmic construction and the

spiritual content if the fine differences in the harmonic construction are not apparent. Remember that Beethoven, Mozart, Haydn and others used practically the same harmonic formulae, those of the diatonic system.[116]

César Saerchinger's essay "The Truth about Schoenberg" from the same volume similarly uses Mozart as a symbol through which to distance the Second Viennese School from its earlier radicalism. He describes his experience of arriving in Vienna not long after the war determined to seek out Schoenberg and "to acquire the last word in morbid modernity and to breathe the air of musical wickedness." Instead of these images of trespass, he finds a scene of aristocratic calm, "the master surrounded by his pupils—the advance guard of young Viennese composers—on a Sunday afternoon. He waited for outrageous sounds; but all he heard was Mozart. Performances of Mozart quartets, under the pedantically severe surveillance of Schoenberg himself!"[117] Leibowitz develops many of the arguments advanced by the three composers in their own writings to claim that the members of the Schoenberg school "have the right to consider themselves *the most traditional of contemporary composers*."[118] As Webern does in *The Path to the New Music*, Leibowitz structures his book to demonstrate the historical inevitability of both the break with tonality and twelve-tone composition, so that the music of Schoenberg, Berg, and Webern is defined as representing the most complete realization of historical processes inherent in the earliest stages of Western music.

Many factors led to this reawakened interest in the Viennese classical tradition, most importantly the pronounced shifts in Schoenberg's, Berg's, and Webern's own compositional aesthetics toward a renewed interest in traditional forms and genres as a means of ensuring comprehensibility. Their image as isolated radicals also came increasingly into conflict with the realities of their professional successes and ties to the musical establishment as a result of Schoenberg's position at the Prussian Academy of Arts in Berlin, Webern's conducting career, and Berg's new stature with *Wozzeck*. The changing political landscape of the interwar period played an important role as well, as the label of revolutionary became associated with bolshevism and anarchy.[119] Many writings from the school during the 1920s and 1930s stress their allegiance to the German tradition, most explicitly Schoenberg's "National Music" from 1931, in which he traces his lineage from Bach and Mozart through Beethoven, Wagner, and Brahms.[120] The sensitivity of the national issue is touched upon in Wellesz's book, where he deals with the problem of Schoenberg's comparative early success in Holland, England, and Russia. He attributes the opposition Schoenberg faced among German-speaking peoples to their "continuous and great musical past," which made it "more difficult to approach a novelty than nations that have just begun to develop an intensive musical life." Yet he goes on to stress that it is also due to this same musical heritage that Schoenberg only met with deep understanding by small circles in Vienna, Prague, and Berlin, in contrast to the lack of "real penetration into his work" among his adherents in other countries.[121] Perhaps the clearest example of the importance of the political context is Webern's lectures on *The Path to the New Music* from early in 1933, after Hitler's election to the chancellorship. By demonstrating the inevitability of their compositional developments and their links to the tradition of Beethoven and Brahms, Webern tries to refute the label of " 'cultural Bolshevism' . . . given to everything that's going on around Schoenberg, Berg and myself (Krenek too). Imagine what will be destroyed, wiped out, by this hate of culture!"[122]

A further factor affecting every aspect of the definition of the Second Viennese School in the 1920s and 1930s was the explosion of competing movements and schools. Roger Sessions's 1933 essay published in the Armitage collection characterizes the interwar period as a time of crisis due to this "confusion of tongues."[123] Armitage's introductory chapter, "Transition," similarly describes the "multiplicity of contradictions" as evidence of an "uncrystallized age": "Former standards, even the old bulwarks of measurement are gone. It is essentially a time of transition; the world is unresolved. Every element of swift change is manifest. The decline of an older culture, the rise of a new world-form, the insistence of manifold new attitudes, the presence of clashing incongruities, all are irrefutable evidence."[124] The perception of competing movements and schools was much less strongly pronounced in the years before and immediately following the First World War. One sign of this was in the programming of the Society for Private Musical Performances. Consistent with the statement in the prospectus that there would be no "one-sided consideration of any particular 'school,' " concerts included works by Debussy, Ravel, and Stravinsky. Wellesz's 1925 biography similarly demonstrates that divisions that later became very important were not yet in place. Among the composers he cites as showing "tendencies approximating to his" are not only Schoenberg's pupils, but "artists like Busoni, Ravel, and Stravinsky," who all appear "to be striving after some common goal."[125]

Yet with the many slogans and trends circulating in these years around such terms as neoclassicism, polytonality, *Gebrauchsmusik*, and *Neue Sachlichkeit* and with the direct challenges from the younger generation such as Krenek, Hindemith, and Weill, it became necessary to stake out a clearly defined party platform.[126] The disappearance of the earlier tolerance is evident in Webern's *Path to the New Music*, where the new music is defined as twelve-tone composition, "for everything else is at best somewhere near this technique, or is consciously opposed to it and thus uses a style we don't have to examine further, since it doesn't get beyond what was discovered by post-classical music, and only manages to do it badly. The greatest strides have been made by the very music, the very style, that Schoenberg introduced and that his pupils continued."[127] As this passage suggests, part of the strong emphasis noted earlier on the twelve-tone technique in writings by Schoenberg, Berg, and Webern was its importance in differentiating those who did and did not belong to the school.

Schoenberg's Three Satires, Op. 28 (1926), even more explicitly defines the boundaries between his school and the "quasi-tonalists" and those who "nibble at dissonance" without drawing the full conclusions; "those who allege to aspire to 'a return to . . . ' "; folklorists; and "all ' . . . ists,' in whom I can see only mannerists."[128] Leibowitz, to cite only an extreme example from later writers, similarly stresses the independence of Schoenberg, Berg, and Webern from all other movements. Stravinsky is derided for never escaping the limitations of "obsolete ideas," and Bartók and Milhaud represent a "dead end," while the neoclassicists "merely tried to warm up a few musical left-overs."[129]

That Schoenberg sought in effect to position his school against all other contemporary trends clarifies why it became so important to lay claim to the one true path of the Viennese classical tradition. Thus Armitage writes that "out of diversity of idioms, the contradictions, and the false starts of modern music, emerges Schoenberg" standing apart as a beacon of stability against the "ruffled surface waves of his generation." In marked contrast to his earlier reputation as the wild man of music, Schoenberg becomes the symbol of classical perfection and restraint: "The beauty of Schoenberg's music is austere. Its scholarly background, its mathematical, constellation-like form, its startling abridgments, its penetration."[130] Using similar language, Leibowitz compares the rejection of the "difficult path of Schoenberg" by many musicians and the public to the turn away from the "seriousness, austerity and complexity of Bach and Rameau," resulting in the "eyesore" of the *style galant* with its dependence on a number of "pleasant and sterile formulae," a detour that was not corrected until the later works of Mozart and Haydn. He identifies the same "predilection for facility and compromise" in "the *style galant* of our day—a style which characterizes most of our composers, from Stravinsky and Hindemith down to those of the lowest rank, many of whom are tremendously successful."[131]

Yet just as the image of youthful rebellion proved a liability for Schoenberg, Berg, and Webern, the establishment of such strong ties to the Viennese tradition and such impermeable boundaries with contemporaneous movements has contributed to the caricature of the Second Viennese School as old-fashioned and out of touch with the modern world. The rejection of Schoenberg's twelve-tone works by the post–Second World War avant-garde, the polarity of Schoenberg and Stravinsky, the notion of a great divide between all three composers and mass culture, and many other deeply ingrained habits of thought can be traced to this construction of the Second Viennese School.

There is no doubt that Schoenberg, Berg, and Webern belong together in any account of music in the twentieth century, but we must be aware of how the notion of the Second Viennese School has shaped the writing of history as well as the historical developments themselves. It is time for the conception of the school represented by the cover of the *New Grove* volume to be rethought. By filling in the historical background around the isolated figures and adding new faces to the group portrait, we might lose the image of "the center of gravity

. . . encircled by shining satellites,'' but we will more clearly show the extent to which the Second Viennese School is a complex and shifting historical construct that has been formed and contested throughout the century.

NOTES

I am grateful to Bryan Simms and Klaus Kropfinger for their careful readings of this chapter and to Matthew Bietz for his help in assembling the source materials.

1. Oliver Neighbour, Paul Griffiths, and George Perle, *The New Grove Second Viennese School* (New York: W. W. Norton & Company, 1983).

2. Egon Wellesz, ''Schönberg et la jeune ecole viennoise,'' *Société internationale de musique* 8, no. 3 (1912–13): 21–26. An article from the same year by Hugo Fleischmann in the *Neue Zeitschrift für Musik* challenges the use of the term ''Jung Wiener Schule'' for Schoenberg and his students. Hugo Robert Fleischmann, ''Die Jung Wiener Schule (Eine musikalische Zeitfrage),'' *Neue Zeitschrift für Musik* 79, no. 39 (26 September 1912): 539–40.

3. See, for example, ''The School of Vienna,'' in *Larousse Encyclopedia of Music*, ed. Geoffrey Hindley (Secaucus, NJ: Chartwell Books, 1971, 380: ''The composers of the modern school of Vienna like those of the classical school, certainly form a well-defined group with shared aims, but their inspiration and achievements were quite different from, and their music as individual as those of their great predecessors, Haydn, Mozart, and Beethoven.''

4. *Oxford Dictionary of Music*, 2nd ed., ed. Michael Kennedy (Oxford and New York: Oxford University Press, 1994), 795.

5. Norman Lebrecht, *The Companion to 20th-Century Music* (New York: Simon & Schuster, 1992), 315. For controversies around the definition of the ''first Viennese School,'' see ''Wiener Schule'' in *Das grosse Lexikon der Musik*, ed. Marc Honegger and Günther Massenkeil, vol. 8 (Freiburg: Herder, 1982), and Reinhold Brinkmann, ''Einleitung am Rande,'' in *Die Wiener Schule heute*, ed. Carl Dahlhaus, Veröffentlichungen des Instituts für Neue Musik und Musikerziehung, Darmstadt, vol. 24 (Mainz: Schott, 1983), 12–13.

6. Schoenberg, ''The Blessing of the Dressing,'' in *Style and Idea: Selected Writings of Arnold Schoenberg*, ed. Leonard Stein, trans. Leo Black (Berkeley and Los Angeles: University of California Press, 1984), 386.

7. The origins and significance of the proliferation of ''schools'' in twentieth-century music merit further consideration. Important existing studies include Susan C. Cook, *Opera for a New Republic: The Zeitopern of Krenek, Weill, and Hindemith* (Ann Arbor: UMI Research Press, 1988); Stephen Hinton, *The Idea of* Gebrauchsmusik: *A Study of Musical Aesthetics in the Weimar Republic (1919–1933) with Particular Reference to the Works of Paul Hindemith* (New York: Garland, 1989); and Scott Messing, *Neoclassicism in Music, from the Genesis of the Concept through the Schoenberg/Stravinsky Polemic* (Ann Arbor: UMI Research Press, 1988).

8. Important sources for this study include Brinkmann, ''Einleitung am Rande''; Frank Schneider, ''Die Wiener Schule als musikgeschichtliche Provokation,'' *Beiträge zur Musikwissenschaft* 32 (1990): 1–6; Otto Kolleritsch, ''Die Zweite Wiener Schule und Beethoven,'' in *Beethoven und die Zweite Weiner Schule*, ed. Otto Kolleritsch, Studien

zur Wertungsforschung, vol. 25 (Vienna: Universal Edition, 1992), 213–220; and the special issue devoted to the Viennese School of the *Österreichische Musikzeitschrift* 16 (1961). For further commentary on the early formation of the idea of a Schoenberg school, as well as extensive documentation of the reception of Schoenberg's music in Germany before the First World War, see Martin Thrun, *Neue Musik im deutschen Musikleben bis 1933* (Bonn: Orpheus Verlag, 1995), 85–260.

9. Berg's *Wozzeck* lecture is reprinted in Douglas Jarman, *Alban Berg: ''Wozzeck,''* Cambridge Opera Handbooks (Cambridge: Cambridge University Press, 1989), 154.

10. Arnold Schoenberg, cited and discussed in Brinkmann, ''Einleitung am Rande,'' 9 (my translation).

11. Carl Dahlhaus, ''Schoenberg's Poetics of Music,'' in *Schoenberg and the New Music*, trans. Derrick Puffett and Alfred Clayton (Cambridge: Cambridge University Press, 1987), 74–75.

12. Arnold Schoenberg, letter of 1 June, 1938, Schoenberg Collection, Library of Congress. Cited with permission of Lawrence Schoenberg.

13. *Der Merker* 2, no. 17 (June 1911). An issue devoted to a single composer was very rare for the journal and attests the degree of attention that Schoenberg had attracted by this time.

14. *Arnold Schönberg in höchster Verehrung von Schülern und Freunden* (Munich: R. Piper Verlag, 1912; reprint ed., Wels, Austria: Duckerei Welsermühl, 1980).

15. *Arnold Schönberg zum fünfzigsten Geburtstage 13. September 1924*, Sonderheft der *Musikblätter des Anbruch* (Vienna: Universal Edition, 1924), 272 (my translation).

16. Arnold Schoenberg, ''How One Becomes Lonely,'' in *Style and Idea*, 41.

17. Joan Allen Smith, *Schoenberg and His Circle: A Viennese Portrait* (New York: Schirmer Books, 1986), 36.

18. Schoenberg, ''How One Becomes Lonely,'' 41. It was perhaps in reaction to such charges that Schoenberg penned these lines in 1923 in the short essay ''The Young and I'': ''Even as a stimulus I am greatly overrated. My pupils can confirm that I tend rather to discourage. And, in fact, of all the very many who learned from me, as is now known even elsewhere, only three have become composers. All the others understand just enough to make it impossible to compose as badly as one must in order to be a modern master.'' *Style and Idea*, 93.

19. Otto Besch, ''Arnold Schönberg, der Mann der Zukunft,'' *Allgemeine Musik-Zeitung* 39, no. 12 (1912): 309.

20. Adolf Weissmann, *The Problems of Modern Music*, trans. M. M. Bozman (1925; reprint ed., Westport, CT: Hyperion Press, 1979), 212.

21. Ibid.

22. Hugo Leichtentritt, *Music, History, and Ideas* (Cambridge, MA: Harvard University Press, 1958), 257–58.

23. Martin Vogel, *Schönberg und die Folgen: Die Irrwege der neuen Musik*, vol. 1, *Schönberg* (Bonn: Verlag für systematische Musikwissenschaft, 1984), 9. See also the exchange of letters with Berg from 1913 about claims that Schoenberg was financially dependent on his students in Juliane Brand, Christopher Hailey, and Donald Harris, eds. and trans., *The Berg-Schoenberg Correspondence: Selected Letters* (New York: Norton, 1987), 166–73.

24. René Leibowitz, *Schoenberg and His School: The Contemporary Stage of the Language of Music*, trans. Dika Newlin (New York: Philosophical Library, 1949, [reprint, New York: Da Capo Press, 1979], xvi.

25. Arnold Schoenberg, "The Task of the Teacher," in *Style and Idea*, 389. See Smith, *Schoenberg and His Circle*, for useful biographical notes on many of these figures, as well as important material on the differences in Schoenberg's approach to teaching at different stages of his life. For more on the impact of Schoenberg as a teacher, see Walter Szmolyan, "Das Fortwirken der Wiener Schule in der Österreichischen Gegenwartsmusik," in *Bericht über den 2. Kongreß der Internationalen Schönberg-Gesellschaft. Die Wiener Schule in der Musikgeschichte des 20. Jahrhunderts*, ed. Rudolf Stephan and Sigrid Wiesmann (Vienna: Verlag Elisabeth Lafite, 1986), 213–18; Harald Kaufmann, "Die zweite Generation," *Österreichische Musikzeitschrift* 16 (1961): 290–96; Brinkmann, "Einleitung am Rande," 13; Mathias Hansen, "Arnold Schoenberg und seine Berliner Schüler," *Bericht über die 2. Kongreß der Internationalen Schönberg-Gesellschaft*, 219; Frank Schneider, "Von Gestern auf Heute: Die Wiener Schule im Schaffen von Komponisten der DDR," *Bericht über die 2. Kongreß der Internationalen Schönberg-Gesellschaft*, 122–28.

26. Schoenberg, "The Task of the Teacher," 390.

27. Willi Reich, *Schoenberg: A Critical Biography*, trans. Leo Black (New York: Da Capo Press, 1981), 29.

28. Oliver Neighbour writes, "Naturally he took what steps he could to make up for his lack of formal musical training, but neither his haphazard reading, nor other odd crumbs of instruction (he is known, for instance, to have heard Bruckner lecture at the academy), nor even Zemlinsky's constant help, could alter his feeling that he never profited from what he was taught unless he had already discovered it for himself: tuition could at best only awaken him to his own knowledge." "Arnold Schoenberg," *The New Grove Second Viennese School*, 19.

29. The image of the satellite is strikingly anticipated in the 1908 "Testamentsentwurf" (Sketch of a will), where he compares the activities of merely clever and talented artists to an attempt to reach heaven by means of an airship with an electrical guide that can only fly in a circle around a tower. Archives of the Arnold Schönberg Center, Vienna.

30. Arnold Schoenberg, *Theory of Harmony*, trans. Roy E. Carter (Berkeley: University of California Press, 1978), 1.

31. Theodor Adorno, "Berg and Webern: Schönberg's Heirs," *Modern Music* 8 (1931): 30. Joan Allen Smith formulates this very well: "It is one of the ambiguities of Schoenberg's nature that he should be sensitive to the inner direction of his students and yet dictatorial about their work and lives to the point that even his closest disciples felt the need to escape him in order to complete their work free of his influence. This conflict became even more apparent with the announcement of the twelve-tone method. Schoenberg wanted to take total credit for the method but expected even Berg and Webern, now mature composers, to adopt it. That these composers were willing and able to do so without violence to their own creative needs is tribute both to their admiration for Schoenberg and the excellence of the training that they received from him." Smith, *Schoenberg and His Circle*, 137.

32. Arnold Schoenberg, "Anton Webern: *Klangfarbenmelodie*," in *Style and Idea*, 484.

33. Arnold Schoenberg, "Attempt at a Diary," trans. Anita Luginbühl, *Journal of the Arnold Schoenberg Institute* 9, no. 1 (1986): 39.

34. Arnold Schoenberg, "Problems in Teaching Art," in *Style and Idea*, 366.

35. Schoenberg, "Attempt at a Diary," 36.

36. Schoenberg, *Theory of Harmony*, 3.

37. Wellesz, "Schönberg et la jeune école viennoise," 26.

38. Fleischmann, "Die Jung Wiener Schule (Eine musikalische Zeitfrage)," 539.

39. Schoenberg, *Theory of Harmony*, 3.

40. Ibid., 407.

41. For further repercussions of this event on the relationship between Berg and Schoenberg, see Brand, Hailey, and Harris, *Berg-Schoenberg Correspondence*, 166–72.

42. Indeed, Rudolf Stephan has suggested that the idea of a "school" belongs above all to the time of the Society for Private Musical Performances (1918–22). See "Wiener Schule" in *Das grosse Lexikon der Musik*, 364.

43. Arnold Schoenberg, "Alban Berg" (2), in *Style and Idea*, 475.

44. Anton Webern, *The Path to the New Music*, ed. Willi Reich, trans. Leo Black (Vienna: Universal Edition, 1975), 44.

45. Ibid., 48.

46. Berg's letter is reprinted in Brand, Hailey, and Harris, *Berg-Schoenberg Correspondence*, 334–37.

47. Adorno's many writings, including *Philosophy of Modern Music*, are, of course, fundamental to the creation of the idea of the Second Viennese School. For an interesting commentary on Adorno's relationship to the school, see Brinkmann, "Einleitung am Rande," 14–15. For more on the importance of the school for his philosophical writings in general, see Max Paddison, *Adorno's Aesthetics of Music* (Cambridge: Cambridge University Press, 1993), 49–52.

48. Adorno, "Berg and Webern: Schönberg's Heirs," 29–38.

49. Ibid., 30.

50. Ibid., 29. See also Carl Dahlhaus, "Developing Variation," in *Schoenberg and the New Music*, 80.

51. Adorno, "Berg and Webern: Schönberg's Heirs," 31.

52. Ibid., 32, 35.

53. Ibid., 38.

54. Leibowitz, *Schoenberg and His School*, 61.

55. Ibid., xv.

56. There are clear connections between this image and the important iconographical symbol of three heads arranged to create an allegory of past, present, and future, as, for example, in Titian's *Allegory of Prudence*. See Erwin Panofsky, *Meaning in the Visual Arts* (New York: Doubleday, 1955), 146–48. I owe special thanks to Klaus Kropfinger for pointing out this relationship.

57. Leibowitz, *Schoenberg and His School*, 190.

58. Eric Salzman, *Twentieth-Century Music: An Introduction*, 3rd ed. (Englewood Cliffs, NJ: Prentice Hall, 1988), 38.

59. Hans Mersmann, *Die Moderne Musik seit der Romantik*, vol. 5 of *Handbuch der Musikwissenschaft*, ed. Ernest Bücken (Potsdam: Akademische Verlagsgesellschaft Athenaion, 1928), 144–47.

60. Stephan makes this point in "Wiener Schule," in *Das grosse Lexikon der Musik*, 364.

61. See Brinkmann, "Einleitung am Rande," 10–11.

62. Brand, Hailey, and Harris, *Berg-Schoenberg Correspondence*, 260.

63. Leibowitz, *Schoenberg and His School*, 186.

64. Ibid., 210.

65. Ibid., 266.

66. Dahlhaus, ''Schoenberg's Poetics of Music,'' 74.

67. ''Weiner Schule,'' *Brockhaus Riemann Musiklexikon*, ed. Carl Dahlhaus and Hans Heinrich Eggebrecht (Wiesbaden:F. A. Brockhaus, 1979), 702 (my translation).

68. Schoenberg, *Theory of Harmony*, 12.

69. Berg, lecture on *Wozzeck*, Reprinted in Jarman, *Alban Berg: Wozzeck*, 154.

70. Arnold Schoenberg, ''Composition with Twelve Tones,'' in *Style and Idea*, 217.

71. Schoenberg, *Structural Functions of Harmony*, rev. ed. (New York: W. W. Norton & Co., 1969), 193–94.

72. Webern, *Path to the New Music*, 44.

73. Ibid., 41.

74. Leichtentritt, *Music, History, and Ideas*, 257.

75. William Thomson, *Schoenberg's Error* (Philadelphia: University of Pennsylvania Press, 1991), 36–37. Besch, ''Arnold Schönberg, der Mann der Zukunft,'' 309–10.

76. Schoenberg, ''Heart and Brain in Music,'' in *Style and Idea*, 54.

77. Weissmann, *Problems of Modern Music*, 182–83.

78. Ibid., 176.

79. Leichtentritt, *Music, History, and Ideas*, 261.

80. Schoenberg, *Theory of Harmony*, 411.

81. Schoenberg, ''Blessing of the Dressing,'' 386.

82. Weissmann, *Problems of Modern Music*, 182–83.

83. Leichtentritt, *Music, History, and Ideas*, 258.

84. James Francis Cooke, *Standard History of Music* (Philadelphia: Theodore Presser, 1936), 268.

85. Arnold Schoenberg, ''My Evolution,'' in *Style and Idea*, 91–92.

86. Schoenberg, ''Composition with Twelve Tones,'' 244–45.

87. See especially Schoenberg, ''Composition with Twelve Tones,'' 214–45.

88. Arnold Schoenberg, ''On Revient Toujours,'' in *Style and Idea*, 108–9.

89. Erich Steinhard, ''Die Kunst Arnold Schönbergs,'' *Neue Musik-Zeitung* 33 (1912): 376.

90. Harry T. Finck, ''The Musical Messiah or Satan,'' *Nation* 101 (1915): 635.

91. See Schoenberg, ''Composition with Twelve Tones,'' 216–18.

92. Webern, *Path to the New Music*, 53–54.

93. Gyorgi Ligeti, ''Metamorphosis of Musical Form,'' *Die Reihe* (1960) 5–19. See also Klaus Kropfinger, '' 'Schoenberg est mort'?—Rückfragen an einer Paradigma,'' in *Über Musik im Bilde*, ed. Bodo Bischoff, Andreas Eichhorn; Thomas Gerlich, and Ulrich Siebert (Köln: Verlag Dohr, 1995): 2: 535–56.

94. Hartmut Krones, ''Wiener Symbolik? Zur musiksemantischen Traditionen in den beiden Wiener Schulen,'' *Beethoven und die Zweite Wiener Schule*, 51–79.

95. *Arnold Schoenberg Letters*, ed. Erwin Stein, trans. Eithne Wilkins and Ernst Kaiser (Berkeley and Los Angeles: University of California Press, 1987), 29.

96. Ibid., 104.

97. Ibid., 277.

98. Hermann Bahr, quoted in Peter Selz, *German Expressionist Painting* (Berkeley: University of California Press, 1974), 149.

99. Stein, *Arnold Schoenberg Letters*, 32.

100. Brand, Hailey, and Harris, *Berg-Schoenberg Correspondence*, 170.

101. See subsequent chapters in this volume and Carl E. Schorske, *Fin-de-Siècle Vienna: Politics and Culture* (New York: Vintage Books, 1981). An article from the same

year by Hugo Fleischmann in the *Neue Zeitschrift für Musik* challenges the use of the term "Jung Wiener Schule" for Schoenberg and his students, a term that he says has lost its original harmless status and has almost become a battle cry. Fleischmann argues that the term "Young Viennese School" is better reserved for the generation of young composers such as Richard Stöhr, Alexander Zemlinsky, Franz Schreker, Karl Weigl, and Walter Klein. While he includes Schoenberg in this group, calling him the "banner carrier of modernist music," he proposes that the group of his pupils are better called "Schönbergianer" and leaves it to the future to bestow on them the appropriate name. Fleischmann, "Die Jung Wiener Schule (Eine musikalische Zeitfrage)," 539–40.

102. Egon Wellesz, *Arnold Schönberg*, trans. W. H. Kerridge (New York: E. P. Dutton, 1925; reprint, New York: Da Capo, 1969), 20.

103. Ibid., 24.

104. Ibid., 51, 106.

105. Ibid., 115.

106. Charles Villiers Stanford, *A History of Music* (New York: Macmillan, 1925), 353–54.

107. Weissmann, *Problems of Modern Music*, 178.

108. Mersmann, *Moderne Musik seit der Romantik*, 132 (my translation).

109. Leon Botstein, "Music and Its Public: Habits of Listening and the Crisis of Musical Modernism in Vienna, 1870–1914" (Ph.D. diss., Harvard University, 1985), 1078–79.

110. Christopher Hailey, "Die Vierte Galerie: Voraussetzungen für die Wiener Avantgarde um 1910," in *Bericht über die 2. Kongreß der Internationalen Schönberg-Gesellschaft*; 242–47.

111. Ernst Krenek, "Arnold Schoenberg," in *Schoenberg*, ed. Merle Armitage (1937; reprint, Freeport NY: Books for Libraries Press, 1971), 87.

112. See Andreas Huyssen, *After the Great Divide: Modernism, Mass Culture, Postmodernism* (Bloomington: Indiana University Press, 1986), 53–54.

113. Brand, Hailey, and Harris, *Berg-Schoenberg Correspondence*, 8.

114. Theodor Adorno, quoted in Paddison, *Adorno's Aesthetics of Music*, 105.

115. Alban Berg, "Credo," *Die Musik* 22, no. 4 (1930): 264–65.

116. Adolph Weiss, "The Twelve-Tone Series," in *Schoenberg*, ed. Armitage, 76–77.

117. César Saerchinger, "The Truth about Schoenberg," in *Schoenberg*, ed. Armitage, 90–91.

118. Leibowitz, *Schoenberg and His School*, 264. Emphasis in the original.

119. For more on the political aspects of neoclassicism, see Richard Taruskin, "Back to Whom? Neoclassicism as Ideology," *19th Century Music* 16 (1993): 286–302.

120 Arnold Schoenberg, "National Music," in *Style and Idea*, 174.

121. Wellesz, *Arnold Schönberg*, 7.

122. Webern, *Path to the New Music*, 19.

123. Roger Sessions, "Music in Crisis," in *Schoenberg*, ed. Armitage, 11.

124. Merle Armitage, "Transition," in *Schoenberg*, ed. Armitage, 1.

125. Wellesz, *Arnold Schönberg*, 151.

126. See Messing, *Neoclassicism in Music*, Cook, *Opera for a New Republic*, and Schneider, "Wiener Schule als musikgeschichtliche Provokation," 4.

127. Webern, *Path to the New Music*, 32.

128. Arnold Schoenberg, cited and discussed in Messing, *Neoclassicism in Music*, 144.

129. Leibowitz, *Schoenberg and His School*, 71.

130. Armitage, "Transition," 5.

131. Leibowitz, *Schoenberg and His School*, 287–88.

2 MUSICAL CULTURE IN VIENNA AT THE TURN OF THE TWENTIETH CENTURY

Margaret Notley

Even the barest recitation of facts hints at an accelerating transformation of Vienna and its art worlds toward the end of the 1890s. The rivalry between Anton Bruckner and Johannes Brahms came to an end with the deaths of the former in October 1896 and the latter in April 1897. In the spring of 1897, forty members of the city's Künstlerhaus (Artists' House) resigned and formed a new association, the Secession, an instantaneous emblem of modernism to be invoked in discussions of new musical trends. After having been elected on a Christian Social platform that blended populism and anti-Semitism with revitalized Catholicism, Karl Lueger took office as mayor of Vienna that same spring, bringing to an end three decades of Liberal political domination in the city. In a contradiction characteristic of the time and place, the Jew Gustav Mahler assumed leadership of Vienna's preeminent cultural institution, the Hofoper (Court Opera), six months later.

The final two facts may suggest that the crucible of political crisis conditioned the changes taking place in Viennese culture, as Carl E. Schorske has observed,[1] but also that politics and culture could interact at cross-purposes: while avowed anti-Semites had gained control of the city government, Jews dominated Vienna's cultural life more than ever. There were other paradoxes. In Vienna, as elsewhere in Europe, the advent of modernism was linked with the beginning of mass democracy and the waning of Liberal—that is, classic middle-class—culture. Particularly explosive strains of mass politics had developed in Vienna. But elements of the Liberal *Weltanschauung* persisted well after the Liberal party had faded, and the institutions that supported Liberal musical culture in the city proved unusually resistant to change.

Anton Webern (1883–1945). Courtesy of the Arnold Schoenberg Institute.

During the final two decades of the nineteenth century, Wagnerism had been a broadly influential force, its disciples seeking to transform Viennese politics and culture. The writings and music of Richard Wagner had served as partial inspiration for the style and substance of the major new parties on both the right and left that coalesced out of the chaotic anti-Liberal politics in the 1880s, and the city's music circles had reflected the polarization between the Liberals and their enemies. After Wagner's death in 1883, Bruckner became the symbolic leader of Viennese Wagnerism. The ensuing conflict between the factions around him and Brahms acquired a strong political cast: Brahms was closely connected with the Liberal establishment under siege, whereas Bruckner attracted many disciples who belonged to the insurgent parties, especially those on the right.[2]

"The politics of Wagnerism" eventually triumphed in 1897.[3] Yet, for example, the Vienna Conservatory, perhaps the most backward of the city's musical institutions, still excluded Wagner's technical innovations as a composer from consideration in the classroom. Even after the political eclipse of the Liberals, the epigonous classicism seen by some as the artistic expression of Liberalism continued to hold sway at the Conservatory, despite the fact that Brahms was no longer around to validate the classicizing style through his transmutations of it. The Viennese classical heritage itself might appear to have fostered inferior academic art in the city where the classical composers had flourished, but the Wagnerites, too, claimed that legacy as their own, for it gave rise to a wide range of responses and interpretations in Vienna.

The character of turn-of-the-century musical culture was thus overdetermined by various and sometimes conflicting factors: a residue of Liberal assumptions, institutional conservatism, Wagnerian infusions into local politics and art, and the power of the native classical tradition. While the factionalism of the previous decades also continued to mark Viennese musical life, many of those active in music circles would begin to see a need to renounce the cliquishness of the past in a gradual adjustment to the sociopolitical sea change and nascent modernism of the city's present.

THE POLITICAL SITUATION

During the final two decades of the nineteenth century, activists of various stripes had called into question basic beliefs and privileges of the Liberals: their faith in reason and progress, their economic power, and their cultural elitism. The Liberal party represented the interests of a minority, the city's *Bildungsbürgertum* (the educated, culturally formed middle and upper-middle classes), and had stayed in power in Vienna by denying the vote to the lower-middle and working classes. The essential political reality in late-nineteenth-century Vienna was the transition toward universal male suffrage that enabled an effective challenge to Liberal hegemony.

From the welter of anti-Liberal politics emerged three parties that would remain important into the Austrian Republic after the First World War: Lueger's

Christian Socials, the Pan-Germans, and the Social Democrats. Adam Wandruszka has observed that "the further one traces back the pedigrees of the three camps the more intimate become the points of contact and mutual entanglement of the movements and their leading personalities, until one finally finds the 'founding fathers' of all three camps—and thus of Austrian party and domestic history in the 20th century—gathered together in a single circle around the young Georg von Schönerer."[4] Thus Lueger and also the future Social Democratic leaders Viktor Adler, Heinrich Friedjung, and Engelbert Pernerstorfer had originally been acolytes of Schönerer and his embryonic Pan-Germanism. Anti-Semitism, populist politics, and jingoistic pride in German culture—all supported and in part inspired by Wagner's writings—had bound the early group together. It eventually split over the first issue. Although most Viennese Jews, like most Viennese Gentiles, belonged to the city's desperately poor lowest classes, widely held stereotypes connected Jews with capitalism and Liberalism. For Adler, Friedjung, and Pernerstorfer, anti-Semitism meant anticapitalism and anti-Liberalism: they framed their bias in cultural terms (the first two men were themselves Jewish). The circle began to break up after Schönerer declared the racial basis of his own prejudice in the early 1880s;[5] the left-wing Social Democrats and right-wing Christian Socials both became formal parties in 1889.

The anti-Semitism that formed a fundamental part of Wagnerism could be bent in several directions, and Wagnerism was otherwise subject to a variety of emphases and renderings. While Wagnerian ideas were central to the Pan-German outlook, the party did not develop a comprehensive cultural program as the Social Democrats would later do, but put all of its energy instead into rabble-rousing politics. What Lueger retained from his association with the early group around Schönerer seems to have been precisely the new, emotionally manipulative rhetorical style suitable for addressing the masses, the "politics in a sharper key" that Friedjung and Pernerstorfer had envisioned under the influence of ideas from Wagner and Friedrich Nietzsche.[6]

Certainly, Lueger's anti-Semitism, unlike that of Schönerer, has most often been interpreted as a matter of expediency rather than personal bias, a pragmatic tool that he adopted to appeal to a new group of voters, the lower-middle class, by exploiting its resentment toward the philo-Semitic Liberals.[7] The conduct of Vienna's affairs by the Christian Social majority in the early twentieth century, moreover, has been seen as not sharply different from that by the Liberals.[8] The fact remains that Lueger was the first European mayor elected as an open anti-Semite and that his rhetoric helped create a climate in which the aggressive expression of prejudice became acceptable: in the years around the turn of the century racial anti-Semitism gained increasing currency in Vienna, as did the equally intense venting of antipathy toward the Slavs, for the Austrian half of the empire, of course, included regions later incorporated into Italy, Poland, the former Yugoslavia, and the Czech Republic. (Lueger also played the German nationalist card when a political strategy appeared to call for it.)[9]

On 6 April 1897—during, it is clear, a most eventful spring—the Austrian premier, Count Kasimir Badeni, sparked a crisis by decreeing that the Czech and German languages would have the same status in Bohemian public life and in official communications between Bohemia and Vienna. The justness and common sense of such a measure may seem self-evident, but Badeni enacted it abruptly, which had the unfortunate effect of invigorating Schönerer's Pan-German movement, radically anti-Slavic as well as anti-Semitic.[10] Although Badeni resigned in November 1897, to be succeeded eventually by the much more skillful and diplomatic Count Ernst von Koerber in 1900, the Pan-Germans continued to gain adherents during the first years of the twentieth century and to stir up trouble well after their numbers had begun to decline.

At times the turn-of-the-century political turmoil caused by the problems of the multinational empire and the tensions between Jews and anti-Semites spilled over directly into Vienna's musical life. Mahler had had difficulty obtaining a position in the city because of anti-Semitism[11] and then, as director of the Hofoper, had to endure endless attacks couched in explicitly racial terms, especially during the few years (1898–1901) in which he also conducted the Vienna Philharmonic. His decision in the fall of 1897 to stage Bedřich Smetana's *Dalibor*, an opera associated by some with Czech nationalism, provoked particular outcries by German supremacists.[12] Even in 1900 a critic felt compelled to note that the Philharmonic's performance of Antonín Dvořák's symphonic poem *Holoubek* (The wild dove*) could "arouse only divided sympathies in the present political situation" because the work's "artlessly charming melodic style" sounded "unadulteratedly Czech."[13]

The Christian Socials generally took little interest in cultural matters; nevertheless, they could not have approved of Mahler's prominence in the city's music world. In January 1899 the Philharmonic proposed a performance to benefit the many needy people in Vienna, the projected site for the concert being an auditorium in the City Hall. The Viennese daily *Neue freie Presse* reported that the City Council refused to approve the concert if it were to be conducted by Mahler:

> A festive concert in City Hall under Mahler would have been an official recognition by the municipality that this conductor is a splendid artist, and that was impossible for the present majority in the City Council. . . . Mr. Mahler was thus not found worthy of bestowing a plentiful revenue upon Vienna's poor.[14]

As a party, the Christian Socials restricted their own work in "highbrow" culture to such ventures as the unofficial backing of a *völkisch* (populist, nationalistic, anti-Semitic) theater. This enterprise in so-called Aryan theater lasted only from 1898 to 1903, proving aesthetically as well as politically controversial; the building erected for it, the Kaiserjubiläums-Stadttheater, thereafter housed the Volksoper in existence to this day.[15]

While Lueger's Christian Social party drew support from the recently enfranchised lower-middle class, the Social Democrats represented the interests of the workers, who did not enjoy the right to vote until 1907. Like the Liberalism in decline by then (1889, when the party came into existence), Social Democracy held as basic principles Enlightenment beliefs in reason and equality before the law (and they took the latter more seriously, advocating the franchise not only for working-class men, but also for women of all classes). In contrast to the Christian Social party, Austrian Social Democracy stressed the connection between politics and art, no doubt because such significant figures in the party as Adler and Pernerstorfer remained ardently committed to both Wagner's ideas and his music.[16] This emphasis made the issue of *Volksconcerte*, concerts (especially symphonic concerts) with tickets set at prices that most could afford, centrally important for the Social Democrats. Not one to shy away from controversy, Mahler made no secret of his sympathy for the workers' party,[17] as well as his allegiance to the more broadly supported cause of *Volksconcerte*.

If their view that politics and art went together gave a theatrical tinge to the political conduct of the Social Democrats that was alien to the sobersided style of the Liberals, they still constituted the most natural heirs to the Liberals among the new parties. Through their advocacy of *Volksconcerte*, furthermore, the Social Democrats showed that they neither questioned the fundamental merit of the *Bildung* cherished by the Liberals nor rejected the great musical creations of nineteenth-century middle-class culture. Because of the Wagnerian influence, however, they conceived *Bildung* as less a matter of intellect than of emotion, an education of the soul, and, of course, they wished to extend this privilege to more of the people. Social Democracy, like Liberalism, offered a totalizing *Weltanschauung*, but one formulated more consciously and programmatically. Although the Social Democrats did not gain control of the government until after the First World War, they began to prepare for a utopian future in 1905 by inaugurating the Arbeiter-Symphoniekonzerte (Workers' Symphonic Concerts).

THE VIENNESE MUSIC CRITICS

In an essay of 1946, Schoenberg reminisced about the expertise shared by musicians in the Vienna of the 1890s:

> In my youth, living in the proximity of Brahms, it was customary that a musician, when he heard a composition for the first time, observed its construction, was able to follow the elaboration and derivation of its themes and its modulations, and could recognize the number of voices in canons and the presence of the theme in a variation. . . . That is what music critics like Hanslick, Kalbeck, Heuberger and Speidel and amateurs like the renowned physician Billroth were able to do.[18]

While Schoenberg used this aside as part of an argument in favor of "idea" over "style," he also in this passage implicitly allied himself with Brahms's circle, which included Theodor Billroth and a group of Liberal critics with similar tastes, the defenders of absoluteness and logic in music, the latter loosely exemplified by the techniques mentioned in the passage. All four critics listed by Schoenberg had opposed Wagner, the perceived enemy of absolute music, and all except Ludwig Speidel had written derisively about Bruckner; Speidel, earlier a friend and admirer of Brahms, had turned against him and had become an advocate for Bruckner's music in the 1880s.

Although Speidel is an important exception, support in Vienna for the illogical progressivist Bruckner and the logical classicist Brahms had tended, as already noted, to break down along political lines. Because of his musical proclivities, his ties to such elite Viennese cultural institutions as the Philharmonic and the Gesellschaft der Musikfreunde (Society of Friends of Music), and his friendships with establishment critics and other members of Vienna's *Bildungsbürgertum*, Brahms had come to be seen in the city as not just a Liberal, but a virtual Jew as well; after Wagner's death in 1883, members of the anti-Semitic right-wing parties had promoted Bruckner as an archetypal "German" (specifically non-Jewish) composer.[19] With other key events in the late 1890s, the deaths of Brahms and Bruckner themselves changed the configuration of the city's musical life, with Mahler now at the very center of it. In the altered cultural and political climate Mahler was controversial three times over: as an ethnic Jew in an important public position, as a supporter of the opposition party, and as a new kind of musical progressivist.

Schoenberg's mid-twentieth-century comments are subject to various interpretations, but in any case they raise intriguing questions. We know that Eduard Hanslick and Brahms himself had advocated Mahler's appointment to the Hofoper[20] and that Richard Heuberger had recognized Schoenberg's talents in the mid-1890s and encouraged him to devote himself to music.[21] How strong were the connections between the Liberal circle around Brahms and the modernists Mahler and Schoenberg? More to the point, since they were artistically conservative critics, how did Hanslick, Heuberger, and Kalbeck respond to innovative trends in music after the deaths of Bruckner and Brahms?

In April 1899 Maximilian Muntz of the *Deutsche Zeitung* offered a partial answer in his review of Mahler's Second Symphony. Immoderate in his opinions as Muntz was, he nonetheless assessed the situation with some accuracy. According to him, the "clique" around Mahler consisted "for the most part, strange to say, of those who had formerly been opposed to Bruckner and the direction represented by him."[22] A month later, in a survey of the concert season then coming to a conclusion, Muntz mounted a direct attack on Mahler and the critics who supported him. His immediate target was a review of Mahler's Second that had appeared in the *Neue freie Presse* the month before.

A longtime Liberal organ and culturally the most influential newspaper in Vienna, the *Neue freie Presse* had bowed to the new political realities and had supported the Social Democratic candidate for mayor in 1897.[23] Like the newspaper itself, its music critics, Hanslick and Heuberger, seem to have been accommodating themselves, of necessity, to the changed Viennese scene. As

Muntz suggested, the critics of the *Neue freie Presse* had been among those most vociferously opposed to Bruckner and progressivist tendencies in general. Yet if, in his review of Mahler's Second, Heuberger offered considerable criticism, he still projected a basically favorable position toward the work and its composer.

According to Muntz, Heuberger's relative open-mindedness toward Mahler's innovations stood in complete contradiction to the aesthetic point of view previously articulated by Hanslick and himself:

> In the absence of the top party boss of the critics [Hanslick], his substitute, the best-known operetta composer in Vienna [Heuberger], carried out for Mahler's benefit the necessary hara-kiri on the critical inclinations hitherto cultivated by the previously mentioned gentleman. He smashed to pieces the aesthetic yardstick of the Viennese Hofrat of music [Hanslick], with which, up until now, all musical products were measured, cracking it on his head and that of the Hofrat with commendable self-abnegation.[24]

In Muntz's peculiar mixture of metaphors, Heuberger had disemboweled Hanslick's standards and had also managed to smash the latter's ''aesthetic yardstick'' on the heads of Hanslick and himself. Muntz proceeded to contrast this colorfully described behavior with the antagonism that the same critics had maintained toward Bruckner, ending with the requisite anti-Semitic slam (the *Deutsche Zeitung* was a mouthpiece for the Christian Social party and had an additional strong German-nationalist slant):

> If he [Heuberger] had executed this sudden change of course in his critical convictions for the benefit of Bruckner or a genius of like talent, it would have been understandable to every musician. In the case of Mahler, however, a completely different conclusion is reached, which is this: that the doctrine ''Vom musikalisch Schönen,'' earlier unfailingly antithetical to a musician of genius, must simply be turned on its head before the might of Jewry.[25]

Considering their previous hostility toward Wagner and Bruckner, these men were indeed surprisingly well disposed toward Mahler's brand of progressivist music. Theodor Helm, the Viennese correspondent for the *Musikalisches Wochenblatt*, characterized Brahms's biographer Max Kalbeck, also mentioned by Schoenberg, similarly as ''a Viennese critic especially inclined to be friendly to the composer [Mahler] (on the other hand, however, falling with real rage on Liszt and Richard Strauss, at times also Wagner and Bruckner).''[26] How are we to account for their receptiveness to Mahler's music? By itself their respect for him as a conductor could scarcely have accounted for their openness to his own compositions. Ideological continuities must have played a part, for the critics do appear to have been trying, with difficulty, to reassess their ''aesthetic yardstick'': obscure as his intentions might seem to them, the Liberal critics assumed that Mahler knew what he was doing.

These older critics could not, of course, endorse his modernism as unreservedly as a younger critic like Ludwig Karpath,[27] who did not bring with him as much baggage from the previous century, but they did at least recognize and attempt to come to terms with problematic aspects of this new music, giving Mahler the benefit of the doubt that they had not allowed Bruckner. Both Hanslick and Kalbeck, for example, went carefully through their many objections to Mahler's First Symphony after its Viennese premiere in 1900. Henry-Louis de La Grange has noted the strangeness of seeing "an intelligent and lucid critic [Kalbeck] here discovering, one by one, some of the 'clues' to Mahler's music, without in any way understanding its essential nature":[28] Kalbeck could decode the individual elements of Mahler's art, stemming as they did from a musical language that he knew, but he could not construe a possible meaning from them. Still, both he and Hanslick withheld final judgment on the merit of the symphony.

After the deaths of Brahms and Bruckner, (slightly) left-of-center politics and one strain of musical progressivism would appear—at least for the moment—to have come into a closer alignment in Vienna, a seemingly more natural state of affairs. But there were limits to what many of the critics could accept. Julius Korngold, Hanslick's successor at the *Neue freie Presse*, offered wholehearted support to Mahler. He was, however, speaking as much for himself as for Vienna's Rosé String Quartet when he noted that Arnold Rosé had been an unqualified advocate for Schoenberg's early chamber music—his quartet performed the works through the Second String Quartet, Op. 10—but that "he had gently detached himself from the Schoenberg sliding into the atonal abyss."[29]

The convergence of progressivist politics and music is unambiguous in the case of David Josef Bach, the reviewer for the *Arbeiter-Zeitung*, the organ of the Social Democratic party. He had in fact been a friend of Schoenberg from youth, after that becoming perhaps Mahler's strongest critical advocate, as well as later on a champion of composers who worked with atonal idioms. Schoenberg had taught him to love Brahms's chamber music,[30] but he valued Mahler even more, assigning him the lofty position of Beethoven's twentieth-century counterpart in the symphony. With other articulators of the Austrian Social Democratic creed, Bach believed in mixing art with politics, seeing art as "an important, indeed essential means for liberating the proletariat, for freeing humanity."[31] Like a number of the other critics, Bach had more than one role in Vienna's music world: beginning in 1905, he helped organize the Arbeiter-Symphoniekonzerte.

It is true that certain critics, most notably Robert Hirschfeld, did not adhere to any straightforward party line. Hirschfeld, who wrote for Liberal newspapers and was a longtime active supporter of *Volksconcerte*, had admired Brahms, Bruckner, and Wagner, but had little use for more recent developments in music.[32] Still, much of the criticism in the city fit into a clear ideological framework in which musical tastes lined up with political affiliations, at least within the context of the newspapers for which the reviewers wrote. This comes through with special force in the case of the previously mentioned veteran critic Theodor Helm, as does the paradoxical situation in Vienna, a city with an expressly anti-Semitic political party in power but a musical culture in which Jews more than held their own. Helm's ongoing reports in the Leipzig-based *Musikalisches Wochenblatt* offer a detailed and for the most part evenhanded account of the Viennese music scene. To the outside world represented by the readership of the *Musikalisches Wochenblatt*, he could deplore the fact that many Viennese would not forgive Mahler for his Jewish lineage.[33] After Joseph Hellmesberger took over the directorship of the Philharmonic from Mahler in 1902, Helm could note wryly that Hellmesberger "appeared almost anxiously eager to want to prove already in the first Philharmonic program through the combination [of pieces by Beethoven, the Czech Dvořák, and Karl Goldmark, a Hungarian Jew by birth] that he—even though part of the audience had demonstratively greeted him as an 'Aryan-German' conductor—belonged to no (national or religious) party."[34]

Yet in Vienna itself Helm shared the job of writing musical criticism for the *Deutsche Zeitung* with Muntz, and while the Christian Social party might not have a program for musical culture, an anti-Semitic, German-nationalist organ had certain expectations of its music critics. Even within the empire, Helm showed one side to the readers of that Viennese daily and another to the Liberal Hungarians who read the *Pester Lloyd*, for which he also wrote music reviews. In December 1902 Karl Kraus's well-known journal *Die Fackel* sarcastically noted that Helm had reviewed an opera by Goldmark in both newspapers and that the two evaluations contradicted each other:

> Differences of opinion between critics are not uncommon. . . . Not so often does the situation present itself in which one and the same theater reviewer has two different kinds of opinion. The music critic Helm—Ludwig Speidel once said "a helmet [*Helm*] without a head"—of course understood that in the *Deutsche Zeitung* he should judge the musical production from the standpoint of anti-Semitism and in the *Pester Lloyd*, strike up hymns to Goldmark. The variation in the display of convictions here was explainable by the tragic conflict of professional interests.[35]

AESTHETIC ISSUES IN THE RECEPTION OF MODERNIST MUSIC

Early in his tenure at the Philharmonic Mahler caused predictable convulsions among the critics by conducting his own version of Beethoven's String Quartet in F minor (Op. 95) arranged for string orchestra. Mahler's arrangement raised a long-standing issue of genre: both logically and by tradition, the distinction between the chamber and symphonic media (the former several individual "voices," the latter a collective) had far-reaching implications that he chose to ignore. Calling Mahler's mixing of instrumental categories a "deplorable mistake," Helm quoted Adolf Bernhard Marx, as a Beethovenist, on the subject: "An outpouring of the heart by a group: can one take it seriously?"[36] Hanslick, in contrast, accepted Mahler's point that the original medium simply did not work in the modern concert hall: "What he intended was only 'an ideal presentation of the quartet.' "[37] Following the lead of "the Master," Wagnerites like Helm tended to have essentialist conceptions of the traditional instrumental genres, the medium determining the inherent nature of each one,[38] and to believe, furthermore, that these genres had attained their ultimate realization in the symphonies, string quartets, and piano sonatas of Beethoven. But the chief concern for Hanslick, as for most other Liberal critics, was the inviolability of absolute music and of the musical logic, especially the thematic-motivic work, that justified its existence; orchestrating a string quartet neither made the music less absolute nor sullied its logic.

In his review of Mahler's Second Symphony, Muntz brought up a related contentious point, inspired invention as opposed to logical elaboration, the issue that had formed the ostensible, aesthetic core of the Bruckner-Brahms dispute:

> Mahler after all brings almost no motives and ideas of his own to his symphony, but rather gets these without scruple from the most pronounced musical antipodes. One finds next to each other elements from Weber, Bruckner, Wagner and—Volkmann [a Jew] dissolved and released, swimming in the sea of noise. Bruckner naturally comes off the worst in the act. This purely analytical, thematic work gives the piece an unmistakable quality of musical decadence.[39]

By then referring to "Jewish decadency [*Decadententhums*] in music," Muntz spelled out ideological implications that had usually remained submerged in the critical attacks on Brahms: lacking the true (German) creativity of a Bruckner, a Jew like Mahler (or honorary Jew like Brahms) could use only his rational intelligence.

Issues from the past thus lingered at the turn of the century. More current questions often turned on the literary bases of much of the newer music. The critics sometimes found fault with the texts that composers chose and, even more frequently, complained about the discrepancy between the (sometimes humble) literary sources and their (often-grandiose) musical settings. Helm, for example, wrote of *Das klagende Lied* by Mahler: "One took offense above all—and was justified in doing so—in the musical treatment of a simple, perhaps almost shabby ballade topic with such enormous means à la Berlioz, aiming for the most part at the most powerful frescolike effects."[40] From another part of the musical spectrum, Kalbeck criticized this work in much the same way, for having "brought into play so large and complicated an orchestra as if it treated not a homely tale but rather the end of the world."[41] The Wagnerite critic Max Vancsa likewise noted of Alexander Zemlinsky's *Die Seejungfrau* (The mermaid) that "[Hans Christian] Andersen's small, charming poem seemed inordinately inflated by three whole symphonic movements."[42] Helm, a fervent admirer of Richard Strauss, wrote of his "only misgiving" about the *Sinfonia domestica*, his doubt that it was necessary for Strauss "to summon up such a gigantic mass of instruments for the musical illustration of so cozily familial a story,'' which was, he had to admit, ''not completely allayed even by the otherwise thrilling total effect of the performance.''[43]

Not every Wagnerite accepted program music as a justifiable genre; almost all of the defenders of program music, however, came from the Wagnerian ranks. Thus Vancsa and Helm did not doubt the basic validity of program music, focusing rather on its artistic requirements. But for most Liberal critics, the very use of a literary source posed aesthetic problems. Sometimes they professed difficulty even in assigning certain texted works to existing genres. In a measured review of an 1899 performance of orchestral songs by Mahler (from *Lieder eines fahrenden Gesellen* and *Des Knaben Wunderhorn*), Hanslick wrote of these ''Gesänge,'' ''neither lied nor aria nor dramatic scene, they have something of each.''[44] In a critique from 1900 of *Das klagende Lied*, which he subtitled ''A Contribution to the Aesthetics of the Present Time,'' Kalbeck likened Mahler's work to a singing ostrich, a creature that cannot be found in nature. Claiming that he could not classify the piece within traditional categories, he finally found the appropriate loaded diction and called it a symphonic poem—most Liberal critics, of course, rejected this genre outright—with some of the words of its program sung (most commentators label it a cantata).[45]

Mahler's symphonies broke rules basic to that more traditional genre in the estimation of Kalbeck, since he saw the symphony as absolute music and therefore dependent upon the logical elaboration of themes and motives, an inconsistent feature in Mahler's work (Muntz notwithstanding). ''Episodic'' functioned as an approximate opposing adjective to ''logical'' in Kalbeck's reviews. In a discussion of Mahler's Fourth Symphony, for example, he asserted that the ''strength of the symphonist, like that of the dramatist, does not lie in the episode but rather in the development of the motive.''[46]

Kalbeck cast his criticism of Mahler's First Symphony in slightly different terms, after characteristically tempering his remarks: ''That his youthful work still pleases him today does not surprise us; for it pleased us to an extraordinary degree in many of its details, if we also allow ourselves to deem it no masterpiece of absolute music.'' Among other things, Kalbeck objected to Mahler's use of the melody from his song ''Ging heut' morgen über's Feld'' as the primary theme of his opening Allegro, on the grounds that it had been poetically rather than musically motivated and was not suited for symphonic development: ''His otherwise so charming partiality for the folk-song-like accounts for the at times quite severe shortage of thematic work.'' Giving the First the title ''Sinfonia ironica,'' Kalbeck observed that the ''destructive sharpness of the irony appears to have produced the work's episodic character.'' In his searching critique of this symphony, Kalbeck took issue with the distance that the composer (or his symphonic persona) maintained from the work, for he believed that this was inimical to the genre: ''The symphonist should be a dramatist overflowing with lyric poetry, who stands always in the middle of the scene, even if it changes as quick as lightning around him; he should not reflect, but rather feel and act.'' Thematic work creating an effect of logical necessity would presumably come with this total immersion in the symphonic process. Kalbeck then brought up his central concern, the corrupting effect of words upon music: he considered irony to be "foreign to absolute music" and music capable of irony only "in immediate or indirect connection with words." (Mahler's minor-mode version of "Frère Jacques" in the third movement would exemplify an "indirect connection with words.") He concluded this argument by calling absolute music "the noblest of arts because it cannot say the opposite of what it means."[47]

For the Viennese premiere of his First Symphony, Mahler not only had suppressed his own original program based on Jean Paul's *Titan*, but also had not allowed even the usual program notes: since he had decided to present the symphony as absolute music, it should stand on its own. Kalbeck, however, believed that this work, more than most others, required introductory notes and a few musical examples. Helm, on the other hand, saw the problem to lie in the decision to remove the programmatic text, claiming that Mahler overestimated his audience and that he "also forgot that what was originally conceived as program music can never again be completely satisfying absolute music, in any case losing poetic charm through the simple erasing of the programmatic explanation."[48]

That same season Helm in a sense contradicted this position in the way that he chose to promote Strauss's *Ein Heldenleben*, after first taking a swipe at certain unnamed critics (we know who they are):

> On some of these gentlemen—*nomina sunt odiosa*—the mere name "program music" already had an effect like that of a red cloth on a bull. Besides, I found that it must definitely be admitted that *Ein Heldenleben* also succeeds as absolute music because of the logically compelling course of the masterly thematic work.[49]

Helm will have it both ways, defending the work as program music, but at the same time pronouncing it a logical piece of absolute music: absoluteness had powerful ideological claims.

The thread of programmatic versus absolute runs throughout the journalistic music criticism around the turn of the century. The Liberal critics complained about the lack of musical clarity that programmatic works seemed to entail and, conversely, about the episodic nature of certain works without programs that seemed to demand programmatic explanation. Hanslick lamented the turn late in life toward the symphonic poem by Dvořák, one of his favorite composers, writing that a narrative program like that associated by Dvořák with *Holoubek* "is a misfortune for the composition because it is ambiguous and—unfortunately—essential":[50] the numerous discontinuities in the music otherwise made no sense.

Heuberger greeted a performance of *Verklärte Nacht* in 1902 with similar misgivings, yet again showed an unexpected receptiveness to this new music, praising what Schoenberg had managed to accomplish in spite of his unfortunate decision to base the string sextet on a poem:

At the same time, next to the intentionally confused and ugly, much that is moving, stirring, much that overcomes the listener with irresistible force, that presses into the heart and senses. Only a serious, deep nature can find such sounds, only an unusual talent can throw light in such a way on so dark a path.[51]

Because various opera composers had used musical means similar to those chosen by Schoenberg to portray a star- or moonlit night, Heuberger believed that even listeners who did not know the program would be able to decode Schoenberg's depiction of the physical setting for the narrative, as well as the expression of "anxiety, sultriness, the longing and pain of love." But he marveled that Schoenberg should credit music with "such precise capability of expression" that it could convey the complicated narrative in Richard Dehmel's poem, dryly noting that "a composer had to renounce all claim to representing the overly tolerant two-father system" of the poem (these critics took obvious pride in their wit). Heuberger had no quarrel with Schoenberg's choice of a chamber rather than an orchestral medium; the issue was the music's nonabsolute nature and the problems that seemed to create:

Program music, which already more than once began a semblance of life and is again celebrating a temporary resurrection, now appears to want to encroach upon chamber music. There is no real reason to oppose this expansion of its domain—if one composes unclear orchestral music, one can just as well—or just as ill—also create unclear chamber music. The means with which one expresses oneself incomprehensibly are of no importance.[52]

For the Social Democratic critic Bach, the supposed obscurity of program music had a sociopolitical dimension that motivated him and the other organizers to avoid it completely in the earliest Arbeiter-Symphoniekonzerte. Unlike the absolute genres—so this line of thinking went—program music was "bound to the time and social stratum of its origins" and therefore required that listeners have a certain level and kind of education: "not high, but rather narrow precisely because seeming so comprehensive. . . . [This *Bildung*] demands the whole of the human intellect, not of the heart."[53] Again showing continuity with Liberal views but giving them one kind of Wagnerian inflection,[54] Bach conceptualized absolute music as timeless, universal, capable of communicating with all classes because its wisdom did not entail "an intellectual, but rather a soulful [*gemütlich*] process."[55]

THE STUDY OF MUSIC AT THE UNIVERSITY AND CONSERVATORY

If such critics as Hanslick, Kalbeck, Heuberger, Bach, and Helm remain interesting because of their biases and what these tell us about the competing ideologies of the day, the musicologist Guido Adler proves a valuable on-the-spot observer of musical events in turn-of-the-century Vienna because of his open mind and level head; while no less a person of his time than the others, Adler seems to have consciously cultivated a broad perspective as an Austrian citizen and as a musician and scholar. In a survey of contemporaneous musical practice in December 1906, Adler described the many historical styles that could be heard in performance, noting that the "total picture offers us a super- and juxtaposition of layers of musical culture from past centuries,"[56] a diversified scene to which he had certainly contributed. The discipline of musicology had grown rapidly during the 1880s, with Adler playing a central role in the course it took. His style-based construction of music history entailed the consideration of many compositions; concomitantly, he favored the preparation of editions geared toward the actual performance of music from the past.

In 1898 Adler had succeeded Hanslick, a man of much narrower tastes, as professor at the University of Vienna. Hanslick had little affinity for music before Haydn and Mozart, and he felt decided antipathy toward Wagner as both person and composer. Although Wagner's music dramas had from the beginning met with much resistance from Hanslick and other Viennese critics, with the exception of *Tristan und Isolde*, they had never lacked regular presentations at the Hofoper and, around the turn of the century, were receiving highly praised performances by Adler's friend Mahler. Unlike Hanslick, Adler admired Wagner's music. He had, in fact, been a founding member of the Wiener Akademischer Richard Wagner-Verein (Viennese Academic Richard Wagner Society) in 1873, but left the group in 1888,[57] probably because Wagnerism had by that time become closely associated in Austria with extreme forms of German nationalism. In a series of lectures at the university in 1904, Adler characteristically tried to disengage Wagner's achievements as a composer from his most controversial essays and from the even more polemical interpretations of those writings by such latter-day Wagnerites as Houston Chamberlain;[58] Wagner's music was to be kept separate from the explosive ism that bore his name.

Adler appears to have shown a receptive yet also clearheaded attitude in all his scholarly endeavors. At the university he founded the Musikwissenschaftliches Institut, where he gave the study of music history a fresh orientation that recognized the different beauties of historically distant musics, regarding these compositions as something more than steps in the evolution toward classical style. Still, Viennese classicism remained the standard of perfection in the city where it had come to full flower, perhaps more so than anywhere else, serving as a central cultural symbol as well.

In 1906 Adler gave a public talk at the university to celebrate the 150th anniversary of Mozart's birth. By way of introduction, he made the point that the particular quality of Austrian culture came through most clearly in its music, and he referred to Mozart's art—"like all true art"—as *völkerverbindend*, serving to unite peoples. The *Neue freie Presse* published an excerpt from the speech, accompanied by an article entitled "The Significance of the Academic Mozart Festival," in which an unnamed professor at the university isolated and expanded these two comments. He focused first on Adler's use of the word *völkerverbindend: ''Völkerverbindend!* Therein lies the secret for the future of Austria.''[59] Noting that German-nationalist organizations had initiated the Mozart Festival, but that the entire, diverse student body had celebrated it, he saw in the conduct of the students at the festival evidence of music's power to bring people together.

Adler's ''colleague'' quoted him a second time, ''Mozart's art, like that of all classical Viennese music, mirrors Austrian culture in the noblest, most distinguished, most imperishable way,'' and then elaborated on the remark: ''Austria is thus not merely a conglomerate of nations protected and secured by a military . . . it is also an artistic manifestation with a distinct physiognomy. One recognizes its features most clearly in the works of that art that is bound to no specific language.'' In a rhetorical leap, he imagined the music of the Viennese classical composers as a model for the conduct of Austria's internal affairs: ''Thus, as the customs of the Austrian peoples are interwoven in the works of the classical composers of music, as the motivic material is taken from the national stores, which the artists . . . work up into classical structures, so may a higher statescraft join the particularities of the various peoples into a higher unity.''[60]

In this passage the ''anonymous'' professor both acknowledged the various elements of Austrianness and celebrated it as something more than those individual components. Elsewhere the article referred to divisive political activity at the university, to which the stress upon the multinational specialness of Austrian culture was obviously intended as a response. Although Pan-Germanism had peaked around 1900 and had gone into decline by 1906, student radicals continued to agitate for its cause. The twist that Adler's ''colleague'' gave to the implied ''universality'' of classicism (as an amalgam of many national styles), an assumption that more often presented German culture as the unmarked and therefore superior norm, became part of a plea for tolerance and unity in the Vienna of the early twentieth century.

The idea of absoluteness, as we have already seen, had a firm hold on much of the Viennese music world. With these remarks by Adler and his colleague and the earlier ones by Bach, the local appeal of a ''universal language'' that could transcend barriers of nation and class begins to come into focus; moreover, the centripetal force of the classical legacy, as the ultimate realization of absoluteness in music, begins to seem a conservatism that is, in part, beneficial. Might not the skeptical attitude of critics like Hanslick, Heuberger, and Kalbeck toward music tied to one particular language, including their own German, be less a matter of narrow-minded formalism than an idealistic, if also overly optimistic, response to the Austrian situation?

Adler himself seems to have consistently displayed an ecumenical outlook. Through the advocacy of such influential musicians as Hanslick and Brahms, he had secured financial support from the Austrian government for undertakings that included the series of editions Denkmäler der Tonkunst in Oesterreich (Monuments of music in Austria) and the founding of the *Vierteljahrsschrift für*

Musikwissenschaft (Quarterly journal of musicology), which "was to be conducted in a nonpartisan manner"; his original plan for the *Vierteljahrsschrift* had called for publishing the best work by scholars from many nations, who would have been allowed to write in English, French, or Italian, as well as German.[61] Schorske has noted similar governmental backing that the Secession obtained through Koerber, the Austrian premier between 1900 and 1904, and his minister of culture, Wilhelm von Hartel, ascribing the state's interest in supporting the group to its cosmopolitan point of view: "A Secession spokesperson had explained her commitment to the movement as 'a question of defending a purely Austrian culture, a form of art that would weld together all the characteristics of our multitude of constituent peoples into a new and proud unity.' "[62] While Adler had begun to receive funding for his work well before Koerber's tenure as premier and the advent of the Secession, his own nonnationalistic perspective surely figured in the government's continuing support for his projects.

Adler taught a number of the young modernist composers at the university;[63] his catholic tastes drew students to him and served to broaden their own range of interests. At the Conservatory, on the other hand, an unreflecting classicism had become the fixed basis of the curriculum many decades before, which meant that the professors did not address the revolutionary features of Wagner's musical style in the classroom, forcing the composition students to write one way for their teachers and another for themselves. In the Conservatory Viennese classicism was not one among many historical styles, nor did it have the symbolic resonance that Adler found in it; this "universal" style had become a compendium of concrete and rigid rules for composition.

By no means peculiar to the Vienna Conservatory, the enshrinement of classical style was bound up with the very institution of the conservatory. Stefan Kunze has indeed observed a close three-way connection between the nineteenth-century establishment of conservatories in Europe, the taking of classical works as compositional models, and the development of new kinds of music theory. Earlier music theory had focused on the teaching of craft, namely, thoroughbass and species counterpoint; the nineteenth-century *Melodielehre* and *Formenlehre* sought to impart a total understanding of, and ultimately prescription for, composition. According to Kunze, the new theory derived its rules from the close analytical study of masterpieces, and "that these were principally works of the Viennese classical composers can scarcely be disputed." In what initially might seem like a contradiction, this led to a split between theory and composition: "As the teaching of composition erected its structure on the basis of actual pieces of music, the paradoxical fact followed that the teaching of composition lost its connection to composing. For it rested on a music taken from the past but viewed as eternally valid and exemplary."[64]

Classicism does seem to have become more thoroughly entrenched at the Vienna Conservatory than elsewhere. Brahms helped perpetuate this situation by supporting Robert Fuchs's appointment as a teacher of counterpoint in 1890 and then of composition in 1895 (Fuchs had previously taught only *Harmonielehre*, the third new kind of theory).[65] From 1880 Brahms had been a member of the directorate of the Gesellschaft der Musikfreunde, which oversaw the Conservatory (as well as the Singverein, a choral society presented by the Gesellschaft in a regular series of concerts). Although his own name is associated with both academicism and classicism, and although he had many friends at the Conservatory, Brahms disagreed with much that went on there. One object of his disapproval was, naturally, Bruckner, who taught counterpoint and harmonic theory at the Conservatory until 1891 and at the university until 1892. Brahms's censure of Bruckner the teacher would have had only an indirect connection to his low regard for Bruckner the composer, since for Bruckner theory and composition had little to do with each other, the so-called Bruckner problem.[66] That very estrangement between theory and practice would most likely have particularly incensed Brahms, who set great store by the venerable crafts of figured bass and species counterpoint as a basis for actual composition.

Like Schoenberg after him, Brahms also believed in using classical models as preparation, but not as a prescription for composition. Under the extended tenures of Fuchs and Hermann Grädener at the Conservatory, the teaching of composition congealed in the early twentieth century into classicizing formulae that would scarcely have pleased Brahms had he lived to see this state of affairs. A former student recalled the uninspiring pedagogical approach two decades later:

> The composition instruction of twenty years ago had alienated itself from contemporary developments. . . . Many teachers went so far as to require composing exactly according to certain Classical examples. Thus a theory teacher in Vienna once gave the assignment of composing a piano sonata after the model of the *Spring* Sonata, with even the same number of measures, only the key should be C minor!![67]

In 1904 Adler worked with Hartel, the minister of culture, on a plan for the government to assume control of the Conservatory, with Mahler as the new director, from the Gesellschaft der Musikfreunde. The reorganization did not, however, take place immediately or exactly as planned because Hartel died in 1907, and Mahler left for New York the same year. The longtime director of the Conservatory, Richard von Perger (another associate of Brahms), nonetheless resigned in 1907 and was replaced by a musician from Mannheim, Wilhelm Bopp. Two years later the Conservatory became the state-run Akademie (today Hochschule) für Musik und Darstellende Kunst (Academy of Music and Representational Art). One of Bopp's pressing concerns after the institutional reorganization was to force retirement upon Fuchs and Grädener, a step he finally accomplished in 1912. In the report in which he recommended this action, he cited Fuchs's lack of interest in Wagner and more recent composers: "Fuchs does not know and does not want to know the later works of Richard Wagner and prides himself on knowing nothing of *Tristan*. Richard Strauss, Max Reger,

Gustav Mahler; the innovators Debussy, Schoenberg, Scriabin are certainly only known to him by name.''[68]

Bopp then pointedly connected ''true love and true appreciation of the Classical composers'' with ''an unbiased attitude toward modern musical art,''[69] pressing the classical legacy into rhetorical service for a new agenda.

THE AKADEMISCHER RICHARD WAGNER-VEREIN AND THE TONKÜNSTLERVEREIN

Adler, again our witness, wrote in 1904 about the cliquishness of Vienna's music circles, observing that the various musical societies (*Vereine*) of the day had

> essentially degenerated into a cult of individuals. In Vienna we have a Wagner-Verein, a Hugo Wolf-Verein, more recently have seen an Ansorge-Verein. The Viennese Tonkünstlerverein was for a long time a Brahms-Verein; in the last fifteen years the Wagner-Verein could have laid claim to the supplementary title of a Bruckner Verein. These associations have in the last decades stamped the physiognomy of Viennese music life.[70]

Of the four groups mentioned by Adler, the Wagner-Verein and the Tonkünstlerverein (Society of Musicians), formed, respectively, in 1873 and 1885, were by far the most significant. The members of the Tonkünstlerverein, as the name indicates, were all professional musicians of one kind or another: composers, performers, scholars, and teachers, many of them associated with the Conservatory. The Wagner-Verein, on the other hand, was made up of Wagnerites, whether musicians or not. Both groups sponsored a number of semipublic musical evenings, with revealing differences in the repertory represented in the concerts given by each.

As Adler's remarks may suggest, the two groups had come to be aligned with the opposing sides in the politicized Bruckner-Brahms division that developed in the 1880s. Wagnerism became a much more important phenomenon after ''the Master's'' death in 1883. Since his ideas had helped shape the style and content of the new politics, and he died at a time of increasing polarization in the city, the Wagner-Verein's agenda of promoting his music and writings inevitably took on more pronounced extramusical implications thereafter. During the 1880s the society included on its roster several leaders from the developing anti-Liberal movement: Schönerer, Victor Adler, and Pernerstorfer, along with the later Christian Social politician Robert Pattai. The numbers in the Wagner-Verein swelled during the 1880s, with many members favoring both overt involvement in the radical antiestablishment politics of the day and the complete exclusion of Jews from membership in the society. When the Wagner-Verein decided against becoming politically active as a group in 1890, the more militantly anti-Semitic Wagnerites left and formed their own organization, which they dedicated as much to Schönerer's cause as to that of Wagner.[71] Enrollment in the Wagner-Verein went down in the 1890s, becoming more or less stable by the end of the decade.

The Wagner-Verein had come into existence blandly enough. In the first year (1873) a duet by Brahms and in 1878 two of his lieder were even performed in the group's *Interne Abende* (Internal evenings), or semipublic concerts, before the society had yet programmed anything by Bruckner. Brahms's name did not, however, reappear in the society's programs.[72] Works by the New German School, in the latter part of the nineteenth century the central-European avant-garde in music, naturally made up the core repertory of the group's evening concerts. A study of the works performed between 1873 and 1910 reveals, along with the expected partiality toward Wagner, Bruckner, Liszt, and Wolf, continuing devotion to a canon of standard works by Bach and Handel, the Viennese classical triumvirate, Weber, and Schubert. By the turn of the century, little music that we now consider ephemeral appeared in the programs because the organizers had for the most part quit taking chances on new composers well before then. The repertory of the Wagner-Verein had become more frozen than that of the Philharmonic: the erstwhile musical counterculture had itself turned into a stodgy establishment.

Since Wagner, Liszt, and Bruckner had tended to cultivate genres requiring large numbers of performers, and the Wagner-Verein usually had only a small space and limited forces at its disposal, what kinds of music did it favor in its concerts? To present the orchestral repertory, the society did not by any means look down on piano arrangements of various kinds (for two or four hands at one instrument, or for two pianos). Because it had formed its own chorus in 1881, the group could also perform the big vocal works by the New German composers in versions with piano accompaniment. In its choice of other choral repertory, the Wagner-Verein showed the antiquarian tendencies of the time. The four semipublic performances in 1901, for example, presented choral music by Bach, Schubert, Peter Cornelius, Liszt, and Bruckner, but also by Luca Marenzio and Jean-Baptiste Lully. Although the most frequent venue for the evening concerts, the 500-seat Bösendorfer Hall, was considered ''acoustically almost ideal'' for chamber music,[73] for many Wagnerites chamber music had ended with Beethoven,[74] enjoying only brief resurrections in the solitary String Quintet of Bruckner and, apparently with some reservations, works by Weber and Schubert. Vienna's Hellmesberger Quartet had begun to perform Schubert's chamber music at midcentury, but the Wagner-Verein scheduled these pieces rarely, focusing instead on his lieder and other vocal music; the society likewise preferred Weber's other compositions over his chamber music. The chamber repertory therefore consisted largely of sonatas by J. S. Bach and various works by the Viennese classical masters, along with the Bruckner Quintet.

With Guido Adler and several others, Bruckner had helped found the Wagner-Verein, but the organization did not make concerted efforts on his behalf until after Wagner's death in 1883.[75] The society named Bruckner an *Ehrenmitglied* (honorary member) in 1885 and also began to present frequent performances of the Quintet, the choral music, and piano arrangements of his symphonies in the semipublic concerts and, less formally, within the confines of the society; on several occasions, moreover, it sponsored public orchestral performances of the symphonies and drew further attention to Bruckner through lectures about him and his music. In 1891 Helm aptly referred to the Wagner-Verein as having become a "mini-Bayreuth for Bruckner."[76]

As Adler later noted, the Tonkünstlerverein was for many years almost a Brahms-Verein. Unlike Bruckner, Brahms, of course, did not need the backing of a musical society—he received plenty of performances elsewhere. The Tonkünstlerverein was a "Brahms Society" because his tastes and personality dominated it. Three professors of applied music at the Conservatory, Jacob Epstein, Josef Gänsbacher, and Theodor Leschetitzsky, had formed the society in the fall of 1885, and Brahms joined shortly thereafter, becoming honorary president in 1886 and remaining an energetic participant in the society's activities during the final decade of his life.[77] With some exaggeration—since, for instance, a number of people did belong to both groups, and the Wagner-Verein certainly drew members from the constituency of the Liberal party—the Tonkünstlerverein can be viewed as the Wagner-Verein's Liberal complement, and Jews, as we know, were associated with Liberalism. In 1887 Schönerer's scandal sheet *Unverfälschte deutsche Worte* (Unadulterated German words), a periodical not given to halftones or other subtleties, listed some of the members of the Tonkünstlerverein, remarking on how Jewish (*verjudet*) the society had become in the year or so of its existence: "This list of names at the same time gives a short summary of the completely Jewish-dominated state of art in Vienna, in the Conservatory, and in the music shops. By rights, though, the Viennese Tonkünstlerverein should really be called Cohnkünstlerverein."[78] While this kind of coarse rhetoric helped bring about the political collapse of Liberalism, it seems to have had little effect on institutions like the Tonkünstlerverein that tended to support Liberal musical culture: a public ballot, after all, did not determine the course of those institutions.

Just as the Wagner-Verein never presented the classicizing chamber music of Schumann, Mendelssohn, or Brahms, the Tonkünstlerverein never performed Wagner or Bruckner and rarely programmed Liszt or Wolf (occasional lieder by both and piano works by the former).[79] Because the standard repertory of chamber and vocal music received frequent performances elsewhere in the city, only obscure or simply under-performed works by Bach, Schubert, and the Viennese classical composers appeared on the Tonkünstlerverein's programs. The stated purpose of the society was "the most extensive promotion of music, as well as of the spiritual and material interests of musicians,"[80] and its own (private) *Musik-Abende* included a large number of new chamber works, many of them by now-forgotten composers. The yearly report for 1900–1901 stated the twofold policy in choosing works for performance:

In compiling the programs for our fourteen musical evenings, we are again proceeding according to the dual motives established some years before: on the one hand, to cultivate the newest creations, native and foreign, in the areas of chamber and vocal music; on the other hand, however, to bring to light little-known or forgotten works of the past from under today's layer of culture and, where possible, perform them in the original version.[81]

During that same year, between November 1900 and November 1901, the "little-known or forgotten" music from submerged "layers" of culture (the same geological metaphor Adler would use in 1904) included arias by Bach, a flute duet from Beethoven's early years in Bonn, two divertimenti by Haydn, and two men's choruses with guitar accompaniment by Schubert. That season Richard Strauss was the most performed contemporary composer, with his violin sonata, cello sonata, and nine lieder distributed over four of the evenings (the Wagner-Verein also programmed works by Strauss), but the newer music played in the Tonkünstlerverein tended more often to be by such composers as Edvard Grieg, Antonín Dvořák, and various professors at the Conservatory.

Along with a number of academic composers, the Tonkünstlerverein included notable performers and musical scholars among its members; the roster in 1900–1901 in itself suggests the wide range of musical talent and activity in Vienna at the turn of the century, for it included Guido Adler, the theorist Heinrich Schenker, and the pianist Arthur Schnabel, as well as Schoenberg and Zemlinsky. Although the Tonkünstlerverein had programmed several of Zemlinsky's early works, including the Brahmsian Clarinet Trio (later published as Op. 3) that won a prize in one of the society's competitions, he and Schoenberg would soon leave the group. Schoenberg's personal mythmaking included the story that the Tonkünstlerverein had refused to perform *Verklärte Nacht* "because of the 'revolutionary' use of one—that is *one* single uncataloged dissonance."[82] Yet several years later the Rosé Quartet and two guest artists played that very work in one of the Tonkünstlerverein's private concerts.[83]

Schoenberg overstated the conservatism of the Tonkünstlerverein; still, its limitations—and those of the Wagner-Verein—stand out clearly enough. Both societies centered on one or two stellar figures, and each refused to acknowledge important composers and bodies of work. The latter is especially noticeable in the Wagner-Verein's treatment of the contested genre of chamber music; since the Tonkünstlerverein rarely programmed piano arrangements of any kind, the Liberal aversion toward such genres as the symphonic poem does not come through as obviously (and the Tonkünstlerverein did eventually present the programmatic *Verklärte Nacht*). More important, though, the two groups were as insular in their functions as in their tastes, each directed inward rather than toward the Viennese public.

Around the turn of the century many attempts were being made to change the tenor of the city's musical life. The primary aim was often to broaden the audience for elevated art music, especially instrumental music: the Viennese were understood to like trivial music too much, and most of them in any case had few opportunities to hear the great chamber and orchestral literature. But the writings supporting these efforts frequently also stressed the need both to rise above the factionalism that had tended to characterize the Viennese scene and to refashion the connection between the musicians and their audiences, making it more immediate and also more specifically didactic. These common aims linked new groups as otherwise varied in significance and intent as the Erstes Wiener Volksquartett für Classische Musik (First Viennese People's Quartet for Classical Music), the Wiener Konzertverein (Viennese Concert Society), and the Vereinigung Schaffender Tonkünstler in Wien (Alliance of Creative Musicians in Vienna).

THREE REPRESENTATIVE NEW MUSICAL ORGANIZATIONS

With the first series of public concerts given by the Hellmesberger Quartet in the 1849–50 season, a new era of Viennese chamber-music performance had begun. A half-century later, the city had a number of additional quartets in residence, including those with Arnold Rosé, Rudolf Fitzner, and Carl Prill as first violinists and namesakes, along with the Wiener Damen-Streichquartett and another whose name was a particular sign of the times: the Erstes Wiener Volksquartett für Classische Musik. August Duesberg founded this string quartet in 1890, and it remained active into the twentieth century.

In 1892 Duesberg published a pamphlet that explained the quartet's goals. Using utopian language typical of musical activists in Vienna during this period, he advocated improving the musical tastes of the people as a whole and "the complete dislodging of the trivial"[84] and did not neglect to appeal to the self-interest of the more privileged members of Viennese society:

> Music is the most powerful and best-qualified means for creating an ennobling effect on the human spirit. If we endeavor to make music well known and liked by the people, to make it a necessity, it will be a diversion for the discontented and the revolutionary minded from dark thoughts, a safeguard from their own souls.
>
> I therefore call upon those who share my convictions to work for this good cause, to support us in our striving for strength, to become in this way benefactors of humanity, pioneers for a better future.[85]

Duesberg noted that the name of the quartet had caused some consternation. Addressing observers troubled by the phrase "für Classische Musik," he asked, "Doesn't that little word 'Classical' in itself sum up everything suggestive of the beautiful, serious, and noble?" He marveled at those bothered by the word *Volk*, as if it signified only "vagrants, cut-throats, pickpockets, ragged bums, and their consorts." To Duesberg, "all ranks and classes belong to the *Volk*, for all together create a people and represent a sovereign."[86] Like many other evangelists for music at that time, he believed that the tastes of the upper classes had become degraded, which made the forging of new audiences important for musical art itself,[87] and he expressed pleasure at the diversity of those who had attended the Sunday concerts of his quartet: ''Not only simple laborers, seamstresses, or laundresses with Sunday off appeared there; not only students, painters, young musicians, both male and female, middle-class citizens, and civil servants, but also those of noble and princely rank appeared frequently and in large numbers at these concerts.''[88]

As befits someone with so inclusive a vision, Duesberg was associated with both the Wagner-Verein and the Tonkünstlerverein, appearing on their rosters in various seasons around the turn of the century.[89] The repertory of his quartet represented not only the common heritage of Haydn, Mozart, Beethoven, and Schubert that each society believed it understood best, but also tastes peculiar to each one. The Volksquartett played chamber music by Mendelssohn and Schumann, works that were never performed in the musical evenings of the Wagner-Verein, as well as pieces by such classicizing composers within the Tonkünstlerverein as, for example, Fuchs, Grädener, and Julius Zellner. The quartet also played those chamber rarities by New German composers that did exist, Bruckner's String Quintet and Liszt's *Angelus* (*Gebet an die Schutzengel*), an andante for string quartet that had surfaced in the 1880s. Clearly striving to diminish the factionalism of Viennese musical life, Duesberg also aimed at creating a different kind of connection with the new audiences. Seeing the ''almost personal communication'' that had developed between the public and the performers, he inaugurated a system that allowed audiences to vote on the programming for subsequent Sunday concerts.

The same interest in expanding the audience for the highest instrumental genres led to the founding of the Wiener Konzertverein (called the Comité von Musikfreunde at first), which guided the formation of the Neues Philharmonisches Orchester in the 1899–1900 season, the culmination of several decades of efforts to establish a second orchestra in Vienna. Every year since 1842 the Hofoper orchestra had regrouped as the Wiener Philharmoniker on occasional Sunday afternoons to perform a meager schedule, usually eight subscription concerts plus one ''popular'' benefit performance. This paucity of symphonic concerts was a central factor in the extreme exclusivity of the city's musical life.[90] To be sure, by the last years of the nineteenth century, large numbers of amateur orchestras and military bands had come into existence,[91] but there was still no permanent, professional conduit for the serious orchestral literature to most of the Viennese populace.

Echoing the complaints of many Viennese, Helm (in his persona as critic for the *Musikalisches Wochenblatt*) summed up the situation as it had long stood:

> If only the Philharmonic concerts were not so expensive! How often, over how many years have we had to listen to this complaint right in the circles of our most musical Viennese middle class! To which is usually then added: If we had at least one other

acceptable symphonic orchestra performing at affordable prices and secure in its continuing existence.[92]

In 1890–1900 alone, three new orchestras aimed at remedying the problem had come into existence, including one led by the former military band conductor Carl Stix that soon became the Neues Philharmonisches Orchester. Stix's undertaking had gained substantial financial backing, which enabled its transformation from a typical series of popular performances given in spacious "refreshment rooms" at the beginning of the season into one of six symphonic concerts at "very cheap" subscription prices, presented between January and March 1900 in the large hall of the Musikverein building (home of the Vienna Philharmonic and the Gesellschaft der Musikfreunde) under the eminent conductor Ferdinand Löwe. Despite several setbacks (including the death of Nicolaus Dumba, a member of both the Wagner-Verein and the Tonkünstlerverein and one of the orchestra's most generous benefactors), the Neues Philharmonisches Orchester flourished, later becoming the Wiener Symphoniker active to this day.

Helm saw a symbolic reconciliation in the programming for the initial season of concerts, which featured symphonies by both Bruckner and Brahms, observing that this was the first time that the Brahms Symphony in C minor had worked with a Viennese audience: he had heard seven previous performances of Brahms's First in the city, but none had succeeded before this one conducted by Löwe, a former student and close associate of Bruckner. A rapprochement between previously antagonistic parties can also be inferred from the fact that while the Bruckner disciple Löwe was the orchestra's conductor, the committee working to ensure the group's future included two of the most vocal opponents of Bruckner's music, Kalbeck and Heuberger. If Kalbeck and Heuberger did not share many of Helm's inclinations in either music or politics, the three critics could at least agree on the need for both another orchestra and easier access to the symphonic repertory for more of the Viennese people. The report on the next season specifically stated the committee's determination that "the undertaking must be guided by the elimination of every factional inclination; no artistic direction may be excluded, but also none dominate one-sidedly; the purely artistic, impartial goal must be strictly maintained."[93]

Like the Volksquartett, the Wiener Konzertverein accepted the *Bildungsfunktion* that supposedly autonomous instrumental music historically had implied, in fact, again like that organization, making edification an explicit purpose. Because new, mostly middle-class audiences were being exposed to the symphonic repertory in the Konzertverein concerts, "the classical must predominate," according to Helm; thus all nine Beethoven symphonies appeared "in strict chronological order" in the 1900–1901 season (four in the Tuesday series, four in the Wednesday series, and the Ninth in a so-called extraordinary, or nonseries, concert).[94] The same didactic motive led Löwe to repeat Brahms's Fourth Symphony, also in an extraordinary concert, after it was received less than enthusiastically in one of the subscription concerts, his aim, of course, being to give the public a chance to get to know it better.[95] In 1905 the new orchestra became the first vehicle for one of the great accomplishments of Austrian socialism, the previously mentioned Arbeiter-Symphoniekonzerte, which extended to broader classes of citizens than ever before the cultural prerogative of elevated orchestral music.

It is against the background of such ongoing attempts to reform the city's musical life that the creation of the Vereinigung Schaffender Tonkünstler in the spring of 1904 should be understood. The primary purpose of the group, whose members included Schoenberg and Zemlinsky, was to promote contemporary music in a city viewed as antipathetic to the new, "in flagrant contradiction to Vienna's history as a musical trendsetter." But a by-now-familiar pedagogical impulse underpinned their plans, as evidenced in the organization's manifesto:

> All musical appeal rests on an intrinsic relationship between work and listener, for the realization of which not only the quality of the work but also that of the listener are of decisive significance. . . . Thus, if the musical public is to secure a relationship to the music of the present, familiarity with the peculiar features of the latter is above all necessary, just as the public's receptiveness to the music of the classical composers was only made possible by thorough knowledge of it.[96]

"The public" may refer to the Philharmonic audiences, perhaps, or to those more recent initiates whose listening education had been programmatically grounded in the classical repertory; in any case, the classical heritage clearly functioned as a constant point of reference in Vienna during this period.

Like the Volksquartett and the Konzertverein, the Vereinigung aspired to create a less distant, more interactive relationship with audiences, its manifesto proposing that composers

> must emerge from their indirect, removed connection to the general public and strive to secure an immediate relationship to it. . . . The majority of Vienna's composing musicians have therefore decided to form an alliance with the purpose of bringing about that immediate relationship between it and the public, to prepare a fixed place for encouraging the music of the present in Vienna, to keep the public continuously informed about the current state of musical creation.[97]

Again like those groups, the new one declared itself in principle against the cliquishness that had divided Vienna's music world:

> No type of style, no "direction" will be given special preference in the choice of works to be performed. Since the artistic quality of a composition has nothing to do with affiliation with any direction or school, works of the classicizing as of the New German school, of the Apollonian as of the Dionysian direction should be performed, as long as a powerful artistic personality expresses itself in a formally impeccable manner in them.[98]

In an article greeting the Vereinigung, Guido Adler explained the group's tolerance for "Apollonian," in other words, classicizing, music by noting that its proposed program could not indeed be "completely detached from traditional art" in Vienna, "the classically consecrated site" for music, for though the "artistic receptiveness" of the city's concert public could not be disputed, that audience "nevertheless has its own definite taste, which rests on tradition." Adler acknowledged that in most essentials the musical inclinations of the Viennese did not differ from those of audiences in many German cultural centers, seeing the primary distinction to lie precisely in the attitude of the Viennese public toward the city's musical past: "That the Viennese cling to this does not have to do so much with the law of inertia characteristic of everything human, as with reverence before the hallowed tradition of classical art and ancestral love for Austria's musical dynasty." Adler cited the recently founded Konzertverein as friendly to contemporary music, but believed that the "historical institutions of the Gesellschaft der Musikfreunde [and] the Philharmonic can only permit the new to a limited extent, for here the conservative public is united." He considered the group of composers to be "breaking away from the presently existing organizations and forming a musical Secession, as has happened in the field of fine arts in Vienna and for music already in several German cities."[99] In reviews of the first concert sponsored by the Vereinigung, commentators almost unanimously invoked the Secession analogy, which well before then had become a staple of music-critical discourse.

THE SECESSION ANALOGY

What did references to the Secession add to the lexicon of Viennese music criticism? In his review of the concert of orchestral songs by Mahler in 1900, Hanslick applied the metaphor of the Secession to express his own partly resigned expectation of a specifically twentieth-century musical orientation: "Now, at the beginning of a new century, it is advisable to say after each new work of the musical 'Secession' (Mahler, Richard Strauss, Hugo Wolf, and so on): It is very possible that the future belongs to them.[100] The word seems to mean something along the lines of "modernist school." For a critical chameleon like Theodor Helm, the analogy could take on positive or negative connotations according to the journalistic context and the composer under consideration. Thus he used it approvingly to compare the controversy that surrounded Strauss when he conducted his own music in 1901 during a return visit to Vienna with the different reaction that he had elicited from Viennese audiences in 1895: "No note by Strauss himself, however, was heard then, nor was he yet at that time the daring musical Secessionist of today, over whose artistic significance a whole world quarrels at length in passionately heated pros and cons."[101] But Helm's stance toward Mahler, as we know, was far more convoluted; hence the metaphor of the Secession took on a variety of nuances in his reviews of that composer's music. In the *Musikalisches Wochenblatt* Helm called attention to "a very curious thing, this Fourth Symphony of our hypersecessionistically gifted opera director.''[102] When he employed the analogy again in the same journal to describe *Das klagende Lied*, he focused on the orchestrational complexity that helped stamp turn-of-the-century compositions as modernistic: ''In setting this uncanny story Mahler lets the orchestra play by far the chief role; he handles it with a brilliance, an array of color, a Secessionist refinement.''[103] A similar application of the word in the *Deutsche Zeitung* had a more ambivalent tone: in a review of Mahler's First symphony, Helm questioned the need for the Philharmonic to program a work ''revealing at best a certain Secessionistic deftness in the orchestral technique, with still so many debts of honor to be paid off to Bruckner, Liszt, Rich, Strauss, and other masters.''[104]

The fine-arts Secession had more basically meant institutional change; therein lay the supposed likeness between it and the Vereinigung Schaffender Tonkünstler in Wien. Certainly, the organizers of the new musical alliance made its name analogous (at least in German) with the official title of the Secession: Vereinigung der Bildenden Künstler Oesterreichs (Alliance of Austria's Fine Artists). The first concert given by the group, an orchestral performance, took place on 23 November 1904. Mahler, the honorary president of the organization, conducted the Wiener Konzertverein orchestra in a program of works, all text based, by Strauss, Siegmund von Hausegger, and Hermann Bischoff: the existence of a second professional orchestra enabled not only an expansion of the audience for the standard repertory, but also the performance of adventuresome contemporary works.

Helm wrote that the Vereinigung ''represents what one could call 'Musical Secession,' ''[105] and Bach, the critic of the *Arbeiter-Zeitung*, affirmed that ''the similarity between the two artistic organizations was patent.[106] Vancsa elaborated on the analogy in the *Neue musikalische Presse*, beginning with this observation: ''It can safely be said that both institutions originated from a deeply felt need.'' After describing the previously petrified state of the fine arts in Vienna, which according to him had been at more or less the same place in 1895 as in the 1870s, Vancsa noted that the present situation in music was by no means as dire as it had been in other arts seven years ago, before the establishment of the Secession: ''The monopolization of musical activity has already been broken by the founding of the Konzertverein and other enterprises.''[107]

Yet if a second orchestra (and a string quartet, the Rosé) willing to perform difficult contemporary music already existed, and if, unlike the fine-arts Secession, ''the fight of the musical Secessionists,'' as Bach noted, ''does not at all go against any endeavors whatsoever by other musicians,''[108] does the analogy have any real meaning beyond that casually assigned to it by Hanslick and Helm? If not, why did so many of the critics enthusiastically endorse the comparison with the fine-arts Secession? Perhaps the institutional framework in the music world did not, after all, closely resemble that in the fine arts. Elitism had been a problem particular to Viennese musical culture—virtually anyone had long been able to visit the city's museums and galleries—but the situation had begun to improve. Protracted battles between opposing directions had taken place in Vienna's music world before those in other artistic circles; the tendency in music was now, as we have seen, toward reconciliation. Institutional change had come most slowly in the teaching of composition at the Conservatory. A number of commentators appear to have seen the crisis to lie precisely in the state of musical art, where they indeed wished for an advance of Secessionistic importance.

In 1899 the music critic Otto Keller had discussed at length the significance of the Secession in other areas:

> Secession—a modern word, which was flung out into the world like a burning torch and signified a declaration of war against everything previously existing. What is Secession? I certainly do not believe that it is necessary to explain the word and its meaning. The Secession captured the field of painting, graphic arts, decorative arts, fashion; it stands for a withdrawal from the former direction, a new path, a new orientation, that became dominant and set the standard everywhere.[109]

Keller did not believe that, in this sense, a contemporary Secession had taken place in music. What he and the critics who hailed the creation of the Vereinigung five years later wished to advocate was, it seems, a radically new direction in musical composition. The classicizing style associated with Liberal culture had long since become an obvious dead end, and some critics had also begun to question whether the innovations introduced by the New German School could be taken any further.

Keller, for one, expressed doubts about the continuing validity of that longstanding musical counterculture, which he limited in his discussion to its recent manifestations in the symphonies of Bruckner and Mahler, Strauss's tone poems, and Wolf's lieder, writing that these works did not merit the designation "Secession," for "only that direction can be called Secession that systematically tries to achieve new effects with old means, with received materials."[110] He saw the listed compositions as extreme in style yet retrospective, final offshoots in categories that could be taken no further, but he did believe that the stylistic mannerisms might somehow prepare the way for a true Secession in music. In his review of the Vereinigung's first concert, Bach asserted along similar lines that for some time music "more than perhaps all other arts has been in a crisis-ridden state of transition," and that had made it "not just a useful, but rather a necessary deed to offer the composers of the present the possibility of hearing their works performed."[111] Like Keller, Bach and Vancsa wanted music as innovative as the works of the more extreme Secession artists, all three critics concluding that the early excesses of that movement had led to the development of a mature modern art. Viewing musical composition as at an impasse, they awaited a Secessionistic breakthrough.

The musical Vereinigung did not, in truth, have much of an impact on musical life in the city, lasting only one season. The advanced orchestration and the reliance on literary texts in turn-of-the-century modernistic compositions do not appear to have formed a sufficient basis for a new music, and the alliance did not manage to foster a Secessionistic vision like that which, only several years later, Schoenberg would have. Still, the hopes that it raised suggest again the variegated quality of Viennese musical culture, facets of which were changing, if at different rates. In most respects the city's famous conservatism appears less than monolithic and also multivalent: Brahms and Fuchs, for instance, presented different inflections of late-nineteenth-century classicism. Schoenberg himself would later claim Brahms as an influence and also, in effect, align himself with the critics around Brahms who upheld the ideal of absolute music and the principle of musical logic challenged by fin-de-siècle modernism. The sticking points for these Liberal critics, moreover, become understandable in view of Austria's peculiar status, absolute music offering, as the Secession's spokesperson said of her own group, "a form of art that would weld together all the characteristics of our multitude of constituent peoples into a new and proud unity."[112] For if Adler attributed the supposed conservatism of the Viennese public to its respect for the classical legacy, as he himself made clear, this same tradition could be used to justify not only the most hidebound, but also the most worthy and, ultimately, even progressive agendas.

NOTES

The author gratefully acknowledges support from the American Philosophical Society during the preparation of this chapter.

1. Carl E. Schorske, *Fin-de-Siécle Vienna: Politics and Culture* (New York: Vintage Books, 1981), xviii and *passim.*

2. Margaret Notley, "Brahms as Liberal: Genre, Style, and Politics in Late Nineteenth-Century Vienna," *19th-Century Music* 17 (1993): 107–23.

3. For this phrase, see the introduction to *Wagnerism in European Culture and Politics*, ed. David C. Large and William Weber (Ithaca, NY: Cornell University Press, 1984), 18.

4. Adam Wandruszka, "Oesterreichs politische Struktur," in *Geschichte der Republik Oesterreich*, ed. Heinrich Benedikt (Munich: R. Oldenbourg, 1954), 292–93; translated in William J. McGrath, *Dionysian Art and Populist Politics in Austria* (New Haven: Yale University Press, 1974), 166.

5. Herwig [Eduard Pichl], *Georg Schönerer und die Entwicklung des Alldeutschtumes in der Ostmark: Ein Lebensbild*, 4 vols. (1912–23; reprint, Oldenburg Berlin: Gerhard Stalling, 1938), 2:59.

6. McGrath, *Dionysian Art and Populist Politics*, 201.

7. See, for example, Schorske, *Fin-de-Siècle Vienna*, 133–46.

8. John W. Boyer, *Culture and Political Crisis in Vienna: Christian Socialism in Power, 1897–1918* (Chicago: University of Chicago Press, 1995).

9. Andrew G. Whiteside, *The Socialism of Fools: Georg Ritter von Schönerer and Austrian Pan-Germanism* (Berkeley and Los Angeles: University of California Press, 1975), 147.

10. Ibid., 160–87.

11. See, for example, Ludwig Karpath, *Begegnung mit dem Genius*, 2nd ed. (Vienna: Fiba Verlag, 1934), 140.

12. Sandra McColl, *Music Criticism in Vienna, 1896–1897: Critically Moving Forms* (Oxford: Clarendon Press, 1996), 94–100.

13. Theodor Helm, *Musikalisches Wochenblatt* 31 (1900): 100.

14. "Antisemitische Strömung," *Neue freie Presse*, 10 January 1899.

15. Richard S. Geehr, *Karl Lueger: Mayor of Fin de Siècle Vienna* (Detroit: Wayne State University Press, 1990), 192–97.

16. Johann Wilhelm Seidl, *Musik und Austromarxismus: Zur Musikrezeption der österreichischen Arbeiterbewegung im späten Kaiserreich und in der Ersten Republik*, Wiener Musikwissenschaftliche Beiträge, vol. 17 (Vienna: Böhlau Verlag, 1989), 11–25.

17. See David Josef Bach, "Viktor Adler und Gustav Mahler," *Kunst und Volk: Mitteilungen des Vereines "Sozialdemokratische Kunststelle"* 1, no. 10 (November 1926): 6: "Gustav Mahler always held himself aloof from political life and everything party-like. That his politics were socialist, everyone who came in contact with him knows, and he showed it publicly. In the 1901 elections, the 'Imperial and Royal Director of the Imperial and Royal State Opera' Gustav Mahler openly cast his ballot for the Social Democratic candidate in his ward. The candidate was named Viktor Adler. The Christian Socials raged, the *Deutsches Volksblatt* [an anti-Semitic daily] could not come up with enough abuse."

18. Arnold Schoenberg, "New Music, Outmoded Music, Style and Idea," in *Style and Idea: Selected Writings of Arnold Schoenberg*, ed. Leonard Stein, trans. Leo Black (Berkeley and Los Angeles: University of California Press, 1975), 121.

19. Margaret Notley, "Bruckner and Viennese Wagnerism," in *Bruckner Studies*, ed. Paul Hawkshaw and Timothy L. Jackson (Cambridge and New York: Cambridge University Press, 1997), 54–71.

20. An article in the *Neues Wiener Journal* of 19 May 1911 mentions the support by Brahms and Hanslick; quoted in *Mahler: A Documentary Study*, ed. Kurt Blaukopf and Zoltan Roman (New York: Oxford University Press, 1976), 189.

21. David Josef Bach, "Aus der Jugendzeit," *Musikblätter des Anbruch* 6 (1924): 319. Heuberger was not alone in these efforts.

22. Maximilian Muntz, *Deutsche Zeitung*, 11 April 1899: 2.

23. Kurt Paupié, *Wien*, vol. 1 of *Handbuch der österreichischen Pressegeschichte, 1848–1959* (Vienna: Wilhelm Braumüller, 1960), 148.

24. Maximilian Muntz, "Die Wiener Concertsaison von 1898/99: Rückblicke, Ergänzen, und Betrachtungen. II," *Deutsche Zeitung*, 19 May 1899: 3.

25. Ibid.

26. Theodor Helm, *Musikalisches Wochenblatt* 32 (1901): 204. See Sandra McColl, "Max Kalbeck and Gustav Mahler," *19th-Century Music* 20 (1996): 167–84, for a thoughtful treatment of Kalbeck's reception of Mahler.

27. Ludwig Karpath wrote, for example, a thoroughly favorable review of Mahler's Second Symphony in the *Neues Wiener Tagblatt* of 10 April 1899.

28. Henry-Louis de La Grange, *Vienna: The Years of Challenge (1897–1904)*, vol. 2 of *Gustav Mahler* (Oxford: Oxford University Press, 1995), 311.

29. *Das Rosé Quartett: Fünfzig Jahre Kammermusik in Wien. Sämtliche Programme vom 1. Quartett am 22. Januar 1883 bis April 1932*, with an introduction by Julius Korngold (Vienna: n.p., n.y.), 9.

30. Bach, "Aus der Jugendzeit," 318.

31. David Josef Bach, "Der Arbeiter und die Kunst," *Kampf* 7 (1913/14): 41; quoted in Seidl, *Musik und Austromarxismus*, 42.

32. For Hirschfeld and for other critics not discussed here, see Leon Botstein, "Music and Its Public: Habits of Listening and the Crisis of Musical Modernism in Vienna, 1870–1914" (Ph.D. diss., Harvard University, 1985); also see McColl, *Music Criticism in Vienna*.

33. Theodor Helm, *Musikalisches Wochenblatt* 30 (1899): 526.

34. Theodor Helm, *Musikalisches Wochenblatt* 33 (1902): 39.

35. Karl Kraus, "Antworten des Herausgebers," *Fackel* 4, no. 123 (December, 1902): 26.

36. Theodor Helm, *Musikalisches Wochenblatt* 30 (1899): 133: " 'Eine Herzensergiessung compagnieweise: kann man die ernst nehmen?' "

37. Eduard Hanslick, *Neue freie Presse*, 17 January 1899.

38. See Margaret Notley, "*Volksconcerte* in Vienna and Late Nineteenth-Century Ideology of the Symphony," *Journal of the American Musicological Society* 50 (1997): 421–53.

39. Maximilian Muntz, *Deutsche Zeitung*, 11 April 1899: 2–3.

40. Theodor Helm, *Musikalisches Wochenblatt* 32 (1901): 143.

41. Max Kalbeck, " 'Das klagende Lied' von Gustav Mahler: Ein Beitrag zur Aesthetik der Gegenwart," *Neues Wiener Tagblatt*, 23 February 1901: 1–2.

42. Max Vancsa, *Neues Musikalische Presse* 14 (1905): 42.

43. Theodor Helm, *Musikalisches Wochenblatt* 35 (1904): 895.

44. Eduard Hanslick, review from *Neue freie Presse*, reprinted in Eduard Hanslick, *Aus neuer und neuester Zeit (Der modernen Oper IX. Teil): Musikalische Kritiken und Schilderungen* (Berlin: Allgemeiner Verein für Deutsche Litteratur, 1900), 76.

45. Max Kalbeck, *Neues Wiener Tagblatt*, 23 February 1901: 1.

46. Max Kalbeck, *Neues Wiener Tagblatt*, 16 January 1902: 2.

47. Max Kalbeck, "Gustav Mahler's *Sinfonia ironica*," *Neues Wiener Tagblatt*, 20 November 1900: 2.

48. Theodor Helm, *Musikalisches Wochenblatt* 32 (1901): 204.

49. Theodor Helm, *Musikalisches Wochenblatt* 32 (1901): 116.

50. Eduard Hanslick, review from *Neue freie Presse*, reprinted in Hanslick, *Aus neuer und neuester Zeit*, 85.

51. Richard Heuberger, *Neue freie Presse*, 24 March 1902: 5.

52. Ibid.

53. David Josef Bach, "Die Kunststelle," in *Kunst und Volk: Eine Festgabe der Kunststelle zur 1000. Theateraufführung* (Vienna: Verlag Leopold Heidrich, 1923), 116; quoted in Seidl, *Musik und Austromarxismus*, 139.

54. For Wagner's own complex and changing stance toward absolute and program music, see "The Idea of the Musically Absolute and the Practice of Program Music," in Carl Dahlhaus, *The Idea of Absolute Music*, trans. Roger Lustig (Chicago: University of Chicago Press, 1989), 128–40.

55. Bach, "Die Kunststelle"; quoted in Seidl, *Musik und Austromarxismus*, 139.

56. Guido Adler, "Feuilleton: Musikalische Kulturprobleme unserer Zeit," *Neue freie Presse*, 17 December 1906. For Adler, see Volker Kalisch, *Entwurf einer Wissenschaft von der Musik: Guido Adler* (Baden-Baden: Verlag Valentin Kouner, 1988); and Botstein, "Music and Its Public."

57. This information is from the *Jahresberichte* of the Wagner-Verein for 1873 and 1888.

58. Guido Adler, *Richard Wagner: Vorlesungen gehalten an der Universität zu Wien* (Leipzig: Breitkopf und Härtel, 1904). See also Guido Adler, *Wollen und Wirken: Aus dem Leben eines Musikhistorikers* (Vienna: Universal-Edition, 1935), 78–79.

59. Reported in the *Neue freie Presse* of 27 January 1906: 7. Although the article is not signed, according to Edward R. Reilly, the autograph demonstrates that Adler wrote it. See the unpublished list by Reilly, "The Papers of Guido Adler at the University of Georgia: A Provisional Inventory," 12–13. I wish to thank Prof. Reilly for sharing his work with me.

60. Ibid.

61. Adler, *Wollen und Wirken*, 29–30.

62. Schorske, *Fin-de-Siècle Vienna*, 237.

63. Adler's students included Paul A. Pisk, Anton Webern, Egon Wellesz, and Karl Weigl, among others. See Adler, *Wollen und Wirken*, 42.

64. Stefan Kunze, "Klassikerrezeption in den Kompositionslehren des frühen 19. Jahrhunderts," *Schweizer Beiträge zur Musikwissenschaft* 3, ed. Kurt von Fischer, Stefan Kunze, Ernst Lichtenhahn, and Hans Oesch (Bern and Stuttgart: Verlag Paul Haupt, 1978), 151.

65. According to the yearly *Berichte über das Conservatorium für Musik und darstellende Kunst der Gesellschaft der Musikfreunde in Wien*, Fuchs began to teach counterpoint as well as harmony in 1890–91. See also Adalbert Grote, *Robert Fuchs: Studien zu Person und Werk des Wiener Komponisten und Theorielehrers*, Berliner Musikwissenschaftliche Arbeiten, vol. 39, ed. Carl Dahlhaus and Rudolf Stephan (Munich and Salzburg: Emil Katzbichler, 1994), 40: "In 1895, thus two years before his death, Brahms, possibly as a member of the directorate [of the Gesellschaft], had recommended Robert Fuchs to head the joint teaching of theory and composition."

66. See, for example, Robert W. Wason, *Viennese Harmonic Theory from Albrechtsberger to Schenker and Schoenberg* (Ann Arbor: UMI Research Press, 1985), 84.

67. Felix Petyrek, "Franz Schreker als Lehrer," *Musikblätter des Anbruch* 10 (1928): 113; quoted in part in Christopher Hailey, *Franz Schreker, 1878–1934: A Cultural Biography* (Cambridge: Cambridge University Press, 1993), 59.

68. Wilhelm Bopp, quoted in Grote, *Robert Fuchs*, 61.

69. Ibid.

70. Guido Adler, "Feuilleton: Eine neue musikalische Vereinigung in Wien," *Neue freie Presse*, 1 April 1904:1.

71. For this organization, see Notley, "Bruckner and Viennese Wagnerism," 66–67.

72. Most of the information in these paragraphs came from a study of the *Jahresberichte* of the Wagner-Verein for the years 1873 through 1910.

73. Theodor Helm, "Fünfzig Jahre Wiener Musikleben (1866–1916): Erinnerungen eines Musikkritikers," *Merker* 7 (1916): 767.

74. See Willi Kahl, "Die Neudeutschen und die Kammermusik," *Musik* 20 (1927–28): 429–33.

75. See Notley, "Bruckner and Viennese Wagnerism," passim.

76. Theodor Helm, *Deutsche Zeitung*, 17 December 1891: 1, in a review of a performance by the Vienna Philharmonic of Bruckner's First Symphony: "Man befindet sich da [the Wagner-Verein] in einer Art Klein-Bayreuth für Bruckner."

77. See Richard Heuberger, "Brahms als Vereinsmitglied," reprinted in *Erinnerun-*

gen an Johannes Brahms: Tagebuchnotizen aus den Jahren 1875 bis 1897, ed. Kurt Hofmann (Tutzing: Hans Schneider, 1976), 173–82.

78. "Vom Wiener Tonkünstlerverein" (signed "r."), *Unverfälschte deutsche Worte*, 16 March 1887: 94. The same inflammatory pun reappeared in another article in the same periodical, "Wiener Musik Verhältnisse" (signed "n."), 1 December 1888: 295.

79. No full file of the *Berichte* for the Tonkünstlerverein appears to have survived. I have looked at reports from these years: 1888–89, 1892–99, 1900–1901, 1907–1908, 1909–12.

80. *Rechenschafts-Bericht des Ausschusses des Wiener Tonkünstler-Vereins für das 25. Vereinsjahr vom 1. November 1909 bis 1. November 1910*, 2.

81. *Rechenschafts-Bericht des Ausschusses des Wiener Tonkünstler-Vereins für das 16. Vereinsjahr vom 1. November 1900 bis 1. November 1901*, 8.

82. Arnold Schoenberg, "Criteria for the Evaluation of Music," in *Style and Idea*, 131.

83. La Grange, *Vienna: The Years of Challenge*, 692.

84. August Duesberg, *Ueber Hebung der Volksmusik in Hinsicht auf das "Erste Wiener Volksquartett für classische Musik"* (Vienna: Lesk und Schwidernoch, [1892]), 3.

85. Ibid., 23.

86. Ibid., 16. Duesberg's Quartet was a particular favorite of the right-wing *völkisch* press. In the group's program notes, he substituted Teutonic neologisms for standard German words derived from other languages, a practice espoused by the Pan-Germans. See Eduard Hanslick, *Fünf Jahre Musik (1891–1895)*, vol. 7 of *Die Moderne Oper* (Berlin: Allegmeiner Verein für Deutsche Literatur, 1986), 286–87, for a sarcastic commentary on Duesberg's program notes.

87. Duesberg, *Ueber Hebung der Volksmusik*, 5.

88. Ibid., 11.

89. According to the *Jahresberichte* of the Wagner-Verein, Duesberg became a member in 1886, left in 1888, but returned in 1898; according to the *Rechenschafts-Bericht* of the Tonkünstlerverein, he became a member in 1892.

90. See, for example, Notley, "*Volksconcerte* in Vienna."

91. Bach noted in "Aus der Jugendzeit," 317, that outdoor concerts by military bands "for most of us offered the only opportunity actually to hear a little music."

92. Theodor Helm, *Musikalisches Wochenblatt* 31 (1900): 139.

93. *Jahresbuch des Wiener Konzertverein über das Jahr 1900–01* (Vienna: n.p., 1901), 6.

94. Theodor Helm, *Musikalisches Wochenblatt* 32 (1901): 158.

95. Ibid.

96. Reprinted in *Neue musikalische Presse* 13 (1904): 178–79, at 179.

97. Ibid.

98. Ibid., 1.

99. Adler, "Feuilleton: Eine neue musikalische Vereinigung in Wien."

100. Eduard Hanslick, review from the *Neue freie Presse*, reprinted in Hanslick, *Aus neuer und neuester Zeit*, 77.

101. Theodor Helm, *Musikalisches Wochenblatt* 32 (1901): 116.

102. Theodor Helm, *Musikalisches Wochenblatt* 33 (1902): 69.

103. Theodor Helm, *Musikalisches Wochenblatt* 32 (1901): 143.

104. Theodor Helm, *Deutsche Zeitung*, 20 November 1900: 7.

105. Theodor Helm, *Musikalisches Wochenblatt* 35 (1904): 894.

106. David Josef Bach, ''Feuilleton: Sezession in der Musik,'' *Arbeiter-Zeitung*, 2 December 1904: 1.

107. Max Vancsa, *Neue musikalische Presse* 13 (1904): 341.

108. Bach, ''Feuilleton: Sezession in der Musik,'' 1.

109. Otto Keller, *Deutsche Kunst- und Musikzeitung* 26 (1899): 60.

110. Ibid.

111. Bach, ''Feuilleton: Sezession in der Musik,'' 1.

112. See note 62.

3 *WIENER MODERNE* AND THE TENSIONS OF MODERNISM

Dagmar Barnouw

> I have learned more from you, perhaps, than is permissible if I want to preserve my independence.
>
> —Arnold Schoenberg's dedication in the copy of his *Harmonielehre* sent to Karl Kraus.[1]

Schoenberg's admiring words addressed to Karl Kraus are only a small indication of the multiplicity of connections that link the work of the Second Viennese School to the nonmusical arts, letters, and sciences that flowered in Vienna early in the twentieth century. The intellectual legacy of Kraus, Adolf Loos, Ludwig Wittgenstein, Sigmund Freud, Ernst Mach, and Robert Musil proved so prophetic and distinctively Viennese that it has since been termed *Wiener Moderne*—Viennese modernism—a term like Second Viennese School that embraces the diverse, though coherent, outlook on the future that characterizes the music and artistic perspective of Schoenberg, Berg, and Webern. So important is the legacy of *Wiener Moderne* that I turn in this chapter away from music per se in order to analyze the phenomenon in its own right and to describe the highly complex set of conditions under which it thrived. Analogies with the musical modernism of the Second Viennese School, described in other chapters of this book, will be obvious.

Schoenberg, Berg, and Webern freely admitted to the stimulus that they received from outside of music. Schoenberg, for example, found in the poetry of the German Stefan George the catalyst that he needed finally to move beyond the late romantic style of Hugo Wolf, Richard Strauss, and Max Reger into the uncharted realm of atonality. Webern's student Frederick Dorian recalled his teacher's dictum, paraphrasing Kraus, that the fate of humanity could well depend on the correct placement of a comma. Berg almost never missed a lecture that Kraus gave in Vienna, and his correspondence with Schoenberg and Webern is filled with discussions of these events, which he found sometimes troubling but always ingenious. Adolf Loos was so close, both personally and professionally, to those of the Second Viennese School that he can virtually be counted as one of its members. He polemicized on their behalf, attended their concerts, and was always ready to use his fists to silence protestors at these occasions. Although not as initimate with the Second Viennese School, Karl Kraus was a constant presence in their minds. They all read his journal, *Die Fackel*, and Schoenberg attentively imitated his style of writing and polemical tone in his own aphorisms and brief essays. Perhaps surprisingly, the three composers had only limited contact with Freud or his psychoanalytic circle. But they all pondered the role of the unconscious mind in musical creativity, and a work such as Schoenberg's *Erwartung* clearly reveals in the actions of its hysterical protagonist an awareness of Freud's analysis of psychosis.

The phenomenon of *Wiener Moderne*, or, as some cultural historians prefer, *Wiener Avantgarde*, has intrigued many critics with its wealth of new developments in many areas of high culture, especially literature and the arts.[2] In a recent essay, ''Die Position der jüdischen Intelligenz in der Wiener Moderne,'' Steven Beller has argued strongly for a dominating role of Jews in Viennese liberal high culture around 1900: ''If one assumes that ''Wiener Moderne'' is a product of the 'liberal,' 'educated,' and bourgeois class, is it not important to recognize that this liberal, educated, bourgeois class was two-thirds Jewish?''[3] His list of important Jewish participants in *Wiener Moderne* is, expectedly, impressive: not only did they contribute a large majority of the ''leading'' writers, critics, journalists, and dramatists, they also did important work in such areas as music, philosophy, medicine, and progressive politics. It is ''unthinkable'' for Beller to speak of *Wiener Moderne* ''without mentioning Josef Popper-Lynkeus, Otto Neurath, Hans Kuhn, Karl Popper, and also Ludwig Wittgenstein.''

In Beller's scenario modern Judaism equals Enlightenment equals liberalism. He concedes that Viennese Jews, especially in the area of literature, had been influenced to some degree by Viennese baroque culture with its social and political hierarchy, aestheticism, and determined abdication of responsibility. However, it was Jewish intellectuals who criticized most incisively these aspects of Viennese culture and thus were instrumental in bringing about *Wiener Moderne*: ''Especially Freud, Schnitzler, Schoenberg, Kraus—and also Weininger come to mind here.'' In Beller's view, the animosity toward Jews expressed in Viennese political anti-Semitism affirmed Jews in their ''recognition of the dangers of purely aesthetic, a-ethical, irrational modernity—a recognition that made *Wiener Moderne* particularly important.''[4] He acknowledges that Robert Musil or

Ernst Mach had similar ideas on these issues. Viennese Jews were not the only ones who had "developed" German liberal culture, and they were not alone in criticizing certain aspects of Viennese culture. But even though *Wiener Moderne* signified a complexly multicultural confluence of Jewish, *reichsdeutsch*[5] Catholic, and Slav influences, Beller thinks that Jewish influence was by far the most important, citing here Musil's work, which appears to him completely dominated by it. If Jews seem to play only a small part in the sociopolitical world of Musil's "Kakanian" capital (Vienna), this is for Beller nothing but "camouflage," and he lists Arnheim (Walther Rathenau), Fischel, Feuermaul (Franz Werfel), Tuzzi (Hermann Schwarzwald), and even Agathe (Musil's Jewish wife Martha Heimann): "The cultural world of Musil's Vienna was predominantly Jewish. . . . Musil was part of a world in which Jewish writers were leading and Jews supported the new literature."[6]

If Musil's Vienna was predominantly Jewish—an assertion that remains open to discussion—he clearly did not assign his "Jewish" characters the characteristically Jewish "emancipatory" energies of Beller's scenario: their unwavering "search for a world of equality and freedom" as the "great steam engine driving *Wiener Moderne*."[7] As I will argue, the "great" literary Jewish figures associated with *Wiener Moderne*—Freud, Karl Kraus, and Wittgenstein—flatly contradict Beller's claims. *Wiener Moderne* was driven by many different "steam engines" going in different directions simultaneously, precisely because it reflected so clearly the psychic, social, and political difficulties caused by the emancipatory hopes and demands of Enlightenment modernity: acceptance of an open self and with it cultural openness to other forms of social organization, transformation, mobility, anthropological imagination, multivocalism, tolerance for open conflicts of interest, critique of authority, and psychological and social secularism, to name just a few. Robert Musil, profoundly influenced by Ernst Mach's functionalist concept of the "open self," was arguably the "greatest," that is, the most astute, articulate, and persuasive critic of these difficulties that he saw so clearly and sharply from the hindsight of the Weimar Republic when they had escalated dangerously. Some of his most powerful critical arguments in the *The Man without Qualities* (1932) went into the making of Arnheim (Rathenau)—a *Geistesfürst* (prince of the ideational) and *Grosschriftsteller* (superman of letters) resounding with the seductive vacuities of "progressive" high-cultural syntheses. If his characters were "Jewish," they were so in such differential ways as to make Beller's unifying scenario useless. Beller also overlooked the salient fact that Musil re-created Vienna in a work of fiction, not of sociology, political science, or psychology, though his insights presented in fictional discourse are important for these areas of inquiry. He was in a position to shape his different characters according to the needs of his essayistic-fictional explorations of Kakanian (Weimar) cultural malaise. There is a world of difference between the impeccable high-cultural correctness and economic-political astuteness of the immensely successful Arnheim[8] and the endearingly humdrum common sense of the banker Fischel; between the precisely observed comical self-inflations of the poet Feuermaul and the dry, ironical intelligence of the diplomat Tuzzi.[9]

Kraus, in his different roles as political journalist and dramatist, philosophical socio-linguist and neoidealist poet, was the sharpest and wittiest critic of Viennese *Kulturbetrieb*, the lively business of culture. He admired Otto Weininger's tormented, disturbing talent in *Geschlecht und Charakter* (1902) and did not think much of Freud's ''metapsychological'' mythopoetic constructs. But his own yearning for and celebration of a paradisiacally pure, ''Adamatic'' language, beckoning behind all the corrupted language use he was castigating so brilliantly, shares certain important aspects of Freud's search for the origin: the neoromantic, Neoplatonic descent into the true truth of the self or of language. So does Wittgenstein's desire to define once and for all what can be said by demanding to remain silent about what cannot be said. (Puzzled and intrigued, Bertrand Russell noted in the introduction to Wittgenstein's *Tractatus Logico-philosophicus* that its author managed to speak quite eloquently about what cannot be said.) Wittgenstein, too, admired the young ''genius'' Weininger for his radical perspective on the familiar ''otherness'' of Jews and women.[10] Like Freud's, Weininger's psychological radicalism is mythopoetic and at the same time touches on difficult social-psychological realities. But unlike Freud, he also shared with Kraus, Adolf Loos, and Wittgenstein a preoccupation with drawing clear distinctions in the ''crossover'' multivocal culture of *Wiener Moderne*.[11]

If there is one common strand in *Wiener Moderne*, it is not ''Jewish domination,'' though many Jews contributed to it. As a group, they had done well in Vienna, representing at the turn of the century a large portion of the educated middle classes. The reasons for their success, repeated in Germany, are composite, as they have been for other successful minorities in modern Western cultures. But in the case of Viennese Jews, their ability, as a group, to cope well with certain aspects of modernity that caused great problems for other groups was particularly important.[12] However, as contributors to *Wiener Moderne*, a high-cultural movement that emphasized individual creativity, Jews, though numerous, differed so much among themselves as to make its alleged ''Jewishness'' a moot question: just imagine a literary group portrait of Kraus, Arthur Schnitzler, Freud, Hugo von Hofmannsthal, Theodor Herzl, Hermann Broch, and Franz Werfel. The notion of an overarching significant Jewishness is a product of a post–World War II hindsight perspective, anachronistic, if understandable. It is not a useful tool with which to approach the complexly multicultural phenomenon of *Wiener Moderne* in terms of the contributions of differently acculturated groups, of different critical (ideological) positions, and of different cultural activities.

Instructively, there is no room in Beller's concept of *Wiener Moderne* for the contributions of the fine arts, architecture, and the Arts and Crafts movement that, perhaps more than anything else, shaped an enduring general notion of *Wiener Moderne*. Jews were ''underrepresented'' in this area, though they were great supporters through commissions and purchases. Beller quotes from Kraus's widely read journal *Die Fackel*: "Dear Fackel! A puzzle [*Preisrätsel*]: A lady is sitting in a chair by Olbrich—Darmstadt, she is wearing a dress by Van de Velde—Brussels, ear-pendants by Lalique—Paris, a brooch by Ashbee—London, she is drinking from a glass by Kolo Moser—Vienna, reading in a book published by "Insel"—Munich, printed in type by Otto Eckmann—Berlin, written by Hofmannsthal—Vienna. What is her confession?"[13] It could, of course, be any "confession" or none. Beller's suggestion that the point of the "puzzle" is "le goût juif" is probably right. The issue is Viennese cosmopolitan consumption, frivolous and therefore somewhat suspect in the view of the purist Kraus, who did not care much for novels and paintings, not to mention Hofmannsthal's poetry, pretty clothes, and stylish jewelry.[14] However, presenting the lady as a "contemporary symbol" of "Jewish cultural preeminence" (*jüdische Vorherrschaft*) in *Wiener Moderne*, Beller greatly simplifies the issue.[15] The lady, whoever she was, would have had the good taste and the money to ask Gustav Klimt to paint her in all her culturally correct chic.[16] Like most members of the newly rich European haute bourgeoisie, wealthy Jews were particularly interested in following the latest fashions in "high" art as well as in arts and crafts, and with all the cultural advantages and disadvantages of such preoccupation with the "cutting-edge" attractions of the "coming."[17] Consumption and production are, of course, intimately linked, and the flourishing of certain kinds of painting and of arts and crafts objects in Vienna is attributable to the interest of wealthy buyers, Jewish and non-Jewish. But did Klimt, whose portraits affirmed the sophisticated stylishness of his sitters, some of them Jewish, respond to a particular Jewishness in their self-presentation? How "Jewish" were these rich, cultivated Jews—for instance, the Wittgenstein family? These are extraordinarily complicated questions that have been unduly simplified in the post–World War II period, sometimes to the detriment of a more intelligently critical cultural history of this indeed fascinating "confluence" of different "ethnicities," that is, cultural traditions, practices, and mindsets.[18]

ADOLF LOOS, KARL KRAUS, AND THEIR CIRCLES

In the 1960s, Oskar Kokoschka remembered the Adolf Loos who had supported him in his struggles for recognition when he was a young painter as

> a voice in the wilderness. He was the forerunner of modern architecture: that's why he was not allowed to build. . . . His bible was Vitruvius on Greek architecture—that eternal witness of human dignity. Loos' appearance resembled his behavior. His face was like a portrait by a Flemish master. He was a civilized man. Even the way he dressed was in contrast with Viennese "smartness." . . . In Adolf Loos I always saw the last of the Greeks, the individualist.[19]

Always looking for young talent, for something new and original, Loos had commissioned Kokoschka to paint his portrait and had then persuaded his influential friends to let him paint them—an invaluable entrance to the self-consciously elitist and cliquish Viennese high-cultural scene.[20] Kokoschka also remembered how Loos had rescued him from getting stuck in provincial Vienna, selling "the carpets from his own house to pay for my trip."[21]

The Viennese art scene was not quite "the wilderness" Kokoschka later made it out to be, but he was by no means alone in seeing himself perform a significant role in the theatrum mundi that was Vienna—the world his audience—and complaining about Viennese provinciality. Characteristically, Loos had been fascinated most of all by Kokoschka's acts of rebellion: Kokoschka's room in the 1908 exhibition (*Kunstschau*) organized by the Klimt group that had broken away from the Secession was different. With its four large tapestry cartoons, *Die Traumtragenden*, and a painted clay bust, *Der Krieger*, a self-portrait with wide-open mouth suggesting a passionate scream, it was generally referred to as the "Chamber of Horrors," and the influential, by no means reactionary art critic Ludwig Hevesi of *Neue freie Presse* called Kokoschka *Oberwildling* (super wild man). The paper's readership was comfortably bourgeois, culturally "with it," and largely uncritical—more than enough reasons for Kraus to attack it relentlessly. Loos bought the sculpture and, having made a commitment to the young artist, would, from now on, support him unconditionally.

For Loos and for Kokoschka, greatness in cultural terms derived from the intense individualism of the willed outsider position. In his memoirs Kokoschka speaks of Loos as the most important architect of the modern movement, a source of inspiration to his contemporaries. He sees in him the "radical innovator" who declared "total war" on *Jugendstil*, concerning himself with "man's creation of his total environment." Kokoschka is still, as he was then, in complete agreement with this "total" approach, recounting with admiration how in his lectures and in his writings Loos addressed himself to every aspect of modern life, "right down to the way we walk, sit, stand, lie down and cook." Like Loos, Kokoschka wanted to confront Viennese "retrograde society" to impress on it its need for total reeducation and rebirth.[22]

Loos had increasingly taken on the role of the heroic outsider, especially in his writing, but he was by no means isolated. Like his friend and ally Kraus, he was a highly successful lecturer who commanded his audiences' complete attention and loyalty. But like Kraus, too, he presented himself to his audiences in the role of the lone critic of corrupt social conventions—be it in language or in architecture. Instructively, Kokoschka introduced Kraus in his memoirs as the "editor of the much-feared periodical *Die Fackel*"[23]—feared, that is, by "them," the Viennese philistines, but loved and admired to the point of enslavement by the initiated, Vienna's best and brightest when Kokoschka was young. In 1913, responding to a *Rundfrage* (inquiry) sent out by the respected literary journal *Der Brenner* about the phenomenon Karl Kraus, Kokoschka had simply stated, "Karl Kraus descended to hell to sit in judgment over the living and the dead."[24] The *Brenner* inquiry was directed mainly to established literary figures whose answers emphasized Kraus's unquestionable, indeed unique, cultural significance: the educator who, as cultural conscience, purifier, high priest, prophet, and holy warrior, was weaning the young from their morally flabby preoccupation with aesthetics. The (with one exception) adoring statements say a great deal more about their authors' cultural self-perception than about Kraus's work: it was as easy to agree that he was very good as it was difficult not to honor the great outsider, the "only one" (*der Eine*), whose "mission," in the words of *Brenner*, was fighting contemporary cultural and political corruption reflected in contemporary language use.[25] His—and any true intellectual's—archenemies were the highly successful modern mass media controlled by the likes of Mosse, Scherl, and Ullstein. But his attacks on them were irresistible precisely because his "sublime," "geistig" (spiritual) battles with *Journaille* (Kraus's neologism combining the words "journalism" and "canaille") transcended social and linguistic conventions.

The reason given by *Brenner* to conduct its *Rundfrage* was Kraus's enduring isolation, not only in the world against which he fought—which was for it and its (assumed) readership an entirely expected and indeed culturally significant position—but also in the world that he defended, the world of authenticity and *Geist*. The latter assumption (verified, Brenner thought, by the absence of his name from almost all literary histories) seems quite odd, given the visibility (audibility) of Kraus, the famous lecturer. Characteristically, Thomas Mann declared himself enchanted by the "highly visible" "celebrity" Kraus, whose performance as a lecturer he much admired.[26] But Kraus's followers tended to go straight to the essences: the judging, educating, culturally authenticating properties of his critique of socially corrupt language. They affirmed thereby, beyond the shadow of a doubt, his enormous and indeed unique importance for the better future of a profoundly disturbed present. Protecting authentic cultural values by unmasking contemporary inauthenticity, his work was, in the broadest sense, culturally conservative and thereby, in his and their eyes, authentically progressive. In an essay on the tenth anniversary of *Die Fackel* in 1908, Robert Scheu remembered the enormous success of the first issue—the small red brochure was seen everywhere. People were carrying it, reading in it, all over Vienna, in the streets and the parks, and the journal had to be reprinted immediately in the ten thousands.[27] Largely written by Kraus, exclusively so from 1911 (issue 326) on, this small red brochure would be seen for decades all over Vienna on publication day. There was no self-respecting intellectual who did not read it, and young, aspiring intellectuals carried it around like an identity card.[28]

Critics have remarked how Kraus's use of language became increasingly more complex, his wit more self-referential in unmasking and demolishing the corrupt language of others, but they have been less interested in exploring how this ever more refined verbal sophistication had drawn on Kraus's desire for the origin (*Ursprung*), the paradisiacal stage of linguistic innocence, before the misunderstandings caused by symbolic signification. His preoccupation in his *Ursprung* poems with pure language, *Sprache* itself, that is, a language untainted by human (social) use, which to him meant inevitable misuse, arguably influenced his admirer Wittgenstein's *Tractatus* and also Walter Benjamin's early speculations on language. This neoromantic search for Adamitic language, the prelapsarian, presymbolic identity of signifier and signified set against modern misunderstandings and contradictions, was an important aspect of literary *Wiener Moderne* and central to Freud's development of his "metapsychology." During the Weimar Republic it can be found most clearly in the Frankfurt School's neoidealism, notably the Schopenhauer-influenced split between "progressive" critical and "regressive" instrumental reason; in Ernst Bloch's baroque verbal mysticism, Broch's tautological speculations on cultural value, and Benjamin's "magic gaze" that would become the inspirational core of Adorno's *Negative Dialectic*. After the war it reemerged in late Heidegger (*Time and Being*) and, following him, Jacques Derrida's "postmodern" *différence*.

On some level all these texts share the German romantic impatience with Enlightenment affirmation of the "world out there" as the intellectual's responsibility because it is there. This is also true for Kraus's work, despite its admirable social and political activism, above all the unwavering, stunningly articulate resistance to the "Great War," the first global technological disaster. Kraus was one of the few intellectuals who took this disaster seriously, namely, literally, and the combined *Wörtlichkeit und Entsetzen* (literalness and horror) of his antiwar texts has retained its old power.[29] But much of his social and cultural critique at the time, despite its notorious verbal brilliance, has not.

With rapidly advancing technology and ever more impressive, potentially oppressive technocracy, the "world out there" has become immeasurably more complicated and obscure since 1800. A romantic literary and cultural critic like the young Friedrich Schlegel could still praise, in a highly intelligent appreciation of his cultural contribution, the modern cosmopolitanism of the traveler and intellectual Georg Forster. A hundred years later, the position of intellectuals had shifted: it was now precisely their cultural marginality—Kraus and Loos against the corrupt world—in which the intellectual anchored claims to authenticity and therefore authority. Kraus, Loos, Freud, and Wittgenstein are highly important figures of *Wiener Moderne*, and they all exhibit variations on the tension between the modern and the premodern—going forward with and contributing to the process of modernity, and going back to their roots as the significant *Ursprung*. This duality would remain an important aspect of twentieth-century culture, from the period between the two world wars to our current "postmodern" multiculturalism.[30]

Instructively, Kokoschka distinguished between different kinds of individualism: Loos, despite his interest in American architecture, was "worlds apart from the individualist Frank Lloyd Wright."[31] In actuality, Loos's ingenious and resourceful interior designs, especially for low-budget apartment remodeling, distinctly recalled Wright's interiors in Oak Park.[32] In this early stage of his development, Wright was indeed preoccupied with the single-family dwelling, partly under the influence of Louis Henry Sullivan, partly out of his concern for the well-being of the family, which he thought threatened by the acceleration of technological, industrial modernity.[33] But if it is true that he contributed thereby to the illusion that the suburb could preserve the wholesomeness of small-town America, of the American past, he also acknowledged modern modes of self-presentation. Loos had been interested precisely in these aspects of Wright's interior designs: the attention paid to the needs of the individual family, their comfort and their interaction as a group, the use of materials (open beams, whitewashed walls) and space to support relaxed social intercourse, and the emphasis on drawing the outsider (visitor) into the family dynamics rather than encouraging the family's self-presentation in formal (defensive) perfection.

There was another dimension of Wright's design that was to resonate with Loos: his conception of "the house" as a *Gesamtkunstwerk* in which every detail, including the furniture, the light fixtures, and kitchen appliances, down to the clients' purchases of artwork and clothes, would be subject to the architect's advice, his creative will. This concept betrayed, as a critic put it, "a desire to assume total control over one piece of environment, perhaps a compensation for his failure to achieve any influence over the rest. There was certainly a strong element of defensiveness in his will to determine the character of every detail in the sum total, even to the size and shape of the pieces of glass in the window."[34] However, as Wright himself realized, his very success in asserting his creative vision, though revolutionizing a small sector of architecture, had prevented him from achieving what he outlined in his famous Bull House lecture "The Art and Craft of the Machine" (1901). His sought-after designs of suburban houses had identified him with the anachronistic notion of a suburban asylum for clients who could afford to simply leave behind the increasingly difficult urban conditions they were unwilling or unable to change. He began questioning the individualism of his architectural concepts, and his development underwent dramatic changes.

Loos's development was quite different. His work is generally seen as an early forerunner of modern architectural design, International Style, and his originality has assumed attributes of the solitary and the heroic—as he would have wanted it. Thus Nikolaus Pevsner in his influential work *Pioneers of Modern Design from William Morris to Walter Gropius* has much praise for Loos's 1910 Haus Steiner—with its unmistakable modern features it could be dated around the mid- to late 1920s—and laments the fact that Loos has been neglected for too long a time,[35] but he does not point out the contradictions in Loos's work that might have had something to do with such neglect. In Peter Vergo's view, Haus Scheu (1912), with its stepped-back terraces, is the most modern, "forward-looking" of Loos's buildings, less massive, less fortresslike than Haus Steiner, which he nevertheless admires. But he also points out that by the 1920s, when International Style had prevailed and Loos was recognized as one of its earliest and most important practitioners, the innovative architect had moved backward. Of all the contributors to art in Vienna in the early twentieth century,

Vergo writes, "Loos demonstrates quite clearly that duality inherent in the work of the Viennese avant garde, that tension between radicalism and conservatism which, ultimately, limited the impact of the revolution they had initiated."[36]

But what would that revolution have been like? It seems to me that the inherent "duality" was essential to their "revolution," which reemerged after World War I. Instructively, Loos's early essays around 1900 for *Neue freie Presse* and his own short-lived journal *Das Andere* (1903, subtitled "A Newspaper for Introducing Western Culture into Austria") were much less informed by these contradictions than were his later, more "radical" texts like the much-cited manifesto "Ornament und Verbrechen" (Ornament and crime). Loos was to complain in the Foreword to his 1921 essay collection that he disliked the early pieces for their conciliatory tone of sweet reasonableness: he had lowered his voice too much because of external pressure. This explanation, however, comes from a hindsight perspective on his former self that seems too selective. In 1900 he had just returned from a successful trip to America, happily full of new ideas. His texts of that time offered thoughtful, informative arguments, despite their obvious pedagogical fervor and some gestures toward the prophetic. In "Loblied des Overalls" he described the different American attitude to clothes that seemed to him culturally important; his relations, farming people, were equally comfortable in overalls and fashionably elegant city clothes. Liberated from the "quaint," uncomfortable, dysfunctional *Trachten* (ethnic costume) still worn by their Austrian counterparts, they dressed according to the occasion; they used clothes functionally. In several of the pieces written on the occasion of the 1898 *Jubiläumsausstellung* in Vienna, Loos tried to counteract Austrian provincialism and nationalism with praise for the American and British life-style: culture is defined not only by the beauty of its art and architecture but also by the functionality of buildings, appliances, and utensils, by cleanliness, health, and comfort, by physical well-being. "A home without a bathroom! An impossibility in America!" he writes in "Die Plumber" (1898); or "An increase in water consumption is one of the most urgent requirements of civilization."[37]

In the essay "The Story of a Poor Rich Man" (1900), Loos offers a sensible critique of the then-popular *Gesamtkunstwerk* concept of interior design: too self-conscious, too unified, too perfectionist, too restricting. He may have been referring here to the much-admired Mackintosh tearoom of the Eighth Secession Exhibition in 1900, though he usually supported showing modern English design in Vienna. Besides, his own interior designs for coffeehouses and stores were quite close to C. R. Ashbee's designs included in that exhibition; similarities or influences were noted by contemporary critics. In Loos's satirical account, the poor rich man is caught in the design imposed on him by the Secession architect he has commissioned to build his house. Moving one single object would disturb the artistic effect created by the architect, would, in effect, deny his creative authority. Loos's reasonable plea for functionality (not functionalism) rejects the architect's authorizing power over the house built for clients, presumably taking into account their temperament, habits, and needs. The argument rejects imposition of an artificially complete order, no matter how creative or authentic. But the poor rich man and his wife must have subjected themselves willingly to this imposition; in fact, they must have desired to become part of a *Gesamtkunstwerk*. It was chic, culturally correct, and therefore a priori meaningful. Loos restricted himself to ironical pity on the poor rich man, but the subtext of this piece pointed to his increasingly difficult relationship with the increasingly successful Secession, particularly the sumptuous objects of its offspring, the Wiener Werkstätte, or the correctly equipped lady of the *Fackel* puzzle.

Loos had always acknowledged the importance for his development of Otto Wagner's *Moderne Architektur* (1896), sharing Wagner's admiration for the clean lines and the comfort of British industrial art.[38] Like Henry van de Velde, Wagner was in love with the new building material of steel and became duly famous for his designs of Vienna *Stadtbahn* stations. For Wagner, the importance of machines was social as well as aesthetic, or, rather, aesthetic because of the social impact of machines, not despite it. In contrast, William Morris and his followers, whose concept of "arts and crafts" exercised a profound influence on Wiener Werkstätte (formally constituted in 1903), were hostile to the increasing influence of the machine. Loos, on the other hand, shared their stance against the machine where aesthetics were concerned, but he also had fought from the beginning against attempts to combine arts and crafts. This combination seemed to him and to Kraus harmful since it would cause confusion regarding the question of art status. In a period of lively transformative cultural border crossings and exchange, they thought it absolutely necessary to uphold clear distinctions as the basis for cultural integrity. Sensibly, Loos did not think of his interior and architectural designs as art, but rather as craft, belonging to the intersubjective, interactive social medium rather than the self-authorized sphere of authentic artistic creativity. But the manifesto-style "Ornament and Crime" draws the line between art and craft most dramatically, relying on passionate verbal gesture rather than sustained, rationally accessible argument. This radical stance in support of a pure art, independent of and transcending any broader contemporary concerns, seems reactionary, especially when one considers the context of lively confluences of the most diverse artistic activities that made Wiener Werkstätte such a success. But here the difference between the clarity of the ideological position and the much more muddled reality of practice is quite instructive. Even more so is the fact that Loos did not acknowledge it.

The Arts and Crafts movement as conceived by Morris and John Ruskin was motivated by the desire to create an art for the people by the people set against the anonymous destructive power of the machine. Morris's antitechnology utopia in *News from Nowhere* (1891) portrays a future society in which this goal has been achieved: Beauty is as important to the physical and mental well-being of men and women as food, air, and water, and it cannot be produced by the machine. Morris and his followers reintroduced what they thought beautiful medieval simplicity, throwing out all mechanical devices developed since the

Renaissance. The movement did bring a revival of artistic craftsmanship, for example, the objects created by Ashbee so admired by Loos. But in his last two books on art, especially *Should We Stop Teaching Art*? (1911), Ashbee insisted on integrating into the concept of art the fact that modern civilization rests on machinery. Shrinking from the reality of technological revolutions and their cultural consequences, Morris's movement had simply withdrawn into the rarified realm of poetry and high art, and this position had influenced the credo, more than the practice, of Wiener Werkstätte. It was formulated by the architect Josef Hoffmann, who had created the famous Palais Stoclet in Brussels, which was at the time *the* example of an architectural *Gesamtkunstwerk*: exterior and interior design, fixtures, furniture, plates, glasses, and cutlery were perfectly harmonized because of the cooperation of Wiener Werkstätte artists (1905–11).[39] In his Wiener Werkstätte manifesto Hoffmann took a stance against machine production and for good materials and artistic execution:

> We want to establish an intimate connection between public, designer, and craftsmen, to create good simple articles of household use. Our point of departure is purpose, utility is our prime consideration, our strength must lie in good proportions and use of materials. . . . The value of artistic work and of the idea should once again be recognized and prized. The work of the craftsmen must be measured by the same standard as that of the painter and sculptor.[40]

The echoes of Morris and Ruskin are clear, but Hoffman also invoked here the elegance and simplicity of the "spirit of our time" and with it resonances of Ashbee (originally indebted to Morris's antitechnology position) and Mackintosh. Instructively, the manifesto of Wiener Werkstätte production was much more straightforward and simple than the production itself. The proverbially well-wrought, pleasing, expensive objects made here resulted from the fertile interdependency of crafts handed down through the centuries and modern individualist artistic temperament. An outstanding example was the work of the versatile Kolo Moser, who had learned a number of crafts in his youth and whose exquisite designs depended precisely on such a fusion.[41] Much coveted by style-conscious customers then—the *Fackel* lady is drinking from a glass by Moser—now untouchable art in the showcases of museums, these gorgeous objects were a far cry from the "good simple articles of household use" invoked in Hoffmann's text. Only the wealthiest could buy from Wiener Werkstätte. For instance, the woman sitting for Gustav Klimt, Friederike Maria Beer, whom Klimt painted in 1916, wears a gown designed by Wiener Werkstätte and a fur with the stunning Wiener Werkstätte lining turned inside out.[42] Craft was elevated from the populist realm of "utility" to the refined sphere of art, and beauty was not, as Morris had wished and hoped, for the people by the people, but rather for the moneyed elite by highly trained and artistically talented individuals.

The contrast with Loos's design practice is instructive. Emphasizing the principle of functionality as essential to the machine age and insisting on the separation of art and craft, Loos was an ingenious and resourceful interior decorator for clients of moderate means. Remodeling at low cost, he took his clients to junk shops and street markets and made them buy the then-still-cheap Biedermeier furniture for its soberly beautiful lines. He included the "good" pieces from their old apartments, put in mirrors to enlarge visual space, and, a first among interior architects, used the much cheaper soft wood, which he simply painted white. For comparatively little money and without much fuss, he created comfortable and elegant, sparsely decorated interiors in "the spirit of our time."[43] For his interior designs of stores and his remodeling of coffeehouses, he used brass, linoleum, marble, and glass. In Café Museum (1899) he wanted the beautiful stark proportions to stand out as clearly as possible and thus left it so sparsely decorated, so "bare," that it became known as "Café Nihilismus." Hevesi described the interior of the 1907 Steiner plume and feather store in terms similar to those used in his reviews of Ashbee's designs shown at the 1900 exhibition. On Loos: "An interior of geometric elegance and clinical precision. The whole thing might be a steel safe." On Ashbee: "Everything vertical, at right angles, ninety degrees . . . as if they came from a rectangular planet."[44] The same rectangular precision, clarity, and starkness of line characterize the design of the men's store on the ground floor of Haus Goldman und Salatsch, the notorious Haus am Michaeler Platz (1910).[45] Both Loos, who adamantly opposed the Arts and Crafts movement, and Ashbee, whose creations had benefited from it, embraced the elegance and simplicity that suggested to their contemporaries a modern progressive sensibility.

While Loos's interior designs were commonly thought attractive or stunning, the Haus am Michaeler Platz, from the hindsight of Bauhaus architecture his most important building of the prewar period, caused considerable consternation. An unsigned piece in the *Neue freie Presse* of 4 December 1910 declared that it had provoked stronger universal opposition even than the much-disliked and ridiculed "cabbage dome" of the Secession building (built by Joseph Maria Olbrich), most of all because there was nothing Viennese about it. The building's "blatantly dissonant modernism"—like many other critics, this one, too, singled out the "tasteless" windows without moldings and the jarring lack of ornament—could not possibly blend or harmonize with its historic surroundings, the Michaelskirche and Burg.[46] But Loos had been at pains to do precisely that, and his defense here is instructive: he had used real marble for the columns of the ground floor housing the store because he took the baroque splendor of the church as a point of departure and because imitation of any kind was distasteful to him. He had used simple plaster surfaces for the upper (apartment) stories because the burghers of old Vienna had built simply: "My object was to make the strongest possible separation between store and apartments, and I had always imagined that I had resolved this problem in the spirit of the old Viennese masters, an illusion fostered by another modern artist who was heard to exclaim: 'What! He calls himself a modern architect and designs a building that looks like the medieval Viennese houses!' ''[47]

Before becoming an architect, Loos had learned the craft of a stonemason and, as Kokoschka observed shrewdly, took pleasure in calling himself a stonemason to set himself apart from those architects who worked only with blueprints.[48] Loos habitually emphasized the concreteness and honesty, the authenticity of craft, especially stonemasonry, and valued highly medieval secular architecture. Here he was close to Morris's position. But his negative attitude toward a possible interdependency of art and craft and toward ornamentation was fundamentally different. Confronted with the profuse, often-fertile interchanges and cross-influences in the arts, in literature, and in the sciences, Loos insisted on distinct lines and a clean concept of style in design, and on clear ideas in writing. His constructs, mental and physical, needed to be authentic when, in his view, everyone else was happily and sloppily eclectic, arbitrary, and irresponsible. Kraus shared the position articulated in Loos's designs, which he found all the more persuasive because they could and would be translated into physical constructs—allegories of Loos's and his own moral and intellectual steadfastness. This connection is expressed in his *Fackel* comment on ''Das Haus am Michaeler Platz'':

> He placed an architectural thought before them. But they only feel at ease in front of architectural moods and have therefore decided to confront him with the indispensable obstacles from which he wanted to liberate them. Mediocrity revolting against functionality. The selfless guards of the past who prefer being buried under the rubble of dilapidated houses to living in new ones, are no less enraged than the artistic bricklayers [*Kunstmaurer*] who see a missed opportunity for cutsey fancies and who for the first time feel life staring at them as a tabula rasa. We could have done that, too, they cry, after they have recovered from the shock, while he, confronted with their facades, has to confess that he could never have done it.[49]

Kraus distinguishes sharply between Loos's and others' architectural designs: ''The others are artists of the drawing board [*Reißbrettkünstler*]. Loos is the architect of tabula rasa.'' In contrast to ''them,'' Loos is genuine, that is, the genuinely contemporary architect; the others practice the nongenuine combination of arts and crafts.[50] The ill-defined notion of ''genuine'' (*echt*) had defining significance for Kraus, who divided people (and their cultural contributions) accordingly. Loos, who is ''echt,'' is good. ''The good Loos builds for a bad world with good materials,'' Kraus wrote in a 1918 poem on his friend, ''Marmor-Chronik'' (*Worte in Versen III*).[51] The gulf between good (genuine) architecture and the bad world remains unbridgeable. Celebrating Loos's dedication to the genuine, the authentic, Kraus questions neither his goodness nor the world's badness. Loos represents the same intellectual and moral absolutism Kraus had practised in *Fackel*; Loos's use of good materials equals Kraus's use of language as a judgment of the corrupted language of others whom he ''took at their word'' (''nahm sie beim Wort'') to denounce them mercilessly. ''The fact that someone is a murderer need not be proof against his [verbal] style. But his style may prove that he is a murderer,'' Kraus wrote in the *Fackel* of October 1907, attacking one of his main enemies, the Berlin critic-journalist Maximilian Harden, editor of the influential *Die Zukunft* (1892–1922). Harden was a highly successful player in the intellectual politics of prewar Berlin, in Kraus's view because of his pompous language and intellectually vacuous arguments. Kraus liked to expose Harden by ''translating'' his verbose, inflated statements, and the result was indeed ''deadly.'' So was his method of quoting from the all-powerful *Neue freie Presse*, which he called *Neue feile Presse* in one of his innumerable, inimitable, and, alas, untranslatable puns (much admired by Wittgenstein), here linking by sound association *frei* to *feil* (venal) and demonstrating in overwhelming detail how this pun was fully justified.

Kraus wrote *Die Fackel* to expose the immoral hypocrisy of journalistic language, the fledgling ''mass media'' in their symbiotic relation to the exclusively self-protective desires of the criminally immoral ruling bourgeoisie: the title of a 1908 collection of *Fackel* pieces was *Sittlichkeit und Kriminalität* (Morality and criminality). In his journal he defended whores of all classes who were dragged through the moralistic verbal morass of the press and the legal system, rich adulterers cast out by society, and poor maidservants sentenced to death for murdering their illegitimate babies because society, though it permitted their seduction, did not permit them to give birth. From now on, Kraus wrote in April 1906, he could only be ''amoralisch entrüstet'' (amorally outraged), playing on the bourgeois idiom ''moralisch entrüstet''—a moral outrage that more often than not justified judgment and exclusion without consideration of evidence. His own ''amoralische Entrüstung'' drove him to expose the language of cruel respectability. In the unremittingly precise recordings of their persecutors' voices the victims preserve their painful individuality. At the end of the first decade of the new century, Kraus thought that things were changing for the worse: ''Before, I was often amorally outraged. But morality is taking over everywhere, and one gives it up'' (*Fackel*, March 1909). He became more intensely involved in the fight against a new variation of bourgeois ''liberalism,'' a belief in progress for its own sake that would turn murderous.[52] Kraus was not alone in anticipating a major military conflict, but his fears were concretely intensified by the confused aggressive language he heard all around him. He knew that a catastrophe of terrible dimensions was in the making.

In 1922 he republished, as a storm warning against another, even more terrible war, the pieces that had appeared in *Die Fackel* from 1908 to 1914 under the title *Der Untergang der Welt durch schwarze Magie* (The collapse of the world caused by black magic). Untested, unchecked technological progress is apt to turn into destructive black magic. Very early he saw war for what it was: a competition between modern armament industries specializing in murder for setting up a crop rotation, changing markets into battlefields so that they can become even better markets, and, for that end, seducing and bullying the population to serve as cannon fodder and fertilizer for future trade. The coming war—first or second—would be nothing but "an outbreak of the peace"—certainly not a renewal of *Kultur*, as many members of the academic and artistic German elite had hoped in 1914.[53] In the 1920s Kraus defended the young Austrian Republic against monarchist restorationism as well as socialist reactionism. Together with Alfred Adler and Loos (who became chief architect of the City of Vienna's Siedlungsamt [housing office], his first municipal position), he was very much involved in Austrian post–World War I social democracy, giving lectures before workers and supporting workers' organizations.[54] For a while he and Loos were hopeful that progress could and would be made toward more humane working and living conditions. At the same time, Kraus also demonstrated by satirical, grimly funny analysis of their language how both capitalist and Communist ideologies were guilty of severely reducing such hopes and indeed seemed perfectly willing (and able) to make war again. In contrast, the letters Rosa Luxemburg had written from prison, which he much admired and used for his public readings, exhibited the verbal precision that, in his view, signified the moral-political sincerity and authenticity needed to support a firm stance against war.

Kraus's militant pacifism resonated powerfully in many of his listeners, among them the young student Elias Canetti, who would never forget what he learned from the satirist as "master of horror"—the symbiotic connection of literalness and horror (*Wörtlichkeit' und Entsetzen*).[55] Kraus represented for him a sense of absolute social responsibility, bordering on obsession, that was also absolutely necessary and right. Having his ears opened by Kraus to the voices of Viennese (European) social reality, he could never again close them. The fantastically accurate and diverse "acoustic masks"[56] of aggression created by Kraus would never set Canetti free—as they kept Kraus a prisoner: Kraus's "pandemonium" of voices in his *Fackel* pieces and in his grandiose antiwar "drama" *Die letzten Tage der Menschheit* (The last days of mankind, 1922) found strong echoes in the virtuoso performance of the acoustic masks in Canetti's novel *Die Blendung* (translated into English as *Auto-da-Fé*, 1935). But, as he would later explain, the limitations of this method lay precisely in Kraus's brilliantly agonal concentration on the sentence: the subhuman imperfection of the quotation now fully exposed in the inhuman perfection of the comment. Canetti saw an ultimately dangerous exclusiveness in this putting others' use of language on a trial it could not possibly survive. Kraus's sentences were indeed forming a "Chinese wall"—*Die chinesische Mauer* is the title of the third volume of selected *Fackel* texts published by Kraus in 1910—a perfectly closed structure that had, by its very perfection, sapped the vitality of the empire it was meant to defend: "For the ashlars with which he built were *judgments*, and all that had been alive in that landscape was subsumed by them."[57] The distinctions drawn by Kraus were too powerful, too clear, too unwavering, the judgments based on them too exclusive; and the evidence for this critique was provided by Kraus's enthusiastic audiences, among them Canetti himself.

In the second volume of his autobiography, *The Torch in My Ear* (*Die Fackel im Ohr*), Canetti remembers the first time he heard Kraus read, 17 April 1924, his threehundredth lecture, a big event.

> When he sat down and began to read, I was overwhelmed by his voice, which had something unnaturally vibrating about it, like a decelerated crowing. But this impression quickly vanished, for his voice instantly changed and kept changing incessantly, and one was very soon amazed at the variety he was capable of. The hush in which his voice was received was indeed reminiscent of a concert; but the prevailing expectation was altogether different. From the start and throughout the performance, it was the quiet before a storm. His very first punchline, really just an allusion, was anticipated by a laughter that terrified me. It sounded enthusiastic and fanatic, satisfied and ominous at once; it came before he had actually made his point.[58]

Canetti learned from Karl Kraus that words could be easily twisted and that a man's statements could be readily turned against him:

> He was a master of accusing people with their own words. Which didn't mean that he then spared them his accusation in *his* express words. He supplied both accusations and crushed everyone. You enjoyed the spectacle, because you recognized the law dictating these words, but also because you were together with many other people, feeling the tremendous resonance known as a crowd, in which one no longer bruises oneself on one's own limits. You didn't care to miss any of these experiences; you never skipped a single one. You went to these lectures even if you were sick and running a high fever.[59]

Still, much more important, in Canetti's view, was what Kraus had to teach: "how to *hear*. Everything that was spoken, anywhere, at any time, by anyone at all, was offered to your hearing, a dimension of the world that I had never any inkling of. And since the issue was the combination—in all variants—of language and person, this was perhaps the most important dimension, or at least the richest."[60] But it was also the "message" that stayed with Canetti and with many other listeners. Half a century later, decades after the second, even more terrible world war that Kraus had anticipated in his lectures and writings of the 1920s, Canetti noted down his impressions when rereading *The Last Days of Mankind* (a very long, complex text that he claimed to have known by heart in the 1920s),[61] unsure about the direction his own work was taking: He emerged revived and strengthened by Kraus's *Panzersprache* (armored language), experiencing once more its influence as "inner structuring and hardening."[62]

Kraus's cultural and moral absolutism may have been unique, but it appeared to many contemporaries to be an integral part of *Wiener Moderne* and was claimed by some who worked in different cultural areas—Loos in architecture, Schoenberg and Alban Berg in music, and Wittgenstein in philosophy. In his

1935 obituary for Berg, Soma Morgenstern named Mahler, Schoenberg, Kraus, Loos, and Peter Altenberg as prominent representatives of *Wiener Moderne* who had been Berg's guiding stars.[63] Wittgenstein's friend Paul Engelmann, a disciple of Loos and secretary to Kraus, was referring to them when he characterized Wittgenstein's "attempt to draw a clear line between what can and what cannot be said" as "only one in a series of similar efforts."[64] Instructively, one of Kraus's most often quoted self-definitions includes Loos: "Adolf Loos and I, he literally and I verbally, have only shown that there is a difference between an urn and a chamber pot and that this difference is the space of culture. The others, the positive ones, are divided into those who use the urn as chamber pot and those who use the chamber pot as urn."[65] While painting his portrait, Kokoschka listened to many of Kraus's conversations with Loos and vividly remembered their interaction:

> His [Kraus's] voice had a cutting edge. Loos, whose hearing was failing, caught every word. Kraus's personality was utterly compelling. He would pounce like a wildcat on a red-cover copy of *Die Fackel* and rip a sentence out of it like a chunk of flesh, in order to convince Loos of the absolute accuracy of an expression. Both had forgotten I was there. In their company I came to understand that some men earn the right to criticize society, and to reform it. . . . For Kraus, the spiritual environment of a people was its language; for Loos it was the way a man builds his home.[66]

At that time, the young Kokoschka fully identified with Kraus's and Loos's insistence on authenticity, the quality of *Echtheit* (authenticity) in culture and cultural critique. They had earned the right to castigate most other people for their moral, intellectual, and artistic shortcomings, which they saw as evil cultural laxness. Language and architecture are socially constituted media of expression; both Kraus and Loos—and, following them, the young Wittgenstein—chafed under the implications of that fact. Loos's manifesto "Ornament and Crime," silly in parts, may or may not have been meant to be taken entirely seriously.[67] However, like Kraus, he wanted to be "beim Wort genommen" (taken at his word). Performative speech acts, his utterances were meant to have consequences. In attacking meaningless ornament he followed two highly effective, successful architects of the previous generation, Louis Sullivan and Otto Wagner. But their thoughtful position in this matter was a far cry from his absolutism. Sullivan in his 1892 Ornament in Architecture had suggested temporarily refraining from the use of ornament for the sake of concentrating on structure. After this period of abstinence, he predicted, "we shall have discerned the limitations as well as the great value of unadorned masses." He found desirable ornament in harmony with the unity of design: "We feel intuitively that our strong, athletic and simple forms will carry with natural ease the regimen of which we dream." America seemed to him "the only land on the whole earth wherein a dream like this may be realized; for here alone tradition is without shackles, and the soul of man free to grow, to mature, to seek its own.''[68] Loos seems to agree with him; commenting on the reactionary nature of the 1898 Austrian jubilee procession, he exclaimed in ''Ornament and Crime'': ''Happy America! . . . Stragglers slow down the cultural progress of nations and humanity; for ornament is not only produced by criminals; it itself commits a crime by damaging men's health, the national economy, and cultural development.''[69] The ornament of the day had no human connections; it was sterile. The modern ornamentalist—Loos's example was the highly successful Velde, designer of the dress worn by the *Fackel* lady—was ''a straggler or a pathological case.'' Lack of ornament, in contrast, was ''a sign of spiritual strength.''[70]

Loos's modernism is much more narrow and exclusive than Wagner's or Sullivan's and, like Kraus's, it has a culture-transcending, religious dimension. In a 1908 essay, ''Die Überflüssigen'' (The superfluous ones), he attacked the designers of Deutscher Werkbund for employing the new functional forms, for their interest in machine production, and for their attempts to gain new impulses from exploring interdependencies of arts and crafts.[71] Their concept of mediation was to inform Bauhaus design as a laboratory for combining handicraft and standardization. Walter Gropius would represent a fertile combination of ideas and impulses from Morris as well as Velde and Hermann Muthesius, the influential propagator of *Maschinenstil.* Notwithstanding his considerable achievements in modernist design and architecture, Loos arrested his development by excluding these possibilities. In 1919 he responded to an inquiry regarding the connection between art and craft: ''For twenty years I have been preaching the difference between art and craft and denying the validity of either artistic handicraft [*Kunsthandwerk*] or applied art. In contradiction to all my contemporaries.''[72] He insisted on the immortality and spirituality of the art work in absolute contrast to the transient, temporal materiality of the crafted object. Both, he conceded, have their historically defined place, and any useful crafted object, for instance, a well-made button, yields important information about the general cultural development of a people: ''God created the artist, the artist creates the [his] times, the times create the craftsman, the craftsman creates the button.''[73] This was an orderly and transcending hierarchy of cultural value.

In his 1933 obituary for Loos, Kraus praised his uncompromising insistence on bringing cosmic order to the desperate mess of social compromises and political irresolution. Both Loos and Kraus had been inexorable in their intolerance for compromises—*No Compromise* is the fitting title of an American selection of Kraus texts.[74] But so had the radical right, at least in its decisionist rhetoric that seemed attractive to its confused and anxious listeners at the end of the Weimar Republic. The search for such order has been an important aspect of modernism, going back to romantic reaction to difficult Enlightenment challenges, and comes in a great variety of shapes denied by our current infatuation with cutting-edge ''postmodernity.'' ''Rede am Grab, 25. August 1933'' was published in the same slim *Fackel* issue that contained Kraus's notorious poem ''Man frage nicht,'' his poignant, much-misunderstood reaction to Hitler, who managed to silence the arguably most articulate cultural critic in (and of) the German language.[75] The loss of Loos at that time was particularly devastating to Kraus. Creating a ''harmonious correlative between the internal and the external,'' Loos had been able, in Kraus's view, to deal with the ''higher, trans-temporal meanings'' of life, but not with the people responsible for social confusion (''soziale Verwirrer''): ''Because you were immortally linked with future generations [*das Zukünftige*], for them you prepared life, cleansing it and making it habitable.''[76]

Emphasis on the future meanings of Loos's contributions fitted the occasion, but it also pointed to Kraus's and Loos's too-pure, too-rigid modernism. Would not the *Zukünftigen* have to fight their own battles, try to extricate themselves from their own social messes, and create their own fragile, temporary attempts at establishing some degree of order and sanity? Loos had been, in Kraus's words, ''a disruptor of disorder'' (''Störer der Unordnung,'' a pun on the arch-German felony *Ordnungsstörung*). Yet neither Loos nor Kraus was willing to consider potentially creative, progressive aspects of their contemporary disorder, that is, to accept conditionally some of the existing partial, tentative solutions to the overwhelmingly complex problems of cultural modernity. Kraus might have tried to debunk Hitler, despite knowing for certain that he would not be able to ''crush'' him with satirical language, no matter how brilliantly pointed, and that this time he would be defeated by this new variety of corrupt language. But he was also so certain of defeat because for him there could be no partial success. In their misunderstanding and disappointment over Kraus's position in 1933 and again in February 1934, when he supported the conservative Dollfuß to fend off the extreme right, his followers turned against him with a vengeance that destroyed him.[77] He had taught them to unmask, under his guidance, the less-than-admirable motivations of others, but rarely their own. Yet if they needed to destroy him because he had left them needing him too much, they had been, as Canetti observed in the mid-1920s, too needy, too ''hungry'' for complete answers, solutions, and successes.

LUDWIG WITTGENSTEIN

Ludwig Wittgenstein met Loos through the editor of *Der Brenner*, Ludwig von Ficker, in the summer of 1914 when he was working on what would become the *Tractatus Logico-philosophicus*.[78] Contact with Ficker had been established by Wittgenstein's asking his advice about the distribution of a large sum of money among artists and intellectuals, one of them Loos, because of Ficker's writings about Kraus and Kraus's praise of the singular integrity, the *Echtheit*, of *Der Brenner*.[79] A great admirer of Kraus—he had *Fackel* sent after him when he went to Norway in 1913 to work on Russell and Gottlob Frege—Wittgenstein would become as interested in Loos's architecture as in his cultural critique. His friend Engelmann was convinced that Kraus's and Loos's ''way of thinking . . . exercised a decisive and lasting influence on the objectives of his philosophical activity.''[80] In Engelmann's view, the three ''creative separators'' were united in their endeavor to separate and divide correctly and also in provoking fierce resistance to their work, ''since their endeavor runs counter to the deepest (and justified) instinct of their age which seeks to overcome division in all fields.'' He agreed with the three ''separators'' that this instinct needed to be corrected, because a new unity could only be built on ''fresh foundations, never through an indiscriminate mixture of polluted and deformed debris, the detritus of once living cultural values.''[81] Engelmann was right to point out Kraus's, Loos's and Wittgenstein's preoccupation with such ''fresh foundations,'' but he did not consider the cultural meanings of their belief in the autonomy of a new order created by going back to the origins, the mystic-individualist ahistorical, asocial, and indeed amoral dimension of their thought. A highly important energy in *Wiener Moderne* and also in Weimar modernity and late-twentieth-century ''postmodernity,'' this dimension sets them apart from the secular tendencies of their time that affirmed human temporality and historicity, the processual nature of modern culture.[82]

The philosophical solipsism of Wittgenstein's position in the *Tractatus*, which was developed under the influence of Loos and Kraus, emphatically denies the temporality and historicity of the philosophical self: ''Was geht mich die Geschichte an? Meine Welt ist die erste und einzige!'' (What do I care about history? My world is the first and only one!), Wittgenstein noted in 1916. ''I want to report how *I* found the world. . . . *I* have to judge the world, to measure things. The philosophical self [*Ich*] is not the human being, not the human body or the human soul with its psychological properties, but the metaphysical subject, the border, (not a part) of the world.''[83] Wittgenstein's concern that we cannot say anything about the world as a whole had its source in that solipsism that, in its yearning for a paradisiacally clear and complete language, excludes other speakers. From his position of ''logical atomism,'' projection or portrayal of the facts (*Tatsachen*) that constitute the world was possible only through the sign-facts of language based on the assumption of a logical form shared by world and language. Wittgenstein was not interested in understanding the existence of objects (*Dinge*), that is, ontological questions. He wanted to understand, rather, the existence of facts by understanding the determinate way in which objects are connected in a state of affairs (*Sachverhalt*), namely, the structure of a state of affairs (proposition 2.032). The way to understand such structures was to use models that Wittgenstein described in subpropositions to proposition 2 (2.1, 2.14, 2.141, 2.151). But these models did not solve the problem that was so profoundly disquieting to him at the time: we cannot portray the form itself—language itself—of the world. This is impossible, because to do so we would have to assume a position outside the world—or language—and then the world would cease to be the whole world—or language—for us. Wittgenstein's attempts at solving this problem led him to propose 2.171, ''The picture can represent every reality whose form it has'' (''Das Bild kann jede Wirklichkeit abbilden, deren Form es hat''), and 2.172, ''The picture, however, cannot represent its form of representation; it shows it forth'' (''Seine Form der Abbildung aber kann das Bild nicht abbilden; es weist sie auf''). The form itself of the world can only reveal itself in the logical structure of its portrayal that cannot portray itself. There is an obvious tension, then, between the stretching of the philosophical *Ich* to the world's boundary and its receptive attention to what might be revealed concerning the form of the whole world.

The conclusion reached by Wittgenstein already in the second of the seven propositions contains the central motive of his philosophy: the suspicion that all metaphysical propositions—that is, propositions about totalities—are meaningless. ''Metaphysical'' refers here not only to propositions (*Sätze*) dealing with ontological questions but also to propositions about propositions, attempts at a systematic analysis of language:

> **4.12** Propositions [*der Satz*] can represent the whole of reality, but they cannot represent what they must have in common with reality in order to be able to represent it—logical form. / In order to be able to represent logical form, we should have to station ourselves with propositions somewhere outside logic, that is to say outside the world.[84]

Wittgenstein is very close here to Kraus's mystical concept of language in his *Ursprung* poems: hypostatization of ''the word'' and the revealed authenticity of its source.[85] In his introduction to the *Tractatus*, Russell pointed to certain potentially problematic aspects of this attitude toward language and reality as they concerned the reader. He was ready to accept Wittgenstein's conclusion that the teaching of philosophy had to confine itself to the propositions of the sciences, stated with the greatest possible clarity and exactness, and to proving that philosophical assertions are meaningless. He pointed out, however, that Wittgenstein does manage to say a great deal about what he says cannot be said:

> The whole subject of ethics, for example, is placed by Mr. Wittgenstein in the mystical, inexpressible region. Nevertheless he is capable of conveying his ethical opinions. His defense would be that what he calls the mystical can be shown, although it cannot be said. It may be that this defense is adequate, but, for my part, I confess that it leaves me with a certain sense of intellectual discomfort.[86]

Russell was not so much troubled about Wittgenstein's silence—the seventh (concluding) proposition consists of one sentence: ''What we cannot speak about we must pass over in silence''—as about his way of speaking: his verbally expressed insistence on both the impossibility of communicating totalities (for instance, ethical questions) and the existence of such totalities that can reveal themselves. Proposition 7 itself is ''meaningless'' to the philosopher; it is also centrally important to Wittgenstein's intellectual position at that time.

This tension moves the ostensibly philosophical discourse of the *Tractatus* toward poetic discourse. Wittgenstein was aware of that situation, as is clearly indicated in his letters about his intentions in the *Tractatus* to Ludwig von Ficker in 1919 and to Paul Engelmann in 1918. Writing to Ficker about the difficulties of finding a publisher for his text, Wittgenstein described it as "strictly philosophical and at the same time literary; but there is no rambling" ("es wird aber doch nicht darin geschwefelt").[87] The second letter on that matter, accompanying the manuscript, is meant to guide Ficker in his reading of the text. There are two parts of the work: one is the text of the manuscript; the other, more important one has not been written. Wittgenstein quotes for Ficker the key sentence of the preface and comments: "What can be said at all can be said clearly, and what we cannot talk about we must pass over in silence. The whole meaning of the book could be summarized in this sentence." The meaning of the text is "ethical," but the realm of the ethical, that part of the book that has not been written but passed over in silence, is marked and limited from the inside ("von Innen her begrenzt"): "All the *ramblings* of the *many* today [Alles das, was *viele* heute *schwefeln*] I have defined in my book, by passing them over in silence. And therefore, if I am not very much mistaken, the book will say much of what you want to say yourself, but you will perhaps not see that it has been said. I would suggest you read the preface and the conclusion, since they express the meaning most immediately."[88]

Ficker is one of the exclusive, select audience addressed in the first paragraph of the Foreword, just as Kraus's listeners saw themselves in exclusive, select company no matter how large and crowded the lecture hall and how tumultuous the applause. "Perhaps this book will be understood only by someone who has himself already had the thoughts that are expressed in it—or at least similar thoughts.—So it is not a textbook.—Its purpose would be achieved if it gave pleasure to one person who read and understood it." The mode of the text is not discursive; its accessibility depends on the reader's deeper sympathy for Wittgenstein's attempt, as he says in the Preface, "to draw a limit to thought," that is, to accept silence as the fullness of meaning.[89]

Wittgenstein was very much aware of the paradox of silence as discourse.[90] More conclusively than his much-quoted statement in the letter to Engelmann of 26 October 1918 that philosophy really ought to be written like poetry,[91] proposition 4.121 points to his understanding of philosophy as embedded in an essentially neoromantic poetic discourse: "Propositions cannot represent the logical form: this mirrors itself in the propositions. That which mirrors itself in language, language cannot represent. That which expresses *itself* in language, *we* cannot express by language. The propositions *show* the logical form of reality. They exhibit it." ("Der Satz kann die logische Form nicht darstellen, sie spiegelt sich in ihm. Was sich in der Sprache spiegelt, kann sie nicht darstellen. Was *sich* in der Sprache ausdrückt, können *wir* nicht durch sie ausdrücken. Der Satz *zeigt* die logische Form der Wirklichkeit. Er weist sie auf."[92]

In the *Tractatus*, as in Kraus's *Ursprung* poems, "language itself" exists in its mysteriously creative connection with a world that it significantly reveals by concealing it. Loos, who once said to Wittgenstein, "You are me,"[93] celebrated authentic form, emerging spontaneously, revealed to the artist. There is no way in which such authenticity might be articulated by the consensus of an artistic community, since it is given, shown to the artist. Instructively, Loos had no interest in architectural developments in the 1920s, for example, the *Neue Sachlichkeit* movement: ''New forms? How dull! It is the new spirit that matters. Even out of old forms it will fashion what we new men need.''[94] But where did these ''new men'' and their authentic needs come from? The ''new man'' sentiment and rhetoric that had dominated the images and forms of *Jugendstil* at the beginning, the ''dawn'' of the century, had reemerged with full force after World War I: the utopian hope that men and women would be reborn out of the fires of that catastrophic destruction, thereby to reveal its meaning. That hope was still characterized by what Vergo rightly refers to as the ''duality inherent in the work of the Viennese avant garde, that tension between radicalism and conservatism.''[95] But it did not so much, as Vergo thought, ''limit'' the ''impact of the revolution they had initiated'' as it enlarged it in unforeseen ways by remaining static. In the postwar period of extraordinary technological and therefore social changes, and of growing cultural plurality, the enduring modernist duality of ''back to the roots'' and ''forward with modernity,'' arguably the most important aspect of the success of national socialism, diverted attention from the difficult reality of those new developments, and so did the modernist, highly idiosyncratic Marxisms of Weimar intellectuals like Benjamin, Bloch, and Theodor Adorno.[96]

Younger than Kraus and Loos, Wittgenstein was to develop misgivings regarding the paradoxical silences imposed by such rigorously pure language (art), which he later understood to be caused by its independence of the historical specificity and diversity of language use. In Kraus, the search for an authentic social order interdependent with authentic language led to the most richly complex if instructively flawed contribution to literary *Wiener Moderne*. In its religious cultural exclusivity and its hard-hitting, highly intelligent secularism, its neoromantic glorification of the one pure, prelapsarian, unmediated language, and its superb command of postlapsarian tainted linguistic plurality, it documents powerfully the tensions of modernism that were to dominate this century.

FREUD: FROM SELF TO PSYCHOANALYSIS

Ever since it was questioned by Rousseau and, following him, the first generation of German romantic intellectuals (who could be seen as the first modernists), the process of modernity has been a shifting composite of Enlightenment encouragements and (neo)romantic allurements: the Enlightenment equation of identity as open-ended processes of transformation fed by curiosity about what is different and therefore questionable, and the romantic desire for final transformation into identity, for rebirth into the unquestionably true self. The tensions inherent in modernist reactions to increasing cultural complexity and plurality could lead, as we have seen in Kraus's work, to the usurpation of other voices, denying their alterity, their contradictory and elusive nature, which has been an explicitly modern cultural concern since the great explorative voyages of the seventeenth and eighteenth centuries.[97]

The seductive floating of signifiers that neoromantic Derridian literary theorists have passed on to ''postmodernist'' cultural critics indicates a seriously abridged and confused notion of signification and an instructive misunderstanding of Saussure's position. The issue for Ferdinand Saussure was the arbitrariness of the sign in connection with its historicity: language use as convention both upheld and circumvented by individual speakers in speaking to others, as continuity and rupture, sameness and change, concealment and disclosure. Precisely this historicity, namely, recognition of the role of temporality and contingency in human affairs, has been one of the great challenges to modern cultural critique. With the increasing fragmentation, incompleteness, ambiguity, and obscurity of modern (verbally transmitted) knowledge, modernist originality in a literal (''poetic'') sense has had a strong appeal for many intellectuals. This explains the often-puzzling enduring influence of writers particularly mistrustful of cultural plurality, namely, the presence of other voices, from their aggressive appropriation and prosecution by Kraus, their silencing by Wittgenstein, and their ''conquistadorial'' control by Freud in his mappings of their unconscious, via Benjamin's rewriting (German) literature as its first and only critic,[98] to the late Heidegger's and Derrida's esoteric poetics of selectively revealed meaning.

Images and concepts of German romanticism can be found all through Freud's writings, and their influence on his ''metapsychology'' is easy to detect, even if he never acknowledged it. Though he often used literary examples for clarification, Freud notoriously insisted on an absolute originality of psychoanalysis that would ipso facto contradict any formative influence of the ideas or the stories of others. Only after his own ''discoveries'' had been established, ''patented,'' as it were, would he sometimes admit to certain similarities, and then ''off the record.''[99] His modernist break with a culturally predominant (excluding the sciences), idealist concept of consciousness led him to develop a model of the self that would prove to be more extensively controlled than most other variations (e.g., neo-Hegelian ones) on the romantic triad.[100] Freud's constructions of the self from its ''prehistoric'' origins (the area of the unconscious) came to seek a completeness of argument and validity that would defy the modern historic experience of ambivalence, conflictedness, and fragmentation. Authored and authorized by him, all stories of the self carry within themselves their irrefutable meaning or ''solution'' (*Lösung*) from beginning to end. The clinician Freud, who in the early stages of psychoanalysis saw reasons to doubt his effectiveness as a healer, connected the completeness and consistency of stories of the self with a desired scientificity of his highly speculative approach. But it was to be the constructedness itself that most attracted him because it implied most clearly the analyst-as-author's literal authority. The modern preoccupation with the puzzle of the mind, in which Freud shared, has been sublimated in many of his best-known and most influential case histories into solutions so intricate and final as to block the modern impulse to go on asking questions. I will trace here the beginnings of the psychoanalytical method by documenting the genesis of Freud's conceptual and narrative strategies used in *The Interpretation of Dreams*, written in 1877–99 just before the beginning of the new century. Reflecting the analyst-as-author's ingenious collusion between receptivity and interpretive control, explorative and normative impulses, these strategies show quite clearly the tensions of modernism.

The Interpretation of Dreams, Freud's favorite among his books, has become, especially for professional readers in the field of general (literary) cultural criticism, one of the classic texts of the twentieth century. Since there seems to be unmediated access to the world of dream images as a rich arsenal of fragments of experience in the most varied stages of metamorphosis, these readers seem to feel that they share with Freud an expansive, confusing text. The dream book with its colorful but firm charting of the ways in which the self unravels appears to be a guidebook to its evocative, chaotic refractions. No other work of Freud has sought to create such a strong sense of understanding between author and reader. Going back with Freud to the origins of psychoanalysis, the reader participates in the grand adventure of charting the self. Seemingly able to follow the author's simultaneous operations on different levels, the reader is asked to retrace with the author the cartographer's rendering of "the first crude map" of "the psychical territory" and the archaeologist's recovery and interpretive reconstruction of the self.[101] It will appear to the reader that access has been granted to a work in progress as gigantic as it is intimate.

Such is the readerly illusion created by conceptual and narrative strategies that emerged fully for the first time in the dream book. In *Studies on Hysteria*, published jointly with Josef Breuer in 1895, Freud had reflected on the novellalike character of many of his case histories when retelling his patients' stories of the self constructed under his guidance.[102] He had admitted then the apparent lack of scientific rigor of this method but also assured the reader of its efficacy. Such "poetic" representation of psychic processes—"such as we are accustomed to find in the works of imaginative writers [*Dichter*]"—interspersed with a few psychological terms would enable the reader to gain at least some insight into cases of hysteria.[103] Freud was to go beyond such modest goals very soon. In a lecture on the "Aetiology of Hysteria" delivered in April 1896 before the Vienna Verein für Psychiatrie und Neurologie he introduced his newly developed "psychoanalytic" method. In contrast to Breuer's "cathartic" method, it would, he said, no longer be content to simply "remove the symptoms of hysteria and obsessions" but seek a "genuine cure."[104] The cure sought depends on going back to the origins of the story of the self: the true aetiology of hysteria "is to be found in childhood experiences, and once again—and exclusively—in impressions concerned with sexual life."[105] It was the completeness of the construction from the origin with which Freud justified the claim of psychoanalysis to scientificity—an all-important claim in view of his professional goals. But in the eyes of critical readers, this claim has been undermined precisely by the degree and kind of conceptual and narrative control needed to achieve such completeness.

Notwithstanding its richly, spontaneously evocative material, *The Interpretation of Dreams* works with strictly regulated narrative sequences that contradict claims to experiential method. There is little or no tolerance for unresolved conflict. Narration of the puzzle of the self cannot be meaningful without its irrefutable solution. As a clinician, Freud had profound self-doubts about his effectiveness as a healer, but in the act of constructing the self, which importantly integrates dreams, he came to rely on strategies that clearly indicate the desire to produce a self that is whole and unassailable.

Freud admitted quite openly the constructedness of the healed self and the control of the analyst in this process. In his most elaborately and ingeniously assembled case history, the 1918 analysis of the Wolf Man, he stressed both the central importance of the infantile material, that is, of its complete recollection, for this as for any story of the self, and the fact of self-conscious construction in this process of retrieving that might lead to a cure: "So far as my experience hitherto goes, these scenes from infancy are not reproduced during the treatment as recollection, they are the products of construction." They are "divined," "constructed," he reiterates, "gradually and laboriously from an aggregate of indications" under the guidance of the psychoanalyst.[106]

In writing the self, Freud is concerned with the thorough retrieval and articulation of its prehistoric layers, the primal scene. The completion, coherence, and decisiveness of the resulting fiction necessitates his "masterly marshalling and orchestrated arrangement of literally countless clinical details," as one of his reluctantly admiring readers puts it.[107] It also necessitates his unmistakable presence in the story he tells the patient about himself. In each case he writes this story from beginning to end unconcerned about the historical nature of culture and the cultural nature of the individual. It is no surprise, then, that Freud's analysis of the self as its construction from the origins is moving in a closed hermeneutic circle. Noteworthy, however, is the centrality of this circle to the method of psychoanalysis. Arguably, it has been precisely the emphasis on autonomous and authentic creation from the regained origins claiming revolutionary progress in moving back to the beginnings that has made Freudian thought attractive to cultural and literary criticism.[108] Claims to its scientificity or at least significant interdependencies with scientific thought have further enhanced its legitimacy and validity.

Freud developed psychoanalysis in the years 1895–97 when he was moving from psychotherapy to metapsychology.[109] He started writing fictions of the self from the material of psychic activities "brought up" from hitherto-inaccessible locations in the unconscious and constructed under his guidance. This included, most importantly, the materials recovered by his self-analysis, because it was here that the pragmatic nexus between conscious conflict and its role in the ecology of the unconscious became most clearly visible. The metapsychological writing of the self, based on a distinct separation between the conscious and the unconscious and on its symbiotic collusion, is made possible by authorial strategies that rely on and thrive on such paradoxical simultaneity. Their development can best be traced in the letters Freud wrote to the Berlin physician and biologist Wilhelm Fliess around the turn of the century (1887 to 1902), because he speaks here with remarkable clarity of the sources and origins of what would become his normative poetics of the self.

For Wilhelm Fliess, who was during those years of professional isolation and, in Freud's and many Freudians' eyes, earth-shaking discoveries, his highly significant emotional and intellectual "Other" and first reader,[110] Freud charted the first descent into the self, his self-analysis. It was for Fliess that Freud drew "the first crude map" of the "psychical territory," expressing his delight with certain aspects of this exotic mindscape, notably the absence of negation in the unconscious that was to become centrally important to metapsychology. In the important letter of 21 September 1897, the first of eleven letters written in the last four months of 1897 that chronicle his initial charting, he unveiled the "great secret" that he no longer believed in his "neurotica," that is, the origin of neurosis in the early concrete traumatic experience of seduction. Among several reasons given is "the definite realization that there is 'no indication of reality'[111] in the unconscious, so that it is impossible to distinguish between truth and emotionally-charged fiction."[112] But where do these fictions come from? The next sentence in the letter suggests a hunch, at that stage very tentative, that was to develop into the Oedipus complex: "(This leaves open the possible explanation that sexual fantasy regularly makes use of the theme of the parents.)"[113] He was ready, Freud wrote, to abandon both "the complete solution of a neurosis"—a goal on which he had concentrated for the last years in nearly total professional isolation[114] and with the "conquistador's"[115] single-minded drive and exorbitant hopes—"and sure reliance on its aetiology in infancy." But, instructively, the professionally devastating "doubts" do not make him depressed. Can they be only "an episode on the way to further knowledge?" he asks, and at the end of the letter he affirms: "In the general collapse only the psychology has retained its value. The dreams still stand secure, and my beginnings in metapsychology have gone up in my estimation. It is a pity one cannot live on dream interpretation, for instance."[116]

As it turned out, he could. His developing metapsychology enabled him to chart the conscious and unconscious and present his topography of the mind in the interpretation of dreams based on fictions of the self written according to his own specifications. If the trauma could not be found in the experience of a real event, it could be located in fantasy and desire, and as dreams were determined in the unconscious, that is, where they were safe from the negation of the conscious, they stood indeed secure. They were secure with respect to the patterns into which they were fitted by the purposeful explorer as cartographer of the self. Freud's doubts regarding the reality of the primal scene of being seduced in childhood did turn out to be an episode on the way to "further knowledge." He had been working with constructions of the self all along, elaborating the primal importance of sexuality for the model of the mind that, listening to his patients, he had found in the material brought up under his guidance. But the focused adventure of self-analysis (as he charted it in the letters to Fliess and *The Interpretation of Dreams*) enabled him to collapse the exploratory, purportedly open dialogue of the self with itself carried on by the patient in the presence of the analyst into an intricately and rigidly structured explanatory monologue. The key that unlocks the secret to all neuroses is the expected treasure found in the descent into the self and the reward for him who undertook it. Not only does Freud not question and postpone writing the self, but he writes it immediately, insisting on a poetics controlled by himself as "the chief patient,"[117] the analyst of the self as its author.

In the next letter, written twelve days later (3/4 October 1897), after one of Freud's short visits with Fliess in Berlin that were very important to him in these years of professional difficulties and shifting ambitions, he referred to his self-analysis "as indispensable for clearing up the whole problem." Self-analysis had been making "progress in dreams and yielding the most valuable conclusions and evidence. At certain points I have the impression of having come to the end, and so far I have always known where the next night of dreams would continue." He had concluded that the "primary originator" of his neurosis was his nursemaid, ugly and elderly but clever, that his "libido towards *matrem*" was aroused between the ages of two and two-and-a-half on a journey with her from Leipzig to Vienna where he must have seen her "*nudam*,"[118] and that he was jealous of his younger brother, whose early death left "the germ of guilt" in him. The nursemaid, he remembered, instructed him "in sexual matters," and in the dream she washed him in "reddish water in which she had previously washed herself (not very difficult to interpret; I find nothing in my chain of memories, and so I take it for a genuine rediscovery)." This dream image signified for him the "*experimenta crucis*" that his reading of the dream was not just "fantasy projected into the past" but rather "determined by the past."[119]

Freud's explanatory narration of this dream is highly important to an understanding of the nature of his self-construction. In the first part of his letter he had spoken of his gratitude to the memory of the old woman "who provided me at such an early age with the means for living and surviving" because he expected resolving "my hysteria" from the "scenes which lie at the bottom of all of this." This was in spite of the fact that she, as the dream told him, had induced him to steal money for her, suggesting "bad treatment" as the topic of the dream work, that is, his misgivings about his success as a healer. It would be impossible to give Fliess "any idea of the intellectual beauty of the work," because the model worked like a miracle, fitting the distant "buried" part of the self into its present conscious "area."[120] Signifying a crucial lost and regained memory, the dream image "reddish water" seems to carry a rather heavy interpretive burden, but Freud appeared unconcerned.

Freud had to abandon the father aetiology of neurosis because it had continuously frustrated his attempts to "bring a single analysis to a real conclusion," and because of the surprising and disturbing fact that "in all cases, the *father*, not excluding my own, had to be accused of being perverse—the realization of the unexpected frequency of hysteria, with precisely the same conditions prevailing in each, whereas surely such widespread perversions against children are not very probable."[121] The nurse has displaced the father; fantasized or dreamed seduction has displaced the real perversion of child molestation. I am not interested here in the problem of Freud's relationship with his father, nor in the question of Freud's possible suppression of evidence regarding concrete sexual aggression against children,[122] but I would like to draw attention to Freud's increasingly clear departure from the experiential clinical mode. Doubting the "truth" of the material brought up by his patients and disappointed about their "lies,"[123] he seized the opportunity to alter and expand the primal scene to the point where it becomes itself a fiction. It is not, then, a question of the motivation for his models, but, rather, a question of their intention. What we are told in the letters of 21 September, 3/4 October, and 15 October 1897 suggests precisely the problem of "fantasy projected into the past," mentioned by Freud himself but dismissed too easily. The dream image "reddish water" to which he simply ascribes the confirmation value of the "crucial experiment" is, to say the least, ambiguous in its associations. Moreover, as I will argue later, the connection between this image and the primal scene suggested so emphatically by Freud is by no means the most convincing of the referential possibilities. For his own "conquistadorial" reasons, Freud organized his reading of this dream around the theme of "bad treatment," accepting the dream image of "reddish water" as signifying, beyond all doubt, his arrival at the prehistoric origin of the neurotic self, which would make possible the progress of self-analysis to a "real conclusion."

Self-analysis was for Freud at this stage "the most important thing that I have in hand and promises to be of the greatest value to me when it is finished," he wrote on 15 October; it was for him like an unfinished book from whose completion he expects, with great hopes, the longed-for success, *The Interpretation of Dreams*.[124] With the conclusion of the self-analysis and the solution of his neurosis, the division of the self into patient and physician could be neutralized. Fliess was also told repeatedly during these months that Freud could concentrate on his self-analysis because his practice was so slow. Concluding the self-analysis was seen as the necessary condition for the conclusion of analyses in general and thereby the growth of his practice. A completed analysis as completely fitting self-construction had eluded him as long as he was working with the notion of a real primal scene. The self-analysis negated this notion and could therefore proceed, supported by the highly useful displacement strategy of the dream. In this period of intense self-doubt as healer, when he felt himself caught in the role of the patient, plagued by severe phobic symptoms and mood fluctuations, Freud needed to see his friend as the decisive, charismatic "healer" and "magician."[125] But he also needed to present to him fictions of the self that would make it whole and thereby affirm himself as healer in his own right. The result of an analysis brought to a "real conclusion" from the prehistoric origin of the neurosis is the timeless history-transcending self in the state of a new, unassailable innocence. Metapsychology is built on the grid of a neoromantic triad.[126] From lost to regained paradise it proceeds irresistibly to the solution of all conflict and contradiction.

Patients (himself included) can lie, but not their dreams, for Freud reads them in the role of the author. In the letter of 15 October 1897 he mentions that he had asked his mother regarding the recent dream material, that she had affirmed it, and that therefore it was all the more valuable.[127] It is true that the dream deviated from past actuality: it had not been he who, led by her, had stolen; the old woman herself had been the thief. But this does not at all change the interpretation of the dream, because "the dream really means that she stole herself. For the dream-picture was a memory that I took money from a doctor's mother, i.e. wrongfully.[128] The real meaning is that the old woman stood for me, and that the doctor's mother was my mother. I was so far from being aware that the old woman was a thief that my interpretation went astray."[129] However, the interpretation "bad treatment" stands secure. The dream image "reddish water" supports the needed linkage with the infantile material of the primal scene that replaced the father with the nurse; money and theft refer to Freud's bad treatment of his patients, that is, the disturbing awareness of his shortcomings as a healer. It is a significant affirmation of the closed self-referential nature of the dream as text that Freud does not recover here the much more probable historic rather than prehistoric "meaning" of the dream image "reddish water," an event that I will discuss later. But precisely this self-referential completeness of his model would convince readers of the dream book, because it enabled Freud to impose a seductive fantastic order on an overwhelming chaos of fragmented images and references.

In the long letter of 15 October 1897 Freud emphasized again the difficulties of descending into the self, but "being totally honest with oneself is a good exercise," and besides, it yields "universal" regularities. He has found in his case, too, "love of the mother and jealousy of the father," believing this to be "a general phenomenon of early childhood, even if it does not always occur so early as in children who have been made hysterics."[130] This is the first mention of the "Oedipus complex,"[131] "brought up" as a universal model from a self-analysis based largely on readings of dreams. Once such universality has been established, it does not matter anymore that Freud had started the "voyage" as a patient. Significantly, after this presentation, however incomplete, of the psychoanalytical model in the letters to Fliess, the relationship with him in important ways came to an end. Freud as the first cartographer of the "psychical territory" is more and more looking at the self from the outside, and he finally drops his self-analysis "in favor of the dream book."[132]

A few months earlier, on 14, November 1897, Freud had announced to Fliess the birth of the "theory" of the repression of sexuality and the resulting compulsions and anxieties, stressing his interest in the part played in repression by "something organic"—the physiological level—and reminding Fliess of his connecting the release of sexuality with "a kind of secretion, which we correctly perceive as an internal state of libido."[133] It was, however, not the idea of linking an organic secretion that really excited him. He had been thinking in terms of a "hydraulic" mental model for some time—hence the 1895 "Project for a Scientific Psychology"—even if his ideas about the arrangements of feedback systems aiding in the building up and discharge of sexual tension would become more specific (pinpointing the exact quantity and quality of "psychical libido") and his negative feelings about masturbation more intense.[134] The important aspect of the new formulation of repression based on a synthesis of somatic and psychical libido, its "main value," as he wrote to Fliess, "lies in its linking together the neurotic and normal processes."[135] The "discovery" of this linkage was essential to the success of Freud's search because it was the foundation on which he could build a general, metapsychological model of the mind.

At the end of the letter Freud mentions that his self-analysis is "still interrupted" and makes the following important observation: "I can only analyse myself with objectively acquired knowledge (as if I were a stranger); self-analysis is really impossible, otherwise there would be no illness."[136] Quite apart from the illusionary concept of an "objectively acquired knowledge" in the case of the analyst, namely, the question of his control over the material brought up by his patients and over his linking this material with material brought up by himself, he cannot, without greatly compromising the validity of his constructions, assume the role of "stranger" in the territory of his own self. Nor can he be simultaneously the patient, the ill, fragmented person, and the physician, the healer. But even if he gave up self-analysis "in favor of the dream book," here too, as in all his texts to follow, his fictions of the self have been troubled by unacknowledged falsifying collusions between the "discourse of familiarity," the "outsider-oriented discourse," and the discourse of the outsider.[137] In the unknown and familiar territory of the self Freud has played the role of informant and observer without ever working through the epistemological difficulties involved in such a position. Provocatively but wrongly he has thought himself free to write the self autonomously, normatively, and completely. "Linking together the neurotic and normal processes,"[138] he built a model of the mind that disregarded the social experience of the self with its language of familiarity, of silences, ellipses, and lacunae that defies such rigorously complete articulation.

Freud referred to the unknown, obscure parts of the mind as a "psychical territory" of which he was drawing a first crude map with the help of dreams. Exploring and trying to chart that territory he dealt with puzzling fragments of a system of signs that indicated great systemic complexity and that could therefore be read in many different ways; it called for interpretation. The peculiar literalness in Freud's usage of "territory" and "charting" reflects both the physician's reading of "signs and symptoms" and the conquistador's drive to appropriate and control access. Interpretation of dreams for Freud was pragmatic in the sense of, for instance, pragmatic historiography; it served a specific purpose. He wrote his own text, *The Interpretation of Dreams*, out of the difficult fragmented ''text'' of dreams, his own and others'. He read in order to write, to be an author and to authorize.

Dreaming as ''another kind of remembering—subject to the conditions that rule at night,''[139] dreaming as construction, frees the interpreter from the conflicted historic reality of the self. The dream that ''revealed'' to Freud the ''Secret of Dreams'' on 24 July 1895 (as he would tell Fliess on 12 June 1900)[140] is the specimen dream analyzed in Chapter 2 to elucidate the new ''scientific procedure'' of interpreting dreams. It is a dream into which he reads his own preoccupation with being a good healer in spite of and because of his particular psychological approach, referring to and disguising in his interpretation an episode that had been a most traumatic experience in the spring of 1895 and the most awkward issue in his correspondence with Fliess during March and April. One of Freud's patients, Emma Eckstein, under treatment for hysterical abdominal symptoms, was operated on by Fliess in late January or early February 1895 at Freud's suggestion, because Freud was at that time under the influence of his friend's highly speculative theories concerning a distinct calculable periodicity in women and men and the importance for it of the nasal chambers and sinuses, which Fliess understood to be linked to sexual organs. Fliess came from Berlin for the operation—he also gave Freud one of his nose treatments, which eased his neurotic symptoms—but did not stay for Emma's aftercare.

Freud at first attributed the patient's complaints about pain, malodorous secretions, and bleeding to her hysteria, but finally another specialist was called in who found that Fliess had accidentally left a half-meter of gauze in a cavity that he had created by removing the turbinal bone and opening the sinus. The patient had a severe hemorrhage when the gauze was removed and went briefly into shock. Freud, who was present during this procedure, became sick and had to leave the room. The patient was dangerously ill for many weeks and recovered very slowly; her face was permanently disfigured. Freud waited for a day before writing a long letter to Fliess, describing the incident, protesting his unshaken trust in him, and blaming himself for making Fliess come to Vienna. He blamed the hemorrhage on the other specialist, because it could have been avoided if the procedure had taken place in a hospital (instead of the patient's home), where the wound could have been widened before removal of the gauze.[141] The letters of the following weeks (13, 20, 23, and 28 March and 11, 20, 26, and 27 April) repeat Freud's and Emma's complete trust in Fliess, informing him of Emma's continuing severe hemorrhages, with occasional hints about Freud's fears regarding the outcome of the disastrous affair. On 26 April Freud wrote that Emma, ''my tormentor and yours,'' was finally better. In the preceding letter he had shown himself offended by Fliess's request for a testimonial certificate from Vienna for his rehabilitation occasioned by his medical malpractice: ''I wanted to pour forth my tale of woe and perhaps obtain your advice concerning E., not reproach you with anything. That would have been stupid, unjustified, and in clear contradiction to all my feelings.''[142]

These letters clearly reveal, as Freud's physician Max Schur pointed out in an unpublished essay, ''The Guilt of the Survivor,'' his ''desperate attempts to deny any realization of the fact that Fliess would have been convicted of malpractice in any court for this near fatal error.''[143] Freud saw the whole frightening situation exclusively in his own terms, expecting his naturally apprehensive friend to accept his reassurances as a solution to the problem. He needed to defend Fliess's identity as healer because he felt so vulnerable in this respect himself. Despite his strong emotional ties to his friend, he could not put himself in Fliess's place. After Emma's partial recovery he proceeded for a while with her analysis and kept Fliess informed of the results. On 26, April 1896 he wrote that he had come to the conclusion that Emma's hemorrhages had always been hysterical, had probably always been connected with her periods, and had been caused by longing and desire; she resisted his request to give him the dates of her periods, but he was quite certain. With this conclusion he and Fliess were rehabilitated as healers. He had been right to interpret the patient's complaints as hysterical; Fliess's operation had nothing to do with her suffering. On 4 May 1896 he analyzed Emma's feeling during the near-fatal hemorrhage of 6 March 1895 as the fulfillment of a wish: she was now, in her illness, loved by him.[144]

On the day before the dream of 23/24 July 1895 Freud had a visit from a junior colleague and old friend, Otto, who had been staying with a patient of Freud's, Irma, and her family at their country resort and who told him, ''She's better but not quite well.''[145] He had noticed that his friend's tone had annoyed him, as it seemed to indicate reservations that were shared by her family regarding his treatment of Irma. In the evening Freud wrote out Irma's case history with the idea of giving it to Dr. M., a common friend and at the time the leader in their circle, in order to justify himself.

In his dream he was in a large hall, receiving guests, among them Irma, who had complained bitterly in a letter to him about pain and choking. He first reproached her for not having accepted his ''solution,'' putting the blame for her pain on herself, but looking at her, he became concerned, thinking that she must have some organic trouble. She looked pale and puffy and, when he examined her, showed reluctance to open her mouth, as if she had artificial dentures. He found, in the examination, white and grey patches and scabs and ''some remarkable curly structures which were evidently modeled on the turbinal bones of the nose.'' The other physicians present were Dr. M., who had been called in by Freud, and his friends Leopold and Otto. Dr. M. repeated and confirmed the examination, and Leopold found dull places, metastases; Otto was just present. Dr. M. diagnosed an infection and gave a prognosis. They all, including Freud, were aware of the source of the infection: Otto had given her an infection. Freud saw the formula ''printed in heavy type. . . . Injections of that sort ought not to be made so thoughtlessly. . . . And probably the syringe had not been clean.''[146]

In the detailed analysis Freud first discusses the dream figure of the patient and concludes that she is a displacement collage for the real Irma of several patients, among them a young woman with hysterical choking and another one who shared the name Mathilde with Freud's eldest daughter and who had died under his care, poisoned by medication he had considered harmless. The dream figure of Dr. M. is a fusion of M.'s real self and Freud's elder brother; the reason for the fusion is that both had rejected a certain suggestion that Freud had made to them recently. Otto and Leopold are relations, both in the same field of specialization and therefore in competition. Both had acted for years as Freud's assistants when he was in charge of the neurological outpatients' department of a children's hospital; Otto had been quick, Leopold slow but sure. The analysis of Dr. M.'s seemingly nonsensical prognosis yields its intention to be a consolation for Freud, who had (perhaps wrongly) used a psychological diagnosis, and the explanation of Freud's attitude toward such consolation coming from Dr. M.: "derision at physicians who are ignorant of hysteria." Like Irma, Dr. M. had not agreed with Freud's "solution."

One of the ingredients in the formula for the injection made by Otto, trimethylamin, establishes the crucial connection to Fliess, an (unnamed) "friend who had for many years been familiar with all my writings during the period of their gestation" and had "at that time confided to me some ideas on the subject of the chemistry of the sexual processes." Trimethylamin was one of the products of sexual metabolism. Freud's interpretation: "Thus this substance led me to sexuality, the factor to which I attributed the greatest importance in the origins of the nervous disorders which it was my aim to cure."[147] Freud then mentions that Irma and the choking patient were young widows and gives a short description of the importance of Fliess for him during the time when he felt so isolated with his opinions about the role of sexuality. Fliess, he states, had drawn "remarkable connections between the turbinal bones and the female organs of sex (cf. the three curly structures in Irma's throat). I had had Irma examined by him to see whether her gastric pains might be of nasal origin."[148] The sentence "Injections of that sort ought not to be made that thoughtlessly" he interprets as made directly against his friend Otto, whom he had on occasion advised to give the drug orally rather than by a more risky injection. The tragic episode with his patient Mathilde is brought up again by this part of the dream: "Here I was evidently collecting instances of my own conscientiousness, but also of the reverse."[149]

The "meaning" of the dream—note here the use of quotation marks—was "borne in upon" Freud while he was carrying out the interpretation, trying to keep at bay

> all the ideas which were bound to be provoked by a comparison between the content of the dream and the concealed thoughts lying behind it. I became aware of an intention which was carried into effect by the dream and which must have been my motive for dreaming it. The dream fulfilled certain wishes which were started in me by the events

of the previous evening. The conclusion of the dream, that is to say, was that I was not responsible for the persistence of Irma's pains but that Otto was. . . . The dream represented a particular state of affairs as I should have wished it to be. *Thus its content was the fulfilment of a wish and its motive was a wish.*[150]

The analysis of the specimen dream that establishes the model for the interpretation of dreams ends with the assertion: ''*When the work of interpretation has been completed, we perceive that a dream is the fulfilment of a wish.*''[151]

The complete interpretation of dreams unlocks the ''meaning'' of all dreams to be wish fulfillment. The wish itself is not conscious; dream images refer to wish fulfillment, and the intermediate link that establishes the connection between the not-yet-conscious wish and its fulfillment has to be inferred by being attentive to the dependency of the recent wish on prehistoric material.[152] There are, then, no limits to the ingenuity and authority of the interpreter because his fictions of the self are based on wish fulfillment: the healing, completing narration of unconscious fantasizing that is ''subject to the conditions that rule at night'' and thus unable to contradict the author who tells its story. As Freud reminds the reader of the Wolf Man story with its elaborately fantasizing dream, ''No does not exist, and there is no distinction between contraries'' in the unconscious.[153] In the dream book he had simply stated that ''a contradiction to my theory of dreams produced by another of my women patients (the cleverest of all my dreamers) was resolved more simply, but upon the same pattern, namely that the nonfulfilment of one wish meant the fulfilment of another.''[154] There is negation as the process of repression—the resistance to his story by his patients as dreamers who in this ''behave'' like children[155]—but never as the process of falsification pursued by a group of conscious, critical subjects, the author's peers.

The status of ''patients'' in medical treatment has always been based on such ''inequality'' brought about by their enforced passivity, ostensibly for their own good. But Freud, having always longed for ''philosophical knowledge,'' had left medicine to fulfill this longing through his ''metapsychological'' model with its a priori constructions.[156] The choice of the specimen dream is highly significant in this respect; it resolves Freud's conflict over ''bad treatment''—being held to the responsibility of the healer as expert physician instead of expert storyteller—in the synthesis of wish fulfillment: ''For consciousness and memory are mutually exclusive.''[157] The interpretation of this, as of all dreams, as wish fulfillment and the linking of the inferred wish to infantile, prehistoric material releases him, too, from the obligation to remember the history of his relationship with his patients: particularly those parts of their ''case histories'' that do not fit his stories. Instructively, diagnosis and prognosis, central to medical practice, play an important part in the interpretive strategies of the Irma dream. The medical disjunction of signs, to be read and interpreted as fully as possible by the expert physician whose authority can be questioned by another expert, the ''second opinion,'' and symptoms, experienced and partly articulated by the patient, changes dramatically in Freud's metapsychological scenario. The physician whose expert judgment can be questioned is now the authoritative reader as writer whose stories, by their very nature, will not be questioned.

Critical readers of the dream book have been intrigued but also troubled by the seemingly infinite number of possible instances of distortion, displacement, and condensation[158] that control the moves of ''clever'' dreamers because the game of wish fulfillment was so obviously rigged. In Freud's topography of the unconscious the fulfillment of a wish can be, as well, its negation. The reversal of a wish, so often found in fairy tales, does reflect an awareness of the psychological simplification of real-life situations inherent in wishing. But Freud uses it to secure his inexorably abstracting model into which, in the end, all these clever moves reflecting the conflicted practice of the past day simply disappear. The patient as analysand becomes an allegory of the subject's complete submission to the author's authority. Freud's desire to fend off questions because his stories needed to be complete to be successful fictions has been turned into a structural a priori: the denial itself of their historic truth has become their affirmation as fiction. The ''theory'' of wish fulfillment is indeed the single most brilliant move in his writing career. But what does that say about its validity as an interpretive tool in a larger sense, for example, where it concerns responsible cultural criticism that needs to account for conscious subjects in their historicity?

In Freud's reading, the Irma dream articulates his anxieties at a crucial stage of the development of metapsychology, and it asserts his desires. Like the charmed hero of the fairy tale, he wishes to go on wishing. He wishes to read the self so that he can write it completely undisturbed by those memories that have not been explicitly sought out by the writer as the origin of his construction. Freud's interpretation of the dream image ''reddish water,'' the searched-for and therefore unmistakable link to infantile sexuality that enabled him to proceed with his self-analysis, did not retrieve from his unconscious the memory of Emma's life-threatening hemorrhages, a traumatic experience that he shared with another person, his patient. It enabled him, rather, to proceed with the development of his fictional strategies in cartographing and defining the psychic territory as ''timeless,''[159] that is, community- and history-transcending. On his own rather than his patients' authority he wrote the completely articulated, determinate stories of the prehistoric, unconscious self as models to be superimposed on the historic, conscious self. But these models, which he asked his patients to accept as solutions to their own incomplete, fragmented, conflicted stories, deny what has been the cultural experience of modernity. This experience has been one of self-conscious fragmentation, conflictedness, negotiation, and pluralism where cultural value, meaning, and identity are concerned. The profound duality characteristic of modernist cultural activities has its roots in the experience of the self as both deprived of the guidance of authority and released from its control. This, clearly, has also been Freud's experience, which he transcended into fictions that affirmed rather than questioned the author's authority and that therefore could not be negotiated. In turn-of-the-century Vienna, this quality may have been helpful to some of his patients, most of them women, some of whom found it increasingly difficult to be relegated to the passivity of an adoring audience of *Wiener Moderne*. Emma Eckstein, however, was not one of them. As Freud repeatedly complained to Fliess, she "perversely" continued to withhold information that would enable him to complete and thereby, once and for all, resolve her story.[160] As solution had become the metapsychological end in itself, he read more and more selectively in order to write more completely. His disregard for the analysand as author of her own story—the cleverest dreamers who could not persuade him, Emma whose life-threatening hemorrhages did not convince him—became the basis for both his authorship and the authority of his model. It is no wonder that Freud's "discovery" of the reader as authoritative writer of others' texts made around 1900 has proved eminently persuasive to cultural critics who at the end of the twentieth century find themselves more than ever embattled by the perplexities of modernity.

ERNST MACH AND ROBERT MUSIL

In the summer of 1900 the sale of the dream book, on which Freud had placed such high hopes, was going slowly, with only a "short, friendly and uncomprehending review," Freud complained to Fliess on 16 May 1900.[161] But comparing his book to "the latest psychological books (Mach's *Analyse der Empfindungen*, second edition, Kroell's *Aufbau der Seele*, etc.) all of which have the same kind of aims as my work," he professed to be "delighted as the dwarf in the fairy tale because 'the princess doesn't know' " the secret of dreams.[162] There may have been some similar general interests regarding the field of inquiry, but Ernst Mach's approach was distinctly different, and it is significant that Freud not only disregarded that difference but thought that his metapsychology had beaten Mach at his own game. For Mach, psychological inquiry would not have turned on a sudden revelation lighting up demarcations and distinctions that would enable him to draw the only valid map of heretofore-virgin psychical territory. His concept of scientific method in this area of study differs dramatically from Freud's because he insisted on the falsifiable consistency and plausibility of a theory open to questioning by a critical community of inquiry, which included the inquirer's articulated awareness that his theory needed to be a theory of shared practice.

The physicist, philosopher, and psychologist Ernst Mach, probably the single most important influence on Robert Musil's intellectual development, defined his approach in *Erkenntnis und Irrtum* (Knowledge and error, 1905) as "nothing but a scientific methodology and epistemological psychology, (*Erkenntnispsychologie*).[163] In his 1914 review of Walther Rathenau's *The Mechanism of the Mind*, Musil pointed out the lack in the German (Austrian) tradition of such a composite intellectual approach to the process of living, of consciousness: "In our culture artistic and scientific thought do not touch. The problem of mediation between the two remains unresolved.''[164] Musil's essayism is focused on the difficulties of this mediation. It concerns the interdependent modification of scientific and—in a broad sense—literary discourse with the goal of articulating more fully and more precisely human potential in experience. Such an attempt at modification is not served by literary or cultural critics' all-too-easy metaphorical approximations of scientific questions.

Musil, who had studied engineering, mathematics, philosophy, and psychology, had written a dissertation on Mach, and had held a postdoctoral position in behavioral psychology, was one of the rare cases in which a superb verbal talent combined with scientific training and capability and with extraordinary social and psychological intelligence. His early novel *Young Torless* (1906) dealt with his own intellectual and sexual awakening, touching on some of the issues central to *Wiener Moderne*, though he wrote the text while studying engineering in Germany. That short text, a sort of intellectual autobiography, contained in its brief span many of the questions that would concern him all his life and that he would refine over the many decades of writing the philosophical novel *The Man without Qualities*. But already the early text, notwithstanding the young writer's self-absorption, is shaped by the insight that since he deals with conscious subjects, the writer's strategies are informed by his responsibility to the world, which he does not inhabit alone and therefore cannot (re)write and authorize autonomously.[165] The essay fragment ''On the Essay,'' written in the early 1920s, defined these strategies as striving for an appropriately flexible precision where a concept of scientific precision was meaningless.

In ''Der mathematische Mensch'' (1913)[166] Musil ironically debunked intellectual tendencies to radical simplification of an increasingly complicated modern technocratic sociopolitical reality, which cannot be really understood without mathematics but also cannot be fully explained by it. If intellectuals simply deny modern complexity or try to co-opt it metaphorically, mathematics, as Musil points out, is both too complex and too simple to shape and understand life-world decisions. It would be even more catastrophic for the human beings affected by their strategies if successful military leaders were indeed, as they are often said to be, ''mathematicians of the battlefield''—anticipations of the mutually beneficial relations between General von Stumm and the industrialist Arnheim in *The Man without Qualities*, published two decades later. The passionately extreme economy of thought that is characteristic of the practitioners of mathematics does not accommodate the more wasteful, groping, uncertain nature of thinking in most life-world situations. But that is not, as Musil was quick to point out, the fault of the mental discipline of mathematics. In fact, it was among its practitioners that he found ''analogies'' for future men and women who would reaffirm the enlightened rationalism of thinkers like Diderot or d'Alembert and who would continue, beyond their professional expertise, processes of essayistic reflection shaped by the acknowledged force of emotions, desires, and intentions. They would be able to do so precisely because the mathematical discipline of thinking would have made them more sensitive to the ''second dimension of thought''[167] that enables gradations of abstraction, of the subjective shaping of objectivity—anticipations of Ulrich, the intellectual protagonist of *The Man without Qualities*.

Since the Enlightenment, modernity has meant a shared responsibility to understand our natural-cultural environment, the ''world out there,'' which very much includes the sciences and technology. When Musil refers in ''Der mathematische Mensch'' to the ''terrifyingly credible . . . presence of an automobile,''[168] he does so to induce his contemporaries to submit themselves to the indeed vast modern interdependencies of mental processes—(post)modernist chic calls for invoking, but not for dealing with them—and the reality principle of a critical community, that is, the modern concept of truth as trust in evidence. His concept of ''essayism'' in these early essays and *The Man without Qualities* is based on an uncertainty of meaning that is close to the psychologically informed epistemology of the eighteenth-century philosopher David Hume, the ironical pillar of the Scottish Enlightenment.

Hume's critical remarks on the premature certainties of philosophical abstraction where questions of ethics and knowledge are concerned in the 1739 *Treatise of Human Nature, Being an Attempt to Introduce the Experimental Method of Reasoning into Moral Subjects* struck a deep chord of response in Musil. He copied them into the draft of the introduction to a planned volume of essays with the working title *Versuche einen anderen Menschen zu finden* (Attempts to find an alternate man)—that is, attempts to find alternate ways of cultural morals and knowledge.[169] But Musil's essayistic writing is also close to Friedrich Schleiermacher's early-nineteenth-century romantic hermeneutics that works with a concept of linguistic understanding as accommodation of the fullness of language use: it occurs at a particular moment in the development of the user, to which language contributes, and a particular moment in the development of language, to which the user contributes. For Schleiermacher, grasping the fullness of this moment can be no more than a utopian direction.[170] The life of the language and the life of the person using it combine in the moment of speech into an infinite horizon to which the speaker, trying to make himself understood, and the listener, trying to understand, are inevitably drawn and that inevitably defeats them. But this defeat is part of the inevitable and necessary hermeneutic circle that is helped by the modern dialogical agreement to keep open, clarify, and refine an admittedly difficult, often-elusive process of meaning rather than the neoromantic ''postmodern'' monological desire to stage inexorable ruptures. Since the Enlightenment, the ability to speak has been seen as rooted in the fact that memory is shareable imagination and imagination is shareable memory—hence the multivocal, mediating, unfinished, self-transforming discourse of modernity.

Musil was interested in certain essayistic aspects of German romanticism, notably its sensitivity to the cosmopolitan discourse of irony practiced by Enlightenment intellectuals like Diderot, Voltaire, Samuel Johnson, George Lichtenberg, and Georg Forster, but not in the erotic dissolution by romantic poet-critics of all discourse into *Transzendentalpoesie, progressive Universalpoesie*.[171] His texts are notoriously open to a modern plurality of voices, a diversity of discourse, and, in that, they are eminently contemporary to the late twentieth century. Musil's superb use of language in the construction of his ironical perspective—his intricate shaping and shading of truth—supported the rare honesty of his cultural critique. Speech (writing) is for him an infinitely complex social (political) phenomenon, the reality of other voices,[172] and therefore not to be "mastered" but to be attempted and accommodated. The utopian dimension of his essayism signifies its processual dialogical clarifications: to make room, in retreating, for the other voice to be heard, the phenomenon to become visible, with all its modern contradictions, confusions, and obscurities. Thus he emphasized in his 1918 "Skizze der Erkenntnis des Dichters" (Sketch of poetic cognition) the importance for the poet of the "structure of the world" shared with others over the "structure of his own particular talents."[173] Much of his cultural criticism of the 1920s was a modern analysis of the reemergence after the war of early-twentieth-century political and cultural modernisms.

In "Helpless Europe" (1922) he argued that the problem with postwar European culture was not, as many intellectuals complained, an overweening rigid rationalism (the postmodernist bogey of "logocentrism") and too little "soul" (postmodernist "spirituality") but that questions concerning the "soul" were not reasoned intelligibly.[174] He admonished his readers traumatized by World War I and threatened by the accelerated complications of Weimar modernity that the most plausible cultural reaction would be to return to a positive, shared interest in evidence, the testimony of the senses and of reason. He strongly suggested intellectual and political sobriety and advised against a wild-goose chase after truth. If there was a cultural crisis—though he preferred to think in terms of perplexity and potential—it had to do with faulty contemporary understanding of modern experience rather than, as was often argued, lack of spiritual focus or strength, of a unifying philosophy, of a "true" identity. His contemporaries might have yearned for it, but their cultural reality, like ours, did not support such coherent constructs.[175] He also argued that the age-old metaphysical questions—the "mystery of consciousness"—might benefit from being posed in the realm of the modern empirical sciences (*Tatsachenwissenschaften*).[176] "Facts" are of course "made" in the mind; the issue is how. In his hilarious 1921 review of Oswald Spengler's best-selling *Decline of the West* for readers "who had survived it," Musil satirized Spengler's determination not to have his flights of fancy dragged down by evidence,[177] but he also showed how Spengler's text reflected his readers' hunger for "the truth" of the inevitable decline of "the West" rather than their desire for informed inquiry into the complex nature of their current troubles.

One of the reasons for these difficulties given in "Helpless Europe" was the fact that, thinking and acting, we do not really involve ourselves, the persons we are always in the process of becoming.[178] Convinced by Mach's finding that "the object and the self [*Ich*] are provisional *fictions* of the same kind,"[179] Musil referred here to the involvement of a temporary, shifting ego construct that focuses thoughts and actions so that they can be meaningfully questioned. He set the "open," provisional *Ich* against the tendency that he found prevalent in twentieth-century technocratic mass societies to simply "go with the times" and embrace energetically any and every "cutting-edge" position. Such cultural and political indeterminacy—a common and potent ingredient in cultural politics—means that events, acts, actors, and the ideas associated with them flow past consciousness rather than being passed through it. The result is the spongy, all-embracing white noise of the "spirit of the time," the obvious and yet elusive *Zeitgeist*.

Most clearly and urgently in the *The Man without Qualities*, the ethically assertive question "How are we to live?" as naturally cultural beings presupposes for Musil the epistemologically cautionary question "How can we know?" This eminently modern dilemma is at the root of his difficulties in completing the huge project of the novel. In one way or another, all modern writers have experienced this dilemma, certainly since the Enlightenment, and they have contributed to the explosive duality inherent in modernist positions. In Musil's view, all the author could do was to insist that he had stated as clearly as possible the meanings of his fictions, that he had used a shared language to the best of his individual ability. Alerting the reader to the particular, partial, and always-changing "truth" of his fictions, he relinquished their significance. Whether persuaded or not, readers would be able to judge, in reproducing it, their construction. They would come away with the political and psychological contradictions and conflicts unresolved, the cultural confusion intact, if intelligibly analyzed. They would be at liberty to agree or disagree with the novel's characters, who are based on Musil himself and on people he knew directly or indirectly: generals and politicians, industrialists and academics, poets, artists, and philosophers, all of them agents in his and their contemporary culture. In what he considered important cases, he retained their "reality," that is, their sociopolitical individuality, most notably and strikingly in the figure of Rathenau-Arnheim, the man with qualities, constructed to complement Ulrich's open self. But as their author, he could not fully know their lives, the lives of his ideas; there were, as he knew, many uncharted areas, many doubts and uncertainties, or, at best, probabilities.

Musil's narration acknowledges the fragmentary existence of these lives symbiotically entwined with his ideas, their probing rather than predictive nature. It presents those parts that were accessible to him and that he wished to communicate to the reader, because, as contemporaries, they were all together in this. But this essayistic narrative also meant a formidable challenge to the writer who needed to reach an audience of general, educated readers to survive physically (financially) and intellectually. His writing was explicitly situated within a shared contemporary experience out of which had grown the lives of his ideas in his particular use of shared language. But would his readers, ever hungry for the *Totallösungen* of complete stories, appreciate this commonality?

The instability of significance (not signification), its potential for adaptation, ironical connection, and transformation in the absence of fixed ''qualities,'' was functional. It was meant to tempt the reader with the potential of the text, in the tradition of Enlightenment writers like Hume, Diderot, Lichtenberg, Voltaire, Johnson, and Forster, but also some early romantics like Friedrich Schlegel and Novalis. Working through the many versions of the first part of the novel, Musil understood that the discourse of irony that had carried the cultural (political) criticism of his essays would also have to be of major importance for his narrative strategies. When he looked back on the first two volumes in 1938, an exiled writer more than ever separated from his readers, the first volume seemed to him the most accessible because of its particular ironical mode. Irony balances the passions of the intellect and negotiates distances between world and writerly self as ''protagonist of his ideas'' who lacks a sense of belonging—or not belonging—anywhere.[180] Musil reflected here on the stimulating difficulties of his ''zweiseitig Emigrierender'' (double exile). The cultural distance forced on him by the political situation moved his ironical perspective even more toward linkage and removed the observer even more from a position of certainty that could control distances. The more intense the need to understand, the more poignant the risks of misunderstanding. Irony in this sense is also self-irony; it is ''constructive'' because it integrates the self into the act of constructing the other. This essayistic irony connects rather than separates because it is sustained by sympathy and hostility, by authorial judgment and abdication of omniscience, by merging with a protagonist who is not fully knowable, much less predictable.[181]

As it turned out, irony as affinity for transformation would link the different periods of this turbulent century and thereby undermine the rigidity of historical hindsight. Musil noted in 1938 that the narrated time of the novel was twenty-five years earlier. During the long writing process it had become a historical novel, though it had been conceived as a novel about the present developed out of the past (''ein aus der Vergangenheit entwickelter Gegenwartsroman''). But he need not have worried. His experimental stories would have disturbed the comforts of historical hindsight anyway; his and Ulrich's essayism would interrupt rather than construct historical continuity. It is not that their perspective was ahistorical, but that they saw in any given historical instant also the seemingly random selection between various possibilities. This composite, unstable perspective diverted the flow of narration as history, keeping stories open so that they could be transformed through ironical linkage. What Ulrich and his author experienced in 1913 Vienna was the same failure to mediate between emotional and intellectual energies that contributed to the political collapse of Weimar.[182] The connecting ironical projection was Austrian history as a paradigm for German history as a paradigm for twentieth-century Western modernity. Importantly, irony does not support the inventing—or deconstructing—of history. Unlike his author and alter ego, Ulrich is occasionally tempted by such shortcuts—who would not be, given the mess of modern history? But he learns from General Stumm, who has learned that history, made by the military, is preserved by the filing systems (data bases) of libraries so that the military can go on making it. Stumm's energetic way with modernity is the most far sighted and cost efficient, which does not surprise Ulrich, the ironical link between Stumm and Arnheim and lucid interpreter of their transformations. In the hands of Arnheim, the postmodernist Renaissance man with inflammable soul and cool business sense, Stumm's insight will become even more effective once the meaning of history has been streamlined by the fact that "there is a war on." For Musil, the question "Who is [was] responsible?" is synonymous with the two questions "How are we to live?" and "How can we know?" *Wiener Moderne*, like any explicitly modernist position, could not, for better or for worse, explore the meanings of their connectedness at the turn of the century. In its last "posteverything" decade we can still find, as Musil would point out to us, echoes of the promises and problems of its beginning.

NOTES

1. Schoenberg quoted from this dedication in his response to the inquiry conducted by *Brenner* on contemporary reactions to Karl Kraus. See *Brenner* 3, nos. 18, 19, 20 (1913); Schoenberg's response is reprinted in *Rundfrage über Karl Kraus* (Innsbruck: Brenner-Verlag, 1917), 21.

2. Throughout this chapter I will use the German term *Wiener Moderne* to distinguish the modernist position of this group from the larger issue of early-twentieth-century modernity as a continuation of Enlightenment positions. The term "literature" is used in a broader sense, namely, inclusive of literary and cultural criticism, highbrow journalism, literary and cultural history, and certain kinds of philosophy and psychology. Unless mentioned otherwise, all translations from the German are mine and all emphases the authors'.

3. Steven Beller, "Die Position der jüdischen Intelligenz in der Wiener Moderne," in *Die Wiener Jahrhundertwende: Einflüsse, Umwelt, Wirkungen* ed. Jürgen Nautz and Richard Vahrenkamp (Wien: Böhlau, 1993), 712. See his statistics for the period 1880–1910, which "prove" the decisive role of Jews in Vienna bourgeois culture: 30 percent of all university-bound high-school students (*Gymnasiasten*) were Jews, 80 percent of all *Gymnasiasten* with fathers in business were Jewish, 60 percent with fathers in industry and finance, about 30 percent with fathers in the professions: "*in toto* 65 percent of all pupils with a liberal background came from Jewish families" (ibid., 711). These numbers reflect Jewish domination in the educated bourgeois elite, which Beller, however, equates too smoothly with "liberalism." See also Steven Beller, *Vienna and the Jews, 1867–1938: A Cultural History* (Cambridge: Cambridge University Press, 1989). For a good bibliographical selection of studies in Viennese cultural history, see Nautz and Vahrenkamp, *Wiener Jahrhundertwende*, 897–934. It is useful to consult also older studies not limited by the post–World War II perspective, for example, Sigmund Mayer, *Die Wiener Juden: Kommerz, Kultur, Politik, 1700–1900* (Vienna: R. Löwit Verlag, 1918). See John

Boyer, *Political Radicalism in Late Imperial Vienna* (Chicago: University of Chicago Press, 1981), a sober, informative study of the interaction of different ethnic groups and political anti-Semitism in late-nineteenth-century Vienna, (and my review, "Vienna: History and the Literary Tradition," *German Quarterly* 55 (1982): 465–72.

4. Beller, "Position der jüdischen Intelligenz," 714–15.

5. This term refers to, among others, the philosophers Franz Brentano, Rudolf Carnap, and Moritz Schlick, the psychiatrist Theodor Meynert, Freud's onetime superior, and the surgeon Theodor Billroth, but also to Brahms and Richard Strauss.

6. Beller, "Position der jüdischen Intelligenz," 717.

7. Ibid., 718.

8. Musil was much criticized for an implied critique of Rathenau in the Arnheim figure, but Musil the novelist only took those traits from Rathenau's highly complex personality that fitted the Kakanian context. He did not deal with Rathenau's extraordinary political contributions to the fledgling Weimar Republic, but concentrated on his highly successful pre–World War I essays of reactionary-progressivist cultural criticism.

9. See a drawing of Sektionschef Schwarzwald by Oskar Kokoschka and a verbal description by Robert Scheu that stress precisely this sharp dryness and pointed fact orientation in Karl Corino, *Robert Musil: Leben und Werk in Bildern und Texten* (Reinbek: Rowohlt, 1988), 367. Arguably, Musil "copied" the Austrian rather than the "Jewish" diplomat Schwarzwald. The character of the German industrialist Arnheim who quotes Goethe at board meetings and describes the latest industrial technology at cocktail parties is representative of what Musil thought to be an anachronistic (Jewish and non-Jewish) preoccupation with high-cultural synthesis in the face of a rapidly advancing, insufficiently understood mass technocracy.

10. For contemporary reactions to Weininger, see *Jugend in Wien: Literatur um 1900*, Exhibition of the German Literary Archive in the Schiller National Museum, Marbach 1974 (Munich: Kösel, 1974), 324–31.

11. See Peter Labanyi, " 'Die Gefahr des Körpers': A Reading of Otto Weininger's *Geschlecht und Charakter*," in *Fin de Siècle Vienna*, ed. G. J. Carr and Eda Sagarra (Dublin: Trinity College, 1985), 169–73, on the constructedness of Weininger's argument—"its form, dualism, *is* its content"—and the Neoplatonic dimension of his cultural critique. See also Kraus's highly positive reaction in a letter to Weininger, later printed in *Sprüche und Widersprüche* (1909): "Ein Frauenverehrer stimmt den Argumenten Ihrer Frauenverachtung mit Begeisterung zu." He shares Weininger's view of the a priori "otherness" of women, but, in contrast to Weininger, he adores it.

12. See Boyer, *Political Radicalism in Late Imperial Vienna*, 40–121, on the politically exploitable difficulties of artisans confronted with rapidly increasing machine production.

13. Karl Kraus, *Fackel* 59 (mid-November 1900): 28, quoted in Beller "Position," 710.

14. See Elias Canetti, *The Torch in My Ear* (New York: Farrar Straus Giroux, 1982), 159. Canetti's later wife, Veza, although a great admirer of Kraus, had attempted to convince her husband of Kraus's limitations as a model by showing that wrathful grandiosity was utterly singular and inimitable. Kraus's moral absolutism and verbal "purism" are complex issues and will be discussed later at length. His cultural criticism shares some reactions and goals with Musil's, but Musil lacks Kraus's absolutism and purism.

15. Beller, "Position der jüdischen Intelligenz," 710.

16. See Klimt's portraits of women in Viennese high society, among them Ludwig

Wittgenstein's sister Margaret Stonborough-Wittgenstein; see also Peter Vergo, *Art in Vienna, 1898–1918: Klimt, Kokoschka, Schiele, and Their Contemporaries* (London: Phaidon, 1975), 182–83.

17. On Jewish patronage in *Wiener Moderne*, see the informative if too-uncritical Edward Timms, "Die Wiener Kreise: Schöpferische Interaktionen in der Wiener Moderne," in *Die Wiener Jahrhundertwende*, 134–37. Timms (135) quotes Kokoschka on his Jewish customers' greater openness to new developments because they were not as firmly anchored in Viennese society (neither were non-Jewish members of the new and newly rich bourgeoisie) and Loos on enviable Jewish cultural curiosity and energies: "The Jew gets much more out of his life than we. But that is not his fault. We are the indifferent ones. Jews go to the best theatre performances, they read the best books. They take the most interesting trips, and they let me remodel their homes. . . . And then the Christians are angry, when everywhere they are crowded out by Jews."

18. See Carl Schorske, *Fin-de-Siècle Vienna: Politics and Culture* (New York: Knopf, 1980). His Freudian perspective simplifies unduly both the new mass politics (as a revolt of the sons against the fathers) and the new art (as intimately connected with Klimt's midlife crisis). Boyer's *Political Radicalism in Late Imperial Vienna* makes abundantly clear the social and cultural complexities of the new politics (which anticipated in important ways Weimar's problems). Klimt's painterly development was shaped by the increasing exchange of design ideas, material changes, and the influence of arts and crafts, that is, the medium of his art rather than his psyche, which is analyzed by Schorske in entirely predictable Freudian terms.

19. Oskar Kokoschka, quoted in Ludwig Münz and Gustav Künstler, *Adolf Loos: Pioneer of Modern Architecture* (New York: Praeger, 1966), 11–12.

20. The second and third volumes of Canetti's autobiography, *The Torch in My Ear* and *The Play of the Eyes*, give a good sense of the intensity and theatricality, the staging, and the high visibility and competitiveness of Viennese *Kulturbetrieb* (business of culture). More important even than getting commissions for portraits was Loos's introducing Kokoschka to Herwarth Walden, whose influential avant-garde journal *Der Sturm* published Kokoschka's drawings and his drama *Mörder, Hoffnung der Frauen*. The 1909 production caused tumultuous fights in the audience, and Kokoschka was in danger of being arrested for disturbing the peace. However—and this nicely illustrates the contradictions of *Wiener Moderne* regarding cultural authority—he was rescued by the police called by Loos and Kraus, who knew the chief of police.

21. Münz and Künstler, *Adolf Loos*, 11.

22. Oskar Kokoschka, *My Life* (New York: Macmillan, 1974), 35.

23. Ibid., 34. See also Kraus's remarks on Kokoschka, *Fackel* 14, nos. 360–62 (1912–13): 23; Ludwig Erik Tesar, "Der Fall Kokoschka und die Gesellschaft," *Fackel* 12, nos. 319–20 (1910–11): 31–39.

24. *Rundfrage über Karl Kraus*, 38.

25. Ibid., 7–11.

26. Thomas Mann, in *Rundfrage über Karl Kraus*, 15–16. Mann mentioned that he had been to Kraus's *Vorleseabend* (reading) arranged by *Brenner* in Munich, together with his brother Heinrich (whose interest in the theater was well known) and the avant-garde dramatist Frank Wedekind. The latter's response to the inquiry celebrates Kraus's fight for cultural ethics as one of the "greatest treasures of mankind" but finds it regrettable that Kraus has not made any professional use of his extraordinary dramatic talents (ibid., 14–15).

27. *Jugend in Wien: Literatur um 1900*, 297.

28. See Canetti's description of his initiation to Kraus's readings in the early 1920s in Canetti, *The Torch in My Ear* (the German title is *Die Fackel im Ohr*), 65–74. The very title of Canetti's memoirs emphasizes Kraus's extraordinary power, especially over young and impressionable intellectuals. Eventually Canetti would break away from Kraus's influence, but his writerly development was decisively shaped by Kraus's superb talent for listening to the voices of Vienna and making his listeners listen—forming the ''School of Hearing'' that lent itself to the title of a chapter in Canetti's volume.

29. See the selection of translations in Karl Kraus, *No Compromise: Selected Writings of Karl Kraus*, ed. Frederick Ungar (New York: Frederick Ungar, 1977).

30. The position of the architect Loos was somewhat different: his work was seminal for modernism in architecture, a relatively straightforward phenomenon, as has been the reaction to it in postmodernist architecture.

31. Kokoschka, *My Life*, 35.

32. For reproductions, see Münz and Künstler, *Adolf Loos*; H. Allen Brooks, *The Prairie School: Frank Lloyd Wright and His Midwest Contemporaries* (Toronto: University of Toronto Press, 1972).

33. Robert Fishman, *Urban Utopias in the Twentieth Century: Ebenezer Howard, Frank Lloyd Wright, and Le Corbusier* (New York: Basic Books, 1977), 110.

34. Ibid., 112–13.

35. Nikolaus Pevsner, *Pioneers of Modern Design from William Morris to Walter Gropius* (New York: Museum of Modern Art, 1949), 123–24.

36. Vergo, *Art in Vienna*, 177; for examples of the architectural conservatism of Loos's projects in the 1920s, see Münz and Künstler, *Adolf Loos*, 126–29. It is this duality that led to Kraus's—and Loos's and Wittgenstein's—preoccupation with insisting so emphatically on clear distinctions. Nike Wagner, *Geist und Geschlecht*: *Karl Kraus und die Erotik der Wiener Moderne* (Frankfurt: Suhrkamp, 1982), rightly draws attention to this aspect of Kraus's work, but she is, on the whole, too rigidly focused on ''the erotic.''

37. Adolf Loos, *Sämtliche Schriften in zwei Bänden*, ed. Franz Glück (Munich and Vienna: Herold, 1962), vol. 1, *Ins Leere gesprochen, 1897–1900*; vol. 2, *Trotzdem, 1900–1930.* Three of the essays are translated in Münz and Künstler, *Adolf Loos*: ''The Plumbers,'' ''The Story of a Poor Rich Man,'' and ''Ornament and Crime'' (quotations from these essays are from this collection).

38. Otto Wagner, *Moderne Architektur* (Vienna, 1896), 95.

39. Vergo, *Art in Vienna*, 144–46.

40. Josef Hoffman, quoted in Vergo, *Art in Vienna*, 132–33.

41. See the reproduction in Vergo, *Art in Vienna*, 139.

42. See the reproduction in Vergo, *Art in Vienna*, 227.

43. See the reproduction of the interior of Loos's flat in Vienna (1903) in Vergo, *Art in Vienna*, 166.

44. Ludwig Hevesi, quoted in Vergo, *Art in Vienna*, 166, 169.

45. Münz and Künstler, *Adolf Loos*, fig. 35.

46. The unsigned article is quoted in Vergo, *Art in Vienna*, 172.

47. Adolf Loos, quoted in Vergo, *Art in Vienna*, 173.

48. Kokoschka, *My Life*, 35.

49. Karl Kraus, ''Das Haus am Michaeler Platz,'' *Fackel* 12, nos. 313–14 (1910–11): 4–6. See also Otto Stössl, ''Das Haus auf dem Michaeler Platz,'' *Fackel* 12, no.

317 (1910–11): and Paul Engelmann's sonnet celebrating the house, ending with these lines: "Du stehst für dich, gewaltig aufgerichtet, als erstes Zeichen einer neuen Zeit," *Fackel* 12, no. 317 (1910–11): The young architect Engelmann was a friend of the Wittgenstein family and a disciple of Loos and worked as a secretary for Kraus. On his collaboration with Ludwig Wittgenstein on the house commissioned by his sister in 1926, see Bernhard Leitner, *The Architecture of Ludwig Wittgenstein* (Halifax: Press of the Nova Scotia College of Art and Design, 1973), a reverently informative study. See also Werner Kraft, "Adolf Loos," in *Das Ja des Neinsagers: Karl Kraus und seine geistige Welt* (Munich: Edition Text + Kritik, 1974), 166–72, and "Ludwig Wittgenstein und Karl Kraus," in *Rebellen des Geistes* (Stuttgart: Kohlhammer, 1968), 102–34. For more literature on Kraus, see the select bibliography in *Die Wiener Jahrhundertwende*, 897–934.

50. Karl Kraus, *Pro domo et mundo* (Munich: Langen, 1912), now in Karl Kraus, *Beim Wort genommen*, in *Werke*, vol. 3 (Munich: Kösel, 1955), 254.

51. See Peter Altenberg, "Wie ich mir Karl Kraus gewann,"*Vita Ipsa* (1918): "Er war für mich, weil ich 'echt' bin. . . . Keinerlei Konzessionen machen können, selbst wenn es einem noch so sehr schadet . . . ein 'Gerade-Schreiter' sein hinein in den eventuellen Abgrund . . . heißt ein 'Echter' sein" (quoted in Kraft, *Ja des Neinsagers*, 161). Altenberg, a minor writer and professional free spirit ("Sokrates des Kaffeehauses" and "Genie der Nichtigkeit," Kraft, 161), was a well-known figure in *Wiener Moderne*; see Constantin Floros, "Alban Berg und die Wiener Moderne," in *Die Wiener Jahrhundertwende*, 607–18, especially 611–14, on the influence of Kraus and Altenberg on Berg, and also Chapter 5 of this book. Kraus and Loos saw Altenberg as *Echter* because his highly unconventional life-style suggested some sort of identity of art and life. Arthur Schnitzler, always the shrewd and open-minded observer, was intrigued by Altenberg's fluid identity and self-presentation—his pose as free spirit became *Echtheit* and *Echtheit* became pose. See Schnitzler's diary entry, 25 May 1895, on the occasion of the publication of Altenberg's first book, *Wie ich es sehe*, a collection of the short, impressionistic, highly subjective verbal "snapshots" of life in Vienna for which he was to become known (Arthur Schnitzler, *Das Wort*, ed. Kurt Bergel [Frankfurt, 1966], 7).

52. In this context, Kraus's critique was often directed against the Jewish bourgeoisie that wielded considerable influence in Vienna, as the numbers quoted earlier document. To reject such critique as Jewish self-hatred, celebrating, at the same time, Jewish "domination" of the literary scene and Jewish patronage of the arts, seems problematic cultural history because it denies the complex and contradictory past actuality of Jews, as of all groups.

53. In October 1914, ninety-three well-known academics and artists signed an appeal, "An die Kulturwelt," pledging their support to the monarch and the war effort in defense of German culture, which was, in their eyes, profoundly threatened by Western civilization. Among them were men like Ernst Haeckel, Gerhart Hauptmann, Max Liebermann, Max Reinhardt, Max Planck, Wilhelm Roentgen, Karl Vossler, and Wilhelm Wundt.

54. See Timms, "Wiener Kreise," 139–41.

55. Elias Canetti, "Warum ich nicht wie Karl Kraus schreibe," in *Das Gewissen der Worte: Essays* (Munich: Hanser, 1976), 44.

56. Ibid., 43.

57. Ibid., 41.

58. Canetti, *Torch in My Ear*, 70–71.

59. Ibid., 220.

60. Ibid.

61. Ibid., 221.

62. Elias Canetti, *Das Geheimherz der Uhr* (Munich: Hanser, 1987), 26.

63. Soma Morgenstern, quoted in Floros, "Alban Berg und die Wiener Moderne," 607.

64. Paul Engelmann, *Letters from Ludwig Wittgenstein: With a Memoir* (Oxford: Blackwell, 1976), 123.

65. Karl Kraus, *Fackel* 16–17, nos. 388–90 (1914–15): 37.

66. Kokoschka, *My Life*, 39–40. See also Kraus's remark on his portrait in *Pro domo et mundo*, 254: "Kokoschka hat ein Porträt von mir gemacht. Schon möglich, dass mich die nicht erkennen werden, die mich kennen. Aber sicher werden mich die erkennen, die mich nicht kennen" (Kokoschka has painted a portrait of me. Possibly those who know me will not recognize me. But those who do not know me surely will).

67. This is suggested by Vergo, *Art in Vienna*, 172.

68. Louis Sullivan, "Ornament in Architecture," in *Kindergarten Chats and Other Writings* (New York: George Wittenborn, 1947), 190.

69. Münz and Künstler, *Adolf Loos*, 228.

70. Ibid., 229, 231.

71. Loos, *Sämtliche Schriften*, 2: 267–75.

72. Ibid., 2:371.

73. Ibid., 2:372.

74. See note 29.

75. *Fackel* 35–37, no. 888 (1933–36) See also "Nachrufe auf Karl Kraus," *Fackel*, no. 889 (July 1934), a collection of the many negative reactions to the poem.

76. *Fackel*, no. 888.

77. See Canetti's reaction, half a century later, in *The Play of the Eyes*, 287–8: "He was obliterated from my mind and the minds of many others."

78. See Wittgenstein's letter of 14 August 1914 to Ficker, thanking him for having made Loos's acquaintance: Ludwig Wittgenstein, *Briefe an Ludwig von Ficker*, ed. Georg Henrik von Wright, Brenner-Studien 1 (Salzburg: Otto Müller, 1969), 13.

79. Wittgenstein, letter to Ficker, 19 July 1914, *Briefe*, 12: "Als Anwalt meiner Sache wählte ich Sie, auf die Worte hin, die Sie über Kraus schrieben."

80. Engelmann, *Letters From Ludwig Wittgenstein*, 123.

81. Ibid., 131.

82. See Dagmar Barnouw, *Weimar Intellectuals and the Threat of Modernity* (Bloomington: Indiana University Press, 1988), 11–42, and *Critical Realism: History, Photography, and the Work of Siegfried Kracauer* (Baltimore: Johns Hopkins University Press, 1990), 20–52.

83. Ludwig Wittgenstein, *Notebooks, 1914–1916*, ed. Georg Henrik von Wright and G. E. M. Anscombe (Oxford: Blackwell, 1961), 82, 82e.

84. Ludwig Wittgenstein, *Tractatus Logico-philosophicus,* introduced by Bertrand Russell (London: Kegan Paul, 1922).

85. The earliest, most clearly metaphysical of these poems appeared untitled in the 1912 *Pro domo et mundo*, later included as "Zwei Läufer" ("Two Runners") in *Worte in Versen* I (1916). The much later "Mein Widerspruch" ("My Objection," in *Worte in Versen* IX, 1930) relates *Ursprung* more concretely to Kraus's radical position as cultural conservatist. See Jens Malte Fischer, *Karl Kraus: Studien zum "Theater der Dichtung" und Kulturkonservatismus* (Kronberg: Scriptor, 1973), 183–91.

86. Wittgenstein, *Tractatus*, 22.

87. Wittgenstein, *Briefe*, 33.

88. Ibid., 35.

89. Wittgenstein, *Tractatus*, 3. See also Wittgenstein's letter to Ficker, 22 November 1919, *Briefe*, 37: Ficker could not publish the manuscript and wanted to show it to a philosophy professor, but Wittgenstein thought that the professor would not understand a word.

90. See the attempted solution of this paradox in Gottfried Gabriel, ''Logik als Literatur? Zur Bedeutung des Literarischen bei Wittgenstein,'' *Merkur* 32 (1978): 353–62. Basing his argument on Wittgenstein's admiration for Kraus, Gabriel asserts that the significance of the *Tractatus* for Wittgenstein lay in its aphoristic form. In this scenario, ethics and aesthetics are one. But if this were true, Wittgenstein could simply have spoken about ethical issues as Kraus did, often with admirable lucidity and finesse. It is the privilege of the reader to blur the lines between hermeneutics, ethics, and aesthetics, but Wittgenstein, despite his suggestively opaque preface, struggled with the transcendental semantic of the *Tractatus*, which he would later recognize as hermeneutic failure.

91. ''Ich glaube meine Stellung zur Philosophie dadurch zusammengefasst zu haben, indem ich sage: Philosophie dürfe man eigentlich nur *dichten*.'' Gabriel, ''Logik als Literatur?'' 358–59, makes much of this letter.

92. Wittgenstein, *Tractatus*, 26.

93. Engelmann, *Letters to Ludwig Wittgenstein*, 127.

94. Adolf Loos, Engelmann, *Letters to Ludwig Wittgenstein*, quoted in 128.

95. See note 36.

96. See Barnouw, *Critical Realism*, Chapter 2, ''Contemporaneity and the Concept of History.''

97. See Dagmar Barnouw, ''Political Correctness in the 1780s: Kant, Herder, Forster, and the Knowledge of Diversity,'' in *Herder Yearbook*, ed. Wilfried Malsch and Wulf Koepke (Stuttgart: Metzler, 1994), 51–76.

98. Benjamin wrote to his old friend Gershom Scholem (who had tried to get him to come to Jerusalem for years) on 20 January 1930 from Paris that his major goal was to ''récréer comme genre'' literary criticism in Germany and be ''considéré comme le premier critique de la littérature allemande.'' Walter Benjamin, *Briefe*, ed. Gershom Scholem and Theodor W. Adorno (Frankfurt: Suhrkamp, 1966), 2: 505.

99. On Freud's relations to Arthur Schnitzler, see note 165.

100. Freud's more general cultural critique has often been praised for its enlightened secularism set against the entrenched darkness of institutionalized religion. See Ritchie Robertson, ''Freud and Pater Wilhelm Schmidt,'' in *Die Wiener Jahrhundertwende*, 349–59. Robertson, who sees Freud as a lifelong adherent to Enlightenment ideals, lauds his ''public fight against religion'' in *Totem and Taboo* (ibid., 350). But the arguments of the essays collected in this volume are based on the highly speculative Oedipus complex rather than anthropological research. It is precisely the absolute centrality of infantile material to all human development that makes Freud's ''anthropological'' texts and his later mass psychology so problematic. If he appeals, as he often does, to the rule, even the ''dictatorship'' (quoted in Robertson, 350), of scientific reason in the psyche, he means *his* psychoanalytic constructs, which he protected jealously from all critical scrutiny that is central to scientific inquiry.

101. See Freud's letters to Wilhelm Fliess, 9 February 1898, ''The only sensible thing was said by old Fechner in his sublime simplicity: that the psychical territory on which

the dream process is played out is a different one. It has been left to me to draw the first crude map of it,'' And 21 December 1899, ''It is as if Schliemann had dug up another Troy which had hitherto been believed to be mythical.'' Freud here refers to a particularly successful analysis. References to Freud's letters to Fliess by date (and, if necessary, page number) apply to Sigmund Freud, *The Origins of Psychoanalysis: Letters to Wilhelm Fliess, Drafts and Notes: 1887–1902*, ed. Marie Bonaparte, Anna Freud, and Ernst Kris (New York: Basic Books, 1977). The editors of this edition were motivated by the desire to present a thoroughly respectable, scientifically legitimate founder of psychoanalysis. Reference to letters or letter passages excluded by them are to *The Complete Letters of Sigmund Freud to Wilhelm Fliess, 1887–1904*, ed. Jeffrey Moussaieff Masson (Cambridge, MA: Belknap Press of Harvard University Press, 1985), by date and page number.

102. See Freud, ''From the History of an Infantile Neurosis,'' *Standard Edition* (*S.E.*), vol. 17, 50f. (hereafter cited as ''Infantile Neurosis'').

103. Freud, ''Fräulein Elisabeth v.R.,'' in *Studies on Hysteria* (1895), *S.E.*, vol. 2, 135–61. Freud introduces the summarizing ''Diskussion'' of the case history with these reflections.

104. ''The Aetiology of Hysteria,'' *S.E.*, vol. 3, 282. See also Freud's letter to Fliess, 26/28 April 1896, *Complete Letters*, 184: ''A lecture on the etiology of hysteria at the psychiatric society was given an icy reception by the asses and a strange evaluation by Krafft-Ebbing: 'It sounds like a scientific fairy tale.' ''

105. Freud, ''Aetiology of Hysteria,'' 280.

106. Freud, ''Infantile Neurosis,'' 52, 50–51; see also the 1938 ''Constructions in Analysis,'' *S.E.*, vol. 23, 257–60.

107. See the critical discussion of the Wolf Man analysis in Patrick J. Mahony, *Cries of the Wolf Man*, History of Psychoanalysis I (New York: International Universities Press, 1984), 157–59.

108. ''Postmodernist'' readings of Freud are less interested in the partial therapeutic usefulness of his fictions than the significant completeness of their elaborate construction from highly selective materials. See the readings collected in Harold Bloom, ed., *Sigmund Freud* (New York: Chelsea House, 1985).

109. ''Metapsychology'' is first mentioned in a letter to Fliess, 13 February 1896 (*Origins*, 157). It took two more decades for the term to appear in the writings.

110. See Freud's letter to Fliess, 21 May 1894, *Complete Letters*, 1–4; on Fliess's relation to Otto Weininger, who allegedly plagiarized his highly speculative periodicity ''theory,'' see Jacques Le Rider, *Der Fall Otto Weininger: Wurzeln des Antifeminismus und Antisemitismus* (Vienna: Loecker Verlag, 1985), Chapter 4.

111. Sigmund Freud, ''Project for a Scientific Psychology (1895),'' in *Origins*, 429. The title was chosen by the translator; the German title ''Entwurf einer Psychologie'' was chosen by the editor; Freud's uncompleted manuscript is untitled. See also note 151.

112. Freud, *Origins*, 216.

113. Ibid.

114. See Freud's long letter to Fliess outlining his work on the sexual origin of neuroses, 21 May 1894 (*Origins*, 83): ''I am pretty well alone here in tackling the neuroses. They regard me rather as a monomaniac, while I have the distinct feeling that I have touched on one of the great secrets of nature.''

115. After the completion of the dream book Freud wrote to Fliess on 1 February 1900 (*Complete Letters*, 398): ''On the whole I have noticed that you usually over-

estimate me greatly. The motivation for this error, though, disarms any reproach. For I am actually not at all a man of science, not an observer, not an experimenter, not a thinker. I am by temperament nothing but a conquistador—an adventurer, if you want it translated—with all the curiosity, daring, and tenacity characteristic of a man of this sort. Such people are customarily esteemed only if they have been successful, have really discovered something; otherwise they are dropped by the wayside. And that is not altogether unjust."

116. Freud, *Origins,* 218.

117. See Freud's letter to Fliess, 14 August 1897 (*Origins*, 213).

118. Freud, *Origins*, 218–221, 219; on the discrepancies of dating, see Max Schur, *Freud: Living and Dying* (New York: International Universities Press, 1972), 120.

119. Freud, *Origins*, 221.

120. Ibid., 220.

121. Freud, letter to Fliess, 21 September 1897 (*Complete Letters*, 264; *Origins*, 215–16, includes this passage but has one important misreading and one important omission, both corrected in *Complete Letters*).

122. This question is central to the useful if problematic study of Jeffrey Moussaieff Masson, *The Assault on Truth: Freud's Suppression of the Seduction Theory* (New York: Farrar, Straus and Giroux, 1984).

123. See also Masson, *Assault on Truth*, 185–88, on Freud's negative remarks about his patients' truthfulness.

124. Freud, *Origins*, 221.

125. See Freud's letters to Fliess, 20 and 26 April 1895 (*Complete Letters*, 125–27); all the letters containing references to the Emma Eckstein episode (discussed later) have been excluded from *Origins*. In the letter of 26 April Fliess is addressed as "Dear Magician."

126. See Harold Bloom, "Freud's Concept of Defense and the Poetic Will," in Bloom, *Sigmund Freud*, 157.

127. Freud, *Origins*, 221; see, however, "Infantile Neurosis," 14 n. 2.

128. In the preceding letter of 3 October (*Origins*, 218–21), Freud had mentioned his feeling that he ought not to take money from a colleague's wife, but that the colleague had insisted that he take it.

129. Freud, *Origins*, 222.

130. Ibid., 223.

131. See Sigmund Freud, *The Interpretation of Dreams* (New York: Avon, 1965), Chapter 5, "The Material and Sources of Dreams," D., "Typical Dreams."

132. Freud, letter to Fliess, 9 February 1898 (*Origins*, 245).

133. Freud, *Origins*, 232.

134. In his letter of 22 December 1897 (*Origins*, 238–39) Freud informed Fliess, "It has occurred to me that masturbation is the one great habit that is a 'primary addiction,' and that the other addictions, alcohol, morphine, tobacco, etc., only enter into life as a substitute and replacement for it. Its part in hysteria is prodigious, and perhaps my great outstanding obstacle is, wholly or in part, to be found in it."

135. Freud, letter to Fliess, 14 November 1897 (*Origins*, 234).

136. Freud, *Origins*, 234–35.

137. See Pierre Bourdieu, *Outline of a Theory of Practice* (New York: Free Press, 1977), 16–20.

138. Freud, *Origins*, 234.

139. Freud, "Infantile Neurosis," 51.

140. "Do you suppose that some day a marble tablet will be placed on the house, inscribed with these words: 'In this house on July 24th, 1895, the Secret of Dreams was revealed to Dr. Sigmund Freud'?" (Freud, *Origins*, 322).

141. Freud, letter to Fliess, 8 March 1895 (*Complete Letters*, 116–19).

142. Freud, letter to Fliess, 20 April 1895 (*Complete Letters*, 125).

143. Max Schur, "The Guilt of the Survivor," quoted in Freud, *Complete Letters*, 121 n. 3.

144. Freud, *Complete Letters*, 183, 186; see also the letter of 4 June 1896 (*Complete Letters*, 191–92); Masson, *Assault on Truth*, 100–103.

145. Freud, *Interpretation of Dreams*, 138–54 (dream and analysis). For the identity of persons appearing in the dream, see Alexander Grinstein, *On Sigmund Freud's Dreams* (Detroit: Wayne State University Press, 1968), 21–23. "Dr. M." stands for Josef Breuer, Freud's mentor and coauthor of the *Studies on Hysteria*, who irritated him greatly with his reservations regarding his "metapsychological" solutions. Significantly, Freud never mentioned this crucial dream in his letters to Fliess, particularly frequent during that anxious period—very much in contrast to his extensive account of the nurse dream of 3/4 October 1897. But on 24 July 1895, the day on which he analyzed what was to become the specimen dream, he wrote a short note to Fliess, addressing him as "Daimonie" and complaining about his silence.

146. Freud, *Interpretation of Dreams*, 140.

147. Freud, *Interpretation of Dreams*, 149.

148. Freud, *Interpretation of Dreams*, 150.

149. Ibid.

150. Freud, *Interpretation of Dreams*, 151. For an ingenious literary exercise on the occasion of the Irma dream as self-referential jigsaw puzzle, see Jeffrey Mehlman, "Trimethylamin: Notes on Freud's Specimen Dream," in *Untying the Text: A Post-Structuralist Reader*, ed. Robert Young (Boston: Routledge & Kegan Paul, 1981), 177–88.

151. Freud, *Interpretation of Dreams*, 154. Freud used the dream strategy that enabled him to make the connection to Fliess, that is, to sexuality and the primal scene, in "Project for a Scientific Psychology" (*Origins*, 403–6) to exemplify the discontinuous nature of dream formation. Instructively, he started working on this project shortly after the Emma Eckstein episode, which must have caused him to doubt profoundly the clinical validity of his treatment in cases diagnosed as hysteria. However, he was soon frustrated in this attempt "to furnish us with a psychology which shall be a natural science" (*Origins*, 355: the first sentence of "Project"), as he wrote to Fliess on 8 November 1895 (*Origins*, 133–34), and the text remained a fragment.

152. Freud, letter to Fliess, 10 March 1898 (*Origins*, 246–47): "The repetition of experience of the prehistoric period is a wish-fulfilment in itself and for its own sake; a recent wish leads to a dream only if it can be associated with material from that period, if the recent wish is a derivative of a prehistoric wish or can get itself adopted by such a wish. I do not know yet to what extent I shall be able to stick to this extreme theory, or let it loose in the dream book."

153. Freud, "Infantile Neurosis," 81 n. 2.

154. Freud, *Interpretation of Dreams*, 184 (Chapter 4, "Distortion in Dreams").

155. Ibid., 174 (Chapter 4, "Distortion in Dreams").

156. Freud, letter to Fliess, 2 April 1896 (*Origins*, 161–62).

157. Freud, letter to Fliess, 6 December 1896 (*Origins*, 174).

158. See Freud, *Interpretation of Dreams*, Chapters 4 and 6.

159. Freud, "Infantile Neurosis," 11.

160. See Masson, *Assault on Truth*, 105–6.

161. *Origins*, 320.

162. Freud, letter to Fliess, 12 June 1900 (*Origins*, 322).

163. Ernst Mach, *Erkenntnis und Irrtum* (Leipzig: Johann Ambrosius Barth, 1905), VIII.

164. Robert Musil, *Prosa*, vol. 2 of *Gesammelte Werke*, ed. Adolf Frisé (Reinbek: Rowohlt, 1978), 1019.

165. Of the substantial writers of *Wiener Moderne*, Arthur Schnitzler shares this insight to a degree. His scope of psychological curiosity and inquiry, however, is much narrower than Musil's. He contributed to Viennese modernism an intelligent openness to the social meanings of sexuality. Freud thought Schnitzler's dramas, novellas, and novels in certain ways close to his own case histories and therefore considered Schnitzler a competitor whom he tried to "manage." Writing on 14 May 1922 to congratulate the now internationally known writer on his sixtieth birthday, Freud made "a confession which for my sake I must ask you to keep to yourself and share with neither friends nor strangers. I have tormented myself with the question why in all these years I have never attempted to make your acquaintance. . . . The answer contains the confession which strikes me as too intimate. I think I have avoided you from a kind of reluctance to meet my double." Freud presents himself as not "easily inclined to identify myself with another," but when he gets "deeply absorbed in your beautiful creations," he "invariably" finds "beneath their poetic surface the very presuppositions, interests, and conclusions which I know to be my own . . . : your preoccupation with the truths of the unconscious and of the instinctual drives in man, your dissection of the cultural conventions of our society, the dwelling of your thoughts on the polarity of love and death" (*Letters of Sigmund Freud*, ed. Ernst L. Freud [New York: Basic Books, 1975], 339–40). Freud appreciated Schnitzler most of all as the "explorer of psychological depths." Without this particular talent, he wrote, his gift for language would have made him into "a writer of greater appeal to the taste of the masses"—suggesting a shared significant outsider position. But both Schnitzler and Freud had large numbers of readers. Freud disregarded the fact that Schnitzler's fictions, though in some cases similarly focused, were ultimately very different from his because they dealt with the social, that is, shared, meanings of sexual energies. In their representation of "the truths of the unconscious and of the instinctual drives in man" they were not like Freud's closed constructs but remained open for readerly negotiation of different possible meanings. At the time, they were more modern, if less modernist, than Freud's.

166. Musil, *Prosa*, 1004–8.

167. See the essay fragment "On the Essay," in Musil, *Prosa*, 1334–37; the quotation is on 1337.

168. Musil, *Prosa*, 1004–8.

169. Robert Musil, *Tagebücher*, ed. Adolf Frisé (Reinbek: Rowohlt, 1976), 1:663–66; see also 643–45. Mach dedicated his *Erkenntnis und Irrtum*, the text most important to Musil's concept of essayism, to Hume.

170. Friedrich Schleiermacher, *Hermeneutics: The Handwritten Manuscripts*, ed. Heinz Kimmerle, trans. James Duke and Jack Forstman (Missoula, MT: Scholars Press for the American Academy of Religion, 1977), 99–104; see also Schleiermacher's re-

marks on the different combinations of what he calls "grammatical" and "psychological" interpretations suitable for different kinds of texts.

171. Friedrich Schlegel, "Athenaeums-Fragmente" (1798), in *Kritische Schriften*, ed. Wolfdietrich Rasch (Munich: Hanser, 1964), 38.

172. See Walter Moser, "Diskursexperimente im Romantext: Zu Musils *Der Mann ohne Eigenschaften*," in *Robert Musil: Untersuchungen*, ed. Uwe Baur and Elisabeth Castex (Königstein: Athenäum, 1980), 170–97.

173. Musil, *Prosa*, 1029.

174. Ibid., 1092.

175. See Siegfried Kracauer's critique of Benjamin, Bloch, Adorno, and Lukacs in the 1920s and early 1930s in Barnouw, *Critical Realism*, 34–52.

176. Musil, "Helpless Europe," in *Prosa*, 1085.

177. Musil, "Geist und Erfahrung: Anmerkungen für Leser, welche dem Untergang des Abendlandes entronnen sind" (Mind and experience: Notes for readers who have come through the Decline of the West), in *Prosa*, 1042–59.

178. Musil, *Prosa*, 1092.

179. Mach, *Erkenntnis und Irrtum*, 13.

180. Musil, *Tagebücher*, 1:973: "der sich selbst nirgends ganz hin, nirgends ganz fortgehören fühlt."

181. Ibid.

182. Ibid., 2:1148.

Arnold Schoenberg, Self-Portrait. Courtesy of the Arnold Schoenberg Institute.

4 ARNOLD SCHOENBERG

Bryan R. Simms

The music of Arnold Schoenberg (1874–1951) grows from a synthesis of far-reaching opposites. It contains both an extension of the ideas of German composers of the late nineteenth century and, at the same time, such essential innovations as to inaugurate a new era. It was painstakingly constructed upon forms set forward by Bach, Beethoven, and Brahms, but, at the same time, it overthrew the tonal order upon which their music rested. It was music that grew from its immediate past, but remained to be understood in the future.

Other than the Viennese School populated by him and his students, Schoenberg belonged to no larger movement of modern composition. He first gained notice around 1900 as a composer of music in the modernist German style of Richard Strauss, Hugo Wolf, and Gustav Mahler, but by 1905 he had permanently declared his independence from their brand of modernism, moving in an uncharted direction. His adoption of atonality around 1908 was accomplished independently of a contemporaneous and related development in the works of such composers as Béla Bartók, Alexander Scriabin, and Charles Ives. Between the world wars he kept his distance from neoclassicism, the dominant trend in international circles of modern music during those years. At the time of his death in 1951 he was again the outsider, dismissed by such younger composers as Pierre Boulez as a throwback to the romantic period. But Schoenberg's isolation did not at all diminish his relevance to the larger evolution of music in the twentieth century.

Schoenberg's career is most often separated into three periods, a division to which the composer himself subscribed. The first extended until about 1907 and produced music that stemmed from such forebears as Brahms, Wagner, Strauss,

Wolf, and Mahler. The second style, which Schoenberg cultivated from about 1908 to 1915, is usually called "atonal," although the composer rejected this term as misleading. His music of these years does not reveal a consistent tonal center, nor does it use traditional chords, which are replaced by a great variety of dissonant harmonies. The third period, which emerged in the early 1920s following a long period of experimentation, is characterized by his twelve-tone method of composition. Works from this time share with music from the second period a pervasive use of dissonance and absence of tonal center, although the intuitive processes upon which he had earlier relied were now replaced by a systematic compositional method intended to compensate for the lack of tonality.

This threefold division of Schoenberg's career provides a useful outline for its study, especially since the divisions between styles also coincide with important events in his life and major turning points in the general history of the arts in the early twentieth century. At the same time, it obscures transitional phases in the composer's career containing works that do not exemplify the generalities that can otherwise be made. In a broader sense, Schoenberg's creative life can better be understood in two parts, both shaped by a struggle between powerful opposing forces. The years before about 1912 represent a Dionysian phase characterized by a relentless advancement of expression over rule. During this time the composer progressively emancipated his music from traditional or inherited forms, arriving by 1909 at a music of pure expression composed in a virtual stream of consciousness. After 1912 Schoenberg's music gradually entered an Apollonian phase in which new formative ideas gained the upper hand over the intensely subjective expressivity by which he had earlier been driven.

SCHOENBERG'S LIFE

Arnold Schoenberg was one of many leading Viennese intellectuals of the early twentieth century born to Jewish parents who had immigrated to Vienna from the eastern regions of the Austro-Hungarian Empire. For Jewish communities throughout the provinces during the second half of the nineteenth century, Vienna held out the promise not only of cultural and economic enrichment, but also of assimilation into a liberal and seemingly tolerant German society. Schoenberg's father, Samuel (1838–90), was born in the primarily Hungarian-speaking village of Szécsény, a few miles northeast of Budapest. Since his father was born in Hungary, Schoenberg, according to Austrian law, was also considered to be a Hungarian citizen.

As a young man, Samuel Schoenberg resettled in the Jewish district of Vienna, the Leopoldstadt, where in 1872 he married Pauline Nachod (1848–1921) and pursued the trade of shoemaker. Arnold Schoenberg, born on 13 September 1874, was the couple's oldest surviving child. He had two younger siblings, Heinrich and Ottilie.

Unlike many of the more affluent Jewish families in Vienna, the Schoenbergs were not notably artistic. But despite their limited interest in music and modest means, Schoenberg played the violin and began to compose music for this instrument at the age of eight. His formal schooling was vocational and did not involve music. At the age of sixteen, following the death of his father, he was forced to drop out of the local *Realschule*, whereupon he began to work as a bank clerk. But his interest in music only increased, and his independent study and the support that he received from several childhood friends more than compensated for his lack of formal training.

Most important for Schoenberg's development was his encounter with Alexander Zemlinsky (1871–1942). When the two met around 1895, Zemlinsky had already established himself as one of Vienna's leading young musicians, accomplished both as a pianist and as a composer. He had studied composition under Johann and Robert Fuchs at the Vienna Conservatory, and his music had been praised by no less a figure than Brahms. Around 1895 Schoenberg (who by then was playing cello) and several other young Viennese musicians formed an amateur orchestra, called Polyhymnia, which Zemlinsky conducted. The two became close friends, and Zemlinsky informally gave Schoenberg lessons in counterpoint and composition. Zemlinsky introduced Schoenberg to leading Viennese intellectuals and artists, among whom he established a reputation as outspoken and argumentative. Gustav Mahler later called him a "fiery spirit," and Alma Mahler, also Zemlinsky's student, remembered him as one who was "inspired by a youthful rebelliousness against his elders." "Nobody who entered the charmed circle of Schoenberg's spirit," she continued, "could resist his intellectual pre-eminence or the force of his logic."[1]

Musical Vienna in the 1890s was polarized by the division between the neoclassical style of Brahms and the modernist direction represented by Wagner. Both Zemlinsky and Schoenberg were at first advocates of Brahms. "I had been a 'Brahmsian' when I met Zemlinsky," Schoenberg later wrote.[2] Although Zemlinsky was not as doctrinaire in his attitude toward new music, he too was associated with the Brahms camp. He was a mainstay in the Vienna Tonkünstlerverein (Society of Musicians), an organization staunchly committed to the artistic directions represented by Brahms. As a member of the board of the society, Zemlinsky was regularly represented on its concerts as both a composer and a performer. Schoenberg too had his first important performance under the aegis of the society in March 1898, when an early String Quartet in D major was performed.

At about the time that he met Zemlinsky, Schoenberg declared himself a professional musician, a decision that must have seemed foolhardy. The musician's principal sources of income, teaching and performing, were ostensibly unavailable since Schoenberg was not an accomplished performer and lacked even a high-school education. But an intense, independent study of music and a determination to succeed eventually won out. His first employment as a musician was as the conductor of several amateur choral groups, then popular in Vienna. Later, with Zemlinsky's help, he obtained work as an orchestrator of operettas. His essays in composition, including songs, works for piano, chamber pieces, and music for small orchestra, became ever more sophisticated. By his own admission these were squarely based on the style of Brahms, and they culminated in the D-major String Quartet that was performed at the Tonkünstlerverein.

After completing the quartet in 1897, Schoenberg broadened his approach to composing to embrace the new directions represented by such figures as Hugo Wolf and Richard Strauss, then thought to be more progressive and innovative than Brahms. The new orientation suggested the inclusion of programmatic ideas, complex and highly integrated one-movement forms, and an enriched harmonic vocabulary with deliberate freedom from prevailing keys.

Schoenberg's new orientation was provoked not only by his admiration for the works of his musical contemporaries, but also by a heightened interest in modern literature and personal contact with Viennese writers and intellectuals, the latter made possible through his friendship with Zemlinsky. Schoenberg developed a special affinity for the poetry of Richard Dehmel. Following the publication of his *Weib und Welt* (Woman and world) in 1896, Dehmel was esteemed by Viennese intellectuals. The poetic language of this collection was influenced both by symbolist and naturalist styles, as Dehmel crafted an intensely subjective tone and a probing of his own innermost feelings and sensations. The use of erotic themes was pronounced, as was a reliance on figurative language, in which expressions of sensual stimulation were made at the expense of narrative. The rich and colorful verbal ornamentation, syntactic freedom, and intensely introspective tone in Dehmel's poetry provoked Schoenberg to look for similar elements in music, features that he found more readily in works by Wolf and Strauss than in the music of Brahms. In a letter greeting Dehmel on his fiftieth birthday (16 November 1913), Schoenberg reflected on the years around 1897 and 1898, when Dehmel's poetry had plunged him into a new expressive milieu:

> From you we learned the ability of hearing within ourselves while still remaining men of our own time. Even more, because our own time was within, inside of us, not outside in the real world. . . . I think I've already said that at virtually every turning point in our musical development, a Dehmel poem was at hand and that I almost always found a new tone first in your tones, which I then made my own. . . . We learned this tone from your *content*, which we then did not easily understand, but even more from the sound of your verse, which we fully absorbed. I have always approached your work by its meaning as sound, thus more quickly gaining access to its sense meaning.[3]

In the years following his encounter with Dehmel's poetry, Schoenberg composed his first mature and important works, compositions that he later chose for publication and on which he conferred opus numbers. These included several collections of songs (many on poetry by Dehmel), the songlike cantata *Gurrelieder*, the programmatic string sextet *Verklärte Nacht* (1899, based on a poem from Dehmel's *Weib und Welt*), and the tone poem *Pelleas und Melisande* (1902–3, based on the play by Maurice Maeterlinck).

At the turn of the century Schoenberg's interest in Dehmel and in a group of Viennese poets called Jung-Wien drew him briefly toward cabaret culture, then becoming prominent in German artistic circles. Neopopulist in aesthetic and, like symbolism, based on French models, cabaret suggested quite the opposite of the elitist aestheticism for which the symbolists were generally known. In the spring and summer of 1901 Schoenberg tried his hand at writing songs—now commonly referred to as his *Brettllieder*—in a light cabaret style akin to the Viennese operettas that he knew well through his work as an orchestrator. He may have intended some or all of the songs to be performed at a new Viennese cabaret, the Jung-Wiener Theater zum Lieben Augustin, which existed briefly in November 1901 at the Theater an der Wien. The manuscript of one of the songs, a setting of Emanuel Schikaneder's "Seit ich so viele Weiber sah," bears the stamp of the Jung-Wiener Theater, which went out of business after only one week and before any of Schoenberg's music could be heard.

Only a short time before, one of Schoenberg's cabaret songs had also attracted the attention of Ernst von Wolzogen, director of the Berlin cabaret called Überbrettl. Wolzogen says in his memoirs that he met Schoenberg in September 1901, when the Überbrettl troupe was performing on tour at the Carltheater in Vienna. Wolzogen's musical director, Oscar Straus, introduced Schoenberg, who performed his song "Nachtwandler," by which Wolzogen was charmed. According to Wolzogen, Straus sent Schoenberg as his substitute at one of the Viennese performances, but his inexperience as a pianist proved his undoing. Wolzogen recalled: "On that evening he embarrassed himself as an accompanist, so much so that I had to replace him with my second Kapellmeister, Woldemar Wendland. Schoenberg was so stricken by stage fright that the simplest chords eluded him. He was so ashamed of his failure that I never saw him again."[4] On this last point, at least, Wolzogen is clearly in error, for in December 1901 Schoenberg signed a contract as conductor at the Überbrettl, moving during that month to Berlin. Before leaving, he married Zemlinsky's sister, Mathilde (1877–1923). His duties at the Überbrettl, whether as a composer or a conductor, appear to have been minor, and he continued his work in Berlin as a copyist and orchestrator.

Although financially troubled, his sojourn in Berlin yielded important developments in his career. In April 1902 he introduced himself to Richard Strauss, then principal conductor of the Royal Court Opera, who would take a great interest in Schoenberg's music and be helpful to the younger composer on a personal level. With Strauss's recommendation Schoenberg was hired to teach elementary classes in music at Berlin's Stern Conservatory. While in Berlin he also met the music critic Max Marschalk, director of the Dreililien Verlag, who published Schoenberg's early compositions. But in the summer of 1903 Schoenberg decided to return to Vienna. He explained his departure to Strauss in a letter of 10 September: "I am going to remain in Vienna. Some friends have taken trouble on my behalf, so that I can earn my living here to a certain extent. Naturally I have no fixed employment, unfortunately, but I will have a lot of work for Universal Edition, the new Viennese publishing house.''[5]

Upon his return to Vienna Schoenberg resumed the life of a struggling composer and unwilling orchestrator. His brief experience at the Stern Conservatory had evidently fired his interest in teaching, and he now sought to establish his credentials as a pedagogue, despite the professional barriers created by his own limited education. Schoenberg was a skillful, even spellbinding, lecturer with highly original views on musical theory and structure. In 1903 or 1904 he joined Zemlinsky and Elsa Bienenfeld in giving independent classes in music at a new school in Vienna founded by Eugenie Schwarzwald. His students there included several from the musicology program at the University of Vienna, where he had acquired a reputation as an excellent private teacher of theory and composition. Around 1904 several students from the university, including Anton Webern, Heinrich Jalowetz, and Karl Horwitz, became his pupils in composition, and other talented young Viennese music students also entered his private class. Among the latter were Egon Wellesz, who would be Schoenberg's first biographer, and Alban Berg, then nineteen years old and lacking any formal training in music.

Schoenberg's method of instruction was at times highly systematic, as it was with Berg, or flexible for more advanced students. In general, he began the instruction of composition with a thorough investigation of underlying theoretical disciplines. Harmony was studied first, followed by counterpoint, moving then as needed to orchestration, form, and analysis, and finally to free composition. Although Schoenberg did not insist that his students adopt any particular style of composition, his emphasis on motivic development, counterpoint, and richness of harmony produced in their works an advanced musical idiom akin to his own.

As a teacher, he was a master of the revealing analogy, the original and unexpected insight, and the subtle or ironic conclusion. An especially impressive technique, upon which several of his students commented, was his dashing off a large number of continuations at a point in a composition where a student had reached a stumbling block. The student would then be expected to comment on which was the best alternative. His early experiences in teaching led him to contemplate writing pedagogical materials by which his theories of instruction could better be realized. The first result was the publication in 1911 of his *Harmonielehre* (Theory of harmony), which he foresaw as the first installment in a cycle of pedagogical writings later to include books on counterpoint, form, and orchestration. Perhaps reflecting on his own independent training as a musician, Schoenberg rejected the teaching of strict rules, methods, or established techniques. These, he said, could never produce a work of art, which came only from inner necessity.

Schoenberg's personal relations with his students were intense. They were expected to assist in such chores as proofreading and making of arrangements and piano scores and even to help their master in nonmusical duties. Strict formalities were maintained between him and his students, and with them Schoenberg was often patriarchal and censorious. Nonetheless, a great camaraderie, producing the consciousness of a distinct "Viennese School," soon arose among them.

In 1904 and 1905 Schoenberg and Zemlinsky were leaders in the founding of the Vereinigung Schaffender Tonkünstler (Alliance of Creative Musicians), an idealistic organization devoted to the performance of new music by German and Austrian composers. Gustav Mahler, whom Schoenberg had recently met prior to a performance of *Verklärte Nacht*, was named honorary president. In the one year of its existence the society produced two orchestral concerts and four concerts of chamber music and lieder. On the orchestral programs Schoenberg conducted the first performance of his tone poem *Pelleas und Melisande*, and Mahler conducted the first Viennese performance of Strauss's *Sinfonia domestica* and the world premieres of his own *Kindertotenlieder* and two songs from *Des Knaben Wunderhorn*. The Vereinigung was the direct antecedent of Schoenberg's Verein für Musikalische Privataufführungen (Society for Private Musical Performances), which he founded after the end of World War I.

In Schoenberg's life and musical career the years 1907 and 1908 marked a turning point from the end of his first period of composing to the beginning of his second. This was a time of emotional crisis: his marriage underwent a temporary rupture, his most influential supporter, Gustav Mahler, resigned his position as director of the Vienna Court Opera and left Vienna for New York, and performances of his music made clear to him that his works would not in the foreseeable future be accepted by critics, the musical public, or even by fellow musicians whom he admired. The vitriolic reaction by audiences to his String Quartet No. 1 and the Chamber Symphony, Op. 9, is typified by the assessment of Heinrich Schenker, a Viennese theorist and pianist whom Schoenberg much admired. In his diary following the premier performance of the quartet in February 1907, to which he was expressly invited by the composer, Schenker wrote: "Quartet, D minor, by Schoenberg played by Rosé. A singular, extended desecration. If there are criminals in the world of art, this composer, whether by birth or his own making, would have to be counted among them. Without feeling for tonality, motif, proportion, going on simply threadbare, without any technique and at the same time with a great and constant pretense."[6] Schoenberg's students and a few other musicians in attendance, to be sure, had the opposite reaction. Mahler wrote to Strauss, expressing his appreciation of the "important and enormous impression" made by the work.[7] But even Mahler and Strauss could not long follow Schoenberg's development with sympathy or approval.

Schoenberg's feelings of isolation and abandonment reached a point of crisis in the summer of 1908, when his marriage temporarily broke up, an event that had a profound impact on his music of the following years. Very little is known about Mathilde Schoenberg, his first wife. She is said to have been musical, although she was evidently withdrawn, little involved with Schoenberg's professional or social life. Later she became taciturn, even reclusive. In a diary that he kept in 1912, Schoenberg remarked: "Afternoon walk to Zehlendorf with Mathilde. She goes out so rarely that I find it worth mentioning."[8] Both Schoenberg and Mathilde took up painting around 1906 and, shortly thereafter, met the eager and talented young artist Richard Gerstl, who became an informal mentor to their new avocation. Gerstl, now recognized as a major figure in the early Viennese expressionist movement in painting, was virtually unknown when he met the Schoenbergs in 1907. He was notoriously hostile toward the artistic establishment and broadly intellectual, all of which must have made him an attractive addition to Schoenberg's circle, despite his evident tendencies toward psychotic behavior.

Eager to associate with modern musicians, Gerstl moved into an apartment in the same building where Schoenberg lived. In 1907 and 1908 he accompanied the family at their summer retreats, shared with the Zemlinskys, near Gmunden on the Traunsee. The events of the summer of 1908 are known only by anecdote. One account has it that Schoenberg caught Mathilde and Gerstl in flagrante delicto, after which Mathilde left her husband to live with Gerstl in Vienna. Webern and other students talked her into returning. Gerstl's mental condition, never especially stable, apparently declined, as can be judged from the grotesque self-portraits that he painted shortly after the 1908 incident. On 4 November he committed suicide, stabbing himself to death with his head in a noose while seated before the mirror at which he had often painted.

The only known document in which Schoenberg set down his feelings about the affair is a "Testamentsentwurf" (Sketch of a will), undated but probably written between July and November 1908. It is a rambling and, to say the least, curious document.[9] Schoenberg begins with a theme that is familiar from his later writings: he draws a rigid distinction between talent, a lesser quality encountered in the disciple, and genius. Then he turns to his wife's deceptions, which he claims long to have suspected despite her denials. He was "torn apart" by her actions, he says, which brought him to the point of suicide. But the unnamed man with whom she carried out these deceptions was equally deceived by her, equally distressed when she left him, and so distraught when she summoned him a second time that he could only send her away. Schoenberg concludes that his wife may not even truly exist other than as an imaginary apparition that embodies "all that is horrid and adverse."

The Gerstl affair must certainly have represented for Schoenberg not only a profound loss of control but, even more, a deepened sense of rejection. He responded to his dilemma through his art, addressing the crisis in texts that he chose to set to music and writing dramatic works that obliquely embodied and externalized his feelings. The earliest completely atonal compositions were written shortly after the affair, as, for example, passages in the String Quartet No. 2. In July 1908, after having sketched out the first movement and the beginning of the second, he decided to introduce texts into the final two movements, using poetry by Stefan George that speaks of anguish and the fading of "faces that a moment before turned toward me in friendship."

Schoenberg was indeed sensitized to the power of the emotions as never before. "I cried, acted like one in despair, made up my mind, then changed it, had ideas of suicide and almost carried them out, drifted from one madness to another," he wrote in the will. From 1908 until about 1912 the subject of his music became the emotions per se, projected at the expense of the logical unfolding of ideas that heretofore had been one of its leading characteristics. The essential idea of the opera *Erwartung* (1909), he wrote, was the representation of "everything that occurs during a single second of the maximum of spiritual excitement." To Ferruccio Busoni he said in the summer of 1909 that he wished to write music as an "expression of feelings, as our feelings, which bring us in contact with our subconscious, really are," that is, erupting spontaneously and jumbled from the unconscious mind.[10]

Gradually Schoenberg's bitterness toward Mathilde waned, and his music returned to the careful planning and structuring of an earlier time, albeit preserving the liberated dissonance that he now saw as a historical necessity. In the summer and fall of 1923 her health, which was never robust, declined from an ailment later diagnosed as cancer. She died on 22 October, at the age of only forty-six, leaving Schoenberg the single parent of their two children, Georg and Gertrud. The effect on his work was again profound. Virtually nothing was composed for a year, and Schoenberg again turned to the written word to work out his feelings. To Zemlinsky he wrote on 16 November: "Mathilde was so clear and simple in her attitudes. She understood with few words how to unravel complicated problems, always everything done rather silently. . . . Mathilde also always understood how to create peace—not by acting the judge—but by pacifying him who was the most readily pacified. I need someone who at the right time will dare to tell me that I am wrong, even if I am right. There won't ever be another with such authority."[11] The evening before writing this letter, Schoenberg completed the poetic text of a Requiem, which he had begun in 1920 or 1921, as he later told Zemlinsky, as a requiem for himself. The first stanza is filled with bitterness and self-pity ("Pain, rage yourself to a standstill; grief, lament till you are weary! Compassion, open the inner eye. Here lies life that has run its course."). But the remaining eleven strophes, plainly addressed to Mathilde, speak with expressions of love, grief, and hope for the future.[12]

As the crisis of emotionality triggered by the Gerstl affair began to wane, Schoenberg launched a career as an essayist and theoretician. His first important published writings began to appear in print in 1909. These were influenced in style by the Viennese satirist Karl Kraus, much admired by the composer, and in content by the writings of Richard Wagner, who was an influential source of ideas for Schoenberg throughout his life. He also wrote larger works, both poetic musical texts and theoretical or pedagogical treatises.

During his lifetime Schoenberg published some ninety articles, one major theory treatise (the *Harmonielehre* of 1911), several poetic texts, and a collection of essays titled *Style and Idea* (1950). But the true extent of his corpus of writings and the remarkable breadth of his imagination became known only gradually following his death, when his unpublished manuscripts began to appear as books and articles in numbers that soon outweighed the writings that he himself had chosen for publication. A confusing mixture of contemporary and posthumous writings, some decidedly incomplete, has emerged, which can be clarified and updated by consulting the Bibliography of this volume. There are no remaining major unpublished writings by Schoenberg, although many interesting brief and miscellaneous notes will continue to appear in the future.

Schoenberg carried on a very important and extensive correspondence with other musicians of his day, as well as with figures in nonmusical areas. The Bibliography contains citations of the most important and extensive volumes in which this correspondence is published. Although many of the important letter exchanges have now appeared in print, there is one important exception, the letters to and from Anton Webern, which remain largely unavailable. These will be of major significance for an understanding of both composers when they are at last published.

Schoenberg's writings on musical theory were primarily intended for the use of students of composition and arose from his needs as a teacher as well as from his dissatisfaction with existing theoretical and pedagogical doctrines. Schoenberg had a strongly original and independent approach to technical writing on music, although his treatises build upon the doctrines of forebears including Simon Sechter in harmonic theory, Heinrich Bellermann in counterpoint, and Hugo Riemann in doctrines of form. Schoenberg's experiences as a composer are strongly evident in his theoretical doctrines, which argue for a liberal acceptance of dissonant harmony and a skepticism about hard-and-fast rules that might restrain the admission of new ideas into music. Schoenberg nowhere theorized or developed systematic analytic models for his posttonal works. In his textbooks on harmony he refers to such pieces in passing—laws exist here too, he says, but they have not been formulated yet. The composer of such music proceeds instead by instinct, guided by the unconscious mind.

The subjects addressed in his theory treatises—harmony, counterpoint, and form—reflect the traditional steps through which a student of composition advanced. Schoenberg's approach to teaching harmony, as shown in the 1911 *Harmonielehre*, was to have students straightaway compose abstract harmonic progressions, devoid of rhythm or melodic line, in which chords are connected by at least one common tone. More sophisticated progressions are obtained by a gradual enrichment of resources: chords progressing with no tones in common, modulations, secondary dominants, and other liberties. Analysis from the literature plays no role in the 1911 treatise, although Schoenberg's later textbooks add extensive analytic examples from eighteenth- and nineteenth-century classic composers. Few examples are drawn from composers prior to J. S. Bach—music that Schoenberg considered primitive—or from the twentieth-century literature.

The one completed counterpoint text, written during Schoenberg's American period for beginning students, uses a species approach in two to four voices. It differs from the neo-Fuxian doctrines that were common in counterpoint teaching at this time since Schoenberg's examples avoid the church modes. The posthumously published *Fundamentals of Musical Composition* is one of the composer's most successful works, showing a wealth of analytic insight as to how classic composers (especially Beethoven) constructed and presented musical ideas and how the student can compose in similar patterns. These begin with the simplest of forms—the motive and phrase—and progress to various types of themes and, finally, to small and large movement forms.

After Schoenberg began to develop his twelve-tone method, he also drafted aesthetic treatises concerning music as language, seeking to reveal the laws that were common to both traditional and twelve-tone works and thus demonstrating his belief in the necessity of the twelve-tone method. In these writings he planned to address primarily the nature of the musical idea and the possibilities for its coherent, comprehensible presentation. None of these treatises was brought to completion, but his drafts for the most important of them (*Der musikalische Gedanke und die Logik, Technik, und Kunst seiner Darstellung*) have now been published (see the Bibliography).

Schoenberg's literary works originated as texts to be set to music, although some of them (*Der biblische Weg* and the Requiem) developed as independent poetic or dramatic essays. He began to write his own musical texts in a series of fragmentary operatic works, begun around 1902, that were plainly inspired by the Wagnerian model. His first completed opera, *Erwartung* (1909), used a "lyric poem" that Schoenberg commissioned from the amateur poet Marie Pappenheim. After an unsuccessful attempt in 1912 to enlist the collaboration of Richard Dehmel on a new work, he turned exclusively for dramatic texts to those of his own making.

In September 1911 Schoenberg left Vienna for the second time to live in Berlin, where he remained until the summer of 1915. His decision to return to Berlin was primarily financial. Berlin, he said in a letter to Berg dated 19 September 1911, was cheaper and had more opportunities for making a living. He was heartened by the prospect that Max Reinhardt might stage his operas *Erwartung* and *Die glückliche Hand*—the latter still incomplete—at Berlin's Deutsches Theater. Although the project with Reinhardt was not realized, Schoenberg lived in Berlin in reasonably comfortable circumstances with the assistance of several patrons. He gave lectures once again at the Stern Conservatory and continued his private teaching, although without the large number of devoted students he had had in Vienna.

After his first year in Berlin, he received a tempting offer to return to Vienna—an appointment to the faculty of Vienna's Akademie für Musik und Darstellende Kunst (Academy of Music and Graphic Arts). Only two years before, Schoenberg had arranged employment as an outside lecturer at the academy. Now he was to be a regular member, the successor to Robert Fuchs, the teacher of a whole generation of Viennese composers. But the politics lying behind the offer were treacherous, and Schoenberg may have believed that he was not the first choice. On 29 June he declined the position, apparently with many misgivings. To Berg he explained: "The main reason is my aversion to Vienna. I still don't know whether I did the right thing, for I'm certainly in no way provided for here. But at any rate I immediately felt much better."[13]

Schoenberg may also have hoped that the move to Berlin would stimulate him artistically. After an outburst of productivity in 1908 and 1909, coinciding with the beginning of his atonal period, his completion of new works grew ever slower and more sporadic. External circumstances—his financial state, teaching and theory projects, and then the onset of World War I—were partly to blame, but it is also likely that the composer had arrived at an artistic impasse involving atonal composition. He was acutely aware of his difficulty in composing, mentioning it repeatedly to Berg. "I'm not composing anything at all right now," he commented on 21 December 1911. "I'm not satisfied with anything any more. I see mistakes and inadequacies in everything. Enough of that; I can't begin to tell you how I feel at such times."[14] The beginning of his work on *Pierrot lunaire* in March 1912 temporarily brought the wind back into his creative sails. "This morning I was in the mood to compose, after a very long time! I had already considered the possibility that I might never compose again," he confided to his diary on March 12.[15] But *Pierrot* represented a temporary upswing in his creative pace, which slowed again in 1913, not to revive until the early 1920s, when he began to compose according to the twelve-tone method.

While residing in Berlin, Schoenberg worked methodically to increase the acceptance of his music. The completion and performance of *Gurrelieder* was a central element in his plan. This work, composed in 1900 and 1901 in a familiar, Wagnerian style, had been left incomplete in orchestration. Schoenberg now returned to it, completing it by November 1911 and urging his publisher, Emil Hertzka of Universal Edition, to arrange for its premiere. Schoenberg was certain that the work would be a great success, which he saw as a key to the acceptance of his more recent music. *Gurrelieder* was at last performed in Vienna in February 1913, conducted by Franz Schreker with the Vienna Philharmonic Chorus, and, as Schoenberg predicted, it was a complete triumph—the greatest one that Schoenberg would ever have. But his hopes that it would lead to an acceptance of his atonal music were dashed by a concert in Vienna only weeks later. On 31 March 1913, under the aegis of Vienna's Akademischer Verband für Literatur und Musik, Schoenberg himself conducted an evening of orchestral pieces including his own Chamber Symphony, with works by Zemlinsky, Mahler, Webern, and Berg also on the program. The audience in the large hall of the Musikverein was spoiling for a confrontation, both with the modern works that they were hearing and with proponents of such music who were seated in their midst. Whistling, laughter, shouts, and insults were traded, fist fights erupted, and, following the playing of Berg's Orchestral Song, Op. 4, No. 2, the concert was prematurely ended and the hall cleared by the police. This scandal was unprecedented in the history of music, anticipating by about two months the near riot at the premiere in Paris of Stravinsky's *Rite of Spring*.

The outbreak that occurred at the concert was all the more disappointing for Schoenberg because the composer expected that the occasion would advance his credentials as an orchestral conductor. Schoenberg had relished the work of the conductor since he had led amateur choruses in Vienna in the 1890s. His prospects of being a professional orchestral conductor were brightened in 1912 when he conducted *Pelleas und Melisande* in Prague, acting on an invitation from Zemlinsky, who was the new music director there at the Deutsches Landestheater. With the help of an agent in Munich, Emil Gutmann, other conducting engagements were obtained. In October Schoenberg led the premiere of his melodrama *Pierrot lunaire* in Berlin, followed by a tour to several other German cities. In the winter of that year he traveled to Amsterdam and St. Petersburg, where he again conducted *Pelleas*.

In the spring of 1915 Alma Mahler attempted to assist Schoenberg in the development of his credentials as a conductor of the classical repertory as well as of the modern. Joining with some of her wealthy friends, she organized a benefit concert on 25 April at the Musikverein, at which Beethoven's Ninth Symphony would be performed using Mahler's revised orchestration. But even before the concert Schoenberg had cooled to the idea. To Berg he confided: "I would have liked to conduct a classical work for the first time in my life. Today I am rather more indifferent to that sentimental prospect."[16] The concert further disillusioned Schoenberg about a career as an orchestral conductor, since the players apparently ignored his ideas concerning Beethoven's music, especially the flexible and rubato tempos that he considered necessary. Any further development of his theories concerning performance would have to wait until the conclusion of World War I.

Shortly after the Beethoven concert in 1915, Schoenberg returned permanently to Vienna, expecting to serve in the Austro-Hungarian army during the war that had erupted the previous summer. Like others in his circle, he was highly patriotic, convinced of the necessity of preserving the Hapsburg Empire. At the age of forty-one, he volunteered for military service. At first he failed a physical examination due to an asthmatic condition, but later he passed and, on 15 December, entered an Austrian Hoch- und Deutschmeister regiment as a citizen of Hungary. Fearful for his safety, his students and other Viennese musicians immediately petitioned for his release, which took place the following summer. As Austria's prospects in the war diminished, Schoenberg was called up a second time in September 1917, but he was permanently released shortly thereafter.

Following the conclusion of his military service, Schoenberg settled in the Viennese suburb of Mödling, continued his teaching, and revived his interest in performance and its place in the acceptance of new music. At the instigation of his student Erwin Ratz in the summer of 1918, Schoenberg coached a series of ten public rehearsals of his Chamber Symphony, Op. 9. The results were gratifying. The substance of the music was at last accurately and clearly rendered following exhaustive rehearsing, its ideas were better communicated by its repeated hearings, and it was well received by a sympathetic audience of subscribers. Schoenberg was all the more convinced by the experience that the key to acceptance of his music would rest on three factors: clear and accurate performances following adequate rehearsal and coaching, repeated hearings if a work was new or unfamiliar, and the presence of a trained and sympathetic audience.

In the fall of 1918 Schoenberg set about to apply these lessons in a more general way by founding the Verein für Musikalische Privataufführungen (Society for Private Musical Performances). This was conceived of as a concert society devoted to new music, which would be presented under very controlled circumstances, with the ultimate objective of creating in Vienna an audience for new works. As in the open rehearsals of the Chamber Symphony, thorough preparation and rehearsal were insisted upon, and new pieces would be accorded repeated hearings. Except for a few public "propaganda" concerts, only members of the society were allowed to attend its evenings. There could be no reviews, and even applause was forbidden.

Before its demise in December 1921, the society presented over 100 concerts, and more than 250 modern compositions were performed or rehearsed. Works by Reger, Debussy, and Bartók were the most frequently taken up, although music by many little-known composers was also heard. Schoenberg at first declined to have his own music performed, but following the first season, several of his works were presented. Webern, Berg, and Edward Steuermann were at first the principal coaches, and a work could be performed only when they were satisfied with the adequacy of its preparation.

The society could not afford to hire a large orchestra, so modern orchestral pieces were performed in arrangements for keyboard or chamber ensembles. The idea of reducing the full romantic orchestra to a smaller medium had long appealed to Schoenberg, since reduced media held the promise of the greater clarity and accuracy that he now found indispensable. His students, especially Erwin Stein and Anton Webern, now set to work reinterpreting the symphonies of Bruckner, Mahler, and others, bringing them down to chamber proportions. In 1921 the society sponsored a competition for the best new work for chamber orchestra. Although the submissions were found disappointing, a prize was given to Fritz Heinrich Klein, a student of Berg, for *Die Maschine*, Op. 1.

The war, its dismal aftermath for all Austrians, and Schoenberg's own military service marked a profound change in the composer's attitudes toward religion and the consciousness of his Jewish identity. Earlier he had been indifferent to religion, once describing himself as a "nonbeliever." Like many assimilated Jews in turn-of-the-century Vienna, Schoenberg had lost touch with the Jewish faith and its customs. In 1898, at the urging of his friend Walter Pieau, he was baptized and declared himself a Protestant. But his readings in Balzac and

Strindberg around 1912 provoked a new interest in religious questions and a wish to bring them into his music, which to that time had been entirely secular. In December 1912 he wrote to Richard Dehmel and proposed a collaboration on an oratorio that would reflect his own religious ambiguities. Its subject, he wrote, would be "modern man, who has passed through materialism, socialism, and anarchy and, despite having been an atheist, still has in him some residue of ancient faith (in the form of superstition), wrestles with God (see also Strindberg's *Jakob ringt*) and finally succeeds in finding God and becoming religious. Learning to pray!"[17] Certainly, the "modern man" mentioned in the letter is the composer himself.

The reawakening of Schoenberg's religiosity manifested itself by an interest in Old Testament theology. Schoenberg apparently found a connection between stories from the Old Testament and his long-standing philosophical and aesthetic beliefs, even his view of his personal role in present and future musical culture. His often-stated idea, borrowed from Wagner, that a composer needed to follow his sense of destiny, composing out of necessity rather than choice, echoed stories from the Pentateuch in which an acceptance of authority was demanded. His view of the musical genius as a figure of unquestionable authority—its origins were in Nietzsche rather than the Bible—now found a parallel in the role of Moses as a giver of the law. Even his own fate as a creator of new musical ideas that seemed eternally lost on the public of his day reminded Schoenberg again of Moses, leading a recalcitrant people to a promised land.

Given his tendency to mix the Bible with his musical aesthetics and personal history, it is not surprising that Schoenberg expressed his religious reawakening in new compositions. The symphonies of Mahler were almost certainly his models since they too expressed their composer's personal life and religious philosophy. Schoenberg during the war undertook a series of religious programmatic and dramatic compositions in which the narrator or protagonist represents Schoenberg himself and speaks the composer's own mind concerning his personal destiny as individual and artist. The immediate precursor of these autobiographical religious works was the one-act opera *Die glückliche Hand* (1910–13), based on the composer's own brief text. Here the main character, called simply the "Man," enacts Schoenberg's recent life experiences, including the breakup of his marriage, his desire for public acceptance, and his continual failure to achieve recognition despite his superiority as an artist.

As Schoenberg reawakened to spiritual matters and as his interest in Judaism grew ever larger, this tendency to dramatize his personal situation and philosophy took on a biblical dimension. In 1914, before his return to Vienna from Berlin, he began to sketch a large Mahlerian symphony with voices, a work closely related to the oratorio that he had outlined to Dehmel two years earlier. From his manuscripts it is clear that the program of the symphony was based on Schoenberg's personal spiritual journey. The movements, which were to use texts by Rabindranath Tagore, Dehmel, and the Bible, as well as the composer's own writings, had these programmatic headings:

Turning Point in Life: retrospective, look to the future (gloomy, defiant, restrained)

Lust for Life

The Bourgeois God

Unsatisfied—the bourgeois god does not suffice

Psalm

Death Dance of Principles (fundamentals): funeral, funeral oration, death dance, prayer

Faith of the Disillusioned Man: a simple joining of skeptical realism with faith

Early in 1915 Schoenberg broke off work on the massive symphony and turned instead to its final section, which he reconceived as an independent oratorio for solo voices, choruses, and large orchestra. Its text, written by the composer, was completed in 1917 and titled *Die Jakobsleiter*; its music remained incomplete. Here Schoenberg's journey as an artist is reinterpreted in biblical terms. The archangel Gabriel stands on the road that connects earth to heaven and urges groups of souls onward toward a higher level of attainment. Schoenberg casts himself most evidently in the role of the genius, called the "Chosen One," whose duties are to uplift the others and to be "an image of the future."

In the drama *Der biblische Weg* and the incomplete opera *Moses und Aron*, the merger of artistic theory, religion, and personal history is made complete. *Der biblische Weg* (1926–27), originally a musical text that Schoenberg subsequently transformed into a spoken drama, concerns the migration of Jews to a homeland, led by Max Aruns, a modern-day Moses.[18] The hero is ultimately killed by his own people. In the opera *Moses und Aron*, based on Schoenberg's own three-act libretto, Moses is animated by an idea that he cannot enunciate to his people. He relies for this on his brother Aron, who is gifted with the word, but by the end Aron's formulations betray the idea, and Aron is struck dead. Schoenberg, the isolated prophet unaccepted in his own time, plainly stands behind both Aruns and Moses.

During the early 1920s Schoenberg's career and reputation steadily grew, with ever more important performances throughout Europe. His works were heard at most of the important festivals of modern music, events that came to characterize the culture for new music in Europe between the world wars. In 1922 the Second String Quartet was performed with great acclaim by Paul Hindemith's Amar Quartet at the Salzburg modern music festival that led to the founding of the International Society for Contemporary Music. In 1924 the Serenade, Op. 24, was heard at the Donaueschingen Chamber Music Festival. Schoenberg's name was a fixture in new journals devoted to contemporary music, the most important being *Musikblätter des Anbruch*, edited by his publisher, Universal Edition, and *Melos*, published by the rival firm Schott. He continued to be a celebrated teacher, and his students—Alban Berg, Anton Webern, Erwin Stein, Josef Rufer, Heinrich Jalowetz, Karl Rankl, Edward Steuermann, Rudolf Serkin, and Rudolf Kolisch among them—were now themselves involved in major careers as composers, conductors, and performers. His contact with the Viennese violinist Rudolf Kolisch (1896–1978) proved especially important. Kolisch had been a mainstay in the concerts of the Society for Private Musical Performances and, with a quartet that he founded in 1922, was central to the interpretation and appreciation of Schoenberg's chamber music. In August 1924 Schoenberg married Kolisch's sister, Gertrud. The couple would have three children: Nuria (b. 1932), Ronald (b. 1936), and Lawrence (b. 1941).

Although by the mid-1920s Schoenberg's music was receiving more attention than ever, it was clear that his works were distant from a newly emerging international style of modern music. This style, now called neoclassical or objectivist, was French in origin and led by Igor Stravinsky. After World War I it rapidly spread throughout the world, enlisting such adherents as Aaron Copland in America, Manuel de Falla in Spain, and Paul Hindemith, Ernst Krenek, and Kurt Weill in Germany and Austria. Their idiom seemed to represent a rejection of Schoenberg's essentially romantic aesthetic. It was dispassionate rather than expressive, direct rather than complex, and eclectic rather than homogeneous. Prior to 1925 Stravinsky and Schoenberg had good relations, despite their different aesthetic positions. They had met in 1912 in Berlin, where Stravinsky, there to attend performances by the Ballets Russes, heard a rehearsal of *Pierrot lunaire*, a work that he later deemed a masterpiece. Stravinsky's music was often performed by the Society for Private Musical Performances and was much admired by members of Schoenberg's circle, especially by Webern.

But in 1925 Schoenberg read a newspaper interview that Stravinsky gave while on tour in the United States. Here Stravinsky was quoted as saying:

> Outside of jazz, however, I despise all of modern music. I myself don't compose modern music at all nor do I write music of the future. I write for today. In this regard I don't want to quote names, but I could tell you about composers who spend all their time inventing a music of the future. Actually this is very presumptuous. How does it remain genuine? I have listened to experiments of this kind. They sound like very ordinary music, or a bit worse.[19]

Schoenberg interpreted these words as an attack upon himself, and the bad feelings that they aroused boiled over shortly thereafter. In September 1925 both composers were in Venice participating in the yearly festival of the International Society for Contemporary Music. Schoenberg ran over his allotted time in rehearsing his Serenade, Op. 24, and defended himself by declaring that he was the only significant composer at the gathering. An unpleasant confrontation ensued between supporters of the two figures. When Schoenberg returned to Mödling, he composed the Three Satires for chorus, Op. 28, now taking his revenge on Stravinsky and other neoclassicists by way of a musical parody. In the introduction to the published score of the Satires (1926), he explained that the parody was aimed at all contemporary composers who mix tonal and atonal elements, proclaim a return to earlier music, or adopt musical folklore—in other words, any who follow the directions of Stravinsky.

Ironically, Schoenberg's music of the 1920s and 1930s contains many concessions to the new style, although in his essays and lectures of these years he has nothing but criticism of this "New Music," his own sarcastic designation for it. He fired his first literary broadside against the idiom in his essay "Gesinnung oder Erkenntnis?" (Opinion or insight?), which appeared in the widely read 1926 yearbook of Universal Edition.[20] Here he attacked the eclectic mixing of traditional musical features associated with tonality—triads, familiar cadences, ostinati, and pedal points—with more modern elements associated with the emancipation of dissonance. This was pure whim, a juggling of styles, he said, done by composers who expressed only their own "opinion" about what music was. A composer would better exercise "insight" into the historical development of music, by which it would become apparent that musical ideas can only be expressed through cohesive and comprehensible forms, suggesting a homogeneity of style. Any mixing of tonality and atonality, he concluded, was a "grave sin."

In 1924 Schoenberg's professional fortunes improved significantly. With the death of Ferruccio Busoni, a position as leader of a master class in composition at the Prussian Akademie der Künste (Academy of the Arts) in Berlin was opened. The master classes at the Berlin Academy had long been among the most prestigious teaching positions for composers in the German-speaking world. Leo Kestenberg, musical advisor to the Prussian Ministry of Science, Culture, and Public Education, had brought in leading musicians to conduct them. Busoni and Hans Pfitzner were appointed in 1920, joining Georg Schumann, who had led a master class since 1913. Kestenberg now arranged for an offer to be made to Schoenberg. The conditions of the appointment were excellent: a good salary, only six months of teaching per year, a title of professor, and the promise of a highly visible position in the musical life of Berlin.

For a modernist composer, Berlin in 1925 had advantages that Vienna could not offer. The whole life and reputation of the Prussian capital seemed geared to modernism in a way that made Vienna seem a mere bastion of tradition. The Berlin Philharmonic Orchestra, led by Wilhelm Furtwängler, often performed modern works, Bruno Walter had just arrived in 1925 as conductor of the Städtische Oper, and Franz Schreker had been brought in earlier as director of the innovative Hochschule für Musik. In 1927 the Ministry of Culture established a new opera company, the Kroll Opera, specifically devoted to new ideas in operatic staging. It was led by Otto Klemperer, who was joined by Alexander Zemlinsky as a resident conductor. In the same year Paul Hindemith arrived to teach composition at the Hochschule.

Schoenberg unhesitatingly accepted Kestenberg's offer and moved to Berlin in January 1926 to begin his teaching duties. In his seven years at the academy he assembled a group of students that rivaled his private class in Vienna. Winfried Zillig and Josef Rufer followed him from Vienna, Rufer later being named his teaching assistant. Other students came from around the world, including Walter Goehr, Adolph Weiss, and Roberto Gerhard. Americans were also in his class, including Marc Blitzstein and, briefly, Henry Cowell.

Schoenberg's prestigious teaching position brought ever greater attention to his music, and he now traveled repeatedly to performances throughout Europe, often being invited to lecture as well as to conduct. He generally spent the summers in seaside resorts in France and Spain, where he composed and sought relief from a worsening asthmatic condition. Two performances in his hometown of Berlin took on special importance, not only because of the position occupied by Berlin as a center of new art, but also because they epitomized the new and complex relation of Schoenberg's music with the modern music community. The first was the premiere of the Orchestral Variations, Op. 31, by Furtwängler and the Berlin Philharmonic on 2 December 1928, and the second, a staging of his two one-act operas, *Erwartung* and *Die glückliche Hand*, at the Kroll Opera beginning on 7 June 1930.

Wilhelm Furtwängler was one of the few conductors to garner Schoenberg's admiration. His interpretive approach and an ample use of rubato conformed to Schoenberg's own tastes and practices, and his choice of repertory and close analytic study of the masterpieces, guided by his long-standing contact with Heinrich Schenker, appealed to the composer. Most important for Schoenberg was Furtwängler's regular programming of new works. On 2 November 1928, a month before the Variations premiere, Schoenberg wrote to Webern to express a grudging admiration for the conductor: "I have been keeping closely in touch with Furtwängler, who is giving the premiere of my Orchestral Variations on December 2. I really do like him a lot. It's amazing how often I am at first irritated by people who later behave very well toward me."[21]

Schoenberg did not attend the concert on 2 December since he was then on leave from his teaching position, residing in the South of France. But the concert itself marked a disturbing return to earlier public attitudes toward his music, following a period of greater acceptance. The performance was disrupted by a part of the audience, who essentially hooted it down, and its critical reception was pervasively negative. This reaction was especially distressing because Schoenberg had expected Berlin to be tolerant of his music, as audiences in Amsterdam, Frankfurt, and Prague had been, unlike the blind intolerance that he had faced in Vienna. Increasingly after 1928 Berlin would be little different from his native city, on which he had bitterly turned his back.

The same reaction greeted Schoenberg in an even more crucial situation, a staging of *Erwartung* and *Die glückliche Hand* at the Kroll Opera in the summer of 1930. The Kroll Opera, a division of the Berlin Staatsoper, was an outlet for new and classical operas presented in an innovative manner. Otto Klemperer was brought in from Cologne as the artistic director, Hans Curjel was the dramaturge, and the artist Ewald Dülberg oversaw the mise-en-scène. The stagings were especially modernistic, as works were reinterpreted in an abstract and visually contemporary manner. Leading regisseurs, such as Gustav Gründgens, and painters of the day, including László Moholy-Nagy, Oskar Schlemmer, and Giorgio de Chirico, were brought in, and an experimental spirit reigned in which works were transformed by the artistic temperament of the 1920s. Klemperer's taste in modern music was also attuned to the 1920s, leaning decidedly to neoclassical and objectivist stage works by Stravinsky, Krenek, Hindemith, and Weill. Schoenberg now found himself outside of this circle and a representative of an outdated expressionism rather than a contemporary New Objectivity. Klemperer had occasionally conducted Schoenberg's music, but not nearly enough to please the composer. All the same, Schoenberg was assured that his operas would be presented at Kroll, and *Erwartung* was even announced for the first season, only to be postponed.

Finally, on 12 April 1930, the intendant at Kroll, Ernst Legal, contacted Schoenberg to say that both *Erwartung* and *Die glückliche Hand* would be presented in June as part of the Berlin Kunstwoche festivities. He invited the composer to share his thoughts about staging and direction. On 15 April Schoenberg wrote a lengthy reply in which he expressed his fears—no doubt based on Kroll's reputation for reinterpretive stagings—that his operas would be given in a "stylized" manner. The stage design for *Erwartung* was assigned to Teo Otto, *Die glückliche Hand* to the renowned Bauhaus artist Oskar Schlemmer, and the regisseur for both would be the well-known Arthur Rabenalt. Zemlinsky would conduct *Erwartung*, and *Die glückliche Hand* would be led by Klemperer himself.

Schoenberg was invited to attend rehearsals, at which he essentially declared war against the modernist artistic taste of the 1920s. His displeasure was directed primarily against Oskar Schlemmer's set design and staging for *Die glückliche Hand*, which were squarely in the cubist manner of the Bauhaus. Schoenberg's position was typically "romantic" in that he, as the work's creator, wished to control every aspect of its realization. The reigning spirit at Kroll was instead one of collaboration and reinterpretation, ruling out the staunch individualism upon which Schoenberg insisted. At the dress rehearsal Schoenberg was literally dismissed from the theater by Curjel, an extraordinary act considering Schoenberg's position at the academy. Finally, Curjel agreed to a special all-night rehearsal at which a measure of cooperation was restored. The performances were again not well received and seemed to confirm that Schoenberg's reception by the public at large, which had experienced an upturn following World War I, was again headed into a period of bitter antagonism, now with new enemies from among the very modernists whom Schoenberg had once considered his allies.

Following the debacle at Kroll, Schoenberg was increasingly dissatisfied with his life in Berlin. Its northern climate had exacerbated his chronic respiratory condition, and he now saw little difference in the acceptance of his music between Berlin and the Vienna that he so greatly disdained. The overtness of anti-Semitic incidents and insults in Berlin was increasingly an issue. In May 1932 he wrote to Joseph Asch in New York, asking for him to arrange an annuity from Jewish patrons so that he would "not have to go back to Berlin among the swastika-swaggerers and pogromists."[22]

Schoenberg's response to the racially charged atmosphere in Berlin had been developing for a long time. Even during his service in World War I he felt unaccepted by his fellow soldiers because he was a Jew. In the summer of 1921 Schoenberg, accompanied by his family and several students, had encountered an especially overt expression of anti-Jewish sentiment in the vacation town of Mattsee near Salzburg. His reactions to these provocations boiled over in his communications with Vasili Kandinsky, the painter with whom Schoenberg had enjoyed close and cordial relations since 1911. In April 1923 Kandinsky inquired whether Schoenberg might be interested in teaching in Weimar, where Kandinsky taught at the Bauhaus. But the composer had heard, probably from Alma Mahler, that Kandinsky was anti-Semitic. Schoenberg pointedly accused Kandinsky of this attitude in his response to the painter. Kandinsky wrote a conciliatory reply—better to be simply a human being than a Jew or a Russian, he said. But Schoenberg was not to be placated. On 4 May he wrote Kandinsky a long, angry letter, imputing to him flagrantly anti-Semitic attitudes and also noting perceptively that the current form of anti-Semitism in the world would inevitably lead to acts of violence.

When Hitler took office as chancellor of the German government in January 1933, Schoenberg was well aware that he would soon be forced to emigrate from Germany. On 1 March the president of the Academy of Arts, Max von Schillings, reported that the new Nazi minister of education, Bernhard Rust, had commanded that the "Jewish influence" at the academy be eliminated. In a letter to the academy of 20 March Schoenberg offered to resign and to return to Vienna, asking for payment of his contracted salary. On 17 May he left instead for Paris with his wife and infant daughter, ostensibly still on leave from the academy but without clear plans for the future. He now enthusiastically addressed Jewish issues, officially reconverting to Judaism on 24 July and conjuring plans to generate support for German Jews. In September, while residing in Arcachon, he was contacted by the American cellist Joseph Malkin, who offered him a teaching position at his new private conservatory in Boston. A contract was concluded, and Schoenberg left Europe for New York—his future still highly unsettled—arriving on 31 October.

Schoenberg's first year in America was exceedingly difficult for him, as he was plagued by poor health, communicating in a foreign language, and an unfavorable teaching schedule. To increase his number of students, he agreed to hold classes both in Boston and New York, where he had rented a room at the Ansonia Hotel. To Webern he confided:

> The most annoying thing is the weekly trip to New York. I give only 4–5 lessons, but it takes a long time getting there. Everyone with whom I have spoken has told me they don't know how I have kept it up. . . . I leave every Sunday at 5:00 PM, arrive at the hotel [Ansonia] at 10:45, teach on Monday from 9:30 to 12:00 and 2:00 to 4:00 (during

my lunch break people always "have to" talk with you), then travel back at 4:30, arriving home at 10:00. This may not sound as bad as it really is.[23]

Due to his poor health Schoenberg decided not to remain on the East Coast after his first year, despite prospects for a teaching position at the Juilliard School of Music. With no immediate offer of academic employment, he moved to the Los Angeles area in California, residing temporarily in Hollywood in the midst of a growing community of German and Austrian émigrés. At first he taught privately, then, for one academic year (1935–36) and two summers, at the University of Southern California as a part-time and visiting appointee. In the fall of 1936 he began a regular faculty appointment at the University of California at Los Angeles, where he remained until his retirement in 1944. Also in 1936 he purchased a house in the Brentwood district of Los Angeles.

Schoenberg's American teaching revived his long-standing plan for a cycle of pedagogical writings on compositional crafts, now geared to the American student without an extensive background in music. Only *Structural Functions of Harmony* (published in 1954) was completed in his lifetime, but he also compiled extensive drafts for books on counterpoint and form, which were completed and published after his death in 1951. As he had done in Vienna and Berlin, he began to assemble a devoted group of students, including Dika Newlin, Leonard Stein, Gerald Strang, Patricia Carpenter, Richard Hoffmann, and, briefly, John Cage and Pauline Alderman.

Following the end of the war, he reestablished contact with many of his European relatives and former students and was accorded honors both from within the United States and abroad. Schoenberg continued to compose major new works until 1947, despite declining health. He suffered a serious heart attack in the summer of 1946, but he continued to work on compositions and essays. His final musical work was begun in October 1950, a setting for chorus, speaker, and orchestra of a "Modern Psalm" whose text he had written himself.

The disposition of his huge library was one of his final concerns. From about 1908 or 1909 Schoenberg had meticulously preserved materials documenting his music and his personal interests. At that time he began to save virtually all of his correspondence, including many carbon copies of letters to others. All musical manuscripts, including sketches and fragments, were carefully preserved and usually clearly dated. He wrote voluminous notes on subjects that concerned him, entered extensive critical marginalia into books that he read—often dated, sometimes typed—and periodically kept diaries. By 1951 his library of correspondence numbered over 18,000 items, and in June of that year he donated it—"copies of all my letters and letters which I received partly from friends, partly from enemies"—to the Library of Congress, to which he had earlier sold a few musical manuscripts.

Less than a month later, on 13 July 1951, Schoenberg died from heart failure. Ironically, his passing occurred at the beginning of a great revival of interest in his music and in his twelve-tone method. Stimulated by a postwar attitude that forcefully rejected the neoclassical past, young composers in both America and Europe now looked to Schoenberg and others from his circle for usable and relevant models. Schoenberg's belief in the future and his own role in it was realized, probably more quickly than he would have expected. The twelve-tone method became a common starting point for new music that aspired to the complexity and richness of Schoenberg's own compositions.

The knowledge and appreciation of his music has continued to grow to the present day, despite the many changes in musical taste that have appeared since the 1950s. Among the monuments to this continued vitality were the premier performances of his two great unfinished masterpieces, *Moses und Aron* in Hamburg in 1954 and *Die Jakobsleiter* in Vienna in 1961. A general knowledge of Schoenberg's music was greatly advanced by the beginning in 1966 of a complete edition of his entire oeuvre. The founding in 1974 of the Arnold Schoenberg Institute in Los Angeles, the repository for his personal library and papers, further reinforced the bond between Schoenberg's musical legacy and culture of the later twentieth century and beyond.

SCHOENBERG'S MUSIC: AN OVERVIEW

Prior to composing the song ''Dank'' in 1898, which Schoenberg later selected as his Op. 1, No. 1, he had written more than fifty pieces. A complete accounting of these early works is impossible since the composer did not keep a record of them and gave many away. Some of his earliest compositions, primarily juvenalia, were given to his cousin Hans Nachod; a group of the earliest songs was presented to his friend David Josef Bach; others may well have been lost or destroyed.[24]

The genres and media of the early works are typical of the aspiring composer of the late nineteenth century. Most are songs, although works for orchestra, chamber ensembles, chorus, and piano were also attempted. Schoenberg's most important early instrumental composition is a String Quartet in D major, composed under the tutelage of Zemlinsky in 1897. This is a twenty-minute work in four movements whose first version was extensively revised upon Zemlinsky's recommendations. (The original second movement, a Scherzo in F major, still exists; it was replaced in 1897 or 1898 by an Intermezzo in F♯ minor.) The key of D came to have special significance for the composer, who returned to it time and again and apparently used it as a personal motto. The quartet has the proportions and overall form of a work by Brahms or Dvořák, both cited by the composer as among his models at this time. Although its extensive development of motives is characteristic of Schoenberg's later music, the texture and part writing have none of the complexity that later became typical.

Schoenberg was composing songs by 1893, at first to verses written by friends, later to poetry by minor nineteenth-century writers. The youthful composer seemed content at first to deal with simple and mundane poetic ideas rather than grappling with those of major figures or modern writers. One of the most handsome of the early songs is "Waldesnacht" from 1897, a setting of a poem by Paul Heyse. Like the D-major Quartet, the song shows the thinking of a mature and accomplished composer. It is strophic in design, its melody only slightly varied through three stanzas, and the listener is immediately attracted to the effortless and graceful melodic line that aptly communicates the narrator's contented sentiments. Every aspect of the song—its structure, harmonic language, and relation of music to text—could have been written by a German composer of the 1840s or even before. The work is no less skillful for its traditionalism; indeed, its melodic line has the fresh attractiveness that is the equal of many mature songs by Schumann or Brahms.

In the summer of 1903, just before leaving Berlin, Schoenberg signed a contract with Max Marschalk's Dreililien Verlag, by which his music would, for the first time, be published. At this major turning point in his career, he apparently followed a plan for presenting his music to the public according to which he first reached back to earlier songs whose texts and musical style were reasonably familiar and traditional. Only later did he publish his more recent compositions, which were more advanced in musical structure and modern in poetic content. For Op. 1 (appearing in October 1903), he selected songs that he had composed in 1898, settings of Karl von Levetzow's "Dank" and "Abschied." The poems were drawn from Levetzow's *Höhenlieder: Gedichte und Aphorismen*, a copy of which the author sent to Schoenberg upon its publication in 1895, adding in a note his "wishes for success." The music for the two Levetzow settings departs strikingly from such earlier works as "Waldesnacht" in its greater length and complexity of form. Schoenberg evidently wished to present himself to the public first with monumental songs, similar to Brahms's longer songs such as the much-admired "Von ewiger Liebe." The piano is no longer mere accompaniment, but, in the Wagnerian manner, central to the working out of musical ideas. Its part is filled with bombast, imitating a complex orchestral texture, and it is the source of all important themes and the stratum where they are developed and recapitulated. The melodic ideas grow organically from one another in a perpetual development that Schoenberg later termed "developing variations."

The songs published as Opp. 2 and 3 were composed between 1899 and 1903 and reveal a more advanced harmonic language and subtlety of expression. Settings of poetry by Richard Dehmel are prominent in these two publications, and Dehmel's enriched and provocative poetic style evidently inspired Schoenberg to deepen his musical language. "Erwartung" (Expectation), the first of Four Songs, Op. 2, is an example. The boldness and originality of Dehmel's poem leave far behind the verse of Heyse, Levetzow, and most of the other writers whom Schoenberg had earlier addressed. Its expressive freedom and highly ornamental and figurative language were matched by a new tonal and harmonic freedom in the music, a subject to be addressed again later in this chapter.

Schoenberg's discovery of the poetry of Dehmel around 1897 also inspired him to compose programmatic instrumental music. *Verklärte Nacht* (Transfigured night, 1899), a string sextet based on a poem from Dehmel's *Weib und Welt*, is the composer's first major large-scale instrumental composition. It is a rare example of an overtly programmatic chamber work, a genre that was usually interpreted by German romantic musicians in a more classical and absolute manner. Dehmel's poem, printed as a preface in an early edition of the score, describes a man and woman walking in the woods on a cold, moonlit night. The woman confesses that she is bearing the child of another man; her friend is full of forgiveness as they are both transfigured by love.

Schoenberg's music is cast into a multisectional, one-movement form that suggests the nineteenth-century tone poem. According to the composer's own program notes written in 1950, various sections of the score correspond to episodes in the poem. But Schoenberg adds that the music "does not illustrate any action or drama, but was restricted to portray nature and to express human feelings."[25] The form of the work is irregular, although its intense development interspersed with reprises has been interpreted as evidence of sonata or rondo forms. The texture of the sextet is dense and its rhythm unsettled and often turbulent, swinging quickly in mood between the emotional and serene. The key of D (minor) is again chosen, possibly an indication that Schoenberg himself shared in the powerful emotions of love expressed by Dehmel's protagonists.

The tone poem *Pelleas und Melisande*, composed for large orchestra during Schoenberg's sojourn in Berlin (1902–3), is a companion work to *Verklärte Nacht*. It is based programmatically on Maurice Maeterlinck's symbolist drama, the same one used by Debussy in his opera, first heard in 1902. The work again has a one-movement form and, also like *Verklärte Nacht*, is in D minor. But more than the sextet, its harmonies are freed from underlying tonal progressions, and its part writing becomes dense, sometimes even turgid. In notes from 1949 concerning *Pelleas*, Schoenberg emphasized the programmatic aspect of the music: "It is inspired entirely by Maurice Maeterlinck's wonderful drama. I tried to mirror every detail of it, with only a few omissions and slight changes of the order of scenes. Perhaps, as frequently happens in music, there is more space devoted to love scenes."[26]

The formal elements of *Pelleas* were assessed by Alban Berg in 1920 in a "short thematic analysis," part of a longer analysis by Berg that was first published only in 1994.[27] Berg labels themes according to characters and situations in Maeterlinck's drama, but he stresses that the symphonic aspect of the work was more essential than its descriptive relation to the play. According to Berg's often-repeated formal conception, the one movement contains a succession of sections that correspond to parts of a sonata-form movement (exposition, development, and reprise) and, at the same time, to the four movements of a classical symphony. This formal amalgam has antecedents in such earlier works as Schubert's *Wanderer* Fantasy and Liszt's Piano Sonata, and it was used again in Schoenberg's String Quartet No. 1 and the Chamber Symphony, Op. 9, as well as in works by others in the composer's circle.

Gurrelieder (Songs from Gurre, 1900–1903, completed in 1910–11) is

Schoenberg's most often performed early work. It was begun as an entry in a competition for new songs held by the Vienna Tonkünstlerverein in 1899 or 1900. It has been shown by Walter Frisch that Schoenberg's original plan was for a cycle of nine songs for tenor alternating with soprano, accompanied by piano.[28] Around April 1900 Schoenberg decided to expand the song cycle into a massive cantata in three large parts for solo voices, chorus, speaker, and large orchestra. The original nine songs were placed at the beginning, were linked continuously by orchestral interludes, and were greatly expanded by additional movements. The new composition was finished in March 1901, and its orchestration was begun. This work was interrupted during Schoenberg's first sojourn in Berlin and was completed only in 1911.

The text by Jens Peter Jacobsen was written in Danish around 1869, but was not published until 1886, following the author's death. By this time Jacobsen's verse had become highly esteemed, especially in Germany. The poetry deals ostensibly with material from a medieval Scandinavian legend concerning King Waldemar, his beloved Tove, and her death at the hands of the jealous Queen Helwig. Waldemar curses God and calls his vassals from out of their graves, whereupon they ride nightly seeking Tove. He senses her presence in nature, with which he will be united regardless of death or the will of God. The conclusion is an apostrophe to the summer wind, which, like Waldemar and his ghostly band, appears as a force that embodies the spirit of nature and love. Schoenberg—by his own admission seeking to extend and reinterpret the Wagnerian idiom—must have been attracted not only to the Wagnerian flavor of Jacobsen's texts, but also to their modernity, asserting, as they do, the supreme power of love and its emanation in nature.

The music of *Gurrelieder* mixes several styles and forms. The Wagnerian element is strongly represented by the presence of an elaborate web of leitmotifs, a huge, expressive orchestra, and an enriched harmonic language that makes prominent use of diminished and half-diminished chords. The form of *Gurrelieder* mixes the open shapes of Wagnerian opera with closed, concentric forms typical of song and with highly descriptive orchestral interludes. In the concluding "Wild Hunt of the Summer Wind" Schoenberg makes his first use of "melodrama," a popular musical genre in the nineteenth century in which the speaking of a poem is accompanied by instrumental music.

The music that Schoenberg composed near the end of his first period, primarily songs and chamber music, continued earlier directions, although two works, the String Quartet No. 1, Op. 7 (1904–5), and the Chamber Symphony, Op. 9 (1906), stand out as both a culmination of the first period and a harbinger of things to come. Schoenberg himself underscored the importance of the First String Quartet, which represented a "direction more my own" where earlier tendencies toward large forms, expansive melodies, counterpoint, new harmonies, and thematic unity were fully realized.[29] The formal plan of the work is similar to that in *Pelleas und Melisande*, that is, a single movement consisting of principal sections that simultaneously represent the four movements of a classical quartet and the main parts of a single movement in sonata form. The work is a monument to Schoenberg's idea of developing variations, as its themes grow from one another, each one paraphrasing earlier melodic ideas but at the same time persistently introducing new melodic shapes. The quartet carries to an extreme point other aspects of style that had been introduced earlier in *Verklärte Nacht* and *Pelleas und Melisande*, including intense counterpoint, freedom of surface harmonies from underlying tonal progressions, and an irregularity of beat and meter that suggests, to use the composer's term, "musical prose."

Although Schoenberg claimed to have abandoned program music in this work, a sketchbook for it contains a verbal outline that may have guided him in an early stage of the work's conception.[30] The outline conveys disjunct thoughts of joy and despair, possibly associated with love, and, at the end, an allusion to a dream in which a departed lover returns home to those whom he had abandoned, producing feelings of contentment. Any interpretation of it is problematic. First of all, it is far from certain that these thoughts pertain to the quartet at all or, if they do, in what manner. It is also unclear when they were written, since they were set down on a sheet of paper glued to the inside cover of the sketchbook, not entered into the book itself. The notes may record personal feelings that Schoenberg himself experienced, possibly concerning his own marriage, which by 1905 was probably entering a state of stress. But the references to a man's abandonment of loved ones and his ultimate return do not correspond to anything known about Schoenberg's personal life, although his wife, Mathilde, briefly in 1908 abandoned her family, to which she subsequently returned. The existence of a personal subtext in the quartet is plausible all the same, but barring the discovery of additional information, no conclusion can be reached.

The Chamber Symphony, scored for fifteen wind and string instruments, followed on the heels of the quartet. The composer referred to it as the "climax" of his first period of composition.[31] In 1906 the genre of the chamber symphony was new, although not unprecedented. Ermanno Wolf-Ferrari had written a *Sinfonia da camera* in 1901, and Ernst Toch also wrote a *Kammersymphonie* in 1906—works that are, like Schoenberg's, harbingers of a turning away from the large romantic orchestra by twentieth-century composers. The orchestrational style—spartan, unpadded, and crystal clear—owes much to the late symphonies of Gustav Mahler. Schoenberg was at first critical of Mahler's music, but on hearing the Vienna premier performance of Mahler's Third Symphony in December 1904, about a year before beginning the Chamber Symphony, he was converted into a passionate adherent. Schoenberg, like Mahler, pushes the instruments to the limits of their ranges and calls for special or extended playing techniques. Mahler, although using the large romantic orchestra, emphasized chamberlike subdivisions in which doublings were kept to a minimum.

The influence of Mahler is also encountered at the very beginning of the Chamber Symphony. The first four measures constitute a slow introduction, which, like the first-movement introductions in Mahler's symphonies—the Symphony No. 3 is an example—contains embryonic ideas for the remainder of the composition. In this case the ideas are not so much motivic as they are harmonic and tonal. In the first two measures the orchestra slowly unfolds a six-note fourth chord (G C F B♭ E♭ A♭), followed by a five-note whole-tone chord (E G♭ A♭ B♭ C), finally arriving on an F-major triad. This succession of three configurations of pitches—quartal, whole-tone, and diatonic—introduces a basic premise of the piece that is worked out with endless invention throughout. The introduction also suggests a close relation between the keys of F, suggested by the F-major triad at the end of the introduction, and the principal tonality of the whole work, E major, which is first established by a cadential progression that begins with the dominant chord in measure 8. The juxtaposition of two tonalities a semitone apart is often found in Schoenberg's music at this time (*Pelleas und Melisande*, for example, frequently brings the keys of C♯ and D into contact). Although the relation of the two keys has a distant analogy in tonal music—a harmony on F can prepare the dominant of the key of E—the direct juxtaposition of the two regions here serves to weaken rather than to reinforce a sense of traditional tonality. Indeed, the elements of harmonic progressions needed to establish the centrality of E major are so elliptical and so distant from one another that it is virtually impossible to hear them controlling the harmonic dimension of the music.

The elliptical and ambiguous style of harmony and tonality in the Chamber Symphony was greatly extended in music of Schoenberg's second period (1908–22). Indeed, traditional tonality is absent after 1908, except for occasional vestigial allusions to it, and the harmonies become pervasively dissonant, almost entirely avoiding traditional triads and seventh chords. Notes throughout the chromatic scale are used equally, the seven tones of any one major or minor scale no longer having priority. For this reason, Schoenberg abandoned key signatures in his music after this time. Together these features create a style that is termed "atonal," which will be analyzed in greater detail later in this chapter.

Schoenberg normally discussed his atonal music as a homogeneous body of works. While this is true in a general sense, a close study of his music written during the second period shows several very distinct styles and differing approaches to musical structure. It also casts a measure of doubt on the claim—made repeatedly by all figures of the Second Viennese School—that atonal music differs from romantic music only in harmony and tonality. The earliest atonal works do, in fact, remain close to Schoenberg's own late tonal pieces. Their harmonic language is largely the same, although references to triads within a key and conclusions on a tonic triad, characteristic of the late tonal style, are missing. The atonal works that Schoenberg composed from about 1909 to 1912, however, have very little in common with the late romantic idiom. In fact, these pieces are among the most innovative and experimental by any major composer in the twentieth century. Schoenberg delved at this time into stream-of-consciousness composition, which was characterized by extreme brevity and concentration, a renunciation of motivic work or development, and even a reinterpretation of conventional notions of musical meaning. Around 1912 he began gradually to return to earlier compositional and aesthetic norms while still maintaining the pervasive dissonance that characterizes the atonal language.

Music of the second period is distinguished from the first also in the composer's selection and interpretation of genres. Songs continued to be central to his oeuvre, but he deemphasized chamber music and began to write solo piano works, the latter absent in his earlier music. He also began to write operas—of a very original type—whereas he had been unsuccessful earlier in completing an opera in a conventional genre. His attitude toward programmatic music was ambivalent. Overt programmatic gestures, such as they existed in earlier works such as *Verklärte Nacht* and *Pelleas und Melisande*, are now entirely removed, but beneath the surface the music continues to be intensely poetic and expressive, linked covertly to his personal life and his philosophical ideas. His model in this transformation of the programmatic spirit was clearly Mahler, whose symphonies after 1900 were meticulously purged of outward programmatic details, although the music itself continued to express the composer's own narratives and ideas.

The genre of song continued to occupy a central place in Schoenberg's creative life of this period, as it had earlier. Schoenberg later commented that he often felt an even greater need than before for a poetic text, since other purely musical principles of structure associated with tonality were now avoided. The turn toward atonality around 1908 coincided with Schoenberg's adoption of poetry by Stefan George (1868–1933), just as his turn toward Wagnerian modernism a decade earlier had been prompted by his discovery of the verse of Richard Dehmel. In his essay "How One Becomes Lonely" (1937), Schoenberg underscored the inspiration that he found in George for a new musical language: "I was inspired by poems of Stefan George, the German poet, to compose music to some of his poems and, surprisingly, without any expectation on my part, these songs showed a style quite different from everything I had written before. . . . It was the first step towards a style which has since been called the style of 'atonality.' "[32]

Although the influence of French symbolist poetry is evident in some of Dehmel's work, his verse is far more eclectic in style and theme than is George's, who was a strict and devoted interpreter of the French idiom in German letters at the turn of the century. It is not known when Schoenberg discovered George's poetry, although, given the composer's interest in modern literature and the importance attached to George by such Viennese writers as Hugo von Hofmannsthal, it is likely that he was well aware of it from the 1890s. Song treatments of George's texts, generally not encouraged by the writer himself, had been made by the Berlin composer Conrad Ansorge and performed in Vienna in 1904. Albrecht Dümling has argued that Schoenberg was drawn to George since the topics that the poet addressed—the pure isolation of the artist, for example—struck a sympathetic chord in Schoenberg around 1907 and 1908.[33]

Schoenberg's first George setting was the song "Ich darf nicht dankend an dir niedersinken'' (I cannot kneel before you in thanks), Op. 14, No. 1. It was completed only a week following Mahler's departure in December 1907 from Vienna for the United States, and the sentiments of the text plainly refer to this important occasion. Schoenberg next turned to George while working on the Second String Quartet, Op. 10, in the fateful summer of 1908. The quartet was begun as a multimovement instrumental composition, but as the work came ever more to embody the powerful feelings of isolation and abandonment that weighed upon the composer, he changed his initial plan for it and introduced texts into its last two movements. This daring and unprecedented transformation of the quartet genre recalls the composer's reinterpretation of the sextet genre in *Verklärte Nacht*, which he made into an explicitly programmatic medium of expression. Schoenberg used George's poems ''Litanei'' (Litany) in the third movement and ''Entrückung'' (Rapture) in the fourth movement of the quartet. These texts together outline a narrative of death and transfiguration in which the narrator breaks free from his earthly misery to soar above the clouds, becoming but a spark in a holy fire. The quartet fluctuates between moments of tonal and atonal construction, suggesting, among other more autobiographical interpretations, that Schoenberg associated the adoption of atonality with a spiritual and artistic freedom.

In 1908 and 1909 Schoenberg turned decisively to George to capture the atmosphere of the new atonal style. In his cycle of fifteen songs drawn from George's anthology *Das Buch der hängenden Gärten*, Schoenberg created a narrative of initiation to love, its consummation, and its ultimate destruction—sentiments that had special poignancy for him in 1908. The George cycle contains Schoenberg's earliest consistently atonal compositions. When they were first performed in 1910, he wrote in program notes that the songs and their new style represented the bypassing ''of every restriction of a bygone aesthetic'' toward which he was led by an ''inner compulsion'' that outweighed the force of traditionalism exerted by his training and the tastes of his contemporaries.[34]

After the George songs of 1908–9, Schoenberg moved on to other poets and to a greater variety of themes as well as to reinterpretations of the song genre itself. His *Herzgewächse*, Op. 20 (1911), a setting of a poem by Maurice Maeterlinck in German translation, exhibits a flamboyantly coloratura part for soprano and an accompanimental ensemble of harp, celesta, and harmonium. The Four Songs, Op. 22 (1913–16), combine voice with large orchestra (also used earlier in his Six Songs, Op. 8) to set poetry by Ernest Dowson and Rainer Maria Rilke.

Pierrot lunaire, Op. 21 (1912), embodies an even more radical alternative to traditional song. This is a cycle of twenty-one recitations of poems by Albert Giraud in a German version by Otto Erich Hartleben, accompanied by chamber ensemble. Here Schoenberg returned to the genre of melodrama, which he had earlier used in *Gurrelieder* and also in the choral music of his opera *Die glückliche Hand* (1910–13). The work was commissioned in January 1912 by the Berlin actress and singer Albertine Zehme, who specifically requested settings of the Hartleben version of Giraud's poetry.

Schoenberg bypassed the simple recitation that Zehme must have expected, instead casting the voice part in what he termed *Sprechmelodie* (speaking melody). In this style the speaker must observe a strict rhythm, although the pitches indicated by the composer are only to be approximated. The composer insisted that the speaker must avoid singing the line, although his intentions otherwise have been open to differing interpretations. In the earliest performances Zehme dressed in a Pierrot costume to declaim the poems, which tend to be grotesque, even decadent.

The two atonal operas, *Erwartung*, Op. 17 (1909), and *Die glückliche Hand*, Op. 18 (1910–13), were intended by Schoenberg to be performed as a pair. The text of *Erwartung* was by an amateur poetess, Marie Pappenheim, who referred to the work as a "monodrama" since it involved only one character. She was introduced to Schoenberg during his summer retreat in the vacation village of Steinakirchen in the summer of 1909. He asked her to write an opera text for him, and she quickly produced a "lyric poem" that Schoenberg shortened and set to music in less than two weeks. The text is a remarkable precursor of literary techniques later associated with expressionist theater: it is in one short and intense act and speaks from the irrational, inner forces of life. Its one nameless character, called simply the Woman, is awaiting her lover. In a panic she races through a dark forest, blurting out disjointed thoughts and recollections that suggest a nightmare of fear, jealousy, and resentment. Reaching a clearing in the woods, she rests on a bench, whereupon her foot touches a bleeding corpse, the body of her lover. In lines that Schoenberg struck from the text, Pappenheim intimated that the Woman had murdered her lover in a jealous rage, only to efface the crime from her memory in a hysterical state.

Pappenheim's narrative is susceptible to several different interpretations. It was probably influenced by the analysis of hysteria put forward in the 1895 *Studien über Hysterie* by Sigmund Freud and Josef Breuer. Symptoms of this psychotic condition are evident in the Woman's actions and language. Schoenberg himself does not appear to have been especially interested in Freudian theory, and his own interpretation of the libretto turned more to the Woman's jumble of emotions, which he tried to capture in the music.

The musical language of *Erwartung* is an example of a brief and highly experimental style that Schoenberg began using in 1909. He composed quickly, with virtually no sketching or preplanning, and he avoided traditional features of structure such as motivic exposition and development, leitmotifs, or virtually any overt recurrence of musical materials. Instead, he closely followed the text, creating an orchestral sonority that reflected its images and a flexible vocal line that subtly moved back and forth between recitation and lyricism.

Shortly after completing *Erwartung* in September 1909, the composer consulted with Oskar Kokoschka concerning the text for a companion opera for the diminutive monodrama. Schoenberg was an admirer of Kokoschka at this time—later he described him as "the greatest living painter"—and was influenced by Kokoschka's dramatic writings. In the summer of 1909 Kokoschka's play *Mör-*

der, Hoffnung der Frauen had been presented in Vienna, and its theme of gender conflict is shared with the text that Schoenberg himself was to write in *Die glückliche Hand*, the companion work of *Erwartung*. This one-act "drama with music," whose text was completed in 1910, deals with the plight of the artist in a bourgeois society and is, as already mentioned, distinctly autobiographical.

The music, which was completed only in 1913, does not return to the stream-of-consciousness technique that had appeared in the monodrama. It uses instead a more conventional and methodical compositional strategy in which there are many sketches and revisions, sectional and thematic recurrences, and other traditional elements of form.[35] One especially innovative scene contains a "light crescendo," in which the Man's rising emotions and the presentiments of horror that attend his fate are conveyed by a steadily intensifying display of colors that seem to emanate from him, moving steadily from dull red to green to blood red and finally to a blinding yellow.

Vocal works such as *Erwartung* and *Die glückliche Hand* were central to Schoenberg's atonal style, although he also wrote a smaller amount of music, mostly of an experimental nature, for orchestra and for piano. The atonal piano music consists of two collections of "pieces," Opp. 11 (1909) and 19 (1911). The first and second pieces of Op. 11, among his earliest atonal works, are reasonably traditional in form and style, except for their dissonant harmonies and lack of traditional tonal progressions. The third piece of Op. 11, composed in the summer of 1909 at the same time as *Erwartung*, stands apart from the other two by virtue of its greater complexity, intense counterpoint, and lack of traditional formal symmetry and motivic development. The Six Little Piano Pieces, Op. 19, are also far more experimental than the early pieces of Op. 11, especially in their brevity. These are prime examples of a brief experiment that Schoenberg made with "aphoristic" music, more associated with Webern than with Schoenberg. Such pieces are very concise—four of the six in Op. 19 are confined to only nine measures in length—and exhibit a highly recondite and elliptical treatment of motives. The last of the Little Pieces of Op. 19 is especially haunting in its sonority and somber in mood. It was written a month after the death of Gustav Mahler and is thought to be a reflection upon Mahler's funeral, attended by the composer and some of his students.

The aphoristic style of the Little Piano Pieces is also evident in Schoenberg's orchestral music of the same period. It appears in three character pieces for chamber orchestra that the composer wrote in 1910, works that were first published in 1962 under the title Three Pieces for Chamber Orchestra. The second of these dwindles to a mere seven measures in length. The aphoristic element is also found in Schoenberg's Five Orchestral Pieces, Op. 16 (1909), each of which has a duration of three minutes on average. These pieces were originally written for large orchestra, although Schoenberg approved of their arrangement for numerous smaller media. They are often identified by intentionally cryptic subtitles, which Schoenberg reluctantly drafted at the request of the editor Henri Hinrichsen in 1912, although, he said, "if words were necessary, they would be in there.''[36] In the third piece, for example, Schoenberg suggested the title *Farben* (Colors). Gradual changes of color are indeed a prominent feature of the sound and substance of the piece, so much so that many writers have found in it a manifestation of *Klangfarbenmelodie* (tone-color melody), a notion that the composer later mentioned at the end of his *Harmonielehre*. Successions of different tone colors, he speculated, could create units of musical thought in the same way that successions of pitch create melodies.

Music of Schoenberg's third period (1923–50) is characterized by his twelve-tone method of composition. The origins of the method reach back to the years near the beginning of World War I, a relatively fallow period for him compositionally but rich in experiment and reassessment of his position in the evolution and future of music. Technical features of the method will be discussed later in this chapter.

The music of this period contains a transformation of style in which earlier characteristics are brought together with new ideas having a distinct relevance to European musical culture in the 1920s. For example, the music continues to be atonal, pervasively chromatic, highly contrapuntal, and dissonant, but a classical and traditional element is also newly apparent. Schoenberg began to write extended instrumental works in classical genres such as the concerto, variations, suite, and string quartet. Classical forms—rondos, sonata forms, and ternary plans, among others—reemerge, and Schoenberg even occasionally availed himself of exact sectional repetitions, almost entirely absent in his music before this time. The twelve-tone pieces generally avoid the aphoristic brevity apparent in works such as the Little Piano Pieces, Op. 19, readopting instead schemes involving thematic exposition, transition, development, and reprise, all destined to produce music of Beethovenian length. The rhythm of his new compositions exhibits a regularity that was not evident in his middle period, and textures become less dense than before. In certain late works Schoenberg even began to retreat from a homogeneous style based on the emancipation of dissonance. In pieces such as the *Ode to Napoleon Buonaparte*, Op. 41, he mixes triads at major cadences with dissonances, thus betraying an eclecticism that he had earlier described as a ''grave sin'' in music. He also wrote many artistic arrangements of earlier pieces, including folk songs and music by Bach, Handel, and Brahms, thus endorsing a type of music much in favor among neoclassicist composers of the 1920s and 1930s. A few pieces intended for student performers composed after he immigrated to the United States make use of tonality.

Schoenberg's twelve-tone oeuvre is about equally divided between vocal and instrumental genres, as the composer was no longer compelled to rely on texts for formal coherence. The lyric impulse, basic to his music heretofore, is now considerably diminished. With the exception of the Three Songs, Op. 48, the genre of song is entirely banished from Schoenberg's twelve-tone oeuvre, as the composer clearly turned toward more monumental genres—choruses, works for speaker, operas, and oratorios—as more appropriate uses of the voice. The texts that he chose are also different. They avoid the subjective and symbolist style encountered in Dehmel and George and turn instead to poetry that is more often didactic, monumental, and religious than emotional.

Works for orchestra came to occupy a considerably larger place in Schoenberg's oeuvre during his third period, especially after he immigrated to the United States, where the orchestra occupied a central position in musical culture. Schoenberg's principal works for orchestra of the third period are the Variations for Orchestra, Op. 31 (1926–28); *Accompaniment to a Film Scene*, Op. 34 (1929–30); Suite for String Orchestra (1934); Concerto for Violin, Op. 36 (1934–36); Chamber Symphony No. 2, Op. 38 (1906–39); Concerto for Piano, Op. 42 (1942); and Theme and Variations, Op. 43 (1943, original version for wind band). Additionally, there are orchestral arrangements of music by Bach, Handel, and Brahms.

Music for piano was important only to Schoenberg's transition to twelve-tone composition. Two suitelike works—Five Piano Pieces, Op. 23 (1920–23), and Suite for Piano, Op. 25 (1921–23)—document the final stages in the experimental phase leading to the method. The last of the Five Piano Pieces, "Waltz" (1923), is a completely twelve-tone composition, and Schoenberg pointed to the Suite, Op. 25, as the first major twelve-tone work. In many respects it too can be considered transitional, especially its Prelude and Intermezzo, which do not reveal aspects of serialization that Schoenberg later considered basic to the method. After the maturing of the method, Schoenberg returned to the medium of solo piano only in two brief Piano Pieces, Op. 33a (1928) and Op. 33b (1931), the latter written for publication in Henry Cowell's series New Music. Schoenberg's only completed composition for organ is the Variations on a Recitative, Op. 40 (1941), one of several works composed in America that intermingle triadic harmonies, aspects of tonality, and elements derived from the twelve-tone method.

Chamber music was central to Schoenberg's third period. The Serenade, Op. 24 (1920–23), embodies a transitional stage just prior to the maturing of the twelve-tone method. It calls for an ensemble of woodwind, plucked, and stringed instruments and, in the fourth movement, a voice singing a sonnet by Petrarch. The Woodwind Quintet, Op. 26 (1923–24), a tour de force in the quintet literature, exemplifies the classical forms that Schoenberg reapplied in his twelve-tone works. The first movement is cast in sonata form; the second is a scherzo with two trios; the third is ternary; and the fourth is a rondo. Schoenberg's String Quartets No. 3, Op. 30 (1927), and No. 4, Op. 37 (1936), are among his greatest works of this period. Both are in four movements, again using reinterpretations of classical structures. Schoenberg described his String Trio, Op. 45 (1946), as a covertly programmatic work, narrating in musical terms the heart attack that he suffered in the summer of 1946: "The representation is so precise that it even contains my recollection of the pricking of the hypodermic needle. The work is an extraordinarily complex twelve-tone composition. It consists of three main parts that are connected by two episodes. . . .

Passages of wild turmoil alternate with peaceful interludes, recalling my suffering from the disease and its painful moments.''[37]

Even in the classically oriented twelve-tone period, Schoenberg wrote no instrumental sonatas, although one of his last pieces, the Fantasy for violin with piano accompaniment, Op. 47 (1949), resembles the sonata medium. The work is one of Schoenberg's most sympathetic for the resources of the violin, an instrument for which he had a lifelong fondness. He first composed the solo part of the Fantasy in its entirety, only later adding the piano part, which he specifically designated as ''accompaniment.'' The two strata are further distinguished by different applications of twelve-tone materials.

Works for speaking voice are among the most numerous in Schoenberg's third period. The *Ode to Napoleon Buonaparte*, Op. 41 (1942), and *A Survivor from Warsaw*, Op. 46 (1947), are companion pieces, both referring in their texts to the destruction wrought by the Nazis. The first, a setting of a poem by Byron for speaker, piano, and string quartet or string orchestra, makes allusions to the tyrannical Buonaparte and, musically, to Beethoven's Fifth and *Eroica* Symphonies. Its twelve-tone technique, as in other late pieces by Schoenberg, is extensively reformulated in comparison to its classical conception in the 1920s and 1930s. The other works involving speaker—*Kol Nidre*, Op. 39 (1938), and *Modern Psalm*, Op. 50c (1950)—use religious texts in conjunction with chorus.

The chorus is indeed Schoenberg's preferred medium for texted music in the third period, comparable to the solo voice in the earlier two periods. The major compositions for chorus, in addition to those with speaker already enumerated, are Four Pieces, Op. 27 (1925); Three Satires, Op. 28 (1925); Six Pieces, Op. 35 (1930); *Dreimal tausend Jahre*, Op. 50a (1949); and *De profundis*, Op. 50b (1950). Additionally, Schoenberg arranged German folk songs for chorus in his Op. 49 (1948), revising arrangements that he had already made in 1929 for solo voice and piano. He also called on a mixed chorus to sing without words in his Prelude, Op. 44 (1945), suggesting a prelude to the story of the Creation from Genesis. The texts of these choral works, almost entirely by Schoenberg himself, deal primarily with religious and aesthetic issues.

An exception is the Three Satires, Op. 28, in which Schoenberg launched a satiric attack upon neoclassical composers, primarily upon Stravinsky, the ''Little Modernsky'' alluded to in Satire No. 2. Schoenberg was indeed ambivalent about neoclassicism, rejecting it outright in his writings but partly adopting some of its features in his music and revealing more than a touch of envy for the success of composers, such as Stravinsky, who were its leading representatives. This ambivalence is nowhere more evident than in his two operas from the third period, *Von heute auf morgen* (From one day to the next), Op. 32 (1928–29), and *Moses und Aron* (1928–32). The text of *Von heute auf morgen* was written by Schoenberg's wife, Gertrud, in 1928. It followed on the heels of the phenomenal success of Ernst Krenek's opera *Jonny spielt auf*, a work celebrating contemporary life and squarely in the objectivist and eclectic musical style that

Schoenberg disdained. The composer and his wife found their primary model for their essay in the newly popular genre of *Zeitoper* in Richard Strauss's *Intermezzo*, which they had seen performed in Berlin two years before. Schoenberg was enthusiastic about the libretto of *Intermezzo*, written by Strauss himself in a light and utterly non-Wagnerian idiom. On 3 May 1926 Schoenberg wrote to Webern about it: "I recently heard *Intermezzo* by Strauss and must say that, to my great surprise, it was not at all unpleasant. Especially the text, although it is full of the most ponderous and inconceivable errors (12 scene changes, each connected by a long, interlude played to a darkened house). Still, Strauss shows himself here more sympathetically than I would have believed possible."[38]

Strauss's text was based on comic episodes from his stormy domestic life with his wife, Pauline. Suspicions of liaisons outside of their marriage make both partners jealous, although they finally put aside their misgivings and find happiness with each other. Gertrud Schoenberg's libretto is similar to Strauss's, but Schoenberg only partly followed the Straussian model in his music. As is true of the Strauss work, Schoenberg's is a number opera in which arias alternate with recitatives. Both make full use of leitmotifs, and Schoenberg even avails himself of one of the Wagner quotations that lend Strauss's score its distinctively comic tone. But Schoenberg also saw the opera as an opportunity to demonstrate the flexibility of his twelve-tone method, showing that it could produce music that was light and melodious. Since *Von heute auf morgen* is one of Schoenberg's most rarely performed works, he may well have miscalculated the affinity of such inherently divergent ideas.

At the same time that he composed *Von heute auf morgen*, Schoenberg wrote the text of an oratorio, *Moses und Aron*. In the spring of 1930, shortly after the premiere of the comic opera in Frankfurt, he revised it as an opera libretto in three acts and began to compose its music. He had finished two acts by the summer of 1932, when events leading to his emigration caused the work to be put aside, leaving it permanently incomplete. Even as a two-act torso, it is one of Schoenberg's very greatest compositions.

The opera is shaped as a succession of tableaux, freely based on the biblical books of Exodus and Numbers, concerning Moses, his brother and spokesman Aaron, and the Hebrew people. In Schoenberg's treatment, Moses is the bearer of an ineffable idea that will sustain his people in their journey to the Promised Land. But he cannot win their support since he cannot communicate this idea to them. For this he relies upon Aaron, who uses words and images deftly but who ultimately betrays the idea and leads the people back to their slavery of pleasure. Appropriately, the role of Moses is recited in *Sprechmelodie*, while Aaron is a lyric tenor.

In its biblical theme the opera is plainly related to earlier projects based on Old Testament subjects and to Schoenberg's own religious reawakening, but it differs from these earlier works in that Schoenberg now adds a bitter and mordant commentary upon his contemporaries—the advocates of a false artistic modernism. Clearly, Moses speaks for Schoenberg himself, confident in his idea and its relevance to the people and only too conscious of his inability to win their support. The traitor Aaron is probably meant to represent Stravinsky and other neoclassicists, who have won a measure of acceptance and prerogative only by exploiting and cheapening the eternal idea of art.

ATONALITY

When the term ''atonal'' began to appear in musical journalism in Germany prior to World War I, it did not have an especially concrete meaning. It was used broadly to describe modern music that seemed dissonant, unmelodious, devoid of key, or otherwise lacking a sense of traditional beauty. In the present day, a measure of the same vagueness still attends the term and its cognates. The word ''atonality'' is generally used by modern writers to designate a style of twentieth-century music evincing three primary characteristics: the absence of traditional key or tonality, equal use of the full chromatic spectrum of pitches rather than according priority to seven tones of a diatonic scale, and the presence of harmonies that are largely dissonant rather than based on triads or triadic extensions. The phenomenon of atonality has proved to be one of the chief stylistic innovations in music throughout the twentieth century. Like all major developments in the history of music, it was the outcome of a gradual evolution to which many composers contributed. Schoenberg was a central, though not exclusive, figure in its emergence.

Given its vagueness and pejorative connotation, it is not surprising that most early-twentieth-century composers rejected the term for their own music. In the third edition of his *Harmonielehre* Schoenberg took note of the term—still new when this edition was prepared in 1921—and dismissed it as illogical. Since tonality, he wrote, spoke to the relations that inevitably exist within a succession of tones, the antithesis suggested by the term ''atonal'' had no conceivable meaning. In the first edition of the *Harmonielehre* (1911) he alluded to a related phenomenon that he called *aufgehobene Tonalität* (suspended tonality), which he found in passages of late romantic tonal music (he mentioned works by Bruckner and Wolf) having no fixed sense of key. This phenomenon, he said, comes from a pervasive use of ''vagrant'' chords—chords that could theoretically take on functions in several different keys. ''The classical development sections are not too far removed from this,'' he concluded. But Schoenberg never settled upon a term to describe the type of music that others called atonal.[39]

The historical process by which music freed itself from key reaches back to the end of the nineteenth century or even before. Music from the 1890s by Claude Debussy represented an especially crucial stage in this development. Although Debussy's music from this decade remains largely diatonic and triadic, chords are not always assembled into a syntax by which harmonic progressions establishing a key can be inferred. Sometimes Debussy lays out the chords in parallel streams or brings the music to a cadencelike pause on degrees that do not strongly suggest the functions of tonic, dominant, or dominant preparation.

Example 4.1
Claude Debussy, Sarabande (1894), Measures 1–8

An example is the opening phrase of his Sarabande for piano, in its original version of 1894 (Example 4.1). The music is almost entirely diatonic and the harmonies are triads and seventh chords, but the order in which the chords occur and their placement at the beginning and end of phrases do not confirm the key of E major or C♯ minor, suggested by the operative diatonic pitch collection. The G♯ triad at the cadences in measures 2 and 4 may well be a minor dominant of C♯, but there is no support for this interpretation in the context in which these chords arise, no beginning on a tonic nor moving through a succession of chords that traditionally prepare a dominant. Schoenberg concisely assessed Debussy's innovations: "His harmonies, without constructive meaning, often served the colouristic purpose of expressing moods and pictures. Moods and pictures, though extra-musical, thus became the constructive elements, incorporated in the musical functions; they produced a sort of emotional comprehensibility. In this way, tonality was already dethroned in practice, if not in theory."[40]

A more pervasive chromaticism and more strongly dissonant harmony arose mainly in German music at the end of the nineteenth century, although these features also appear in works of the same time by modernists elsewhere, including Alexander Scriabin in Moscow, Charles Ives in America, and Béla Bartók in Budapest. Schoenberg's songs composed between the years 1897 and 1908 provide excellent examples of the gradual emergence of the three features that characterize atonality: absence of tonal harmonic functions, structural equality of the full chromatic collections of tones, and predominant use of nontertian harmonies. These features grew ever more prominent in Schoenberg's music

Example 4.2
Arnold Schoenberg, "Erwartung," Op. 2, No. 1, Measures 1–2

during the early years of the century, converging around 1908 to produce fully atonal works.

The last of the three features emerged clearly in the Dehmel songs from 1899. In "Erwartung," Op. 2, No. 1, a rich, nontertian chord (E♭ A D G♭ C♭) is placed front and center at the beginning of the song (Example 4.2). Our attention is drawn to it more than to the tonic E♭ triad, which is relegated to the status of a mere eighth-note upbeat. Clearly enough, the five-note chord is an embellishment of the triad, to which it is connected by common tones and stepwise voice leading, but its far greater duration and metric emphasis create the impression that it, not the triad, is the central and referential sonority. The five-note chord, furthermore, is not one of the familiar seventh chords that heretofore had characterized the enriched harmonic surface of romantic music, but instead a more pungent sonority appropriate to the exotic and mysterious images of the poem.

The song "Lockung," Op. 6, No. 7 (1905), was cited by Schoenberg as an example of tonality stretched to its limits. The work reveals two devices mentioned by the composer by which key was weakened: the simultaneous presence of two keys (E♭ major and C minor) and the avoidance of progressions that conclude explicitly on either tonic. The central key is E♭ major, which is established in the first phrase by an incomplete harmonic progression that begins on a mediant harmony on G in measure 1, passes then through a succession of other chords preparing the dominant, and arrives finally on the dominant seventh chord in this key in measure 13. Schoenberg asserted that most of these chords could also support an interpretation of C (minor) as the tonic, since the chords are largely "vagrants," that is, altered chromatically so as to allow multiple although ambiguous functions in several keys.[41] The ambiguity of key in the song is heightened by the absence of a coherent bass line connecting diatonic chords.

It is clear from these examples of extended tonality that the exact point at which atonality is reached is to some extent arbitrary. Schoenberg himself alluded to the George songs, Op. 15 (1908–9), as the earliest major atonal pieces. These were indeed his first published works to dispense with key signature, indicating that the composer did not consider their referential pitch collections to be diatonic scales but instead the full chromatic scale. No longer are the chords consistently referable to tonal functions, and the harmonies themselves are overwhelmingly dissonant. Schoenberg's own definition of the new style spoke concisely to these features: it "treats dissonances like consonances and renounces a tonal centre."[42] In a letter of August 1909 to Ferruccio Busoni he added, "I have long been occupied with the removal of all shackles of tonality. And my harmony allows no chords or melodies with tonal implications any more."[43]

The music of the George songs and other pieces composed between approximately February 1908 and August 1909 embody the first of three distinct styles of composition that Schoenberg developed under the more general umbrella of atonality. The song "Das schöne Beet" (The beautiful flower bed), the tenth piece in the George cycle, contains most of the characteristic features of this earliest atonal idiom, which mixes traditional features of form and poetic expression with a new harmonic vocabulary. The song has the same developmental ternary shape that Schoenberg had used in his songs since the 1890s, but its harmonic vocabulary is different from the earlier music in its scarcity of triads and seventh chords. Triads are not entirely banished. In fact, this song begins with a prominent reference to a triad on D, Schoenberg's motto. As seen in Example 4.3, the opening is comparable to a tonal composition that begins by prolonging its tonic triad through stepwise bass motion and free melodic embellishing tones in the upper voices. But soon it becomes apparent that this triad leads to no other functional chords that consistently suggest a key. The triad is an expressive allusion, probably to the composer himself, rather than a central structural entity. The chords that dominate the work are very often four-note figures, many of which contain a major or minor triad but avoid familiar seventh-chord sonorities. Whole-tone tetrachords (i.e., harmonies with four different tones drawn from a whole-tone scale) and pentatonic subsets are also common. There is no evidence that these were chosen or linked together according to system. In fact, Schoenberg repeatedly spoke of atonal harmony as being the product of pure intuition.

The second phase of Schoenberg's atonal period began in July or August 1909 during a summer retreat in the village of Steinakirchen in lower Austria and extended approximately until the spring or summer of 1912. During this time Schoenberg completed the Three Piano Pieces, Op. 11, and Five Orchestral Pieces, Op. 16, both begun earlier, and composed the opera *Erwartung*, Six Little Piano Pieces, Op. 19, and the song *Herzgewächse*, Op. 20. The music of this phase is highly experimental, differing radically from any that Schoenberg composed either before or after. He outlined his new approach in correspondence with Ferruccio Busoni during the summer of 1909, when the experimental idiom was apparently foremost in his mind.[44] He used the words "freedom" and "expression" repeatedly to characterize his thoughts to Busoni. Henceforth, he said, he would reject all aspects of traditional musical cohesion, including motivic

Example 4.3
Arnold Schoenberg, "Das schöne Beet," Op. 15, No. 10, Measures 1–6

Source: Schoenberg, *Das Buch der haengenden Gaerten*. Copyright 1914 by Universal Edition. Copyright renewed. All Rights Reserved. Used in the world excluding the United States by permission of European American Music Distributors Corporation, agent for Universal Edition.

work, architectonic form, and harmony as a structural component. Everything would be of the utmost brevity, based on the unconscious intuition and rapidly changing emotions. He wished nothing "to inhibit the stream of my unconscious sensations."

His music during this phase indeed appears to have been composed in a stream of consciousness, with little in the way of sketching, thematic exposition and development, or forms based on sectional recurrence. Much more than in the George songs, the chords lack coherence and often appear as the confluence of an intricate polyphonic texture. An example of this experimental style is provided by the Piano Piece, Op. 11, No. 3, completed on 7 August 1909. The music—improvisatory, highly fragmented, and linearized—well embodies the program that he announced to Busoni, to whom he further described this particular piece: "I find it goes a considerable way beyond what was successful in the other two [pieces of Op. 11]. At any rate, as far as the above-mentioned variegation [of figures without melodic character]. But also in the 'harmony'—if one can speak so architecturally here—there seems to be something novel in it. In particular: something more slender, more linear.''[45]

Schoenberg's reliance upon intuition apparently led him into a creative impasse, as his completion of new works gradually dwindled after 1909. In the melodrama *Pierrot lunaire*, composed between March and July 1912, he set out upon a new course in which the outré experimentation of the second phase of the atonal period was moderated by the return to more traditional techniques, materials, and formal principles. *Pierrot* thus begins the third phase of atonality, which also marks a transition to twelve-tone composition. The music of the third phase is not as brief as before nor as romantic and naïvely expressive as that from the first atonal phase. A consciousness of form and its logical employment is its trademark.

Examples of the new style are found in *Pierrot lunaire*, but before turning to them we will first examine one of Schoenberg's least-known works, the orchestral song ''Seraphita,'' Op. 22, No. 1, completed in November 1913. The song is relatively long (about six minutes in duration) and fiercely complex. Judging from the numerous sketches for it, it was composed after an extensive period of planning and delving into the resources of the work's materials. The form is based on a familiar ternary shape, and the central integrating factor is a small motif, a three-note figure presented at the outset in the principal line as F G♭ A. This figure is used in a much more pervasive fashion than were motives in works such as the George songs. The three-note motif is, in fact, virtually ever present, embedded into both lines and chords and hidden by transpositions, inversions, and reorderings. The texture is far more complex than in any music of the first phase, and the chords now regularly span six or more tones rather than the simple four-note harmonies in the George works.

In ''Seraphita'' Schoenberg deployed the full chromatic collection of tones more fully than heretofore. He also found ways to unify both vertical and horizontal dimensions of the musical space. A striking example of these phenomena is seen in measures 14–15, near the end of the orchestral introduction (Example 4.4). The violins play a six-note chord while the clarinets state a line made from the same chord transposed so that it has no notes in common with the violins. Schoenberg has thus used forms of a single six-note collection to unify the texture and to produce total chromaticism. Although the systematic chromaticism and multidimensional integration exemplified by this passage are isolated phenomena in ''Seraphita,'' they are symptoms of a new thinking that Schoenberg would continually expand and refine in his music over the next ten years.

THE TWELVE-TONE METHOD

With the beginning of the third phase of atonality in 1912, Schoenberg had set out on a path that led him ultimately to twelve-tone composition. In some movements of *Pierrot lunaire*, written in the spring of that year, he began to dispense with the intuitive, text-based technique of composing atonal music that

Example 4.4
Arnold Schoenberg, "Seraphita," Op. 22, No. 1, Measures 14–15 (Piano Reduction)

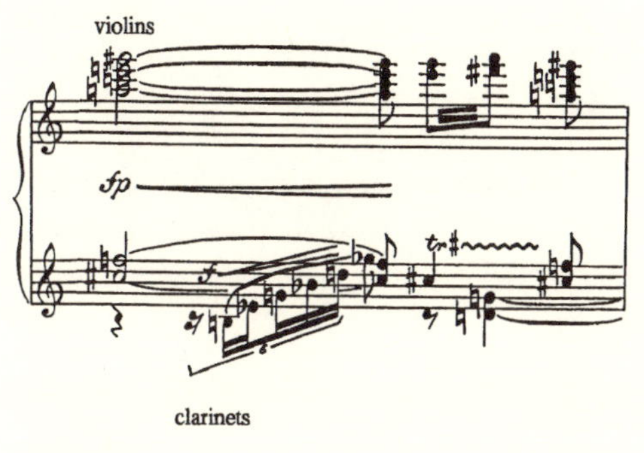

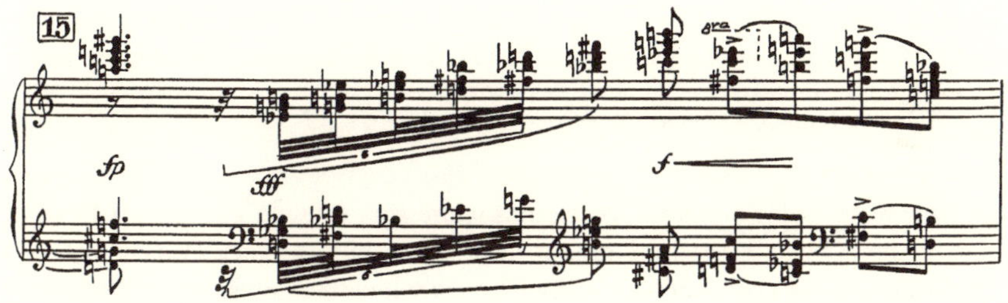

Source: Schoenberg, *4 Lieder*, Op. 22. Copyright 1917 by Universal Edition. Copyright renewed. All Rights Reserved. Used in the world excluding the United States by permission of European American Music Distributors Corporation, agent for Universal Edition.

he had used since 1909, and he turned instead toward a more controlled and structured approach. This change marked a great watershed in his creative career, launching him in a direction that would gradually intensify from that point onward.

The new orientation is seen in the eighth movement of *Pierrot lunaire*, entitled "Nacht (Passacaglia)." After a three-measure introduction, the music proceeds as a strict canon (Example 4.5). It is rounded out by developing variations upon earlier motivic material, primarily a three-note figure, E G E♭. The continuous variation of this motif suggests the genre of passacaglia, to which Schoenberg referred in the title of the movement.

For future developments, the structure of "Nacht" is notable in several ways. The application of canon and the continuous variations of passacaglia speak to a new interest in methodical composition and in polyphonic forms from the baroque period. The outgrowth of the music of the entire movement from the introductory motifs in measures 1–3 suggests a renewed organicism. Even more forward looking is the presentation of a central motif, E G E♭, simultaneously as both line and harmony, a technique also observed in "Seraphita." The pattern

Example 4.5
Arnold Schoenberg, "Nacht," from *Pierrot lunaire*, Measures 1–5

Source: Schoenberg, *Pierrot lunaire*. Copyright 1914 by Universal Edition. Copyright renewed. All Rights Reserved. Used in the world excluding the United States by permission of European American Music Distributors Corporation agent for Universal Edition.

by which the motif pervades the entire texture may be seen in Figure 4.1, which shows the pitches of the first three measures placed into six brief, chromatically descending lines according to the registers in which the notes occur. The central motif arises in different ways. It is heard as a conventional melodic element, for example, as E G E♭ in the pianist's left and right hands at the very beginning, and also more covertly in an interlocking succession of transpositions, enclosed in the figure in triangles. These latter presentations interconnect the adjacent chromatic lines, thus integrating and unifying the vertical and horizontal dimensions of the passage. Plainly, the unity of texture created by varied reiterations of the central motif suggests an entirely different objective from the ''variegation'' of figures and chords at which Schoenberg had earlier aimed, as in his Piano Piece, Op. 11, No. 3.

Schoenberg's new structuralist outlook on composition in 1912 was still troubled by questions concerning form. Atonality to that point had been largely an art of rebellion and liberation, in which more attention was drawn to the removal of the old rather than to its replacement with something new. Large-scale form was especially problematic, since tonality, on which the older conception of form was based, was now eliminated. It was uncertain whether a revival of traditional formal patterns, a reliance purely on text, or experimental aphoristic forms would suffice to make the music understood in its new chromatic and nontonal environment. The principal formal process inherited from tonal music—developing variations upon basic motifs—now seemed too free and unstructured to ensure a comprehensible and cohesive presentation of ideas. Schoenberg began to search for a formal principle to replace tonality and to imbue the heretofore ad hoc outlook of atonal composi-

Figure 4.1
Motif Patterns in Arnold Schoenberg, *Pierrot lunaire*, "Nacht," Measures 1–3

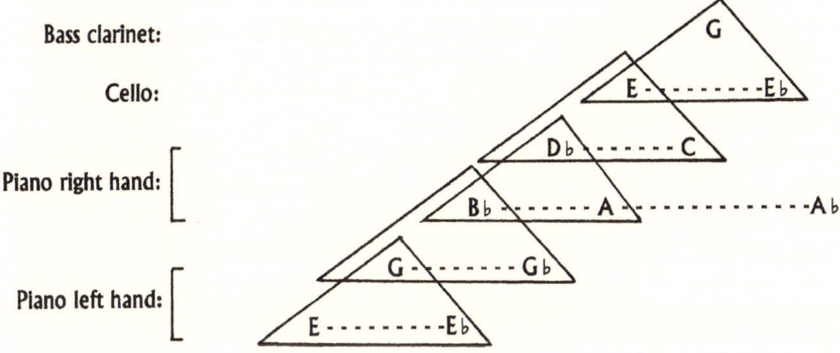

tion with concrete and positive laws. Specifically, the idea of developing variations had to be reformulated to make it more systematic, more in keeping with the spirit of the age.

Schoenberg's new interest in schematizing the creative process must have received psychological reinforcement during and just following World War I as a way of regaining control during a period of great chaos. Following the war, many overt manifestations of structure and restraint became evident throughout the world of art. The geometrical idiom adopted in the paintings of Kandinsky and Piet Mondrian at this time reflects the same grasping for control that motivated Schoenberg. In earlier German music Schoenberg also found support for his new direction. According to a theory of history that he formulated following the war, Schoenberg postulated that musical culture was just then entering a new period, the last of three major eras through which it had unfolded since the Renaissance.[46] The first of these periods, which reached a climax with Bach, was characterized by polyphony. Here a musical idea was contained in a line that was not developed, but instead juxtaposed with iterations of itself in several strands of a contrapuntal texture. The second period, corresponding to the later eighteenth and nineteenth centuries, was characterized by homophony. At this time musical ideas were embodied in themes and motifs that were confined to a single, predominant strand of a texture and continually varied. The accompanimental or harmonic dimension was gradually enriched by an increased use of all twelve tones. Now at the beginning of the third period, Schoenberg envisaged a return to counterpoint, but the chromaticism and motivic development characteristic of the second period would be preserved as well. The new period would thus amount to a great synthesis and summation of what went before, a merger of thematic growth, total chromaticism, and a close integration of the pitch content of lines and chords. "Nacht" from *Pierrot lunaire* was probably the first piece in which Schoenberg could see realized, at least partly, the demands of the new historical period.

Works that Schoenberg began in the decade between 1913 and 1923 reveal a multiplicity of compositional procedures that incorporate total chromaticism, integration of texture, and systems of motivic development. Methods intended to control chromaticism even at this time were widespread. For example, themes constructed from all twelve notes had been used by Franz Liszt in his *Faust* Symphony, Richard Strauss in the "On Science" section of *Also sprach Zarathustra*, and Alban Berg in the Passacaglia (Act 1, Scene 4) of *Wozzeck*, the last composed in 1918 or early 1919. In 1914 Schoenberg himself experimented with a principal theme made from the twelve notes in the Scherzo movement of his fragmentary Symphony. A Viennese contemporary of Schoenberg, Josef Matthias Hauer, had made an especially far-reaching application of the full chromatic collection of tones. In his music after 1919 the twelve notes are continually recirculated, generally in the melodic dimension of a work, from beginning to end. The chords in these pieces usually remained the familiar triads and seventh chords, sometimes suggesting a key. Given Schoenberg's belief in the necessity for an integrated texture, Hauer's music seemed to him to be lacking in artistic integrity.

The integration of harmonic and melodic dimensions indeed seemed imperative to Schoenberg to maintain coherence in posttonal music. He often explained this necessity by asserting that music existed in a unified multidimensional space. The vertical dimension of harmony differed from the horizontal dimension of melody only in the arbitrary perspective of the observer. In his lectures Schoenberg often underscored this perception by drawing attention to his hat, which remained a hat regardless of the direction from which it was viewed. The question that now faced the composer was how to ensure that the entire musical texture would be unified while also being chromatic and motivically interconnected.

One provocative experiment with this objective was conducted in his fragmentary oratorio *Die Jakobsleiter*, composed primarily in 1917. By his own admission he was influenced in the creation of an integrated texture in the oratorio by an article that he had read in *Der blaue Reiter* concerning Scriabin's *Prometheus*. Its author, Leonid Sabaneyev, contended that Scriabin used a collection of six tones— C, F♯, B♭, E, A, D—to unify both lines and chords throughout the work. Sabaneyev wrote: "All melodic voices [in *Prometheus*] are constructed from the tones of the [basic] accompanying harmony, and all counterpoints are subjected to the same principle."[47] In *Die Jakobsleiter* Schoenberg similarly used a collection of six tones—C♯, D, E, F, G, G♯—and its transpositions to create some of the lines of the work, accompanying them elsewhere in the texture by the remaining six tones and thus systematically exploiting the full chromatic collection. This technique, already used in passing in "Seraphita," was applied more frequently in *Die Jakobsleiter* to achieve both total chromaticism and an integration of line and accompaniment.

Finding a methodical alternative to free developing variations upon motifs was apparently more difficult for Schoenberg, as he experimented with various alternatives between 1914 and 1923. Models for a new thematic practice were, to be sure, readily at hand, especially in strict contrapuntal works by Bach. The canons in Bach's *Musical Offering*, for example, sometimes use following voices that duplicate the order of intervals in a leading voice, although they are varied by transposition, inversion, retrograde motion, or a combination of the three. A polyphonic texture containing such strictly imitative forms would also possess the intense integration of dimensions that Schoenberg thought necessary. Schoenberg also looked to the motivic practices of Beethoven, where he found vestiges of the forms inherited from strict counterpoint. In his lecture "Composition with Twelve Tones," Schoenberg cited a motif (G E A♭) from the beginning of the finale of Beethoven's String Quartet in F major, Op. 135, that subsequently reappears in a free retrograde and inversion, although the intervals of these varied forms are not exactly those of the earlier manifestation.

Just as Schoenberg's contemporaries were experimenting in the early 1920s with systems to control the full chromatic spectrum of pitches, they were also proposing new methods for developing themes. One of these was encountered by Schoenberg in a passage from Fritz Heinrich Klein's *Die Maschine* (1921), already mentioned in connection with the Society for Private Musical Performances. A section of this piece, the score of which was sent to Schoenberg just after it was published, is based on a twelve-tone theme. The theme is subsequently developed not by free variations, but mechanistically in a sequential succession of transpositions and intervallic inversions that preserve the order of intervals in the initial line. Klein's experiment suggests that he shared Schoenberg's sense of the necessity for a systematic variational process, but Schoenberg could not have accepted Klein's mechanistic and highly repetitive model for this formal principle.

By 1921 Schoenberg had already begun to experiment with his own ways of renovating and controlling the process of developing variations. Guided by works such as "Nacht" from *Pierrot lunaire* and by even earlier pieces, tonal and atonal, he began to flesh out the notion of a *Grundgestalt* (basic shape)—a means of regulating developmental forms as well as of ensuring integrated textures and total chromaticism. Schoenberg did not extensively write on his notion of basic shape, but reports by his students allow his ideas to be reconstructed. A basic shape is a special type of motif occurring at the beginning of a work that, by an ongoing variational process, governs many of the subsequent melodic and harmonic manifestations. It is different from a traditional motif because it consists purely of a succession of pitches, devoid of rhythm or other musical features. The shape may span twelve tones, as in the mature twelve-tone works composed beginning in 1923, or fewer than twelve, as in works composed between 1920 and 1923.

The basic shape is an abstract entity since it has no musical characteristics except for its succession of intervals. At the beginning of a piece, it is normally embodied in all or part of a theme. This theme then undergoes its own development in a conventional manner, only now controlled on an abstracted level

Example 4.6
Arnold Schoenberg, Piano Piece, Op. 23, No. 3, Measures 1–5

of structure by the presence of the intervallic succession of the basic shape. This succession is present even if it is modified by transposition, intervallic inversion, presentation in retrograde, rotation to begin with an interval other than the first, or all of these combined. The intervals of one such form of the basic shape may be applied directly to a line or, more typically, to several simultaneous lines and chords occurring in a region within the musical texture. Its presence allowed for variety and compositional freedom, both lacking in Klein's mechanistic study, and it also contributed to the multidimensional unity that Schoenberg considered indispensable.

Schoenberg began to apply the concept of basic shape in pieces composed between 1920 and 1923. These are the immediate predecessors of the mature twelve-tone works and are highly diverse in their methods of composition. Those that use basic shapes of fewer than twelve tones represent a transitional technique that the composer called "working with the tones of a motif." Although Schoenberg nowhere precisely explained this procedure, we can deduce its main characteristics by examining a work in which the composer said that it was present, such as the Piano Piece, Op. 23, No. 3, completed in 1923. The opening five-measure section, shown in Example 4.6, reveals a complex and diverse use of the basic shape contained in the tones of the opening theme, B♭ D E B C♯. The shape periodically returns in several of its fundamental forms, for example, transposed to the fifth as F A B F♯ G♯ in the fuguelike answer in the bass line in measures 2–3. An inversion transposed up eight semitones and rotated to begin with the fourth note and end with the third is encountered in the right hand of measure 3, where the tones F E♭ G♭ D C occur in proximity, associated partly by register. But other than these sporadic occurrences, the linear order of intervals of the basic shape is not consistently preserved. The shape in its various forms is more typically encountered in a disordered and partial fashion, its tones scattered into an area within the musical texture, where they are only loosely associated with one another by their proximity. An example is seen in the right hand in the middle of measure 4, where the notes C C♭ E♭ D appear in an inner voice. These tones have the same pitch content as part of the basic shape transposed up one semitone, although as they occur in measure 4, they entirely abandon the order of intervals of the basic shape and are not associated with one another in any distinct musical context other than proximity in a textural strand.

The Piano Suite, Op. 25 (1921–23), represented a turning point in Schoenberg's development of the twelve-tone method. He referred to it as the earliest "larger work" to use this procedure, and it is indeed the first multimovement composition to be strictly based upon a single twelve-tone basic shape or "row." But even in the Suite Schoenberg continues to experiment with differing compositional procedures. The first of six movements, titled Prelude, was the first composed, completed in July 1921. Here the basic shape is not a single succession of twelve tones, but instead a complex of three four-note shapes, together containing the twelve notes. These three are always presented in the same region of the Prelude, thus continually producing total chromatic fields. Different from the Piano Piece, Op. 23, No. 3, the original order of intervals within each tetrachordal shape is preserved in the music, even though the tetrachords themselves are freely shuffled in their order of presentation.

In this Prelude, as in Schoenberg's later twelve-tone works, the composer intended to draw an analogy between his new twelve-tone method and traditional tonality, since he considered the method to be a replacement for the older order. The similarities begin with the classicizing style of the new pieces—clear in rhythm, contrapuntal in texture, and cast into relatively familiar forms and genres. Schoenberg extended the analogy by using forms of the basic shapes to imitate tonal harmonic functions. In the Prelude he treats four forms of the three basic shapes as "tonics" and four others as "dominants," these terms used by the composer himself. The four tonic forms consist of the shapes as initially presented, their inversions transposed to the tritone, and the retrogrades of both. Just as the tonic triad is normally encountered at the beginning and end of a tonal composition, these four forms are used at the beginning and end of the Prelude. Four "dominant" forms are obtained by transposing the four tonic forms all to the tritone, and these dominants are used near the middle, just where a tonal piece might exploit the dominant key.

Beginning with the concluding movements of the Suite, Op. 25 (1923), and continuing until the 1940s, Schoenberg's twelve-tone method entered a mature phase, although, especially in his final works, he continued to experiment with new ways of exploiting his materials. The basic shape in a new work following Op. 25 spanned all twelve tones and became in effect synonymous with what the composer also called the "basic series." A thematic embodiment of it was normally heard at or near the beginning of a work, but later the row or its forms tended to be distributed into several strands of the texture, thus allowing for intervallic variety and freedom as new themes grew developmentally from earlier ones.

A major innovation in the method began to appear in Schoenberg's music from the time of the Three Satires, Op. 28 (1925), as the composer began to exploit a relation, now called "combinatoriality" or "complementarity," that exists between two forms of certain rows. Although Schoenberg himself never coined a term to describe this relationship, it clearly fascinated him, and its application soon became the single most important element of his method. Schoenberg found this relationship among inversionally related forms of a row in which corresponding halves (or "hexachords") shared no notes in common. The row from the Fourth String Quartet, Op. 37 (1936), provides an example. The basic series, which can be extracted from the beginning of the main theme, has these tones: D C♯ A B♭ F E♭ E C A♭ G F♯ B. Their inversion transposed up five semitones has these notes: G A♭ C B E F♯ F A C♯ D E♭ B♭. Clearly, the corresponding hexachords of the two row forms have no notes in common. They are "combinatorial" since the hexachords can be combined compositionally to create fully chromatic fields (now called "aggregates").

By keeping combinatorially related hexachords together in a composition, Schoenberg was able to accomplish two related objectives. The first, by now familiar, was the creation of a more pervasive chromaticism in all areas and dimensions of a piece. The second, related to the first, was the avoidance, to the extent possible, of premature repetition of a note when juxtaposing row forms. These considerations are apparent in the passage from measures 116 to 121 in the first movement of the Fourth String Quartet, part of an episode in a free sonata-form plan (Example 4.7). This passage consists of two principal lines, one in the viola, the other in violin I, accompanied by chords played by the two remaining instruments. Notes of the basic series transposed up two semitones are divided between the two principal lines. The accompanying chords are made from notes of a combinatorial inversional form of this series. By aligning corresponding hexachords of the two row forms, Schoenberg is able to produce an aggregate in the vertical dimension of the texture. This phenomenon is seen, for example, in measures 116–17, in which the first hexachord from the basic form (in violin I and viola) is accompanied by the first hexachord from the inversional form (in violin II and cello). A fully chromatic field results, as it does in the following two measures, where the second hexachords of the two row forms are brought together in a similar way.

Other fully chromatic fields are also present in the horizontal dimension. The unfolding of twelve-tone rows in violin I and viola and in violin II and cello has already been described, and Schoenberg additionally creates twelve-tone rows, not directly related to the intervallic structure of the basic shape, in each of the melodic lines in violin I (measures 117–21) and viola (measures 117–21).

Example 4.7
Arnold Schoenberg, String Quartet No. 4, Op. 37, First Movement, Measures 115–21

The melody in violin I reveals an additional technique that would lead Schoenberg in his later years essentially to reformulate the method. The melody is a developmental outgrowth of several earlier themes and motifs, most closely related to a transitional theme heard in measure 27. In its manifestation in measures 117–21 its intervals are largely freed from those of the basic series, which continues to control its intervallic structure only weakly and very abstractly. The melody arises essentially from a free process of developing variations and conforms to the twelve-tone method primarily by embodying an aggregate. In this and future twelve-tone works Schoenberg struck a balance between the free motivic variations of an earlier period and the stricter motivic practices that guided him originally toward the method. In his twelve-tone works composed in the 1940s this freedom and flexibility are increased, even to the point of allowing him to abandon basic series with any fixed orderings of intervals. Schoenberg's objective of obtaining multidimensional chromatic fields and integrated textures remains, but in these later works he moves toward a much freer concept of intervallic order, in some works even abandoning the use of a basic series altogether.

The new approach is seen strikingly in his *Ode to Napoleon Buonaparte*, Op. 41 (1942). This work makes no pervasive use of a series, but returns essentially to a style that resembles Schoenberg's pre-twelve-tone compositions. Here the return to an earlier and freer compositional outlook is underscored by the use of octave doublings, triadic harmonies, quotations from Beethoven, and, in passing, tonal progressions. In fact, there is very little about the *Ode* that would suggest Schoenberg's earlier twelve-tone method. One of the basic materials of the work, judging from the composer's sketches, is a symmetric hexachord having the pitch content C C♯ E F G♯ A. But only sporadically is it presented as a line or as the basis for creating an aggregate. When it appears, it is freely reordered and usually encountered in incomplete forms.

The *Ode* and other late works from the 1940s represent a summation and retrospective upon Schoenberg's entire accomplishment as a composer. They have little of the doctrinaire about them, none of the spirit of compulsion that led him earlier to declare, as in the text of his Choral Piece, Op. 27, No. 2, "Du sollst nicht, du mußt!" (Not "you may" but "you will"!). His late works touch with a certain nostalgia upon the elements of tonality, atonality, and twelve-tone composition, mixing them with ease. In these pieces we see a letting go of controls, a reversion perhaps to the intuitive practices of earlier times, but now set against a personal and artistic consciousness that had risen above the strict exploitation of system to return to a purer form of self-expression.

NOTES

Abbreviations

ASG Ernst Hilmar, ed. *Arnold Schönberg Gedenkausstellung*. Vienna: Universal Edition, 1974.

BSC Juliane Brand, Christopher Hailey, and Donald Harris, eds. and trans. *The Berg-Schoenberg Correspondence*. New York: W. W. Norton, 1986.

JASI *Journal of the Arnold Schoenberg Institute*.

SI Arnold Schoenberg. *Style and Idea*. Edited by Leonard Stein. Translated by Leo Black. Berkeley and Los Angeles: University of California Press, 1984.

1. Alma Mahler, *Gustav Mahler: Memories and Letters*, third ed., ed. Donald Mitchell, trans. Basil Creighton (Seattle: University of Washington Press, 1975), 77.
2. Arnold Schoenberg, "My Evolution" (1949), SI, 80.
3. The original German text is in Joachim Birke, "Richard Dehmel und Arnold Schönberg,"*Die Musikforschung* 11 (1958): 285. This and all other translations are by the author unless otherwise stated.
4. Ernst von Wolzogen, *Wie ich mich ums Leben brachte: Erinnerungen und Erfahrungen* (Brunswick and Hamburg: Georg Westermann, 1922), 217.
5. *ASG*, 179.
6. Heinrich Schenker, quoted in Hellmut Federhofer, *Heinrich Schenkers Verhältnis zu Arnold Schönberg*, Mitteilungen der Kommission für Musikforschung, no. 33 (Vienna: Österreichischen Akademie der Wissenschaften, 1981), 380.
7. Gustav Mahler, Richard Strauss, *Briefwechsel 1888–1911*, ed. Herta Blaukopf (Munich and Zurich: R. Piper, 1980), 122.
8. Arnold Schoenberg, "Versuch eines Tagesbuches," trans. Anita Luginbühl, *JASI* 9 (1986): 27.
9. The still-unpublished document is the archives of the Arnold Schönberg Center, Vienna.
10. The description of *Erwartung* is found in "New Music," *SI*, 105; the remark to Busoni is from a letter cited in Ferruccio Busoni, *Selected Letters*, trans. Antony Beaumont (New York: Columbia University Press, 1987), 389.
11. Alexander Zemlinsky, *Briefwechsel mit Arnold Schönberg, Anton Webern, Alban Berg, und Franz Schreker*, ed. Horst Weber, Briefwechsel der Wiener Schule, no. 1 (Darmstadt: Wissenschaftliche Buchgesellschaft, 1995), 256–57.
12. The text of the Requiem is found in Arnold Schoenberg, *Texte* (Vienna: Universal Edition, 1926), 31–36.
13. *BSC*, 103.
14. *BSC*, 60.
15. Schoenberg, "Versuch eines Tagesbuches," 39.
16. Schoenberg, letter of 8 April 1915, *BSC*, 233.
17. Arnold Schoenberg, quoted in *Arnold Schoenberg Letters*, ed. Erwin Stein, trans. Eithne Wilkins and Ernst Kaiser (New York: St. Martin's Press, 1965), 35.
18. See the edition and translation of the play by Moshe Lazar, *JASI* 17 (1994): 162–329.

19. Igor Stravinsky, quoted in Leonard Stein, ''Schoenberg and 'Kleine Modernsky,' '' in *Confronting Stravinsky: Man, Musician, and Modernist*, ed. Jann Pasler (Berkeley and Los Angeles: University of California Press, 1986), 322.

20. *SI*, 258–64.

21. *ASG*, 50.

22. *Arnold Schoenberg Letters*, 164.

23. *ASG*, 58.

24. Materials given to Nachod are published in facsimile in John A. Kimmey, Jr., *The Arnold Schoenberg–Hans Nachod Collection*, Detroit Studies in Music Bibliography, no. 41 (Detroit: Information Coordinators, 1979); all of the existing early works will be published in Schoenberg's *Sämtliche Werke* (Mainz and Vienna: Schott and Universal Edition, 1966–).

25. ''Program Notes to Verklärte Nacht,'' published in the booklet accompanying the recording *The Music of Arnold Schoenberg*, vol. 2, Columbia M2S 694 (1963).

26. ''Pelleas and Melisande: Notes'' published in the booklet accompanying the recording *The Music of Arnold Schoenberg*, vol. 2, Columbia M2S 694 (1963).

27. English translations of the short analysis are given by Mark DeVoto, *JASI* 16 (1993): 270–92, and by Derrick Puffett, *Music and Letters* 76 (1995): 250–64. The original, longer analysis is found in Alban Berg, *Sämtliche Werke*, ed. Rudolf Stephan and Regina Busch (Vienna: Universal Edition, 1994), part 3, vol. 1, 97–118.

28. Walter Frisch, *The Early Works of Arnold Schoenberg, 1893–1908* (Berkeley and Los Angeles: University of California Press, 1993), 142–44.

29. Arnold Schoenberg, ''Notes on the Four String Quartets,'' in Ursula von Rauchhaupt, ed., *Schoenberg, Berg, Webern: Die Streichquartette*, program booklet accompanying the recording *Neue Wiener Schule* (LaSalle Quartet), Deutsche Grammophon 419994-2 (1971): 33.

30. An English translation of the outline by Eugene Hartzell is in Rauchhaupt, ed., *Schoenberg, Berg, Webern: Die Streichquartette*, 236–37.

31. Arnold Schoenberg, ''My Evolution'' (1949), *SI*, 84.

32. *SI*, 49.

33. Albrecht Dümling, *Die fremden Klänge der hängenden Gärten: Die öffentliche Einsamkeit der neuen Musik am Beispiel von Arnold Schönberg und Stefan George* (Munich: Kindler, 1981): 198 and passim.

34. Arnold Schoenberg, quoted in Willi Reich, *Schoenberg: A Critical Biography*, trans. Leo Black (New York and Washington: Praeger, 1971), 48–49.

35. See Joseph Auner, ''Schoenberg's Aesthetic Transformations and the Evolution of Form in *Die glückliche Hand,*'' *JASI* 12 (1989): 103–28, and Auner, ''In Schoenberg's Workshop: Aggregates and Referential Collections in *Die glückliche Hand,*'' *Music Theory Spectrum* 18 (1996): 77–105.

36. Schoenberg, ''Versuch eines Tagesbuches,'' 14.

37. *ASG*, 351.

38. *ASG*, 48.

39. In his *Harmonielehre* Schoenberg advanced the term ''pantonal'' as an alternative, and in a lecture from around 1922 he used the term ''twelve-tone music'' (*Zwölftonmusik*), the latter quickly abandoned on account of its similarity to his twelve-tone method. The lecture is published in Rudolf Stephan, ''Ein frühes Dokument zur Entstehung der Zwölftonkomposition,'' in *Festschrift Arno Forchert zum 60. Geburtstag zum*

29. Dezember 1985, ed. Gerhard Allroggen and Detlef Altenburg (Kassel: Bärenreiter, 1986), 296–302.

40. Arnold Schoenberg, ''Composition with Twelve Tones'' (1941), *SI*, 216.

41. Arnold Schoenberg, *Structural Functions of Harmony*, rev. ed., ed. Leonard Stein (New York: W. W. Norton, 1969), 111–13.

42. Schoenberg, ''Composition with Twelve Tones,'' *SI*, 217.

43. Busoni, *Selected Letters*, 395.

44. Ibid., 383–99.

45. Ibid., 396.

46. See especially Arnold Schoenberg, ''New Music, Outmoded Music, Style and Idea,'' *SI*, 113–24, and ''National Music,'' *SI*, 169–72.

47. L. Sabanejew, ''Prometheus von Skrjabin,'' in *Der blaue Reiter*, ed. Wassily Kandinsky and Franz Marc (Munich: R. Piper, 1912), 62.

Alban Berg (1885–1935). Courtesy of the Arnold Schoenberg Institute.

5 ALBAN BERG

David Schroeder

On 1 July 1908 Alban Berg (1885–1935) wrote to his future wife Helene Nahowski about the way he had been spending his time: "In the afternoon I went to the art gallery. . . . In the evening I met Smaragda [his sister] at Altenberg's table in the Löwenbrau beer-cellar, then she went home with Ida [her friend], while I met Karl Kraus—Dr Fritz Wittels was also there, all very nice. At 3 a.m. we all went home, but I ran into Ida . . . and the two of us roistered on for the rest of the night!"[1] Löwenbrau was one of the haunts of the satirist and editor/writer of *Die Fackel* Karl Kraus and the eccentric and iconoclastic writer Peter Altenberg; they could also be found at the Café Central or on occasion at one of the other coffeehouses in Vienna. Unlike Arnold Schoenberg, Berg spent large amounts of time at the coffeehouses, and one should not underestimate the effects of the coffeehouse world on Berg the person and his works.

Vienna, a city of grandness, tradition, and decorum, stumbled into the twentieth century with a fatal sense of nostalgia. Beneath its fondness for the past and obsession with stability lurked menacing forces of disintegration, and out of Vienna's peculiar blend of myopia, sentimentality, and artifice there emerged some of the most extraordinary intellectual and artistic forces of the twentieth century. These individuals and schools of thought were not accidental in a city where they were essentially unwelcome, and much to the chagrin of the establishment they gave Vienna a new cultural reputation. A remarkable amount of this cultural activity took place in coffeehouses, with gurus such as Kraus, Altenberg, Karl Adler, or Gustav Klimt presiding over coteries at closely demarcated tables. The list of writers, painters, architects, composers, and psychoanalysts who populated these tables at the Cafés Imperial, Central, Museum, or Herrenhof reads like a who's who of early-twentieth-century giants: Arthur Schnitzler, Hermann Bahr, Felix Dörmann, Richard Beer-Hofmann, Felix Salten, Hugo von Hofmannsthal, Rainer Maria Rilke, Franz Werfel, Egon Friedell, Max Brod, Franz Kafka (occasionally), Oskar Kokoschka, Egon Schiele, Adolf Loos, Erich Korngold, and Sigmund Freud, to name but a few. Important movements emerged from the coffeehouses, including Jung-Wien (Young Vienna) in literature and the Secessionists in painting and architecture.

Among the writers, the vast majority were Jewish, and in many cases they all but lived at the coffeehouses. Not only did they have access to the best array of international newspapers and magazines the city could offer, good coffee, and a congenial atmosphere, but in space-strapped Vienna they had heated rooms where they could spend all day or night with no pressure to buy coffee or move on.[2] These productive idlers in many instances came from families with wealth; their fathers, having succeeded as merchants or manufacturers, often did not take it amiss that their sons had left that world for a cultured one. Allowances or inheritances in many cases kept them going, and even where extreme breaks had occurred, as with Altenberg, the flow of support did not necessarily cease. While the coffeehouse circles may have been circumscribed—one would not dare to sit at Kraus's table without an invitation, and some would have killed for that invitation—that did not prevent interaction among different schools or individuals. Berg's case was not unusual; he could number Altenberg, Klimt, Werfel, and Loos among his closest friends, as well as Kraus, Schnitzler, and Freud among his acquaintances. In many respects his interests and inclinations were shaped in this subversive, decadent, and defiant world, and that shaping often ran counter to the sterner influence of Schoenberg. Sorting out what Berg and Schoenberg had in common proves to be not entirely straightforward; while Berg presented a public image of unreserved reverence for his musical mentor and a private tone of obsequiousness in letters, his attitude toward Schoenberg at best can be described as ambivalent.

ALBAN BERG'S LIFE

There were times during the life of Alban Berg that money was scarce, such as after his father's death in 1900, during the postwar inflation of the early 1920s, and the last few years of his life when the Nazis prevented the performance of *Wozzeck*. Typically, though, wealth in his household was adequate to allow the young Berg to live a life of relative ease, free to spend his time reading avidly or frequenting coffeehouses instead of enduring the drudgery of employment. During short bouts of bureaucratic employment he could look forward to evenings at coffeehouses for refuge. Berg's father, Conrad Berg (1846–1900), moved in 1867 to Vienna from Nuremberg, where he married Johanna Braun. As an export merchant and bookseller, he fared well enough in business in the last years of the nineteenth century to allow him to purchase an estate in the country, the Berghof on the Ossiachersee in Carinthia. Berg's elder brothers, Hermann and Charley, both pursued careers in business.

Berg and his one younger sibling, his sister Smaragda, were very close and represented the artistic wing of the family (although Charley sang with passion). Both studied the piano with her governess, and both gravitated toward the same coffeehouse denizens, as Berg informed Helene in 1908 that Smaragda, as one of a group of attractive women, frequented the tables of Altenberg and Karl Kraus.[3] Since Helene had had her own strange relationship with Altenberg, these words undoubtedly had special meaning. Relationships with Altenberg could put one very close to the edge, and Smaragda, who eventually acknowledged her homosexuality, may have been better suited than most of Altenberg's women to cope with his peculiarities. Berg himself has interestingly been compared by H. F. Redlich with Oscar Wilde, "whom he curiously resembled in the dionysiac femininity of his features."[4] Redlich does not pursue the idea, but from what we now know of the theme of bisexuality running through Berg's works, as it does for many of his literary and artistic friends and contemporaries, it clearly deserves greater attention, which it will receive later in this chapter.

Some have expressed surprise and others disappointment that for Berg, unlike Schoenberg or Anton Webern, no substantial biography as yet exists, especially considering the linkages that have been drawn in recent decades between Berg's life and works.[5] Douglas Jarman has issued a challenge to the future Berg biographer, and considering the difficulties of getting the information straight from the vast array of resources, placing Berg in his cultural context, and linking the person with the apparently autobiographical elements of his works, it should surprise no one that the task has not yet been completed.[6] Only a tiny percentage of Berg's vast correspondence has been published, and even the large and extraordinarily important Schoenberg-Berg-Webern correspondence, which is available in typescript, may never actually be published.[7]

Beyond the material itself lies the infinitely more challenging matter of making sense of it. Our fascination with secret programs or autobiographical aspects of Berg's works may very well have put us off the track from other considerations, including how real some of these "events" of Berg's life may have been, such as the alleged affair with Hanna Fuchs-Robettin. We may dislike the fact that Berg's wife, who survived him by over forty years, along with former pupils and confidants, may have abridged what they knew to control the impression of Berg that survived, although this should not surprise us when we consider that the same thing had happened with an earlier composer in Vienna, Mozart. Yet Berg himself has presented by far the greater challenge, again just as Mozart did, by wearing exceptionally skillful epistolary masks in his diverse correspondence. If we cannot approach this without bias, we easily fall into the subtle traps that Berg sets. One can almost imagine the delight that Berg would have received from seeing posterity attempting to sort out the confusing and contradictory impressions resulting from his secret programs or letters.

Alban Berg in 1904, Age 19, Vienna. Courtesy of Picture Archive and Portrait Collection, Austrian National Library.

Like many bright adolescents, Berg had considerable difficulty reconciling his own educational aspirations with the stodgy curriculum of his school. From what we know of his appetite for reading, his favorite works tended not to be those in the school syllabus. He appeared also to have an aversion to writing school essays, not, one suspects, because of any lack of ability, which revealed itself amply in his letters from a very early age as well as in his later essays, but probably because of an unwillingness to master the tortured prose taught in school. His friend Paul Hohenberg seemed not to mind these types of exercises, perhaps enjoying the absurdity of the challenge, and on occasions agreed to write Berg's essays for him.[8] The closer Berg came to completing school, the worse matters became; in the end he had to repeat the sixth and seventh levels, finishing school belatedly at the age of nineteen.

The late adolescent years were a troubled time for Berg. The poor health that plagued him for the rest of his life started in 1900 with his first asthma attack, and added to that were bouts of depression that resulted in a suicide attempt in 1903. If one puts together his unstable health and emotions along with his desire to become a poet at this time, immersing himself in the decadent works of Wilde, Maeterlinck, Altenberg, and Wedekind, in many respects creating in himself the spirit of their works, Berg can be seen in his youthful years to be living very much on the edge.

Moving in the Altenberg circle brought Berg into contact with one of the beautiful young women who surrounded the poet at the Café Central, Helene Nahowski. Altenberg had singled her out especially, inventing her for himself in his poems "H. N." and "Besuch im einsamen Park," engendering her with the peculiarly sensual but asexual spiritual features he believed a woman of her appearance should embody.[9] When he observed a more corporeal relationship developing between Helene and Berg, he could not help but take it amiss, lamenting their sellout to physical attraction in "Bekanntschaft." She appeared to be much more conventional than either Altenberg or Berg could grasp, and her preference clearly shifted to Berg, with whom she could imagine some measure of normalcy. Berg had his own illusions about her, but the relationship developed into one of genuine love, even if she continued to play the role of muse for him; until the day they married he could not entirely rid himself of the notion of her as a type of idealized prostitute that Kraus and Altenberg had so elegantly portrayed in literature. The long and intense correspondence between them from their meeting in 1907 until Berg's death almost three decades later gives us one of the richest accounts of Berg's passion for all the arts, his views on his own and others' works, and his opinions of the people around him.[10]

The intrusion of war in 1914 had a profound effect on every Austrian, and certainly on the artistic frequenters of the coffeehouses who had to grapple with its moral implications and the changes to their life-style. Needless to say, opinion was divided, and no one attacked the war effort more relentlessly than Karl Kraus. Berg had originally felt an obligation toward the Austrian cause, but within a short while came over to Kraus's way of thinking. Originally deemed physically unfit for service, Berg wrote to Hohenberg at the front, "I envy you since you can take part in this great cause."[11] Because of the shortage of men, Berg later found himself in a military clerical position, and his attitude quickly changed. Writing to Erwin Schulhoff in 1919, he leaves the impression that he had become an antimilitarist as early as 1914, and he singles out Kraus as his inspiration at that time. During the war years Berg started working on *Wozzeck*, a work that in many respects reflected his attitude to the war: "There is a bit of me in his character, since I have been spending these war years just as dependent on people I hate, have been in chains, sick, captive, resigned, in fact humiliated."[12] Berg's work in composition progressed with excruciating slowness, and prospects for financial security after the war looked dim. Inflation cut into his income from the family estate, and he was forced to sell the beloved Berghof to maintain his apartment in Vienna. It took five years after the war to complete *Wozzeck* and another two to get it performed, but the premiere of this work, certainly the most stunning operatic achievement of the early twentieth century (and probably the entire century), catapulted Berg into international focus as one of the leading composers. He traveled extensively from 1925 until the early 1930s supervising performances and lived securely during this time as the royalties came in.

That security ended in 1933 when cultural policies of the new Nazi government of Germany excluded works such as *Wozzeck* that were deemed to be culturally unfit. Berg completed the short score for his new opera *Lulu* by 1934, but prospects for its performance were even dimmer. This new world, with its linkage of art works with propaganda and its treatment of non-Aryans such as Schoenberg, Paul Pisk, and Hanns Jelinek, plunged Berg into depression that made work all but impossible. His return to financial stability in the late 1920s and early 1930s had allowed him to purchase a new country home, Waldhaus, at Auen near Velden on the Wörthersee. This, along with his purchase of a car (a Ford) in 1930, afforded one of his few pleasures in his last years, allowing some refuge from a world gone mad. Here he composed most of *Lulu* as well as the Violin Concerto. Shortly after completing the Violin Concerto, he became seriously ill, in part because of an insect sting that brought on a carbuncle, and died of general septicemia on 24 December 1935. On hearing the sad news, Schoenberg wrote consolingly to Helene from Hollywood on 1 January 1936: "I still cannot believe that my dear Alban is gone. I still talk to him in my thoughts, as before, and imagine his answers, and it still seems to me as if he were only as far away as Europe is from America. And I can imagine your pain, since I know how affectionately the two of you always lived together. It is terrible, that he had to die so young, particularly from the human, but also from the artistic standpoint."[13]

FRIENDS, ACQUAINTANCES, AND THE AESTHETIC LIFE

Of the various leaders among writers, painters, architects, and other fields, a remarkable number were friends or acquaintances of Berg, including Altenberg, Kraus, Werfel, Schnitzler, Klimt, Kokoschka, Loos, Walter Gropius, Alma Mahler, and Freud. His interaction with these people profoundly influenced his life and works, and one therefore needs to know something about these individuals to chart the nature of their effect on Berg. In a number of cases specific works of theirs provided models or aesthetic direction for certain of Berg's own works, such as the *Altenberg Lieder*, Op. 4. Less overt but nevertheless arguable are Schnitzler for the Three Orchestral Pieces, Op. 6, Kraus for *Wozzeck*, and Werfel for the Chamber Concerto.

Amid these various shaping forces on Berg, one should not look for a single unifying factor that would allow for a particular definition of artistic direction. While decadence or other trends may be apparent, Berg's own interests and inclinations were as diverse and contradictory as those of the people with whom he came into contact (or read), and this multiplicity is reflected in his own works. The influence of Altenberg proved to be especially powerful, as it yielded Berg's first mature work, the *Altenberg Lieder*, with all hints of student exercise now left behind.

Berg's relationship with Altenberg was complex. While the two were friendly and Berg saw him for a time as an artistic mentor, Altenberg's relationship with Helene and his almost slanderous poetic representation of Berg in "Bekanntschaft" proved troublesome. Yet Berg always spoke of him with great respect and even visited the poet at the Steinhof sanitorium during one of his bouts of mental instability.[14] In his personal library Berg had virtually all of Altenberg's books, and some of these, including *Fechsung, Nachfechsung, Mein Lebensabend*, and *Vita Ipsa*, are among the most heavily annotated of all Berg's books. From these works and the person behind them, Berg discovered the possibilities of artistic autobiography, although not in any conventional sense. Rather than creating his works from himself, Altenberg sought to create himself in his works. His world ultimately became an aesthetic one, taking the form of a literary reality, and the person of the artist was created in the aesthetic process. While his links with nineteenth-century romanticism remained strong, his readers were no longer in the position of discovering the person of the artist in the work, since the work itself proclaimed the most vivid artistic and personal reality.

Berg's biographers have not taken kindly to Altenberg. Redlich, for one, looked at him with moral indignation and felt a need to dismiss him as an insignificant dabbler on the lunatic fringe. Redlich believed it necessary to tell us that Altenberg "died in Vienna, half-forgotten, in 1919," and that he "delighted in inventing slightly scandalous texts to picture postcards, in an embarrassing mixture of obscenity and tenderness."[15] Redlich's unwillingness to read the texts seriously parallels a 1913 review that refers to "these gaily nonsensical

Helene Berg, Alma Mahler-Werfel, Franz Werfel, and Alban Berg. Courtesy of Alban Berg Foundation.

postcard texts,'' quoted approvingly by Willi Reich.[16] These are curious dismissals, probably more strategic than ignorant, of the poet who might have won the Nobel Prize for literature had it not been for the outbreak of World War I.[17]

One suspects that Schoenberg also may have regarded the texts with embarrassment and distaste: he not only refused to bolster Berg's confidence after the uproar during the performance of two of the songs of the *Altenberg Lieder* on 31 March 1913 but also took his pupil to task over these songs. Berg seldom discussed Altenberg in his correspondence with Schoenberg, in contrast to his frequent evocations of Strindberg or Balzac, possibly fearing that Altenberg's decadence would not meet with his musical mentor's favor. Altenberg came up more often as a topic in his letters to Webern, who was attracted by aspects of Altenberg's use of language. For Berg, Altenberg appears to have been very close to the heart of his own artistic outlook, and, one can surmise, he was not prepared to expose the intimate nature of this to Schoenberg's possible censure.

For Altenberg, the creation of an aesthetic world went far beyond an indulgence in literature and an intertwining of life and art. The aesthetic world was so pervasive that it required a change of identity, a rejection of his former existence and the formulation of a new reality. The strongest representation of this transformation lay in his name, which he changed from Richard Engländer to Peter Altenberg. While at a resort called Altenberg on the river Danube, he became attracted to the thirteen-year-old tomboyish daughter of the Lecher family, Bertha, nicknamed Peter by her brothers.[18] Throughout his life Altenberg indulged in erotic fetishes, and he had something of a Lolita complex for girls of Bertha's (Peter's) age. More striking, however, was his apparent identification with her (him), a phenomenon described by Edward Timms: "By adopting this boy-girl's name, he was implicitly repudiating the 'masculine' role prescribed for him by society and initiating that cultivation of a 'feminine' sensibility that is so characteristic of his writings."[19]

Altenberg's fragmented literary style, with short pieces in verse or prose poetry in the manner of Baudelaire, covers a wide range of matters pertaining to the soul. Such themes as the blending of masculine and feminine, the cultivation of freespiritedness, and the virtues of isolation are pointedly evident in the passages Berg used from "Texte auf Ansichtskarten" in *Neues Altes* (1911). We should not be surprised by Berg's turn later in his career to Baudelaire in the Lyric Suite and *Der Wein.*

As a creature of urban life, Altenberg looked at nature in a romantic sense: nature could be a salvation from the destructive powers of cities. By experiencing nature and stripping away urban encumbrances, one could go through a cleansing process and be transformed onto a higher level of human and spiritual existence. This notion appealed especially to Berg, who quoted his friend's idea and its relation to nature in various letters to Helene.[20]

The *Frauenfrage* (question of women's rights) was a raging issue at the turn of the century, and Altenberg saw women in much the same way that he did nature, both of them playing an essential role in refining and ennobling the soul. His defense of women and creation of a *Frauenkult* appear to stand in contrast to Otto Weininger's blatant misogyny. Weininger's *Geschlecht und Charakter* was one of the most popular books in Vienna during the first two decades of the twentieth century; Berg heavily annotated his own copy. Altenberg's view has much in common with that of his (and Berg's) friend Gustav Klimt, whose own *Frauenkult* focuses on beauty and the essential need that men have for women. Unlike Weininger, in whose bisexual model femininity represents weakness, Altenberg could not envisage the role of the male poet without integration of the *Frauenseele* (woman's soul).

Among Altenberg's numerous portraits of feminine characteristics, most striking are his treatments of prepubescent girls. In "Zwölf" from "See-Ufer" (*Wie ich es sehe*), the heroine combines "femme fragile" and instinctual animallike features. She has strength, resolution, and vitality, in contrast to older women, and has not yet become jaded or hypocritical. Sexual awareness leads to a loss of innocence, naturalness, honesty, and freespiritedness that can never be recaptured.[21] The poet re-creates this state of innocence and freedom, reentering this dreamlike world and advancing it as a reality more real than the fallen state of the normal, materialistic, adult world. Berg's own subscription to these ideas unfolds, in letters to Helene, through references to "ideal" or "pure" reality as an antidote to "brutal materialism."[22] Those who seek and discover the inner reality of the aesthetic world, according to Altenberg, will surely find themselves at odds with the rest of society, sometimes alienated, sometimes isolated, or at best in solitude. Berg had views on isolation similar to Altenberg's, although he believed that Helene shared this sense of isolation with him.[23]

Altenberg, of course, was not the only literary influence on Berg, and the decadence, bisexuality, and views on nature coming from this quarter are tempered by the more stern realism, precision of language, and social criticism of Karl Kraus. In Berg's letters to Helene, one can see the strength of his feelings about Kraus. A reference to Kraus in 1907 lists him among other literary giants such as Strindberg, Wilde, and Wedekind. On various occasions Berg spoke with great enthusiasm of *Die Fackel* as well as Kraus's ideas and tenacious adherence to principles. His acceptance of Kraus's style and format for his own essay writing stands out especially. Even Schoenberg, the composer perhaps least susceptible to influences this century has seen, admitted the following: "In the dedication of a copy of my *Harmonielehre* which I sent to Karl Kraus, I said, 'I have perhaps learned more from you than one is permitted to learn if one wishes to remain independent.' "[24] Webern, too, who did not share Berg's reverence for Kraus, enthused over the possible application of Kraus's language to music.

Kraus spent his entire adult life in Vienna, and that city gave rise to his biting social commentary and iconoclastic view of the world. In 1899 he published the first issue of his satirical journal *Die Fackel*, which with only minor interruptions appeared on a trimonthly basis until February 1936. In this journal, mostly written by Kraus himself, one finds an extraordinary breadth of subject matter and a highly refined and eccentric writing style. It presents one of the most comprehensive chronicles of Vienna during those years, and the care in writing bestowed on *Die Fackel* by Kraus made it a model not only for other writers but composers as well. Along with satirizing the press, profiteering industrialists, or various peculiar Viennese customs, Kraus also addressed issues such as prostitution, bisexuality, death, nature, and spirituality. Berg followed Kraus's every word, spoken or written, with dogged devotion, running his views on each issue through his own mind as though in a lively exchange of ideas with Kraus himself.

Of Berg's various literary friends and acquaintances, the major writer closest to him was undoubtedly Franz Werfel. The liaison of Berg's dear friend Alma Mahler (affectionately called Almschi by the Bergs) with Werfel began in 1918, while she and Walter Gropius were still married, and they ultimately married in 1929. Werfel soon became a part of the intimate friendship between Alma and the Bergs, and this took a new twist in 1925. Berg visited Prague in 1925, Werfel's hometown, and stayed with Werfel's sister, Hanna Fuchs-Robettin, and her family; at that point the "affair" began. Both Alma and Werfel acted as emissaries between Berg and Hanna, facilitating the exchange of correspondence.[25]

Werfel, a writer of plays, novels, poems, and essays, had an active interest in music; he contributed to the volume commemorating Schoenberg's sixtieth birthday, and he wrote at length about Verdi and Wagner as well as shorter studies of Mahler and Zemlinsky. Music played a crucial role in his own literary works, just as it did for Schnitzler, George, and Strindberg. He frequently discussed music with Berg, leaving Berg occasionally irked by his comments. Aside from music, they shared common views on literature and drama as well. At this time Werfel thoroughly disliked naturalistic drama, which he saw as static and dull. In contrast to it, he praised the type of fantasy so evident in the late works of Strindberg, regarding them as truly "theatrical."[26] On Strindberg, Berg fully agreed with Werfel. Berg's attitude toward Wagner underwent a notable shift around 1920, and Werfel may have had some bearing on this change. In early letters to Helene, Berg expressed only admiration for Wagner, but in 1923 he spoke disparagingly of "this antiquated Wagner music." Werfel had no use for Wagner, attacking him throughout his career. He railed at the length of Wagner's operas, using terms such as "bloated excess" and "garrulous monotony."[27]

If Berg had any doubts about his friendship with Werfel, these did not last long. Some years later Schoenberg entertained the possibility of an opera on a Werfel text and tested the idea of a collaboration with Werfel on Berg. Berg supported the idea enthusiastically, replying to Schoenberg with the following: "From what I know of Werfel (and I know him well) I'm convinced he would consider it a great pleasure and honor to work with you. . . . Should I mention something to him about it?"[28]

Not only did Werfel have strong views on music, but Berg did on literature as well, sometimes providing extended critiques of Werfel's works to the author. The friendship with Werfel remained strong in spite of Werfel's falling out with Kraus. Werfel, for his part, championed Berg's music in spite of his own musical passion for the operas of Verdi. He and Alma would travel great distances to attend Berg's premieres, and in 1937, on the occasion of the world premiere of *Lulu* in Zurich, Werfel gave a lecture entitled "Vorrede auf Alban Berg."

Berg, of course, rubbed shoulders with numerous other writers as well, including great ones such as Schnitzler and the lesser-known Hermann Watznauer and Soma Morgenstern. Watznauer, one of his earliest mentors, who became a father figure for Berg after the death of Berg's own father, undoubtedly led Berg down literary paths he would not otherwise have discovered as quickly. Schnitzler's treatment of Viennese sexual customs, prostitution, and the *Frauenfrage* stood at the highest possible literary level, and Berg appears to have responded to this with his own musical version of "Reigen." Morgenstern did not meet Berg until 1924, but he quickly became one of Berg's principal advisors on the thorny matter of selecting an opera libretto after *Wozzeck*. At one point Berg considered Morgenstern's play *Im Kunstkreis*, a work involving a master-pupil relationship with which he could identify. Another possibility was Solomon Anski's *Dybbuk*, which Morgenstern had seen in a Yiddish production and considered too Jewish for Berg to attempt. Berg proposed that they travel together to Vilna, where Morgenstern could help facilitate Berg's full exposure to Jewish culture; Morgenstern appeared reluctantly willing, but the plan came to nothing when the rights to the play could not be secured.[29]

OTHER LITERARY INTERESTS

Given the number of personal references in both the instrumental and vocal works, one may be tempted to assume that Berg wrote his works to fulfill purely personal purposes. Awareness of these references may add a level of fascination to the works in question, but, at the same time, it has skewed the pursuit of interpretation, leaving the misguided impression that we have discovered the full interpretive essence of the work in question when we know the secret program. If we consider Berg in the context of his contemporaries, and particularly those literary writers whom he idolized, different possibilities emerge. Berg's passion for literature and its effect on him cannot be doubted. Anyone who has read his letters to his wife or his correspondence with Schoenberg and Webern will be struck by the strength of his opinions on various writers and their works. We also have other strong indications of Berg's literary interests, including an extensive set of quotations he prepared while still fairly young, and his own annotations in the books of his still partially intact personal library. The authors whose works he most heavily marked include Strindberg, Baudelaire, Kraus, Goethe, Altenberg, Balzac, Poe, and Weininger.

Some of these writers, to be sure, often created works of a highly personalized nature. Not only did they put forward their innermost spiritual experiences, but they also built into their works their most intimate acquaintances as well as actual experiences. It would, however, be a mistake to assume that they did this for purely individual and cathartic reasons. Strindberg, possibly Berg's favorite writer, undoubtedly represents the extreme example of this type of writer, as he himself makes abundantly clear with the following words: "If you only knew what sort of life this is, in which one must, as a writer must, strip oneself naked in public, how he must like a vampire suck blood from his friends, from his nearest and dearest, from himself! And if he doesn't, he isn't a writer."[30] But clearly he had a higher purpose. In the *Blue Book*, much loved and heavily annotated by Berg, Strindberg notes that "in order to be able to describe life in all its aspects and dangers he [the writer] must first have lived it. . . . A real poet must sacrifice his person for his work."[31] But the sensitive reader will discover, as Evert Sprinchorn has, that "when Strindberg seemed to be most subjective and most personal, utterly lost in himself, he was actually most in touch with world affairs and most deeply enmeshed in the network. His way of anticipating the developing and emergent pattern was to weave himself into it."[32]

Much the same could be said of Berg's other favorite writers. Altenberg affirmed in his *Nachlass*, as Josephine Simpson notes, "that the task of the poet is to aid his fellow beings in the process of self-discovery and fulfillment. His writing, he suggests, has a therapeutic and cathartic function, not only for himself, but more importantly for his readers.''[33] In later years Baudelaire provided the stimulus for Berg that Altenberg had earlier. Berg read everything he could find in German translation, and he also set this poet to music in *Der Wein* as well as secretly in the Lyric Suite. A book on Baudelaire owned by Berg was *Der Leidensweg des Dichters Baudelaire* by François Porché, who observed that ''it was hard for Baudelaire to create characters distinct from himself'' or in any way to separate his life from his works. At the same time, Porché stressed that Baudelaire the critic argued ''that poetry is essentially philosophic, but that it must be so involuntarily.''[34] Even Goethe, much discussed in the Berg-Webern correspondence, did not disguise the fact that his *Pandora* (well known to Berg from Kraus's frequent public readings of it) ''owed its substance to his passion for a girl forty years his junior and that such a passion could find no expression except a sublimated one in the form of art.''[35] At the same time, no one would doubt that *Pandora* serves a much higher, universal purpose. There can be no question that the type of personal/universal duality common to virtually all of Berg's contemporaries also applies to Berg.

We know of the extraordinary breadth of Berg's interest in literature through a number of sources, and one of the most revealing of these is his correspondence. We find this in Berg's earliest letters, written before he reached the age of twenty, to his friends Hohenberg and Watznauer. During the summers of 1903 and 1904 Frida Semler, an American who studied at Wellesley College, resided at the Berghof as a paying guest while her father conducted business in Austria. Since Berg spent his summers there as well, they became close friends, and she was able to report in a memoir on Berg his reading habits during those years. She noted that ''he was reading volume after volume of modern poetry to find words for songs, and he wrote many things that summer that I thought exquisite. . . . In the evenings we read Ibsen aloud with divided parts. In 1903 Ibsen was a discovery. . . . It was in the second summer that we all read—not aloud—Schnitzler's *Reigen* and Wedekind's *Erdgeist*.''[36] In subsequent letters they exchanged, Wedekind, Ibsen, and Wilde were much discussed; in one dated 19 November 1907, Berg made his attitude clear: ''Let us discuss literature a bit: Wedekind and the new school—in modern works the accent is on sensuality. . . . And this is the way it should be. We finally have recognized our error: sensuality is not a weakness, nor is it a loosening of our own free will, but rather a strengthening of our entire being, a force which is within us.''[37]

Berg could not share ideas such as these with Schoenberg, with whom he had been studying for three years by this point. He did not avoid literature in his long letters to Schoenberg, but conscious of his teacher's preferences and sharp disapproval, Berg looked for common ground and praised only those writers where that could be found. Some writers appealed to the sensual and the spiritual, such as Balzac, and when writing to Schoenberg, Berg could enthuse about the spiritual and androgynous *Seraphita*, which Schoenberg intended to incorporate in an oratorio around 1912 and then a Mahlerian symphonic project two years later (neither materialized, but *Die Jakobsleiter* emerged from them). He could also discuss Strindberg and Kraus, both of whom had sufficient breadth to offer something to a moralist as well as a sensualist, with Schoenberg.

Berg could write much more freely to Webern about his literary preferences, Webern being a fellow student and closer to his age, even though Webern too did not necessarily share his views. Once again, they could share enthusiasm for certain writers, although for different reasons, Goethe and Strindberg standing foremost among these. Both composers had a deep admiration for Goethe's *Farbenlehre* (Theory of color), and in 1929 Berg sent Webern a copy. Berg had noted certain passages in the introduction, and Webern was delighted that Berg shared his own views on the work.[38] In general, though, Berg preferred Goethe's more sensuous literary works, including *Faust*, Part I, *Die Wahlverwandtschaften*, and *Pandora*.

For Berg, Strindberg stood as nothing short of a literary god, and Schoenberg and Webern agreed. All three had plans to set works of Strindberg to music, although only Webern actually followed through on this, using a fragment from *The Ghost Sonata* as the text for his song "Schien mir's, als ich sah die Sonne" (Op. 12, No. 3). The influence of Strindberg on writers and musicians in Vienna during the first two decades of the twentieth century should not be underestimated. Strindberg had a champion at this time in Karl Kraus; when Kraus ceased accepting contributions from other writers for *Die Fackel* in 1912, writing the entire journal himself, he nevertheless continued to publish pieces by Strindberg for some time after that date.

An important factor setting Strindberg apart from the other writers admired by Berg was his use of music as the structural or aesthetic basis for some of his plays. While Strindberg drew his musical inspiration from a number of composers, the one who for him towered above all others was Beethoven, and a small number of works by Beethoven had a bearing on his plays. The Piano Sonata Op. 31, No. 2 (first and third movements); the Trio Op. 70, No. 1 (second movement); and the Piano Sonata Op. 10, No. 3 (second movement) stand out. All of these have one feature in common: the key of D minor. Passages from the slow movement of Op. 10, No. 3, are to be played between some of the scenes of *To Damascus*, Part I, a work in which the layout of the scenes as well as the contents of the central scene form a strict palindrome. Schoenberg at one time had planned to set this work to music, and in a letter to Berg encouraging the setting of a dramatic work, his one proviso was that Berg should avoid certain works of Strindberg, including this one, because of his own plans.[39]

The play *Crimes and Crimes* draws on the third movement of Op. 31, No. 2, and Strindberg went so far as to claim that the entire play uses this movement for its structure.[40] While that may be true, a much more direct connection stands out: Strindberg calls for a passage from the beginning of the development to be played during the play. Berg was well aware of this quotation, informing Webern in 1912 that he had just read the play. After quoting Strindberg's directions for the use of measures 96–107, he continues: "I cannot, my dear friend, remember anything of this finale, and since I do not have it along, perhaps you would be so good as to tell me how the first measure and measure 96 go. This relationship of Strindberg to the music of Beethoven is of tremendous interest to me.''[41]

Another play, *The Ghost Sonata*, derives, according to Strindberg, from Beethoven's ''Ghost Trio'' and ''Ghost Sonata.''[42] By ''Ghost Trio'' he refers to Op. 70, No. 1, which was called the ''Gespenstertrio'' during the nineteenth century because of its middle movement. The Beethoven sonata that he labels the ''Ghost Sonata'' is Op. 31, No. 2, and here Strindberg invents his own designation. Once again, Berg was well aware of Strindberg's epithets. Strindberg had used them in a letter to his German translator, Emil Schering, and Berg prominently underscored these remarks with pencil markings in his own copy of the correspondence. In 1925 Berg sent a copy of this volume of letters to Schoenberg as a birthday gift.

While Berg may have felt the need to disguise his true sensualist leanings when writing to Schoenberg or Webern, that was unnecessary in his large correspondence with Helene, herself a member of Altenberg's inner circle. In fact, the sensualist Helene had posed for a picture that Altenberg undoubtedly added to his notorious collection of nude photographs of his favorite women.[43] In Berg's earliest letters to Helene, he identifies Strindberg, Ibsen, Nietzsche, Maeterlinck, Balzac, Dostoevsky, Kraus, Altenberg, Wedekind, Hauptmann, and Wilde as his favorite writers. In 1907 he saw Ibsen and Nietzsche as the giants, and Strindberg stood first among those in the shadow of these two.[44] Within two years he had reordered his priorities, elevating Strindberg to the status of a literary god. While Berg similarly elevated Maeterlinck, he later fell from favor, unlike Strindberg, whose stature never diminished in Berg's estimation. Berg, who was especially fond of Strindberg's autobiographical works, considered him to be one of the most outstanding people of his time.[45]

Berg had a voracious appetite for reading in his late adolescent years, at which time he fully intended to be a poet. The impact of this reading on him was unusual, for in these writers Berg saw the possibility of another realm of existence; through them he found access to an inner world not unlike that already described in relation to Altenberg. Entry into this world involved much more than passive reading, and Berg took active steps to make it a part of his higher reality, both in his own poetic endeavors and in attempts to organize his thoughts on a variety of subjects evoked by the works he was reading. This organization took the form of a collection of quotations from a wide range of authors, among them Goethe, Jean Paul Richter, Kraus, Wedekind, Schopenhauer, Altenberg, and Wilde, entered in twelve neatly arranged notebooks.[46] In all, there are 232 authors listed in Berg's index, including current Austrian and German writers, great writers of the nineteenth century, and writers of the more distant past, reaching back to classical Greece and Rome. By Berg's own numbering there are 2,061 quotations.

In the notebooks he covers hundreds of subjects, sometimes in clusters that are related, but often in no particular order. The quotations are all carefully identified as to author, title, part or section of a book, and page number. Women's issues dominate Book 1, and almost all the quotations are by Goethe. Subjects in Book 1 include poets, mysteries, religion, belief, inner life, spiritual life, art, truth and lying, kissing, longing, and the originality of works.

Each notebook begins with the title "Von der Selbsterkenntnis." This title of the project bears significance, as it implies that the books have special personal importance for Berg, and it gives an early indication of the unusual value he placed on literature. In spite of his filing-cabinet approach to the organization and retrievability of the quotations, it appears that they served a highly personal function. In a lengthy letter to Frida Semler, dated 1907, he professed some knowledge of "human nature in general, and the feminine soul in particular," but admitted that "this knowledge I have learned more from literature than from personal experience."[47] While some might dismiss knowledge acquired in this manner, regarding learning from books as less valid than the actual experience of life, for Berg it was very much the opposite. He believed that his intuition was directly associated with his knowledge of literature, and his repertory of literary quotations could quite rightly be labeled "self-knowledge."

In these notebooks he produced a compendium of thought on virtually every subject important to a young artist searching for meaning, creating an inner world and a sense of himself that resonated with the great literary minds of the past and present. The inclination for such creation would not grow weaker as he became older; if anything, it intensified. That which shaped him early in life determined his works as well and belonged to the inner world that Berg shared with his literary accomplices. Altenberg was clearly one of these accomplices, and in fact the arrangement of Berg's notebooks bears a similarity to the presentation of material in Altenberg's own works, such as *Was der Tag mir zuträgt*, which appeared at about the same time that Berg's literary project began. In the second edition of this book (1902), the second item is a type of autobiographical sketch; it informs the reader that Altenberg's writing is not art but a series of "Extrakte des Lebens" (extracts of life), which in this case covers subjects from the emergence of a new species of man to the transformation achievable through eating easily digested foods.[48]

While Berg's collection of quotations embraces numerous writers, certain authors appear with marked frequency, revealing his cultural and spiritual biases. The fact that Goethe dominates the first book reflects Berg's youthful reading and education. In the case of Ibsen, heavily quoted in the first three books, Berg was enormously taken by him, in part because of Ibsen's dogged adherence to ideals. But enthusiasm for Ibsen did not last. Strindberg, on the other hand, he quotes much less than Ibsen, no doubt because the works of Strindberg (who was twenty years younger than Ibsen) became available in German considerably later than those of the Norwegian playwright, although Strindberg, soon became Berg's favorite writer. Quotations by Kraus can be found in every book but the first. Other writers often quoted by Berg include Altenberg, Franz Grillparzer,

Alban Berg's studio at Trauttmansdorffgasse 27, Vienna. Courtesy of Library of Congress.

Nietzsche, Schnitzler, Theodor Storm, Wedekind, Wilde, Weininger (whose *Geschlecht und Charakter* dominates Book 7), and numerous others from the past and present.

After Berg's death in 1935, Helene survived him by over forty years and continued to live at their apartment at 27 Trauttmansdorffgasse in the thirteenth district of Vienna near the Schönbrunn Palace. Following her death in 1976, the apartment became the base for the Alban Berg Foundation, which has preserved it much as Helene left it. One of the most important aspects of that preservation concerns Berg's library, and the books today remain more or less in the arrangement on the shelves in which Berg left them. This is an exceptionally well-stocked library, with the complete works of various of his favorites such as Strindberg, Goethe, Baudelaire (in George's German adaptation), Georg Büchner, and Poe (also in German), and hundreds of individual volumes by numerous other writers. Not only can one see the range of books that he read, but one also gets a sense of the nature of his reading habits.

Berg read with a pencil in hand, underlining passages and bracketing or marking other passages in the margins, as well as jotting a few words or longer annotations in the margins, responding immediately to the content read. In some books, such as ones by Strindberg, Altenberg, and Weininger, over half the pages of each contain annotations. In others there are annotations on as many as one hundred pages or as few as one. Many books, of course, have no annotations at all. From this material one is overwhelmed by the breadth of his reading, the depth of his penetration, and the focus of his interests.

STUDENT AND COLLEAGUE OF SCHOENBERG

Posterity has developed an image of the young Berg as an idler and dilettante, satisfied with a smattering of knowledge of literature, able to fumble his way through some of the piano repertoire, and too lazy even to write his own school assignments. The myth further has it that he was rescued from amateurishness and indolence by Schoenberg in 1904, when he began to study formally with the man who would give him a rigorous musical education until 1911. From that point on, Berg is seen as the staunchest of Schoenberg's supporters, eternally grateful to and forever a disciple of the man who salvaged him from a misspent youth of coffeehouses and dabbling with art, supplying him, as one study puts it, with "the discipline which Berg vitally needed to develop his character."[49] Some of this, of course, is true. It fails, though, to capture the conflict that Berg experienced as Schoenberg's pupil and later his colleague, attempting to reconcile his own aesthetic views with the foreign ones emanating from Schoenberg. That is not to say that Schoenberg forced his views on Berg or any other pupil, expecting him to follow in the master's footsteps. Schoenberg knew perfectly well that it was bad enough for the world to have one Schoenberg, and the last thing it needed was imitations. He not only encouraged but insisted that his best pupils develop independence and distinctiveness; at the same time, he used subtle means of letting them know if they were straying into regions he found unacceptable, and in the case of Berg he continued this long after the lessons ended in 1911. In the myth we have accepted of Berg's youth, fostered by those who refuse to take writers like Altenberg seriously and look at the early masterpiece the *Altenberg Lieder* exclusively in musical terms, we have very much misjudged Berg's commitment to an aesthetic outlook fundamentally at odds with Schoenberg's. This relationship needs to be understood with that conflict in mind.

As Schoenberg's pupil, Berg encountered not only a rigorous musical regimen, firmly grounding him in musical techniques of the previous two centuries before moving on to composition, but advice and criticism on virtually all aspects of life. Schoenberg, no doubt sensing Berg's inclination toward literary bohemianism, attempted to correct that by assuming a paternal role, hoping to rectify what he perceived as Berg's weakness of character. That included fixing Berg's convoluted writing style as well as getting him to dress properly.[50] The specifics of the musical instruction have been well documented by Rosemary Hilmar:

> It is an established fact that Schoenberg believed in teaching the rules of music with iron discipline until his pupils were masters of the grammar underlying traditional harmony

Alban Berg and Arnold Schoenberg. Courtesy of Alban Berg Foundation.

and counterpoint. He maintained that mastery of these arts was essential if one was to compose successfully. Schoenberg appears to have begun his tuition with the teaching of harmony. This we can see from the dates on Berg's exercises and notes which follow the pattern of Schoenberg's *Harmonielehre* exactly.[51]

Hilmar then proceeds to describe the nature of the tuition and Berg's progress, noting Schoenberg's interventions in blue or red pencil, marking errors in musical grammar. When a student had gained an adequate facility with harmony, instruction shifted to counterpoint, which Schoenberg taught based on the traditional five species even though he claimed that it would be absurd to learn the subject by studying Palestrina. Students were then expected to progress through the great achievements of music of the past, and mastering earlier techniques was a prerequisite to the study of new music. According to Erwin Ratz, ''Schoenberg never spoke about modern music to any student who was not able to, let's say, write a string quartet in Brahms' style well.''[52] Early compositional exercises such as piano sonatas reveal Berg's difficulty in knowing how to keep an idea going; Schoenberg transmitted a sense of musical dialectic—an understanding of the importance and logical unfolding of each note, motive, chord, or passage—bringing Berg to the point where he could in his Piano Sonata, Op. 1, write an entire movement without faltering.

The formal training ended in 1911, when Schoenberg decided to leave Vienna. Schoenberg was just over a decade older than Berg, and both while a student and later, Berg had some difficulty defining the nature of his relationship with this extraordinary force in his life. The age gap was not so great that a reverential deference to the master would be a formality; Schoenberg himself was only thirty when the lessons began. Yet Schoenberg's forceful and overbearing manner demanded something akin to that regardless of his age. Various pupils have given us a sense of this, such as Rudolf Kolisch, who had to admit that Schoenberg intimidated him: ''He was just dominating.'' Marcel Dick put it bluntly: ''Schoenberg talked and you listened. There was no conversation on an equal level.'' That inequality applied even to Berg and Webern: ''He acknowledged Webern and Berg as full-fledged composers of great importance, . . . but Berg and Webern did not feel that they can talk to the master as one would talk to you and you to me. They were always at a distance.''[53]

Writing to Helene in 1909, Berg gives some sense of the struggle he was going through in how to define his relationship with Schoenberg:

> I was looking forward to writing to Schoenberg and getting letters from him, but when I started on one, I realized I couldn't write him the ordinary, conventional letter, ''I've now been a fortnight in the country, the weather is such-and-such, etc.'' I admire him too much for that, and am attached to him with more than ''deep and sincere devotion.'' I realize that they would have to be letters like those I write to you, not as often, but just as profound and as revealing of the depth of my soul. . . . So I'd intended to write him the most beautiful letters, and now I haven't written to him at all.[54]

Until Schoenberg left Vienna in 1911, he saved no letters from Berg. During the student years he wrote no letters to Berg, sending him only the occasional card confirming meeting times for lessons, rehearsals, or concerts. After 1911 the correspondence remained mostly one-sided, with long letters from Berg either not answered at all or with brief replies that all too often betray Schoenberg's sense of exasperation at receiving these long missives. Berg wrote what he regarded as beautiful letters, revealing his soul, discussing literature, and embracing all matters of artistic importance. Schoenberg did not reciprocate: he wished only to discuss business and get information. In 1915, unable to endure Berg's effusive letters any longer, he snapped: "That's why I ask you for: plentiful, factual, and detailed information. One sentence on each point, *clear* and *concise*, and without regard to style, but comprehensive, so I know where I stand. And without forgetting anything! Surely by now you have learned from my letters how to handle such matters!"[55]

Berg received this stinging rebuke, treating him like an adolescent, at the age of thirty, and one notes subtle strategies of response in his letters that follow, not unlike Mozart's letters to his father in 1778. Berg, like Mozart, did not wish to alienate his addressee; he intended only to discover a way of dealing with him. That involved wearing a distinctive epistolary mask for the benefit of that person—or the public in the case of an open letter—showing himself as an adoring and dedicated disciple regardless of how he felt about it. First of all, that meant avoiding discussion of certain topics or people that might invoke censure, such as anything pertaining to Altenberg and the decadent coffeehouse crowd. If he discussed people or matters that provoked tension, he would be sure to present the issue from what he perceived to be Schoenberg's side only.

The most striking example of the latter concerned Alma Mahler. Neither she nor Schoenberg liked the other, but he found himself in an awkward spot since she had supported him as a recipient of a stipend from the Gustav Mahler Trust Fund in 1913, 1914, and 1918. When Schoenberg occasionally expressed his own venomous views about Alma to Berg, as he did in 1915 over a misunderstanding concerning his treatment of some of Alma's scores, Berg presented himself to Schoenberg as her enemy, prepared to tear her down in the most fashionable misogynistic language. To Schoenberg, his dearest Almschi became one who "doesn't think much of us, or possibly anything at all," or worse, "she is, after all, only a woman! . . . But that's why one must measure all her words and deeds *only with the yardstick of a woman* and cannot take her more seriously than she really is."[56] These words completely belie Berg's attitude about women, an attitude that was by no means straightforward, but appealed to Schoenberg's more misogynistic instincts. Berg finally paid her the ultimate insult by invoking Weininger:

> At bottom she knows—as far as a woman can comprehend it at all—*who you are* and she surely desires that these differences be cleared away. It's nothing but capriciousness, born of the moodiness of a woman used to dispensing favor and disfavor according to momentary caprice and whim. For love to turn to hate and hate to love, creatures like that need no *greater* reason than we need to decide between a light and dark tie. Maybe *that* is what Weininger calls the *amorality of woman*. . . . How can a woman's illogic stand up to a man's logic?![57]

In a curious and perverse way Berg was defending her, but clearly not in a way that she would welcome. Only to Schoenberg would he write in such a way about the woman to whom he would dedicate the score of *Wozzeck*.

During the years immediately following the period of formal studies, matters did not always proceed smoothly between Berg and Schoenberg. In his attempt to establish himself as an independent composer, Berg returned to his old friend Altenberg for poetic inspiration, setting five of Altenberg's picture-postcard texts and ordering them in a highly symmetrical pattern that left his personal mark on the texts themselves. At this point Berg stood at the crossroads, now working with Schoenberg no longer looking over his shoulder, and much of his self-confidence for future endeavors rested on the reception of this work. If he thought that Schoenberg's view would be favorable, he would, of course, have been dreaming; the choice of the texts themselves ruled out that possibility. Schoenberg, true to expectation, reacted negatively from the beginning, picking at certain aspects without being forthright about the nature of his disapproval. He objected, among other things, to Berg's visual presentation of the score. But this studentlike error of formatting pales in comparison to the expressive problems: "I find some things disturbing at first; namely the rather too obvious desire to use new means. Perhaps I'll come to understand the organic interrelationship between these means and the requirements of expression. But right now it troubles me."[58] Only the orchestration passed muster at this point. Here was the teacher assigning a grade: it appeared to pass, but barely.

Schoenberg conducted two of the songs at the now-infamous concert of 31 March 1913 in Vienna, where the audience became progressively more unruly and erupted into outright riot during the performance of Berg's songs. Berg may have been hurt by the hostility of the public and the critics, but he was completely shattered by Schoenberg's lack of support. Berg visited him two months later in Berlin, where he received an earful about the extreme brevity of the songs in relation to Berg's expressive nature and an admonition that Berg should write longer and more developed pieces.[59] He may very well have implied, if he did not state it outright, that Altenberg's miniatures would lead nowhere: both their fragmented syntax and decadent sensuality were incompatible with Schoenbergian dialectic. Berg, vulnerable to self-doubt at the best of times, realized that he should have known better than to show these works to Schoenberg at this stage and let them be performed. He tried to put a brave face on it, thanking Schoenberg for his censure, which he knew was intended for his own good; at the same time he could not avoid a convoluted explanation that the censure had left not only self-doubt and pain but an edge of bitterness and depression. To Schoenberg he made it sound as though all of this was good for him. In reality he was deeply wounded and would take a long time to recover. The piece, which more than any other work set the direction for Berg as a composer, was shelved, never to be revived during his lifetime. If Berg learned anything from this, it was—in spite of the pain—to rely on his own instincts.

During the next decade and a half Berg continued to wear what he believed to be the appropriate epistolary mask for Schoenberg, with a tone of respect bordering on obsequiousness. By 1923, when he had written the Three Pieces for Orchestra and *Wozzeck*, a work that would soon establish Berg as the leading opera composer of the century, it became patently clear that this tone was for Schoenberg's benefit and did not reflect his actual attitude. As Berg became more accomplished, Schoenberg appeared to become more envious of his success, as Theodor Adorno has noted,[60] and this added another level of tension. Schoenberg seems to have gone out of his way to keep Berg in his place, and Berg found this insufferable. Helene became the recipient of his annoyed thoughts:

> The Schoenbergs were in good spirits. But it wasn't a pleasant atmosphere, because he kept on finding fault with my Chamber Concerto. He doesn't like the piano in this combination. Only he doesn't know, of course, that it is a *concerto*, not an ordinary octet. And yet he wants me to tell him how the piece is shaping, what sort of thing it will be, and all the time with advice, admonitions, warnings, in fact generally pouring cold water.[61]

Complaints on a host of other matters follow, all of which "goes on with such an air of tutor to apprentice." A few days later there was more: "Then by train to Mödling. Schoenberg was again criticizing everything about me: that I'm still working on *Wozzeck* ('very Karl-Krausish, this eternal correcting'), that I smoke, that I 'shouldn't imagine *Wozzeck* will have any success, it's too difficult', and worst of all that I've still not started on the Chamber Concerto."[62] Berg also found Schoenberg's irascible moods objectionable, lamenting that he "was like a dead weight on the whole company."[63]

Despite Schoenberg's needling about the Chamber Concerto, Berg dedicated the work to him in an open letter published in 1925 in *Pult und Taktstock* on the occasion of Schoenberg's fiftieth birthday. In this letter Berg goes into a detailed description of the piece, indicating the nature and extent of Schoenberg's influence. Toward the end of the letter Berg personalizes it with the following remark: "Secondly, because it is much easier for an author to speak of such structural matters than of the inner processes, though this concerto is surely not poorer in that regard than any other piece of music. I tell you, dearest friend, if anyone realized how much friendship, love, and a world of human-emotional associations I spirited into these three movements, the proponents of program music—if indeed there are still such—would be delighted."[64] Further, he makes it clear that on Schoenberg's birthday he wished to present him with "all good things." These remarks are tantalizing and have led to various types of speculation. One bizarre possibility, documentable through Berg's sketches, has been put forward by Brenda Dalen. She has deciphered references to the names "Mathilde" and "Melisande," both of which can be identified motivically in the work.[65] Mathilde was Schoenberg's first wife, and Dalen postulates that the Melisande reference may invoke her abortive relationship with the painter Richard Gerstl, from which she never recovered, finally dying in 1923. It also led to Gerstl's suicide. This was surely one of the most painful episodes in Schoenberg's life, and if Dalen is right, one can only speculate on Berg's hidden reference to it. He may have felt a need to retaliate against the treatment he received from Schoenberg and opted to achieve this in secret, in a manner no one could identify, carrying on with his public professions of admiration. Similar discrepancies between public and private in other works reinforce the possibility.

In the 1930s the relationship among the three great composers Schoenberg, Berg, and Webern did not go more smoothly. Schoenberg's permanent departure for the United States in 1933, of course, ended any further face-to-face contact among them, and like many other Jewish intellectuals and artists forced to flee Europe, Schoenberg realized in retrospect that the cultural richness he had had to leave could not be duplicated in America. In spite of the tensions, the annoyances, and the inequalities, the world would not see another musical triumverate like these three men. Berg's death at the end of 1935 came as a severe blow to Schoenberg, forcing him to realize how much Berg had meant to him. Rumors of Webern's Nazi sympathies may have been harder to accept than Berg's death,[66] but Schoenberg refused to let even this disturb the sense of extraordinary interaction, friendship, and achievement the three of them had enjoyed. He perhaps best summed it up in his handwritten introduction to the Webern Concerto, Op. 24, published by Editions Dynamo of Liège in 1948 at the urging of René Leibowitz:

> Let us—for the moment at least—forget all that might have at one time divided us. For there remains for our future what could only have begun to be realized posthumously. One will have to consider us three—Berg, Webern, Schoenberg—as a unity—a oneness, because we believed in ideas, once perceived, with intensity and selfless devotion; nor would we ever have been deterred from them, even if those who tried might have succeeded in confounding us.[67]

MUSIC COLLEAGUES

Aside from Schoenberg, one musical association for Berg stands out especially, and that, of course, was with Webern. Unlike most composers who rose to his level of distinction, Berg neither performed in public nor conducted actively, and his association with other musicians therefore remained confined to friendships, teacher-student relationships (to be treated in a separate section), administrative involvement in musical societies, collaborations in the performance of his own works, dealings with music publishers, and coaching or rehearsal conducting. Not having had a conservatory training on any musical instrument, he may have felt slightly insecure in the presence of accomplished performers; after seven years of study with Schoenberg, though, he felt that he could hold his ground with any musician or music scholar, and by his mid-twenties he realized that his own talents were superior to those of most musicians with the type of youthful musical background he lacked. Both publicly and privately he occasionally made his disaffection with other composers known.

As Webern was scarcely more than one year older than Berg, a camaraderie proved possible for them that could not have happened with the older Schoenberg. Berg and Webern came from very different backgrounds and would develop along entirely separate aesthetic lines, but none of this prevented a genuine affection of each for the other, an active interest in the other's ideas and works, and a sense of solidarity in the face of a hostile environment. Webern was also the earliest of Berg's musical friends, as they both began their studies with Schoenberg in 1904. Even at that stage Webern's accomplishments may have seemed somewhat intimidating to the much less disciplined Berg; Webern had studied both piano and cello much more assiduously than the piano-dabbling Berg and had already been studying musicology at the University of Vienna under Guido Adler for two years before coming to Schoenberg. His D.Phil. in 1906 and publication of some of Heinrich Isaac's works in the *Choralis constantinus* placed him in an elite group, and his attempt to pursue a conducting career after 1908 placed him on a level that Berg could only admire. Webern, to his credit, recognized the potential of the youthful Berg, perhaps even more than Schoenberg did, and their shared passion for Goethe and Strindberg cemented a permanent bond. Stronger yet was their shared commitment to artistic ideals, which, in spite of ultimately moving in different directions, remained tenacious in the face of the most extreme opposition. Even the extraordinary intellectuals around them—the coffeehouse writers or the university-educated philosophers—more often than not did not find value in their music.

The surface unfortunately has barely been scratched in publications of the vast correspondence between these two most famous of Schoenberg's pupils. One can only hope that someday the roughly one thousand pages of typescript of their letters to each other will find their way into print, since this represents one of the most extraordinary musical correspondences known—perhaps next only to that of Mozart and his father. Unlike the tortured letters with their obsequious tone sent by Berg to Schoenberg, answered abruptly if at all, the Berg-Webern correspondence shows a relationship of equality in which all subjects could be pursued without fear of censure or dismissal. These letters probe deeply into matters of aesthetics and shared enthusiasm and at the same time always demonstrate a warm regard and concern for the other's welfare. The closeness of this friendship remained firm for over three decades, and Berg's untimely death in 1935 came as a great blow to Webern. Two days after Berg's death Webern commented to his friend and collaborator Hildegard Jone, "You can imagine what I have been through these last days"; his daughter Amalie remembered him weeping uncontrollably that grim Christmas eve.[68]

While Berg could not have developed into the composer he became without Schoenberg's instruction or Webern's encouragement, in the area of opera, which attracted Berg from an early stage, they had much less to offer him. In Vienna Franz Schreker provided a possible influence. Berg knew Schreker's operas well, especially *Der ferne Klang*, having prepared the piano-vocal score. In Berg's estimation, though, Schreker did not measure up to the master composers such as Mahler or Schoenberg. At best, Berg could accept Schreker as a musical journeyman. Normally modest about his own abilities, Berg considered himself a superior musician to Schreker. Concerning the rehearsals for the first Viennese performance of Schoenberg's *Gurrelieder*, Berg could not help displaying exasperation with Schreker's apparent inability to get things right (in spite of the numerous corrections he offered).

Although he thought favorably about Schreker's *Der ferne Klang* and may very well have been influenced by its orchestration, its general musical and aesthetic approaches had less to offer him. In both the libretto and the music this work still displayed more Wagnerisms than Berg could possibly envisage for his own work.[69] Schreker's next opera, *Das Spielwerk und die Prinzessin*, performed in Vienna on 15 March 1913, Berg deemed to be deficient. After the performance he sent Schoenberg his verdict: "It was a great disappointment. With the best intentions and highest expectations, I could scarcely muster any enthusiasm."[70]

Berg brushed shoulders with several of Vienna's more popular composers, such as Franz Lehár (before he became famous), Erich Korngold (before he went to America and became a leading Hollywood composer), Oscar Straus, and even Richard Strauss, meeting them periodically at the Café Museum. His more serious associations, though, were with the members of the Schoenberg circle, people who, like himself, had been drawn by Schoenberg's magnetism and convictions. As fellow pupils of the master, they met during the early stages either in informal meetings to share ideas or in more formal seminars with Schoenberg presiding. As they developed into credible composers, they soon discovered that no suitable forum existed for the performance of their works. Both critics and the musical establishment believed them to be on the lunatic fringe; the famous concert of 31 March 1913, with Schoenberg's Chamber Symphony No. 1, orchestral songs by Zemlinsky, the premiere of Webern's Six Pieces for Orchestra, Op. 6, and two of Berg's *Altenberg Lieder*, was a case in point. Even works of an emerging giant such as Debussy did not get a fair reading in Vienna.

Something clearly had to be done, and Schoenberg took the first step, forming the Verein für Musikalische Privataufführungen (Society for Private Musical Performances). Berg's involvement from the beginning was intensive; Schoenberg entrusted him with writing the prospectus, and he served on the executive committee. Berg's involvement with the society extended well beyond musical matters, as Schoenberg placed him in charge of, among other things, the seating. Felix Greissle, who later married Schoenberg's daughter Gertrud, related a humorous incident of Schoenberg's dissatisfaction with Berg's arrangement of the chairs:

> I remember Schoenberg coming and—horrible, you see. "The chairs are completely cockeyed. This is ridiculous. What did you do here?" So, Berg silently, without saying

one word, took a measure, a tape measure, out of his pocket and measured and said, "You said that you wanted so and so many centimeter; it's really all right; it's a half centimeter more."[71]

The active members of this society, including Webern, Edward Steuermann, Erwin Stein, Paul Pisk, Josef Rufer, Rudolf Wenzel, Felix Greissle, and Rodolf Kolisch, were Berg's real musical friends and colleagues.

As one would expect, Berg had various artistic and business collaborations with performers and publishers who would bring his works into public view. One of his longest relationships, but certainly not the smoothest, was with Emil Hertzka, founding publisher of Universal Edition. Since Hertzka was already Schoenberg's publisher, Schoenberg could exert some influence with him on behalf of his most talented pupils, and this Schoenberg did, although not necessarily at times when Berg felt he most needed it. Hertzka demonstrated an unusual commitment to the cause of new music in Vienna, but at the same time he was a hard-nosed businessman, often irascible, and not about to enter into unprofitable arrangements. As most young writers or composers can attest, dealing with publishers can be frustrating and exasperating, and Berg's experience with Hertzka was no exception.

As early as the beginning of 1910, Schoenberg had written to Hertzka about his "extraordinarily gifted" pupil Alban Berg, explaining how he had taken him from a raw talent incapable of anything other than songs to a composer able to understand instrumentation.[72] This aroused little curiosity on Hertzka's part, but it appears to have led to various types of incidental employment for Berg at Universal, such as commissions to make an index for Schoenberg's *Harmonielehre* or to prepare piano-vocal scores for Schreker's *Der ferne Klang* or Schoenberg's *Gurrelieder*. In a letter to Schoenberg from 1912, Berg registers some of his aggravations related to working for Hertzka:

> I also wrote Hertzka a detailed letter and explained why I was asking for more than he usually pays (. . . I'm curious how far he'll barter me down). . . . And I really let him know what I thought about the "difficulties" of my reductions. For he continually reproaches me that my reductions are so difficult as to be unplayable. Of course he himself doesn't know anything about it and doubtless gets his opinion from Schreker. And Schreker naturally can't play my reductions, as he plays and sightreads very poorly.[73]

In spite of Schoenberg's intervention and Berg's work for Universal, no contracts to publish his works were forthcoming until 1923, and even then they came with difficulty. Berg could finally report with relief to Helene on 14 April 1923 that he had concluded contracts with Hertzka for *Wozzeck* and the Three Pieces for Orchestra. Schoenberg proved to be more a hindrance than a help in securing the contract for the piano-vocal score of *Wozzeck*, and in fact it took some social engagements with Alma Mahler exerting her charms to soften Hertzka up for the agreement. She agreed to secure the shares that Hertzka would not, and earned the dedication from Berg for her efforts. From that point on, the contracts came in more quickly, including those for the Clarinet Pieces and String Quartet in August 1923, after Hertzka heard a performance of the quartet by the Havemann Quartet in Salzburg, and the Chamber Concerto in 1925. All Berg's later works were published by Universal. In spite of Hertzka's manner and reservations, he proved in the end to be one of Berg's most important allies, publishing his works, publicizing the composer, and securing performances of his works.

A number of performers played equally important roles in Berg's ultimate success. About the Havemann Quartet, which Berg traveled to Salzburg to hear, he could write with admiration to Helene:

> In ten minutes we were firm friends. When I saw they knew my *Quartet* nearly by heart, felt it themselves as genuine music, and performed it with all the feeling—my heart opened to them. How well the four of them played together, how perfectly it all works, how happy they are with the printed music! How each of them knows all four parts, in fact keeps a check on the other.[74]

This was, he had to admit, "quite different from the amateur quartet-playing in the Society."[75]

Among his close musical friends, Berg had especially high regard for Steuermann and Kolisch (along with the entire Kolisch Quartet). Steuermann became a close personal friend, meeting Berg at the Café Central aside from professional situations, and the two of them occasionally traveled together for performance engagements. In Frankfurt Steuermann gave Berg a scare when he had a panic attack before going on stage to play the Piano Sonata, but in the end, according to Berg, "everything went marvellously."[76] On the same trip in 1921, Steuermann performed the difficult score of *Wozzeck* as an audition for the heads of the Frankfurt and Darmstadt opera houses. Here was an excellent pianist interrupting his own career to promote the work of a colleague, and Berg recognized his talent and effort. The Kolisch Quartet played the first performance of the Lyric Suite; in 1934 Berg was relieved to learn that for a performance in Venice "the Kolisch Quartet will be playing the *Lyric Suite*, which reassured me like anything; so glad it's not being done by some Italian quartet society."[77]

In spite of the efforts of Steuermann and Hertzka as well as favorable reviews of the score, few conductors expressed genuine interest in taking on *Wozzeck*. That changed with an inquiry from Erich Kleiber, director of the Berlin Opera, who visited Vienna in 1924 and heard Ernst Bachrich's rendition of the work. Kleiber reportedly exclaimed, "It's settled! I am going to do the opera in Berlin, even if it costs me my job!"[78] Kleiber directed the premiere on 14 December 1925, and it almost did cost him his job. These were turbulent times at the Opera in Berlin, and in spite of political interference, the resignation of the chief administrator, and attacks from political factions, Kleiber refused to abandon *Wozzeck*, which soon became the focus of the attacks.

Berg arrived in Berlin two weeks before the premiere and, quickly sensing the precariousness of Kleiber's position, developed a great respect for his musical integrity in the face of looming uncertainty. With one week to go, Berg wrote to Helene that he could not predict if the production would be ready by opening night, but he took comfort in Kleiber's perfectionist tendencies. In this instance all depended on the success of the premiere; consequently, Kleiber had to "have his perfection *in time*."[79] Berg and Kleiber remained firm friends, and no one played a greater role than Kleiber in bringing Berg international recognition: he kept *Wozzeck* in the Berlin repertoire for two seasons, brought out new productions in 1929 and 1933, conducted Berg's music while on tour in the United States in 1930 and 1931, and premiered the *Lulu* Suite late in 1934. As the Nazis were now in power, performing the "degenerate" Berg involved considerable risks, which Kleiber took with characteristic courageousness. This was the last performance of Berg's music in Germany for a decade, and Kleiber resigned his position at the State Opera four days later.

With Hitler's cultural policies in effect, it seemed doubtful that the opera *Lulu* would ever be performed, although that did not prevent Berg from working on it. His progress during 1935, though, was interrupted by a commission for a violin concerto by the young Russian-born American violinist Louis Krasner. At first cool to the idea, Berg soon responded to Krasner's enthusiasm and agreed to write the concerto. They met through a mutual friend, the pianist Rita Kurzmann, in whose home Webern's now-published lectures (*The Path to the New Music*) were given, and Krasner quickly entered Berg's coffeehouse circle. Krasner soon became one of Berg's strongest supporters in the United States, arranging for performances of his works by major orchestras such as the Boston Symphony. Some parts of the Violin Concerto emerged through an unusual type of collaboration, which Krasner recounted with enjoyment:

> We had our coffee and without delay, he asked me to take my violin and play while he busied himself in and out of the music room and about the house. I suggested the Concertos that I was then prepared to play—Glazunow, Brahms, Vieuxtemps, Tchaikovsky. "No", he said, "Keine Konzerte",—"no concertos." "Oh, very well, a Sonata,—which Bach Sonata?" I asked. "Nein, nein, auch keine Sonaten!—no sonatas either. Just play—nur spielen—bitte, präludieren Sie einfach", Berg replied. . . . Since my student days when my teacher scolded me for it, I have always loved to spend my evenings doing just that—playing and improvising for myself. "Noodling", they had called it. . . . I played and played—for hours it seemed—whatever strange figurations, chords, passages, pizzicati and impulsive combinations on the violin—everything that chance brought to my fingers, bow and mind.[80]

Arrangements were made for the premiere of the concerto at the 1937 festival of the International Society for Contemporary Music, an organization for which Berg had served as an Austrian member. After Berg's death, the society asked for the performance a year earlier, at the 1936 festival in Barcelona, with Webern as conductor. All agreed—Webern reluctantly—and the event proved something of a fiasco. Unable to cope with Pablo Casals's orchestra, which lacked experience with new music, Webern withdrew at the last moment. Hermann Scherchen, who had also been a strong advocate of Berg's music, stepped in and performed the work after one rehearsal. Krasner then went on to perform the concerto with Webern in London, and with other conductors in virtually every major center, proving himself to be one of Berg's most devoted and enthusiastic ambassadors.

BERG AS TEACHER

One cannot be certain if Berg took on pupils out of financial necessity or from a genuine desire to teach. On the surface, the latter possibility seems unlikely, considering the view he expressed to Helene in 1912: "But giving lessons is a terrible strain for me, my brain is always quite barren afterwards. I have to think myself completely into my pupils' ideas, to hire myself out, as it were, and it's extremely hard to find my way back from there into my own thinking."[81] Yet Berg is in good company among excellent teachers who find teaching a strain. Being neither an extrovert nor an authoritarian full of conviction in his own ideas, he was forced as a teacher into something much more difficult, namely, the process he attempts to describe to Helene.

Comparisons between his and Schoenberg's teaching are inevitable, and one must point to both similarities and differences. Former pupils have noted that Berg used techniques similar to those of Schoenberg, insisting on a firm grounding in harmony and counterpoint before proceeding, and forcing students to be able to account for the purpose of every note in compositions. Berg's dissimilarity to Schoenberg, though, placed the pupil on a very different footing, which one former pupil, Theodor Adorno, took pleasure in describing: "With loving care he devoted himself to freeing me of my compositional inhibitions, just as—very different from the way Schoenberg treated his students—he always encouraged me; . . . his authority was the total absence of authoritarianism."[82] Schoenberg's pupils found their teacher intimidating and dominating: "Schoenberg talked and you listened. There was no conversation on an equal level."[83] In contrast, students found Berg warm, generous, giving all their ideas serious and meticulous attention, and seeming more like a friend than a teacher.[84]

Among Berg's pupils from 1912 until his death were Gottfried Kassowitz, Hans Erich Apostel, Fritz Heinrich Klein, Julius Schloss, Adorno, and Willi Reich. He treated each one differently, depending on the nature of the person and his background; he took a novice such as Kassowitz through the entire course of harmonic and contrapuntal study, while Adorno, who already possessed a solid musical background, could move directly into composition. Berg appeared to charge little for his lessons, but invariably developed a friendly relationship and put his students to work as assistants or advisors. Both Schloss and Reich served as secretaries or ran errands, and Berg consulted Adorno on compositional and aesthetic matters, including the selection of the text for his second opera. Adorno, who later imagined that he had first directed Berg toward Wedekind's Lulu plays, argued against Gerhard Hauptmann's *Und Pippa tanzt!* Berg was not surrounded by students with great potential as composers, and he recognized this. Adorno stood at the threshold of a brilliant career as a philosopher, but Berg appears to have tacitly relegated his "philosophical bombast to the category he termed 'a bore.' "[85] While Adorno's descriptions may be somewhat idiosyncratic, he gives us one of the most insightful views available of Berg as a teacher, confirming Berg's words to Helene about thinking himself into his pupil's ideas:

> Even as a teacher he responded slowly, almost broodingly, his strength was that of intellectual imagination and an acutely deliberate command of the possibilities, as well as a strong original fantasy in all compositional dimensions; not one among the newer composers, not even Schoenberg or Webern, was so much the antithesis of the ideologically puffed-up musician of that period as he was. Usually he would take a long time looking at what I brought him and then come up with possible solutions, particularly for passages where I had reached an impasse. He never smoothed over difficulties or skirted them with facile answers, but always hit the nail on the head: he knew better than anyone that every properly composed measure represents a problem, a choice between evils.[86]

ESSAYS, GUIDES, AND ANALYSES

Throughout his life Berg remained immensely attracted to the printed word, his inability to face writing school essays notwithstanding. As a youth he imagined his future to be that of a poet, and after exposure to Karl Kraus he saw that all forms of writing could be considered honorable. The idea of a composer as writer on music flourished in the nineteenth century, with Berg's much-loved Schumann leading the way. Another of Berg's favorites, Debussy, was not only a prolific music journalist but a highly polemical one as well, extending no mercy to his opponents. Also, of course, there was Wagner, who fully understood the power of the pen and did not hesitate to wield a poison one if he thought it necessary. The reluctance of some composers to write about music, fearing it might somehow devalue them as musicians, clearly did not apply to early-twentieth-century Vienna. Few composers wrote as much about music as Schoenberg, and when he suggested to Berg that Berg might consider a career as a *Musikschriftsteller*, or writer on music, he intended no insult to Berg's talent as a composer. At one stage, Berg found the prospect decidedly appealing, suggesting to Webern in 1920 in an outline of his future career plans that "I would like to devote myself completely to 'writing about music', and also making piano reductions. . . . In this way it would also be possible—so I believe—to have a regular income. . . . Composing?? Yes, that would be very nice. Perhaps one or two months in the summer!!"[87]

Prior to trying his hand at music journalism, Berg received a number of commissions from Hertzka at Univeral Edition to prepare thematic guides for upcoming performances of some of Schoenberg's works. The first of these came in late 1912 for *Gurrelieder*, for which Berg was already preparing the piano-vocal score. Both Berg and Schoenberg felt a general contempt for this type of guide, pointing to the mind-numbing thematic descriptions served up by Richard Specht or Josef Wöss. Berg doubted that these had any useful purpose and suggested that if the musical examples were removed, a guide written for Mahler's Eighth could just as well be applied to a work by Delius. Schoenberg agreed, but since Hertzka was hell-bent on having one, better it should be by Berg, who understood and loved the work, than by someone like Specht. Berg knew perfectly well that real analysis could not be presented in this type of guide; Hertzka wanted something for the interested concertgoer, not the few initiates who might understand actual analysis.

Expecting a guide in the range of 40 pages, Hertzka became alarmed when Berg approached 100 pages with over 150 musical examples. To his credit (with some prompting from Schoenberg), Hertzka accepted Berg's version, perhaps realizing that this was no run-of-the-mill guide. While thematic material is featured, Berg places it within its formal, harmonic, and contrapuntal context and also reveals its poetic significance.[88] Later guides, for Schoenberg's Chamber Symphony, Op. 9, and *Pelleas und Melisande*, were considerably shorter, the length being determined by Hertzka before they could get out of hand. Berg did write a longer version for *Pelleas und Melisande*, although it remained unpublished until 1994.[89]

If Berg had misgivings about writing thematic guides, he was similarly conflicted about how much energy to put into music journalism. Writing occasional articles presented no problem; these arose spontaneously from issues or concerns and could be written in the heat of the moment, more often than not responding to the barbs of critics or other composers. The first of these polemical pieces, published in 1920 in the *Musikblätter des Anbruch*, was "The Musical Impotence of Hans Pfitzner's 'New Aesthetic' " (Figure 5.1) replying to Pfitzner's attack on modern music in his own *The New Aesthetic of Musical Impotence*. Berg's essay made a considerable stir, so much so that Hertzka, the publisher of *Anbruch* (the house journal of Universal Edition), invited Berg to become editor of the journal. Berg, perhaps in the weakness of the moment imagining himself as the Karl Kraus of the musical world, accepted the offer, taking up his duties in September 1920. On more sober reflection, he realized his incompatibility with such a regular schedule, as well as the fact that this was Hertzka's journal and not his. He expressed these misgivings to Webern a month before starting:

> Believe me, I too regard the near future with fear and trembling. Will I be able to defy all resistance—Hertzka, the publisher's interests . . . avoiding clashes, making no enemies? That's how Hertzka imagines it! Will I be in a position to make absolutely no concessions? That's the negative side! And what about the positive side: Will I really be able to do what is needful . . . just to get the articles together to fill such a book, and a fortnight later another one, and so on twenty times a year! My activity so far has had

Figure 5.1
Table of Contents, *Musikblätter des Anbruch*, 1/2 June 1920.

MUSIKBLÄTTER DES ANBRUCH

HALBMONATSSCHRIFT FÜR MODERNE MUSIK
SCHRIFTLEITUNG: DR. OTTO SCHNEIDER

INHALT DER ZULETZT ERSCHIENENEN HEFTE:

NUMMER 11/12

NUMMER 13

practically no result. Believe me: I've spent so many sleepless nights wishing I had never laid a finger on "Anbruch." . . . Yes! when it comes to writing what suits me and publishing it wherever I can get it accepted!—But, to take over the whole management in such a slippery—almost journalistic—field. Truly, if I didn't *have* to do it, if I didn't stand before the necessity of scraping some means of existence, I would write to Hertzka today and throw the whole thing over, come what might, and spend the winter here and compose my opera . . . so from 1st September I throw myself into the arms of the public.[90]

Trusting his instincts, Berg left this position one year later.

As editor of *Anbruch*, Berg submitted another of his own essays, "Two Feuilletons,'' but it was rejected because it openly attacked certain Viennese critics. Berg apparently decided to test whether or not he could treat *Anbruch* like *Die Fackel* and discovered that he could not. This experience did not put him off from writing other essays or giving lectures dealing with his own works. In these various pieces the spirit of Karl Kraus is never far from view, not only in the relentless adherence to principles and the style of the attacks, but in matters of format as well. Berg's ''The Problem of Opera,'' an essay on his own *Wozzeck*, commences with Kraus's favorite headings ''Pro mundo'' and ''Pro domo.'' In his commentary he not only adopts Kraus's style but directs his barbs at Kraus's prime target as well: the press. Some of Berg's observations seem excessively polemical, but this appears to be for the benefit of journalists and critics, whose glib pronouncements he had learned to detest almost as much as Kraus did. Much the same could be said of his various written defenses of Schoenberg.

STUDENT AND OTHER EARLY WORKS

Schoenberg's teaching may have stressed the individual and independent development of his pupils, but that development should clearly follow the appropriate Schoenbergian path. He accepted the fact that Berg was a gifted pupil, but in 1910 wrote a smug letter to Hertzka of Berg's earlier defects and the effort it took to correct them: ''But the state he was in when he came to me was such that his imagination apparently could not work on anything but *Lieder*. He was absolutely incapable of writing an instrumental movement or inventing an instrumental theme. You can hardly imagine the lengths I went to in order to remove this defect in his talent. . . . I removed this defect and am convinced that in time Berg will actually become very good at instrumentation.''[91] Better, in fact, than Schoenberg ever imagined. What Schoenberg regarded as a defect remained one of Berg's great strengths, and the master did not succeed in turning Berg into something other than a composer of vocal music. As a mature composer Berg wrote only four pieces for instruments alone—the Three Pieces for Orchestra, the Chamber Concerto, the Lyric Suite, and the Violin Concerto—and even in these the evidence of his vocal lyricism remains strong. Two other works, the *Drei Bruchstücke aus ''Wozzeck''* and the *Lulu* Suite, are instrumental arrangements from his operas.

In contrast to his instrumental output, Berg's two most ambitious works were operas, and each of his two sets of orchestral songs, the *Altenberg Lieder* and *Der Wein*, represents a watershed at a critical point in his career. These observations in no way devalue Berg's instrumental works, all of which are extraordinary (in spite of some negative opinion of the Chamber Concerto). They simply point to one more area in which Schoenberg may have misjudged his pupil, who would not abandon his passion for song or his world of sensuality. Adorno probably came very close to the truth when he suggested that Berg ''criticized a want of expressive content in Schoenberg's first twelve-tone compositions.''[92] In contrast, Berg's first major twelve-tone works, the Lyric Suite and *Der Wein*—a vocal work—place expression above all else.

In one respect, of course, Schoenberg was right: when Berg came to him in 1904, he had nothing in his portfolio of compositions but songs.[93] These early songs, of which there are about seventy, reflected his affinity for certain earlier or contemporary composers, such as Schubert, Schumann, Debussy, and Mahler, and perhaps one cannot blame Schoenberg for his comments to Hertzka based on them. Berg himself recognized them for what they were, and except for the ones included in the Seven Early Songs, the Four Songs, Op. 2, and later the first version of ''Schliesse mir die Augen beide,'' he refused to publish any of them. With most of them now available in print, one can only say that Berg's instinct about them was right; they have been subjected to the type of analysis he feared would happen.

Perhaps more important than the music of these early songs, aside from the fact that the lyrical and harmonic richness shows him to be a sensualist like Schubert, Schumann, and Debussy, is the choice of texts. As an avid reader, poet, and even cataloger of literary quotations from before his first meeting with Schoenberg, Berg chose texts that reflect a well-formed aesthetic stance, combining the otherworldliness of romanticism and decadence from the past and the transplanting of that into the coffeehouse world of his time. In his choice of eighteenth- or earlier nineteenth-century poets, one notes an inclination toward some of Schubert's texts, especially in the case of Goethe's ''Erster Verlust,'' ''Grenzen der Menschheit,'' and ''Mignon'' (''Kennst du das Land''). In fact, these three already show an important side of Berg, as ''Erster Verlust'' laments the loss of first love, ''Grenzen der Menschheit'' belongs to Goethe's polarity texts where logic seems intentionally lacking,[94] and ''Mignon,'' an androgynous character from *Wilhelm Meister*, provides an entry into bisexuality. Berg also uses Heinrich Heine and Joseph von Eichendorff, but avoids the more optimistic Friedrich von Schiller. A number of his early literary idols are present, such as Ibsen, Rilke, Hofmannsthal, Dörmann, Detlev von Liliencron, Alfred Mombert, and Otto Erich Hertleben; they did not necessarily retain their elevated position in his estimation. Some friends can be found as well, including Frida Semler, Hohenberg, and Altenberg. With Altenberg he was most in his element and would ultimately find his genuine artistic voice through this poet. In some respects, the songs in general, all relatively short, reflect a similar inclination toward miniatures felt by Altenberg about his literary works.

As one would expect, Berg started to write for instruments as Schoenberg's pupil, and of the student pieces he saw fit to publish the Piano Sonata, Op. 1 (1908), and the String Quartet, Op. 3 (1910). The Four Pieces for Clarinet and Piano, Op. 5 (1913), while composed two years after his formal lessons ceased, belong more to this group than to the works that followed. Other early student works for piano, including sonatas and variations, either were not completed or were not deemed appropriate for publication. The Piano Sonata marked an important breakthrough for Berg because he finally found the means in this work for developmental continuity. Early efforts show his attempts to take an idea forward with the inevitable running aground in what appears to be indecision about what should come next. Now the motives and themes flowed in a tightly structured interweaving, with changes in tempo marking the formal divisions of the sonata. Even though Schoenberg may not have used the term at this stage, it appears that he was now teaching the Brahmsian principle of ''developing variation,'' and that Berg had found his way out of his previous dead ends by applying it.[95]

With the achievement in the Piano Sonata of development on a fairly small scale, Berg was able to transfer that to much larger dimensions in the String Quartet. This was the last piece Berg wrote under Schoenberg's scrutiny, and Schoenberg did not hesitate to recognize the accomplishment, as in the testimonial he wrote just after Berg's death: ''His String Quartet (Opus 3) surprised me in the most unbelievable way by the fullness and unconstraint of its musical language, the strength and sureness of its presentation, its careful working and significant originality.''[96] Some of the musical principles Berg discovered here would serve him well in future works, including *Wozzeck*, such as a motif that uses a portion of the whole-tone scale. He develops the principle of motivic expansion in an extraordinary manner and realizes the possibility of doing that within a symmetrical pattern. Adorno believes this to be the most underrated of all Berg's works: ''With abrupt, violent exertion it seizes full mastery. . . . Nothing remains of the apprentice's self-consciousness, nothing of the emotional decor of *Jugendstil*.''[97] As remarkable as this early achievement may be, it perhaps shows more about Berg's ability to process Schoenberg's instruction than the direction he would ultimately take as a composer. In this respect Redlich rightly sounds a note of caution: ''What it lacks in lyrical tenderness—so characteristic of the Berg of *Wozzeck* and the Violin Concerto—it makes up for in dramatic directness of appeal.''[98] The work touches on the severity that Berg would later find unappealing in some works of Schoenberg.

If the *Altenberg Lieder* suggest a somewhat contradictory approach to miniatures in which the brief temporal units are augmented with a rich orchestral palette, a sensual encompassing of the decadent texts, the Four Pieces for Clarinet and Piano move in the opposite direction, toward miniatures on all levels. Even thematicism gives way here to much smaller motivic ideas or musical cells. Miniatures in music and literature were by no means confined to Vienna, as Busoni and Bartók, among others, enjoyed them. These pieces also show solidarity with Schoenberg and Webern at the time, as Schoenberg's Piano Pieces, Op. 19, provide a type of model, and Webern finds the ultimate conception of the musical miniature in his Six Bagatelles, Op. 9, Five Pieces, Op. 10, and Three Little Pieces, Op. 11. Berg presents his Four Pieces, as Adorno suggests, in the manner of a condensed (or shriveled) four-movement sonata, with each movement transforming its material in new and surprising ways.[99]

THE WORLD OF THE SOUL: THE *ALTENBERG LIEDER*

Berg's *Fünf Orchesterlieder nach Ansichtskarten-Texten von Peter Altenberg*, op. 4 (*Altenberg Lieder*), defined his future direction as did no other of his early works. In spite of the dismal fate of this work during Berg's lifetime, it stands as a stunning achievement, bringing together the diverse and even contradictory elements of this young composer. The texts themselves are of the greatest possible importance, as they underline Berg's relationship with Altenberg and Berg's fascination with women, bisexuality, death, nature, and transcendence as these are presented by Altenberg. Berg's artistic mastery emerges in his control of the musical forces—including a large and complex orchestral score—and his distinctive arrangement of the texts themselves.

''And the Altenberg songs were after all written for you,'' Berg reminded Helene in 1914, two years after he wrote these songs.[100] While all the early pieces from Op. 1 to Op. 5 were dedicated to her, this work was much more than a dedication since its texts, through association with Altenberg's Helene poems, indirectly embrace her as a subject and define the world that Berg believed he shared with her. In removing the individual poems from the context of the ''Texte auf Ansichtskarten'' (from *Neues Altes*, 1911, the same source in which Altenberg published the Helene poems), and in extracting five specific texts and rearranging their order, Berg made them his own, imbued them with meaning for himself, and to some extent gave them significance beyond that which they possessed in their original presentation. This relates closely to Altenberg's view of woman, whose primary role he defines in relation to man, not as one who satisfies physical, material, and social needs but as a provider of spiritual support. In his Helene poems he had placed her in this context of the soul, separated from material concerns, and in spite of her own rejection of this placement, Berg idealized her in the same way. This caused some awkward moments when Berg compared her with Altenberg's (and Kraus's) freespirited and admired notion of prostitutes, whom Altenberg believed had the capability of discovering the inner world and standing closer to nature because they were untouched by the hypocrisy of modern civilization. In his defense of this type of woman and his subsequent portrayal of her in the songs as well as in later works, despite resistance from Helene, Berg saw this model as part of his own being, determining his role as keeper and defender of the feminine soul.

In rearranging the Altenberg texts to suit his own artistic needs, Berg inaugurated an approach that would be evident later in his career, most notably in *Wozzeck* and *Der Wein*. In *Wozzeck* he took a fragmented text and gave it a highly defined structure. The parallel with *Der Wein* comes even closer, involving both structural and aesthetic considerations; in both works, the poems chosen for the center of the set have palindromic implications, which Berg realized in his musical setting. The poet of *Der Wein* (''Le Vin''), Baudelaire, had the single strongest bearing not only on Altenberg's prose-poem style, but also on his world of the soul, of decadence, and on his portrayal of women.[101]

The poem used as the central text of the Altenberg songs, "Über die Grenzen des All," with its arch form provided by the repetition of the first line at the end, alerts one to Berg's symmetrical arrangement of the five texts. Berg in fact ordered the texts to allow for an overall thematic-poetic symmetry, providing them with a formal significance as well as accommodating a narrative flow from beginning to end. The first and fifth texts provide the foundation of a large thematic arch; both treat the images of the soul, snow, melancholy and sorrow, and peace. Woman does not appear overtly in either of these texts, but by implication she stands very much present. Nature is central to the first text, and through the association with water, one of Altenberg's most potent nature images, it positions itself in the fifth text as well. The third text, the apex of the thematic arch, takes the image of the soul to a new height, but at the same time does not avoid conflict. The conflict, apparent in the third line, "Leben und Traum vom Leben plötzlich ist alles aus" (Living a dream of life—suddenly, all is over), a phrase crucial to the narrative, is framed by the repeated first and fourth line, "Über die Grenzen des All blicktest du sinnend hinaus" (Over the brink of beyond musingly wandered your gaze), which in turn reach out to the first and fifth texts. "Über die Grenzen" (beyond the limits) stands as a heightened image of the soul as an otherworldly state beyond the borders of the physical, known universe. In spite of the apparent breakdown in the third line, the third text ultimately draws the poet deeper within his own soul.

The tears that flow in the fifth text, the ability to cry, and the release of unfathomable, measureless sorrow are the voice of the poet, the final goal for Berg of the narrative process. From the first to the second text, snowstorms become rain, beauty and peace triumph, and woman enters. She toys with the soul in the third text, but rejects it in favor of life. In life, however, she finds a void, the "nothing" of the fourth text; the male poet experiences this with her, sharing the agony of her conflict, accepting what he can of her feminine soul. In the fifth text he finds peace, a peace possible because sorrow has been experienced. In the act of releasing sorrow he is most alone, secluded from all humanity, but at the same time, he has found the deepest recesses of his soul and union with nature. In this symmetrical yet narrative arrangement Berg has made the texts his own. In his dual presentation the soul becomes the "significant season," beyond temporal (and hence earthly) association, engendered in symmetrical form. He reaches his goal, however, through the experience of pain—the brushing with reality—a temporal, formless process.

Berg musically constructs the *Altenberg Lieder* with a highly elaborate thematic scheme that determines the organization of individual songs as well as the integration of the cycle as a whole. Certain themes or chords are used in more than one song, and a remarkable correspondence can be found between the musical and poetic themes. Just as the soul, snow, melancholy and sorrow, and peace appear in a symmetrically arranged manner in the text, a number of

Example 5.1
Theme of Alban Berg, *Altenberg Lieder*, Op. 4

the musical themes occur in a similar manner.[102] That is not to say that any of these themes have programmatic/poetic associations; instead, Berg's treatment suggests a parallel process of text and music. The image of the soul—the feminine soul of which Altenberg saw himself as protector—pervades the whole cycle, as does the theme with the pitch outline shown in Example 5.1. Just as the soul moves through certain transformations, partly in relation to a feminine influence, this theme undergoes different permutations and establishes itself in the fifth song as the dominant theme.

Berg wrote this work for soprano and orchestra, and the voice, along with other musical characteristics, suggests a feminine character. In the first song the solo voice does not project above the orchestral texture as a predominant force, but instead emerges quietly as though it were another orchestral instrument, without text, before the first word "Seele" (soul). In the nineteenth-century literary scheme of things, as in Goethe's *Die Wahlverwandtschaften*, solo roles had a male association while piano accompaniments were given to women, although the accompaniment would be considered the primary part. In a work such as this written for a female voice, a new level of gender mixture becomes possible. The feminine role of the accompaniment was heightened through its harmonizing and unifying function, and by extension (as Mahler especially realized) the sensuality of the accompaniment could be enhanced through orchestration.

The instrumentlike voice part does not enter until measure 20, allowing the work to be contextualized by a tone of rich orchestration. For Berg, orchestral depth and color may very well have been comparable to Klimt's color and decorative design. Orchestral color could provide an aural sensuality bordering on the erotic, a profusion of detail, stretching the ear as Klimt's designs enlarge the eye, making possible the fusion of different images (or themes) in a complex of simultaneity. The visual counterpart of this technique can be found in Klimt's *The Kiss* (1907–8), in which the garments of the embracing pair seem to blend together but nevertheless remain distinct through the rectangular design used in the man's clothes and the circles used in the woman's. The two of them are engulfed in a third design that favors the feminine shape and suggests a fusion that leans toward femininity. In the complex density of the instrumental introduction to the first song, with its four primary themes and underlying chords in the piano, Berg seems to achieve a similar end. At the end of the work Berg takes the theme given in Example 5.1 and transforms it into the harmonic accompaniment. In the final statement of this theme, the most persistent of the entire work, now integrated into the harmonic fabric, lies the fulfillment of a distinctly romantic image. Berg's engendering of theme into harmony at the end of the work, also evident in the final six measures of the third song, travels a step further in the transference of feminine characteristics into the poetic/musical process and fuses the ultimate goal of the music with that of the text.

DANSE MACABRE: THREE PIECES FOR ORCHESTRA, OPUS 6

In a letter to Webern dated 29 July 1912, Berg addressed his future compositional plans: "But now to get to Balzac! I must read *Seraphita* again here, I brought it along. You know: this winter I want to write a large symphonic movement, and toward the ending would like to put a boy's voice (high) singing words from *Seraphita*. Naturally it remains—as is so often the case with me—only a plan. But now pleasure—inspiration—for me, the more considering Schoenberg's treatment."[103] A year later, with the fiasco of the *Altenberg Lieder* performance behind him, he had not yet given up on the idea of an orchestral work, especially since Schoenberg had advised him to write such a work, to be dedicated to his mentor for the occasion of his fortieth birthday. Berg tried to write the orchestral suite Schoenberg suggested, but he simply could not make the work develop in that way. That gave him some cause for alarm because of Schoenberg's displeasure with the *Altenberg Lieder* and what he perceived at this time as a moral obligation to do his master's bidding. Once again he lapsed into obsequiousness in addressing his mentor, having just been upbraided by him in Berlin: "You yourself know, dear Herr Schönberg, that I am always conscious of, and never want to be conscious of anything but: being your student. To follow you in every respect, knowing that everything I do in *opposition* to your wishes is wrong. If during these last months I have thought so often and intensely about writing a symphony it is surely because I want to make up for what I would have composed *under you*, dear Herr Schönberg, *had you stayed in Vienna* and because I want to heed your words, 'Each of your students should at some point have written a symphony.' "[104]

Berg intended to write a symphonic work, but not the one Schoenberg had in mind. In fact, considering what he finally did produce, the tone in his letters to Schoenberg seems somewhat suspect. To be sure, he dedicated the Three Pieces for Orchestra to Schoenberg, but had Schoenberg understood Berg's thrust with this work, he would surely not have approved. Berg originally placed the work in relation to Balzac's *Seraphita*, inspired by Schoenberg's grand symphonic project on that subject, but for neither did the project materialize. Mahler was the obvious model for these projects, especially the Ninth Symphony, but Schoenberg soon realized that he could not be Mahler's symphonic heir. His attempt gave way to the oratorio *Die Jakobsleiter*, where the presence of *Seraphita* can still be very much felt. For Berg, *Seraphita* evaporated in the orchestral fragments of 1913.

In the letter to Webern of 29 July 1912 Berg wrote at length about Strindberg, including Schoenberg's interest in *Jacob Wrestling*. While that work had obvious implications for *Die Jakobsleiter*, another one that Berg described in detail, *Advent*, has an even stronger possible bearing on Schoenberg's oratorio. Webern and Schoenberg shared Berg's enthusiasm for Strindberg, although each found something different in this complex and often contradictory writer. Berg also described Strindberg's *Crimes and Crimes* (in German, *Rausch*) in this letter and for the first time expressed his fascination with Strindberg's own attraction to the key of D minor. After describing Strindberg's treatment of Beethoven's Sonata in D minor (Op. 31, No. 2), he emphasized that ''this relationship of Strindberg to the music of Beethoven is of tremendous interest to me.'' Drawing yet another connection, Berg reminded Webern that he had ''said once that Strindberg most likely would have liked Mahler's music.''[105] The key of D minor emerges with some frequency in Berg's music throughout his career as a potent image; its appearance in the Three Pieces for Orchestra may suggest more than a connection with Mahler's Ninth Symphony, invoking perhaps the character of this key as Berg understood it in Strindberg's various literary applications.

Berg wrote the two outer movements, ''Präludium'' and ''Marsch,'' first, completing them in time to send them to Schoenberg for his fortieth birthday on 13 September 1914. ''Präludium'' remains most strongly connected to Mahler's Ninth (the first movement) with its symmetrical shape and almost silent opening with motivic fragments that later develop melodically, as well as the common approach to the building of a climax and the similarities in meter and rhythm. It was this movement by Mahler that had inspired Berg's comment to Helene: ''The whole movement is based on a premonition of death, which is constantly recurring.''[106] When he refers to death appearing ''mit höchster Gewalt'' (with highest force) at the point of the most profound and anguished love of life, followed by resignation, he may very well have been describing his own ''Präludium.''

As for the third piece, ''Marsch,'' George Perle aptly calls it Berg's ''marche macabre'': ''It is not a march, but music *about* a march, or rather about *the* march, just as Ravel's *La Valse* is music in which *the* waltz is similarly reduced to its minimum characteristic elements. In spite of fundamental differences in their respective musical idioms, the emotional climate of Berg's pre-war 'marche macabre' is similar to that of Ravel's post-war 'valse macabre.' ''[107] While this piece points directly to *Wozzeck*, it serves a vital purpose within this work, since the middle piece is a waltz, and both pieces are treated with dark irony directed at the same social, military, or class targets at which Kraus also aimed his barbs.

The middle piece, ''Reigen,'' probably has the strongest literary association, being connected by Berg with the play by Arthur Schnitzler of the same name. Robert Falck, who first noted this connection, stresses that it is not as obvious as it might seem; ''Reigen'' or round dance, after all, was not an unusual name for a piece of music, and it is only through careful comparison of Berg's piece and Schnitzler's play that the link emerges convincingly.[108] The formal similarities are remarkable, and Falck skillfully demonstrates them. Berg had read the play before he was twenty, and one suspects that he was less struck by the banal treatment of sex than by the deception of the men and the forthrightness of the women. The play has ten characters of all classes, ten interlocking scenes with two characters engaging in sex in each, and one common character in each adjoining scene. As such, the play has a symmetrical form, with the whore in the first and the last scenes having moved from a lowly soldier at the beginning to a (military) count at the end.

The center of the work focuses on the deceptions of a married couple. The whore holds the work together, and the other women (a maid, a young wife, a *süsse Mädel*—a young lower-class woman who frequently appears in Schnitzler's works—and an actress) all resemble the whore in one way or another. Like Altenberg's or Kraus's whores, her freespiritedness and amorality place her in a position of admiration. Berg could easily identify with most of the men (a soldier, a young gentleman, a husband, a poet, and a count) and in fact had found himself in comparable sexual situations. Considering his treatment of woman in the *Altenberg Lieder*, this work was a natural extension, one potentially offensive to Schoenberg. But if Schoenberg or anyone else did not suspect the connection with Schnitzler, Berg, who relished secret associations and would plant many more in his works to come, was not about to tell him.

OPERA, APOCALYPSE, AND THE DANCE OF DEATH: *WOZZECK*

Berg appears to have had some inkling of how extraordinary his achievement with *Wozzeck* was when he completed the work in 1922 and finally saw its premiere in 1925, but he could not possibly have known what this work would do to opera in the twentieth century—that some of the finest composers of the century would not even attempt opera because of his accomplishment. One of those composers, George Crumb, in an interview published in 1982, put the matter into perspective: "I tend to be a little frightened at the possibility of ever doing that [writing an opera]. The example of *Wozzeck* is frightening, it's such a tremendous piece. One feels that Berg has kind of wrapped up all the possibilities. I'm sure that's not true, but it just seems that way to composers. Some of them do write operas, but there's nothing that comes close to Berg."[109]

In May 1914 Berg saw the Vienna premiere of Georg Büchner's drama *Woyzeck* and instantly recognized that this was the work on which he would base his first opera. A year and a half earlier Schoenberg had made a remark that strengthened Berg's confidence about such a project: "Have you ever thought of writing something for the theater? I sometimes think you would be good at that! In any case it could be very stimulating for you."[110] After seeing Büchner's drama, Berg immediately set to work on sketches for two scenes for his opera. After this initial burst of energy and enthusiasm, the project could very easily have foundered, as had happened with the recent *Seraphita* symphony. Circumstances prevented any sort of concentrated work on the score. Military service made headway all but impossible, and during periods of leave he accomplished very little. As late as June 1921 he had not yet completed the layout of the scenes.

Berg wrote *Wozzeck* in three acts, with each act carefully divided into five scenes. As the musical basis for the scenes he used forms or processes such as passacaglia, sonata form, and variation. For dramatic purposes at times he used *Sprechstimme* or speech singing. While *Wozzeck* is an atonal work, tonality remains very much a factor, and in fact keys such as C major and D minor are used symbolically. Wozzeck, a lowly soldier, takes abuse from persons in authority such as the Captain and the Doctor and is given to hallucinations and visions. He argues that conventional morality suits persons of wealth, not ''poor people like us''— words used by Berg for a musical leitmotif. The infidelity of his common-law spouse, Marie, along with his own mental instability, drives him to murder her. After the murder he attempts to dispose of the weapon in a lake and drowns himself in the process.

Following the initial euphoria of discovering the right text, Berg was forced to look more soberly at the complexity and purpose of the project. With the war in progress, did he wish his opera to make any type of political or moral statement about the war? Considering the nature of Büchner's text, would he emphasize certain themes such as apocalypse, was there room for optimism in his approach, and how would he structure this highly fragmented work? Also, there were questions to be answered about the function of the music, the nature of the musical language, and the approach to be taken to musical imagery.

Opera in 1914 had reached a crisis point, and the existing operatic models were of little help to Berg. While he still admired Wagner at this time, the solution was not to be found here. Speaking about the completed *Wozzeck* a decade and a half later, he referred to the necessity of achieving a ''variety of musical means by avoiding the Wagnerian recipe of 'through-composing' each scene in similar manner.''[111] Among his contemporaries, associates, and friends, no useful models emerged. Richard Strauss's works were completely foreign to the type of text that Berg had taken on. Schoenberg's operas to date, *Erwartung* and *Die glückliche Hand*, were relatively short monodramas and therefore helped little in planning a large, complex work with different characters, themes, and levels of action. Similarly, Schreker's operas did not help other than in matters of orchestration.

The lack of an adequate operatic model for *Wozzeck* proved not necessarily to be a disadvantage. If music could not provide the model, literature quite possibly could; Berg knew that writers had grappled with and in fact solved many of the problems he saw facing his dramatic work. Here Strindberg stood out; not only did the sense of searching in his plays correspond with Berg's own aspirations, but he had also devised means of using music in both structural and metaphorical ways that Berg found immensely appealing. His fascination with Strindberg's use of the key of D minor has already been noted. Aside from that, Berg was well aware of Strindberg's literary applications of musical forms or processes such as the suite (*Charles XII*), sonata form (*Crimes and Crimes* and *The Ghost Sonata*), or variation form (*A Dream Play*). It can be argued that Berg's use of these forms in *Wozzeck* owed something to Strindberg's treatment of them in his plays.[112] In the case of *Wozzeck*, Kraus may have also pointed in the direction Berg wished to go.

Of Kraus's various works, his monumental drama *Die letzten Tage der Menschheit* probably had the greatest impact on Berg. Writing to Helene on 14 September 1919, he ordered, "Nobody must talk to me now for the next two or three days: the fourth and fifth act of *The Last Days of Mankind* has been published—a whole book, 450 pages."[113] Even for his own composition Berg was unlikely to be so protective of his privacy. His acceptance of Kraus's style and format for his own essays has already been discussed; Kraus's possible effect on Berg's music, the influence on "art and the most sacred things," is a much more delicate matter, but should not be underestimated.[114]

The possibilities for comparison between *Wozzeck* and *Die letzten Tage* unfold in various ways; considering Kraus's publication dates and Berg's progress on his opera, influence from a purely logistical point of view appears possible. Kraus specifically intended his work as a commentary on Austria's involvement in World War I, and finding appropriate language or formats for this proved a major challenge. For Kraus, the solution lay in the presentation of a combination of documentation and imaginative material, a mixture of satire and poetry in what appears as a format of free association. His strongest model for this, as Edward Timms has recognized,[115] may very well have come from the works of Büchner, whose *Woyzeck* presents the elements of an actual legal case in fragmented and bizarre ways.

As Kraus's title implies, an apocalyptic vision stands as a primary feature of his work. The devastation of the war both sharpened his satire and forced him beyond satire as he stood in lonely vigil over the apparent collapse of the human race. While apocalypse is also central to Büchner's *Woyzeck*, Berg interprets the text in a way that brings it more into line with Kraus's irony. *Wozzeck* opens in medias res, lacking a definable beginning, with an explanation from the Captain that time is but a stream of minutes, hours, days, months, and years that need somehow to be filled. Wozzeck has very little to sustain himself, as he receives punishment at every turn. He has little left but the working of his own mind, and even that becomes progressively less reliable. When he is left to his own devices, he engages in a type of sense-making process with his apocalyptic visions, allowing him to imagine that he is "on the track" of something big. Stripped of his dignity in all social and personal relationships, isolated and regarded as a freakish spectacle, he has one remaining hope for reunion with humanity, and that lies in his eschatological vision, a vision of a common end. Even this final chance of escaping the temporal chaos recognized by the Captain evaporates as he inadvertently drowns himself searching for the knife he used to murder Marie.

Dance, especially the waltz, stands as the strongest symbol of Viennese stability and security, and in *Die letzten Tage* this becomes the force that ironically hurls humanity into the abyss. In 1913 Kraus had written in *Tod und Tango* about the bizarre case of a young Viennese bank employee from a good family, an elegant dancer, who murdered his wife. Not only was he acquitted by the authorities because of his dancing prowess, but the bank promoted him as well. The "dance of death" theme takes on a much more grisly aspect in *Die letzten Tage*. Kraus sets a late scene in a ballroom with the social elite who predictably dance. An Austrian says, "Aus Tod wird Tanz," and this leads to a ghastly scene with terrible music, a pile of rotting unburied corpses, and a flock of ravens taking special pleasure in the pickings of men of honor. In "Die letzte Nacht" (the last scene), shortly before the final destruction, hyenas dance a tango around the corpses, and three journalists describe the event using the appropriate society-column language. Complete chaos ensues.

Büchner's play contains dances, but Berg goes much further, toward the possibilities suggested by Kraus. Preceding the apprentices' scene, marked by irreverent and nonsensical outpourings, Berg provides a dance, a slow Ländler, that captures the essence of the breakdown of order, representing, in his own description, musical chaos.[116] In the Act 3 inn scene, Wozzeck dances after murdering Marie, shouting, "Dance, all of you, dance away! Leap, sweat, and reek! For some day soon, he'll fetch you . . . the Devil!" This squalid side of dancing relates to Kraus's woman in Act 3, Scene 3, of *Die letzten Tage*: "If I dance, I sweat. If I sweat, I stink." The polka used in Berg's inn scene compares with Kraus's tango. In Berg's final scene Marie's child and other children play and ride hobbyhorses. One child callously shouts, "Hey! Your mother is dead," while Marie's child says nothing but "hop, hop" to the accompaniment of a children's folk dance.

Even in his use of *Sprechstimme* or *Sprechgesang*, Berg seemed closer to Kraus than to Schoenberg, who had used it in *Pierrot lunaire*. In *Wozzeck* Berg contrasted it with normal bel canto singing for dramatic purposes, and since Schoenberg did not do that until *Moses und Aron*, it appears that the master may have learned from his pupil. An example of Berg's contrast occurs in Act 1, Scene 2, in which Wozzeck uses *Sprechstimme* (in 3/4 time) while his friend Andres sings a folk song in a normal singing voice (in 6/8). Here Wozzeck stands on fertile ground for the outpouring of his apocalyptic vision, and *Sprechstimme* seems appropriate to the nebulous and distorted nature of the vision. Berg altered Büchner's text at this point, making the folk-song text stable and sensible, allowing for the musical contrast between the two voices. This and other treatments in *Wozzeck* suggest Kraus's in "Die letzte Nacht," where a general, in *Sprechgesang*, chastises a dead corporal for not observing proper dress regulations. The complete detachment of his thinking from human decency is aptly set apart by a mode of expression that emphasizes the underlying chaos.

In *Die letzten Tage* poetry emerges as an extremely potent force toward the end of the work, and in this a striking model existed for *Wozzeck*. Most of

Kraus's work uses a satirical mode, but the extraordinary ending defies that language. Beginning late in Act 5, Scene 55, Kraus moves from satirical prose to poetry and remains in verse until the end of the work. The Epilogue, ''Die letzte Nacht,'' entirely in verse, embraces the supernatural and brings about the destruction of this planet. In contrast to the first speaker of the work, who was a news vendor, the last, the Voice of God, quotes the words of Kaiser Wilhelm II from the beginning of the war: ''I did not wish it so.'' In spite of the destruction, this brings a curiously optimistic ending to the work. A god with regrets reaffirms moral and cosmic order. Hope, therefore, remains alive, and Kraus the poet rather than the satirist suggests a possibility of redemption and renewal.[117]

For Berg, there was a model here for the means of transcending ''brutal reality,'' suggesting musical possibilities. Like Kraus's treatment of poetry, Berg uses music in a special way near the end of *Wozzeck*, in the interlude between Scenes 4 and 5 of Act 3. Harry Zohn aptly describes Kraus's Epilogue as a recapitulation of ''many motifs of his play in concentrated, cinematographic form, with actual and allegorical characters appearing in a ghastly operatic procession.''[118] Similarly, Berg's interlude is a reprise of the major themes from *Wozzeck*, described by Berg himself as an epilogue culminating in D minor, which ''should be appreciated as the composer's confession, breaking through the framework of the dramatic plot and, likewise, even as an appeal to the audience, which is here meant to represent Humanity itself.''[119] Berg's discussion of this could not be closer to Kraus's own apparent intention for his Epilogue. Not only in the final interlude but by means of musical assimilation throughout the work, Berg transcended the despair of Wozzeck, offering a sense of hope through a process of integration.

Just as Kraus was able to find meaning in the acceptance of the existing high achievements of language and poetry, so Berg attempted to define the composer's role as one that involved allowing music to rise to those heights it had reached so often in the past. As George Crumb attests, few would achieve it after *Wozzeck*.

THROUGH A MIRROR DARKLY: THE CHAMBER CONCERTO

Berg seldom wrote much about his works, letting them speak for themselves; the exceptions are his ''Lecture'' on *Wozzeck* and the open letter of dedication to Schoenberg on the Chamber Concerto. The possibility exists of either secret or overt programs attached to all Berg's instrumental works. In the Lyric Suite and the Violin Concerto the music itself suggests programs without actually articulating them. As for the Chamber Concerto, Berg leaves no ambiguity about this, referring to the ''friendship, love, and a world of human and spiritual references I have smuggled into these three movements,'' and the delight this should give to adherents of program music.[120] As his comment suggests, different levels of programmatic meaning can be found, and Brenda Dalen's study of one of these, the private reference to Schoenberg's first wife, Mathilde, has already been noted. As for the "world of human and spiritual references," one must seek a more universal interpretation, and here Berg's literary interests prove exceedingly useful.

Of the various striking musical features of the Chamber Concerto, the palindrome in the second movement stands out most prominently both audibly to the listener and visually in the score. In Berg's own words, "The return of the first half of the movement, comprising 120 measures, occurs in retrograde, either as free presentation of the thematic material spooling back, or, for instance during the entire middle part (B), in exact mirror image."[121] This was not Berg's first musical palindrome, but in no earlier work did he present one in such a conspicuous way. One can argue, as I will in the discussion of *Der Wein*, that there were strong literary precedents for Berg's palindromes, found in the works of Goethe, Strindberg, and Baudelaire. In the Chamber Concerto, started in 1923, the palindrome stands so pervasively that a probable model should not only contain mirror images but should also have them as its central theme. Such a work does in fact exist, the drama *Spiegelmensch* (Mirror Man), completed in 1920 by Berg's friend Franz Werfel. Berg read this work shortly after it appeared and in 1921 remarked to Schoenberg that "Werfel is the coming literary giant. He has written 'his *Faust*': *Der Spiegelmensch*."[122]

Werfel designed his drama in three parts: (1) Mirror, (2) One thing at a time, and (3) Window. Its elaborate stage machinery and length (over 200 pages) make it difficult to stage, although it is not as unmanageable as Kraus's much longer *Die letzten Tage* or Goethe's *Faust*. The connection with *Faust* has been noted often, as it was by Berg, and it resembles *Faust* in content as well as the fact that Werfel wrote it in verse. In an oriental setting of indeterminate time, the work has two main characters: Thamal and Spiegelmensch. Thamal, a poet dissatisfied with his meaningless life and the world, withdraws to a Tibetan monastery. There he discovers a large mirror, in which he must confront his own image. A surge of renewed self-hatred compels him to shoot with a revolver at his image in the mirror. An animated figure leaps from the mirror, Spiegelmensch, his alter ego or darker self. After numerous adventures of love and glory led by Spiegelmensch, Thamal must accept death as punishment for his sins, but instead of dying he is transported back to the monastery, where the mirror now reveals a radiant landscape. Freed from his egotism, he can look dispassionately at the world.

Music plays an important role in this work, as the text calls for the performance of music and also includes distinctive rhythms and meters in the treatment of language and verse. Remarkable parallels can be found not only between Werfel's musical designations—especially the use of specific dances—and Berg's, but also in larger structural matters. For Werfel, the mirror necessarily appears in the first part, while Berg's palindrome, with its bearing on the whole work, must be placed as the middle movement. Aside from that shift, the works bear a very close resemblance to each other, with specific musical events in the play happening at similar points in the Chamber Concerto.[123] Rhythm is especially important to both works, and Berg invokes Mahler's death rhythm from the Ninth Symphony referred to earlier, an appropriate reference in association with a work where redemption comes through an acceptance of death.

Palindromes or mirror images play an extraordinarily important role in virtually all of Berg's mature works, and the comparison with *Spiegelmensch* allows interpretive access to the meaning Berg may have intended for his mirrors, as he ties into a long-standing literary tradition. Nineteenth- and early-twentieth-century literature used the mirror extensively as an image, evoking at larger or smaller levels the conflicting sides of the *Doppelgänger*. The forces in opposition are the dual sides of one person, the internal struggle between pure and debased instincts. God and the devil wage a battle for possession, and both sides, as with Faust, must necessarily be experienced. Berg similarly designed his palindrome to fuse symmetry and contrast.

Strindberg's *Road to Damascus*, Part I, is generally recognized as one of Werfel's models for *Spiegelmensch*. Berg knew Strindberg's work exceedingly well and underscored the following line in his copy of it: "Annihilation of the godhead in you. We call that spiritual death."[124] The main character in this palindromic play finds salvation through the discovery of humility and faith. As for *Spiegelmensch*, Walter Sokel aptly suggests that the person "who has truly transcended himself looks out through a window upon true 'higher reality.' "[125] Berg found the journey into this type of Christian mysticism immensely appealing, referring to "an ideal, pure reality of the spirit" as early as 1909.[126] In the early to mid-1920s it was even stronger and determined that his instrumental works would have programmatic associations far exceeding personal or private matters.

DE PROFUNDIS: THE LYRIC SUITE

While Berg informs us of the programmatic possibility of the Chamber Concerto in his open letter to Schoenberg, in the Lyric Suite he does that in the work itself with highly expressive movement headings as well as with musical quotations. Because the six movements of this piece written for string quartet in 1925–26 are designated *Allegretto gioviale, Andante amoroso, Allegro misterioso* (*Trio estatico*), *Adagio appassionato, Presto delirando*, and *Largo desolato*, he clearly expects us to think of nonmusical associations. Those who wrote about the work before 1977 did not miss this expectation, with Redlich referring to the work's programmatic tendencies and Adorno calling it a "latent opera."[127] Two discoveries in 1976 and 1977 changed forever the way this work will be regarded, although we have not yet necessarily grasped which of the two is more important. Douglass Green, examining a manuscript draft of the finale at the Austrian National Library in 1976, was astounded to find that Berg had written in a text. Green succeeded in identifying it as Stefan George's translation of Baudelaire's "De profundis clamavi" from *Les Fleurs du mal* (*Die Blumen des Bösen*).[128] A year later, George Perle tracked down a score of the work privately annotated by Berg for Hanna Fuchs-Robettin, in which Berg professes his passionate love for her.[129] Subsequently his letters to her have surfaced, and they confirm this passion.

Quite aside from the implications of these discoveries for the interpretation of the work, the letters and annotations appear to foster an impression very different from the officially sanctioned one (given in Reich's biography) of Berg's marriage during the last decade of his life. The results have not been pleasant: Helene Berg has been maligned by some for her apparent deception, defenders of the happy marriage have been offended, and disbelievers in such personalizing of works have scoffed. Perle's own approach, waving his discovery like a red flag in the face of a charging opposition, has not helped; by turning Hanna into a conventional lover who jeopardized the marriage to Helene, he entirely missed the mark. Helene more than anyone understood what was happening, and one should not be surprised that she did not like it and preferred that the world should not know the truth. Not only did Helene understand, but in her own way she could tolerate it, knowing that it was crucial for Berg's creativity; in no way did it diminish her love for him.

A somewhat bizarre implication of the discovery of the Baudelaire text has been the assumption that the work should now be performed with the text sung. Perle for one calls the nonvocal version Berg presented an "arrangement,"[130] assuming that he was under some sort of marital duress to suppress the vocal version. As an outstanding composer himself, Perle should know better: composers have the right to change their minds, make revisions, and present works as they see fit. A larger issue arises here concerning the extent to which great works such as the Lyric Suite are purely private and personal expressions or may still offer something more universal. On this matter Berg fully emulated Strindberg, who acknowledged that the writer "must like a vampire suck blood from his friends, from his nearest and dearest, from himself." But, as Evert Sprinchorn noted, when he "seemed to be most subjective and most personal, utterly lost in himself, he was actually most in touch with world affairs."[131] Berg spoke to people other than Hanna with the Lyric Suite, and he probably left out the text to emphasize the work's universality.

The linkage with Baudelaire may in fact be much more important than the existence of a private annotation intended for one person's eyes (and ears) only. Baudelaire's *Les Fleurs du mal* would figure prominently in Berg's next work as well, and even the Lyric Suite may have yet another of his texts associated with it. Among the papers of Berg's pupil Julius Schloss, a collection now at McGill University, lies a copy in Berg's hand of George's translation of Baudelaire's "Herbst" (Autumn), also from *Les Fleurs du mal*, which Don McLean believes is connected to the fifth movement.[132] The text for "De profundis clamavi" has also been entered in a score of the Lyric Suite in this collection.

Baudelaire had been Altenberg's strongest literary influence, and at this point in his life Berg appears to have shifted his strongest poetic affiliation to Altenberg's French model.

In all probability Berg experienced a profound personal crisis around 1924. He had not yet enjoyed the success of *Wozzeck*, Schoenberg felt like a millstone around his neck, and the euphoria of the earlier years with Helene had no doubt worn thin. Yet these external issues paled in comparison to his much more important inner aesthetic world, to what may have now seemed a type of imprisonment of his self, no longer offering him solace from the brutal or aggravating outside world. Quite possibly this inner prison was driving him to a point of isolated despair, one he could certainly not share with anyone else. The solution was to solve it on its own terms, through the resources that had never failed him in the past: poetry. Altenberg had saved him from his personal prison in the past, but Berg's crisis now thrust more deeply than Altenberg could reach; the resources of a greater poet were called for, and Baudelaire came forward in Berg's mind.

Baudelaire had experienced a similar crisis that drove him close to the brink, and Berg, aware of this from his extensive reading of Baudelaire, sought a similar solution. In *Der Leidensweg des Dichters Baudelaire*, acquired by Berg in the early 1930s, François Porché describes the crisis at this time as everything turning "to fetters, the convict's chain and ball."[133] In the *Journaux intimes*, which Berg owned in 1924, Baudelaire speaks of the problem faced by the genius of combining his need for recognition with the need for solitude. Baudelaire's longtime lover, Jeanne Duval, could no longer inspire poems, and a new muse—a Laura or Beatrice, as he called her—was urgently needed. She finally came in 1856 in the form of Mme Sabatier, a prominent salonnière, who quickly became the recipient of love poems and letters from Baudelaire. Jeanne remained important to him until he died, but, as he pointed out about his new muse, "the woman one does not possess is the woman one loves." He did ultimately have sex with her and lost the magic: "A few days ago you were a goddess, which is so convenient, which is so beautiful and inviolable. And now, you are a woman."[134]

Berg did not make the same mistake, and circumstances no doubt prevented it: he was married, unlike Baudelaire, and so was Hanna, unlike Mme Sabatier. Hanna became a necessary muse for Berg, a poetic illusion capable not so much of lifting him from despair as allowing him to transform despair into beauty. Like Baudelaire to Mme Sabatier, he sent professions of spiritual love to her, similarly mastering the requisite epistolary technique, to which she replied in kind. For whatever reason, she was prepared to indulge this need of the man who had just emerged as one of the musical giants, perhaps even with the knowledge of her husband, Herbert, who remained a great friend and admirer of Berg. It is unclear when Helene discovered what was happening, but when she did, she understood it, as we learn from a letter to one of the "conspirators," her dear friend Alma Mahler, sister-in-law of Hanna:

He didn't want too close an association with this woman, as he imagined her in the unheard-of florescence of his artist's fantasy, for fear of disappointment (for Alban was spoiled, mentally and physically). He avoided her. . . . It all comes to *a flight from reality*. In *this* way and *only* in this way could the *Lyric Suite* come to be. I must therefore acknowledge the *sense* of all that has happened—and remain silent. And therefore I can also say that there is no trace of bitterness in me, only emotion and melancholy. And nothing, nothing can dim my love for him.[135]

The creative flow of poems from Baudelaire to his new spiritual lover also worked for Berg: hence the Lyric Suite. Just as Baudelaire could say about *Les Fleurs du mal* that "I have put my whole self into this terrible book," Berg could surely say the same of the Lyric Suite, and his annotated score for Hanna certainly confirms that fact. This, however, should not delude us into thinking that the work came into existence purely as a testament of love to her; the work was conceived to fulfill Berg's innermost poetic needs, and she became the catalyst allowing that to happen. The progression in the Lyric Suite from *Allegretto gioviale* to *Largo desolato* confirms its inner and hence universal application. The despair at the end does not result from something as petty as the impossibility of a union between Berg and Hanna; Helene rightly recognized this. Here we have the ultimate acceptance by Berg of despair as the prime tenet of romanticism; like Baudelaire, he could call himself the "poet of unhappiness," and this he does in the music of the Lyric Suite, in the progression of the programmatic movement headings, in his musical quotations of Zemlinsky and Wagner's *Tristan* Prelude, and in the linkages with Baudelaire's texts from *Les Fleurs du mal*.

The Baudelaire text used by Berg for the finale, "De profundis clamavi" (Out of the depths I call to thee), as well as the one possibly linked with the fifth movement, "Herbst Sonnett" (Autumn sonnet), both underline the sense of despair in a prison of solitude. Both refer to winter or its approach, linking, as in "De profundis clamavi," the abyss and chaos into which the soul has fallen with the dead landscape, darkness, and coldness of winter: "Even the polar land is not so barren." Animals are to be envied their ability to escape it through "the dizziness of a senseless sleep." Similarly, in "Herbst Sonnett" Baudelaire cries, "In my grief I bear only the unenveloped instinct of beasts." Here too there is "torture-chamber pain" as well as "terror, delusion and disgrace." In all probability Berg also knew (or knew about) Oscar Wilde's *De profundis*, Wilde's letters from prison where he was literally in fetters and despised because of his sexual orientation. Both Berg and Baudelaire, conscious of their own feminine characteristics, could experience solitude and create poetic worlds not unlike Wilde's. In the Lyric Suite Berg sinks to the depths, but with the help of his muse he can express this as beauty in perhaps the most beautiful of all his works.

Aside from the short setting of Theodor Storm's "Schliesse mir die Augen beide" in 1925, a recasting of the same poem he had set in a richly romantic version almost two decades earlier, this was Berg's first foray into twelve-tone music. He did not see this mode of composition as a deterrent in any way to expressiveness and may have chosen Storm's text to illustrate that. As Adorno points out, Berg regretted the diminishing of expression in Schoenberg's early twelve-tone efforts and endeavored to avoid this in his own works.[136] To make this clear to the performers of the premiere of the Lyric Suite, Kolisch and his quartet, Berg discussed his technique in his analytical notes for them, placing the unique compositional approach in the context of his aesthetic (or programmatic) objectives:

> The row of the first movement is changed in the course of the [second, third, fifth, and sixth] through the displacement of several notes. (This change is immaterial with respect to the line, but significant with respect to its character—''subjection to fate.'') . . . Connections between the individual movements are achieved—apart from the fact that the twelve-tone row establishes such connections—in that one component (one theme or one row, one section or one idea) is taken over in the movement that follows, and the last reaches back again to the first. Not in a mechanical way, naturally, but likewise in connection with the large unfolding (the continuing intensification of mood) within the *whole* composition (''subjection to fate!'').[137]

Within the row Berg uses a basic four-note cell, B F A B♭ (in German notation, H F A B—Hanna's and his initials); in his annotations he calls her attention to ''our numbers, 10 and 23.'' The significance of these numbers, found in tempo markings or measure counts throughout the work, will be discussed with the Violin Concerto, but even the application of these may owe something to Baudelaire. In his *Journaux intimes* he writes: ''Music conveys the idea of space. So do all the arts, more or less; since they are *number* and since number is a translation of space.''[138] The space in question may have helped release Berg from the inner exile he shared with Baudelaire.

DECADENCE AND D MINOR: *DER WEIN*

Unlike the Lyric Suite, where Baudelaire lurks furtively in the background, Berg set three poems in *Der Wein* (Wine) from *Les Fleurs du mal*, once again from Stefan George's translation/adaptation *Die Blumen des Bösen*. Baudelaire wrote five poems in his *Le Vin* set, and Berg selected three of the four given by George for his concert aria of 1929, commissioned by the Viennese soprano Ružena Herlinger. Berg then rearranged the order of the final two, giving the new order ''Die Seele des Weines,'' ''Der Wein der Liebenden,'' and ''Der Wein des Einsamen.'' His strategic arrangement reminds one of his treatment of the texts in the *Altenberg Lieder* as well as his ordering of the scenes of Büchner's *Woyzeck*.

In *Der Wein* the strongest presentation of the key of D minor in all Berg's works emerges. He had taken special note of Strindberg's fascination with Beethoven's D-minor works, and in the works in question Beethoven always modulates from D minor to C major before reaching the relative major, usually treating C major as the primary second-key area. Despite their aesthetic differences, one can easily get from D minor to C major, and the abruptness of the key change allows the sense of polarity between them to be emphasized. Berg exploits the same relationship in *Der Wein*, placing it in a symmetrical, palindromic context; as in the Chamber Concerto in relation to Werfel's *Spiegelmensch*, the two sides of the mirror image point to primary oppositions. The prime twelve-tone row itself, prominently stated in the opening vocal line, begins with a D-minor scale. C major also appears near the beginning and throughout, and in fact it can be found in the twelve-tone matrix as a fusion of RI_5 and P_7.[139] In *Der Wein* the presence of a text helps to define these oppositions, and parallel poetic ones are invoked, including the focus on the color red as a fusion of a light and dark opposition that Goethe had explained in his *Farbenlehre*.

In keeping with the approaches of Strindberg and Goethe, the Baudelaire poems of *Der Wein* are notable representations of polarity within symmetry. In the first and last poems (in Berg's order), wine claims to bring hope to the disinherited or lonely man. Darkness and light are invoked, as well as colors, most notably red, the color of wine and the vehicle for possible transcendence. Berg places ''Der Wein der Liebenden'' strategically at the center of his work for both formal and metaphorical reasons. This sonnet may be deceptively optimistic, but that should not obscure the illusory sense of possible transcendence, emphasized by the key words ''Feenhimmel,'' ''leuchtende All,'' or ''traume Land.'' Against the projection of hope lurks a sense of impossibility, unreality, and disappointment. The inexorably driven seeker knows full well that any fulfillment will be countered by emptiness, hope will be met with despair, and communion, as we realize in ''Der Wein des Einsamen,'' will not dispel loneliness.[140]

In the central poem of the aria, the rationale for the structure of Berg's work emerges. The middle lines of ''Der Wein der Liebenden,'' ''Durch des Morgens blauen Kristall / Fort in das leuchtende All'' (through the blue crystal of morning, let us follow the mirage), define the search as illusory and therefore subject to despair as well as hope and place it in a twilight state, between darkness and light. The fundamental polarity here is placed in a striking context in the following tercet, where the final line reads ''Beide voll gleicher Lust'' (both filled with the same joy). The last two words, translated from the French ''délire parallèle'' (parallel transcendence), suggest a symmetry or balance, even though Baudelaire refers to the lover as ''sister,'' adding yet another level of polarity since he appears to couch the relationship in incestuous terms. The word *Kristall* presents an image of reflection, this being a favorite word for Goethe when referring to mirror images. For Berg, the nature of the text left no question as to how the music should be shaped. The idea of symmetry in the text gives rise to a strict musical palindrome that has its center at measure 141, just after the completion of the text of ''Der Wein der Liebenden.'' In fact, the surrounding score, measures 112–70, functions symmetrically, but at the same time emphasizes contrast through the relationship of D minor and C major.

There has been a tendency to regard *Der Wein* as an experiment toward the development of the musical language of *Lulu*, rather than to give it the respect it deserves as an independent and self-contained work. While this work certainly played a role in Berg's crafting of *Lulu*, that as a purpose could not have been further from his mind. The themes emerging from the Baudelaire text show him to be grappling with the same conflicting issues as in some earlier works, including isolation, illusion, and despair. The probing of each work, both musically and aesthetically, stands as a monumental achievement in itself and cannot be detached from the poetic issues that drive the work.

PANDORA'S BOX: *LULU*

The apparent gap between Frank Wedekind's ghastly plays *Erdgeist* (Earth spirit) and *Die Büchse der Pandora* (Pandora's box) and Berg's extraordinary music for *Lulu* has not gone unnoticed by those who have written about the opera. Claudio Spies, for one, rails at Wedekind's "abysmally poor" language, its verbal excess and "hot air," and its "raffishness of low-life lingo." Spies seems to think that Berg took care of this with his paring of the text, bringing it down to something manageable as an operatic libretto; beyond that, Spies implies that the text should be ignored and we should get on with the interesting part—the music.[141] Douglas Jarman does not go that far, but still prefers a treatment that concentrates "on Berg rather than Wedekind."[142] Among writers on music these views have been in good company; in various essays on Berg's vocal music one must guess that a text exists, since it is never actually mentioned. Perhaps at the end of the century we are embarrassed by his literary tastes; how could such a great composer be attracted to the dregs of literature? Librettos, after all, the most absurd of all literary genres, have no obligation to make sense. Berg can surely be forgiven his poor choices, just as Mozart, Verdi, and others have been.

But ignoring the text of a work over which Berg agonized during the last five years of his life has its perils. In fact, we pay his intelligence and artistry the supreme insult by suggesting that the libretto to *Lulu* may be inconsequential. Literary critics have been less narrow, and while they have perhaps missed the implications of the music, they have at least been able to point in the direction of reconciling the apparent gap between libretto and music in the case of *Lulu*. No one has done this better than Erich Heller.

Wedekind's Lulu plays might very well have been relegated to the junk heap of literature had it not been for Berg's setting. Despite his crude language, Wedekind had at least one champion in Vienna in none other than Karl Kraus, who appears to have found the language appropriate to the subject matter. Kraus staged a private production of *Pandora's Box* in 1905, when censorship had banned the work from public presentation; Kraus himself took a minor role

(Kungu Poti), and Wedekind played Jack the Ripper. A young Alban Berg, as Tilly Newes (Wedekind's future wife, who played Lulu) recalled some years later, sat in the audience.

The Lulu plays draw on Weininger's peculiar notions of women and bisexuality, with Wedekind's own distinctive twist. Lulu has all the attributes of the sensually liberated woman, free to move among partners and enjoy others while still married. Her amorality identified her as the prostitute type so admired by Kraus and Altenberg, although the mortality rate for her partners sounds Weininger's misogynist alarm. The extreme male-female opposites come together at the end of the work when Lulu, now a common prostitute in London, meets Jack, whose domination of her must be so complete that he kills her in the act of sex; his penetration of her is for his benefit only, and his penis becomes a knife. Between the extremes of Jack and Lulu stand characters who combine male and female characteristics, most notably in the lesbian Countess Geschwitz. Even Alwa, the poet and son of Lulu's discoverer Dr. Schön, proves more companion than lover to Lulu, needing her for his artistic inspiration but also sensitive to her needs.

The Lulu plays attempt to be more than a sordid tale of her sexual exploits and her lovers' grisly demises. The titles, *Earth Spirit* and *Pandora's Box*, invoke not only myth but distinctive treatments by Goethe, the *Erdgeist* being the powerful apparition from the opening of *Faust*, Part I, who shakes Faust away from his musty intellectual world and opens the door of nature to him. The mythical Pandora brings misery to mankind, but Goethe in his incomplete *Pandora* treats her differently. Kraus admired Goethe's version as he did few other works, and one can safely assume that Berg had witnessed at least some of his frequent readings of it. Other references to Goethe can be found in Wedekind, such as Lulu's various nicknames, which include Mignon and Nellie (Helen). Wedekind appears to make a complete mockery of Goethe's sublime works, but neither Kraus nor Berg took his plays that way, preferring the transcendent possibilities that lay beyond his banality.

The transcendent vision—the other side of the coin—lay in Goethe's representation of *Erdgeist* and Pandora, in the acceptance of nature that Berg himself so ardently believed possible. Woman becomes the embodiment of this sense of nature, ultimately effecting salvation through "das ewig Weibliche" (the eternal feminine), the words that bring *Faust* to a close. Goethe inverts the mythical Pandora so that she releases joy, not misery, on the world; the incomplete part of the work was to allow her return, and here an inevitable parallel with Christianity emerges. Love with the highest spiritual and sensual (although not necessarily consummated) union is inexorably driven by nature, and one should not interfere with the force. Death in the sense of romantic fulfillment lies at the end; as Erich Heller reminds us, "All tragic Romantic lovers are blood relations of Tristan and Isolde and die of love."[143] Here lies an explanation for Berg's quotation of Wagner in the Lyric Suite.

Without the projection of Goethe beyond Wedekind, the gap between Berg's music and the libretto for *Lulu* proves all but impossible to bridge. The text confronts us with the raw image of unrestrained sexuality, apparently unleashing a torrent of plagues on mankind; Lulu in the end must be punished in kind for her evil. Yet she is innocent, succumbing to the forces of nature, and while she may not hold the keys to salvation, she points to her sisters Gretchen and Pandora who do. For Berg, the music carries that role, just as the interludes (especially the last one) had offered a sense-making function in *Wozzeck*, comparable to Kraus's poetry in *Die letzten Tage*. In *Lulu* Berg makes no mystery of the fact that he identifies with Alwa, the poet turned composer in the opera, the only man who understands Lulu, who can get the most from her without possessing her, who needs her for artistic inspiration, and who recognizes that he cannot be a complete man or artist without her becoming a part of him. With this understanding he (Berg/Alwa) can transcend Wedekind and create music that becomes the ultimate bisexual and spiritual fusion, reaching the level he had only begun to imagine was possible with the *Altenberg Lieder*.

George Perle has been maligned by some for bringing Hanna into Berg's late works (the "Tritone Lady," as Spies calls her); while Perle may have misplaced her autobiographically, his instinct was nevertheless correct. She was not Berg's Lulu but his Pandora (as Goethe portrayed her) from afar; if this had turned into an affair, the poetry would have been lost. The music plays a highly integrative function and achieves that at levels that will be heard by the audience or can be deciphered only through close analysis. Like many of Berg's other major works, this one has a musical palindrome at its center, accompanying the "film-music" interlude at the midpoint of Act 2. Hearing the work in three acts, with Friedrich Cerha's completion of Berg's almost finished Act 3, is, of course, absolutely crucial to the formal and aesthetic design of the work. Berg himself underlined the importance of this interlude, writing to Schoenberg that "the interlude which bridges the gap between the last act of *Earth Spirit* and the first act of *Pandora* is also the focal point of the whole tragedy. In it begins, after the ascent of the preceding acts and scenes, the descent of the following scenes."[144] A passionate filmgoer, Berg had no doubt seen G. W. Pabst's *Pandora's Box* of 1929, and he may have even taken note of Pabst's use of mirrors at a similar point in his film.

For Berg, this mirror image affects the entire work. In the most obvious representation, Berg allows the same three singers/actors to play different roles in both halves of the opera: the victims (the Physician, the Painter, and Dr. Schön) become the three clients (the Professor, the Negro, and Jack the Ripper) of the second half. The effects of the palindrome ripple far beyond the center of the work, reaching in various ways toward the beginning and the end. On a larger scale, this influences the three-part, ABA structure of the opera, allowing Act 3 to work as something of a recapitulation of material from the earlier part.[145] Highly intricate musical integration exists as well at the level of tone rows and their breaking into component parts or cells, which offer connections, for example, among the various characters of the work. Some have even argued that the work derives from a single row, although that depends on how loosely one is prepared to accept row similarities. Just as the mirror in the Chamber Concerto implied a polarity of opposites as well as integration, the same applies here, as musical dualities point to those in the drama. Clearly Berg's elaborate musical working-out process points beyond the music itself to the issues involving bisexuality and spiritual transcendence that were fundamental to his own existence.

THE RHYTHMS OF LIFE AND DEATH: THE VIOLIN CONCERTO

In 1935, while trying to complete *Lulu*, Berg received a request from Louis Krasner to write a violin concerto. When Krasner finally mustered the courage to make his request, he found Berg not hostile to the idea but nevertheless puzzled by the young violinist's interest, observing that "what you require for your programs are brilliant compositions by Wieniawski and Vieuxtemps—you know, that is not my kind of music." Krasner replied that Beethoven and Mozart also wrote violin concertos, and then played what he imagined to be his trump card: "The attacking criticism of 12-tone music everywhere is that this music is only cerebral and without feeling or emotion. . . . Think of what it would mean for the whole Schoenberg Movement if a new Alban Berg Violin Concerto should succeed in demolishing the antagonism of this 'cerebral, no emotion' cliché and argument."[146] The composer of *Der Wein* and the Lyric Suite must have been bemused by this naïve challenge, but in any event he accepted the commission.

For a composer now into his fifth year of work on an opera, there was little reason to assume that the concerto would be written quickly. Having much earlier in his career recognized his inability to work at a rapid pace, Berg stopped using opus numbers after Op. 7 (*Wozzeck*), embarrassed by the unlikelihood of ever reaching Op. 20. Considering the extraordinary complexity of Berg's works, posterity has not been surprised by the small output. With the Violin Concerto, however, he broke from the pattern by writing it in a mere few months, completing the short score on 23 July and the orchestration in August. On 28 August he described it to Schoenberg: "I myself can report that as of two weeks ago the violin concerto is completely finished. It is in two parts. Each part with two movements: I a) Andante (Präludium) b) Allegretto (Scherzo) II a) Allegro (cadenza) b) Adagio (chorale setting). I chose a very advantageous row for the entire piece (since D major and similar 'violin concerto' keys were of course out of the question), namely: [see Example 5.2] which coincidentally corresponded with the chorale beginning of Bach's 'Es ist genug.' "[147] The unusual opening of the Bach chorale connects to the whole-tone scale at the end of the row, although contrary to what was originally thought, Berg designed the row before he selected the chorale. He may have avoided a key, but the interlocking triads making up the opening of the row

Example 5.2

nevertheless suggest a strong tonal affinity. Krasner had asked for the work to be "lyrical and songful"—catching the essence of the violin—and with this Berg certainly complied.

Shortly after Berg embarked on the work, the eighteen-year-old daughter of Alma Mahler, Manon Gropius, much loved by the Bergs, died, and Berg dedicated the work to her with the inscription "to the memory of an angel." The tone of the concerto, along with the appropriateness of the text from "Es ist genug" (which Berg actually had printed in the score, not unlike Beethoven's "Muss es sein" in the finale of the String Quartet, Op. 135), suggests a type of programmatic eulogy for Manon. As with earlier works, more private programmatic possibilities have also arisen, and these relate to Berg's fascination with the numbers 10, 23, and 28 and their or their multiples' frequent appearance in measure counts or metronome markings (as they also had in the Lyric Suite and *Lulu*). Berg's apparent use of 23 as a personal cipher for himself and 10 for Hanna has led some to believe that this, like the Lyric Suite, stands as another hidden testimony to their love. A closer look at the significance of these numbers suggests other, more universal possibilities.

As early as 1915 Berg had told Schoenberg that 23 was his fateful number, and Schoenberg, himself fascinated by number significance and numerology, had advised Berg to become less dependent on such things. Finding a less-than-sympathetic response from Schoenberg, Berg took another tack, although he abandoned nothing of his "dependence"; completing the Violin Concerto's short score on 23 July 1935 was no coincidence. Perhaps Schoenberg would be impressed by the scientific, medical research into the matter, and Berg tried it out on him:

I must tell you briefly, dear Herr Schönberg—in *this* connection—about a book I had *never* heard of before that I came across *by chance* last summer—which seemed to confirm my old belief in the number 23. It comprises biological lectures by the well-known Berlin [medical] scholar Wilhelm Fliess: *Vom Leben und vom Tod*, in which he espouses the belief that life and divisions in the lives of all living creatures proceed periodically, resulting in periods that are always divisible by 28 and 23. [A detailed demonstration for plants and animals follows.] Similar examples for horses, dogs, etc., then also for humans, but not just for *individuals*, but also for birth and death dates, stages of life, periodicity of illness in whole families, generations, indeed nations; for the *relationship* of birth and death dates of a man and wife within individual families, royal lines, nations, etc.—and the conclusion is that the woman's number is 28, that of the man 23.[148]

Uncertain of how Schoenberg might react, Berg omitted a critical piece of information, and most of those who have written about these numbers in relation to the Violin Concerto have done the same. While the numbers 23 and 28 apply to men and women, respectively, each also pertains to the opposite sex, thereby embracing a numerical conception of bisexuality.[149]

Fliess's mixture of biology and numerology, which had numerous supporters, including Freud and Einstein, fit Berg's purposes perfectly. Not only did these numbers demonstrate convincingly for Berg the bisexual principle he so firmly believed in, but they also provided a rhythm or periodicity for the important events of life and anticipation of death. His subscription to the application of this to the rhythm of life is well known, as he often noted that important things happen on days reducible to the number 23 or attempted to help this process along, ending major works on the 23rd day of the month. If it applied to birth[150] and life, it surely bore on one's death as well, as Berg noted in his letter to Schoenberg. Freud, for a time distressed by his own homosexual attraction to Fliess, had noted that several colleagues had died at the age of 51 and made a famous prediction of his own death at that age.[151] Berg, who knew Freud, may have been struck by the fact that 23 and 28 add up to 51 and possibly anticipated his own death at that age. If that were true, he would have time to finish *Lulu* even with the interruption of the Violin Concerto. He miscalculated by only a few months, dying shortly after midnight on the night of 23–24 December 1935 at the age of 50.

The numbers of the Violin Concerto may invoke Berg and Hanna, but only to the extent that Berg saw Hanna as a gateway to a heightened spirituality he wished to share with the world. The "woman" he had tried to define in other works makes a strong appearance here, the sensuous, freespirited woman, the prostitute, the woman capable of being a muse and achieving the idea of the eternal feminine. Contrary to Weininger, woman did not stand apart from man; going beyond Kraus and even Altenberg, Berg now found the decisive way to portray her as part of man, the ideal male fusing within himself these feminine elements. Through Fliess's numbers the fusion could be achieved in music, and Berg's formal schemata, described by Douglas Jarman in relation to Fliess,[152] demonstrate how the fusion works. Part I may favor 28 and Part II, 23, but the work as a whole ties them together as a unity, just as Fliess considered 23 as the strongest defining feature of a 28-day cycle (23 days being the average interval between the end of one menstruation and the start of the next). For Fliess, "The wonderful exactitude with which the period of 23 or 28 whole days is maintained allows one to presume a profound relationship between astronomical conditions and the creation of organisms."[153]

If one takes a more universal view of the work, the significance of the Carinthian folk song quoted in both Parts I and II need not be as purely personal as some have made it. The text of this now-identified tune speaks of oversleeping in Mizzi's bed, and Mizzi (the diminutive of Marie) has been linked to Marie Scheuchl, the maid at the Berghof whose child Albine Berg fathered as an adolescent. That autobiographical connection may hold here, with Berg looking back over a life that included a relationship of the type so often described by Schnitzler in reference to the *süsse Mädel.* A famous Mizzi at the time, Mizzi Veith, described by Kraus in *Die Fackel* in "Prozess Veith" (October 1908), a prostitute who committed suicide after the arrest of her stepfather, who solicited on her behalf, could be even more important to Berg's discourse. Berg surely sympathized with Kraus's strident defense of her:

> Many a creature destined for love becomes the victim of the great Christian principle of brotherly hatred. They expose themselves to all the arrows which the social world holds ready for those who disavow it, follow the command of nature and are destroyed in the great war of annihilation which represents the most sublime spectacle of this inferior age. What does a public prosecutor know of this? Would he understand it if it were burnt into his brain that whoredom signifies the last heroism of a washed-out civilization?[154]

The *süsse Mädel* and the type of prostitute just described were very much a part of the female essence Berg wished to absorb.

Rather than being a purely personal statement (his own requiem), it seems more probable that Berg intended the Violin Concerto—a work in all likelihood he realized would be his last—as a comprehensive view or a total assimilation of his *Weltanschauung*. All the pieces from the *Altenberg Lieder* or earlier now come together, covering the issues about which he passionately cared: women, bisexuality, love, death, and spiritual transcendence. Indirectly, the voices of Altenberg, Kraus, Schnitzler, Werfel, Wedekind, Strindberg, Goethe, and Baudelaire are all present. While some of the poetry may be hidden, Berg made certain that the overall thrust would not be lost by quoting Bach and including the text of the chorale by F. J. Burmeister in the score:

> It is enough;
> Lord, if it pleases Thee,
> Then indeed put me to rest!
> My Jesus comes;

Now good night, O world!
I travel into heaven's-dwelling,
I depart securely—in peace,
My great misery remains below.
It is enough.[155]

NOTES

1. Bernard Grun, trans. and ed., *Alban Berg: Letters to His Wife* (New York: St. Martin's Press, 1971), 34–35 (cited hereafter by title). Some ideas and passages in this chapter were previously put forward in other articles I have written on Berg: "Berg's *Wozzeck* and Strindberg's Musical Models," *Opera Journal* 21, no. 1 (1988): 2–12; "Berg, Strindberg, and D Minor," *College Music Symposium* 30, no. 2 (1990): 74–89; "Opera, Apocalypse, and the Dance of Death: Berg's Indebtedness to Kraus," *Mosaic* 25 (1992): 91–105; "Alban Berg and Peter Altenberg: Intimate Art and the Aethetics of Life," *Journal of the American Musicological Society* 46 (1993): 261–94; "Berg's *Kammerkonzert* and Franz Werfel's *Spiegelmensch*: Mirror Images in Music and Literature," in *Encrypted Messages in Alban Berg's Music*, ed. Siglind Bruhn (New York: Garland, 1998), 67–90. Research was supported by a grant from the Social Sciences and Humanities Research Council of Canada. I would like to thank Harry Zohn, Robert Falck, and Don McLean for communications they sent me.

2. Harold B. Segel, trans. and ed., *The Vienna Coffeehouse Wits, 1890–1938* (West Lafayette, IN: Purdue University Press, 1993), 14.

3. *Alban Berg: Letters to His Wife*, 34.

4. H. F. Redlich, *Alban Berg: The Man and His Music* (London: John Calder, 1957), 218.

5. The one attempted biography, Karen Monson's *Alban Berg* (Boston: Houghton Mifflin, 1979), while readable and generally accurate, draws on a fairly small percentage of the unpublished letters and other available documents of Berg's life. Rosemary Hilmar's *Alban Berg: Leben und Wirken in Wien bis zu seinen ersten Erfolgen als Komponist* (Vienna: H. Böhlaus Nachf., 1978), as the title suggests, covers only his early life.

6. Douglas Jarman, " 'Man hat auch nur Fleisch und Blut': Towards a Berg Biography," in *Alban Berg: Historical and Analytical Perspectives*, ed. David Gable and Robert P. Morgan (Oxford: Clarendon Press, 1991), 11–23.

7. The Musiksammlung of the Wiener Stadt- und Landesbibliothek now makes its copy of this typescript of some 3,000 pages accessible to readers.

8. Joan Allen Smith, "The Berg-Hohenberg Correspondence," in *Alban Berg Symposion, Wien 1980: Tagungsbericht*, ed. Rudolph Klein (Vienna: Universal Edition, 1981), 189–91.

9. See David Schroeder, "Alban Berg and Peter Altenberg: Intimate Art and the Aesthetics of Life," 266–69.

10. The letters are published in Alban Berg, *Briefe an seine Frau* (Munich and Vienna: Albert Langen and Georg Müller, 1965). The English translation, *Alban Berg: Letters to His Wife*, has been much abridged.

11. Smith, "Berg-Hohenberg Correspondence," 196.

12. *Alban Berg: Letters to His Wife*, 229.

13. Juliane Brand, Christopher Halley, and Donald Harris, eds., *The Berg-Schoenberg Correspondence* (New York: W. W. Norton, 1987), 471 (cited hereafter by title).

14. Ibid., 145.

15. Redlich, *Alban Berg*, 59.

16. Willi Reich, *Alban Berg*, trans. Cornelius Cardew (London: Thames & Hudson, 1965), 40.

17. The two Nobel nominees for 1914 were Arthur Schnitzler and Altenberg. See Andrew W. Barker, "Peter Altenberg," in *Major Figures of Turn-of-the-Century Austrian Literature*, ed. Donald G. Daviau (Riverside, CA: Ariadne Press, 1991), 2.

18. Edward Timms, "Peter Altenberg: Authenticity or Pose?" in *Fin de Siècle Vienna: Proceedings of the Second Irish Symposium in Austrian Studies*, ed. G. J. Carr and Eda Sagarra (Dublin: Trinity College, 1985), 133, and George Lorenz, "How Berta Became Peter," *Austria Today* 2 (1993): 60.

19. Timms, "Peter Altenberg: Authenticity or Pose?" 133.

20. *Alban Berg: Letters to His Wife*, 23, 33, 75, 132.

21. Josephine Simpson, *Peter Altenberg: A Neglected Writer of the Viennese Jahrhundertwende* (Frankfurt: Peter Lang, 1987), 84–85.

22. *Alban Berg: Letters to His Wife*, 90.

23. Ibid., 32, 132–33, 200.

24. Arnold Schoenberg, quoted in Alexander Goehr, "Schoenberg and Kraus: The Idea behind the Music," *Music Analysis* 4 (1985): 64.

25. George Perle, "Mein geliebtes Almschi . . . ," *International Alban Berg Society Newsletter* 7 (1978): 5.

26. See Lore B. Foltin and John M. Spalek, "Franz Werfel's Essays: A Survey," *German Quarterly* 42 (1969): 179.

27. Ibid., 184–85 and *Alban Berg: Letters to His Wife*, 336.

28. *Berg-Schoenberg Correspondence*, 400–401.

29. Joan Allen Smith, "Alban Berg and Soma Morgenstern: A Literary Exchange," in *Studies in the Schoenbergian Movement in Vienna and the United States: Essays in Honor of Marcel Dick*, ed. Anne Trenkamp and John G. Suess (Lewiston, NY: Edwin Mellen Press, 1990), 38–39.

30. August Strindberg, letter to Verner von Heidenstam, quoted in Evert Sprinchorn, *Strindberg as Dramatist* (New Haven: Yale University Press, 1982), v.

31. Strindberg, *Zones of the Spirit* [*A Blue Book*], trans. Claud Field (New York: G. P. Putnam's Sons, 1913), 83–84.

32. Sprinchorn, *Strindberg as Dramatist*, 277.

33. Simpson, *Peter Altenberg*, 18.

34. François Porché, *Charles Baudelaire*, trans. John Mavin (London: Wishart, 1928), 98, 96.

35. R. J. Hollingdale, in the Introduction to Johann Wolfgang von Goethe, *Elective Affinities* (Harmondsworth: Penguin, 1971), 10.

36. Frida Semler Seabury, "1903 and 1904," *International Alban Berg Society Newsletter* 1 (1968): 5.

37. Donald Harris, "Berg and Frida Semler," *International Alban Berg Society Newsletter* 8 (1979): 11.

38. See Hans Moldenhauer and Rosaleen Moldenhauer, *Anton von Webern: A Chronicle of His Life and Work* (New York: Alfred A. Knopf, 1979), 328.

39. *Berg-Schoenberg Correspondence*, 117.

40. Sprinchorn, *Strindberg as Dramatist*, 240.

41. Alban Berg, letter to Anton Webern dated 29 July [1912], Handschriftensammlung, Wiener Stadt- und Landesbibliothek, MS. I.N. 185. 570 (my translation).

42. See August Strindberg, *Briefe an Emil Schering* (Munich: Georg Müller, 1924), 203.

43. I came across this photo in Berg's copy of Altenberg's *Das Nachlass*. I would like to thank the Alban Berg Foundation for placing Berg's personal library at my disposal in 1988 and 1992.

44. *Alban Berg: Letters to His Wife*, 27.

45. Ibid., 72.

46. Berg 100/I–XII, Musiksammlung, Nationalbibliothek, Vienna.

47. Alban Berg, quoted in Donald Harris, "Berg and Frida Semler," *International Alban Berg Society Newletter* 8 (1979): 9.

48. Andrew W. Barker, "Peter Altenberg (1859–1919)," in *Dictionary of Literary Biography*, vol. 81, *Austrian Fiction Writers, 1875–1913*, ed. James Hardin and Donald G. Daviau (Detroit: Gale Research, 1989), 6.

49. John C. Crawford and Dorothy L. Crawford, *Expressionism in Twentieth-Century Music* (Bloomington: Indiana University Press, 1993), 128.

50. Hilmar, *Alban Berg*, 9.

51. Rosemary Hilmar, "Alban Berg's Studies with Schoenberg," *Journal of the Arnold Schoenberg Institute* 8 (1984): 7.

52. Joan Allen Smith, *Schoenberg and His Circle: A Viennese Portrait* (New York: Schirmer Books, 1986), 145.

53. Ibid., 146–47.

54. *Alban Berg: Letters to His Wife*, 95, and *Berg-Schoenberg Correspondence*, 1.

55. *Berg-Schoenberg Correspondence*, 233.

56. Ibid., 238, 242.

57. Ibid., 243.

58. Ibid., 143.

59. Mark DeVoto, "Berg the Composer of Songs," in *The Berg Companion* (Boston: Northeastern University Press, 1989), 51.

60. Theodor Adorno, *Alban Berg: Master of the Smallest Link*, trans. Juliane Brand and Christopher Hailey (Cambridge: Cambridge University Press, 1991), 29.

61. *Alban Berg: Letters to His Wife*, 306.

62. Ibid., 315.

63. Ibid., 330.

64. *Berg-Schoenberg Correspondence*, 337.

65. Brenda Dalen, " 'Freundschaft, Liebe, und Welt': The Secret Programme of the Chamber Concerto," in *The Berg Companion*, 153–71.

66. See David Schroeder, "Was Webern's Death an Accident?" *Musical Times* 137 (June 1996): 21–23.

67. Arnold Schoenberg, quoted in Louis Krasner, as told to Don C. Seibert, "Some Memories of Anton Webern, the Berg Concerto, and Vienna in the 1930s," *Fanfare* 11 (1987): 347.

68. Anton Webern, *Letters to Hildegard Jone and Josef Humplik*, ed. Josef Polnauer, trans. Cornelius Cardew (Bryn Mawr, PA: Theodore Presser, 1967), 453.

69. Carl Dahlhaus, "Schreker and Modernism: On the Dramaturgy of *Der ferne Klang*," in *Schoenberg and the New Music*, trans. Derrick Puffett and Alfred Clayton (Cambridge: Cambridge University Press, 1987), 192–200.

70. *Berg-Schoenberg Correspondence*, 166.

71. Felix Greissle, quoted in Smith, *Schoenberg and His Circle*, 93.

72. Arnold Schoenberg, *Arnold Schoenberg Letters*, ed. Erwin Stein, trans. Eithne Wilkins and Ernst Kaiser (London: Faber & Faber, 1964), 23.

73. *Berg-Schoenberg Correspondence*, 111.

74. *Alban Berg: Letters to His Wife*, 324–25.

75. Ibid., 325.

76. Ibid., 296.

77. Ibid., 422.

78. Erich Kleiber, quoted in Reich, *Alban Berg*, 58.

79. *Alban Berg: Letters to His Wife*, 353.

80. Louis Krasner, "The Origins of the Alban Berg *Violin Concerto*," in *Alban Berg Symposion, Wien 1980*, 111.

81. *Alban Berg: Letters to His Wife*, 158.

82. Adorno, *Alban Berg*, 33–34.

83. Smith, *Schoenberg and His Circle*, 146.

84. Gottfried Kassowitz, "Lehrzeit bei Alban Berg," *Österreichische Musikzeitschrift* 23 (1968): 323.

85. Adorno, *Alban Berg*, 29–30.

86. Ibid., 32.

87. Alban Berg, quoted in Reich, *Alban Berg*, 51–52.

88. Mark DeVoto, "General Remarks about the Guides," *Journal of the Arnold Schoenberg Institute* 16 (1993): 9–10.

89. Alban Berg, "Arnold Schönberg, *Pelleas und Melisande*, op. 5. Thematische Analyse," in Alban Berg, Sämtliche Werke, ed. Rudolf Stephan and Regina Busch (Vienna: Universal Edition, 1994), part 3, vol. 1, 97–118.

90. Alban Berg, quoted in Reich, *Alban Berg*, 52–53.

91. Schoenberg, *Arnold Schoenberg Letters*, 23.

92. Adorno, *Alban Berg*, 29.

93. For a list of these songs, see Nicholas Chadwick, "Berg's Unpublished Songs in the Österrreichische Nationalbibliothek," *Music and Letters* 52 (1971): 123–25.

94. See David Schroeder, "Polarity in Schubert's *Unfinished* Symphony," *Canadian University Music Review* 1 (1980): 25.

95. See Janet Schmalfeldt, "Berg's Path to Atonality: The Piano Sonata. Op. 1," in *Alban Berg: Historical and Analytical Perspectives*, 79–109.

96. Arnold Schoenberg, quoted in Reich, *Alban Berg*, 29.

97. Adorno, *Alban Berg*, 53.

98. Redlich, *Alban Berg*, 50.

99. Adorno, *Alban Berg*, 69.

100. *Alban Berg: Letters to His Wife*, 159.

101. Barbara Z. Schoenberg, "The Influence of the French Prose Poem on Peter Altenberg," *Modern Austrian Literature* 22, nos. 3–4 (1989): 15–32. For a full study of Altenberg's texts in relation to Berg's music, see Schroeder, "Alban Berg and Peter Altenberg."

102. Mark DeVoto identifies the themes in "Some Notes on the Unknown *Altenberg*

Lieder," *Perspectives of New Music* 5 (1966): 40. For the correlation of the musical and poetical themes, see Schroeder, "Alban Berg and Peter Altenberg," 284–86.

103. Letter of Berg to Webern dated 29 July [1912] (my translation).

104. *Berg-Schoenberg Correspondence*, 182.

105. Letter of Berg to Webern, 29 July [1912].

106. *Alban Berg: Letters to His Wife*, 147.

107. George Perle, *The Operas of Alban Berg*, vol. 1, *Wozzeck* (Berkeley: University of California Press, 1980), 18.

108. Robert Falck, "Two *Reigen*: Berg, Schnitzler, and Cyclic Form," in *Encrypted Messages in Alban Berg's Music*, ed. Siglind Bruhn (New York: Garland, 1998), 91–105.

109. Cole Gagne and Tracy Caras, *Soundpieces: Interviews with American Composers* (Metuchen, NJ: Scarecrow Press, 1982), 127.

110. *Berg-Schoenberg Correspondence*, 117.

111. Alban Berg, quoted in Redlich, *Alban Berg*, 267.

112. See David Schroeder, "Berg's *Wozzeck* and Strindberg's Musical Models," 2–12.

113. *Alban Berg: Letters to His Wife*, 247.

114. Ibid., 111.

115. Edward Timms, *Karl Kraus: Apocalyptic Satirist* (New Haven: Yale University Press, 1986), 377. For a more complete discussion of *Wozzeck* and *Die letzte Tage*, see David Schroeder, "Opera, Apocalypse, and the Dance of Death: Berg's Indebtedness to Kraus," 91–105.

116. Alban Berg, "Lecture on *Wozzeck*," in Redlich, *Alban Berg*, 278.

117. Timms, *Karl Kraus: Apocalyptic Satirist*, 379, and Harry Zohn, *Karl Kraus* (New York: Twayne, 1971), 83.

118. Zohn, *Karl Kraus*, 82.

119. Berg, "Lecture on *Wozzeck*," 284.

120. Reich, *Alban Berg*, 148, and *Berg-Schoenberg Correspondence*, 337.

121. *Berg-Schoenberg Correspondence*, 335.

122. Brand and Hailey, "Catalogue of the Correspondence between Alban Berg and Arnold Schoenberg," *Journal of the Arnold Schoenberg Institute* 11, no. 1 (1988): 96.

123. For a detailed comparison, see David Schroeder, "Berg's *Kammerkonzert* and Franz Werfel's *Spiegelmensch*: Mirror Images in Music and Literature," 67–90.

124. Berg's copy can be found at the Alban Berg Foundation.

125. Walter Sokel, *The Writer in Extremis: Expressionism in Twentieth-Century German Literature* (Stanford: Stanford University Press, 1959), 213.

126. *Alban Berg: Letters to His Wife*, 90.

127. Redlich, *Alban Berg*, 185; Adorno, *Alban Berg*, 104.

128. Douglass Green, "Berg's De Profundis: The Finale of the *Lyric Suite*," *International Alban Berg Society Newsletter* 5 (1977): 13–23. Douglas Jarman had also noticed Berg's cryptic but illegible text.

129. George Perle, "The Secret Program of the *Lyric Suite*," *International Alban Berg Society Newsletter* 5 (1977): 4–12; reprinted in *Musical Times* 118 (1977): 629–32, 709–13, and 809–13.

130. George Perle, *The Operas of Alban Berg*, vol. 2, *Lulu* (Berkeley: University of California Press, 1985), 21.

131. August Strindberg, quoted in Spinchorn, *Strindberg as Dramatist*, v, and ibid., 277.

132. Don McLean, ''Schloss und sein Schlüssel: New Documents on Berg's *Lyric Suite*: The Schloss Collection at McGill University,'' unpublished paper, 11.

133. Porché, *Charles Baudelaire*, 132 (the original French title was *La vie douloureuse de Charles Baudelaire*).

134. Ibid., 160, 171.

135. Helene Berg, quoted in Perle, *Operas of Alban Berg*, vol. 2, *Lulu*, 28–29.

136. Adorno, *Alban Berg*, 29.

137. Alban Berg, quoted in Perle, *Operas of Alban Berg*, vol. 2, *Lulu*, 12.

138. Charles Baudelaire, *Intimate Journals*, trans. Christopher Isherwood (San Francisco: City Lights Books, 1983), 87.

139. See Douglas Jarman, *The Music of Alban Berg* (London: Faber & Faber, 1979), 103. For a more complete study of the connection between the music and the Baudelaire/George texts, see Schroeder, ''Berg, Strindberg, and D Minor.''

140. See Enid Peschel, ''Love, the Intoxicating Mirage: Baudelaire's Quest for Communion in 'Le vin des amants,' 'La chevelure,' and 'Harmonie du soir,' '' in *Pre-Text, Text, Context: Essays on Nineteenth-Century French Literature*, ed. Robert L. Mitchell (Columbus: Ohio State University Press, 1980), 121–22.

141. Claudio Spies, ''A View of George Perle's *The Operas of Alban Berg, Volume Two: 'Lulu,'* '' *Musical Quarterly* 71 (1985): 521, 532.

142. Douglas Jarman, review of *Kultur und Natur in Alban Bergs ''Lulu''* by Albrecht von Massow, *Music and Letters* 75 (1994): 296.

143. Erich Heller, ''From Love to Love: Goethe's Pandora and Wedekind–Alban Berg's Pandora-Lulu,'' *Salmagundi* 84 (1989): 106–7.

144. Alban Berg, quoted in Redlich, *Alban Berg*, 176.

145. For more detailed discussions of the music, see Perle, *Operas of Alban Berg*, vol. 2, *Lulu*, Chapters 3 and 4, and Jarman, *Music of Alban Berg*, 198–222.

146. Krasner, ''Origins of the Alban Berg *Violin Concerto*,'' 110.

147. *Berg-Schoenberg Correspondence*, 466.

148. Ibid., 248–49.

149. For useful summaries of Fliess's *Vom Leben und vom Tod* and *Der Ablauf des Lebens*, see Frank J. Sulloway, *Freud, Biologist of the Mind: Beyond the Psychoanalytic Legend* (New York: Basic Books, 1979), 135–70, and Peter Heller, ''A Quarrel over Bisexuality,'' in *The Turn of the Century: German Literature and Art, 1890–1915*, ed. Gerald Chapple and Hans H. Schulte (Bonn: Bouvier, 1981), 87–99.

150. As Geoffrey Poole has shown for Berg in ''Alban Berg and the Fateful Number,'' *Tempo* 179 (1991): 2–7.

151. Sulloway, *Freud, Biologist of the Mind*, 166.

152. Douglas Jarman, ''Alban Berg, Wilhelm Fliess, and the Secret Programme of the Violin Concerto,'' in *The Berg Companion*, 186–87.

153. Wilhelm Fliess, quoted in Sulloway, *Freud, Biologist of the Mind*, 141.

154. Karl Kraus, quoted in Timms, *Karl Kraus*, 86.

155. Translation by Melvin P. Unger, *Handbook to Bach's Sacred Cantata Texts* (Lanham, MD: Scarecrow Press, 1996), 206.

6 ANTON WEBERN

Anne C. Shreffler

Anton Webern's life (1883–1945) and music present a contradictory, even paradoxical picture. Influenced by literary and artistic circles in Vienna, he retained an idealistic individuality. Fiercely loyal to his teacher Arnold Schoenberg and to his friends and colleagues, he could be openly hostile to nonsympathetic outsiders. His music is complex and difficult to perceive, but at the same time fundamentally lyrical and rooted in the classical German-Austrian tradition. He inscribed his most involved twelve-tone sketches with the names of mountain plants and saw no inconsistency in this. He embraced the twelve-tone method, developed by Schoenberg as a means to rationalize and organize musical material, in the spirit of a Goethe-inspired mysticism. Webern's shy and retiring personality did not lend itself to self-promotion, but after his death he was venerated on an international scale. The elevation of his music by the post–Second World War serialists above that of Schoenberg and Alban Berg would have made him very uncomfortable had he lived to see it.

Webern's participation in what later became known as the Second Viennese School—the Schoenberg circle that included Berg, Heinrich Jalowetz, Karl Horwitz, Egon Wellesz, Erwin Stein, Rudolf Kolisch, Edward Steuermann, and others—irrevocably stamped his musical and personal development. Members of this "school," however diverse their personalities and styles, shared a musical tradition based on a synthesis of Brahms and Wagner and a conviction that this tradition should be extended. They venerated Richard Strauss, Hugo Wolf, and Gustav Mahler, who (in fundamentally different ways) had continued from the Wagnerian legacy. The harmonic implications of this legacy were carried even further by Schoenberg, with the consequence, to him inevitable, of breaking the

Anton Webern (1883–1945). Courtesy of the Arnold Schoenberg Institute.

moorings of tonality altogether. Once Schoenberg had "breathed the air of another planet" (as the Stefan George text of his Second String Quartet puts it), his commitment to the new language of atonality thrust him outside the musical establishment, whose sympathy for his music had been none too great to begin with. Berg and Webern soon joined Schoenberg in his tonal experiment, paying the same price of public rejection. The hostility from concertgoers that they continually faced after 1910 was a formative experience for Schoenberg and his pupils. Similarly, their adoption of the twelve-tone method during the 1920s opened the gates of renewed misunderstanding, as they were accused of being cerebral note counters. The public's incomprehension solidified their identity as a group, strengthened their idealism, and caused them to seek new ways to present their music. Belonging to the Schoenberg school therefore irrevocably altered the destiny of its members.

Although he owed much to Schoenberg, Webern achieved a highly individual musical idiom early on. His music is best characterized by extremes. Its extreme brevity—many pieces or movements last less than a minute—seems to defy all laws of musical structure (and to defeat concert programmers). This aphoristic expression represents on the one hand the ultimate compression: as Schoenberg remarked in his Foreword to Webern's Six Bagatelles for String Quartet, Op. 9, "a novel in a single gesture, a joy in a breath."[1] On the other hand, Webern's music seems not so much to compress as to expand from a moment of stillness. When one listens with close attention, time seems to slow down; one can easily understand Webern's overestimations of the lengths of his pieces by 100 percent or more.

The extreme quietness of Webern's music adds to its hermetic character. Many pieces never rise above pianissimo, and the occasional loud passages seem like extraordinary outbursts. Webern paints with the finest of brushes, which allows him to create the most delicate of timbral nuances. The delicacy is not fragility, however, but rather the contained, barely repressed expression of powerful emotion. The philosopher and Berg student Theodor Wiesengrund Adorno recognized this quality of Webern's music when he wrote, "This threefold pianissimo, the softest possible, the threatening shadow of an infinitely distant and infinitely powerful noise: so sounded, in 1916, the cannonfire of Verdun from the Waldchaussee near Frankfurt."[2]

The quality of Webern's music that has received the most attention is its structural complexity. The atonal instrumental works and certain twelve-tone works have invited a steady stream of analyses of their intricate pitch organization. This kind of analysis is rewarding precisely because the composer delighted in subtle procedures that can only be revealed through study. This inward-directed music is a mystery to most of the concertgoing public but standard fare in university seminars.

An equally important aspect of Webern's music is its lyricism. The music's small-scale, nonredundant forms are analogous to those of lyric poetry, in contrast to the more extended "musical prose" of Schoenberg. Moreover, the textures are markedly linear and melodic. Over half of Webern's published output is vocal, and even in the instrumental music the interplay of lines often takes priority over the resulting harmonies. By virtue of its intense expressivity, Webern's music is lyrical in a third and more general sense as well. Although many modern performances belie this feature, ''earwitness'' reports confirm that Webern favored a rubato, highly accentuated performance style. The scores are full of detailed tempo, dynamic, articulation, and expression marks (there can be several performance indications surrounding a single note). The lyrical nature of Webern's music in all three senses holds sway throughout his compositional output.

YOUTH, MUSICAL TRAINING, AND FIRST COMPOSITIONS (1883–1904)

Anton Friedrich Wilhelm von Webern[3] was born on 3 December 1883 in Vienna to Carl von Webern, a member of the minor Austrian nobility and a mining engineer and government bureaucrat, and Amalie, née Geer, a talented amateur musician from a working-class family.[4] Of the couple's five children, only Anton and his two sisters, Maria and Rosa, survived infancy. The family moved to Graz in 1890 and then four years later to Klagenfurt in Carinthia, where they lived until Webern was nineteen. They spent summers and holidays at the Preglhof, a fairly large country estate owned by the family. In the small-town environment of Klagenfurt, Webern attended the Humanistic Gymnasium, where he underwent the standard rigorous course of study emphasizing ancient and modern languages. His true love was music, however; he studied the piano and cello and tried his hand at composition. His main ambition was to become a conductor. Webern's instrumental lessons were supplemented with instruction in music theory from the local composer, teacher, and accompanist Edwin Komauer, whose passion for the ''new music'' of Wagner, Wolf, and Richard Strauss surely infected his pupil. The concert life of Klagenfurt presented a wide range of music, which Webern supplemented by playing cello in the local orchestra and piano four-hand arrangements with his teacher. By the time he finished high school, he was well acquainted with the German-Austrian standard repertory.

After passing his high-school examinations in the spring of 1902, Webern was given a trip to Bayreuth for a graduation present. This was one of the defining musical experiences of his life. After returning home, he made up his mind to become a professional musician. This decision did not please his father, who wanted Anton to study agriculture so he could run the Preglhof. Carl von Webern then called in some musically knowledgeable acquaintances to test his son's aptitude for music. They apparently vouched for Anton's talent. In a compromise probably insisted upon by Carl von Webern, it was resolved that Anton could study music, but at the University of Vienna rather than undergoing practical training at a conservatory (Moldenhauer and Moldenhauer, 52).

Webern's own first modest compositional efforts included pieces for cello and piano as well as song settings on texts of Richard Dehmel and Ferdinand Avenarius. A set of four songs composed between 1899 and 1901 was designated Op. 1: "Vorfrühling," "Wolkennacht" (both Avenarius), "Tief von fern" (Dehmel), and "Wehmut" (Avenarius).[5] The immaturity of these songs is obvious: the static harmonies (underlined by the omnipresent open fifth in the left hand), awkward progressions, and unidiomatic vocal lines are redeemed by the occasional memorable chord or melodic figure (such as the opening vocal phrase of "Vorfrühling"). The simple, transparent accompaniments indicate a modest pianistic ability and perhaps also a gap between the auditory vision and its realization.

Dehmel and Avenarius were especially important to Webern; he wrote eight songs on poems of Dehmel, including the posthumously published Five Songs, which were his last works before his actual Op. 1, and seven on poems of Avenarius. The works of Dehmel were especially favored as song texts by composers whom Webern admired, including Strauss, Zemlinsky, and Schoenberg. The poetry of Dehmel, Avenarius, and Detlef von Liliencron (another poet popular with turn-of-the-century lied composers) may seem sentimental and dated today, but was taken very seriously in cultural circles at the time. These poets cultivated a poetic discourse that emphasized descriptions of nature and overt sensuality. Their works fulfilled a need for the expression of individual subjectivity in the socially restrictive and politically ossified late Austro-Hungarian Empire. Webern even absorbed their language into his personal vocabulary. In his diaries and letters he often quoted from the poems, especially with regard to his love affair with Wilhelmine Mörtl, his cousin and future wife.[6] His own poetic efforts, in which rhapsodic descriptions of nature serve as reflections of the narrator's soul, are clearly derived from Avenarius.[7]

In the fall of 1902 Webern began his studies at the Musicological Institute of the University of Vienna, whose chairman was Guido Adler, a respected scholar and one of the founders of modern musicology. Although Webern found the course of study, which emphasized early music, sometimes dry and tedious, he undeniably benefited from the exposure to new ideas and musical techniques. Moreover, Adler's admiration for Wagner's music and his friendship with Mahler would have struck a sympathetic chord with Webern. He threw himself into his musicology courses while continuing to study piano and cello privately. His studies of harmony with Hermann Grädener and counterpoint with Karl Navrátil laid the foundation for his future compositional technique.

Dozens of composition exercises and short pieces from Webern's years of study have survived, but their chronology is still unclear. The Moldenhauers assume that the short piano pieces in traditional forms (M. 22 through M. 46 in their work list) were university assignments (Moldenhauer and Moldenhauer, 66), but Gareth Cox believes that these were written later, during Webern's study with Schoenberg.[8] Also uncertain is the dating of Webern's orchestrations of Schubert and Wolf songs and Schubert's piano sonatas; his university course probably included orchestrations, but these could have been done for Schoenberg as well. It is likely that most of the student exercises that survive were produced for Schoenberg—these Webern would have been more likely to keep for sentimental reasons—but an exact chronology awaits further research.

In addition to his music studies, Webern also took courses in philosophy and art history. His interests in art were whetted by his first cousin and childhood companion Ernst Diez, who was to become a renowned art historian. After going to Bayreuth together, Diez and Webern traveled to Munich, where they visited museums. Webern's tastes in art at the time were conservative, tending toward the landscape artists Arnold Böcklin, Moritz von Schwind, and Giovanni Segantini. He wrote in his notebook: "We visited the Neue Pinakothek, where there are some glorious pictures. I was especially impressed by Segantini's *Alpenlandschaft*, Böcklin's *Spiel der Wellen*. . . . Lastly we went to the Secession. This was the first exhibition of modern artists I've ever seen. To be honest! none of the paintings made an outstanding impression on me."[9] Although Webern continued to admire Segantini, he would soon develop an appreciation for modern art, especially the works of Gustav Klimt, Oskar Kokoschka, and Egon Schiele.

Webern's personality, later serious and severe, was evidently quite lively and vivacious when he was young. His friend and classmate Wellesz recalled: "Those who knew Webern only during the years after the First World War or especially during the Second—when he was thoroughly disillusioned and emotionally shattered, can hardly imagine the enchanting lightheartedness and cheerfulness that radiated from the young Webern."[10]

While Webern was at the university, his main energies seem to have been devoted less to his studies than to the rich musical life of Vienna. He sang in the Richard Wagner Society chorus and attended concerts and operas almost nightly. Webern reacted to these musical experiences with characteristic intensity. Hardly just an evening's entertainment, concerts were his library and his conservatory. Given that he aimed to become a conductor, he studied the performances with a critical ear and recorded many details in his diary. These experiences were also important for Webern's own composing, since he had not yet found a composition teacher. Works of Beethoven, Liszt, Bruckner, and above all Wagner made the biggest impression on him. In his first year alone he saw the whole *Ring* cycle, *Tannhäuser, Der fliegende Holländer, Tristan und Isolde*, and *Die Meistersinger*, the latter five times. After his Bayreuth experience and first Vienna concert season, Webern tried to compose in a post-Wagnerian style, producing an uncharacteristically extended and pseudodramatic song on the Dehmel text "Nachtgebet der Braut" (The bride's night prayer).[11] Here his debt to *Tristan und Isolde* is painfully clear.

Webern completed his doctoral degree in 1906, four years after he began. He submitted as his dissertation an edition with commentary of Part 2 of Heinrich Isaac's *Choralis constantinus* (the second of three settings of the mass propers). It is tempting to think that the polyphonic complexities in this early-sixteenth-century work influenced Webern's later contrapuntal constructions, especially perhaps the double canon in his chorus *Entflieht auf leichten Kähnen*, Op. 2, composed in 1908. In later years Webern certainly acknowledged his debt to the "Netherlanders," who (according to his view of music history) were the last before the twelve-tone composers to write truly polyphonic music.[12] But according to Wellesz, "It would be a mistake to make too much of a mystique about Webern's work with early 16th-century polyphony." Adler customarily assigned students their dissertation topics, normally choosing editing tasks whose results could be published in his series Denkmäler der Tonkunst in Österreich (as Webern's was).[13] Wellesz remembers: "I never noticed that Webern immersed himself in this epoch any more than what was necessary for the purpose at hand."[14] The dissertation project evidently did not influence Webern's own music of this time, which is not especially contrapuntal. Even if he viewed the task as a routine assignment, however, he later came to value his knowledge of Renaissance music.

Webern's compositional technique improved rapidly after his first year at the university. In contrast to his academic assignments, the songs he composed in these years were probably written on his own. He continued to set the poetry of Dehmel, Avenarius, and Liliencron, along with Goethe and Nietzsche. As Derrick Puffett has shown, many of these early songs bear the unmistakable traces of Hugo Wolf, the late-nineteenth-century lied composer, whom Webern much admired.[15]

The song "Aufblick" (completed in August 1903) on a poem by Dehmel was one of Webern's best accomplishments during these years. The sentiment of the opening line, "Über unsere Liebe hängt eine tiefe Trauerweide," is reflected in descending chromatic harmonies over a pedal tone. The tonality is ambiguous. The tonic C is not reached until the tenth measure and is barely touched on subsequently; the piece ends on a hanging dominant, appropriately for the open-ended last line of the poem, which simply evokes isolated images: "Glockenchöre . . . Nacht . . . und Liebe. . . ." There are some harmonically awkward passages, and, as with other songs, the vocal writing is not very idiomatic, but taken as a whole, "Aufblick" shows how Webern's improved technique allowed him to write a song of great beauty and expressiveness.

Martin Hoyer has shown that two early songs thought to have been by Webern are arrangements instead. The fragment "Zum Schluss" is an orchestration of a song for voice and piano by the composer and conductor Leo Blech (1871–1958).[16] Webern admired Blech's music, devoting a whole page of his 1902–3 diary to a discussion of his chamber music and songs. Likewise, the orchestral song "Siegfrieds Schwert" proved to be an arrangement of a song by Martin Plüddemann (1854–1897).[17] Webern most likely encountered the completely diatonic, folklike ballad in *Der Kunstwart*, where it was published in 1902.

Webern's admiration for Wagner's music influenced not only his compositions, but also his literary taste, his view of music history, and his aesthetic stance. When Webern became acquainted with Wagner's music dramas while still a high-school student in Klagenfurt, he encountered a still-controversial, mysterious, and vaguely dangerous music. (This view of Wagner was beautifully captured in several works of Thomas Mann, including *Buddenbrooks*, in which a young boy's sickliness is associated with his passion for Wagner.) The qualities of sensuality and eroticism manifested by Wagner's music, particularly the hyperchromatic *Tristan und Isolde*, seemed to unlock the deepest layers of the psyche, an impression that made a strong impact on poets, artists, and thinkers in fin-de-siècle Vienna and undoubtedly had some bearing on the thought of Sigmund Freud, who produced his most influential works around the turn of the century.

When Webern visited Bayreuth for the first (and as it turned out, only) time in 1902, he approached the experience in the spirit of a pilgrimage to a holy shrine. He visited the Villa Wahnfried and Wagner's grave and reverently recorded in his diary every detail of the stage sets and performance. Shocked that others in the audience did not seem to take the experience as seriously as he did, he wrote:

> I saw clearly that Bayreuth has already become a fad. What appears to me almost impossible is that the ladies, in their ostentatious finery, with their eternally smiling faces, or these gentlemen in patent leather shoes, displaying the most expensive ties, could have even the slightest notion of where they really are or of what constitutes Bayreuth's enormous significance. . . . There was, on top of it, applause! If people start to applaud after the end of Parsifal it cannot be anything but a display of the greatest rudeness. (Moldenhauer and Moldenhauer, 51)

The attitude that great art is sacred and consequently fully available only to the select few is a common romantic trope, but at the same time it would become a leading idea for the turn-of-the-century Viennese avant-garde.

This was no coincidence, for to be a Wagnerian around the turn of the century was to be an advocate of modern music. In the still-valent Brahms-Wagner controversy, Wagner's lavishly orchestrated music dramas were deemed advanced, Brahms's symphonies with their traditional sonata forms, conservative. This aesthetic judgment belonged to a particular view of music history that saw the "New German School" of Liszt and Wagner and later of Bruckner, Strauss, and Wolf as the true descendants of Beethoven. Enchanted with a performance of Liszt's *Dante* Symphony in February 1903, Webern wrote: "Liszt is probably one of the greatest; for me, the line from Beethoven goes on to Liszt and Bruckner. To be sure, Wagner, as dramatist, stands entirely apart" (letter to Diez, Moldenhauer, and Moldenhauer, 55).

The future of music as Webern saw it around the turn of the century belonged to Wagner's heirs Strauss and Wolf. The program symphonist and the song composer, as different as they may seem, both aimed to combine the world of verbal ideas with that of music (unlike the proponents of "absolute music," who strove to keep them apart). This transference of the specificity of words to the gestic, illustrative powers of instrumental music was the Wagnerian legacy, which Wagner believed to be the logical consequence of the union of words and music in Beethoven's Ninth Symphony. This expanded role for music demanded new forms, a new timbral palette, and (most important for the Second Viennese School) a new, densely chromatic harmonic vocabulary.

The importance of this musical heritage for the members of the Second Viennese School cannot be emphasized enough. Their indebtedness to the post-Wagnerian school can be seen first in Schoenberg's cultivation of the tone-poem genre in *Pelleas und Melisande* and its development in the programmatic chamber piece *Verklärte Nacht.* The most ubiquitous genre in the early part of the century was the lied, of which their idol Wolf was the most recent master and to which Schoenberg, Berg, and Webern all contributed substantially in their early years.

The most crucial element of the Wagner heritage, however, was the idea of musical progress itself. The view that nineteenth-century tonality evolved toward increasing chromaticism ultimately provided the intellectual justification for the move to atonality. Moreover, Wagnerians shared a fierce idealism and the sense of membership in an elite circle. Webern's aesthetic position as a Wagnerian, then, was good preparation for his later position as a member of the Schoenberg camp.

During the summer of 1904 Webern completed his most ambitious piece to date, an orchestral tone poem based on Bruno Wille's poem "Im Sommerwind." The writer, like Dehmel a social philosopher and liberal thinker, was one of Webern's favorite authors at the time. The poem "Im Sommerwind" is "a paean to nature, an impressionistic description of a summer day in woods and fields," a subject certainly close to Webern's heart (Moldenhauer and Moldenhauer, 69). The piece is derivative of both Wagner and Strauss, but nonetheless contains some attractive musical ideas and shows real skill in orchestration.[18] Webern did not choose to produce a massive Wagnerian orchestral sound (or else he was not capable of it); *Im Sommerwind* is orchestrated with a watercolor brush, not a trowel. Many passages feature solo instruments, often marked with the very Webernian designation "sehr leise und zart." Composed after two years of intensive study of harmony, counterpoint, and orchestration, this is still a student piece, but one that displays a high level of competence. Webern now had a major piece of which he could be proud. It marks the end of his first apprenticeship; the second, with Schoenberg, was about to begin.

STUDIES WITH SCHOENBERG (1904–8)

After two years at the university and many years of composing, Webern needed a regular composition teacher. There was apparently no hope of studying with either Strauss or Mahler, both of whom he admired. His next choice was Hans Pfitzner, at the time a well-known and highly regarded composer in the post-Wagner tradition. Webern's friend Josef Polnauer later related how Webern and his fellow student Jalowetz traveled to Berlin to meet Pfitzner, only to leave in disgust when the elder composer made some "disparaging remarks" about Mahler (Moldenhauer and Moldenhauer, 71).[19]

The precise circumstances that led Webern to sign up for private lessons with Schoenberg in the fall of 1904 are not known. Schoenberg, who was only thirty years old at the time (and only nine years older than Webern himself), was not nearly as highly esteemed as the other composers whom Webern had considered. Since his return from Berlin in 1903, Schoenberg had given some classes at the private Schwarzwald School for girls and was actively seeking private pupils. On the basis of *Verklärte Nacht*, he had already acquired a reputation as something of a revolutionary. In the spring of 1904 he, along with Zemlinsky and others, had set up the Vereinigung Schaffender Tonkünstler (Alliance of Creative Musicians), an organization to present concerts of new music. They published an artistic manifesto that could well have been noticed by the university students, especially since Karl Weigl, a classmate of Webern's, was a member.[20] Weigl had apparently brought sections of the manuscript score of Schoenberg's still-incomplete *Pelleas und Melisande* to the institute in the fall of 1902 and shown them to Webern, who had evidently been fascinated.[21]

The most likely catalyst, however, was Guido Adler, who was friendly with Schoenberg.[22] In any case, by the fall of 1904 Webern, along with his university classmates Horwitz and Jalowetz, had begun to study with Schoenberg (Wellesz followed a year later); Stein and Berg soon joined them. It proved to be an illustrious group, the quality of which would never again be equalled in Schoenberg's near half-century of teaching. Berg, as we know, became one of the century's most important composers. Jalowetz had a successful career as a conductor, Stein held prominent posts at Universal Edition (and later Boosey and Hawkes), Horwitz organized festivals of contemporary music (among them the Donaueschingen festival), and Wellesz became a well-known composer and specialist in Byzantine music. The Schoenberg pupils also formed a tight circle of friends. These were the people who were closest to Webern until the 1930s, when the group dissolved due to emigration (Schoenberg, Jalowetz, Stein, and Wellesz) or death (Berg died in 1935; Horwitz had died in 1925).

It is difficult to determine what Webern thought about Schoenberg at the beginning, since his memories were so strongly colored by later events. For example, Webern wrote to Schoenberg in 1907 that *Verklärte Nacht* had made a tremendous impression on him during the concert season 1903–4, but there is no mention of it in his diaries of the time. Nor did Webern record his first meeting with Schoenberg in his diary or in any letter known to me. But even if Webern's relationship with Schoenberg began without much fanfare, it soon assumed great significance.

It is no exaggeration to say that Webern's lessons with Schoenberg, which lasted formally until the autumn of 1908 and informally much longer, changed his life.[23] The encounter had both positive and negative consequences. First (and most crucially), it enabled Webern to develop his technique to the point where he could express himself musically. This is shown by the sophistication of the Passacaglia for orchestra, Op. 1, and the canonic chorus, *Entflieht auf leichten Kähnen*, Op. 2 (both written in 1908), compared to his earlier efforts. Second, this relationship led Webern to follow Schoenberg into atonality, a life-changing decision. There is no reason to believe that Webern would have taken this step on his own. Third, his relationship with Schoenberg allowed him to expand his cultural horizons. Through his teacher Webern became acquainted with Mahler, Karl Kraus, Kokoschka, Vasili Kandinsky, Peter Altenberg, Adolf Loos, and many other leading literary and artistic figures.

A fourth consequence of Webern's study with Schoenberg was less positive. Webern, to an even greater extent than Berg and other students, developed an unhealthy emotional dependence on Schoenberg. All of Schoenberg's students were expected to display devotion and subservience to a degree that seems excessive today. Although it was taken for granted at that time that pupils would correct the teacher's scores and prepare his piano reductions, Schoenberg's pupils did much more: they promoted his music and defended it against attacks, raised money when he needed it, and took care of all kinds of practical business and daily chores (for example, they helped him find housing and even packed up his things when he moved).[24]

Webern seems to have been even more dependent than the others, and the closeness of the tie certainly affected his musical and personal development. In September 1911, for example, after having left a position at the theater in Prague shortly after he had arrived, Webern wrote to Schoenberg: "Above everything: I would like to be with you. I picture the winter thus: I will be in whichever city you are in and will mainly make reductions of your works" (Moldenhauer and Moldenhauer, 148–49). Soon after this, Webern joined Schoenberg in Berlin, where he had no job nor any prospect of one. The possibility of daily contact with Schoenberg was worth the sacrifice. Webern wrote: "The way to Schoenberg is lined with blossoming fruit trees. At night the nightingales sing. . . . In short, it is wonderful here. I am with Schoenberg daily" (letter to Paul Königer; Moldenhauer and Moldenhauer, 156). The amount of psychological damage caused by this dependency, which went far beyond the usual master-pupil relationship typical at that time, is difficult to assess; at the very least, it slowed Webern's progress toward emotional maturity.

The indisputable value of what Webern learned with Schoenberg, though, is apparent from the pieces from this period. Schoenberg was a strict and thorough teacher. It is well known that he did not instruct his students in modern styles, but rather schooled them intensively (even mercilessly) in counterpoint and harmony before they could start to write even short pieces. Webern, having already studied counterpoint and harmony, began right away in the autumn of 1904 (according to Cox) with a series of piano pieces in three-part form (M. 29–46), which were followed by works in variation form (M. 22–24). Only then was he permitted to write "kleine Sätze" in free form.[25] All of these exercises were for piano or string quartet. Webern was apparently not encouraged to continue writing songs (just like Berg) or to attempt anything for orchestra. The exercises are overwhelmingly diatonic; Schoenberg did not allow his students to use chromatic harmony until they had fully mastered basic tonal writing.[26] (Therefore it is misleading to try to order Webern's early works in terms of increasing chromaticism, as the Moldenhauers do.) The composition exercises were supplemented with analyses of traditional works, with special emphasis on Beethoven.

After less than a year of study, Webern was permitted to write extended free compositions (according to Cox, these were the piano pieces in C minor, M. 116, A minor, M. 75, and G major, M. 76).[27] In 1905–6 (his last year at the university) he produced two piano pieces (*Satz für Klavier* and *Sonatensatz—Rondo*) and three extended string quartet movements (*Langsamer Satz*, String Quartet [1905], and Rondo for String Quartet). Schoenberg's tutelage shows in Webern's new mastery of motivic writing. Whereas earlier works display striking musical ideas, the connecting joints are often awkward or too obvious (this is particularly true in a longer work such as *Im Sommerwind*). From Schoenberg, Webern learned how to generate a tightly structured, coherent piece from one or two musical ideas.

The String Quartet (1905), a single large movement composed in the summer, was especially ambitious. Webern's debt to Schoenberg, particularly to *Verklärte Nacht*, is obvious. Like its model, Webern's String Quartet drew its inspiration from specific literary and pictorial sources. The work was inspired by a Segantini painting, the triptych *Werden-Sein-Vergehen* (Becoming-existing-expiring); the music reflects the painting's three-part structure. In the score Webern quotes from Jacobus Böhme, a German mystic of the late sixteenth and early seventeenth centuries. The same quotation, not coincidentally, had served as the opening motto for Wille's novel *Offenbarungen des Wacholderbaums* (which includes his poem "Im Sommerwind"): "In this Light did my Mind forthwith penetrate all Things; and in all living Creatures, even in Weeds and Grass, did I perceive God, who He may be and how He may be and what His Will is" (Moldenhauer and Moldenhauer, 87).

This passage expresses the kernel of Webern's future artistic creed and his deepest religious convictions. Although nominally a Catholic, he held to the pantheistic belief that God was manifested in nature. God's essence, contained in every living and inanimate thing, was also part of human beings and their artistic expressions. If everything manifests the deity, then the surface of a thing must reflect its essence. In a piece of music, there should be no inconsistency between surface and structure, or (as Schoenberg later put it) between style and idea. This unbroken continuum from God to the natural world to the human world and back again is also depicted by the Segantini painting upon which the quartet is based.

If Webern's early development as a composer was marked by his immersion in the post-Wagnerian tradition, then his first maturity resulted from his coming to terms with Brahms. Schoenberg, for whom Brahms was the most important model for his autodidactic training as a composer, was the impetus behind this.[28] As Edward Cone put it, "behind Schoenberg's teaching stands the ghost of

Brahms. The construction of a melody by motivic manipulation, the use of thematic material to create accompaniment figures, the transformation of one theme into another, the devices of foreshadowing and reminiscence—all these are familiar methods of the Old Master.''[29] Webern learned his lesson well, as his tightly motivic Quintet for Piano and String Quartet of 1907 and other works show.

Before coming to Schoenberg, Webern (as a typical Wagnerian) had not shown great enthusiasm for Brahms's music. In his diary from the 1903–4 concert season, he wrote: ''Brahms' Symphony [No. 3] is so restrained, cold and without special inspiration, everything brooding like a frosty November day, badly orchestrated—grey in grey. Wagner's Overture [*Faust*] is full of the deepest passion, of scorching ardor, of uprooting power'' (Moldenhauer and Moldenhauer, 58). Given his earlier attitude, it is ironic that Webern's Passacaglia, his first mature piece (the designation ''Op. 1'' shows that he considered it as such), proved to be such a thoroughly Brahmsian exercise.

The Passacaglia, which was probably completed by the late spring of 1908, is a model for the kind of mastery of tradition that Schoenberg wished his students to attain. The piece is firmly rooted in D minor (a favorite key of Schoenberg and Berg as well) and displays a virtuosic command of late-romantic harmonic vocabulary. Webern builds a large-scale work out of a small amount of thematic material, using the Schoenbergian (and Brahmsian) technique of developing both themes and accompanying material from a limited number of motives. Although Webern follows the strict passacaglia form—a theme with a succession of eight-bar variations—the piece makes a striking effect even if one is not conscious of the form. This is achieved by sculpting the series of variations into larger units, shaped by three climaxes; the piece ends, moreover, with a long, freely composed coda that develops and recapitulates previous ideas. Compared to *Im Sommerwind*, composed four years earlier (the only single movement in Webern's output that is longer than Op. 1), the Passacaglia shows not only a much more fluent handling of tonality, form, and orchestration, but also a decided turn away from a post-Wagnerian style.

Webern's Op. 1 is based not on a Bachian passacaglia, but on the fourth movement of Brahms's Fourth Symphony. The points of contact are numerous and unambiguous. There are similarities in the themes, the character of the corresponding variations, and the overall structure (which in both works combines aspects of sonata form with the passacaglia structure). Yet Webern's apparent homage to Brahms was really an homage to Schoenberg. With the Passacaglia Webern establishes his links to the ''great German tradition,'' emphasizing his roots in it just as he is about to move into a new world.

SWIMMING AGAINST THE TIDE (1908–AUGUST 1914)

The years between Webern's finishing his studies with Schoenberg and the First World War were the most productive of his life and at the same time among the most difficult. During this period Webern found his own distinctive voice as a composer, cultivating and radically transforming the traditional genres of accompanied song, chorus, string quartet, violin sonata, cello sonata, and orchestral piece. These works (which include his Opp. 3–11), like Schoenberg's and Berg's equally ground-breaking music of this time, were greeted with public incomprehension (when they were performed at all). With their move to atonality, Schoenberg, Berg, and Webern in effect seceded from mainstream musical life. The hostile reception by the public to this music reached its climax in the famous *Skandalkonzert* of March 1913, which confirmed the composers' worst fears and at the same time strengthened their resolve. Yet their compositional radicality was also nurtured by their sense of belonging to a larger cultural movement, which manifested itself in literature, arts, and the theater as well as in music.[30] The ideals and aesthetic views of Kraus, Kokoschka, Kandinsky, Loos, and others supported the musicians of the Schoenberg circle and helped them to maintain their course in the face of public rejection. "Nothing is now more important than showing those pigs that we do not allow ourselves to be intimidated," Webern wrote to Schoenberg after the controversial premiere of the latter's Second String Quartet (Moldenhauer and Moldenhauer, 105). In spite of the brave words, the uncomprehending reception had disturbed him greatly and would continue to do so on future occasions.

Webern's inability to reconcile the practical necessities of daily life with his artistic vision led to a personal and professional crisis, which culminated in the autumn of 1913. Aided by psychoanalysis, he returned to composition after a block that had lasted almost two years (from the summer of 1911 until the summer of 1913). His works after his recovery are distinguished by a brevity even more extreme than before; the whispered utterances threaten to shrink to the vanishing point.

Although the years between 1908 and 1914 were marked by unprecedented compositional productivity, this was also a time of bitter struggle as Webern tried to establish himself as a conductor. Season after season he would obtain a post in a theater as a vocal coach or assistant conductor, but virtually every attempt resulted in catastrophic failure. The problem lay not in his musical competence, which was generally acknowledged, but in his emotional instability. In these situations Webern was his own worst enemy. Friends, especially Zemlinsky and Jalowetz, tried to help him, but each time Webern's inability to cope with the daily hustle and bustle of theater life led him to resign or simply to flee.

Webern's attempt to establish a conducting career resulted in eleven different engagements as vocal coach and assistant conductor between 1908 and 1916.[31] During this time he worked only one full season (1909–10 at the Vienna Volksoper); at all other jobs he quit before the season was over or even before it began. During the war several engagements were cancelled or interrupted through no fault of Webern's, although he did leave a job in Prague in 1916 because he felt guilty that he was working as a musician while Schoenberg had to serve in the army (Moldenhauer and Moldenhauer, 215). This zigzag career had a disastrous effect on his financial situation. For years he relied on an allowance from his father, which was all the more necessary once he became responsible for a family.

Webern's impractical idealism made it difficult for him to fit into theater life. How divergent his vision of music theater was from the ordinary practice is shown in his own opera plans of 1908. In a letter to his cousin Diez, who was to write the libretto, Webern made the following conditions: ''*no procession, no combat, nothing of the sort that in any way requires* 'illustration.' I need nothing but a few characters. By no means a theatrical piece. . . . Just get away from everything that is now called theatre. The opposite. . . . Everything else repulses me to the highest degree'' (Moldenhauer and Moldenhauer, 117).

Webern's aesthetic of theater was influenced by the theater pieces of Kokoschka and August Strindberg, both of whom he admired greatly. Another important model was the symbolist poet and playwright Maurice Maeterlinck, whose plays *Alladine und Palomides* and *Die sieben Prinzessinnen* he had chosen for opera libretti himself (though neither attempt went beyond a few sketches). Webern knew and admired Claude Debussy's Maeterlinck opera *Pelléas et Mélisande* as well as Schoenberg's orchestral tone poem on the same subject. Webern's conception of a nonnarrative, nonrealistic theater was bound to clash sharply with the daily fare of operettas and other light entertainment at the theaters at which he worked.

Although Webern did not dislike all operetta—he admired the works of Johann Strauss, Albert Lortzing, and Carl Zeller, for example—he did find most of the pieces he dealt with to be worthless. ''O my God, do I have to perform all this filth? It cannot be. What will become of me? If I think of my ideals—or whatever they are called—I would have to perish!'' (letter to Schoenberg, 25 July 1909; Moldenhauer and Moldenhauer, 106) The litany of woes continued with each job. In 1912 at the theater in Stettin (where his friend Jalowetz was also employed), Webern wrote to Berg, ''As a non-participant, I would flee a theater such as the one where I am at present as if it were a place infested with the plague, and now I myself must help to stir the sauce'' (Moldenhauer and Moldenhauer, 162).

The main reason for Webern's lack of success in the theater, however, was his fundamental belief that the practical and aesthetic spheres were separate and indeed mutually exclusive: ''When people are in business and concern themselves with external things, then they all become hollow inside. No longer is the passionate devotion there. But with me, I assure you, it becomes ever stronger.''[32] The theater represented for Webern the world of commerce, intrigues, and vulgarity. The inner world encompassed not only the spiritual and creative life of an individual, but also family, friends, and nature. Webern described this dichotomy as follows: ''From the excess of diversion and outside activity . . . , I flee in thought to a life that is quieter on the outside but has more movement within. It is strange: I dry out in this flood of music, excitement, and so on. Mahler once wrote that he needed this commotion . . . in order to have a counterweight against his inner turmoil. I suffocate in it'' (letter to Königer, 1 January 1913; Moldenhauer and Moldenhauer, 168).

With each engagement Webern's antipathy to the theater grew and his health worsened. He was released on sick leave from a position in Stettin in January 1913, but in spite of rest cures and vacations his health did not improve. That summer he experienced a major crisis, which caused him to leave a position in Prague abruptly before the beginning of the season. Several doctors he consulted came to the conclusion that there was nothing physically wrong with him and suggested psychoanalysis, a radically new treatment at that time. Webern resisted this suggestion at first, perhaps unwilling to admit that he could have mental problems, but then gave in and undertook a three-month course of psychological analysis with Dr. Alfred Adler in Vienna (Moldenhauer and Moldenhauer, 178).

Webern's failure in the public sphere and his productivity in his own compositions were not coincidental, but bore a basic and interactive relationship with each other. The music he wanted to compose was completely incompatible with the music he worked with daily. While others, including Mahler, were able to separate the psychological space needed for composing from stresses of the outside world, Webern could not. The constant battle between the idealistic radicality of his own work and the compromises necessary when working with other people caused him repeatedly to fall ill. These psychosomatic illnesses, although unconsciously generated, gained him the time and space to compose. His exposure to musical convention and routine practice in the theater perhaps also served as a psychologically useful antipode against which he could rebel in his own music.

Webern's compositions between 1908 and 1914 mark the establishment of an individual voice distinct from that of Schoenberg. During these years he produced a series of brief, sparse, expressionistic pieces that comprise some of his best-known works (Opp. 5–11). In almost every respect—form, length, timbre, melody, harmony, and rhythm—Webern's music of this period questions the most basic principles of Western musical logic. For this reason these pieces have been rightly considered radical. Yet Webern did not wave the avant-garde banner, but rather viewed his music as a direct and inevitable distillation of personal experience. He did not always have confidence in the results and did not dare to place himself on the same level as his idols Schoenberg and Mahler.

The aspect of the Schoenberg circle's music that was greeted with the greatest incomprehension was its abandonment of a tonal center or key. Closely following Schoenberg, Webern took this step in 1908 and 1909, not coincidentally in a series of vocal works. The colorful, hyperexpressive texts of Dehmel and Stefan George contain images that ask for equally vivid and extreme music. At the same time, a poem's verse structure provides a superficial form that the music can follow, although the verbal structure alone does not compensate for the articulative capabilities of tonality.[33]

In the Dehmel setting ''Nächtliche Scheu'' (1907), for example, every important musical event is derived from the first interval in the vocal line, a descending minor seventh. This crucial motive, a ''dissonant'' interval presented in a harmonically ambiguous context, reflects the first word, *Zaghaft* (timorously). Leaps of sevenths and other large intervals create a turbulent mood, appropriate for the poem's theme of an anxious first kiss. For the climactic last line of the poem, ''Mädchen, küsse ich dich,'' the vocal line descends almost two octaves (an expansion of the opening minor seventh), its widest range in the piece.

The later Dehmel songs (''Am Ufer,'' ''Himmelfahrt,'' and ''Helle Nacht,'' composed in 1908) are characterized by even more extended tonality. In ''Am Ufer,'' whole-tone sonorities result in a sense of suspended tonality (what Schoenberg called ''schwebende Tonalität''); a stable tonic (D) is heard only at the end. In ''Helle Nacht'' the dream state depicted in the poem is reflected in the music's ambiguous, whole-tone-based tonality. The song, the last of the set, is open ended: instead of a tonal resolution, the voice closes with two tonally ambiguous tritones and the piano with an augmented triad.

The poems of George, of which Webern set fourteen for voice and piano but published only ten (under the opus numbers 3 and 4), were perfect vehicles for his first attempts at composing without the support of the tonal system. The poems evoke fantastical dream worlds, conjured up in an elevated, pseudo-archaic language; George's poetry evokes a golden, aestheticized world like that in Klimt's paintings. In Webern's settings the vocal line hovers around the low and middle registers, which helps to achieve the soft dynamic level desired. Although the songs are not tonal in the sense of having a single established tonic, certain notes are indeed emphasized from time to time. More often, an entire complex of notes becomes a kind of ''reference sonority'' that opens the piece and returns at the end. In the first song of Op. 4, a prominent major triad (whose tonal associations are weakened, if not undermined, by the dissonant bass) plays such a role. This sonority familiar from tonal music—and its subversion—can be understood as the direct musical counterpart to the ''world of beings'' to which the narrator bids farewell in the poem's first lines.

At a time when Schoenberg was exploring the limits of hyperexpressivity, Webern's music seems to retreat into itself. While the singer in Schoenberg's Second String Quartet proclaims (in George's words), ''I feel the air of another planet,'' Webern's Op. 3 songs begin, ''This is a song for you alone'' (No. 1). The more introspective world implied by the chosen text is reflected in the fragmented canon between the voice and the piano, who seem to ''speak'' (actually to whisper) only to each other.

During Webern's student days his admiration of Mahler's music had steadily increased. This probably coincided with Schoenberg's own growing admiration of Mahler and the latter's support of Schoenberg and his students (Moldenhauer and Moldenhauer, 74–75). If Webern's early works were stamped by Wagner and his student works by Brahms, then his first independent instrumental compositions bear the indelible traces of Mahler's music. As Derrick Puffett put it,

"It is perhaps the coming to terms with the influence [of Mahler] . . . that marks the greatest difference between 'early' and 'later' Webern."[34] Although Mahler's large-scale symphonies might seem far removed from Webern's concentrated utterances, they actually have much in common. One of the most valuable lessons Webern learned from Mahler was that simplicity and profundity are not incompatible. Mahler's example also showed Webern how to combine song and instrumental music, how to use the late-romantic orchestra in a fresh and subtle way, and, most of all, how to express personal ideas and feelings in music.

In a letter to Berg, Webern described how his compositions grew directly out of personal experiences:

> Say, how do you begin to compose? With me it is so: an experience goes around and around inside me until it turns into music: with a very definite relationship to this experience. Often in detail. . . . With the exception of the violin pieces [Op. 7] and some of my latest orchestra pieces, all my compositions from the "Passacaglia" on relate to the death of my mother.[35]

Webern's Six Pieces for Large Orchestra, Op. 6, composed in 1909 (only a year and a half after the Passacaglia), grew out of personal experiences, particularly his mother's death. Webern's orchestration, which employs gongs, bells, harp, and celesta as well as a large brass section (six horns, six trumpets, four trombones, and tuba), is clearly indebted to Mahler's. At the center of Webern's Op. 6, the fourth piece is a Mahlerian funeral march, which, Webern related, described his feelings as he walked behind his mother's coffin on the way to the cemetery. Webern describes how the other pieces of Op. 6 also came out of his grief: "The first piece is to express my frame of mind when I was still in Vienna, already sensing the disaster, yet always maintaining the hope that I would find my mother still alive. . . . The third piece conveys the impression of the fragrance of the Erica, which I gathered at a spot in the forest very meaningful to me and then laid on the bier" (letter to Schoenberg, 13 January 1913; Moldenhauer and Moldenhauer, 126).

Webern's descriptions are not, strictly speaking, "programs," since they reflect only the composer's state of mind during creation and are not necessary in order to understand the work. Like Mahler, Webern never spoke publicly about the personal experiences that lay behind his works. In a 1933 program note about Op. 6, Webern described the piece in more objective terms than he had earlier: "The first expresses the expectation of a catastrophe; the second the certainty of its fulfilment; the third, the most tender contrast . . . ; the fourth, a funeral march; five and six are an epilogue: remembrance and resignation" (Moldenhauer and Moldenhauer, 128). The Six Pieces meant so much to Webern that he had them printed at his own expense (as "Op. 4," in 1913). They received their premiere at the so-called *Skandalkonzert* of 31 March 1913, in which the audience rioted and the police had to be called.

The Two Songs, Op. 8 (1910), on poems from Rainer Maria Rilke's prose work *The Notebook of Malte Laurids Brigge*, were originally scored for an orchestra almost as large as that of Op. 6. (Webern later revised them for voice and nine instruments.) ''Are there not violent reverberations of the soul that are yet very gentle?'' Webern wrote to Schoenberg on 10 August, 1910 about the song. ''What the orchestra possesses in expressive possibilities is limitless'' (Moldenhauer and Moldenhauer, 133).

The Rilke poems form two parts of an interrupted monologue about lovers' inability to express their feelings for each other. Webern's choice of these newly published poems grew out of his intensifying love affair with Wilhelmine. Since they were first cousins, they could not be married in the Catholic church without a special dispensation, and both families were opposed to a marriage outside the church. This was a matter of some urgency, as Wilhelmine had become pregnant that summer. They married in a civil ceremony in February 1911; their first child was born two months later (Moldenhauer and Moldenhauer, 138–40).

Although Webern's atonality was indebted to Schoenberg's model for its very existence, he very quickly turned it in a new direction. He had learned Schoenberg's lesson about nonredundancy all too well; by 1909 his works had reached a state of unprecedented brevity. The extreme concision of Webern's music during these years reflected, on one hand, a tendency to severe self-criticism, and on the other, his receptiveness to the ideas of Kraus and Loos (who in turn had influenced Schoenberg's thought). In his architecture Loos emphasized the ''clean line'' and the need to avoid superfluous ornamentation. The poet and essayist Kraus passionately advocated a simple, nonredundant, and direct form of language. Webern, who had been reading Kraus's journal *Die Fackel* since at least 1911, shared Kraus's convictions about the purity of language and the moral duty of the artist. The aphorisms of Kraus in particular were formative models for Webern's miniatures.

The second and fourth pieces of the Five Movements for String Quartet, Op. 5, composed in 1909, were the most concentrated works Webern had yet composed. In these two extremely slow movements (the eighth note is marked 56 and 58 beats per minute, respectively), Webern eschews forward-directed development in favor of a delicate web of timbres that capture a moment of stillness. The prominent repeated chords, tremolos, and ostinatos contribute to the static effect. Against such backgrounds, fragmentary melodies emerge; their motion seems undirected and often circular. In No. 4, for example, an ascending gesture (heard three times, transposed) begins and ends on a weak beat; played pianissimo and diminuendo, it leads nowhere. If Schoenberg's music suggests ''prose'' (as he himself described it),[36] then Webern's is more analogous to lyric poetry, where language is used not to inform or to narrate, but to allude, to evoke, and to infer.

The Five Movements were originally conceived as a ''First String Quartet, Op. 3.'' Echoes of Schoenbergian technique are still audible, particularly in the continuous motivic development of the first piece and the scherzo quality of the third. Yet Webern's touch is unmistakable, particularly in the aphoristic brevity of the latter four pieces. From this point in 1909 until the First World War, Webern was occupied almost exclusively with very short pieces. While evidently not something that was planned or even desired, this drastic reduction of scale turned out nonetheless to be a fruitful idea: Schoenberg followed suit by drafting some tiny chamber orchestra pieces (1910, published posthumously) and the Six Little Piano Pieces, Op. 19 (1911), as did Berg with his *Altenberg Lieder*, Op. 4 (1912), and Four Pieces for Clarinet and Piano, Op. 5 (1913).

Uncomfortable with the idea that such short pieces could make up a complete opus, Webern added four more pieces in the summer of 1911, calling them "Op. 3 Nr. 2" (these are listed in Table 6.1). Two years later, Webern completed a three-movement string quartet (one movement of which had a vocal part), which he called "Op. 3 Nr. 3." "Op. 3" Nos. 2 and 3 became the Six Bagatelles, Op. 9. "These three groups [Op. 3, Nos. 1, 2, and 3, later Op. 5 and Op. 9] belong together as to content," Webern wrote in 1913. "The pieces of groups [No. 2] and [No. 3] are, moreover, so short that it would not make good sense to perform one of these groups alone" (letter to Schoenberg; Moldenhauer and Moldenhauer 192).

With Op. 9, Webern ventures even further into the realm of aphorism; not a single piece is longer than thirteen measures, and the shortest is eight measures. In Schoenberg's well-known Foreword to the published score of Op. 9, he attributes this brevity not to compression, but to an absence of self-indulgent rhetoric. The text is thoroughly Krausian both in its language and in its meaning:

> Though the brevity of these pieces is a persuasive advocate for them, on the other hand that very brevity itself requires an advocate. Consider what moderation is required to express oneself so briefly. You can stretch every glance out into a poem, every sigh into a novel. But to express a novel in a single gesture, a joy in a breath—such concentration can only be present in proportion to the absence of self-pity.[37]

In the instrumental aphorisms from this period—Op. 5; Four Pieces for Violin and Piano, Op. 7; Op. 9; Five Pieces for Orchestra, Op. 10; and Three Little Pieces for Violoncello and Piano, Op. 11—continuous lines have given way to brief, interrupted melodic fragments. Timbre plays a crucial role; Webern makes liberal use of altered sonorities such as col legno, tremolo, and harmonics. The orchestra is deployed as if it were a collection of solo instruments; like Mahler, Webern uses the orchestra as an extended palette of colors rather than for sheer loudness. Endings fade away rather than close emphatically; the most extreme case of this is found in the first version of the fourth violin piece of Op. 7. Here Webern asks the violin to slide gently down the G string, thus closing the entire set of pieces with a glissando of indistinct pitch (this passage, measures 13–15, was later revised).[38]

Webern's musical aphorisms reflected, in their compressed lyricism, every contour of his personal emotional landscape. The vocal movements that Webern

Table 6.1
Some Early Works of Anton Webern in Prepublication Groupings

Date	Original Title/Instrumentation	Publication or Opus No.
1906	"Ideale Landschaft"	Dehmel I*
1907	Quintet	Quintet**
	"Nächtliche Scheu"	Dehmel IV
1908	Passacaglia	Op. 1
	"Am Ufer"	Dehmel II
	"Himmelfahrt"	Dehmel III
	"Helle Nacht"	Dehmel V
	Entflieht auf leichten Kähnen	Op. 2
1908–9	7 Songs, "Op. 2" (George)	Opp. 3–4, George
	7 Songs, "Op. 4" (George)	songs***
1909	"First String Quartet, Op. 3 Nr. 1"	Op. 5
	Six Pieces for Orchestra, "Op. 4"	Op. 6
1910	Four Pieces for Violin and Piano, "Op. 6 Nr. 1"	Op. 7
	Two Songs (voice and orchestra)	Op. 8
1911	Orchestra pieces	Op. 10/I, IV
	"2nd String Quartet, Op. 3, Nr. 2"	Op. 9/II, III, IV, V
1913	"Three Pieces for String Quartet (with song) Op. 3, Nr. 3"	Op. 9/I, VI
	("Schmerz")	Unpublished
	"Four Pieces for Orchestra, the third with voice, Op. 6" ("O sanftes Glühn der Berge")	Op. 10/III, II, V 3 Orch. Songs****
	stage play *Tot*	Unpublished
1914	"Two songs for Mezzosoprano and Orchestra, Op. 7" ("Die Einsame," "Leise Düfte")	Op. 13/2, 3 Orch. Songs***
	"Kunfttag III" (George)	3 Orch. Songs***
	Piece for Cello and Piano	Cello Sonata
	Three Little Pieces for Violoncello and Piano	Op. 11

*Five Songs after Poems by Richard Dehmel (New York: Carl Fischer, 1966).
**Quintet (Hillsdale, NY: Boelke-Bomart, 1953).
***Four Stefan George Songs (New York: Carl Fischer, 1970).
****Three Orchestral Songs (1913/14) (New York: Carl Fischer, 1968).

originally included in his Op. 9 and Op. 10 ("Schmerz, immer, blick nach oben" and "O sanftes Glühn der Berge," respectively) can provide some insight into the aesthetic world of these pieces. Both poems were written by Webern himself in 1913, a time in which he was especially occupied with writing poetry. In the fall of that year he drafted a stage play, *Tot* (*Dead*), whose immediate impetus was the death of a young nephew, but that certainly also allowed Webern to work through his continued mourning for his mother. Both song texts clearly relate to the death of his mother. "Schmerz" is barely syntactical; it proceeds in a series of isolated words and phrases, culminating in the last lines "Schwer / O Trauer / auf Herz / aus / Mutter" (Heavy / Oh grief / on the heart / gone / Mother). "O sanftes Glühn," which has a more conventional poetic shape, relates a vision of the Virgin Mary as *Gnadenmutter* (Mother of Mercy), seen on a mountain face at sunset.[39] Both songs use *Sprechstimme*, a technique not found in Webern's published songs, in order to convey a hushed intensity that contrasts with the otherwise wide-ranging vocal lines.

The instrumental movements associated with these songs were also engendered by Webern's grief. Of the third of the "Three Pieces for String Quartet" (later Op. 9, No. 6), Webern wrote to Schoenberg on 24 November 1913: "First a word: angel. From it comes the 'mood' of this piece. The angels in heaven. The incomprehensible state after death" (Moldenhauer and Moldenhauer, 192). It is not known if Webern associated similar images with the other string-quartet movements, but it is likely that the first piece of the set (later Op. 9, No. 1) was also part of this conception.

For the Five Pieces, Op. 10, Webern provided titles on the occasion of a performance during the 1919–20 season: (1) "Urbild" (Primal image), (2) "Verwandlung" (Change), (3) "Rückkehr" (Return), (4) "Erinnerung" (Memory), and (5) "Seele" (Soul). In this he was surely following the example of Schoenberg's Five Orchestral Pieces, Op. 16, but the titles also relate to the original ideas behind the work, which had been expressed in concentrated form in the omitted song.

Why did Webern leave out the songs in the published versions of Op. 9 and Op. 10? One reason is that by the time he was able to publish this music—1924 and 1923, respectively—he was already beginning to be involved with the twelve-tone method and was therefore far away from the aesthetic of these expressionistic miniatures. Another reason may have been Schoenberg's disapproval. Webern had carefully prepared calligraphic-quality fair copies of the Three Pieces for String Quartet and the Four Pieces for Orchestra for Schoenberg (the latter as a Christmas present).[40] Schoenberg's response to the quartet pieces was the terse remark "that his erstwhile pupil no longer needed criticism from him" (Moldenhauer and Moldenhauer, 192). A third reason was almost certainly the highly personal nature of the song texts, which, like *Tot*, contain Webern's innermost thoughts on death, religion, and the hereafter. His literary efforts, which were concentrated in the period immediately before and after his breakdown, could even have played a therapeutic role in his healing process. Later, he may not have found these texts, which resemble an emotional diary, to be relevant anymore. When he published Op. 10, he omitted the titles as well.

Webern's aphoristic style reached a point of no return with the three cello pieces of Op. 11, which have nine, thirteen, and ten measures, respectively. Following Schoenberg's urgings, Webern had tried to write a longer piece for cello and piano (published posthumously as the Cello Sonata), but did not finish it. On 16 July 1914 he wrote to Schoenberg defensively:

> I am sending you . . . a copy of what I last wrote [Op. 11]. . . . I beg you not to be indignant that it has again become something so short. I should like to tell you how this happened and thereby try to justify myself. . . . When I was fairly far advanced with the first movement [of the Cello Sonata], it became more and more compellingly clear to me that I had to write something else. I felt with complete certainty that I would leave something unwritten if I suppressed the urge. Thus I broke off the major work, although my progress in it had been smooth, and quickly wrote these small pieces . . . and rarely have I felt so certain that something good has come into being. (Moldenhauer and Moldenhauer, 202–6)

This letter shows the sense of necessity with which Webern regarded all his works. He did not set out to create a new genre of expressionistic aphorism, but rather felt himself ''forced'' to do so by the demands of his materials. In the earliest atonal music a compression was inevitable, since the repetitions that are built into tonal music (in the form of reprise and variation) were no longer available. Without repetition, it is difficult to produce periodicity and a sense of hierarchical organization, both of which contribute to a tonal piece's form and therefore its length. It is possible, however, to retain the phrase structure and rhetorical gestures of tonal music while using nontonal pitch material; Schoenberg's music often does this.

The extreme brevity of Webern's music from this period resulted precisely from his refusal to employ traditional musical rhetoric. Adorno observed that Webern's music goes even further than poetry in realizing a timeless, compressed lyricism, without the lengthening devices of narrative or musical form: ''But music has been held in thrall of its architectural nature, the received notions of form. . . . Therefore music has never completely realized the idea of the lyric, which is nevertheless irrevocably present within it. Webern—one might almost say: only Webern—achieved this.''[41]

THE FIRST WORLD WAR (1914–18)

The outbreak of war in August 1914 disrupted Webern's life both personally and professionally. Swept up in the patriotic tide, Webern volunteered for the army and in spite of his age (thirty-one), nearsightedness, and small stature served almost two years. The immediate professional consequences were severe: the theater in which he was engaged closed, and the contract he had signed with Universal Edition to publish his music was put on hold. Because of the wartime chaos, he was able to compose only sporadically, completing nine pieces (all songs) between the fall of 1914 and the summer of 1918.

During this period, and in fact for the next ten years, Webern occupied himself with vocal music almost exclusively, perhaps because reading poetry and writing songs were activities well suited for a time of relative isolation.[42] He turned to his previous favorites, Peter Rosegger, Strindberg, and Kraus, in addition to newer interests such as Goethe, Hans Bethge, and Georg Trakl. Webern never tried to write his own song texts again. In choosing these authors, he showed his independence from Schoenberg, who had not used any of them except Goethe for musical settings.

Through his encounters with poetry, Webern entered into a phase of musical experimentation. His expressly stated goal was to write longer pieces. He did this not by simply using the texts as scaffolding for a larger musical structure, but by redesigning his musical language. New models of motivic development helped him to write the longer melodic lines required by these texts. Counterpoint returns in these songs, resulting in thicker textures. The pieces from this period are in many ways ''atypical'' Webern: they are (relatively speaking) long, are densely textured, and employ loud dynamics.

The texts Webern chose during these years are at first glance bewilderingly diverse. The four poems of Op. 12 alone span centuries and nations. One, ''Der Tag ist vergangen,'' is an imitation Austrian folk song (Rosegger), one, ''Schien mir's, als ich sah die Sonne,'' is from a stage play by the Swedish author Strindberg, and one is a translation from the Chinese by Bethge (''Die geheimnisvolle Flöte''). Only the Goethe poem ''Gleich und gleich'' corresponds to the traditional notion of a lied text. The same hodgepodge quality characterizes the texts of Op. 13, which combine two modern Austrian poets (Kraus and Trakl) with two Bethge translations.

Webern's choice of the Bethge poems is easily explained through their connection with Mahler, who had used Bethge's Chinese texts in *Das Lied von der Erde*. Webern loved this piece intensely; after learning it in a piano arrangement, he, along with Berg and Paul Königer,[43] had traveled from Berlin to its posthumous premiere in Munich in 1911. The Moldenhauers rightly characterize this visit as ''one of the high points of [Webern's] life'' (150). For Webern (and probably for Mahler as well), the Chinese origins of the poems were far less important than the simplicity and clarity of the German poetic diction. The poems Webern chose—''Die geheimnisvolle Flöte,'' Op. 12, No. 2; ''Die Einsame,'' Op. 13, No. 2; ''In der Fremde,'' Op. 13, No. 3; and ''Nächtliches Bild'' and ''Der Frühlingsregen'' (fragments)—contain images of a serene natural beauty that would have appealed to him.

Simple language and nature images are also characteristic of the Rosegger and Goethe texts. Peter Rosegger, an Austrian *Heimatdichter* who was quite popular in the early part of the century, created stories and poems in the style of folk tales.[44] Webern set Rosegger's poems many times (Op. 12, No. 1; Op. 15, Nos. 1 and 3; Op. 17, Nos. 1 and 2; and Op. 18, No. 1), although he usually identified them only as ''Volkslied.'' The light-hearted Goethe poem ''Gleich und gleich'' (Op. 12, No. 4) comes from a collection designated by the author as ''Lieder.'' The short lines, strophic construction, and nursery-rhyme character belie the subtle wit that informs the underlying sexual metaphor.

> Ein Blumenglöckchen vom Boden hervor
> war früh gesprosset in lieblichem Flor;
> da kam ein Bienchen und naschte fein:
> Die müssen wohl beide für einander sein.[45]

It is likely that Webern knew Wolf's setting of this poem, since there are many musical similarities.

After Webern produced the minute Op. 11 pieces in 1914, his main concern was to write longer ones. In January 1915 he completed two songs (later Op. 12, Nos. 1 and 3) that are still quite brief. ''Der Tag ist vergangen'' (No. 1) imitates the folklike character of the poem with its periodic phrasing and allusions to tonality. ''Schien mir's'' (No. 3) captures the poem's ecstatic tone with its extreme range and rapid juxtaposition of loud and soft dynamics. In 1917 Webern added two more songs, ''Die geheimnisvolle Flöte'' (No. 2) and ''Gleich und gleich'' (No. 4).

Webern made his first sketches on Trakl poems in early 1915, leaving two extensive fragments (''In der Heimat'' and ''In den Nachmittag geflüstert''). ''In der Heimat,'' even in its incomplete state, is longer than ''Der Tag ist vergangen''; it would have been about twice as long if it had been completed. In these fragments Webern attempted to draw all the motivic material for the piece from the elaborate vocal lines, which he apparently sketched first (after sketching an instrumental introduction). He approached here the more linear, contrapuntal textures that would be prominent after 1917. The double canon ''Fahr hin, O Seel' '' (composed in 1917, Op. 15, No. 5) represents the epitome of this tendency.

The modern poets Kraus and Trakl confronted Webern with much more complex syntax and images than had the folklike poems of Rosegger or Goethe. During the war years Webern occupied himself intensively with Kraus's and Trakl's poetry, sketching many more songs than he ultimately finished. A few of these sketches present complete drafts, while others are only a few bars. The importance of these poets for Webern is therefore not shown by the published works alone.

The preoccupation with Trakl's poetry was to continue without interruption until 1921. It resulted in the orchestral song ''Ein Winterabend'' (Op. 13, No. 4, composed in 1918) and the Six Songs on Poems of Georg Trakl, Op. 14 (1917–21). Webern was undoubtedly attracted by the images of the Austrian countryside, as well as the beauty of the language and the images of decay and destruction that are prominent in Trakl's verse.[46] The depiction of a transcendentally peaceful Holy Communion scene in ''Ein Winterabend'' (because of its hopeful tone an atypical Trakl poem) obviously spoke to Webern. His primary interest, however, lay in the disjunct syntax of Trakl's poetry. A Trakl image usually has no fixed reference point, but can refer to many other images in the poem simultaneously. A complex web of relationships results. To set these texts, Webern developed a similarly complex, contrapuntal web of motives, which can refer forwards and backwards to several points at once (elsewhere I have referred to this phenomenon as "multiple reference").[47] In Trakl's poetry seemingly unrelated ideas are bound together by elaborate rhyme schemes, which Webern tried to reflect in his music.

The Four Songs, Op. 13, settings of Bethge, Kraus, and Trakl for soprano and small orchestra, represent a collection of loose ends. The presence of numerous extended song sketches on texts of these poets suggests that Webern intended to have separate Kraus and Bethge cycles, as well as an orchestral Trakl cycle, but did not complete enough songs to realize this plan. "Die Einsame" (No. 2, Bethge), composed in 1914, belongs to Webern's aphoristic style; he originally paired it with an orchestral song on his own text, "Leise Düfte," in a set called "Two Orchestral Songs, Op. 7" (see Table 6.1). "In der Fremde" (No. 3, Bethge) features the coloristic orchestration—solo strings often played pizzicato or on the bridge and the prominent use of celesta and harp—characteristic of the set as a whole. In "Ein Winterabend" (No. 4, Trakl) Webern creates a continuous three- and four-voice contrapuntal texture in which the instrumental parts are derived from the voice (in the original version the texture is even thicker than in the published version). The vocal line (particularly at the melisma "Golden blüht der Baum der Gnaden," measures 14–15) takes on a new cantabile quality missing in the aphoristic prewar songs.

Like many others, Webern reacted to the outbreak of war with an intense surge of nationalistic feeling. He wrote to Schoenberg on 11 August 1914: "I implore Heaven for victory for our army and that of the Germans. It is really inconceivable that the German Reich, and we along with it, should perish. An unshakable faith in the German spirit, which indeed has created, almost exclusively, the culture of mankind, is awakened in me" (Moldenhauer and Moldenhauer, 209). On 8 September he wrote: "I can hardly wait any longer to be called up. Day and night the wish haunts me: to be able to fight for this great, sublime cause. Do you not agree that this war really has no political motivations? It is the struggle of the angels with the devils. . . . Lord, grant that these devils will perish. God indeed ordains it already" (Moldenhauer and Moldenhauer, 210). In the same letter Webern rails against the Russians, the French, and the English in turn. While he had previously been suspicious of Protestant Germany, he writes, now he regards it more favorably than Catholic France, which has "raged against Germans and Austrians like cannibals." Even two years later, after serving in the army (although only in support functions), and after the war had already brought on unprecedented destruction and loss of life, Webern wrote to Schoenberg in June 1916: "I am striving for the keenest, most exact understanding of the obligations that have now become necessary, to relate everything to them, to live in the most pious submission only to this: to the rescue and the victory of our fatherland'' (Moldenhauer and Moldenhauer, 216). Only in November 1916 did Webern become disillusioned, writing to Schoenberg: ''I have completely lost my earlier optimism. . . . It is really as if Christ had never existed. 'Eye for eye, tooth for tooth'—the ancient law of the Old Testament alone has validity'' (Moldenhauer and Moldenhauer, 218).

Whereas many artists and intellectuals, including Schoenberg and Berg, were (at least at the beginning) in favor of the war, Webern's pan-Germanic patriotism knew no bounds. Whereas all were deceived by biased and misleading news reports,[48] Webern swallowed all the official wartime propaganda, no matter how outrageous. He was even dimly aware that he was being manipulated, writing: ''I do not know at all any more how peacetime really was. Where was this dreadful hatred hidden before?'' (letter to Schoenberg, 11 August 1914; Moldenhauer and Moldenhauer, 209)

Two factors that contributed to Webern's nationalistic frenzy were his belief in the superiority of German culture and his almost pathological reverence for authority. The first he shared with many others, including Schoenberg. Although Webern had admired French music, especially that of Debussy, he believed in a central Germanic line of music history that reached from Bach through Mozart to Beethoven, then through Wagner and Brahms to Schoenberg.[49] This belief would intensify as he (following Schoenberg's lead) later came to understand the history of music as the history of counterpoint and form.

The second characteristic, Webern's respect for authority, was excessive even by standards of the time. This was manifested most clearly in his idolization of Schoenberg, which Webern seemed to need more than Schoenberg did. Although Webern could not tolerate being subservient to people whom he did not respect (such as various theater directors), he revered authorities whom he considered deserving of it. True to his upbringing, Webern never questioned the legitimacy of what he considered to be the highest authorities: God, nation, and Kaiser.

As the war dragged on, even Webern became disillusioned with the senseless and unprecedented loss of life and the seemingly irresolvable stalemates characteristic of trench warfare. With Austria's ultimate loss and the collapse of the Austro-Hungarian Empire (the Kaiser Franz Josef had died in 1916 after a sixty-eight-year reign), the world Webern had grown up in had changed beyond recognition. This crumbling of the old society, which had been anticipated for so long, was a tremendous strain on individuals and institutions alike. In response, the postwar period was to see rapid changes in the arts, giving rise to neoclassisicm, dada, surrealism, epic theater, *Neue Sachlichkeit*, and the twelve-tone method.

Webern's choice of song texts after 1916, many of which treat themes of destruction and death, reflect his disillusionment with the war.[50] Rosegger's ''Fahr hin, O Seel' '' (composed in 1917, later Op. 15, No. 5) is a dirge; in the original novel it is sung at a funeral procession. Kraus's ''Wiese im Park'' (composed in 1917, later Op. 13, No. 1) at first depicts a beautiful park landscape, representing an idyllic life complete with leisurely Sunday promenades. Kraus's narrator stops himself, however ("nicht weiter will ich, / eitler Fuβ, mach' halt!") and suddenly recognizes the cold reality: "Ein toter Tag schlägt seine Augen auf / und alles bleibt so alt."

Many Trakl poems, particularly the later ones that Webern set exclusively after 1916, reflect an obsession with morbidity and decay. This reflects, first, Trakl's indebtedness to the French symbolist tradition of Charles Baudelaire and Stéphane Mallarmé, and second, his own tortured life (which included incest, drug addiction, and depression and ultimately ended in suicide).[51] One example of Trakl's deep pessimism is "Klage," which Trakl wrote shortly before his suicide in the autumn of 1914. This poem confronts the horrors of war (he wrote it while on the front), which here are depicted as forces that are capable of destroying mankind itself. Webern tried to set this poem in 1918, the last year of the war, but did not complete it.[52]

Trakl's three-part poem "Abendland" (The Occident) paints a similarly dystopian picture of the end of Western civilization. Webern set all three parts of the poem; they form the central core of his Op. 14 set (Nos. 2, 3, and 4). He began, however, with the third part, "Abendland III," in June 1917. This poem invokes the urban and rural geographies of an unnamed civilization—mighty cities, bare trees, distant rivers—that is populated by homeless and dying people (lines 4–6, 12). The romantic image of the sunset has been transformed into something horrifying and threatening (lines 9–11); the twilight at day's end stands for the end of civilization itself. The rhythmic emphasis of the poem's short lines reinforces its impact. This poem, written before the war, anticipates the imminent destruction with remarkable prescience.[53]

Ihr groβen Städte	Ye great cities
Steinern aufgebaut	Built up from stone
In der Ebene!	In the plain!
So sprachlos folgt	Just as speechless,
Der Heimatlose	The outcast follows,
Mit dunkler Stirne dem Wind,	With darkening brow, the wind,
Kahlen Bäumen am Hügel.	Leafless trees on the hill.
Ihr weithin dämmernden Ströme!	Ye distant twilit torrents!
Gewaltig ängstet	Shuddering, the sunset
Schaurige Abendröte	Stirs up violent alarm
Im Sturmgewölk.	In the thunderheads.
Ihr sterbenden Völker!	Ye dying peoples!
Bleiche Woge	Bleached-out wave
Zerschellend am Strande der Nacht,	Crashing on the beach of night,
Fallende Sterne.	Falling stars.

Webern's setting of "Abendland III" introduces a contrapuntal density not seen in his works since the Passacaglia; the E♭ clarinet, bass clarinet, and cello all play practically without pause, resulting in a continuous four-part texture including the voice. A forte, staccato sixteenth-note figure in the E♭ clarinet opens the piece and is spun out into a motoric background that is heard in almost every measure. This figure gradually stabilizes into a three-note ostinato in the bass clarinet, paralleled by shorter ostinatos in the other instruments. At the same time, the tempo accelerates and all parts crescendo to forte; this underlines the vivid textual images ("Gewaltig ängstet schaurige Abendröte im Sturmgewölk"). After this climax the ostinatos dissolve and the tempo slows. At "Ye dying peoples," the music of the opening lines is recalled, but the original motives are fragmented and extremely soft. It is as if only tattered shards of the musical material were left, reflecting the whispered desperation in the poem's last lines.

Webern's preoccupation with Trakl and Kraus during the last years of the war shows that he had moved beyond his earlier unreflected patriotism. By repeatedly drafting settings of their poems (of which only a few were completed), Webern engaged in a kind of musical "close reading." Some use overt tone painting, others display a more abstract relationship to the text, but in all these fragments Webern aimed to find musical counterparts to the ideas and images that were so powerful to him. These texts may have helped him to work through his complex feelings toward the war and ultimately even to temper his optimism. Webern's attitude toward the First World War should be judged not only by the early enthusiasm shown in his letters, but also by the works he produced during these years. These were not battle symphonies or nostalgic reminiscences of a vanished past, but (particularly "Wiese im Park" and "Abendland III") small-scale, intensely lyrical evocations of despair.

A PRIVATE UTOPIA: WEBERN AND THE SOCIETY FOR PRIVATE MUSICAL PERFORMANCES (1918–22)

After the war the defeated suffered from shortages of food and fuel, inflation, and social unrest. The citizens of Vienna had to adjust further to living in an ordinary middle-sized city rather than the capital of an international empire. The Webern family suffered from the same extreme material hardship that affected almost everyone in Vienna. Having left his position at the theater in Prague in April 1918 to follow Schoenberg to Mödling, Webern found himself again in a financially precarious situation. During the winter of 1919 a fourth child was born, a daughter, Christine. Food and fuel were in such short supply that the Weberns were forced to send their three older children (Amalie, Maria, and Peter, born in 1911, 1913, and 1915, respectively) to stay with relatives for about six months. Raging inflation, which lasted until 1924, wiped out what was left of the Webern family's savings.

During the fall of 1918 Webern also took the first step toward independence from Schoenberg; after a quarrel, Webern instigated a break of some six weeks. The falling-out was apparently set off by Schoenberg's impatience with Webern's continuing complaints about his conducting career (Moldenhauer and Moldenhauer, 224–25). This experience must have made Webern realize that Schoenberg could not serve as a father figure forever. The death of Webern's actual father in 1919 broke the last parental tie. Now in his middle thirties, Webern was slowly becoming more self-aware and emotionally mature.

His music was beginning to be performed and recognized. His Passacaglia, Op. 1, *Entflieht auf leichten Kähnen*, Op. 2, *George-Lieder*, Op. 3, Five Movements, Op. 5, and Four Pieces, Op. 7, were published by Universal Edition (after a long delay due to the war), making it possible for these works to be performed outside the immediate Schoenberg circle. The Passacaglia was played regularly in Europe, sometimes with Webern conducting.[54] In 1922 Op. 5 was played at the International Chamber Music Festival in Salzburg by the Amar Quartet, of which Paul Hindemith was the violist. The resulting scandal was reported in the international press. The next day the work was presented in a private performance for fifty invited musicians, including Arthur Honegger, Francis Poulenc, and Jean Wiéner, where it was well received (Moldenhauer and Moldenhauer, 248–49).

Webern finally began to establish a reputation as a conductor during these years. Rather than pursuing theater work, which he abandoned after one last aborted engagement at the theater in Prague in the fall of 1920, he carved out a niche in Vienna as a conductor of modern music. A successful performance of Mahler's Third Symphony in the Arbeiter-Sinfonie (Workers' Symphony Orchestra) concert series in May 1922 marked the beginning of a continuous twelve-year association with that ensemble and its chorus, the Singverein (Workers' Choral Society) (Moldenhauer and Moldenhauer, 244–45). In 1921 Webern also took over the directorship of the Mödlinger Männergesangverein (Men's Chorus of Mödling), which he led for five years.

Nevertheless, the familiar pattern of failure continued sporadically, especially in situations where he had no control over the program or the number of rehearsals. After his success with Mahler's Third, Webern was invited to guest-conduct four concerts for the Wiener Konzertverein (Viennese Concert Society). The first two concerts went well, although he was allowed only one rehearsal for each, but during a rehearsal for the third concert there was open rebellion from at least one member of the orchestra, after which Webern resigned. "Alas, these people absolutely do not want to rehearse," Webern lamented (Moldenhauer and Moldenhauer, 250–51). Compared to the intensive rehearsal style customary in the Society for Private Musical Performances, the exigencies of practical orchestra rehearsal frustrated Webern. He had had a similar experience with the Wiener Schubertbund, a men's chorus he had been invited to conduct in 1921; he had resigned after five months because the members had found his rehearsal style too demanding.

In spite of the material and emotional hardships, the years after the war were among the happiest in Webern's life because of his work in Schoenberg's Society for Private Musical Performances. Webern throve in this serious, idealistic environment; here, for the first time in his life, he was able to prepare thoroughly rehearsed performances of music he respected.

Schoenberg's idea for the society grew out of profound dissatisfaction with the normal concert business, which had not served the members of the Schoenberg circle well. The society created a new model for the concert environment (which has since been imitated many times) that took into account the increased difficulties of performing and perceiving modern works. It was not by any means a showcase for the Schoenberg school: works of Debussy, Scriabin, Reger, Milhaud, Stravinsky, Mahler, Josef Hauer, and many others appeared on the programs more often than the works of the Schoenberg circle.[55] The society broadened the Schoenberg circle even as its intensive activities brought the core members even closer together. During the society's four seasons (1918–22) Webern formed and cemented friendships with Edward Steuermann, Benno Sachs, Rudolf Serkin, Rudolf Kolisch, and many others.

Webern's work as *Vortragsmeister* (coach) in Schoenberg's society satisfied him as no other work had, although it only afforded him a tiny income. The coaches, who prepared the musicians for the weekly concerts, were responsible for the quality of the performances. The coach and the musicians, as Berg wrote in the society's prospectus, should aim for ''maximum clarity.'' The musicians were not to indulge in any ''virtuosity that does not correspond to the intention of the work.'' Presumably the coaches were discouraged as well from imposing their personal interpretations upon the works: ''The only success that the composer should experience here is that which must be the most important to him: to make himself understood.''[56] The ''workshop'' atmosphere of the rehearsals was carried over into the concerts in the form of introductory lectures and the repetition of works. Webern's self-effacing personality and his passion for thoroughness, the same qualities had probably hindered him in his theater work, were perfectly suited to the society's practices.

An important part of the coaches' work consisted of making reductions of orchestral works so that they could be played by the society's smaller forces. String quartet, piano, and harmonium constituted the preferred ensemble, although many works were arranged for piano four hands. Although there were clearly practical reasons for these arrangments, there were important musical ones as well. These are articulated in another version of Berg's prospectus, which bears the unmistakable stamp of Schoenberg's thinking at the time:

> [Through arrangements] it is possible to hear and to judge modern orchestral works after they have been shorn of all the sonic effects, all the sensual aids that only the orchestra can produce. Then the common complaint that this music is effective only because of its lavish and unusual instrumentation becomes irrelevant; one can no longer say that it doesn't have the characteristics that good music has had up to now: melodies, harmonic richness, polyphony, completion of form, architecture, etc.[57]

Therefore the reduction becomes a virtue rather than a necessity, allowing the essential elements of the music to be heard without the distraction of coloristic variety.

The dethroning of timbre as a structural element marked a decisive change from Schoenberg's earlier views. In his *Harmonielehre* of 1911 he had called for composition with tone colors,[58] but by 1925 he had come to believe that "the true product of the mind—the musical idea, the unalterable—is established in the relationship between pitches and time-divisions."[59] Even within the Schoenberg circle, this position was viewed as extreme; Zemlinsky, for example, once expressed his concern that piano reductions or arrangments, even if well rehearsed, might not be the best way to present modern compositions to a public.[60]

Webern made reductions of his orchestra works (Passacaglia, Op. 1; Six Pieces, Op. 6; and Five Pieces, Op. 10), as well as Schoenberg's opera *Die glückliche Hand*, his Four Songs, Op. 22, and—for a special "Propaganda-Abend"—Johann Strauss's *Schatzwalzer.* Of these only his arrangements of his own Op. 6 and the Strauss waltz have survived.[61] The society arrangement of Op. 6 represents an important stage in the work's history, an intermediate step between the original version for large orchestra and the revised version for standard orchestra, which he prepared in 1928 and considered definitive. Reducing the piece from approximately eighty instruments to eleven (flute, oboe, clarinet, string quartet, contrabass, harmonium, piano, and percussion) forced Webern to focus on the essential musical content. He took great care, nevertheless, to preserve the basic timbral design.[62] The task may have made him think not only about the impracticalities of such a large orchestra, but also about how to refine and clarify his musical ideas. By 1928 he had come to regard the first version's lavish orchestration, which included alto flute, six trombones, and contrabassoon, as "extravagant. . . . Now I can represent all this much more simply," he wrote to Schoenberg on 20 August 1928 (Moldenhauer and Moldenhauer, 128).

Webern's experiences in the society also changed the way he thought about his earlier works. When Universal Edition finally began publishing his music in 1920, he edited and revised everything he had composed up to that time (Opp. 1–13). At the same time, he grouped his works into opus numbers, finalizing the number and order of pieces (see Table 6.1).[63] At this stage the fourteen *George-Lieder* were reduced to ten and divided into two groups (Op. 3 and Op. 4). He finalized the number of movements in the string-quartet pieces (Op. 5 and Op. 9) and orchestra pieces (Op. 10), removing the songs "Schmerz, immer blick nach oben" and "O sanftes Glühn der Berge" in the process. He gave up on the idea of an orchestral Trakl cycle, moving "Ein Winterabend" into Op. 13. Of the "Two Orchestral Songs, Op. 7," "Die Einsame" likewise moved into Op. 13, while "Leise Düfte" was not published. The two Rilke songs were published together as Op. 8. Many pieces in the early opus-number groupings did not therefore originally belong together, but resulted from the exigencies of publication. When seeking evidence for musical connections between works within an opus, then, one should take the original groupings into account.

In revising his works, Webern often made far-reaching changes in orchestration, vocal lines, and texture, in addition to clarifying and simplifying the notation. He seldom altered pitches, although there are a few striking exceptions.[64]

Webern consistently reduced the size of the instrumental ensemble. The Two Songs, Op. 8 (1910), were originally conceived with an orchestra of about forty players. Over the course of the next fifteen years, Webern reduced the ensemble to nine instruments. Although he was certainly aware of the increased practicability of a smaller ensemble, the reduction of forces was only one aspect of a thorough rethinking of the piece: motivic relationships were strengthened, the formal structure was clarified, and the work was made more unified.[65] In other words, Webern brought the piece stylistically closer to his current compositional practice.

Webern undertook a similarly thorough revision with ''Ein Winterabend'' (1918, Op. 13, No. 4). The most striking feature of this revision is the breaking up of instrumental lines into shorter melodic fragments; in the more pointillistic texture that results, the interplay of motivic cells becomes more audible.[66] In ''Die Einsame'' (1914, Op. 13, No. 2), Webern smoothed out the vocal line and refined the orchestration. Among other things, he replaced extreme registers with comfortable ones: for example, he changed the bassoon in a high treble register to the trumpet, which can play easily in this range.[67]

In his revisions Webern aimed above all for increased clarity, whether of motivic structure, orchestration, or vocal writing. This is apparent as well in the frequent removal of playing techniques that cloud the pitch, such as col legno or fluttertongue. By reducing the number of ''noisy'' sounds Webern clarified pitch structures but also sacrificed some timbral variety.

Webern revised not only for practical reasons (although his conducting experience had sharpened his craftsmanship), but also because his compositional aesthetic had changed. Compared to the extravagant expressionism characteristic of the prewar works, especially in their original versions, Webern's works after 1918 are more taut, streamlined, and contrapuntal. The verbal programs and song movements that had accompanied some instrumental pieces were removed, as they did not correspond to Webern's increasingly rational aesthetic, in which *Fasslichkeit* (comprehensibility) was valued above all. The earlier, more personal aesthetic was gradually being replaced by a more ''classicist'' thinking, which was to culminate in the twelve-tone works of the late 1920s. This shift in aesthetic orientation, which paralleled Schoenberg's own during these years, was brought about at least in part because of Webern's work in the society.

During these busy years Webern was able to compose only during his summer vacations, completing the Trakl songs, Op. 14, in 1921 and Five Sacred Songs, Op. 15, in 1922. Both works use small ensembles of solo instruments; Webern did not finish any more songs with orchestra after he started working with the society, although he continued to sketch them until 1920.[68]

After years of reading Trakl and making many fragmentary sketches, Webern finally had a breakthrough and finished four of the six songs, Nos. 2, 3, 5, and 6, in one month during the summer of 1919 (he had finished No. 4 in 1917).[69] The three-part poem "Abendland" was finished and placed at the center of the collection. "Nachts" (No. 5) was placed first, and "Gesang einer gefangenen Amsel" (No. 6) at the end. Webern evidently then considered the work finished, since he gave it a title page—"5 Lieder mit Begleitung von Solo-Instr., Op. 14 (15)"—and circulated the manuscript.[70] Only in 1921 did he set "Die Sonne" (No. 1) and put it at the head of the cycle.

These songs are much more difficult to sing and to play than their predecessors. The vocal lines in Op. 14 feature the wide leaps and extreme range characteristic of the later vocal works. (The fifth song, "Nachts," begins on a high B, a register in which articulation of words is impossible.) Yet the vocal writing and the dense counterpoint in the instruments together produce a vivid impression of Trakl's poetry. Rather than seeking to reflect individual words and phrases in music, Webern provides a musical analog to the richly complex verse. He does this by creating an equivalent shape based on the interaction of small motives, which reflect the fractured syntax and multiple meanings of the Trakl texts.

After the Trakl songs were completed in the summer of 1921, Webern did not set any more modern poetry until 1933, when he began to focus exclusively on the poetry of Hildegard Jone. In the meantime he chose either folklike verse (by Rosegger or from *Des Knaben Wunderhorn*) or sacred verse (from Lutheran chorales or from the Catholic liturgy). (Webern had already set Rosegger's "Der Tag ist vergangen," Op. 12, No. 1, in 1915.) Although these choices reflect Webern's increasing piety, a tendency shared by many artists and intellectuals during the postwar years, these texts also were of great personal significance. Webern prized them because they expressed eternal human values in a "simple," comprehensible form, the same goals he aspired to in his music.

In the summer of 1921 Webern completed "Das Kreuz, das musst' er tragen" and "In Gottes Namen aufstehn" (Op. 15, Nos. 1 and 3) on Rosegger texts (which, however, he referred to as "old sacred chants").[71] He grouped these together with another Rosegger setting he had composed four years earlier, "Fahr hin, o Seel' " (later Op. 15, No. 5) to form a set he called *Drei geistliche Lieder*. The first two songs feature wide-ranging, disjunct lines in all parts; the voice takes on the character of the instruments, although text painting on words like "Himmelreich" and "himmlischen" show the sincere reverence that lay behind Webern's choice of the religious poems. "Fahr hin, o Seel' " is a contemplative double canon; the conjunct vocal writing, the strict counterpoint, and the continuous instrumental lines contrast with the jagged, fragmented intensity of the other, more current, songs of the group.

Webern continued to be preoccupied with religious verse. The next summer he set two chorale texts, "Morgenlied" and "Mein Weg geht jetzt vorüber" (later Op. 15, Nos. 2 and 4), which in spite of their small dimensions he considered to be part of a planned "sacred cantata."[72] In "Mein Weg," composed on 26 July 1922, he made his first twelve-tone sketches, but he did not develop them in the finished piece. The row is preserved as the first twelve notes of the vocal line, but the rest of the piece was freely composed. Webern must have learned about twelve-tone composition from Schoenberg, who had completed his own first fully twelve-tone pieces the previous summer and had communicated at least some aspects of the method to his students in the meantime.[73] Webern's failure to use the technique in "Mein Weg"—although his sketches show an understanding of its basic possibilities—points to a conceptual clash between the motivic, text- (and voice-) based composition that he had increasingly refined over the years and the more abstract thinking about pitch relationships necessary in twelve-tone composition. Over the next three years he devoted himself to making the new technique his own.

NEW FRONTIERS (1923–27)

Whereas the years immediately after the First World War were centered around the private utopia of the Society for Private Musical Performances, the 1920s brought Webern a heightened public role and increased confidence in his compositional direction. His conducting career blossomed as he continued to work with the Workers' Symphony Orchestra and the Choral Society. Through the efforts of Universal Edition Webern's music became increasingly widely performed, although performances were still often greeted by public incomprehension and rejection. His income was further augmented by a job teaching piano at the Israelitic Institute for the Blind and by several private composition pupils, including Reich, Ludwig Zenck, Leopold Spinner, Erwin Ratz, and Moritz Kaplan.

After 1925, when Schoenberg took on a post at the Prussian Academy of the Arts in Berlin, Webern was left again without his mentor's direct guidance. He handled Schoenberg's absence much better than he had before, bouyed up by an independent professional life, a close relationship with his family, and frequent retreats into his beloved mountains. Personal and professional growth was accompanied (and perhaps even spurred on) by new developments in his compositions. Between 1923 and 1927 Webern reached a musical turning point in two senses: first, he developed an individual twelve-tone language that differed in significant ways from that of Schoenberg. Second, after more than a decade of writing vocal works, he returned to instrumental composition with the String Trio, Op. 20 (1927). This work, the first extended piece of instrumental music since Op. 6 almost twenty years earlier, nonetheless marks the culmination of the dense motivic style characteristic of the "vocal decade."

In February 1923 Schoenberg called his pupils and friends together in order to explain the principles of his new method of composing "with twelve tones related only to each other." Webern, who, as we have seen, had already experimented with the method, was apparently not entirely persuaded by Schoenberg's arguments.[74] Although Webern never doubted that he should adopt the method, his path to twelve-tone composition was hardly a smooth one. This is not surprising, since for him, as for Berg, the method did not come as a natural stylistic development, but rather was imposed upon him from outside.

After first attempting to compose with twelve-tone rows in the summer of 1922, Webern did not compose anything for a whole year. During the next summer he produced only three canons on Latin texts for voice, clarinet, and bass clarinet (Op. 16, Nos. 2, 3, and 4). The canons gave Webern the opportunity to explore aspects of serial technique without actually adopting the twelve-tone row. (In the summer of 1924 he made row sketches for "Crucem tuam," Op. 16, No. 5, but did not realize them in the piece.) The canonic structure itself is a perfect laboratory in which to investigate transposition, inversion, and invariance. The first occurs whenever a following voice imitates at any interval other than an octave: in No. 4, for example, a canon at the half step, each gesture is heard at the original pitch and then immediately a minor ninth higher. All of the other four canons have an inverted voice as well, which produces consistently symmetrical relationships with the original voice.[75]

The vocal demands of Op. 16 exceed those of any previous work. Leaps of more than an octave are common (No. 5 ends with a leap from G♯ to A more than two octaves above). The new virtuosity came about in part because of the canon form: since all parts have the same music, the voice is challenged to behave like a clarinet. But Webern still did not wish to write purely instrumental canons, however practical that might have been, because he valued the sound of the human voice and especially its capability of semantic expression. Webern was clearly captivated by the Latin texts. He related to Schoenberg on 30 July 1923 how, planning a cycle of sacred lieder, he had borrowed a breviary from the priest: "It contains everything: hymns, psalms, and so forth. The breviary is a glorious work" (Moldenhauer and Moldenhauer, 272). He evidently did not consider Op. 16 to be an etude, whatever technical skills he had honed working on it.

Webern completed his first twelve-tone pieces in the fall and winter of 1924. The *Kinderstück* for piano (published posthumously) and the song "Armer Sünder, du" for voice, violin, clarinet, and bass clarinet (Op. 17, No. 1) represent two quite different approaches to twelve-tone writing. The former, planned as part of a cycle of children's pieces commissioned by Universal Edition, features a simple and audible row technique. The single twelve-tone row is almost always presented melodically. The beginnings and endings of the row statements are marked by accents or repeated notes.[76]

In contrast to this transparent, linear row technique, in "Armer Sünder, du" the row is broken up among the parts to the point where it is not even identifiable, much less audible.[77] In the third song of Op. 17, on the other hand, the vocal line follows the row, while the instruments respond with fragments of the row moving in kaleidoscopelike fashion. Two years earlier, Webern had derived the row from a vocal melody and conceived of it primarily as a linear entity.

Rather than systematically exploring the many possibilities of twelve-tone technique, such as retrograde, transposition, and inversion of a row or combination of different row forms, he had instead aimed for greater freedom. Breaking up the row and distributing bits of it to the voice and to the instruments allowed him to compose motivically, much as he had done before. Indeed, all three songs of Op. 17 give the impression of dense chromatic chaos rather than serially controlled order.

Only in the spring of 1925, when he began sketching his String Trio and Op. 18 songs, did Webern regain the momentum he had lost three years earlier. Though the relative dry spell had been due in part to his busy conducting schedule and to revisions of earlier works, absorbing the implications of the new method certainly also slowed his pace.

With the Three Songs, Op. 18 (1925), Webern showed his new mastery of twelve-tone technique. Each of the three songs applies the method in a different way: the first uses one row in a single form, the second employs another row in the four available transformations (prime, retrograde, inversion, retrograde inversion), while the third (employing still another row) combines two or more forms simultaneously throughout, using all four transformations. The increased complexity over the course of three songs does not reflect Webern's learning process—his sketches show that he was acquainted with these procedures even when he wrote Op. 17—but rather the poetic content of the texts.[78] The three texts, "Schatzerl klein" (Rosegger), "Erlösung" (*Des Knaben Wunderhorn*), and "Ave regina coelorum" (Marian antiphon), "form a complete whole," according to Webern; they pay homage to the Virgin Mary in her three roles, "Virgin, Mother, Queen of Heaven."[79] The different row techniques here serve as metaphors for the theological progression depicted in the poems.

"Twelve-tone technique is now completely clear to me," Webern wrote to Berg in 1925, "and this work gives me pleasure like practically nothing before."[80] In his earliest twelve-tone works Webern viewed the row in an almost metaphysical way. He believed that its very presence provided subconscious unity; therefore, the surface of the music could be as chaotic as desired. (This notion is at odds with Schoenberg's early conception of the technique, in which the row should function as an audible organizing principle.) Webern's almost religious faith in the row's power to unify gave him the freedom to construct music of unprecedented motivic density.

These features are evident in the songs of Op. 17 and Op. 18 as well as in the Two Songs for Chorus, Op. 19, of 1926. The culmination of Webern's early twelve-tone style was reached in his String Trio, Op. 20, completed in 1927. In no other work of Webern is the dichotomy between underlying structure and the music as perceived so great. By using the complete coloristic palette of the three string instruments, he creates a constantly shifting mosaic of sounds. The bowed continuous lines characteristic of string instruments occur relatively seldom, and when they do, they disintegrate into pizzicato or harmonics. The extreme ranges of the instruments are brought into play, so that they do not stay in their traditional registers, but overlap constantly. These characteristics, together with the fragmentary melodic figures and harmonies saturated with dissonant sevenths and ninths, make the work difficult to follow. The work's many performances over the next several years by Kolisch, Eugen Lehner, and Benar Heifetz were greeted with even more incomprehension and invective than usual (Moldenhauer and Moldenhauer, 322–23).

Yet in this work Webern followed traditional forms very closely; the first movement (originally the second) is a rondo, and the second (originally the first) is in sonata form. (Webern had planned to have three movements.) The sections of the music are articulated by different forms of the row; in the sonata movement, for example, the recapitulation occurs when the prime row forms return. The second theme uses a different group of row forms, which recur at the corresponding place in the recapitulation, now appropriately transposed down a perfect fifth. There is a slow introduction, an exposition repeat, and a coda.[81]

Although these features are clear upon studying the score, they are not easy to perceive aurally. Stravinsky is said to have remarked about the first movement, "The music is marvelously interesting, but no one could recognize it as a rondo."[82] This is because Webern did not follow the thematic characteristics of the traditional forms, but relied upon the row structure to articulate the overall shape. In the recapitulation of the sonata, for example, the "first theme" of the exposition is not repeated melodically. Only the identity of the rows relates the two passages. Since row structure is generally not perceptible except after studying the score, the music's traditional formal organization is difficult to hear. For Webern at this time, the mere presence of the row guaranteed coherence: "I can also work without thematicism, that's to say much more freely, because of the unity that's now been achieved in another way; the row ensures unity."[83] The structuring device of a preexisting form would provide even more unity. Therefore, it was not necessary to emphasize thematic features in the surface of the composition; in fact, Webern seems to have tried to blur or even negate them. In works after the String Trio he would resolve the tension between clear row structure and athematic surface in favor of a new, more audible comprehensibility.

Webern's reputation as a composer continued to grow, extending beyond Vienna into Germany, Switzerland, and the United States. Two important events at which Webern's music was played were the Donaueschingen festival in July 1924 and the International Society of Contemporary Music (ISCM) festival in Zurich in June 1926. The former, a festival for contemporary chamber music founded by Prince Max Egon zu Fürstenberg, had only been in existence three years but had already achieved considerable renown. Here Webern's Bagatelles, Op. 9, and Trakl songs, Op. 14, finally received their premieres. Two years later Webern was invited to conduct his Five Pieces, Op. 10, and Schoenberg's Wind Quintet, Op. 26, at the Zurich ISCM festival.[84] Webern continued to conduct his Passacaglia, his most accessible work, throughout Europe. Kolisch and Steuermann became advocates for the Four Pieces, Op. 7, while Kolisch's quartet played the Five Movements, Op. 5, and the Bagatelles, Op. 9. While a few works achieved an independent performing tradition in Webern's lifetime, his music was usually programmed along with that of other composers of the Schoenberg circle. He was therefore known mainly in connection with that circle, even, as one critic put it, as "the incarnation of Schoenbergian discipleship."[85]

The Workers' Symphony and the Workers' Choral Society were part of the Social Democratic party's cultural wing, which was led by Schoenberg's close friend David Josef Bach. From 1922 until 1934 Webern led the chorus and conducted the orchestra regularly. In this capacity he made respected contributions to the city's musical life, for which he was awarded the Prize of the City of Vienna in May 1924. Webern's success as a conductor during these years is confirmed by reports outside the Schoenberg circle as well as within it. By this time he had apparently learned better how to rehearse within a limited time frame, how to compromise his fanatic perfectionism, and how to motivate musicians.

A high point of Webern's tenure with the Workers' Choral Society was his performance of Mahler's mammoth Eighth Symphony on 18 and 19 April 1926. Bach had chosen this spectacular work to mark the occasion of the two hundredth Workers' Symphony concert, at which leading Socialist politicians were present. The concert was reviewed widely: the Berlin journal *Die Musik* reported that Webern had certain technical problems as a conductor, but that his passion for the music came across all the same.[86] Even the Viennese critics were impressed with what Webern had achieved with amateur choruses, for example, the *Wiener Zeitung*: "With this accomplishment, Webern, up to now known only as one of the most outspoken and rigid leaders of modern composition, has shown himself also to be a conductor of the first rank."[87]

Reports of Webern's conducting of the Workers' Symphony and Choral Society over the years are mixed. Reviews from colleagues or people sympathetic to the Second Viennese School praise his work extravagantly, often comparing his conducting with Mahler's.[88] Others were generally much less complimentary, if they mentioned Webern's contribution at all. A picture emerges of a conductor with impeccable musicianship and extremely high standards who nonetheless did not have a conducting technique adequate to realize all of his musical ideas. His obsession with perfection, which caused him to rehearse at a painstakingly slow pace, often led to resentment among the musicians; one can imagine that his lack of humor and his ego presented further obstacles. Another problem was his difficulty handling stress; what was eventually diagnosed as a "nervous condition" sometimes caused him to cancel rehearsals or even concerts at the last minute (Moldenhauer and Moldenhauer, 383).

Nevertheless, Webern's activities as a conductor brought him respect in many quarters. In the area of modern music his achievements were undisputed. In addition to Mahler, whose music became something of a specialty, Webern regularly conducted works of Schoenberg, Berg, Krenek, Reger, and Hanns Eisler. Wellesz later recalled Webern's crucial role in the Viennese modern music scene: "It is my sincere hope that, before it is too late, a chronicler may be found to record how much Vienna owed to Webern, in the years between the wars, for his activities in maintaining the contact with contemporary music, while those whose duty it was to keep up these contacts failed to fulfill their obligations."[89] Wildgans even maintained that the Workers' Symphony Concerts under Webern's direction "became practically a branch of the International Society of Contemporary Music."[90] (In 1932 Webern became president of the Vienna section of the ISCM.)

Webern's relatively successful conducting career during the 1920s and early 1930s may seem surprising given his previous track record. His greater maturity and experience certainly helped, but so did the guidance of Bach, who became a close friend during these years, and the particularly sympathetic working conditions within the Workers' Choral Society. Rehearsing an amateur chorus, whose members for the most part could not even read music, required teaching each part by rote. Such concentrated, repetitive work played into Webern's strong suit. As in the Society for Private Musical Performances, he could shape his performances down to the minutest detail. The ultimate goal—for himself no less than for the participants—was complete internalization of the music. Knowing pieces "by heart" was a guiding principle of the Schoenberg school's performance practice.[91] When the conditions were right, Webern was apparently able to achieve impressive results.

In spite of his professional affiliation with groups supported by the Social Democrats, Webern never belonged to the party and did not even consider himself a Socialist.[92] (In fact, while he was employed by the Social Democrats, he belonged to two nationalistic, pro-German organizations.)[93] He took on the work because he needed it and because of his personal loyalty to David Josef Bach. His nonetheless-sincere conviction that music should be available to the working classes stemmed as much from his belief in the moral qualities of high art as from any sense of political egalitarianism.[94] He was expected to program music by Socialist composers regularly; this he resisted only when he considered the music to be completely worthless.[95] He apparently liked the music of Eisler, who had strong left-wing beliefs, and conducted several of his overtly political works (Moldenhauer and Moldenhauer 335).

Webern did not shun all political involvement: his signature appears on a letter protesting cuts in Vienna's culture budget, published in the *Arbeiter-Zeitung* (the Social Democratic party's newspaper) before the parliamentary elections in 1927. The letter, which was also signed by Freud, Alma Mahler, Wellesz, and others, articulates a view with which Webern surely sympathized: "The intellectual and cultural idealist stands between and above social classes. He cannot submit to any political dogma because it is the mind and spirit alone that create the new realities, which politics only later puts into force."[96] This is consistent with Webern's own belief that "art has its own laws; it has nothing to do with politics."[97]

Webern made a political statement of a more personal nature when he resigned his position with the Men's Chorus of Mödling in 1926 because the group had objected to him bringing in a Jewish soloist (Moldenhauer and Moldenhauer 292). Given Webern's small and irregular income during these years, this move entailed considerable sacrifice.

RETURN TO ORDER: *FASSLICHKEIT* (1928–38)

The decade after 1928 brought considerable upheaval to Webern's life as well as a shift in his compositional direction. After the Nazis came to power in Germany in 1933, many in his circle of friends and acquaintances were forced to emigrate; Schoenberg's sudden departure for New York in October of that year was especially painful and disorienting.[98] The suicide of his friend Rudolf Ploderer and the death of Loos later the same year were further blows. With Berg's death two years later, Webern lost his closest friend and very nearly suffered a nervous breakdown as a result.[99] Wellesz reports, "The lights went out for Webern when Schoenberg left Europe and Berg died. From then on he seems to have walked in a dark cloud."[100] These losses were only partly compensated for by new friendships with the singer Josef Hueber, the poet Hildegard Jone, and her husband, the sculptor Josef Humplik. Webern's family, always the focal point of his emotional life, began to assume greater importance than ever.

On the other hand, between 1928 and 1938 Webern's reputation as a composer was at its peak. Well-known musicians such as Hermann Scherchen and Otto Klemperer propagated his work. He was invited to conduct his own music in Barcelona, Berlin, Frankfurt, and London. The first all-Webern concert took place in Vienna in 1931. In 1933 Webern's fiftieth birthday was celebrated with concerts in Vienna, Copenhagen, Winterthur, and Brussels as well as with special issues of Universal Edition's *Musikblätter des Anbruch* and Reich's journal *23*. However, there were no commemorative events in Germany because of the new National Socialist artistic policies.

After the Social Democratic party was declared illegal in 1934, Webern's music was rarely played in Austria either, and after the *Anschluss* by Germany in 1938, local performances stopped altogether. London became a particularly important venue. Due in part to the efforts of Erwin Stein, who after migrating there had a position with Boosey and Hawkes, Webern's music was performed in London relatively frequently. In 1938 alone, English audiences heard Webern's Opp. 5, 7, 11, 14, 20, 21, 26, and 27 and his arrangement of Bach's *Musical Offering* (Moldenhauer and Moldenhauer, 503).

Webern's music was also performed in the United States. Serge Kussevitsky conducted the Five Pieces, Op. 10, in New York a few months after their premiere in June 1926; in the same year, Leopold Stokowski presented the Passacaglia in Philadelphia (Moldenhauer and Moldenhauer, 295). The Five Sacred Songs, Op. 15, were played in New York in 1926 by the International Composers' Guild, which had presented the American premiere of Schoenberg's *Pierrot lunaire*. Webern's Symphony, Op. 21, received its world premiere in New York on 18 December 1929 as a commission by the League of Composers (Moldenhauer and Moldenhauer, 326). The next year his song Op. 17, No. 2, was published in Henry Cowell's series New Music. In 1932 Webern showed his gratitude by conducting a program of American music (including music of Ruggles, Ives, Copland, and Cowell), which he organized together with Cowell (Moldenhauer and Moldenhauer, 377–78). Six years later his String Quartet, Op. 28, was commissioned by the American patroness Elizabeth Sprague Coolidge and received its premiere at the Berkshire Festival of Chamber Music by the exiled Kolisch String Quartet (Moldenhauer and Moldenhauer, 490).

The international recognition gave Webern special satisfaction, especially as he became more and more disillusioned with conditions in Vienna. After the Social Democrats were removed from power in 1934, the Workers' Choral Society and the Workers' Symphony were disbanded, leaving Webern without his main sources of income. From May 1928 until 1935 he was occasionally invited to conduct radio concerts, but this work was sporadic and ill paid. Webern's long association with the Social Democrats, however apolitical he may have been, had irreparably damaged his Viennese conducting career. "No one asks me to conduct anymore," he wrote to Adorno in June 1937.[101] Aside from a part-time job as director of the Freie Typographia Chorus (chorus of the typesetters' union) after 1934, teaching was the only way left to support his family. Webern had a few private pupils, including Stefan Wolpe, Philipp Herschkowitz, and Humphrey Searle, but given his policy of charging only what students could pay (which in some cases meant free lessons), he did not earn much. His part-time teaching position at the Israelitic Institute for the Blind (which ended in 1931) also did not pay enough to live on. He gave some courses in a private home in Vienna in 1932 and 1933, which brought in some income (these lectures were recorded in shorthand and published posthumously as *The Path to the New Music*). Webern's letters of the 1930s are full of urgent requests for introductions and invitations; he eagerly followed up job possibilities in Frankfurt, Berlin, and even New York, none of which led to anything.[102]

Perhaps as a compensatory mechanism, Webern threw himself into composition during these years. He became increasingly concerned with clarity and comprehensibility (which he called *Fasslichkeit*). His efforts to control his musical materials were balanced by attempts to create the most possible variety within the self-imposed limitations. As he gained ever-increasing control over his twelve-tone technique, inventing different kinds of variation, canon, and symmetry, he continued to draw his inspiration from nature. Regular mountain-climbing trips not only restored his mental equilibrium but also provided images and sounds that he tried to realize in his compositions. He produced larger works again, focusing on traditional genres such as the symphony (Op. 21), concerto (Op. 24), piano variations (Op. 27), and string quartet (Op. 28). After several works of only two movements (Op. 20, Op. 21, and Op. 22), with Op. 24 he was finally able to write works of three movements or longer, which he viewed as a breakthrough. Vocal works, which had been neglected for eight years, returned as Webern began an intensive encounter with Jone's poetry, composing first some songs with voice and piano (Op. 23 and Op. 25) and then a cantata, *Das Augenlicht* (Op. 26).

The immediate compositional problem that Webern faced after the String Trio, Op. 20, was how to shape the infinitely malleable twelve-tone method. One solution was to adapt traditional musical forms such as sonata, rondo, and variations. Here Webern followed Schoenberg's and Berg's lead; many of Schoenberg's first twelve-tone works, including the Suite, Op. 25, the Wind Quintet, Op. 26, and the Suite, Op. 29, had employed forms borrowed from tonal music, as had long stretches of Berg's (not-yet-twelve-tone) *Wozzeck*. Another solution was to systematize the twelve-tone method itself. The wide-ranging freedom with which Webern had handled the rows in Op. 20 was not something he wanted to repeat. In his subsequent works Webern explored different and ever more complex ways of organizing the prime row and the relationships between row forms.

The Symphony, Op. 21, completed in August 1928, shows Webern's new preoccupations. The aural contrast with the String Trio is unmistakable; instead of a chaotic, rapidly changing, mosaiclike texture, the Symphony projects a clear, quiet symmetry. The first movement's sonata form, unlike the String Trio's, is audible as such because the various parts (first theme, second theme, development, and recapitulation) are marked by caesuras and thematic changes as well as by repeats (of the exposition and the development-recapitulation together, as in early classical sonatas). The row itself is a palindrome; Webern takes advantage of this property by building an elaborate structure of palindromes at various levels (this is especially true of the second movement, which is in variation form). The row structure—the beginnings and ends of important groups of rows, the return of rows at their original pitch level, and so on—is completely consistent with the external, audible form of the music.

Webern's first experiments with twelve-tone composition had grown out of a vocal line; here he explores the linear possibilities of the method in a quite systematic way. In the first movement four row forms proceed in canon, which is however not audible as such because the voices are distributed among several instruments and cross frequently. More audible is the harmonic structure of the exposition, where each note is heard in a fixed register; the result is a static sonority, in which each successive sound fills out a bit more of the background chord. The piece's contrapuntal structure is enhanced by a "chamber-symphony" performance with solo strings (with the clarinet, bass clarinet, two horns, and harp, nine instruments in all), which Webern sanctioned.[103]

Webern's next work, the Quartet for violin, clarinet, tenor saxophone, and piano, Op. 22 (completed in 1930), explores two different approaches to twelve-tone technique. (There is no hint of jazz, whose popularity among serious composers of that time probably inspired the choice of the saxophone.) The first movement is similar in many ways to the first movement of Op. 21; both present a clearly audible two-part sonata form (with both sections repeated), both use rows canonically, and both are (as a result) rewarding to analyze. The second movement of the Quartet, however, "seems almost to be the work of another person," as Kathryn Bailey put it.[104] The rows are deployed freely: sometimes only one row is distributed among the instruments, while at other times up to four rows occur simultaneously. While there are occasional brief canons and palindromes, they do not last long enough to orient the listener. Yet the music does not sound chaotic; the movement's fast tempo, short quarter-note and eighth-note motives, and plentiful grace notes give it a scherzolike quality. One hears contrasting sections that support Webern's designation of rondo form, although, because the row structure does not always coincide with the audible sectional divisions, analysts do not agree on the exact boundaries of the sections.[105] After the "meticulous order" of the Symphony,[106] the Quartet's second movement explores the twelve-tone technique's potential for openness and multiplicity.

Webern's manipulations of the row and the elaborate, often-inaudible constructions in his music would seem to be inconsistent with his conviction that music must be *fasslich*. Yet Webern's conception of *Fasslichkeit* related to what he viewed as music's "laws" (*Gesetze*), not to its sound. These "laws" control musical material in the same way that the laws of nature control natural phenomena.[107] It is not even necessary for an artist to be conscious of the laws, because the true genius will recognize them intuitively. Yet some of the laws have been discovered; the twelve-tone technique, for example, is "a wholly natural outcome of the ages."[108] This technique ensures a "deeper unity" that at the same time allows greater variety than in any previous music. The twelve-tone structure might not be immediately perceptible, but "something surely sticks in the ear, even if one's unaware of it."[109]

Webern's ideas, which draw from Goethe's writings on nature and on color theory, belong to the organicist thinking of his age. Yet since adolescence Webern had believed that nature and art shared the same laws. His passions for mountain climbing and gardening were much more than hobbies; his love for nature was indissolubly connected to his aesthetic world.

Often Webern began a composition by jotting down images from nature and from life. During the composition of the second movement of Op. 22, for example, he made a diagram of the rondo form, associating each section of music with an idea or image; the first section, for example, is designated "Coolness of early spring (Anninger [a hill near Mödling], first flora, primroses, anemones, pasque-flowers)"; the return of the main theme, "Dachstein [a mountain], snow and ice, crystal clear air" (Moldenhauer and Moldenhauer, 423). Whatever the relationship between verbal notes and composition might have been, it is clear that Webern viewed these "programs" as private; he did not include them in his published scores and never talked about them with students or performers.

Yet these remarks are much more than mementos of pleasant mountain excursions: they point to Webern's belief in a cosmic order that rules the metaphysical as well as the physical world. The twelve-tone row is a manifestation of this order in the aesthetic sphere, just as, according to Goethe's theories of plant metamorphosis, the shape of an individual leaf reflects the larger order in the natural sphere. The variety produced by the row and its forty-eight permutations corresponds, for Webern, to the immense variety of shapes and colors in plants, which are all based on the single model of biological organization that Goethe called the *Urpflanze* (primeval plant).[110] For Webern, therefore, "there is no essential contrast between a product of nature and a product of art."[111] Just as every living thing reflects nature's laws, which, however, can be comprehended only after close study, works of music reflect its laws, which need not be immediately perceptible. The two contrasting movements of Op. 22—one orderly and symmetrical, the other disorderly and free—are both manifestations of the same "law."

For Webern, beauty in nature and in music was not a spontaneous, superficial phenomenon; rather, it could only result from the laws governing both. In a letter to Berg he emphasized the immense importance of the natural world to his composition:

> The significance of this flora, unfathomable: that is the greatest magic to me. I perceive an unimaginable idea behind it. And I can say: to reproduce musically what I perceive there, for that I have struggled my whole life. A greater part of my musical production can be traced back to that. Namely: just as the scent and shape [*Gestalt*] of these plants—as a model given by God—come over me, that is what I want from my musical shapes [*Gestalten*] also. If it does not sound too presumptuous; then I immediately add: vain struggle to grasp the ungraspable [*das Unfaßbar zu fassen*].[112]

Webern's arrangement of the six-part Ricercare from Bach's *Musical Offering* (1935) bears further witness to his understanding of *Fasslichkeit*. He took the work's sophisticated fugal structure as a given and did not attempt to bring out the entries of the subject or other obvious contrapuntal features (Moldenhauer and Moldenhauer, 442). Instead, he broke up Bach's melodic lines into small cells. Yet this fragmentation was not intended to disfigure the work, but on the contrary "to reveal the motivic coherence," as Webern wrote to Scherchen (Moldenhauer and Moldenhauer, 444). The orchestration is also a study in tone color; every instrument, every register, and every performance indication was carefully chosen to fit into the larger design. Here Webern uses exactly the same procedure as he did in his Symphony and other works: disguising the contrapuntal structure by distributing small fragments of the melodic lines among different instruments. The work's *Fasslichkeit*, which is ensured by the contrapuntal structure, is not disturbed, but rather strengthened from the new motivic unity that is revealed.

In Hildegard Jone (1888–1958) Webern found a collaborator and the closest friend of the last part of his life. Her poetry combined everything that Webern valued most: nature images, elaborate structures, and mystical Christian rhetoric. He asked her for a cantata text as early as 1930[113] and ended up writing three (*Das Augenlicht*, Op. 26, and the two Cantatas, Opp. 29 and 31), as well as two sets of songs (Opp. 23 and 25, composed in 1933–34). He corresponded with her and her husband, the sculptor Josef Humplik, from 1926 until his death.[114]

Webern's friendship with Jone and his attraction to her poetry is understandable, given their many shared beliefs and values. As Lauriejean Reinhardt has pointed out, there were three main points of intersection: their mutual belief in the "lawful nature of art" and in "the spiritual nature of art," as well as their conviction that the "future of modern art [was] based on Western tradition."[115] The apparent stylistic gulf between their works—Jone's work is considered to be conservative, Webern's to be modern—is illusory, since both were committed Neoplatonists who believed that an abstract underlying order controlled both the aesthetic and the natural world. Dismissing Jone as an "imitation Goethe," as Boulez has done,[116] is irrelevant and unfair for two reasons. First, Webern could have set Goethe's poetry and chose not to, and second, he clearly benefited from the exchange of ideas with a living poet.

The texts of Op. 23 and Op. 25, which Webern selected from Jone's *Viae inviae* cycle, reflect the poet's mystical Christian philosophy and reverence for nature. In "Das dunkle Herz," Op. 23, No. 1, the "dark heart" perceives the spring not only in its scent of flowers, but also deep in the earth, where the plants are rooted. Just as the flowers and trees reach up to heaven, so do the dead who rest beneath the earth.

> Das dunkle Herz, das in sich lauscht, erschaut den Frühling
> nicht nur am Hauch und Duft, der durch das Leuchten blüht;
> es fühlt ihn an dem dunklen Wurzelreich, das an die Toten rührt:
> Was wird, legt sich mit zarten Wurzeln an das Wartende im Dunkel,
> trinkt Kraft und Stille aus der Nacht, eh' sich's dem Tage schenkt,
> eh' es als Liebeskelch zum Himmel duftet
> und eh' aus ihm zu ihm ein goldnes Flattern Leben trägt.

> The dark heart [,] which hearkens to itself, perceives spring
> not only by the breeze and scent which blossom through its glow;
> it feels spring in the dark realm of roots, which reaches to the dead.
> That which grows lays its tender roots against that which waits in the dark;
> it drinks strength and repose from the night before it gives itself to the day,
> before as a chalice of love it sends its fragrance to heaven,
> and before from heaven a golden flutter bears it life.[117]

In "Herr Jesus mein," Op. 23, No. 3, the narrator relates how "there are no walls between us and God," since "He touches us with every gust of wind and every branch.''[118] Jone communicates her ideas in a simple language, with regular meters and rhyme schemes. If her metaphors sometimes seem self-conscious and even forced (such as, for example, ''Stars, you silver bees of the night / around the flower of love'' from Op. 25, No. 3),[119] they nevertheless provide vivid images that Webern used to good effect in his music.

Jone's texts also indirectly provided the impetus for Webern's largest project of the early 1930s, the Concerto for Nine Instruments, Op. 24. The Concerto's first movement, which was composed in fits and starts between 1931 and 1934, was completed only after Webern had written the three songs of Op. 23 and sketched a choral fragment on a Jone text, ''Wie kann der Tod so nah der Liebe wohnen.'' Writing the simpler vocal pieces helped him to overcome some obstacles in the instrumental work, which almost did not get finished at all.[120]

Webern worked for a long time on the Concerto's row, trying to arrive at an equivalent to the Latin word-square palindrome

S A T O R
A R E P O
T E N E T
O P E R A
R O T A S

which reads the same left to right (from the top), right to left (from the bottom), downwards (from the top left), or upwards (from the bottom right). Webern's row, though not itself a palindrome, is extremely economical and tightly knit. Each trichord (three-note group) is either a retrograde, inversion, or retrograde inversion of each of the other trichords. The row is furthermore constructed so that certain transpositions yield trichords with the same pitch-class content. The resulting redundancy provides countless interrelationships within and among rows, but makes it difficult to achieve variety. Webern struggled with this problem for a long time, taking over three years to sketch the row and the first twenty-six measures of the first movement.[121] Once he worked that out, however, the rest of the movement and two further ones followed quickly. The work's trichord-based row and recurring rhythmic figures have led some commentators to view it as an anticipation of post–Second World War total serialism.[122] However, much as the work's minimalist play of trichords might indicate a high level of abstraction, the Jone texts that Webern set during and around the Concerto (one of which, the choral fragment, uses the same row) suggest the possibility of a parallel and equally relevant programmatic reading.

Das Augenlicht (1930) for chorus and orchestra, which is actually a cantata, though it does not bear that title, is Webern's first large-scale setting of a Jone text. Here, in sharp contrast to the immediately preceding works, Webern indulges in a free, even chaotic treatment of the twelve-tone rows. There are no symmetries, palindromes, or canons. The disposition of the rows does not always coincide with the musical structure, and, atypically for Webern, there is no discernible pattern in the choice of row forms and transpositions.[123] On the other hand, *Das Augenlicht* is one of Webern's most accessible works (and one of the few that has been consistently well received from its premiere on) (Moldenhauer and Moldenhauer, 500–502). Its effective, idiomatic choral writing reflects Webern's long experience conducting choruses. The text, here as elsewhere, served as the point of departure. As so often with Jone's poetry, an image is projected onto different levels: the "light of the eyes" that, in a loving glance, penetrates the heart is transmuted into the sun, the light of the heavens. The work's extended form is created by alternating homophonic and polyphonic sections built around the central verse "O Meer des Blickes mit der Tränenbrandung!" (Oh, the ocean of a glance with its surf of tears!), which plays off the contrasting scale of the human and natural worlds. The tightly woven text and Webern's clearly audible sonic architecture result in an immediately perceptible *Fasslichkeit.*

With his next two works, the Variations for piano, Op. 27 (1935–36), and the String Quartet, Op. 28 (1936–38), Webern continued to develop his twelve-tone technique. Both works use elaborately constructed rows with special properties. Both feature contrapuntal devices such as canon and fugue, which are usually, however, carefully disguised. Both contain extended movements in variation form, a form inherited from tonal music that Webern thought particularly adaptable to the special conditions of twelve-tone composition.

In October 1935 Webern sketched the beginning of a solo piano work entitled "Klavier-Variationen." This movement, which became the third movement of Op. 27, does indeed correspond to the familiar variation form: a recognizable theme using the prime forms of the row is followed by five sections of equal length. After finishing the movement in July of the next year and beginning to sketch subsequent movements, Webern wrote to the Humpliks, "The completed part is a movement of variations; what is evolving will be a kind of 'suite' " (Moldenhauer and Moldenhauer, 482). Yet a week later (in a letter to Polnauer), he seemed to change his mind: "[I] now see that the *variations go on further* [*sic*], even if they turn into movements of most diverse types" (Moldenhauer and Moldenhauer, 482). This statement has perplexed analysts for decades, since what became the work's first and second movements, an ABA form and a two-part canonic scherzo, respectively, do not appear to be in variation form (although many analysts do believe this to be the case).[124] One explanation lies in the multiple meanings of the word "variation": it can indicate, first, a particular musical form, and second, development in a more general sense. In twelve-tone music "variation" in the broader sense—what Schoenberg called "developing variation"—is ubiquitous, since everything is derived from the prime row and its transformations.[125] In this sense, the first two movements of Op. 27 are "variations" as well, although in a different way from the formal variations of the third movement. Given that all three movements explore different kinds of symmetry—horizontal and vertical, perceptible and imperceptible—the "variations" of the title could refer to variations of a process rather than of a theme.

With the String Quartet, Op. 28, Webern chose that most Beethovenian of genres in order to pay homage to the German musical tradition. In his own analysis of the piece, recorded in a letter to Stein in 1939, Webern explained the two main constructive principles of that tradition: the "horizontal," or homophonic ("the classical cyclic forms [such as] sonata, symphony, and so forth"), and the "vertical," or polyphonic ("canon, fugue, and so on") (Moldenhauer and Moldenhauer, 753). In his String Quartet, his first in over twenty years, he sought to combine these two principles. Each movement is built upon a contrapuntal row scheme: the first uses a linear presentation of rows, the second is canonic, and third is based on fugue. Each movement also belongs to a "classical" form: first, variations, then a scherzo ("in miniature"), concluding with ternary form ("*subject-development-reprise*") (Moldenhauer and Moldenhauer, 753).

For this work Webern created "the most perfectly symmetrical of all [his] rows."[126] Based on the B-A-C-H tetrachord (itself a symmetrical motive), the row has only twenty-four forms (the prime form is the same as the ninth retrograde inversion). It is possible to elide the last tetrachord of one with the identical first tetrachord of another, creating "chains" of rows. Webern makes full use of the row's symmetrical properties, creating an intricate interlocking structure. He was very happy with the results: "Within the work [the third movement] must be the 'crowning fulfilment,' so to speak, of the '*synthesis*' of '*horizontal*' and '*vertical*' construction (Schoenberg!)" (Moldenhauer and Moldenhauer, 753).

Just as Webern was finishing Op. 28, German troops marched into Austria. On that day Webern wrote to the Humpliks, "I am totally immersed in my work and cannot, cannot be disturbed." Did Webern use his work as a refuge? Although direct connections are difficult to draw, the notion that Webern's increasing isolation after Schoenberg's emigration and Berg's death bore some relationship to his growing preoccupations with abstract twelve-tone constructions is suggestive. As the world grows more and more incomprehensible, one can retreat into art and artifice, which is much more readily controlled. Adorno was one of the first to criticize Webern for overemphasizing row manipulations: "In his late works Webern shies away from the formulation of new musical forms. It is anticipated that such forms would be external to the pure essence of the row. His final works are schemata of the rows translated into notes."[127]

Adorno's harsh judgment, which was based on study of the scores rather than actually hearing the works (moreover, the works after Op. 28 were unknown to him), is understandable but one-sided. Although Webern did explore how far he could go with twelve-tone technique during this period, he cared first and foremost about the music's sound. He composed (and conducted all his composition lessons) at the piano (Moldenhauer and Moldenhauer, 511). His sketches, which for the later works become increasingly numerous, show fastidious concern for every detail; rhythm, articulation, dynamics, and expression marks are sketched and revised and revised again. The balanced proportions, the sense that there are no wasted notes, and (most of all) the sheer beauty of Webern's characteristic ''bassless'' sound bear witness to this process.

We also know from contemporary accounts that Webern wanted expressive, rhythmically flexible performances of his music. Peter Stadlen, who premiered Op. 27 and received extensive coaching from the composer, published his rehearsal score with Webern's markings and verbal remarks.[128] From this source and from other accounts it is evident that Webern expected performers to bring much more to the music than what was written in the score.[129] Their interpretation, however, was not to be based on the work's twelve-tone construction, as Stadlen related:

> Throughout all those weeks of instruction and preparation Webern never once touched on the serial aspect of his Piano Variations. Even when I asked him, he declined to go into it with me—because, he said, it was important that I should know how the work should be played, not how it was made . . . Indeed, he acted as if he himself were not aware of the serial aspect of his work, or at least never thought of it when playing or discussing it. (Moldenhauer and Moldenhauer, 485)

One can get some idea of Webern's performance aesthetic from his performance of Schubert's *German Dances*, which he had orchestrated in 1931.[130] The constant rubato (excessive by today's standards) lends each phrase an individual shape; the extreme rhythmic and dynamic flexibility gives the impression of a living, breathing organism. He apparently played his own music the same way (according to his pupil Arnold Elston): ''Such a performance was always a revelation of the élan, of the intensest expressivity which infused every note, so that one experienced a living presence, and all questions of tone-row manipulations and constructive devices seemed totally extraneous'' (Moldenhauer and Moldenhauer, 508). Evidently Webern made a clear distinction between a work's compositional technique and its interpretation. First came the intricate and self-contained twelve-tone structure of a work, known only to the composer and the analyst. The next level, the music's sounding surface, may reflect the underlying order but is not identical with it. With both of these aspects Webern sought clarity, order, and logic to a degree unprecedented in his earlier works. For the final realization of the piece, yet another level, interpretation by a performer or a reader of the score, is necessary; the final score is a detailed road map, not the landscape itself. ''When one actually performs,'' Webern wrote to Reich, ''then there must also be the right sensory impression. Revel in sounds, you conductors, then you do right!''[131]

ISOLATION, WAR YEARS, AND LATE WORKS (1938–45)

Bereft of virtually all of his old friends, after the *Anschluss* in March 1938 Webern lived in increasing poverty and isolation until his death. His new situation became fully apparent when he was denied permission to travel to the London ISCM to hear the premiere of *Das Augenlicht* in July 1938; the Austrian ISCM, over which Webern had presided, was deemed not in compliance "with Third Reich doctrines" (Moldenhauer and Moldenhauer, 500). His publication contract with Universal Edition was not renewed; Op. 27 was the last work published in Vienna in his lifetime. After the outbreak of war in September 1939, his last remaining radio work stopped. His private pupils scattered to the four winds, removing his only remaining source of income. He scraped by doing piano reductions and odd jobs for Universal Edition, relying too on the financial help of his now-grown children.

Whereas before the war Webern had traveled a lot, during this period he left the country only twice. Both times he went to Switzerland, where performances of his music were organized by his exiled former pupil Reich and sponsored by the wealthy Winterthur patron Werner Reinhart. In February 1940 the Passacaglia was played in Winterthur, and the Basel ISCM programmed songs from Opp. 4 and 12 (Moldenhauer and Moldenhauer, 523–24). Three years later Webern again went to Winterthur to hear the premiere of his Variations for Orchestra, Op. 30, under Scherchen. This would be the last concert performance of his music that he would hear (Moldenhauer and Moldenhauer, 550). Webern's sixtieth birthday in December 1943, which passed without public notice in Vienna, was commemorated by a concert in Basel (Moldenhauer and Moldenhauer, 554).[132]

Webern corresponded with his exiled friends until the war made that impossible. In his letters to Schoenberg, which continued at least until March 1941, Webern repeatedly reassures him of his loyalty. There is no reason to doubt Webern's sincerity in this regard despite his growing Nazi sympathies (discussed later). In a letter to a pianist pupil who had emigrated to New York, Webern wrote in 1939: "Remember and always keep before your eyes *solely* that there exists music by Schoenberg. He who thinks otherwise or does not muster the energy to overcome the outside resistance must *by way of natural law* remain stranded on the 'track' " (Moldenhauer and Moldenhauer, 520).

Webern remained loyal to his other Jewish friends as well, even when social contact with Jews was officially forbidden. The morning after *Kristallnacht*, the anti-Jewish pogrom on 9–10 November 1938, Webern sought out his friends Polnauer and Bach to make sure they were unharmed (Moldenhauer and Moldenhauer, 516). He continued to invite Polnauer for dinner on Friday evenings and made efforts to help him escape to England (which did not, however, come to pass) (Moldenhauer and Moldenhauer, 531). When the Bach family left for London in 1939, Webern and his wife helped them pack; as a parting gift

Webern gave Bach a manuscript of his String Trio (Moldenhauer and Moldenhauer, 517). Webern taught the Russian-Jewish composer Herschkowitz for free until he was able to flee in September 1939.[133] Although one might simply take for granted that someone whose artistic idols were Schoenberg and Mahler could not become anti-Semitic, this was by no means self-evident in the poisoned climate of the times.

Whereas in 1933 Webern had been decidedly anti-Nazi, due to his shock at Schoenberg's emigration and the forced dispersion of his friends and colleagues,[134] he later warmed considerably to fascist views. Given his fanatic reverence for authority, his extreme pan-German nationalism, and his conviction that the music of the Second Viennese School was the culmination of the great German musical tradition, it was perhaps predictable that he would share in the delusion of a great German Reich. He had ample opportunity to be exposed to Nazi thought; several members of his immediate family were devoted Nazis, as were two of his closest friends, Josef Hueber and his former pupil Ludwig Zenck. Letters to Hueber, cited at length in Moldenhauer and Moldenhauer (526–30), document an ongoing discussion about Hitler and the Nazi regime. Although Webern himself never joined the Nazi party, his enthusiasm is unmistakable; in March 1940, after reading *Mein Kampf*, he commented: "The book has brought me much enlightenment." A couple of months later, Webern wrote: "This is Germany today! But the *National Socialist* one, to be sure! Not just any one! This is exactly the *new* state, for which the seed was already laid twenty years ago. . . . Created by this unique man!!!" (Moldenhauer and Moldenhauer, 527).

In 1992 Fred Prieberg published new evidence that shows Webern's willingness to become more deeply involved with Nazi cultural politics. First, Webern did in fact join the Reichsmusikkammer (Reich Music Chamber); since membership was expected of all working musicians, this is neither remarkable nor especially damning.[135] But on 9 November 1940 Webern wrote to the Reich Music Chamber asking for a grant from the Künstlerdank, a fund for impoverished musicians. In his letter he outlined his desperate financial situation, which had occurred in spite of his outstanding qualifications as a musician. He concluded, "I still find myself, in spite of my readiness to cooperate, in complete isolation, which I can only explain as a result of the peculiar situation in Viennese musical life, which I have had to suffer under for years!"[136] The officials noted that "Anton von Webern is artistically quite eccentric [*reichlich verschroben*], but doubtlessly filled with conviction about his work and high ideals." They concluded that even though his compositional style was undesirable, Webern himself was politically acceptable; after all, his son had become a member of the Austrian Nazi party when it was still illegal. In light of his special situation, he received a onetime payment of 250 marks.[137]

Webern's sympathy for the Nazi regime went at least as far back as 1936. Louis Krasner, the American violinist who premiered the Berg Violin Concerto, traveled with Webern on the way to the Barcelona concert. Other members of the group had taken the route through Switzerland, but Webern had insisted on traveling through Germany so that he could see what "conditions there were like under Hitler" (Moldenhauer and Moldenhauer, 455). Krasner relates the admiration with which Webern spoke of the German regime. After they had stopped at the train station in Munich for a beer, Webern asked, "Look, Krasner, did anyone do anything to you?" He thus implied that all the stories about German anti-Semitism were just propaganda.[138]

Among Webern's musical sketches, along with notes about his children's birthdays and other family events, we find the remark "incorporation of Austria into the German Reich" and the date of the *Anschluss*, which we now know he greeted with enthusiasm (Moldenhauer and Moldenhauer, 477). As late as 1943 Webern was apparently still loyal to the Nazi regime; during his concert tour of Switzerland, he wrote to Hueber how happy he was that the German consul, the consul of his homeland, had greeted him.[139]

Webern's readiness to become a loyal Third Reich composer was apparently stymied only by the Nazis' refusal to accept him. Even worse, his motives must be characterized as idealistic and not merely opportunistic (as in so many other cases), given how remote his chances of profiting from them were. Neither did he appear to modify his views as the war dragged on. Webern's case, however, can be seen as "bizarre" and even "tragic," as Michael Kater has characterized it.[140]

First, the fact that Webern himself saw no contradiction between his political loyalties and his compositional style shows an astonishing capacity for self-delusion. Whereas Schoenberg after March 1933 immediately grasped the musical ramifications of the new political situation, Webern continued to believe that their music was true "German music," in spite of unmistakable and continuing evidence that the Germans themselves did not think so.[141] Webern's delusions verged on the pathetic; even after Schoenberg's forced exile, the banning of Berg's operas, and the inclusion of all three of them in the exhibit "Degenerate Music," Webern could still say that "one should attempt to convince the Hitler régime of the rightness of the twelve-tone system" (Moldenhauer and Moldenhauer, 474).

Webern was an extremely stubborn person; he was just as tenacious about his compositional direction and his loyalty to Jewish friends as he was about his pro-Nazi beliefs. The strength of all three of these loyalties prevented him from seeing that the first two were fundamentally irreconcilable with the last (which, of course, the Reich Music Chamber had recognized right away).[142] Webern's sympathies cannot be explained away or excused. As Stephen Tipton Miles has written, "Though it would be comforting to find in Webern a completely integrated man and artist, such was obviously not the case."[143]

It is also not possible to claim that Webern's art was completely separate from his political views, as the Moldenhauers do. On the contrary, Webern strove during these years to create music that could take its place in the great German musical tradition, which was represented, indeed aggressively marketed, by the Third Reich. His whole compositional development had been based on the principle that the Schoenberg school grew from and advanced the tradition of German music. Until 1933 Schoenberg himself had tirelessly advocated this view.[144] Their music combined, Webern believed, the two main historical tendencies: the polyphonic, represented by Bach, and the homophonic, represented by Beethoven. With these two giants behind him (and Schoenberg at his side), Webern felt invincible in his march to a great German future. That the cultural powers in Germany envisioned a different musical future does not alter Webern's intentions.

In his last three works, each longer than any since the Passacaglia, Webern was able to achieve the balance of structural complexity and freedom that he had aimed for since he started composing with the twelve-tone method. Perhaps since the de facto ban on his music ''freed'' him from the necessity of thinking in terms of specific performers or performance venues, he could now write for ''impractical'' large forces (in fact, neither of the two cantatas was performed in his lifetime). If Webern's immediately preceding works do not always jump off the page, his last three efforts display a richer musical surface: the resources of the full orchestra (and, in the cantatas, chorus and vocal soloists) are exploited to achieve a much broader range of textures and tone colors than before. His increasing virtuosity with the twelve-tone technique is not meant to dazzle (in fact, most of it is not perceptible without analysis), but rather to serve his conviction that these musical ''laws'' reflect nature's divine order; all three works are in this sense deeply religious.

In the First Cantata, Op. 29, completed in November 1939, the two outer movements provide a choral ''frame'' for the soprano solo's inner movement (in the third and last movement, the solo voice joins the chorus at the end). The orchestra presents the main musical ideas; the chorus and the solo vocal line both derive their material from the instruments.[145] Webern arranged the text from diverse excerpts from Jone's poetry. Therefore, he was at least partly responsible for the shaping of the text. Instead of setting the text first with a vocal line, as he had done in his earlier songs, Webern worked from the basis of the twelve-tone row. The text's image of the winged maple seed (''Kleiner Flügel Ahornsamen,'' second movement) serves as an analogy to the row; just as the tiny seed floats to the ground and is reborn as a tree, so does the row generate every aspect of the piece. (The metaphor also clearly refers to the Christian doctrine of resurrection.) As Webern described it to Jone, ''But however freely it [the maple seed/row] seems to float around . . . it is the product of a regular procedure more strict, possibly, than anything that has formed the basis of a musical conception before.''[146] Webern's music does not ''set'' the text in the sense of expressing its individual words, but instead by translating its central metaphor directly into the twelve-tone structure. The very one-dimensionality of Jone's poetry allowed the composer to follow the twelve-tone ''laws'' while being faithful to the text.

The Variations for Orchestra, Op. 30 (1940), represents the culmination of

Webern's efforts to put forms associated with tonal music at the service of twelve-tone variation. Here, as in the String Quartet, a three-part ABA form is superimposed upon the variation form. The symmetrical row is made up entirely of half steps and minor thirds (the second hexachord is a retrograde inversion of the first). Its construction from four identical overlapping tetrachords allows "chains" of partially overlapping rows. The work begins with a series of four-note figures that move, kaleidoscopelike, among different instruments in subtly varied forms. Webern viewed the process of musical variation as directly analogous to Goethe's conception of metamorphosis in nature. About this work, he wrote to Jone: "Imagine this: 6 notes are given, in a shape determined by the sequence and the rhythm, and what follows . . . is nothing other than this shape over and over again!!! Naturally in continual 'Metamorphosis' (in musical terms this process is called 'Variation')—but it is nevertheless the same every time."[147] The process of variation is extended beyond pitches to rhythms and timbres as well. The work has a distinct sound because of the many doublings and the relatively bass-heavy orchestration (Webern uses contrabass and tuba for the first time since Op. 10).

If the Variations for Orchestra were Webern's answer to Beethoven and Brahms, the spirit of Bach hovers over the Second Cantata, Op. 31 (1941–43). The work's six movements—composed in the order 4, 5, 6, then 1, 2, 3—can be viewed as two groups of three movements, each group following the Bachian formal scheme of recitative, aria (with chorus), and chorus. Webern designated the last movement as "a sort of chorale" (Moldenhauer and Moldenhauer, 577), which makes sense because of its apparently simple four-voice strophic construction. After he finished the piece, he was delighted to see parallels to a "Missa Brevis": the first movement, he wrote, can be considered a "Kyrie," the second a "Gloria," the third a "Credo," the fourth and fifth a "Benedictus" and "Sanctus," and the sixth, "Agnus dei."[148]

If the Bach of the cantatas and the B-minor Mass provided Webern's main inspiration for the Second Cantata, then the Bach of the *Art of the Fugue* guided his hand. In a piece that sounds completely comprehensible and even transparent, Webern created his most elaborate contrapuntal structures. He described the fourth movement (the first composed), for example, as a "recitative," but also "a four-part canon of the most complicated kind."[149] Although this canon is imperceptible, the canon in the sixth movement is equally complex but completely audible. Similarly, one can easily follow the unfolding of the row in the vocal line of the second movement ("Sehr tief verhalten"), although the "cycling" of the row chains by successive whole steps until the beginning is reached again is perceptible only through analysis. "It's all even stricter, and for that reason it's also become still freer," Webern wrote of this movement. "That's to say, I move with complete freedom on the basis of an 'endless canon by inversion.' By variation, diminution, etc.—rather as Bach does with his theme in the 'Art of Fugue.' "[150]

During the war Webern sought solace and pleasure in his garden, lavishing nearly as much attention upon it as he did upon his compositions. In letters to friends he described in great detail the types of plants he had, the condition of the soil, and the direction of the sunlight. He wrote about the garden in the same style, and with the same degree of enthusiasm, as he did about his music, for example: "I believe that my garden will *represent something completely different* from next spring on!!! If everything turns out the way I have figured (after very thorough reflection and taking into account blossom time, *colours*, etc.), I believe that you, too, will rejoice in it!" (letter to Hueber, 16 October 1942 in Moldenhauer and Moldenhauer, 547).

After completing the Second Cantata, Webern immediately began sketching a third, which he would not be able to finish as the war intensified.[151] In April and May 1944 Webern was drafted into the Luftschutz-Polizei (air-raid police), although he was soon released after the intervention of Universal Edition and several friends. At this time Webern made futile inquiries about emigrating to Switzerland (Moldenhauer and Moldenhauer, 591–92). In February 1945 Peter, his son, died in battle. This was a blow from which Webern and his wife never recovered. In March 1945, as the bombing intensified and Soviet troops approached Vienna, the Weberns fled on foot to Mittersill, where their daughters Maria Halbich and Christine Mattel were living with their children.

After the war ended two months later, the Weberns could not yet return to their home in Vienna, which was in the Russian zone of occupation (Mittersill was in the American zone). The extreme hardship of the postwar months was somewhat alleviated for the Webern family by the black-marketeering activities of their son-in-law, Benno Mattel, a former member of the Nazi party. On 15 September 1945, while American soldiers were attempting to arrest Mattel for illegal trading, Webern was shot and killed in an accident that will probably never be fully explained. He had gone outside to smoke a cigar (one of the fruits of Mattel's labors) when he scuffled in a dark hallway with Raymond Bell, an army cook who was participating in the arrest. Bell felt himself to be attacked and "fired three shots 'in self defence,' " according to the army report (Moldenhauer and Moldenhauer, 634). Webern's death has been the subject of much speculation, ranging from questions about the extent of Webern's knowledge of Mattel's "business activities" to the far-fetched theory that his death was essentially a suicide.[152] It would be a mistake, however, to dramatize Webern's death as a symbol of his destiny, either as victim or as enraged Nazi. This event, like countless others during the chaotic postwar months, was a senseless accident. It brought down the composer at the height of his powers, far away from his garden in a world he no longer understood.

NOTES

I am very grateful to Felix Meyer, Felix Wörner, and Kathryn Bailey for their helpful comments on the text and for many interesting discussions about Webern and his music.

1. Arnold Schoenberg, Foreword to *Six Bagatelles for String Quartet, Op. 9*, by Anton Webern (Vienna: Universal Edition, 1924/1952), n.p.

2. Theodor W. Adorno, "Anton von Webern," in *Gesammelte Schriften*, vol. 16 (Frankfurt.: Suhrkamp, 1978), 118. All translations are mine unless otherwise noted.

3. After titles of nobility were forbidden in 1918, Webern wrote his name without the "von." At the time when Friedrich Wildgans, Webern's student and first biographer, knew him, the composer always called himself simply Anton Webern. See Friedrich Wildgans, *Anton Webern: Eine Studie* (Tübingen: Rainer Wunderlich Verlag, 1967), 17. Moreover, Webern published all his music under the shorter version of his name.

4. Much of the information upon which my discussion of Webern's life is based is drawn from Hans Moldenhauer and Rosaleen Moldenhauer's landmark biography *Anton von Webern: A Chronicle of His Life and Work* (New York: Knopf, 1979), which is valuable not least because it includes many letters and other documentary evidence not published elsewhere. References to this work are so frequent that they will appear in the text in parentheses (authors, page number). "M." numbers refer to the Moldenhauers' work list, 700–705.

5. Two songs were published posthumously: "Vorfrühling" in *Three Poems for Voice and Piano* (New York: Carl Fischer, 1965), and "Tief von fern" in *Eight Early Songs* (New York: Carl Fischer, 1965.) Other early songs came out posthumously in *Three Songs after Poems by Ferdinand Avenarius* (New York: Carl Fischer, 1965).

6. In an effusive diary entry of 1905, for example, Webern quoted two lines from "Heimgang in der Frühe" by Liliencron, which he had set in 1903: "What the night gave to me, will long make me tremble" (Moldenhauer and Moldenhauer, 78).

7. See Susanne Rode-Breyman, " '. . . Gathering the Divine from the Earthly . . . ': Ferdinand Avenarius and His Significance for Anton Webern's Early Settings of Lyric Poetry," in *Webern Studies*, ed. Kathryn Bailey (Cambridge: Cambridge University Press, 1996), 1–31.

8. Gareth Cox, *Anton Weberns Studienzeit: Seine Entwicklung im Lichte der Sätze und Fragmente für Klavier* (Frankfurt: Lang, 1992), 126.

9. Anton Webern, cited in Rode-Breyman, " '. . . Gathering the Divine from the Earthly . . . ,' " 11–12. Rode-Breyman also points out here how Webern's tastes in art were probably influenced by the Avenarius-led periodical *Der Kunstwart*, which had published reproductions of these three painters' works.

10. Egon Wellesz und Emmy Wellesz, *Leben und Werk*, ed. Franz Endler (Vienna: Paul Zsolnay Verlag, 1981), 39.

11. This song was published posthumously in *Three Poems for Voice and Piano.*

12. Anton Webern, *The Path to the New Music*, ed. Willi Reich, trans. Leo Black (London and Vienna.: Universal Edition, 1975), 27.

13. Heinrich Isaac, *Choralis constantinus. Zweiter Teil*, ed. Anton von Webern, Denkmäler der Tonkunst in Österreich 32 (Vienna, 1905–6).

14. This and the earlier quotation are from Wellesz and Wellesz, *Leben und Werk*, 39.

15. Derrick Puffett, "Webern's Wrong Key-Signature," *Tempo* 199 (January 1997): 21–26. Puffett makes a particular case that Webern's "Aufblick" was modeled on Wolf's "Lebe wohl" from the *Mörike-Lieder* (21–22).

16. Martin Hoyer, "Neues zu Anton Weberns frühen Liedern," *Mitteilungen der Paul Sacher Stiftung* 5 (January 1992): 32.

17. Ibid., 34. Wildgans, to his credit, speculated thirty years ago that "Siegfrieds

Schwert'' was so atypical of Webern that it could well be an orchestration of another's composition (Wildgans, *Anton Webern*, 27).

18. Derrick Puffett offers an extended analysis of the piece and reprints the poem in ''Gone with the Summer Wind; or, What Webern Lost,'' in *Webern Studies*, ed. Kathryn Bailey (Cambridge: Cambridge University Press, 1996), 32–73.

19. Webern confirmed this story in a letter to Schoenberg a few years later: ''[In 1904] I wanted to go study with Pfitzner in Berlin, but I hardly just arrived when it became clear to me that this was nonsense and that I had to go back to Vienna to become your pupil.'' Letter from Webern to Schoenberg, 2 September 1907, in *Anton Webern, 1883–1983*, ed. Ernst Hilmar (Vienna: Universal Edition, 1983), 61.

20. The circular is given in full in Willi Reich, *Schoenberg: A Critical Biography*, trans. Leo Black (New York and Washington: Praeger, 1971), 16–19.

21. Letter from Webern to Schoenberg, 2 September 1907, in Hilmar, *Anton Webern, 1883–1983*, 61.

22. Wildgans believes that Guido Adler recommended Webern to Schoenberg; see his *Anton Webern*, 36.

23. It is possible that the lessons had ended by the autumn of 1907. Webern wrote to Schoenberg on 2 September of that year: ''Am I perhaps now at the end of my regular study time with you? Since you allow it, I would like to come to you whenever I have composed quite a bit'' (Moldenhauer and Moldenhauer, 102). On the other hand, Webern said that he composed his chorus Op. 2 (written in the autumn of 1908) ''under [Schoenberg's] direct guidance'' (letter from Webern to Schoenberg, 10 June 1914; Moldenhauer and Moldenhauer, 101). Since Webern continued to show Schoenberg his music for many years, there was probably no clear line of demarcation between his study period and later.

24. Wildgans, *Anton Webern*, 39.

25. Cox points out that this follows Schoenberg's ordering of subjects in his text, *Fundamentals of Musical Composition* (London: Faber and Faber, 1967). Cox, *Anton Weberns Studienzeit*, 126.

26. Walter Kolneder speaks of a ''diatonic rest-cure'' in *Anton Webern: Genesis und Metamorphose eines Stils* (Vienna: Elisabeth Lafite, 1974), cited in Cox, *Anton Weberns Studienzeit*, 124.

27. Cox, *Anton Weberns Studienzeit*, 126.

28. See Walter Frisch, *The Early Works of Arnold Schoenberg, 1893–1908* (Berkeley and Los Angeles: University of California Press, 1993), 5.

29. Edward Cone, ''Webern's Apprenticeship,'' in *Music: A View from Delft: Selected Essays*, ed. Robert Morgan (Chicago: University of Chicago Press, 1989), 273.

30. See Carl E. Schorske, *Fin-de-Siècle Vienna: Politics and Culture* (New York: Vintage, 1981), especially Chapter 7, ''Explosion in the Garden,'' 322–66.

31. These, at theaters in Innsbruck, Vienna, Danzig, Stettin, and Prague, are described in detail in Moldenhauer and Moldenhauer, *Anton von Webern*, Chapters 6 and 8–13.

32. Letter from Webern to Schoenberg, 28 November 1910, in Hilmar, *Anton Webern, 1883–1983*, 63.

33. See Anne C. Shreffler, *Webern and the Lyric Impulse: Songs and Fragments on Poems of Georg Trakl* (Oxford: Oxford University Press, 1994), 7–12.

34. Puffett, ''Gone with the Summer Wind; or, What Webern Lost,'' in 62–63.

35. Letter of Webern to Berg, 12 July 1912, in Hilmar, *Anton Webern, 1883–1983*, 65–66.

36. Schoenberg, "Brahms the Progressive," in *Style and Idea: Selected Writings of Arnold Schoenberg*, ed. Leonard Stein, trans. Leo Black (Berkeley and Los Angeles: University of California Press, 1984), 414–16.

37. Schoenberg, Foreword to *Six Bagatelles for String Quartet, Op. 9*, by Webern.

38. Felix Meyer and Anne Shreffler, "Performance and Revision: The Early History of Webern's Four Pieces for Violin and Piano, Op. 7," in *Webern Studies*, ed. Kathryn Bailey (Cambridge: Cambridge University Press, 1996), 166–68.

39. See Felix Meyer, " 'O sanftes Glühn der Berge': Ein verworfenes 'Stück mit Gesang' von Anton Webern," in *Quellenstudien II: Zwölf Komponisten des 20. Jahrhunderts*, ed. Felix Meyer (Winterthur: Amadeus, 1993), 11–38.

40. These manuscripts are now in the Pierpont Morgan Library, New York.

41. Adorno, "Anton von Webern," 112.

42. The only purely instrumental sketches Webern made between 1915 and 1924 were a fragmentary string quartet in 1917–18 and seventeen measures of a string trio in 1920.

43. Königer, also a Schoenberg pupil, was Webern's brother-in-law (he had married Wilhelmine's sister) and close friend.

44. Rosegger can perhaps best be compared to the current American author and raconteur Garrison Keillor. For more on Rosegger, see Anne Shreffler, " 'Mein Weg geht jetzt vorüber': The Vocal Origins of Webern's Twelve-Tone Composition," *Journal of the American Musicological Society* 47 (1994): 325–28.

45. "A little bell-flower had sprung early / in full bloom from the ground; / along came a little bee and nibbled delicately: / Those two must be made for each other."

46. Shreffler, *Webern and the Lyric Impulse*, 20–38.

47. Ibid., 159.

48. For example, Schoenberg, Webern, and others had strongly condemned the Belgian poet Maeterlinck, whom they had previously admired, on account of his anti-German remarks, but they did not know about the atrocities by the German army that had brought on those remarks. See *Alexander Zemlinsky: Briefwechsel mit Arnold Schönberg, Anton Webern, Alban Berg, und Franz Schreker*, ed. Horst Weber (Darmstadt: Wissenschaftliche Buchgesellschaft, 1995), 127.

49. See Arnold Schoenberg's essay "National Music" (1931) in *Style and Idea*, 169–174.

50. Shreffler, *Webern and the Lyric Impulse*, 25–27.

51. See Herbert Lindenberger, *Georg Trakl* (New York: Twayne, 1971).

52. See Anne C. Shreffler, "A New Trakl Fragment by Webern: Some Notes on 'Klage,' " *Mitteilungen der Paul Sacher Stiftung* 4 (1991): 21–26.

53. Georg Trakl, *Sebastian im Traum* (Leipzig: Kurt Wolf Verlag, 1915) (my translation).

54. For a performance in Düsseldorf in 1922, Webern wrote a detailed program note, reprinted in Rudolf Stephan, "Weberns Werke auf deutschen Tonkünstlerfesten: Mit zwei wenig beachteten Texten Weberns," *Österreichische Musikzeitschrift* 27 (1972): 121–27.

55. The programs are listed in Walter Szmolyan,"Die Konzerte des Wiener Schönberg-Vereins," *Musik-Konzepte* 36 (1984): 101–14.

56. Alban Berg, "Prospekt des Vereins für musikalische Privataufführungen," *Musik-Konzepte* 36 (1984): 5.

57. Alban Berg, quoted in Willi Reich, *Alban Berg: Leben und Werk* (Zurich: Atlantis, 1963), 46.

58. Schoenberg, *Harmonielehre* (Vienna: Universal Edition, 1911), 471.

59. Schoenberg, "Mechanical Instruments," in *Style and Idea*, 326.

60. Zemlinsky, *Alexander Zemlinsky: Briefwechsel mit Arnold Schönberg*, 209.

61. The Moldenhauers record the Op. 10 arrangement as having survived, but the location of the manuscript is unknown. All the arrangements were for chamber ensemble except the Passacaglia, which was for two pianos, six hands.

62. Felix Meyer, "Anton Webern und der Verein für musikalische Privataufführungen: Notizen zur 'Kammerfassung' der Sechs Stücke für groβes Orchester op. 6," *Dankesschrift für Ernst Lichtenhahn*, ed. Patrick Müller et al., forthcoming; and Nicolaus A. Huber, "Zu Weberns Kammerorchesterbearbeitung seiner Sechs Stücke für Orchester op. 6 für den 'Verein für musikalische Privataufführungen,' " *Musik-Konzept* 36 (1984): 65–85.

63. These revisions followed an earlier round carried out before 1914, when Universal Edition had first promised Webern a publication contract (Op. 7 and Op. 8, and perhaps others, were substantially revised during this time).

64. For example, the last chord of Op. 7, No. 1, in the right hand, which was changed from an augmented triad to a major one. See Meyer and Shreffler, "Performance and Revision," 151–54.

65. Felix Meyer, "Im Zeichen der Reduktion: Quellenkritische und analytische Bemerkungen zu Anton Weberns Rilke-Liedern Op. 8," in *Quellenstudien I*, ed. Hans Oesch (Winterthur: Amadeus, 1991), 53–100.

66. Felix Meyer and Anne Shreffler, "Webern's Revisions: Some Analytical Implications," *Music Analysis* 12 no. 3 (1993): especially 363–77.

67. Felix Meyer and Anne Shreffler, "Rewriting History: Webern's Revisions of His Early Works," in *Revista de Musicologia*: XVI (1993 [1997]), 32–43. (Actas del XV Congreso de la SIM).

68. Op. 13 was finished in 1918, but revised in 1922.

69. Shreffler, *Webern and the Lyric Impulse*, 68.

70. In an early article Egon Wellesz refers to Op. 14 as having five songs only: see "Anton von Webern: Lieder opus 12, 13, 14," *Melos* 2 (1921): 38–40.

71. Shreffler, " 'Mein Weg geht jetzt vorüber,' " 321.

72. Ibid., 324.

73. Ibid., 286–87.

74. As reported by eyewitness Felix Greissle, in Joan Smith, *Schoenberg and His Circle: A Viennese Portrait* (New York: Schirmer Books, 1986), 198. For a further discussion of this meeting, see Shreffler, " 'Mein Weg geht jetzt vorüber,' " 284–86, 298. In an unsent letter to Josef Matthias Hauer of August 1922, however, Schoenberg refers to "some lectures" that had already taken place "several months ago" at which he communicated the main points of the new method to certain students; see Bryan Simms, "Who First Composed Twelve-Tone Music, Schoenberg or Hauer?" *Journal of the Arnold Schoenberg Institute* 10 ([1987]) 122.

75. Shreffler, " 'Mein Weg geht jetzt vorüber,' " 303–4.

76. Ibid., 309–12.

77. For the correct form of the row, see Shreffler, " 'Mein Weg geht jetzt vorüber,' " 313.

78. Ibid., 330–35.

79. Letter to Emil Hertzka, 2 February 1926, in Hilmar, *Anton Webern, 1883–1983*, 76.

80. Letter of Webern to Berg, 8 October 1925, in *Opus Anton Webern*, ed. Dieter Rexroth (Berlin: Quadriga, 1983), 91.

81. Kathryn Bailey, *The Twelve-Note Music of Anton Webern: Old Forms in a New Language* (Cambridge.: Cambridge University Press, 1991), 155–63.

82. Igor Stravinsky, quoted in Bailey, *Twelve-Note Music*, 237.

83. Webern, *Path to the New Music*, 55.

84. The young philosopher and Berg pupil Theodor Wiesengrund Adorno wrote his first of several articles on Webern's music on the occasion of this performance: "Anton Webern: Zur Aufführung der fünf Orchesterstücke in Zürich," reprinted in *Musik-Konzepte: Sonderband Anton Webern I* (Munich: Edition Text+ Kritik, 1983), 269–71.

85. Report from *Der Wiener Tag* of 15 April 1931, cited in Hilmar, *Anton Webern, 1883–1983*, 143.

86. Webern did not, for example, use a podium, but conducted from the floor, which led to ensemble problems. See Hilmar, *Anton Webern, 1883–1983*, 140–41.

87. Hilmar, *Anton Webern, 1883–1983*, 139.

88. See, for example, the review of a Workers' Symphony Concert in 1931 by Alfred Rosenzweig (*Der Wiener Tag*) in Hilmar *Anton Webern, 1883–1983*, 143.

89. Hans Moldenhauer, comp., and Demar Irvine, ed., *Anton von Webern: Perspectives* (Seattle: University of Washington Press, 1966), 109.

90. Wildgans, *Anton Webern*, 83.

91. The Kolisch Quartet caused a stir when it carried out this practice not only in rehearsals, but in concerts as well.

92. In 1929 Webern turned down a job with the Austrian radio because he would have been expected to represent the Social Democratic party. Letter to Schoenberg, 18 April 1929, in Hilmar, *Anton Webern, 1883–1983*, 83.

93. The Alpenverein and the Südmark. See Hanspeter Krellmann, *Anton Webern in Selbstzeugnissen und Bilddokumenten* (Reinbek bei Hamburg: Rowohlt, 1975), 92.

94. Ibid., 92.

95. For example, the music of Rudolf Réti; see Christopher Hailey, "Webern's Letters to David Josef Bach," *Mitteilungen der Paul Sacher Stiftung* 9 (1996): 37.

96. Ernst Glaser, *Im Umfeld des Austromarxismus: Ein Beitrag zur Geistesgeschichte des österreichischen Sozialismus* (Vienna: Europaverlag, 1981), 19.

97. "Kunst hat ihre eigenen Gesetze, sie hat mit Politik nichts zu tun." Anton Webern, *Der Weg zur neuen Musik*, ed. Willi Reich (Vienna: Universal Edition, 1960), 21. This passage was omitted from the English version.

98. Jalowetz, Kolisch, Steuermann, Wellesz, Stein, Reich, and Bach also emigrated between 1933 and 1938.

99. In April 1936 Webern was supposed to conduct the posthumous world premiere of Berg's Violin Concerto in Barcelona. He resisted this assignment from the beginning. Obsessed about the requiem character of the work, he was afraid that he would not be able to take the emotional strain of conducting it. His worst fears were realized when he became ill from stress the day before the concert. The performance was saved by Hermann Scherchen (Moldenhauer and Moldenhauer, 454–57).

100. Moldenhauer and Irvine, *Anton von Webern: Perspectives*, 109.

101. Anton Webern, "Briefe an Theodor W. Adorno," in *Musik-Konzepte: Sonderband Anton Webern I*, 21.

102. For example, in March 1934 Webern wrote to Adolf Weiss about the possibility

of a job in the United States, for which he would have been prepared to emigrate (Moldenhauer and Moldenhauer, 408–9).

103. The early Viennese performances were all done by the Kolisch Quartet in the chamber version (Moldenhauer and Moldenhauer, 327).

104. Bailey, *Twelve-Note Music*, 48.

105. Ibid., 242–49.

106. Ibid., 242.

107. Webern, *Path to the New Music*, 10–11.

108. Ibid., 41.

109. Ibid., 55.

110. Ibid., 53. Barbara Zuber's book, *Gesetz+ Gestalt: Studien zum Spätwerk Anton Weberns* (Munich: Musikprint, 1995), treats in detail Webern's relationship to Goethe's thought.

111. Webern, *Path to the New Music*, 10.

112. Letter of Webern to Berg, 8 October 1925, in Rexroth, *Opus Anton Webern*, 90–91.

113. Hilmar, *Anton Webern, 1883–1983*, 84.

114. The letters, which are in the Österreichische Nationalbibliothek in Vienna, were unfortunately published with cuts and heavily edited. See Anton Webern, *Letters to Hildegard Jone and Josef Humplik*, ed. Josef Polnauer, trans. Cornelius Cardew (Bryn Mawr, PA: Theodore Presser, 1967).

115. Lauriejean Reinhardt, " 'From Poet's Voice to Composer's Muse': Text and Music in Webern's Jone Settings" (Ph.D. diss., University of North Carolina at Chapel Hill, 1994), 463.

116. Pierre Boulez, *Stocktakings from an Apprenticeship*, ed. Paule Thévenin, trans. Stephen Walsh (Oxford: Clarendon Press, 1991), 300.

117. Unattributed translation from CD booklet, Boulez, *Webern: Complete Works* (Sony SM3K 45845).

118. "nur keine Wände zwischen uns und Gott. / Er rührt uns an mit jedem Wind und Zweige."

119. "Sterne, Ihr silbernen Bienen / der Nacht um die Blume der Liebe!"

120. These difficulties and their solutions are described in Kathryn Bailey, "Symmetry as Nemesis: Webern and the First Movement of the Concerto, Opus 24," *Journal of Music Theory* 40 (1996): 245–310.

121. Bailey, "Symmetry as Nemesis," Appendix 3 (304–6), gives a chronology of work on the first movement.

122. Karlheinz Stockhausen, "Weberns Konzert für neun Instrumente," *Melos* 20 (1953): 343–48.

123. Bailey, *Twelve-Note Music*, 56–60.

124. See Kathryn Bailey, "Willi Reich's Webern," *Tempo* 165 (1988): 18–22, and the response by Regina Busch, "Letter to the editor," *Tempo* 166 (1988): 67–69.

125. Bailey, *Twelve-Note Music*, 195. For a detailed discussion of Webern's understanding of variation form, see Neil Boynton, "The Combination of Variations and Adagio-Form in the Late Instrumental Works of Anton Webern" (Ph.D. diss., Cambridge University, 1993).

126. Bailey, *Twelve-Note Music*, 24.

127. Theodore Adorno, *Philosophy of Modern Music*, trans. Anne G. Mitchell and Wesley V. Blomster (New York: Seabury Press, 1980), 110. Since Adorno completed

this part of the book in 1941 while in American exile, he could not have known the still-unpublished First Cantata or Variations for Orchestra, and the Second Cantata had not yet been written.

128. Anton Webern, *Variationen für Klavier, Op. 27*, ed. Peter Stadlen (Vienna: Universal Edition, 1979).

129. See Robert W. Wason, ''Webern's Variations for Piano, Op. 27: Musical Structure and the Performance Score,'' *Integral* 1 (1987): 57–103.

130. The performance was recorded in Frankfurt in 1932 and reissued in the Boulez's CD recording, *Webern: Complete Works*.

131. Webern, letter to Reich, 4, September 1942, in *Path to the New Music*, 63.

132. In the United States Webern's birthday was commemorated by an article on him and his music by his former pupil Kurt List; see ''Anton von Webern,'' *Modern Music* (November–December 1943): 27–30.

133. Krellmann, *Anton Webern*, 93.

134. In his *Path to the New Music* lectures, for example, Webern declared, ''What's going on in Germany at the moment amounts to the destruction of spiritual life! . . . What idea of art do Hitler, Goering, and Goebbels have?'' *Path to the New Music*, 19.

135. Fred Prieberg, *Musik und Macht* (Frankfurt: Fischer Taschenbuch, 1991), 261. The author points out that this does mean that Webern's music was not officially banned, which is a moot point in my opinion since it was in any case not performed. Michael H. Kater, in *The Twisted Muse: Musicians and Their Music in the Third Reich* (New York and Oxford: Oxford University Press, 1997), states that membership in the Reich Music Chamber was ''compulsory for all professionals'' (17).

136. Prieberg, *Musik und Macht*, 263.

137. Prieberg believes that this was an unusually large grant (*Musik und Macht*, 263). Kater points out, however, that it was only a little more than what Webern normally earned each month, which was barely enough to live on (*Twisted Muse*, 74). Prieberg claims that efforts were made to help Webern by appointing him to the Musikakademie in Vienna, but that these plans came to nothing when it became clear that Webern would still teach the Schoenberg school (*Musik und Macht*, 264).

138. Louis Krasner and Don Seibert, ''Some Memories of Anton Webern, the Berg Concerto, and Vienna in the 1930s,'' *Fanfare*11 (1987): 337.

139. Krellmann, *Anton Webern*, 94. During the same trip, however, Webern had evidently made anti-Nazi comments to Reinhart. Krellmann, *Anton Webern*, 96–97.

140. Kater, *Twisted Muse*, 72.

141. See Constantin Floros, ''Die Wiener Schule und das Problem der 'deutschen Musik,' '' in *Die Wiener Schule und das Hakenkreuz: Das Schicksal der Moderne im gesellschaftspolitischen Kontext des 20. Jahrhunderts*, ed. Otto Kolleritsch (Vienna and Graz: Universal Edition, 1990), 35–50.

142. Webern never realized, for example, that Steuermann, who had emigrated to New York, broke off their friendship after Webern had written ''Deutsches Reich'' on the return address of his letters. See Webern's still-clueless last letter to Steuermann in Regina Busch, ed., ''Aus dem Briefwechsel Webern-Steuermann,'' *Musik-Konzepte: Sonderband Anton Webern I*, 47–51.

143. Stephen Tipton Miles, ''Anton Webern and the Politics of Historicism'' (D.M.A. thesis, University of Illinois at Urbana-Champaign, 1990), 98.

144. See Schoenberg, ''National Music,'' in *Style and Idea*, 169–74. In this essay of

1931 unpublished until 1975, Schoenberg used overtly military metaphors to explain the "hegemony" of German music, his own included.

145. Bailey, *Twelve-Note Music*, 272.

146. Webern, *Letters to Hildegard Jone and Josef Humplik*, 37. Bailey explains the work's twelve-tone structure in *Twelve-Note Music*, 272–302.

147. Webern, *Letters to Hildegard Jone and Josef Humplik*, 44. Arnold Whittall, who suggests that the Variations can be seen as "a religious text," has explored the parallels between this work and Goethe's philosophy; see "Music—Discourse—Dialogue: Webern's Variations, Op. 30," in *Webern Studies*, ed. Kathryn Bailey (Cambridge: Cambridge University Press, 1996), 264–97.

148. Webern, *Letters to Hildegard Jone and Josef Humplik*, 52.

149. Webern, Letter to Reich, in Webern, *Path to the New Music*, 62.

150. Webern, Letter to Reich, in Webern, *Path to the New Music*, 64.

151. On the "Third Cantata," see Larry Todd, "The Genesis of Webern's Opus 32," *Musical Quarterly* 66 (1980): 581–91.

152. Krasner and Seibert, "Some Memories of Anton Webern," 345–46; David Schroeder, "Was Webern's Death an Accident?," *Musical Times*, 137 (June 1996): 21–23.

7 THE LEGACY OF THE SECOND VIENNESE SCHOOL

Jonathan W. Bernard

Schoenberg's "emancipation of the dissonance" and the working out of its implications in his compositions and in those of his two best-known pupils, Berg and Webern, eventually had many far- and wide-reaching effects upon European and American music. But well before the last of these three composers had passed away, the Second Viennese School had become famous (or at least notorious) principally for one contribution: the twelve-tone method. Accordingly, this chapter is devoted mainly to examination of the ways in which knowledge of this method spread throughout Europe and the United States, and examination as well of the sometimes curious, sometimes astonishing mutations that twelve-tone practice underwent over time and distance. The story is told here through a focus upon representative, exemplary figures of twentieth-century compositional history without any attempt at comprehensive coverage and with little attention to the more far-flung locales into which intelligence of dodecaphony and, later, serialism at length penetrated (such as South America, Scandinavia, the Soviet Union, Japan, Australia, and so forth), reflecting the present author's preference for rendering what might be termed the central experience of Western musical culture in its response to the massive stimulus that emanated from Vienna during the first decades of the twentieth century.

DISSEMINATION OF THE TWELVE-TONE METHOD TO 1945

One of the most important factors shaping the legacy of the Second Viennese School was the way in which the initial dissemination of Schoenberg's ideas came about. In retrospect, the fact that Schoenberg himself published absolutely nothing about his "method of composing with twelve tones related only to one another" until 1949—by which time others' conjectures as to the workings of the method had taken on a life of their own—is truly astonishing.[1] How can this long delay be explained? Partly it must reflect a certain ambivalence on Schoenberg's part about his great discovery—not so much as a method for himself as a method that might be misunderstood and misused if it were publicized. His somewhat rueful comments in 1936 about the course that developments had taken were not published until long after his death:

> At the very beginning, when I used for the first time rows of twelve tones in the fall of 1921, I foresaw the confusion which would arise in case I were to make publicly known this method. Consequently I was silent for nearly two years. And when I gathered about twenty of my pupils together to explain to them the new method in 1923, I did it because I was afraid to be taken as an imitator of Hauer. . . . I could show that I was on the way to this method for more than ten years and could prove so by examples of works written during this time. But, at the same time, already I did not call it a "system" but a "method," and considered it a tool of composition, but not as a theory. And therefore I concluded my explanation with the sentence: "You use the row and compose as you had done it previously."

Unfortunately,

> What I feared, happened. Although I had warned my friends and pupils [not] to consider this as a change in compositional regards, and although I gave them the advice to consider it only as a means to fortify the logic, they started counting the tones and finding out the methods with which I used the rows. Only to explain understandably and thoroughly the idea, I had shown them a certain number of cases. But I refused to explain more of it, not the least because I had already forgotten it and had to find it myself. But principally because I thought it would not be useful to show technical matters which everybody had to find for himself and could do so.[2]

Schoenberg's first lectures on the twelve-tone method, and the publication that eventually developed out of them, did not take place until after his emigration to the United States in 1933. Even before then, however, some of his students had taken it upon themselves to explain the method to the musically inclined reading public. Ernst Krenek has asserted that the first such explanation to reach print was Erwin Stein's "Neue Formprincipien," which appeared—perhaps ironically, in light of Schoenberg's own desires in this matter—in a special number of *Musikblätter des Anbruch* issued in honor of Schoenberg's fiftieth birthday in 1924.[3] From Schoenberg's account, quoted earlier, of the circumstances under which he divulged some of the details of the twelve-tone method, one may gather that instruction in this method neither had been nor subsequently became part of the curriculum that Schoenberg offered, and in this respect things seem to have remained the same throughout his life, to judge from the accounts supplied by some of his American students.[4] Thus it is not surprising that, in the United States at any rate, knowledge of the method was largely a matter of rumor until the early 1930s, when articles by Stein and another former pupil, Adolph Weiss, appeared in *Modern Music*.[5] Later in that decade, much more detailed information would be supplied in a book by Ernst Krenek and in a widely read and cited article by Richard Hill.[6]

What all these writings had in common was a focus upon the melodic or polyphonic properties of the twelve-tone series—if not to complete exclusion of harmonic considerations, at most with relatively little attention paid to them. This is entirely understandable; after all, the very idea of a series seemed to imply that temporal order was the principal, if not the sole, factor distinguishing one row from another. Further, Schoenberg's deliberate abandonment of tonality suggested that he had attempted the overthrow of the hegemony of harmonic progression as practiced during the past few centuries. Anyone who cared to examine a Schoenberg twelve-tone score could see that when it came to chords, no single principle of order (for instance, top to bottom, or vice versa) obtained with respect to order of the series or any of its classical transformations. Krenek, for one, saw the interdependence of horizontal and vertical in twelve-tone music as opposite in condition from that of tonal music: whereas harmony ruled in tonal music, in twelve-tone music that role fell to the motivic function of the twelve-tone series, simply because a harmonic system like that of tonality "would no longer be possible" under these new conditions.[7] Indeed, Krenek saw an analogy between the present (1937) and the beginning of the polyphonic era, in that as musicians looked for a center of balance in a "systematic order of harmonic relations" to replace what was lost with the passing of tonality, they looked "exactly where the ancients looked for it when they began to submit disorderly harmonies to an organized principle, namely, in the sphere of polyphony and counterpoint."[8] Stein, in 1924, had said much the same thing: since with the superseding of traditional harmony "all vertical combinations have now become possible," there was now opened up "a vista of new, highly differentiated harmonic effects." However, "An organizing principle . . . has not yet been found; nor is it likely to emanate from the theory of harmony, but rather from counterpoint and from practical experience. It was, after all, in this way that the dissonance came to power—as a result of polyphonic part-writing (see Schoenberg's *Harmonielehre*)."[9]

Both Krenek and Stein made it clear in their expositions of the twelve-tone method that the series was not to be regarded as tantamount to *theme*, but that it functioned rather as a source of *motifs*. For Stein, the row, whether twelve-tone or not,[10] bore an important relation to the *Grundgestalt*: "The most significant feature of the new method is the introduction of a succession of notes, a *basic shape* as Schoenberg calls it, which carries the form of a piece." But if "the succession of notes will amount to one or more motifs whose formative power is likewise based on their restriction to a selection and a certain order of notes," one must keep in mind that any such entity "is a *motif* in the most literal and original sense of the word. . . . It is but a defined melodic shape without rhythmic articulation.'' Furthermore, ''Its possibilities of variation . . . are more numerous and various than those of a motif in the usual sense''—that is, than in music governed by the old laws of tonality.[11] Krenek, for his part, warned his readers that ''themes which give a work its unique figure and really carry the emotional expression are in no sense identical with the twelve-tone series''; but, on the other hand, neither is the twelve-tone series ''particularly suitable for the purposes of functioning as a motif in the old sense of the word. Such a series is simply too long and contains too many elements . . . to form a significant, easily grasped figure.'' Therefore, motifs could only be extracted from a series, in Krenek's view; but even so, the fact that the polyphonic exigencies of new music could force employment of the twelve-tone series in several voices at the same time was ''a phenomenon which weakens and modifies the motif functions of the series to a considerable extent.''[12] We see from this stance that for Krenek the series had begun to assume a more general and hence more abstract character in relation to the actual compositions that came out of it.

Among the first compositions written outside the circle of the Second Viennese School to exhibit any form of serial organization that might be traced, at however many removes, to an acquaintance with Viennese developments is Wallingford Riegger's *Dichotomy* (1932) for orchestra. Long alleged to be the first American twelve-tone work, *Dichotomy* is actually no such thing, being rather, as George Perle has noted, ''a set of free variations on two nondodecaphonic 'tone-rows' employed thematically against a nonserial harmonic background.''[13] The two rows, identified as A and B in the prefatory matter to the score and with their incidences in prime, inversion, and the retrogrades of both clearly marked throughout in the music, consist respectively of eleven tones (with no duplications) and thirteen tones (with three duplications). The variations alluded to by Perle include, at various points, doubling in parallel intervals, truncation, extension, and fragmentation. Such procedures clearly belong within the realm of traditional thematic treatment. Riegger evidently had grasped something of the twelve-tone technique thanks to his contact with Adolph Weiss, but it is unlikely that by this time he knew much of Schoenberg's or his pupils' music well.[14]

Riegger was in this respect to have many emulators (conscious or not), including composers whose own working methods, by the time they encountered the twelve-tone technique, were already firmly established but who tried incorporating rows as a way of ''freshening up'' their style—the sort of thing that Peter Evans has described, unkindly but accurately, in the music of the 1950s as ''those essentially twelve-note successions introduced by composers seeking, anxiously or facetiously, to dispel the charge of being behind the times.''[15] Not that this was always the motivation, especially earlier on, before serialism was in any sense in vogue. Another good example of ''thematic serialism'' can be found in the third movement of Walter Piston's Partita for Violin, Viola, and

Example 7.1
Walter Piston, Partita for Violin, Viola, and Organ, Third Movement, Measures 85–90

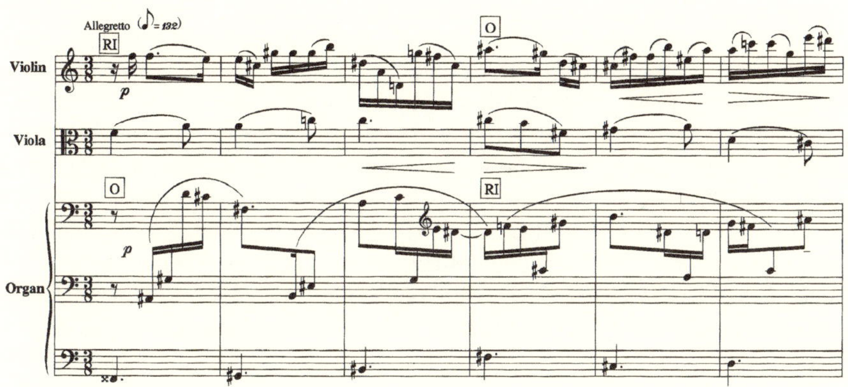

Organ (1944), where the prime and retrograde inversion (marked "O" and "RI," respectively, in Example 7.1) are used twice simultaneously, with parts exchanging between the first incidence and the second.[16] Again, this is hardly "twelve-tone music," for the accompanying parts are freely composed. Such usages lend credence to the hypothesis that even for well-educated and cosmopolitan composers like Piston, the twelve-tone technique was generally associated at that time with the old contrapuntal devices, such as canons in inversion or in retrograde (crab), which certainly could and did occur with added parts not derived by any such specific device.

Even among generally sympathetic and knowledgeable commentators, the twelve-tone method in these relatively early years came in for some not entirely supportive criticism. Richard Hill, in his article "Schoenberg's Tone-Rows and the Tonal System of the Future," went further than had Stein or Krenek in explaining and classifying the different ways in which, in Schoenberg's works, the row might be combined with transpositions of itself or with its retrograde, inversion, or retrograde inversion in various ways and in various kinds of textures ranging from contrapuntal to homophonic. Among the "rows whose intervals are so composed that the notes of different sections are somehow allied," Hill identified the type that in present-day terminology would be called inversionally semicombinatorial—that is, "the row is divided into two six-note groups, the first of which in the prime contains the same notes as the second half of the mirror [inversion], but in a different order, the other halves necessarily being related similarly."[17]

The brilliance of this revelation, never before discussed in print—that collections of all twelve tones could be formed by parts of different row forms in combination, as well as by single forms—was, however, somewhat overshadowed by Hill's assertion that in presenting his row forms as he had done in many of his more recent compositions, Schoenberg had effectively misused his own invention. Because row order was not reflected in the temporal order of events in the music, "the motival significance of the row has been completely destroyed."[18] This criticism, growing out of the misguided notion that "motival significance" resides wholly in the strict adjacencies of tones in the row, and that therefore it was necessary to be able to "identify the row" aurally in order to make sense of any composition based on it, was to exhibit remarkable tenacity throughout subsequent decades; indeed, as has been pointed out, it has persisted in some quarters, along with the misunderstanding that generated it, right up to the present.[19]

Hill's criticisms may well have convinced some that Schoenberg's method was unworkable, but they also persuaded others that the salvation of the twelve-tone method would lie in its eventual modification. Already in 1937 Krenek had envisioned the "strict" twelve-tone method only as a stage in development and expected that sooner or later it would become more flexible. "In the future, one will no longer use the whole series continuously, but will choose characteristic groups from it; one will allow certain variations within that chosen series." He professed to see such a tendency toward free treatment in some of Schoenberg's more recent twelve-tone works.[20] Krenek's article "New Developments of the Twelve-Tone Technique," written after his emigration to the United States and in light of his exposure to Hill's critique, revealed a considerable willingness to extend the technique into regions of contrapuntal and harmonic structuring only remotely related to Schoenberg's original method.

Effectively taking up Hill's challenge to composers to find a "modal" interpretation of the row that would overcome the inadequacies (in Hill's view) so far displayed in its handling, Krenek invented "two six-tone groups which together form a twelve-tone series," but then, instead of treating them as a series in the Schoenbergian sense, proceeded to form "diatonic" and "chromatic" modes from them. For the former, he rotated the contents to produce six ordered scales for each hexachord, each hexachord in each of the two sets of six containing the same tones as the other five but starting on a different tone. To form chromatic modes, each member of the group of six diatonic modes, embodying six different orders of intervals, was transposed to begin on the same note, thus "eventually us[ing] all twelve tones in various six-note combinations" (see Example 7.2). In composing his *Lamentatio Jeremiae Prophetae* (1942), Krenek treated the six-note groups as internally unordered but externally ordered, always observing their respective positions in the form of the original twelve-note collection.[21] Around this same time, paradoxically, Krenek also took the "breaking down [of] the integrity of the series"—in which Schoenberg had supposedly engaged in such works as his Violin Concerto, Op. 36—even further. In the Symphonic Piece for String Orchestra (1939) he built up the twelve-tone series from various smaller-sized groups of notes, extracted new motives from contoural extremities, dissolved the series into new segments and reordered them, and so on.[22]

Example 7.2
Ernst Krenek, Modes for *Lamentatio Jeremiae Prophetae*

O=Original J=Inversion
I=First; II=second half of the basic tone-row
△=Diatonic; ×=chromatic six-tone patterns

Although perhaps neither of them realized it at the time, the ideas of Krenek's youthful pupil George Perle, twenty-four years old when he first went to Krenek in 1939, had even more radical implications for the twelve-tone method. The story of how Perle came by these ideas is a notable example of the combined

Figure 7.1
George Perle's Matrix of Dual Circle-of-Fifths Rows

P:	C	F	G	B♭	D	E♭	A	G♯	E	C♯	B	F♯
R:	F♯	B	C♯	E	G♯	A	E♭	D	B♭	G	F	C
I:	C	G	F	D	B♭	A	D♯	E	G♯	B	C♯	F♯
RI:	F♯	C♯	B	G♯	E	D♯	A	B♭	D	F	G	C

effect of two circumstances: the general lack of availability of scores by Schoenberg, Berg, and Webern even in large cities like Chicago, in and around which Perle grew up; and the reluctance of Schoenberg to teach or publish anything about the twelve-tone method or even to talk about it much. Into this vacuum flowed a great deal of speculation, much of it inaccurate. Two years before taking his first composition lesson with Krenek, Perle had attempted on his own to induce the workings of Schoenberg's method from the score of Berg's Lyric Suite, being unable to obtain any scores of Schoenberg himself. He came up with the interesting idea that a twelve-tone row worked to structure the composition based on it by making available to any given tone, as its next move, any tone following it in the prime, the inversion, or their retrogrades. This idea was so interesting, in fact, that when Krenek eventually gave him the straight (Schoenbergian) story, Perle found it actually rather disappointing, "primitive" by comparison to what he had himself invented: "I had thought that the series must be something like a scale, functioning as the background structure of a piece, even though, unlike the diatonic scale, it was specific to that piece. The Schoenbergian series was simply a disguised ostinato twelve-tone motive. It was almost like defining the tonality of a piece in E major by simply playing the scale of E major over and over again."[23]

Of course, Perle's invention did not explain Berg's technique either. He had no way of knowing (since no one else at the time did either) that the first movement of the Lyric Suite was based on not one but three rows, only one of which was a "series" in the Schoenbergian sense.[24] Still, Perle was encouraged by Krenek's characterization of his idea as "a discovery," and two years later he set forth a "twelve-tone modal system," effectively his later "twelve-tone tonality" in embryonic form. In this early formulation Perle developed his system out of a single order of tones that he called "*the* twelve-tone scale": the circle of fifths traced in both directions at once, in alternation. Under this definition, "the row is no longer a motive in itself, but has become instead a source of material in a more general sense." It was thereby freed from a task to which, in Perle's view, it was not particularly well suited anyway, a task that in fact placed heavier demands on the row—"to result in a totally unique organization for each individual work"—than it was, in the final analysis, capable of supporting. From the four ways of negotiating the circle of fifths in opposite directions simultaneously (see Figure 7.1), Perle derives pairings of prime with each of the possible transposed forms of the inversion, and vice versa, then constructs matrices of the neighboring tones for each pair. These become usable chords and other groupings of notes in actual compositional settings. This system, already rich in potential, was further augmented over the years, to the point that eventually, Perle became impatient with the tendency to classify him as a "serialist" or "twelve-tone composer," since he had come to regard his methods as quite different from anything else under that label.[25]

DEVELOPMENTS IN EUROPE AFTER THE SECOND WORLD WAR

Any dissemination of the twelve-tone method, owing to the "secret" having gotten out, that might have progressed to a general level of awareness of its tenets among musicians in Central Europe and elsewhere came essentially to an abrupt end with the accession to political power by the Nazis in Germany in 1933 and the emigration of Schoenberg to the United States. Berg's sudden death at the end of 1935 and the forced withdrawal of Webern from public musical life from the time of the Austrian *Anschluss* in 1938 until his death in 1945 were, of course, further disruptions to any natural course of development. By the time the war ended, the musical scene in Europe had drastically changed, and it proved to be up to individuals with little if any contact with the originators of the twelve-tone method to rekindle the flame, as it were.

Olivier Messiaen was certainly to play a crucial role in the early going.[26] Repatriated to France in 1942 after internment in a German prisoner-of-war camp, Messiaen took up an appointment as teacher of harmony at the Paris Conservatoire. The following year he commenced a private, supplementary class, devoted to analysis and composition, open to his regular conservatory students (but meeting, of necessity, extramurally, since his appointment in the Conservatoire did not permit him to teach composition). Here works of Stravinsky, Schoenberg, Berg, and others were studied. Among Messiaen's pupils by 1944 was Pierre Boulez, who particularly remembers analyzing *Le sacre du printemps* and Messiaen's own music.[27] In 1944 Messiaen also published his *Technique de mon langage musical*; his treatise exposed an already-intricate rhythmic practice that gave every indication of rivaling pitch for status as a primary, autonomous component of musical structure.[28] Boulez actually studied with Messiaen for only one year, and while he is quick to disavow any influence from Messiaen's compositions (he strongly disliked everything Messiaen wrote before around 1950), he allows that from his contact with him he took "what could be of service to me—namely, his work on rhythmic cells and their modification, interpolation, partial augmentation, diminution, and so on."[29] It does seem clear that Messiaen's tutelage had a great deal of influence on one of Boulez's longest and best-known analytical essays, "Stravinsky Remains," completed by 1951, which delves in great detail into the rhythmic character of

Le sacre from the point of view of rhythmic cells and their manipulation and modification.[30]

By his own recollection, Messiaen encouraged his students (undoubtedly including Boulez) to think of ways in which the ordering principles of twelve-tone music could be extended: "In 1944 . . . I had spoken out forcefully against the universal tendency of composers to prospect solely in the domain of pitch. And I had already pronounced the words: 'series of timbres,' 'series of intensities,' and, above all, 'series of durations': being a rhythmicist myself, this [last] was closest to my heart."[31] Again, one must bear in mind that Messiaen was apparently speaking of pitch serialization without benefit of access to many scores that actually exhibited it: of the two works that he mentions in this context, *Pierrot lunaire* is not twelve-tone at all, and the Lyric Suite he found "serial . . . only for brief moments," which only shows that its twelve-tone organization remained as opaque to him as it had to Perle and other Americans a decade earlier. But it was this propensity for thinking of serialism in multiple domains that made it possible, when scores by Webern finally became available shortly after the end of the war, to see a nascent control of domains other than pitch by means of serial mechanisms in certain of the late works. This circumstance, in fact, set the entire tone for the reception of Webern in Europe in the late 1940s and early 1950s. "Webern was the 'real' serial composer; Schoenberg and Berg were the precursors," Messiaen said in 1967; it was Webern who had taken the notion of *Klangfarbenmelodie* (tone-color melody) only advocated by Schoenberg, and actually realized it.[32]

Another important teacher and promulgator of the twelve-tone method in Paris immediately after the war was René Leibowitz. Boulez, fascinated by a performance of the Schoenberg Wind Quintet that he heard in 1945, learned of Leibowitz's past connection to the Second Viennese School (he had studied briefly with Webern in 1930–31 and with Schoenberg in 1932) and organized a group of Messiaen's pupils for a weekly class with him.[33] Leibowitz's curriculum apparently concentrated on Schoenberg, with some excursions into Berg and Webern; he became much better known in the years afterward, owing to his courses at the Darmstadt summer school in 1947–48, where he taught many future serial composers; to his notable career as a conductor of the twelve-tone repertory; and, perhaps above all, to his books *Schoenberg et son école* (1947) and *Introduction à la musique de douze sons* (1949).[34] For many readers, these books were undoubtedly the first relatively reliable and abundant source of information about the Second Viennese School they had yet encountered. Leibowitz did tend to emphasize Schoenberg's contribution, especially in the *Introduction*; only a few works of Webern are analyzed in any detail, and there is hardly anything useful about Berg at all. If this balance of treatment was also reflected in his classes, it may have fueled Boulez's impatience, soon to develop, with an approach he found overly dogmatic and with the harking back to tradition that he had begun to notice more and more in Schoenberg's music—particularly in his employment of classical forms such as the sonata—and in

Berg's. Later (1955) he would write: "Whereas Schoenberg and Berg ally themselves to the decadence of the great German romantic tradition, and in such works as *Pierrot lunaire* and *Wozzeck* round it off by the most luxuriant, flamboyant means, Webern—via Debussy, one might say—reacts violently against all inherited rhetoric, in order to rehabilitate the powers of sound."[35]

Still, it was thanks to Leibowitz that Boulez got to know his first Webern scores, the Symphony (Op. 21) and the Concerto for Nine Instruments (Op. 24),[36] and began to develop an appreciation for the power of the row when it was used in a deliberately "athematic" way to generate the briefest of motives and "a certain texture of intervals," as he put it in his conversations with Célestin Deliège.[37] Moreover, it was the deepening involvement of Messiaen's pupils in matters dodecaphonic, as well as the work that Pierre Schaeffer had begun to do in the new musique concrète at the Radiodiffusion-télévision française (RTF) studios in Paris—work that seemed to promise an exactitude of control previously impossible to achieve over domains other than pitch—that stimulated Messiaen to push his own rhythmic and durational researches even further than he had outlined them in the *Technique*. A number of pieces notable for their innovations in this respect resulted from his efforts, but it was *Mode de valeurs et d'intensités* (1949), for piano, that represented the real breakthrough. Messiaen had never written a piece like this, and he never would again: *Mode de valeurs* organized the twelve pitch classes into a tripartite arrangement of thirty-six pitches, each of the three divisions making use of all twelve pitch classes but occupying a different part of the piano's range (high, middle, and low, with some overlap). Each of the divisions, considered as a succession of pitch classes, could be interpreted as a row, but this was not the way Messiaen employed them: each pitch was assigned a particular duration, loudness, and mode of attack, out of a total range of twenty-four, seven, and eleven possibilities, respectively. No rules governed the order of pitches, durations, dynamic levels, or attack modes, nor was there any prior stipulation of relative frequency of occurrence; there were also no explicit rules regarding interrelation of divisions, which proceeded in apparently linear-contrapuntal manner, each independent of the other two and, as if to emphasize that relationship, each notated on a separate staff (Example 7.3). The work gave the impression (which is different from saying that it had actually been composed that way) of embodying a set of precompositional decisions that had then been set in motion and allowed to take their course, almost as if on autopilot.

Was Messiaen, with this piece, on the verge of becoming, not a "twelve-tone composer," but a serialist, one who had found a viable way of organizing all the domains of musical sound into a single, ruled system? Observers at the time might have thought so, but as it turned out, *Mode de valeurs* was only the most extreme of a group of pieces that Messiaen wrote during a relatively brief "experimental" period (1949–52) and that served collectively as a transition to a definitively mature style in which elaborate rhythmic/durational schemes played a major role.[38] However, the idea of a precomposed "mode" incorporating pitch

Example 7.3
Olivier Messiaen, *Mode de valeurs et d'intensités*, First Page of Score

Mode de valeurs et d'intensités

Olivier MESSIAEN

Source: © 1950 Durand S.A. Used by permission. Sole representative U.S.A. Theodore Presser Company.

with other domains mightily impressed Boulez (and, later, Karlheinz Stockhausen), among numerous others, and it became a point of departure for their further efforts.

The first certifiable compositional ''effects'' of Messiaen's bold experiment came from two of his students who had been with him at Darmstadt the summer he composed *Mode de valeurs*. During 1950–51 the Belgian Karel Goeyvaerts and the Frenchman Michel Fano both wrote pieces for two pianos that exhibited the same sorts of preoccupations with serial organization of all four domains. Their manifestly modest talents have been largely forgotten today, but the fact that Boulez knew their pieces before he began work on his own two-piano *Structures* suggests that their position in history is of some significance.[39] Goeyvaerts's and Fano's works are, as well, harbingers of the rapidity with which the idea of "total" or "integral" serialism spread throughout Europe; for them, like many young composers to follow, this was soon the only way to write music. In 1952 Boulez would proclaim: "Any musician who has not experienced . . . the necessity of the dodecaphonic language is USELESS"—and by "dodecaphonic" he meant the Viennese Three only as historical forerunners.[40] By then, the avant-garde had even stepped over Webern, "the threshold."

Boulez, by the time he saw the score of *Mode de valeurs* in 1950, was by no means unprepared to absorb its lessons. Immediately after he commenced his studies with Leibowitz, his own music began to reflect a growing acquaintance with the twelve-tone method. Particularly important in his development during the late 1940s are the Sonatine (1946) for flute and piano and the Second Piano Sonata (1948). The first of these combines what he had learned of Schoenberg's and Webern's methods in thematic and athematic writing, together with recognizably Messiaenic rhythmic techniques.[41] The Second Piano Sonata shows a greater development in the direction of motivic fragmentation and the use of intervals to define space and texture—the legacy of Webern, including pitches frozen in register during certain passages.[42] Two pieces from Boulez followed soon after his exposure to *Mode de valeurs: Structure 1a*, for two pianos, and *Polyphonie X*, for eighteen instruments, both in 1951.[43] The latter now has the status of a withdrawn work, but it has continued to have a kind of influence through some of Boulez's more technical prose, which makes use of the work as illustration. For *Polyphonie X*, a twenty-four-note row in quarter tones is pulled apart into two twelve-note rows in semitones, which are then further transformed according to criteria invented, apparently, for the specific occasion of this piece, resulting in fourteen rows in all, some in quarter tones, others semitonal, which become the polyphonic components. The rhythmic organization, independently arrived at, is based on three cells, their combinations, and their further transformations according to a notably prolix collection of possibilities. These are coordinated with the pitch series and given instrumentation, such that "the complexity of the rhythm is a function of the complexity of the series or the instrumental formation."[44]

In *Structure 1a* Boulez took things even further, extending the serial principle to arrive at twelve of everything: besides pitch and duration, dynamics and mode of attack are at least potentially twelvefold. The piece is in a way an homage to *Mode de valeurs* in that the row is taken over from the pitches of Messiaen's Division I (but treated, of course, as an ordered set of pitch classes), and the durational series is constructed out of values from one to twelve thirty-second notes in length (the same range of values as were assigned to Division I). As for dynamics and mode of attack, Messiaen's ranges are simply augmented to

Example 7.4
Pierre Boulez, *Structure Ia*, First Page of Score

Source: Pierre Boulez, *Structures*. Copyright 1958 by Universal Edition (London) Ltd., London. Copyright renewed. All Rights Reserved. Used by permission of European American Music Distributors Corporation, sole U.S. and Canadian agent for Universal Edition (London) Ltd., London.

make up the required quantities. But Boulez's procedure diverges sharply from Messiaen's in that no single mode is constructed, with all four domains inflexibly linked at every point; rather, the row is treated in classical twelve-tone fashion, and from the order-number matrices defining its prime and inverted forms the matrices for the other domains are derived but are compositionally applied independently (Example 7.4).[45] Once all this precompositional work had been done, one gathers, the actual writing went extremely quickly, if Boulez is

Example 7.5
Row Divided into Segments

to be believed when he says that he composed *Structure 1a* "in a single night."[46] One gathers also that the "automatic" impression given off by Messiaen's piece had impelled Boulez to build the sort of compositional engine that he could simply set in motion—what he later referred to, borrowing Barthes's phrase, as "the zero degree of writing."[47]

Although what resulted from this experience—effectively a *tabula rasa* as far as compositional technique was concerned—is probably not one of the enduring masterpieces of Western music, Boulez's next work, *Le Marteau sans maître*, may rightly be accorded such status. For this piece, the precompositional apparatus became far more elaborate than it had been even for *Structures*, though the details were not generally known until more than three decades after its premiere.[48] In *Le Marteau* Boulez introduced the technique of pitch-class multiplication, greatly magnifying the row's power to generate harmonic/contrapuntal structures while also, paradoxically, greatly diffusing that power, since most of the new structures bore only the remotest of relationships to the original row. Under this technique, the row was divided asymmetrically into segments of one to four tones; these segments were then "multiplied" with one another to generate pitch-class groups of varying size, which were then assembled into matrices.

For example, a row might be divided as in Example 7.5. To multiply the first and second segments, it helps to imagine both as chords, even though ultimately all the members of both are treated as pitch classes that can appear in any spacing and any register. In the matrices used to do this, as reconstructed by Lev Koblyakov, the first segment appears as a minor seventh (F-E♭), the second from bottom to top as B-D-B♭-C♯. Then the interval structure of the first segment is superimposed repeatedly upon the pitches of the second, building a minor seventh above each of its four tones. Once the octave duplications have been eliminated, the result is B-D-A-B♭-C-C♯-A♭. A segment can also be multiplied by itself; for the first segment, the result of this operation is F-E♭-D♭. Further possibilities, and completely different matrices, can be obtained by partitioning the row in new ways, and by partitioning the inversional form of the row. The 5 × 5 matrices of pitch groups that emerge from these multiplications are then "navigated" by the composer in various patterns, generating chords, lines, and combinations of the two, in ensemble creating a mosaic of the pitch groups. Analogous methods are used to organize the durational, dynamic, and attack-mode domains as well.

Karlheinz Stockhausen came to the lessons of Messiaen somewhat later than Boulez—he heard *Mode de valeurs* first on a recording at Darmstadt in 1951 and did not study with its composer until the following year—but as his compositional history shows, he was quick to catch up with these latest developments. Stockhausen had "discovered" the twelve-tone method by that time and had even written a dodecaphonic violin sonatina, but his studies of scores by Schoenberg, Berg, and Webern had not brought him to any special awareness of a difference between Webern and the others before his encounter with Goeyvaerts at that same Darmstadt summer course. It may also have been in the summer of 1951 that Stockhausen heard a Webern work for the first time; later he would speak in this connection of "the sheer excitement of the musical experience."[49]

The effect of all these new stimuli within such a short time must have been intense, judging from *Kreuzspiel*, a piece that marked a radical shift in Stockhausen's style. It was composed during the autumn of 1951 and premiered over Cologne Radio in December of that year. Returning to Cologne from Darmstadt, Stockhausen had brought a copy of *Mode de valeurs* to Herbert Eimert, who dubbed it "punktuell." Thus, apparently, was the musical term "pointillist" born, as a descriptor not only of Messiaen's piece but of much music written in emulation of it, including Stockhausen's *Kreuzspiel* and *Punkte* (1952), as well as Boulez's *Structures* (Book 1) and *Polyphonie X*. Stockhausen explained:

> Pointillist—Why? Because we hear only single notes, which might almost exist for themselves alone, in a mosaic of sound; they exist among others in configurations which no longer destine them to become components of shapes which intermix and fuse in the traditional way; rather they are points amongst others, existing for themselves in complete freedom, and formulated individually and in considerable isolation from each other. Each note has a fixed register, and allows no other note within its preserve; each note has its own duration, its own pitch and its own accentuation.[50]

It was Messiaen, furthermore, who helped cement Webern's stature as the greatest of the Viennese Three. Stockhausen recalled that

> on the basis of a few analyses [Messiaen] had demonstrated as early as 1952 that Webern was seeking not only a greater complexity of the serial principle as applied to melody and harmony, but also an actual unification of the sort he had found in his studies in music history . . . the principle of *talea* and *color*, that organization of form by means of interlaced techniques involving both the rhythmic-metrical and the melodic-harmonic aspects of music. To the question of where Webern's artistic development would have led had his life not been tragically cut short, Stockhausen replies with the greatest confidence: Webern would have achieved complete structural integration.[51]

In an analytical article a few years later, Stockhausen would show at some length just how he saw Webern striving toward this goal.[52]

More or less inescapably, however, the adoption of *Mode de valeurs* as a

Figure 7.2a
Stockhausen, *Kreuzspiel*, First Two Transformations of the Row

0	1	2	3	4	5	6	7	8	9	10	11
1	2	3	4	5	11	0	6	7	8	9	10
2	3	4	5	10	0	11	1	6	7	8	9

Figure 7.2b
Stockhausen, *Kreuzspiel*, Final Transformation of the Row, Showing Original Hexachords in Reverse Order

6	7	8	9	10	11	0	1	2	3	4	5

model meant that composers would fix primarily upon the linear, polyphonic aspect of the row as far as purely pitch-class matters were concerned, allowing harmony mostly to take care of itself. In this sense, Messiaen's piece was not as much of a break with his past as it is sometimes made out to be: his *Technique* shows far more of a tendency to codify rhythmic than harmonic matters, and what codification of harmony there is in that book relies mainly upon adherence to the contents of other modes, those he called "of limited transposition." *Kreuzspiel*, for example, certainly reflects primarily linear structuring, even while it also shows an original and fertile mind at work. The "crossplay" of the title is worked out in several ways, as Jonathan Harvey has shown in his comprehensive analysis.[53] To take just the first section as an example (measures 1–91): the three pitched instruments in the ensemble, piano, oboe, and bass clarinet, together project a twelve-tone row that is systematically permuted through twelve occurrences, each time with the first and last tones "crossing" to the middle but with this middle expanding concentrically. The first two transformations are shown in Figure 7.2a; numbers denote order positions (0 to 11) in the row. This process is carried through the first six row statements, then effectively reverses, yet what happens in statements seven through twelve is not exactly a mirror image of one through six, for in the final row the order of hexachords is exactly reversed (crossed), as shown in Figure 7.2b. Throughout this process the eleven-complementary order pairs (0, 11; 1, 10; 2, 9; and so on) are held symmetrically positioned with respect to the center. Another kind of crossing occurs with respect to register: the piano plays only in the extreme high and low registers, the oboe and bass clarinet in medium-high and medium-low registers, respectively. The first section begins and ends with piano; when it is over, the six tones initially in the highest register have become the six lowest, and vice versa.

As for durations, they are subject to a serial structure in part linked to, in part independent from, pitch. *Kreuzspiel* resembles *Mode de valeurs* in that each pitch class is paired with a duration, and these twelve pairings remain fixed throughout the work. Stockhausen's work departs from its ostensible model, however, in having two other, independent durational schemes projected by percussion parts, in two differently crossing patterns that are both also different from the crossing pattern of the pitches.

Like Boulez, Stockhausen eventually found the pointillist approach too confining, but in moving away from it he took a route toward generalizing the serial principle that was notably different from Boulez's. Two among many aspects of this revision are especially worthy of mention. First, Stockhausen discovered that points could be replaced by groups with no loss of serial rigor; the beginnings of this process of discovery are evident in *Kontra-Punkte*, which in its first version was a "points" piece (*Punkte*) but soon was rewritten in a completely different style. Stockhausen thus gives us to understand that the new title means not only "counterpoints" but "against points."[54] The second crucial development was a reconsideration of the relationship between pitch and duration. The "additive" approach of Messiaen (and Boulez) began to seem to Stockhausen arbitrary and, in terms of perception, actually false: since scales of pitches do not work on an additive principle, why should scales of durations? For the chromatic scale, for instance, it is not equal increments in the frequency (cycles per second) from one tone to the next that make the steps sound equal in size, but rather the equality of ratio between adjacent tones $x{:}y$ and adjacent tones $y{:}z$. The entire scale, of course, fits into the 1:2 ratio of an octave. By contrast, within the 1:12 ratio postulated by an additive range of durations from, say, one thirty-second to one dotted quarter, the ratio of thirty-second to sixteenth (first two terms) is vastly different from that of quarter-plus-dotted-sixteenth to dotted quarter (last two terms). Building on this observation and on the closely related one that where perceptible duration ends (about one-sixteenth of a second), perceptible pitch begins (around sixteen cycles per second) Stockhausen laid out a theory for unifying the two compositionally in what may well count as his most significant essay, ". . . wie die zeit vergeht . . ." (". . . how time passes . . .").[55] A twelve-tone row, in addition to or even instead of serving as a source of pitch material, could serve equally well as a source of durational proportions or successive tempi.[56]

In *Gruppen* (1955–57), for three orchestras, one of the great works to come out of the 1950s, none of the row's functions duplicates those it would have in classical twelve-tone music. A chart of the twelve successive transpositions of the row, many with some segmental reordering and the twelfth really detectable only in aggregate, is used to control shifts of tempi between one group structure and the next, connecting the ratio representing the interval between adjacent tones to a ratio between tempi. For example, the first two tones of the row are G and D♯, (enharmonically) a major third, or 5:4. With G's corresponding tempo arbitrarily set at metronome marking (MM) 120 (group 1), D♯ will correspond to about MM 95, which is the tempo of group 2. Ratios between adjacent tones are also used, more cryptically, to control the duration itself of each group. The actual pitch range of each group is treated as a field, filled more or less densely (in terms of both pitch and temporal space). The upper and lower pitch limits of each of the fields are determined by the retrograde of the chart of rows mentioned earlier.

The foregoing description, though of course inadequate for a comprehensive grasp of the compositional processes involved, will at least give some idea of the remarkable powers of invention that were stimulated in Stockhausen by the serial concept, powers that continue to serve him well although they have been applied in many different ways in the dozens of pieces he has written since *Gruppen*. In an interview conducted in the early 1970s he gave some indication of just how far the serial concept had taken him, and how much further it was likely to take him yet:

> Serialism means nothing but the following: rather than having everything based on periodic values in any parameter, what we do is use a set, a limited number of different values—let's say 1, 2, 3, 4, 5, 6. And a series which is based on a scale of different values is simply the permutation of these individual steps in a given scale. We have two conditions to follow. In order to have a serial sequence of individual values—whether it's pitch, timbre, duration, the size of objects, the color of eyes, whatever—we need at the base to have a scale with equal steps. . . . Chromatic music is the most neutral kind because it doesn't seem to belong to any particular style, it incorporates all the other scales within itself—you use all the steps with equal importance. In serial composition, we use all the notes within a given scale of equidistant steps. . . . But we have to use them, statistically speaking, with an equal number of appearances so that there's no predominance, no one tone becomes more important than the other. And we don't leave out notes. . . .
>
> [Interviewer:] But you're not using the serialization of music parameters in your recent compositions, are you?
>
> [Stockhausen:] Certainly. Only *more* than previously. Which means that since the end of the 1950s, I've no longer applied the serial technique to the *quantitative* differences of things—of inches in duration or of decibels in dynamics—but to the *qualitative*. I give a value to what I perceive as a unified expression of a certain sound event. . . . And next to it I put another unified event which has certain things in common with it. There's nothing in the world that doesn't have something in common with any other thing.[57]

As an appendix to his book *Die Komposition mit zwölf Tönen* (1952), another important contribution to general dissemination of the serial method, Josef Rufer included comments that he had solicited from various contemporary composers "on their experiences of composing with twelve notes."[58] Reading these autobiographical statements, most of them from composers born in the first decade of the twentieth century, one is struck by the great diversity of interpretations to which the twelve-tone idea had already been put by then. The approaches described by Boris Blacher, Wolfgang Fortner, Roberto Gerhard, Hanns Jelinek, Rolf Liebermann, Mátyás Seiber, and others suggest that most, if not all, of the European composers of that generation who were drawn to the twelve-tone method arrived at a personal vantage point upon it by a combination of creative brilliance, score study (where possible), intellectual effort, and sheer inspired guesswork—more or less, that is, as their American counterparts had done around the same time.

Luigi Dallapiccola, also included in Rufer's appendix, deserves special mention as a composer whose twelve-tone work rose to considerable prominence after the war and who stood as an example and inspiration to the next generation of Italian composers. Dallapiccola, compared to some aspirants to the twelve-tone method, had even less access to vital information; around 1950 he recalled the "singularity" of his position during the 1930s, "having adopted the twelve-note technique at a time when I had no contact with the masters of the Viennese school (Schoenberg, Berg, Webern), nor with their disciples." More or less coinciding with the rise of fascism, "in the first period of my activities as a composer (from 1934 to 1939) . . . series of twelve notes began to make their, undeniably timid, appearance in my works." He added, significantly, "In some cases they were used for purely coloristic purposes, in others with exclusively melodic intent."[59] Elsewhere, he has said: "The twelve-tone system intrigued me, but I knew so little about it! Nevertheless, I based the entire composition [*Canti di prigionia*, 1938] on a twelve-tone series and, as a symbolic gesture, counterpointed a fragment of the ancient liturgical sequence, 'Dies irae, dies illa.' "[60] In this we see again the early tendency of composers outside the Viennese circle to interpret the twelve-tone method as a primarily or even exclusively contrapuntal technique.

Other accounts suggest that the Italians during the fascist period may not have been quite as isolated as Dallapiccola has implied. Bruno Maderna, for instance, supplies this insight:

> Before the war, we Italians didn't know the music of the Vienna school very well, but we still knew it better than the Germans did. In fact Mussolini had a great friend, the futurist Marinetti; Mussolini himself was not very intelligent, but he listened enough to Marinetti, who drew him towards modernity and progress in all the arts. By this means we were not completely separated from the rest of Europe; composers such as Dallapiccola and Petrassi, the generation before ours, could keep in touch with the music of Bartók, Stravinsky, and the Viennese, certainly more than was possible for German composers.[61]

Yet the problem of lack of access to the Viennese composers' scores must still have been (mostly) insurmountable until the end of the war. (Dallapiccola has said flatly that Schoenberg's scores were "unobtainable" before then.)[62] At any rate, soon after 1945 Dallapiccola's music began to reflect greater familiarity with Schoenberg's method in works like *Due studi* (1946–47), with textures composed entirely from the row and its transformations.

This is not to say that Dallapiccola at this point became some "loyal partisan" of the Second Viennese School. Although he never took up serialism in the sense of that term in the music of Boulez, Stockhausen, and their followers (and he inevitably suffered some criticism for that), his music bore ample testimony to the fact that the twelve-tone method imposed no standard style on all its practitioners. Apparently without any idea that Berg had done the same thing, Dallapiccola occasionally used multiple rows, as in the opera *Il prigioniero* (1944–48); this tendency went essentially into eclipse during the 1950s, only to reemerge later in his career, as in *Tempus destruendi/Tempus aedificandi* (1971), where at least a dozen intricately related yet distinct rows are spun out of a systematic reordering process.[63] His great attraction to canonic devices, firmly entrenched in his adoption of the twelve-tone method from the beginning, also led him into rhythmic innovations that are certainly structural if not exactly serial in derivation: in composing the *Canti di liberazione* (1951–55), Dallapiccola recounts, " 'Metrical cells' . . . were set forth simultaneously on one single note by all four voices in unison at four different speeds. . . . I elaborated canonic developments in which two or three tempi were superimposed one on the other."[64]

More of a divergence from the Second Viennese line is represented by Dallapiccola's widely noted preference for rows that embed triadic or more generally "modal" elements,[65] a tendency that at one time tended to draw scorn upon him: "He is dismissed either as the infiltrator of 'Italian lyricism' into the twelve-tone system, or the 'serialist' who makes it all sound like pink clouds."[66] Such elements clearly do not in themselves make a piece tonal, or even reminiscent of tonality, though Schoenberg himself seems to have avoided rows of this kind lest just this sort of confusion develop. But for Dallapiccola, they may well have served as a kind of substitute:

> I came to the conclusion that if, in the twelve-note system, the tonic had disappeared, taking with it the tonic-dominant relationship, and if, in consequence, sonata form had completely disintegrated, there still existed, nevertheless, a power of attraction, which I will call *polarity*. . . . I mean by this term the extremely subtle relationships which exist between certain notes. These relationships are not always easily perceptible today, being much less obvious than that of the tonic to dominant, but they are there, all the same.
>
> The interesting point about this polarity is the fact that it can change (or be changed) from one work to another. One series can reveal to us the *polarity* that exists between the first and twelfth sounds; another that which exists between the second and the ninth; and so on.[67]

If such ideas seemed positively heretical, striking at the very root of "twelve tones related only to one another" by privileging certain ones among the twelve, they perhaps paled even so by comparison to some of the other things that were being done in the name of dodecaphony or serialism at the time. Once Schoenberg was dead—and not merely in the physical sense, as Boulez had emphasized—anything might happen.

Another Italian, Luigi Nono—Dallapiccola's junior by a generation—emerged in the 1950s as one of the more talented members of the Darmstadt School. His earliest acknowledged composition, the *Variazioni canoniche* (1950)

Example 7.6
Luigi Nono, *Il canto sospeso*, Row

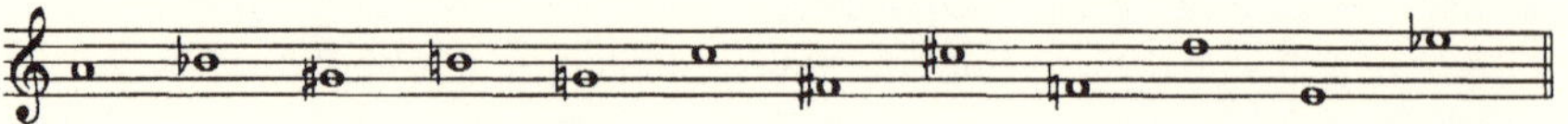

on a twelve-tone series of Schoenberg, is already in a recognizably pointillist style (in marked contrast to the Schoenberg work, *Ode to Napoleon Buonaparte*, Op. 41, from which its series was taken), with a fragmentary presentation of the row that does not coalesce into full statements until near the end. Nono did not leap into serialization of nonpitch domains with the alacrity of some of his fellows: *Polifonica—Monodia—Ritmica* (1951), for instance, exerts only modest precompositional control over duration and dynamics. By 1955, however, he was writing works like *Incontri*, in which by his own account the fundamental pitch series remains unchanged throughout but the series for duration and dynamics undergo permutations such that no tone in the pitch series ever has the same duration or dynamic level twice in succession.[68] This kind of thinking also clearly informs what may be Nono's best-known piece, *Il canto sospeso* (1956), with its oft-analyzed second movement. The pitch series is of extremely simple design, the "wedge" type that unfolds in progressively larger intervals, alternately above and below an initial pitch (Example 7.6). It is never transposed, retrograded, or inverted; it never occurs in more than one statement at a time.[69] By contrast, the durational structure is quite elaborate, consisting as it does of a proportional series and its retrograde based on Fibonacci numbers (1, 2, 3, 5, 8, 13 / 13, 8, 5, 3, 2, 1) that are applied to four different units of duration (eighth, triplet eighth, sixteenth, quintuplet sixteenth) by multiplication. For example, in the first presentation of the twelve-tone row (see the score, Example 7.7), pitch A receives the duration of an eighth (eighth × 1), B♭ the duration of a triplet quarter (triplet eighth × 2), G♯ the duration of a dotted eighth (sixteenth × 3), and so on. This suggests that the units of duration are also treated serially; however, as the second movement continues (and even before the first statement of the twelve-tone row is complete), this turns out not to be the case, for when the values in the proportional series get shorter again, as they do in the retrograde, each newly entering duration is simply placed where there is "room" for it, temporally speaking. In the first presentation of the twelve-tone row, the quintuplet sixteenth gets used more often than the others just because this value, when it occurs multiplied by 8 in the retrograde, runs out before the other three durational multiples present in the texture at the same time do. Nono, in general, seems bent on keeping all four durational units in play at all times, but there is some freedom in his scheme, as can be gathered from the momentary "drop-outs" that do occur (by interposition of rests). A further permutational influence (and source of further unpredictability) comes with each cycle of proportional series and retrograde, as individual values that "should" occur are omitted (1

Example 7.7

Luigi Nono, *Il canto sospeso*, *II*, First Page. The measures are numbered continuously in this piece through all the movements; the second movement begins with measure 108. The row involves all the parts at once: A in m. 108, Contralto 2; B♭ in Soprano 2; A♭ (G♯) in Soprano 1; B in Contralto 1; G in Contralto 2 (second note); and so forth.

is left out at the beginning of the second cycle, 2 near the beginning and near the end of the third cycle, and so on). This, of course, ensures that the cycle of durations goes out of phase almost immediately with the twelve-tone row.

By all accounts, Nono did not continue writing music this way for very long; indeed, the second movement of *Il canto sospeso* is already atypical for being much more "transparent" to analysis than any of the others. This circumstance suggests a larger point: part of the reason why the dissemination of serial methods diffused so quickly into many individual approaches had to do with the relative lack of ease with which serial procedures could be inferred solely from examination of scores—that is, without benefit of "inside information" as to what those procedures were. Such difficulties were, of course, already an issue even with Webern, whose rows tended not to be thematic in presentation and lent themselves to analytical reassembly from fragmentary motives in at least several potential ways. This was actually regarded as a virtue, indicative of an evolutionary step for the twelve-tone method toward the greater complexity and power that would be associated with serialism. As Henri Pousseur put it: "If in Schoenberg the series is still a solid thematic entity, endowed with sufficient rigidity to function as an *actual* musical figure, . . . if one must always begin by exposing it, in Webern, to the contrary, its function is secret and virtual, it is never anywhere present in a 'best' or, more specifically, 'original' form, it is too general (not in the sense of *too little*, but of *too powerful*) to be expressed, exhausted, by any one of its actualizations."[70] With the introduction of serialization to domains other than pitch, the challenge rose exponentially in level of difficulty; even a composer who did know the workings of some serial procedures might be forgiven for concluding that he might just as well make up his own. Naturally, the cachet of "originality" also provided considerable incentive for adopting such a strategy.

Pousseur, a serial composer of marked originality himself, is actually an excellent example of a system builder whose musical results, even if supplemented by verbal explanation, can on occasion stubbornly withstand an outsider's attempts to retrace the compositional process that led to them. Pousseur gave expression to his high regard for Webern in the *Quintette à la mémoire d'Anton Webern* (1955), in which he used the row from Webern's Saxophone Quartet (Op. 22) as an organizing principle. Not, however, in the sense of simply "borrowing" it: the row remains even more "secret and virtual" in his piece than it was in Webern's (see Example 7.8). Following upon ideas exposed in his analysis of the first of Webern's Bagatelles, Op. 9,[71] Pousseur sets a premium upon chromatic connection in his own piece by filling (conceptually) the intervals of Webern's row with semitones and using the resulting segments of the chromatic scale across a range of eight temporal density distributions, from a quarter note to a double whole note in duration (that is, the chromatic sets are projected onto a temporal grid whose largest division is four measures long in 2/4 time). This, at least, is the gist of Pousseur's published explanation.[72] Actually identifying these segments, however, proves very difficult—even though, owing to rhythmic stratification, each segment appears to be confined to a single

Example 7.8
Henri Pousseur, *Quintette à la mémoire d'Anton Webern*, First Page of Score

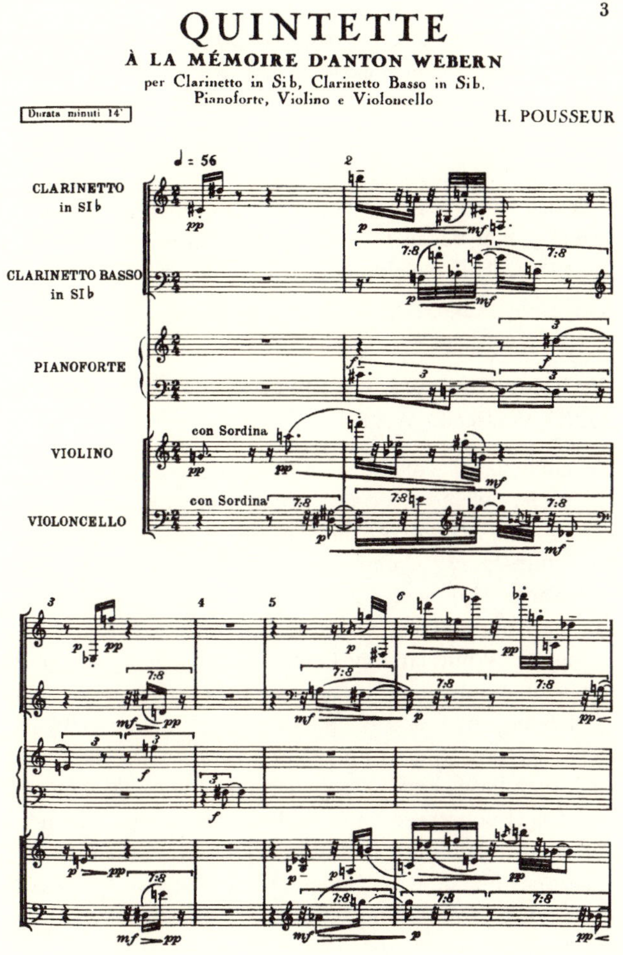

part—for the pitches constituting them may occur in any combination of registers and may also be interspersed with rests; the total duration of a given segment is thus not always clear. Furthermore, it seems that pitches can be omitted from segments, although Pousseur does not explicitly mention this possibility. In short, the completed score gives evidence of a great many compositional decisions having been made supplementing, or even independently of, the basic serial framework. Pousseur does provide some hint of this; speaking of the chromatic filling of Webern's row intervals as "partials," he says:

> The serial succession of these completely included "partials" is left free, but in the course of composition it has to be fixed so as to give, on the one hand, the best "vertical"

superimpositions (particularly those of notes belonging to different polyphonic strata), i.e. the best "harmonic fields," and equally, on the other hand, the best successive forms, i.e. the best "melodic figures" (these depend on various factors, including the mobility and particular technique of the individual instruments). In the same way, the register distribution of the notes of the groups is left free; the resultant harmonic fields are thus the result of an apparently empirical mode of working.[73]

Clearly we have come a long way from the "automatism" of Boulez's *Structure 1a.* But the loss of transparency of procedure with the accretion of so many "empirical" decisions was one of the factors contributing to a certain disaffection from serialism that began to overtake many European composers toward the end of the 1950s. This development will be discussed at length later in this chapter.

DEVELOPMENTS IN THE UNITED STATES AFTER THE SECOND WORLD WAR

Among the contents of volume 3 (1950) of the *Journal of the American Musicological Society* were reviews of two of René Leibowitz's books and the *quatrième cahier* of *Polyphonie*, this last including the first publication of Schoenberg's lecture-essay "Composition with Twelve Tones."[74] The reviewer was Milton Babbitt, who here served notice that the postwar reception of Schoenberg in the United States would be very different from what it was, and would be, in Europe. While chiding Leibowitz for making inappropriate assertions of historical continuity and for engaging in not much more than description of the works of Schoenberg and his pupils, "uncritical empiricism" that "appears to accept any deviation from, or extension of [twelve-tone] principles merely because such cases exist in actual composition," Babbitt made it clear that as far as he was concerned "the twelve-tone system," as he preferred to call it, was different in kind, not simply in degree, from the tonal system: "The tonal motive assumes functional meaning within a context, and becomes, in turn, a vehicle of movement within this context; the twelve-tone set, however, is the instigator of movement, and defines the functional context."[75]

Thus Babbitt took as much exception to the analogies Schoenberg himself made between his twelve-tone transformations and the motivic transformations in Beethoven's Op. 135 as he did to Leibowitz's comparisons of twelve-tone procedures to those of tonal counterpoint. To Babbitt, however important Schoenberg's essay might ultimately prove to be in charting Schoenberg's personal development, "as a statement of the nature of the twelve-tone system it must be adjudged disappointing."[76] The significance of the twelve-tone system went far beyond Schoenberg's ability to explain it. It even went beyond what Schoenberg had shown of its possibilities in his own compositions—not that Babbitt himself found Schoenberg's music inadequate as music, of course. He evinced no discomfort at the qualities members of the European avant-garde were beginning to dislike in Schoenberg, what they heard as dwelling on the (tonal) past, for to Babbitt's mind the twelve-tone system could not, by definition, have anything to do with that past.[77]

Although few people at the time knew anything about it, Babbitt had by 1950 already expended considerable effort at formalizing the twelve-tone system, laying out its compositional assumptions "in a rigorous statement" and "examin[ing] the implications of these assumptions as the basis for a deductive, yet applicational, theory of the system." Babbitt's study, "The Function of Set Structure in the Twelve-Tone System," from which the preceding quotation was taken, was complete by 1946 but not put into public circulation until forty-six years later.[78] Here we already find many (if not most) of the ideas that inform his later, though much sooner published, work: the different types of twelve-tone rows (called by Babbitt, by preference, "sets") and their properties; the conditions under which a set may acquire combinatorial potential, and what degrees of combinatoriality there are; the construction of aggregates; and the definition of a special class of all-interval sets. Here is manifest a level of understanding of the twelve-tone method that not only embraces both Schoenberg's and Webern's practice but could include a great deal more, and that is far beyond the reach of the Europeans at the time. More to the point, perhaps, is that this kind of understanding of the twelve-tone method had not taken root in Europe—as is obvious enough from Babbitt's critique of Leibowitz—and that its absence there would force European composers to find alternative ways of making their music "serial." Also not to be discounted is the impact of Schoenberg's American works, with their semicombinatorial feature, on Babbitt's developing sensibilities in the 1930s and 1940s, an impact that was felt only slightly or not at all in Europe owing to the extreme difficulty or impossibility (depending on where in Europe one was) of obtaining such important scores as the Violin Concerto and the Fourth String Quartet.[79]

The music that Babbitt was writing by the late 1940s already reflected his sophisticated grasp of the twelve-tone method. The first of his *Three Compositions for Piano* (1947), the very first composition he now acknowledges (see Example 7.9), is based on a row built out of one of the all-combinatorial hexachords, 6–8: [0, 2, 3, 4, 5, 7] or (transposed so that the lowest note in this normal order is B♭) B♭-C-D♭-D-E♭-F.[80] This, as is explained both in "The Function of Set Structure in the Twelve-Tone System" and in his earliest publications on the subject,[81] is a first-order all-combinatorial hexachord, meaning that there is exactly one transposition and one each of the other three transformations of that hexachord that will supply the other six notes from the universal twelve-note collection. The complete form of the row (P_0) is stated in measures 1–2 of Example 7.9, in the left hand; an additional feature of this row is its all-interval property, meaning that among the eleven intervals between adjacent pairs of notes in the row there is one each of all intervals within the compass of an octave (excluding, of course, the octave itself), from minor second to major seventh.[82] In the right hand of these same measures, the transposition up a tritone

Example 7.9
Milton Babbitt, *Three Compositions for Piano*, I, Measures 1–12

Three Compositions for Piano

of the same row is to be found. A quick inspection will reveal that its first six notes are precisely the ones not in the first hexachord of the left hand. The contents of measure 1 are thus an aggregate: a collection of all twelve pitch classes, each occurring only once, that comes about as an interaction (usually expressed as a simultaneity) between row forms, but is not in itself a row form. (It follows inexorably from this circumstance that the contents of measure 2 form a second aggregate.)

Also evident on this first page of Babbitt's composition is the serialization of duration, which by this date no European composer had yet attempted. The durational series comprises just four elements, defined at first in terms of number of successive attacks at sixteenth-note intervals without any intervening durations. Thus the left hand of measures 1–2 expresses the series 5, 1, 4, 2, while the right hand (effectively in canon) does the same, but in a different rhythm. The intention here seems to be to produce an analogue to pitch relationships, in which transposition (same interval order at a different pitch level) becomes "same durational order in a different rhythm." This is already, let it be pointed out, quite different from what Boulez would do four years later in *Structure 1a*, where the serial schemes of pitch and duration are deliberately kept as independent from each other as possible while they are nominally "connected" by matching the twelve pitch classes with twelve durations and by running them off the same pair of 12 × 12 matrices.

The reader may wish to inspect measures 3–4 of Babbitt's piece and ascertain that the left- and right-hand parts, devoted to retrograde-inverted (RI) and retrograde (R) transformations, respectively, of the twelve-tone row, are projected (again respectively) by RI and R forms of the durational row.[83] In measure 9 the durational series within the unbroken stream of sixteenth notes is defined by phrasing marks: again the P (prime) form 5, 1, 4, 2 to go with P_0 in pitch classes. Beginning in measure 10 this new definition of duration is combined with series of single durations measured in multiples of sixteenth-note values. Hence the right hand of measures 10–11 reads: 2, 4, 1, 5; 1, 5, 2, 4.

From this analysis, it is clear that the idea of extending the serial concept to domains other than pitch was an interesting and, in a sense, sufficiently natural idea to have occurred to avant-gardists independently on both sides of the Atlantic. As George Perle has pointed out, however, for Americans this kind of structuring had precedents in work done earlier in the twentieth century among the so-called experimentalists. Of particular interest in this connection is the String Quartet (1931) of Ruth Crawford Seeger, which makes use of recognizably serial transformations in the first movement and, especially, in the fourth movement, where aspects of both pitch and duration are serialized.[84]

In the pitch domain, Babbitt soon began to generalize upon the two-dimensional row/aggregate structure he had inherited from Schoenberg. If one could obtain musically rewarding results from an arrangement of simultaneously deployed row forms that formed "columnar" aggregates with each of two pairs of hexachords, why would it not also be possible to invent a row that could be deployed in four simultaneous forms in which each of four successive quartets of trichords would form aggregates, all the while preserving the hexachordal-aggregate feature within each of the two pairs of rows? With rows exhibiting a certain kind of internal (hexachordal and trichordal) structuring—intimately bound up with the all-combinatorial property, of course—this did indeed prove possible, and it led Babbitt along what Andrew Mead has termed the "trichordal pathways" of his first period as a composer (to 1960).[85] It is here, fairly early on in Babbitt's career, that we find ideas gleaned from Webern joining those from Schoenberg. Babbitt was, of course, aware of Webern's practice of forming his rows out of smaller "cells" (often trichords), such that one cell would "generate" the others by way of the transformations R, I (inversion), and RI (as, famously, in the Concerto for Nine Instruments, Op. 24), and also such that the "original" row order was often absorbed into the structure of the piece in a way that made it more difficult to discover than Schoenberg's more thematically oriented rows, but also less crucial, and even less interesting, to discover in order to make sense of the piece musically.

Babbitt's response to Webern was not particularly emulative; he has said of the Concerto for Nine Instruments, for example, that it is "one of my most unfavorite pieces—it's too literal for me." But he did admit that it was "fundamentally suggestive" to him.[86] The constituent trichords of the row in *Composition for Four Instruments* (1948), for example, are revealed in Babbitt's analysis to be based on the same set of transformations of the same trichord type as in Webern's concerto. Moreover, the fact that the relevant segmentation of the opening unaccompanied clarinet line is registrally based reminds one of many of Webern's twelve-tone works with pitch class "frozen" in register. Babbitt took the idea of rows made up of trichordal components a step further in constructing what have come to be called *arrays*, the multidimensional row/aggregate structures alluded to earlier. Sometimes he would shuffle the order of trichords in a way not available through any of the classical transformations (something, actually, that Webern also did in a few of his late works), thereby producing a *derived set*. Eventually, Babbitt's practice expanded further, to the production of *all-partition arrays* (which work through all the possible partitions of the twelve-tone set within pre-fixed limits on size of components of each partition) and, within the past twenty years, to *superarrays*, effectively "arrays of arrays" that generate awesomely large and elaborate contrapuntal networks.[87]

With regard to matters of rhythm and duration, Babbitt did eventually expand the four-term durational rows of *Three Compositions for Piano* into "additive" twelve-term rows. This will inevitably remind the reader of Boulez's practice in *Structure 1a*, but the resemblance is actually quite superficial, for the use of these rows tended to be tied quite closely to pitch structure, and in ways that actually reinforce one's hearing of hexachordal boundaries (as in Babbitt's Second String Quartet). In any event, Babbitt soon became dissatisfied with such strategies and moved on to devise the *time-point* system, an important innovation that originated in his work with the RCA Synthesizer.[88] In this system durations were controlled through application of a modulus, a fixed time span subdivided into twelve units of equal length. The modulus was applied to duration of the pitches in a twelve-tone row by repeating it over and over again as many times as were necessary to spin out the pitches' locations with respect to the modulus. For example, if the P_0 form of a row began C, E♭, E, B♭, D, translated into pitch-class numbers as 0, 3, 4, 10, 2, the corresponding time-point row would place an attack at time-point 0 (beginning of the modulus), another attack three units later, a third only one unit later (since time-point 4 immediately succeeds time-point 3), a fourth six units later, and a fifth four units later, which occurs in the second cycle through the modulus. Thus the intervals of the twelve-tone row become, not individual durations, but actual temporal intervals. This device did not make perfect the correspondence between pitch and time: the problem remained that there was no intrinsic reason to limit durations to twelve in number. Babbitt seems to have realized fairly early on in his work with this system that there was accordingly little reason, in a compositional context, to "track" the two domains exactly with each other, and correspondingly more reason to be content with a looser, analogous relationship. That his approach has resulted in music of great elegance and power that is also utterly distinctive in style is, of course, undeniable.[89]

The postwar impact of serialism in America is measurable not only in the rapidity with which its influence spread among younger composers, but (as in Europe) also in the ways it affected the music of those whose working methods—not to mention compositional philosophies—were already well established by 1945. The best-known manifestation of such influence is the late career of Igor Stravinsky, who by the early 1950s was surely the world's most famous living composer.[90] For any composer already seventy years of age upon first coming into intensive contact with the works of Schoenberg, Berg, and Webern, such a transformation would be remarkable; that it happened to Stravinsky essentially guaranteed that to the twelve-tone corpus would be grafted a major new limb.

Over the past nearly half-century there has been much talk of Stravinsky's "change of life," as he (and Robert Craft) called it, in terms of a "conversion" to an eventually astringent serialism from the familiar, even comfortable neoclassicism by which he had been known since the early 1920s. There has also been a certain amount of innuendo about the timing of this change, as though Stravinsky had deliberately waited until Schoenberg, his great rival, had died (in 1951) so as not to give him the satisfaction of seeing Stravinsky accede to the necessity of composing with twelve tones. But first of all, if indeed this was a conversion, it was hardly of the sudden, religious kind. Even by the time Robert Craft first began to chronicle it, in an article published in 1957, it was far from completed.[91] Second, it seems irrefutable, from Craft's account as well as various statements of Stravinsky, that even at the time when Stravinsky began to sense the need for a change of direction on his part, Schoenberg's music alone would not have made a twelve-tone composer out of him. All of the Schoenberg pieces that Stravinsky truly liked were well in the past, all but one in the atonal period.[92] Otherwise, for Stravinsky there was a great deal not to like in Schoenberg: his texts were "appallingly bad," his expressionism naïve, his heart/brain distinction unconvincing, his late tonal works dull. Pieces like the Violin Concerto (Op. 36) were suffused with the "pathos" of the nineteenth century: "Harmonize the second movement in a purely Brahmsian manner—you have only to move a few notes over a bit—and the theme is happily restored to its true habitat."[93] Rather, Stravinsky's path to twelve-tone composition was clearly marked out by Webern, with whose music in 1952–55, as Craft has said, "no composer can have lived in closer contact."[94] For Stravinsky, the inability to continue after 1951 in the vein of *The Rake's Progress* was one of the two great crises of his life as a composer, severe enough to have forced him to turn down the possibility of setting another libretto by W. H. Auden that, as a sequel to *The Rake*, would have demanded a similar style of music. It seems likely that the onset of this crisis in the year of Schoenberg's death was simply a coincidence.

Exactly what was it about Webern's music that Stravinsky found so compelling? The historical record is curiously opaque on this matter. Even Stravinsky's own words, or Craft's transcriptions of them, reveal relatively little, for Stravinsky in his praise tended to be general, reserving his specificity for negative criticisms. By compensation, in a way, we have the famous "transparency" of Webern's sonorities and textures, his "leanness of utterance" and gesture.[95] It was to these characteristics, so different from anything in Berg or Schoenberg, that Stravinsky evidently felt drawn, these characteristics in which he sensed a new, essentially "contemporary sensibility and style."[96] It could hardly have escaped Stravinsky's notice either that Webern's serial practice was emphatically polyphonic, in ways decidedly reminiscent of music of the Renaissance and even earlier in its incorporation of elaborate contrapuntal devices. Webern, of course, was notably versed in such repertoire, having earned a doctorate in musicology from the University of Vienna for his edition of masses by Heinrich Isaac. Stravinsky, for his part, evinced an "appetite during the early stage [of his adoption of serialism that] extends with as much zeal to the polyphonic masters of the Renaissance as to the twentieth-century serialists." Pieter van den Toorn notes that in Stravinsky's works of this period "the serial presence, twelve-tone or other, is linked to a very traditional Renaissance-like part-writing."[97] Still, Stravinsky kept his distance from Webern in some ways: he found himself "ultimately less interested in the construction of the row, *per se*, than is Webern," and commensurately more interested in the row as a thematic entity, like Schoenberg.[98]

Stravinsky's progress through various manifestations of nondodecaphonic serialism to a full-blown twelve-tone technique has been well charted elsewhere, but a brief (and selective) recapitulation may be useful at this point.[99] (1) The tenor solo in the central Ricercar II of the Cantata (1952) exhibits an eleven-note, six-pitch series in prime, retrograde, inverted, and retrograde-inverted forms, carefully bracketed in their overlapping occurrences by the composer though not labeled as such, eventually occurring in transpositions of P_0 as well as in canon with instruments of the ensemble. (2) The Septet (1953), in its Passacaglia and Gigue movements, is based on a sixteen-note series (using eight pitch classes) combined contrapuntally with itself in different rhythmic patterns, at different transpositional levels, and eventually (in the Passacaglia) in all four serial transformations simultaneously and (in the Gigue) in paired fugues that present the series both inverted and retrograded as well as in original order—sometimes all at once. (3) *Three Songs from William Shakespeare* (1953) and

In memoriam Dylan Thomas (1954), by contrast to the earlier two works (which combined serially and nonserially derived material), are each built entirely out of a nondodecaphonic row (of four and five notes respectively, though with no pitch-class duplications among these) and its three classical transformations. (4) In *Canticum sacrum* (1955) we find Stravinsky's first use of twelve-tone series: one in "Surge, aquilo," another in "Ad tres virtutes hortationes" and "Brevis motus cantilenae." As in his earlier serial usages, these movements reveal a largely contrapuntal ("linear") disposition of the ordered elements, but unlike any previous works, this one does occasionally give evidence of serialism having affected harmonic thinking, as, for instance, at the opening of "Surge, aquilo" (see Example 7.10), where the three tetrachords of the row appear as three actual chords, in the order of the retrograde. *Canticum sacrum* also consolidates the gain in serial rigor represented by the two works preceding it in that all notes in these three inner movements are row derived.

The next work to be completed, *Agon* (1957), bears more of a resemblance to the Cantata and the Septet in its serial practice than to its immediate predecessors, largely because Stravinsky actually began composing it in 1953: serial features do not appear until the sixth of the twelve movements, and from then on (except for the final coda, which is tonal, like the beginning of the work) the series varies in number of elements from six to twelve to concatenations of four-note groups. The first fully twelve-tone work is *Threni* (1958); later, in works from *A Sermon, a Narrative, and a Prayer* on, Stravinsky made use of an adaptation of Krenek's rotated hexachords.[100] What Stravinsky did in these late works was to assemble Krenek's permutations in an array, or, rather, four pairs of 6 × 6 arrays, corresponding to the two hexachords in the prime form of the row and each of its three transformations. For example, the "classical" 12 × 12 row array for *The Flood* (1962) is shown in Figure 7.3a (G♯ = 0). Observe the diagonal of zeroes running from the upper left to the lower right. In the "rotated" array of the first hexachord of the prime form of the row (Figure 7.3b), that diagonal becomes the leftmost column, with all other diagonals parallel to it arranged in order to the right. Thus the second column consists of the (five-element) diagonal immediately to the right of the zeroes, plus the "round-the-corner" element in the far left position (the lower left corner of the 6 × 6 block corresponding to the first prime-form hexachord); the third column takes the second (four-element) diagonal to the right of the zeroes plus the two-element diagonal to the right of the lower-left-corner element; and so on. These new columns (apart from the zeroes), as Babbitt has pointed out, bear an intimate correspondence to the intervallic content of the original hexachord: the second column displays, in order, the intervals between the first and second elements, the second and third, and so on; the third column, the intervals between the first and third, the second and fourth, and so on; and so on.[101] These columns of intervals, then, were interpreted by Stravinsky as harmonies, for which purpose they were ideal, being drawn from the row but not directly dependent on its pitch-class content. This turned out to be one of Stravinsky's

Example 7.10
Igor Stravinsky, *Canticum sacrum*, "Surge, aquilo," First Page

ways of maintaining a distinction between the linear and vertical dimensions, which connected convincingly with his past compositional practice.

Among other older American composers who began to feel the pull of the serial principle after the Second World War, Roger Sessions is surely notable for the gradual transition he underwent, as reflected both in his compositions and in his writings, from the steadfast opposition of his earlier years to an interestingly "personalized" adoption of the twelve-tone method from the early 1950s on. Milton Babbitt, who encountered Sessions as a composition teacher in the late 1930s, remembers him as being "very anti-Schoenberg,"[102] an ori-

Figure 7.3a
Igor Stravinsky, *The Flood*, Row Array

0	11	1	2	6	8	9	7	10	4	3	5
1	0	2	3	7	9	10	8	11	5	4	6
11	10	0	1	5	7	8	6	9	3	2	4
10	9	11	0	4	6	7	5	8	2	1	3
6	5	7	8	0	2	3	1	4	10	9	11
4	3	5	6	10	0	1	11	2	8	7	9
3	2	4	5	9	11	0	10	1	7	6	8
5	4	6	7	11	1	2	0	3	9	8	10
2	1	3	4	8	10	11	9	0	6	5	7
8	7	9	10	2	4	5	3	6	0	11	1
9	8	10	11	3	5	6	4	7	1	0	2
7	6	8	9	1	3	4	2	5	11	10	0

Figure 7.3b
Igor Stravinsky, *The Flood*, Rotated Array for First Hexachord of Prime Form of the Row (after van den Toorn, *The Music of Igor Stravinsky*, 442)

0	11	1	2	6	8
0	2	3	7	9	1
0	1	5	7	11	10
0	4	6	10	9	11
0	2	6	5	7	8
0	4	3	5	6	10

entation that certainly would seem to go with the attitudes expressed in an early essay: "The 'twelve-tone system' has often been decried as a purely cerebral construction; and there is no question that some of its features are extremely dogmatic. It cannot be too much stressed, however, that a system of this kind has no real existence apart from the works which embody it." However, later in the same essay Sessions asserts, "One may reject many of Schoenberg's ideas and modes of procedure while acknowledging not only his historical position as the initiator of even more in contemporary music than is usually accredited to him, but also his work, and that of some of his followers, as in itself an important and fundamentally unassailable element in the music of this time.''[103] Here one detects considerable respect for Schoenberg the artist but none at all for his impulse toward system building. In Sessions's view the twelve-tone method was ''a system which seems to claim more than empirical validity; a system, that is, in which the works seem to be almost of secondary importance in comparison with the theory behind them.''[104]

Sessions, in fact, seemed to reserve his harshest criticism for Schoenberg's apologists rather than for Schoenberg himself—for those, in other words, who translated the inner necessity to which Schoenberg had responded in adopting the twelve-tone method into an outer one, as if it were inevitably the direction in which music had to go. The following passage, from a review of Krenek's *Über neue Musik*, is typical:

> One takes exception . . . not to the fact that the twelve-tone composers are conscious and reflective in their methods, but to the intensely abstract nature of their thought. In a remarkable passage Krenek demands not a ''natural'' (*Naturgegebenen*) but an intellectually determined basis (*geistesbestimmten Voraussetzungen*) for music. This writer's antipathy for the twelve-tone system is expressed precisely in these terms, provided that by ''nature'' is understood not physics but the response of the ear and spirit to the simplest acoustic facts. . . . Such elementary musical phenomena as the fifth, and the measurably qualitative distinction between consonance and dissonance, are psychological as well as physical facts, out of which a whole language has grown, and which even in music based on the twelve-tone system seem often more powerful binding forces (*Relations-momente*) than those inherent in the system itself.[105]

By the mid-1940s there are some signs that this uncompromising stance was softening somewhat. An essay written in 1944 holds out the interesting possibility that Sessions, a composer with more than a passing involvement in pedagogy himself, may have become impressed with Schoenberg's reputation as a teacher: ''For one who has never been his pupil, the striking feature of his teaching is precisely that it is systematic without ever becoming a 'system' in any closed sense; that it is almost fanatically rigorous in its ceaseless striving after mastery of resource; logical and clear in its presentation of materials, but as free as teaching can be from any essential dogmatic bias.''[106] In the meantime, throughout the late 1930s and the 1940s Sessions's own music showed a steady development away from the firmly tonal qualities of his first mature work. By 1952, the year in which he wrote the Sonata for Solo Violin, his first twelve-tone composition, Sessions had arrived at a new understanding of the method, one that was diametrically opposed to that of Babbitt:

> What Schoenberg achieved, . . . with the formulation of the twelve-tone method, was to show his followers a way toward the practical organization of materials. The true significance of the twelve-tone method, and of Schoenberg's immense achievement, cannot possibly be understood if more than this is demanded of it. . . . For it is, precisely, *not* a new harmonic system: it does not seek to contradict or deny, but to make possible the exploitation of new resources.[107]

Thus, for Sessions, the twelve-tone method was a way of supplementing or making more effective a compositional technique that was already well and fully formed; it could not be a world unto itself. It is this coming to terms that probably best explains the wide variety of purposes to which Sessions put the twelve-tone method in his music from then on, ranging from the relatively "strict" application of it in the solo violin sonata and the Six Pieces for Violoncello (1966), and its "thoroughgoing" use in the String Quintet (1958), to pieces like the Fourth Symphony (1958), where the row is "very tenuous" because he "didn't want to depend on [it] for any thematic material," or the Ninth Symphony (1978), where two rows are used, a technique that Sessions does not distinguish in any hard-and-fast way from variations upon single row forms not defined by any of the classical transformations, as in the Sixth and Seventh Symphonies (1966, 1967).[108] In the opera *Montezuma* (1963), by Sessions's account, such derivational procedures often involve reordering trichords (characteristically, a technique he had thought up as early as the 1930s), analogously to hexachordal procedures. "I formulated my ideas about the row, and the kind of liberties you can take. . . . You can take no liberties with one hexachord and use the other one very freely, and so forth. And the greatest liberty of all is just using the twelve tones very freely and shuffling them around."[109]

None of this should be taken to suggest that Sessions used the row in a simplistic or ad hoc fashion, or that he could have gotten essentially the same compositional results without it. Rather, he had assimilated the twelve-tone method in a way that enabled him to internalize the mechanical aspect of using it as far as possible: his remarks to the effect that "I sort of discover the row as I go on" and "I forget the row always afterwards. It's very important when I'm working" are quite characteristic.[110] It is clear, too, that he saw himself as a subscriber, if still a slightly skeptical one, to the Schoenbergian "thematic" philosophy of the row. We understand this partly from his assessment of Webern's music as "the intensive cultivation of one phase of Schoenberg, to whom he always remained essentially and consciously subject," partly also from his ironic, momentary pose, in an interview, as the precompositionally inclined type of composer: "Now here's a good row, what am I going to do with it? Well now, by what criteria is this a good row? I don't think there is any such thing in the abstract. . . . One has to find a row that's good for what one wants. In that sense it's got to come out of some musical impulse."[111] This philosophy, of course, did not rule out for him—any more than it did for Schoenberg—the possibility of constructing a "symmetrical" row, that is, employing a semicombinatorial hexachord, his usual procedure.[112]

Another American whose later music can be even more loosely (and, at that, only partially) construed as twelve-tone is Aaron Copland. Like those of Sessions, Copland's first impressions of the Second Viennese School were negative, but his antipathy, unlike Sessions's, stemmed more from an aesthetic reaction than a compositional-methodological one. Throughout the 1930s and the early 1940s it was the *style* of Schoenberg and his pupils that kept Copland at bay:

"The expressive quality of their music took precedence over their method, which wasn't clearly understood until much later anyway. . . . It never occurred to anybody to disconnect the method from the aesthetic, which seemed to be basically an old Wagnerian one. The later works of Webern hadn't been written. His cool approach was completely unknown." It became clear only after the war, thanks to the example of Boulez and others, that "you could keep the method while throwing away the aesthetic."[113] One can well appreciate how repugnant that aesthetic must have been to a young composer whose sensibilities, to the extent that they responded to European culture at all, were mildly Francophile but strongly anti-German—especially during the 1930s, when a nationalistic spirit took hold of many American composers, Copland among them. That such issues were still alive for Copland even by the end of the 1940s is attested by his review of Leibowitz's *Schoenberg and His School*:

> Nowhere in his book does the author speak of the special world—Vienna at the turn of the century—that so strongly influenced the aesthetic ideals of the music of Schönberg and his school. The declining romanticism of that period, with its tense emotionality and its love of complexities, powerfully influenced the new revolutionary music. Its principal adherents, even today, are those who feel a natural affinity with the language of an exaggerated romanticism.[114]

Nevertheless, even at the same time he was pointing out that "it is one of the ironies of the twelve-tone system that its supporters should be so anxious to prove that they are in the main line of musical tradition" and waxing indignant at the fact that "Leibowitz in particular grovels before tradition in a way that is most unsympathetic to the American mind," the seeds of doubt were already being sown. Elsewhere, he has written: "I must admit that we of the older generation were taken by surprise" at the strength of the twelve-tone method's appeal to younger composers right after the war. By 1950, he himself was "involved" and, in his Piano Quartet, had "first consciously tried my hand at twelve-tone composition."[115]

Again, as for Stravinsky and Sessions, *conversion* is a misleading way to express what happened. From the start, for Copland, the twelve-tone method was an extension of his own tonal language, which was by then well developed. "The attraction of the method for me was that I began to hear chords that I wouldn't have heard otherwise. . . . This was a new way of moving tones about. It freshened up one's technique and one's approach."[116] His first steps in this new direction already show that he conceived of the row not as the "source" of all his musical material, but more as an entity along the lines of a theme. The row of the Piano Quartet's first movement is initially (first subject) only eleven notes in extent—apparently to avoid too great a sense of closure at the outset—and is retrograded to produce a contrasting theme but completed with the twelfth note only at the end of the movement.[117] This sort of approach surfaces again in the Piano Fantasy (1957), where Copland describes the pitch material as consisting initially of "ten different tones of the chromatic scale," with the remaining two notes held in reserve, as it were, for cadential purposes.[118] The subsequent working out, however, owes little to any recognizably Schoenbergian twelve-tone technique and much more to traditional "thematic" development. *Connotations* (1962) for orchestra reveals a much more thoroughgoing use of the row than Copland had attempted in the Piano Fantasy, but the attitude toward serial rigor is much the same (that the row is viewed subjectively may well be signaled by the title): as Peter Evans points out, Copland "can regard a twelve-tone series as simultaneously a generator of precisely determined note relationships and a spur to almost improvisatory fantasy."[119] Interestingly, Copland recognized in his (cautious) embrace of the twelve-tone method the picking up of an older thread of his development, one that may have predisposed him to becoming a serial composer, after a fashion, eventually. In the 1960s he could look back to the Piano Variations (1930) as "the start of my interest in serial writing"—in this case with only seven principal tones, "stay[ing] with them throughout in what I hope is a consistently logical way."[120] One thinks, too, of the *Statements for Orchestra* (1935), in which the theme of the first movement ("Militant"), in its inexorable, angularly chromatic way, quickly (by measure 9) exhausts the stock of twelve tones.

In all, Copland's encounter with the row may be accurately termed a catalyzing experience, one that broke him out of a tonal (or, at least, exclusively tonal) frame of reference but did not much alter many of his fundamental compositional reflexes. For this reason, Copland found it quite possible to continue writing tonal pieces alongside his serial ones late in life, as had Schoenberg, though for Copland it was perhaps less a case of *On revient toujours* and more one of *On n'est jamais parti.*

REACTION AND DISSENT

> I thought there were eighty-eight tones.
> You can quarter them too.
>
> —John Cage

In 1955 Milton Babbitt reported that "the number of twelve-tone composers here [in America], as elsewhere, continues to increase." Five years later, George Perle provided an update: "Twelve-tone composers are now so common, in America and elsewhere, that the label no longer guarantees one recognition as a member of the *avant-garde.*"[121] The rapid and widespread acceptance of the serial idea effectively guaranteed, rather, that signs of dissatisfaction with it would eventually appear. Although the fact that this happened as soon as it did apparently surprised some observers at the time, it should not surprise us now in retrospect. For if serialism was well established by the mid-1950s, so was the indispensability of an avant-garde, in music as in the other arts. Once serialism was no longer a revolutionary idea, other worlds to conquer would have to be found. This part of the Second Viennese School's "reception history" wore from the beginning a different aspect in Europe by comparison to America, but in both places there were basically two sources of reaction and dissent: composers who at one time had been deeply committed to the new twelve-tone method (one could call them, only half-facetiously, apostates); and other composers, in the main younger ones, for whom the tug of serialism had had only the slightest effect, or none at all, on their creative lives.

Among the pupils at the Darmstadt summer school in its earliest years was Hans Werner Henze, then barely out of his teens. In an autobiographical essay Henze recalls Leibowitz as "a marvelous teacher" who "taught me a great deal" about the twelve-tone method, then a topic of burning interest to him and his peers. "We very quickly realized that dodecaphony and serialism were the only viable new techniques: fresh, and able to generate new musical patterns."[122] But at the time there were hardly any scores or recordings available, a problem that persisted for some years. Partly for that reason,

> Renewed or first encounters with the works of the Viennese trinity Schoenberg/Berg/Webern had made a particularly strong impression on me. The freshness and beauty of some of these works had a great impact on us young composers, while others were especially attracted by the possibilities, implicit in these scores, of the total rationalization of musical creation. In the following years it was, indeed, chiefly this aspect that served as a model, and pointed towards the new types of serial creation.[123]

Within half a dozen years of his first summer at Darmstadt, Henze would be sufficiently well known himself as a twelve-tone composer to be asked to contribute to the appendix being compiled by Josef Rufer for his book on twelve-tone composition—the youngest among the thirteen who recounted their experiences there.[124] This rapidity of rise to prominence may not have been exactly common, but it was probably more often witnessed than it would have been under any conditions other than those that prevailed after the war. The premature deaths of Berg and Webern, the emigration of Schoenberg to a distant location, along with many other (especially Jewish) musicians, and the deaths of many others all left European music with very few senior figures of any real authority, those few who remained alive and were not by that time discredited or superannuated. Into this vacuum stepped Messiaen, Leibowitz, Herbert Eimert and not much later came Boulez and Stockhausen, whose extreme youth would otherwise probably have frustrated their ambitions at that point to form a new movement with themselves as its spokesmen.

In retrospect, it is clear, Henze is ambivalent about the effects of the power exerted at the time by these few, young and old:

> We were assured by senior composers that music is abstract, not to be connected with everyday life, and that immeasurable and inalienable values are lodged in it (which is

precisely why the Nazis censored those works which strove to achieve absolute freedom). . . . Everything had to be stylized and made abstract: music regarded as a glass-bead-game, a fossil of life. Discipline was the order of the day. . . . Discipline enabled form to come about; there were rules and parameters for everything.[125]

This led to Darmstadt becoming a kind of nerve center for "the technocratic conception of art, dodecaphony's mechanistic heresy, which became official doctrine there at the beginning of the 1950s, and which for many years dominated radio networks and composers." Henze left Darmstadt's precincts for a while, then returned in 1955 to give a composition class with Boulez and Maderna, by which time "things had become pretty absurd." Seeing how dismissively Boulez treated anything not written "in the style of Webern," Henze realized that "my antipathy was directed not against Webern's music, but against the misuse and misinterpretation of his aesthetic and, indeed, of his technique and its motivation and significance." Disillusioned at what he regarded as distortion of the meaning of music that had in important ways symbolized freedom to him and others, and as well at the replacement of that sense of freedom with a new orthodoxy, Henze began to distance himself from the serial circle. His music soon followed suit, to the point that in 1958, at the premiere of his *Nachtstücke und Arien* at Donaueschingen, "after the first few bars, Boulez, Stockhausen, and also my friend Nono, got up together and left the auditorium, making sure that everyone saw them."[126] In turning away from Darmstadt, Henze had also reconnected his music to "everyday life" and had begun to incorporate unabashed references to popular culture and the romantic "art music" of the past. This kind of stylistic pluralism remained anathema to composers who adhered, more or less, to serial principles, whatever other changes their styles underwent in the years to follow.

Two others, Italians who were at least nominally in the serial camp from the early 1950s onwards, soon made it clear that serialism would be only a relatively brief and passing phase in their development. From his studies with Dallapiccola, Luciano Berio gained a healthy respect for twelve-tone principles, but the "impeccable musical geometries" of Webern and his emulators left him cold, as did his teacher's fondness for canon.[127] Thus even in such early pieces as *Chamber Music* (1953), the row was not only designed to evoke, if fleetingly, tonal associations (though it is hard to hear the first seven pitches of P_0 or I_0 in Example 7.11 and not immediately think "A major") but was also used rather "loosely"—sometimes in fragments, sometimes with notes out of order or missing entirely. In *Cinque variazioni* for piano, of the same year, the variation process is run in reverse (similarly in this respect to the *Variazioni canoniche* of Nono, previously discussed), such that the serial working out often consists of a generalized filling out (or "using up") of the chromatic scale.[128]

The next steps in Berio's development were his meeting Maderna (also in 1953); his involvement with him in getting the first Italian electronic music studio, the Studio di Fonologia Musicale, started in Milan; and his first visit to

Example 7.11
Luciano Berio, *Chamber Music*, Prime and Inverted Forms of Row

Darmstadt in 1954. Berio's first work growing out of that experience was *Nones*, which already showed a desire to generalize the serial principle beyond twelve of everything: the row is a thirteen-note series (Example 7.12a), symmetrical about a central A♭ such that the tritone transposition of P_0 is equivalent to the retrograde of I_0, and there is a subsidiary, derived series (Example 7.12b) obtained by starting with the first and last notes of the original series and working inwards (omitting duplication of the D). On the first page of the score (Example 7.13), the interested reader may trace the principal row unfolding simultaneously with three of its transpositions. The first nine notes of P_0 occur entirely within the harp part. P_8 begins with G in the timpani, moves to the electric guitar (B♭, F♯, E♭, C, B, E), then migrates to timpani (A, measure 6) and flute (A♭, measure 6). P_6 begins with the violins' chord (ordered F, A♭, E), moves to cello (D♭, B♭), then to vibraphone (A), timpani (D), and oboe (G). P_{11} begins with the trombone/tuba B♭, moves to clarinet D♭ and A, then to contrabass F♯, celesta E♭ and D, then to oboe G. Further, instead of constructing durational, dynamic, or mode-of-attack series as such, Berio assigned these domains various numerical values and ensured, in distributing them throughout his score, that for each note the ordinal position in the series plus the value of its other domains would add up to at least nine (in keeping with the title, taken from a poem by W. H. Auden).[129] All of this may seem quite "proper," serially speaking (except for the thirteen-note row), but before long "exceptions" begin to crop up, fragments of both original and derived rows appear in analytically confusing juxtapositions, and so forth. In short, for Berio the trip to Darmstadt resulted in no "baptism in the faith"; his ingrained impatience with strictly observed systems remained intact. "One consequence of this," as David Osmond-Smith points out, "is that the analyst will often find in Berio's scores only hints or remnants of a 'system' which has in effect been consumed in the process of composition."[130]

Berio's critique of serialism, delivered nearly a quarter of a century after his experience with it, hinged on the separation of musical domains and the dangers that it posed. He noted that in some ways (though not in its consequences), it was comparable with "the separation of dramaturgical 'parameters' in Brecht's theatrical work. A sort of *divide et impera* in other words." Such separation worked well enough for analytical purposes, but problems arose "when, inevitably, people began going in the opposite direction, taking unattached pieces, separate 'parameters,' and putting them together under the indifferent and uniform light of abstract proportions, and then waiting for the unveiling of the

Example 7.12
Luciano Berio, *Nones*, Prime and Derived Row Forms

piece (or the non-piece . . .).'' Speaking of his own somewhat half-hearted attempts to impose total organization using a Webernian ''magic square'' in his *Serenata* (1957), Berio described the ''only weakly directional conglomerations that were then filtered by selective rhythmic models . . . and by durational proportions. . . . The filter could be a series of durations, a sequence of notes, of intensities of instrumental colors, etc.; in other words, anything could be symbolically quantified.'' He continued, ''There was a danger in all this of a certain abstractness or excessive interchangeability between acoustic parameters.''[131]

Nevertheless, one may judge that Berio's encounter with serialism was relatively benign, not only because it enabled him to write some pieces that he still acknowledges as worthwhile, but also because, as he turned away to find his own voice, he took certain lessons from serialism that helped him speak more clearly. Even the interchangeability of domains ''contained the seed of something fundamentally important—something that I believe to be 'universal' whose nature continues even now [1980–81] to condition my musical conduct.''[132] In a 1968 interview he spoke of having just finished composing *Sinfonia*, with its long section ''based on the third movement of Mahler's Second Symphony. Mahler's entire harmonic and formal structure is always present, but in a proliferation that distinguishes it from Mahler. This would not have been possible for me to do in this fashion without the experience of serial thought.''[133] In all, this experience made possible ''an objective enlargement of musical means, the chance to control a larger musical terrain.''[134] It was also immensely helpful in coming to grips with the challenges of the electronic medium and its initially bewildering range of possibilities for the creation and transformation of sounds. One could use serialism as a tool to analyze the complexity of these sounds, to select certain aspects of them, and to connect them in ways that avoided preestablished conceptions of (musical) language.[135] This remark serves to point out that in fact the electronic medium must have been very attractive to many serialists for just this reason: it held out the tantalizing possibility of control over all domains of musical sound, enabling the composer to impose the same degree of exactitude upon timbre and dynamics that was already (mostly) available to pitch and rhythm with acoustic instruments. Further, in Europe at any rate, it seems that widespread interest on the part of serialist composers in working in electronic studios had a good deal to do with the rapid diffusion and generalization of the serial principle beyond the twelve-tone row, with effects on both electronic and acoustic music.

Example 7.13
Luciano Berio, *Nones*, First Page of Score

Bruno Maderna's experience with serialism was in many ways akin to that of Berio. Maderna did not study with Dallapiccola, but like his countryman Luigi Nono he had become acquainted with some of that older composer's earlier twelve-tone works, such as the *Sex carmina Alcaei* (1943), and admired them greatly, as a 1949 letter to Dallapiccola attests.[136] Maderna received his first tutelage in the twelve-tone method from Hermann Scherchen, in whose company (along with Nono) he first journeyed to Darmstadt in 1950. Once Berio had caught up with Maderna, and thanks to their collaboration on the Milan studio mentioned earlier, the two of them worked through some of the stages of serialism more or less at the same time (Maderna's "magic-square" piece *Quartetto per archi in due tempi* [1955] was written only a year before Berio's *Serenata*). Like Berio's, Maderna's early twelve-tone works are actually, by dodecaphonic standards, rather freely composed: in the *Tre liriche greche*, for example, a row is plainly evident, but so are many freely derived other parts; there is really no single principle uniting everything.[137] In interviews conducted toward the end of his life, Maderna looked back with some regrets—"I believe that famous serial consistency has been one of the worst diseases"—though also in defense: "[In the early 1950s] it was necessary to be unilateral, even fanatical, because we had to create a new stock of possibilities to have at our disposal." He also made it clear that the twelve-tone method had never taken with him as it had with Dallapiccola:

> Even when I was a member of the earliest dodecaphonic groups . . . I never believed that serialism was the only road open. Personally, I thought that serialism offered musicians more possibilities than the, let's say, "traditional" technique. But I never felt like poor old Leibowitz (a very kind, civilized person, to be sure, well in touch with the world), nor yet like Dallapiccola, enclosed within his rock-crystal.[138]

Other Europeans, only slightly grazed by the impact of serialism, either ignored it entirely or made light of its historical importance. Krzysztof Penderecki belongs in the former category and is typical of his 1930s-born contemporaries: while an acquaintance with the sounds of Boulez's and Nono's scores, on a more or less intuitive level, is evident in such early works as *Emanations, Threnody to the Victims of Hiroshima*, and *Strophes*, there is no discernible recourse to serial technique per se in those pieces.[139] As for Iannis Xenakis, when he was asked in 1974 whether he thought that the music-compositional world was now in a "postserial" period, he answered that even if that were true for those who had at one time written serial music, it made no sense for all the others (who, he implied, were much more numerous) to speak of a postserial period.[140] Xenakis's training in mathematics, engineering, and architecture had undoubtedly made him at least a bit contemptuous of the kind of quantitative manipulation he saw displayed in the pages of *Die Reihe*; he noted that the serial system was "only one particular case" whose possibilities "are very slender when I compare them with those I meet in my own field."[141] As early as 1955, in fact, Xenakis had written on "the crisis of serial music," pointing out that in light of the vast horizons of musical composition opened up by electronic means, the achievements of the Second Viennese School seemed rather narrowly confined, and although Messiaen had helped a great deal by bringing rhythm and duration, previously slighted, to a "place of honor" on a par with that occupied already by pitch, his followers had proved unable to expand the serial idea further, having been brought up short by the linear definition of the series, its limitation to twelveness by the tempered chromatic scale, and its tendency to dissolve into incoherence when used polyphonically.[142]

György Ligeti, finally, is a rather special case. Writing his first works in a kind of post-Bartókian style in Hungary during the postwar years of the Iron Curtain, he yearned to be let in on the secrets of the advanced music that he could barely hear sometimes, through the Communists' jamming, on the late-night programs from Cologne Radio. But when he finally did flee to the West, during the 1956 revolution, he soon discovered that the resources made available by this liberation had come too late, for his own development had already proceeded in quite a different direction. Some of this disappointment, which would soon coalesce into scathing criticism, is evident in the first assignment he undertook for the editors of *Die Reihe*, an analysis of Boulez's *Structure 1a*. Quite clearly appalled at the arbitrary way in which the serialized domains had been arrived at and combined, Ligeti nonetheless plunged gamely into the task of exposition, interspersing commentary in which he tried to explain the workings of this piece in terms of his own emerging compositional preoccupations.[143] One year later, Ligeti made his unhappiness with serialism explicit in "Metamorphoses of Musical Form."[144] This article echoes some of Xenakis's criticisms but goes much further in pointing out that the supposedly desirable equalization of domains in totally organized music was achieved at great cost: the more or less inescapable flattening out of the musical result. Here Ligeti has identified a paradox: the more a composer concentrates on determining the result, the order and relationship of elements, the less can actually be controlled. "For the degree of indeterminacy of the structure increases in proportion to the number of directives that are issued." The piling up of polyphonic layers into dense textures simply makes the ear less sensitive to intervals. In short, "Total, consistent application of the serial principle negates, in the end, serialism itself."[145]

It was Ligeti's observation that "it is no longer primarily the intervals that constitute the structure but relations of density, distribution of registers and various displacements in the building up and breaking down of the vertical complexes,"[146] combined with his developing individual traits as a composer, that led him, as I have written elsewhere, "to a key realization: if the qualities he had noted were in fact the true determinants of aural shape in new music, why not engage them directly, instead of through compositional methods that could not control such qualities, except more or less serendipitously?"[147] Thus emerged a group of composers (never in any sense a "school," however) who worked in textures and densities of sound, defined often in pitch (as opposed to pitch-class) space and greatly dependent upon the articulative powers of duration, timbre, and dynamics.[148] But there was another outcome possible from this crisis too, one that in fact was already taking shape: an acknowledgment that the ends of the avant-garde might be as well, or even better, served by forms that left the realization of a work, whether compositionally or in performance, to a greater or lesser extent governed by "chance" or aleatoric procedures. To give Boulez some credit, he seems to have realized several years earlier that the integral approach to serialism would eventually prove self-defeating. In 1954 he asked: Are we at the verge of the Promised Land, or of Babel? "Webern only organized pitch; we organize rhythm, timbre, dynamics; everything is grist to this monstrous, all-purpose mill, and we had better abandon it quickly if we are not to be condemned to deafness."[149] Of course, Boulez had been one of that mill's principal architects, and for a while it seemed as though everyone wanted to work there. Looking back in 1980, Berio could see what had happened: composers' separation of domains and their attempts to glue them back together, once "organized," to form pieces "helped to institute a certain indifference between material and form, and to suggest that an inert, 'functional' material, devoid of creative necessity, is worth just as much as material enriched by musical experience and intentions. . . . That indifference . . . finally broke down into a total absence of relationship between the conceptual and the physical, between project and result. This produced a sort of 'meta-aleatoricism.' "[150] The embrace of aleatoric music that followed, on however limited a basis, may well have continued to satisfy Stockhausen's very broad requirements for a serial principle (in a piece like his *Klavierstück XI*, after all, the performer still had to make a series of choices), but only in the very remotest of terms could the resulting music be said to have any connection at all with the Second Viennese School.[151]

In the United States, meanwhile, the currents of reaction and dissent flowed in somewhat different channels. Aleatoric music had already made its appearance on the American avant-garde musical scene by the early 1950s, in a form considerably more radical than it would take in Europe in the late 1950s; ironically, it was an ex-pupil of Schoenberg's, John Cage, who was primarily responsible. Cage can be considered one of the apostates, but as such, his trajectory is unique. Like many other American composers in the 1930s, he had started writing a kind of twelve-tone music even before he met Schoenberg, working according to the sketchy information about the method available to him at the time, and continued to do so until 1938 despite the fact that Schoenberg would neither accept him as a composition student (Cage attended his classes in harmony, counterpoint, and analysis at the University of Southern California and the University of California at Los Angeles from 1935 to 1937) nor reveal to Cage the basis of his (Schoenberg's) twelve-tone method. Cage's earliest twelve-tone efforts assign fixed ranges of two octaves to two or three equal parts. Thus each part has a repertory of twenty-five pitches; the principal rule organizing them is that no part may use a pitch over again until the other twenty-four have occurred, but even this rule is not always observed. In any case, there is no series, although it is possible to follow a kind of contrapuntal development based on such devices as a constructed subject and countersubject, the occasional use of retrogradation, and so forth. When Cage started using actual twelve-tone rows in 1935, the row was treated as a source of intervals, deployed in concatenated small groups, and as a regulator of transpositional level for the next group of intervals in the concatenated series of groups.[152] Cage did this, according to his own testimony, in order to avoid making the row too "noticeable" as an entity; his practice is, as might be expected, still very far from Schoenberg's.

Cage's development as a twelve-tone composer was soon to be interrupted, though not yet quite for good, by a burgeoning interest in percussion music instilled in him by his other important teacher, Henry Cowell. This instrumental medium was inviting to Cage and others as a vehicle for, among other things, the exploration of structures free of the influence of Western harmony. (Cage had taken very much to heart Schoenberg's judgment upon him that he had "no feeling for harmony" and had therefore decided that his destiny as a composer lay elsewhere.) During the long period that followed, some of what Cage had learned from his self-styled dodecaphonic techniques can be discerned, though at least as important are the influences of the American experimentalist school, including Cowell and Ruth Crawford Seeger as well as William Russell and Lou Harrison. A much bigger change, of course, was in store for Cage at the end of the 1940s: the turn to aleatoric music, the formation of the New York School, and the forging of links with painters and other artists eventually stole the avant-garde limelight from the twelve-tone composers, who were meanwhile on their way to becoming the "establishment."

However, in the United States there were some daunting obstacles standing in the way of such acquisition of prestige. In New York City, for instance—still at that time the undisputed center of the American musical world—there were two figures of considerable status who offered serious competition to the twelve-tone movement: Edgard Varèse, who was openly hostile; and Stefan Wolpe, scarcely less so even though he had studied with Webern for a time in the early 1930s and had written some pieces (such as the Passacaglia of 1935) in a row-based technique of his own devising. Even stiffer resistance came from the large number of neotonal composers, who ranged from such highly visible and glamorous individuals as Leonard Bernstein, to the aging yet still-vigorous Paul Hindemith, to the countless denizens of music departments in colleges and universities everywhere. There had been no *tabula rasa* in America comparable to that of Europe; while the days when a composer could be fired for teaching twelve-tone music (as Ernst Krenek had been, at Vassar College in 1942) were probably past, the ascension of serialism—focused within institutions of higher learning, since they were the only places where meaningful support of advanced music would ever be found in the United States—would be a very gradual process. George Rochberg offers a useful perspective on these developments:

> The problems of Europe were too unreal perhaps, certainly too distant, to have made a dent in the more naive, sometimes brasher, souls of American writers or composers. The Atlantic, which divided the two continents physically, also kept the cultures apart spiritually. This may or may not explain, in part at least, why the American composers of the early twenties and thirties looked upon Schoenberg as something of an aberration. Certainly they rejected both his approach to composition and its emotional, psychological base and impulses. It was not until the late forties and early fifties, not till after Americans

had been deeply involved physically and emotionally themselves with the European cataclysm of World War II, that a new generation of American musicians allowed themselves to be influenced and affected by Schoenberg.[153]

By the time George Perle could announce that to be a twelve-tone composer was not necessarily to be avant-garde, the 1960s had begun and other developments were on the horizon. The next avant-garde movement turned out to be a new form of neotonality called minimalism, whose principal proponents, educated in twelve-tone composition, had grown up to reject it.

The postwar history of American twelve-tone music did finally produce one genuine apostate. George Rochberg, like other young composers of his day, worked through a succession of models (Hindemith, early Stravinsky, Bartók) before settling on the twelve-tone Schoenberg in the early 1950s (this thanks to his contact with Luigi Dallapiccola). An essay written in 1955, in indignant response to Boulez's assertion ("Schoenberg Is Dead") of Schoenberg's loss of relevance to modern serialism and also in response to the European elevation of Webern, praised Schoenberg at the expense of Webern. "Webern's music leaves his followers no new, unexplored territory. He completely exhausted one side of the spectrum of twelve-tone possibilities. . . . Schoenberg, on the other hand, left much to be done. In discovering the principle of the mirrored hexachord he opened a vast unexplored area in which creative personalities can yet stake their claims."[154] Throughout, Rochberg's emphasis is on the narrowness of Webern, both technically and expressively. "Webern's music creates a tiny, precious world of thin, wired sounds which spark and crackle occasionally, but which, for the most part, possess a feeling of *already completed action*. This develops an overall feeling of 'motionless motion.' " By contrast, "Schoenberg's sense of dramatic, urgent power," where rhythm controls instead of being controlled, reveals "a supreme artist and equally supreme thinker-in-tones who opened a new world, to Webern and to us."[155] Note the close agreement with Copland's assessment and the complete opposition to Stravinsky's.

By 1972, however, Rochberg had drastically changed his tune. His "Reflections on Schoenberg" criticizes Schoenberg's followers as much as it does the composer himself, but it is clear where Rochberg places the ultimate blame. "In his essay, 'Brahms the Progressive,' one senses how intensely devoted [Schoenberg] is to the idea of linear change, how much value he attached to it. He undoubtedly saw his own work as a necessary extension of the past, an inevitable motion in the historical development of music and its materials. So did his followers and his latter-day apologists." But Rochberg himself had ceased to believe in this idea of progress, for he saw the brain usurping the function of the ear in order to bring it about. Rochberg suggested that Schoenberg

became too self-conscious about the historical value of his work and lost touch with the primitive instinct of the musician's ear which had guided him through his early tonal works and even during the works of the atonal period. Once embarked on the twelve-tone works he succumbed to abstraction and rationalization. . . . His twelve-tone music often comes out conflicted—crabbed and strained—where the early tonal and atonal music is large-gestured, without strain in its realization, although intense in projection.[156]

Schoenberg still comes across as a figure to be respected, but also to be feared and, in the end, shunned.

What had happened to Rochberg during the intervening years to precipitate such a crisis of faith? Partly it may have been an inability to make the (Schoenbergian) twelve-tone method convincingly his own; Rochberg's music of the early 1960s reveals newfound enthusiasms for Webern and Varèse. A personal tragedy in 1964 may have had a catalytic effect, but it can hardly be taken to explain everything. Another important piece of the puzzle is supplied by Rochberg's evident failure to establish himself as a significant contributor to the theoretical and analytical literature that had begun to grow up around the twelve-tone method and the music of the Second Viennese School. His book *The Hexachord and Its Relation to the 12-Tone Row* (1955) had been soundly panned by George Perle two years later; and although Rochberg attempted, in a later article, to make amends for the shortcomings Perle and others had identified, it was already obvious only a year after that, with the publication of the second of Babbitt's three ''instantly classic'' twelve-tone articles, that Rochberg's would not stand as the definitive formulation.[157] By 1965, in works such as *Contra mortem et tempus*, Rochberg was beginning to stray from strict ''structural'' definitions of musical coherence by quoting other composers' works as well as his own. In 1972 came a much greater change, in the form of his Third String Quartet, a piece ''framed'' by harshly atonal writing (in its outer movements) that is slowly transformed toward the central movement, a set of variations in A major written in a hypertrophic, heavily romanticized version of Beethoven's late style. In an odd and somewhat ironic way, this development (which was soon continued by three more quartets written entirely in a tonally emulative style) also followed Schoenberg's dictates, for this kind of writing executed on a grand scale the ''model composition'' that Schoenberg had required of all his students. (As he is reputed to have said to his class on at least one occasion, ''There is still plenty of good music to be written in C major.''[158])

Finally, the Second Viennese School's legacy had other, subtler forms of influence too. For some American composers during the 1950s, the opportunity at long last to study scores came as a revelation that, even if it did not precipitate a complete change in style or working methods, clarified certain basic issues and suggested new ways to solve compositional problems. Elliott Carter, for one, had reached his maturity in the early 1950s in a state of fundamental mistrust of the Viennese influence. His activity in the International Society for Contemporary Music had brought him into contact with William Glock, then director of the Dartington summer music school in England. Glock recounts:

Two years after the [1955 ISCM] Baden-Baden Festival I asked him to take a class at Dartington, and to include an analysis of the Schoenberg Variations, Op. 31. He was in his fiftieth year, but it proved to be Elliott's first encounter with twelve-tone music. [Quoting Carter from correspondence:] "I was at first taken aback by your suggestion. Still, the idea has acted as a challenge to me and I must say that I welcome the stimulus to find my way around in the twelve-tone literature, much of which I have enjoyed without bothering to count to a dozen."[159]

Carter's next two works, the Second String Quartet (1959) and the Double Concerto (1961), reveal a working out of pitch materials that takes the twelve tones as a kind of frame of reference without in any way imposing a serial structure, through the complementary relationships of certain specific groups of intervals constituted by fewer than twelve pitches. Although he has never become a "twelve-tone composer," Carter's experience with Schoenberg's Variations did help open up a new and astonishingly fertile field for exploration for him—an exploration that even now, forty years later, is still not over.[160]

THE SECOND VIENNESE SCHOOL AND THE MODERN RISE OF MUSIC THEORY

Ever since the dawn of modernism in the early twentieth century, it has been characteristic of every new artistic movement to begin generating quantities of verbal commentary soon after its inception. Even Schoenberg, however close-mouthed he remained himself, could not keep his close associates from writing voluminously about the twelve-tone method. In turn, the efforts of Erwin Stein and others in this respect were far outstripped after the Second World War, with the rapid proliferation of serialism on two continents.

In Europe most of the writing that appeared was either by composers about their own methods, aesthetics, and philosophies or by others who tended to focus on the music of specific composers. Several influential books published during the decade after 1945 were of the latter variety: the two volumes by Leibowitz, previously discussed, came first, followed in short order by those of Herbert Eimert (1950) and Hanns Jelinek and Josef Rufer (both 1952).[161] All except Eimert concentrate on Schoenberg, with some side excursions to Webern and Berg—or, in Jelinek's case, to his own music. Eimert, by contrast, opts for a more "theoretical" presentation with relatively few examples from the literature. Of some historical interest are his comments on all-interval rows and the circle-of-fifths transformation, the latter discussed here apparently for the first time in print and of considerable importance to subsequent developments in twelve-tone technique.[162] Later publications, especially those appearing in the periodical *Die Reihe* (1955–62), follow the same pattern, but with the significant difference that Schoenberg now falls into comparative neglect as Webern's status rises in inverse proportion (the second issue of *Die Reihe* is devoted entirely to him). Here the writing, even when it is not concerned with the technical intricacies of composing in the first, primitive electronic music studios, tends to reflect an interest in quantifying almost every aspect of musical production and is abundantly supplemented with charts and graphs of various kinds.

The language often verges on the impenetrable, cluttered as it is with terminology borrowed from mathematics, acoustics, and linguistics, sometimes assigned new meanings in the transfer. (Stockhausen was a prime offender in this respect.) But for all the apparent recourse to abstraction, very little of this work was directed toward genuinely theoretical aims, at least in the general sense. Intricate systems were often devised to compose or analyze a single work, to be dismantled thereafter in preparation for the next such task.

In the United States after the war, writing about the music of the Second Viennese School and its heirs got off to a slower start and eventually took on a much different character. Aside from Krenek's short manual on the twelve-tone technique (1940), which with admirable concision covered all the basic "facts" of the method as it was then understood, with writing exercises based on all four transformations of the series, no book about twelve-tone composition was published there before 1945.[163] The demise of *Modern Music* in 1946 meant that until *Perspectives of New Music* was launched in 1962, there was no American journal during the postwar years devoted exclusively or principally to the music of the twentieth century; before *Perspectives*, one made do with *The Score* and *Tempo* in England, and with sporadic coverage in other British and American periodicals. But already by 1960, with Babbitt's first two articles on twelve-tone theory, Rochberg's book and article on the properties of hexachords, and Perle's various contributions (especially in *The Score*) to discussion of twelve-tone issues, a distinctive American critical profile appeared to be taking shape. By contrast to the Europeans, Americans remained interested mainly in twelve-tone matters specifically. To the extent that their work was analytical at all, it tended to deal mainly with Schoenberg, secondarily with Webern—Berg ran a distant third—and hardly at all with the author/composer's own music. But its main focus resided elsewhere: Babbitt dealt extensively with the property of combinatoriality and the various ways in which and intensities with which it could be manifested; with the property of invariance between the various transformations of the row and its implications for composition; and with isomorphisms between pitch and order—in short, with the very structure of the twelve-tone system itself, which here came under far more intense scrutiny than it had ever received before.

This sort of study had practically no appeal for the Europeans, for whom twelve-tone music, in the "strict" sense, had been a far more temporary phase. But their at best only thinly veiled contempt for "mere twelve-tone music," expressed on many a page of *Die Reihe*, had a response from the Americans in 1962, when in the very first issue of *Perspectives of New Music* appeared a review by John Backus (entitled, with pointed irony, "A Scientific Evaluation") of the first four issues of *Die Reihe*, by then issued in English translation. With an evident mixture of glee and distaste, Backus enumerated many of the elementary errors in quantitative reasoning and in the use of scientific and mathematical terminology, reserving his sharpest barbs for Stockhausen's article in No. 3, ". . . how time passes . . ." The signal that the American approach would be on a different tack altogether could not have been clearer.[164]

Babbitt's pathbreaking troika of articles, completed with a 1961 appearance in the *Journal of Music Theory*,[165] brought in their wake a host of others by an ever-increasing number of authors; the literature of twelve-tone theory and analysis in English is now vast and is still growing. Perle, meanwhile, remained a "twelve-tone composer" in a very special and individual sense; his compositional methods and scholarly interests, from a very early stage, engaged in only the most tangential fashion the "classical" row-based techniques of Schoenberg and Webern, upon which most of the literature alluded to earlier was founded. Perle's take on twelve-tone structure bore a much stronger relation to that of Berg; thus it was that his articles on *Lulu* started appearing during the 1950s, eventually to be synthesized into a book on that opera, as were, more recently, other writings of his on the Lyric Suite.[166]

Though the body of writing that began to accumulate on twelve-tone theory was not explicitly analytical in aim, in a sense it could not help but be implicitly "about" the fixed repertoire of pieces that had been written by Schoenberg, Webern, and Berg. This circumstances seems to have acted eventually as a stimulus to interest in their earlier, atonal compositions—at first referred to, significantly, as "preserial," that is, imperfect creations symptomatic of the difficulties that had led to Schoenberg's creative paralysis for some years before he arrived at the "solution" represented by the twelve-tone method. Thus his works of the years 1908–23, along with those of his pupils about the same time, had been consigned to a sort of limbo, where they received the occasional curious glance but no real attention. Most musicians apparently did not think them worth the trouble, in what often seemed their enigmatic brevity, gnarled or knotty textures, and highly concentrated expressionism—the last in particular decidedly not in favor during the war years and immediately afterwards, when this quality carried associations with the German hysteria that had led to the rise of Hitler. It took the better part of two decades for these associations to wear off, but when they finally did, in the early 1960s, it became clear that the standards set by Babbitt's work in twelve-tone theory would shape in significant ways the approach to be taken to the atonal repertoire.

Two very different ideas as to the most fruitful approach surfaced around the same time. One, in 1963, came in Perle's *Serial Composition and Atonality*, which at least recognized that the atonal works of Schoenberg, Berg, and Webern were worthy of study. Discussion of them, however, was confined to a chapter of 27 pages (out of the total of 150 in the book) entitled " 'Free' Atonality." Its first sentence has remained unchanged through the six editions of this book to date: "The 'free' atonality that preceded dodecaphony precludes by definition the possibility of a statement of self-consistent, generally applicable compositional procedures."[167] By this statement, as one subsequently learns, Perle does not mean that any individual atonal work, as an artistic product, is necessarily inferior to the later, twelve-tone works. But his chosen mode of presentation does suggest that Schoenberg and his pupils were at the time groping toward a goal that could be glimpsed only dimly, if at all, and, furthermore, that reaching that goal was absolutely essential to their future as composers. Despite the considerable sensitivity and insight displayed in his analyses, Perle does judge the atonal repertoire, as a whole, inferior to what followed, precisely because no twelve-tone principle, or anything analogous in structural power, can be induced from it.

A little later, in the second issue of *Perspectives of New Music*, there appeared an article by Allen Forte on the atonal Piano Pieces, Op. 19, of Schoenberg.[168] Forte was not only not known as a twelve-tone or serial composer; he was not a composer at all, which, as it turned out in his case, meant that he brought to the atonal repertoire the same level of theoretical, analytical, and general musical interest and the same spirit of inquiry that he had previously brought to other subjects, such as tonal music and other (non-Viennese) twentieth-century music. Forte, as was evident from the beginning of his work on atonal music, had been mightily impressed with Babbitt's twelve-tone theory and aspired to formulate something of equal rigor for a repertoire that at the time had been much neglected and maligned. He also found highly suggestive for his own work two compact articles from early issues of the *Journal of Music Theory* by David Lewin, a composer and theorist possessing considerable background in mathematics. These articles deal with ''collections of notes'' for the first time as what would later be called unordered pitch-class sets, with different emphases from those that would eventually be adopted by Forte. Although Lewin's ''interval function'' was not incorporated under its general definition into Forte's work, the ideas of interval relations between a collection and itself, and between a collection and its complement, were so incorporated and turned out to be very important indeed.[169]

The approach taken in Forte's first ''set-theoretic'' article is, as the title suggests, highly contextual and is also highly tentative in its assertions and conclusions. Yet the scope of the author's ambitions already foretells the shape of things to come, with the adaptation of (mathematical) set terminology to define groups of notes bearing specific relationships to a single referential dyad (G–B) and to show the systematic nature of inclusion relations between these groups. Analyses of this sort were important first steps for Forte toward a formal theory, but it was largely to get away from the single-piece context and to attempt a generalization of the kind of ''cellular'' formations and relations that Perle had written about in his book that led to Forte's first essay on the set-complex, published in 1964.[170] Here, the set—always a group of specific pitch classes in the Op. 19 analysis—was generalized into a *set class* (although this term was not yet employed), under which all possible transpositions and inversions of a given set were considered equivalent. This of course bears a distinct analogy to the transposition and inversion of twelve-tone rows and was in fact modeled on twelve-tone theory in this regard, except that retrogradation and other matters of order did not arise in set-complex theory, since by definition the *pitch-class set*, as it would henceforth be called, was unordered. Over the next decade the theory was ''tested'' in analytical application, and further refinements were made toward a definitive version, published in 1973 as *The Structure of Atonal Music*, a book that remains a standard reference in the field of music theory.[171]

Forte's work on pitch-class sets and their relations, both abstractly considered and in actual pieces, represented a confluence of two distinct strands of twentieth-century music-theoretical thought. One of these strands was twelve-tone theory, as previously discussed. The other had a much longer history, stemming as it did from turn-of-the-century efforts to categorize the vast and (at the time) bewildering variety of note combinations, especially harmonies that had begun to arise in new music in seeming defiance of the old principles of tonal functionality. (One of the earliest contributors to these efforts, in fact, was Schoenberg himself in his *Harmonielehre* of 1911.) Many attempts were made from then on to account for "all possible chords" in the chromatic universe, with varying degrees of success.[172] By 1960 the most recent such accounting, and the one that would bear the closest resemblance to Forte's own list of set classes (largely because, like Forte, the author had adopted the principle of inversional equivalence), was Howard Hanson's in his *Harmonic Materials of Modern Music*.[173] This book, however, showed little inclination on the part of its author to venture much beyond mere taxonomy. From the musical illustrations supplied from a stylistically diverse variety of sources in the literature, it could be seen that Hanson regarded his "harmonies" as both horizontal and vertical constructs (as, of course, rows and segments thereof were regarded in twelve-tone theory), but apart from that he gave no indication as to how they might be compositionally exploited. Certainly there was no hint of any necessary connection to the more advanced tendencies of twentieth-century composition. Quite the contrary: Hanson's distinct antipathy toward the atonal and twelve-tone repertoire probably alienated many potentially sympathetic readers.

Forte's most important contribution, then, was twofold. First, he provided a sound theoretical footing in his adaptation of set theory, not simply for the enumeration of chord or harmony types, but for their interrelation by way of inclusion, degree of similarity of interval content, and complementation literally or abstractly expressed. Second, and equally important, he showed that this conceptualization could be concretized in its application to a specific analytical problem, the music of the Second Viennese School of the fifteen years or so preceding the dodecaphonic period. In fact, several of the most interesting features of Forte's theory seem to have been arrived at by a process of extrapolation backwards in time from the relatively well understood phenomena of twelve-tone music. It is hard to explain otherwise the appearance of inversional equivalence, invariance, and complementation in pitch-class set theory, and how they could have borne such abundant fruit in their transplantation. Finally, really only as a kind of sidelight in *The Structure of Atonal Music*, Forte provides a few brief analytical examples from music by composers other than the Viennese as added food for thought. Other analysts, following Forte's lead and making use to a greater or lesser extent of his methods, have found, in these examples from Stravinsky, Ives, Ruggles, Bartók, Scriabin, and Busoni, much to chew on. Thus has this part of the legacy of the Second Viennese School continued to prove nourishing, sometimes in unexpected ways.

In closing this section, it would be well to take note of the other method Schoenberg has left us, the one he did talk about a great deal to his students in the context of tonal composition and analysis: the general principle of the *Grundgestalt*, or basic shape, of which the twelve-tone method was in a sense a specific outgrowth, and from which its "necessity" derived.[174] Schoenberg did not publish prolifically on this idea of musical inception and development, even as it pertained to tonal music, although his pedagogical works, such as *Fundamentals of Musical Composition*, and his late essay "Brahms the Progressive" contain some useful exposition.[175] Perhaps just because of its vast generality of significance to musical coherence, the *Grundgestalt* has evidently proved a difficult platform upon which to build a theoretical or analytical apparatus; but since Schoenberg's death a few of his former pupils, notably Josef Rufer and the American Patricia Carpenter, have succeeded in keeping the idea in circulation. With the recent publication, in a bilingual edition coprepared by Carpenter, of Schoenberg's treatise on the subject of the musical idea, we may have an actual revival of Schoenberg's contribution to tonal theory and analysis to look forward to.[176]

THE SECOND VIENNESE SCHOOL TODAY: AN ASSESSMENT

To the question that Ernst Krenek posed in the title of an article nearly half a century ago—"Is the Twelve-Tone Technique on the Decline?"—we can now answer that, strictly speaking, as a living compositional practice it has indeed declined, more or less to the verge of extinction.[177] It is safe to say that hardly any young musician these days with a desire to compose desires to do it as a serialist; the twelve-tone method, once nearly universally taught, is now on the required curriculum for composition students mainly, if at all, for the sake of its historical interest. Never, even in its heyday, wildly popular with performers, audiences, or newspaper journalists (a fate it shares, of course, with much other serious music written in the twentieth century), twelve-tone music has had only a slight long-term impact on the concert scene; now, with the exception of an occasional late work by Stravinsky or the Berg Violin Concerto, it is conspicuous in its absence from programs everywhere. Even in America one could probably count the active composers who still consider themselves twelve-tone or serial in their methods on the fingers of one hand; in Europe, that number may well have reached zero by now.

Yet as the twelve-tone method and its associated repertoire dwindle to invisibility, one must recognize that in another and very real sense, the Second Viennese School and all of its music are everywhere, for they are absolutely central to the Western musical experience of the twentieth century. Schoenberg, Berg, and Webern grew up in the waning years of the tonal period; their native nineteenth-century sensibilities also provided the impetus to step beyond them. Their first radical compositions were spawned in the hothouse atmosphere of early modernism, out of the belief that the old ways were exhausted and that new ones had to be found if the arts were to survive. This crisis, which gave us atonal music, was succeeded by another in some ways even more severe: Schoenberg's years of silence—a terrible experience for Schoenberg at the time, no doubt, but in the long run highly beneficial to his influence, for such artistic crises followed by prodigious spates of activity were entirely in keeping with the modernist image of perpetually renewed revolution manifested as a spasmodic series of upheavals. The musical world could not help but be fascinated as soon as word got out about the twelve-tone method, and no sooner had this begun to happen than its musical products were banned in the countries of their origin and their originators were silenced or forced into exile, a turn of events that only increased the fascination all the more. During the 1930s it seemed that there was no middle ground when it came to the twelve-tone method: one either hated or loved the idea of it. What remains amazing, in retrospect, is that so many composers did try to discover, or rediscover, the twelve-tone method on their own. It is a circumstance that bespeaks a certain desperate longing for progressive musical activity, especially in the United States, where the native experimentalist movement had begun to peter out and an extremely conservative neoclassicism was taking its place.

Once the war was over, and the music of Schoenberg, Berg, and Webern became readily available, it was probably inevitable that, as modernism's second wave swept the musical world, the twelve-tone method would rapidly begin to seem old hat. Yet it was precisely at this time that just what the legacy of the Second Viennese School would be began to come into focus. It is misleading today to take the measure of that legacy in terms of the number of composers who are still writing "twelve-tone music," or in the number of their students who are following in their footsteps—or even in terms of the number of certifiably twelve-tone works that are played by major symphony orchestras throughout the world. For while the twelve-tone method has certainly not "replaced" common-practice tonality as the universally shared musical ground, it has given many composers, faced with the frightening abyss of sheer intuition in an era of utter fragmentation of compositional practice, some sort of toehold in the conscious acquisition of technique—a standard, in other words, against which to assess one's own efforts, for better or for worse, and also to assess one's own originality.

On the American scene, for example, it seems that among truly well known living composers born before, say, 1940, only Milton Babbitt and Charles Wuorinen these days are willing to admit that they are still writing twelve-tone or serial music; everyone else either never has or no longer does, and the list is long and diverse: Elliott Carter, Mario Davidovsky, David Del Tredici, Donald Martino, George Perle, Ralph Shapey, and Ellen Taaffe Zwilich, among many others—not to mention the likes of Philip Glass and Steve Reich.[178] Yet not one of these individuals, including the last two named, can claim not to have been touched in some way by the Second Viennese School; no one can claim to have learned nothing from the experience.

We have already read Berio's testimony about serialism and its importance to him. Here is what Ligeti, in a 1971 "interview with himself," said he had learned:

> There are aspects of serial thinking that I have felt to be promising for the development of my own working methods, above all, the principle of selection and systemization of elements and procedures, as well as the principle of consistency: postulates, once decided upon, should be carried through logically. . . . I did find it feasible—while rejecting a uniform treatment of *all* postulates—to build a compositional structure consisting of a heterogeneous repertory of elements. . . . All that was necessary was to ensure that elements and procedures, once tested and fixed, would then be applied completely and consistently in the area in which their viability had been proved. In this way, my compositional working method could be regarded in a very general sense as serial, though not a single series had been employed.[179]

In other words, as the serial influence has become diffused, no longer strictly associated with a specific repertory of pieces, so also has it been generalized, almost into a philosophy of compositional process. Consequently, it is not really such a stretch to trace this influence down to the present day. Within the past few years one of New York's most radical and iconoclastic "downtown" composers, John Zorn, has said in an interview, while discussing his recent projects: "There's not one moment on the *Cobra* record, *Archery*, my Kurt Weill tribute, my Monk tribute, or my *Spillane* piece that I can't justify in terms of why it belongs there and why, if you took it out, the whole piece would fall apart. I mean, that was my uptight twelve-tone upbringing, where everything had to have its place. And that transferred itself even into my free improvisations. Everything has to have a reason for being there."[180] It would be difficult to imagine anything further from the sensibilities of Schoenberg than the startling, disorienting jump-cut juxtapositions and wild improvisations of Zorn's music, yet here is the Second Viennese influence, in the last decade of the twentieth century, still, in a strange way, making itself felt.

NOTES

1. Arnold Schoenberg, "La composition à douze sons," trans. René Leibowitz, *Polyphonie: Revue musicale trimestrielle* 4 (1949): 7–31. This essay appeared for the first time in English as "Composition with Twelve Tones," in Arnold Schoenberg, *Style and Idea*, trans. Dika Newlin (New York: Philosophical Library, 1950), 102–43.

2. Arnold Schoenberg, " 'Schoenberg's Tone-Rows' " (1936), in *Style and Idea*, ed. Leonard Stein, trans. Leo Black (London: Faber & Faber, 1975), 213–14.

3. Erwin Stein, "Neue Formprincipien," *Musikblätter des Anbruch* 6 (1924), special issue, *Arnold Schönberg zum fünfzigsten Geburtstag*, 286–303; trans. Hans Keller

as ''New Formal Principles,'' in Stein, *Orpheus in New Guises* (London: Rockliff, 1953), 57–77.

4. See, in particular, the very detailed recollections of Dika Newlin in her book *Schoenberg Remembered* (New York: Pendragon, 1980), passim.

5. Erwin Stein, ''Schoenberg's New Structural Form,'' *Modern Music* 7, no. 4 (1930): 3–10; Adolph Weiss, ''The Lyceum of Schoenberg,'' *Modern Music* 9, no. 3 (1932): 99–107. Also see George Perle, ''Atonality and the Twelve-Note System in the United States,'' *Score* 28 (1960): 51–66.

6. Ernst Krenek, *Über neue Musik* (1937), trans. Barthold Fles as *Music Here and Now* (New York: Norton, 1939); Richard S. Hill, ''Schoenberg's Tone-Rows and the Tonal System of the Future,'' *Musical Quarterly* 22 (1936): 14–37.

7. Krenek, *Music Here and Now*, 176–77.

8. Ibid., 168.

9. Stein, ''New Formal Principles,'' 58–59.

10. Stein's article treats the nondodecaphonic serial aspects of Schoenberg's Opp. 23 and 24, as well as the fully twelve-tone series in Op. 23, no. 5, Op. 24, no. 4, and all of Op. 25.

11. Stein, ''New Formal Principles,'' 62, 65.

12. Krenek, *Music Here and Now*, 176, 175.

13. Perle, ''Atonality and the Twelve-Note System in the United States,'' 60n.

14. Wallingford Riegger, ''Adolph Weiss and Colin McPhee,'' in *American Composers on American Music: A Symposium*, ed. Henry Cowell (1933; reprint ed., New York: Frederick Ungar, 1962), 36–42. See also Stephen Spackman, *Wallingford Riegger: Two Essays in Musical Biography*, I.S.A.M. Monographs no. 17 (Brooklyn: Institute for Studies in American Music, 1982), 38. Although some of his later works employ ''strictly'' dodecaphonic rows, Riegger's compositional technique never came much to resemble the twelve-tone practice of the Viennese. See Richard Goldman, ''The Music of Wallingford Riegger,''*Musical Quarterly* 36 (1950): 39–61.

15. Peter Evans, ''Compromises with Serialism,'' *Proceedings of the Royal Musical Association* 88 (1961–62): 6.

16. This example is taken from Elliott Carter, ''Walter Piston,'' *Musical Quarterly* 32 (1946): 354–75, reprinted in *Elliott Carter: Collected Essays and Lectures, 1937–1995*, ed. Jonathan W. Bernard (Rochester: University of Rochester Press, 1997), 174. The row labels are Carter's annotations.

17. Hill, ''Schoenberg's Tone-Rows,'' 25–26.

18. Ibid., 31.

19. See Martha Hyde, *Schoenberg's Twelve-Tone Harmony: The Suite Op. 29 and the Compositional Sketches* (Ann Arbor: UMI Research Press, 1982), Chapter 1 (1–23), and in particular n. 50 (153–54). That Hill's article represented a significant step both forward and backward in musicians' understanding of the twelve-tone method is clear enough from the fact that it was this article that impelled Schoenberg to write (though not publish) the rueful response quoted from earlier (see note 2).

20. Krenek, *Music Here and Now*, 189.

21. Ernst Krenek, ''New Developments of the Twelve-Tone Technique,'' *Music Review* 4 (1943): 81–97. As I have remarked elsewhere, Krenek's ideas represented a significant step in the realization of the *collectional*, or setlike, implications of the row. See Jonathan W. Bernard, ''Chord, Collection, and Set in Twentieth-Century Theory,'' in

Music Theory in Concept and Practice, ed. J. M. Baker, D. W. Beach, and J. W. Bernard (Rochester: University of Rochester Press, 1997), 11–51 (especially 41–43).

22. Krenek, ''New Developments of the Twelve-Tone Technique,'' 87–89. See also Robert Erickson, ''Krenek's Later Music (1930–1947),'' *Music Review* 9 (1948): 29–44.

23. George Perle, *Perle on Perle: The Composer Recalls His Life in Music in an Interview by Dennis Miller* (Boston: League/ISCM Publications, [1987]), 9. This excerpt from the interview is also quoted in Perle, *The Listening Composer* (Berkeley and Los Angeles: University of California Press, 1990), 133.

24. Perle, *Perle on Perle*, 10.

25. George Perle, ''Evolution of the Tone-Row: The Twelve-Tone Modal System,'' *Music Review* 2 (1941): 273–87. Perle's later, more comprehensive system is exposed in his book *Twelve-Tone Tonality* (Berkeley and Los Angeles: University of California Press, 1977). A brief and highly readable summary of twelve-tone tonality can be found in Perle, ''Symmetry, the Twelve-Tone Scale, and Tonality,'' *Contemporary Music Review* 6, pt. 2 (1992): 81–96.

26. The following synopsis draws mostly on Peter Heyworth, ''The First Fifty Years,'' in *Pierre Boulez: A Symposium*, ed. William Glock (London: Eulenberg, 1986), 3–39; and Dominique Jameux, *Pierre Boulez*, trans. Susan Bradshaw (Cambridge, MA: Harvard University Press, 1991), especially 9–19.

27. Pierre Boulez, *Conversations with Célestin Deliège* (London: Eulenberg, 1976), 13.

28. Olivier Messiaen, *Technique de mon langage musical*, 2 vols. (1944), trans. John Satterfield as *The Technique of My Musical Language* (Paris: Leduc, 1956).

29. Boulez, *Conversations with Célestin Deliège*, 14.

30. Pierre Boulez, ''Stravinsky Remains,'' in *Stocktakings from an Apprenticeship*, trans. Stephen Walsh (Oxford: Oxford University Press, 1991), 55–110. This title is the natural complement of (and consequent to) a much shorter essay immediately predating this one, ''Schoenberg Is Dead.''

31. Olivier Messiaen, in Antoine Goléa, *Rencontres avec Olivier Messiaen* (Paris: Julliard, 1960), 247 (my translation).

32. Claude Samuel, *Entretiens avec Olivier Messiaen* (1967), trans. Felix Aprahamian as *Conversations with Olivier Messiaen* (London: Stainer & Bell, 1976), 116, 25.

33. Heyworth, ''First Fifty Years,'' 10–11.

34. René Leibowitz, *Schoenberg et son école* (1947), trans. Dika Newlin as *Schoenberg and His School* (New York: Da Capo, 1975); Leibowitz, *Introduction à la musique de douze sons* (Paris: L'Arche, 1949).

35. Boulez, ''The Threshold,'' in *Die Reihe*, no. 2 (*Anton Webern*), English ed. (Bryn Mawr, PA: Theodore Presser, 1958), 40–44.

36. See Gerald Bennett, ''The Early Works,'' in *Pierre Boulez: A Symposium*, 41–84.

37. Boulez, *Conversations with Célestin Deliège*, 14.

38. For further information on Messiaen's experimental period and developments thereafter, see Robert Sherlaw Johnson, *Messiaen*, new ed. (Berkeley and Los Angeles: University of California Press, 1989); Paul Griffiths, *Olivier Messiaen and the Music of Time* (Ithaca, NY: Cornell University Press, 1985).

39. One suspects that these two composers would have been forgotten entirely had not an admirable article by Richard Toop asserted their status as the ''missing link'' between Messiaen and his two now much more famous pupils. See ''Messiaen / Goey-

vaerts, Fano / Stockhausen, Boulez,'' *Perspectives of New Music* 13, no. 1 (Fall–Winter 1974): 141–69.

40. Boulez, ''Possibly . . .'' (1952), in *Stocktakings from an Apprenticeship*, 113.

41. Bennett, ''Early Works,'' 57–62.

42. Bennett, ''Early Works,'' 77–81; Boulez, ''Proposals,'' in *Stocktakings from an Apprenticeship*, 47–54.

43. *Structure 1a* was eventually joined (1952) by *1b* and *1c* to constitute a complete Book 1. (Book 2 would follow some ten years later.) *Polyphonie X* was written, or at least finished, between *Structure 1a* and the rest of Book 1. See Boulez, *Conversations with Célestin Deliège*, 58.

44. See Boulez, ''The System Exposed,'' in *Orientations*, trans. Martin Cooper, ed. Jean-Jacques Nattiez (Cambridge, MA: Harvard University Press, 1986), 135; also in its original form, as letters to John Cage (30 December 1950 and August 1951), in *The Boulez-Cage Correspondence*, ed. Jean-Jacques Nattiez (Cambridge: Cambridge University Press, 1993), 80–90, 98–103. Further information on the rhythm appears in ''Possibly . . . ,'' especially 121–26.

45. The durational matrices are essentially the pitch matrices turned upside down and backwards, with order numbers (of the pitches) interpreted as durations. The other two domains are derived from diagonals of the pitch matrices, with fewer available series and only ten distinct elements in each. Thus, in practice, Boulez does not make use of a full twelve dynamic levels or modes of attack in *Structure 1a*. See György Ligeti's comprehensive analysis, ''Pierre Boulez: Decision and Automatism in *Structure 1a*,'' in *Die Reihe*, no. 4 (*Young Composers*), English ed. (Bryn Mawr, PA: Theodore Presser, 1960), 36–62.

46. Boulez, *Conversations with Célestin Deliège*, 55.

47. See ''From the Domaine Musical to IRCAM: Pierre Boulez in Conversation with Pierre-Michel Menger,'' trans. Jonathan W. Bernard, *Perspectives of New Music* 28, no. 1 (1990): 10.

48. Boulez was already thinking about pitch-class multiplication (see the following discussion) in 1952, as is clear from some of the examples in ''Possibly . . .'' (128–30; originally published as ''Eventuellement . . .'' in *Revue musicale*, May 1952); other relevant material appeared in *Boulez on Music Today*, trans. Susan Bradshaw and Richard R. Bennett (London: Faber & Faber, 1971), 38–41. But the condensed and cryptic character of Boulez's presentation baffled most readers' attempts to understand the procedures at work: see, for instance, Bayan Northcott's review of the latter book, ''Boulez's Theory of Composition,'' *Music and Musicians*, no. 232 (April 1971), 32–36. Some years later, Lev Koblyakov published a partial ''solution,'' but his article appeared in an obscure journal with many editorial and production deficiencies, and it was not until publication of Koblyakov's *Pierre Boulez: A World of Harmony* (Chur and London: Harwood, 1990) that his ideas became generally known. Some problems with formalization of basic concepts—and with interpretation of some aspects of the matrices—that remained in this book were resolved in Stephen Heinemann, ''Pitch-Class Set Multiplication in Boulez's *Le Marteau sans maître*'' (D.M.A. diss., University of Washington, 1993).

49. Karlheinz Stockhausen, quoted in Karl H. Wörner, *Stockhausen: Life and Work*, introd. and trans. Bill Hopkins (Berkeley and Los Angeles: University of California Press, 1976), 78.

50. Stockhausen, quoted in Wörner, *Stockhausen: Life and Work*, 81.

51. Ibid., 78–79.

52. Stockhausen, "Structure and Experiential Time," in *Die Reihe*, no. 2, 64–74.

53. Jonathan Harvey, *The Music of Stockhausen* (Berkeley and Los Angeles: University of California Press, 1975), 14–20.

54. Ibid., 21.

55. Karlheinz Stockhausen, ". . . how time passes . . . ," in *Die Reihe*, no. 3 (*Musical Craftsmanship*), English ed. (Bryn Mawr, PA: Theodore Presser, 1959), 10–40. Also of relevance is Stockhausen, "Die Einheit der musikalischen Zeit," trans. Elaine Barkin as "The Concept of Unity in Electronic Music," in *Perspectives on Contemporary Music Theory*, ed. Benjamin Boretz and Edward T. Cone (New York: Norton, 1972), 214–25.

56. Actually, Stockhausen's idea for unifying pitch and duration was not new: a quarter-century earlier Henry Cowell had proposed an analogy for compositional purposes between the ratios of pitch intervals and the same ratios expressed as polyrhythms in *New Musical Resources* (1930; reprint ed. with introduction and notes by Joscelyn Godwin, New York: Something Else Press, 1969), 45–108. This circumstance in no way detracts from Stockhausen's achievement, which was arrived at quite independently and by a completely different route from Cowell's and produced very different compositional results.

57. Jonathan Cott, *Stockhausen: Conversations with the Composer* (New York: Simon & Schuster, 1973), 100–102. Jerome Kohl has shown in great detail how Stockhausen's music of the 1960s continued to be serial, to what extent, and in conjunction with what other methods. See "Serial and Non-Serial Techniques in the Music of Karlheinz Stockhausen from 1962–1968" (Ph.D. diss., University of Washington, 1981).

58. Josef Rufer, *Composition with Twelve Notes Related Only to One Another*, trans. Humphrey Searle (New York: Macmillan, 1954), Appendix 1, 177–201.

59. Luigi Dallapiccola, "On the Twelve-Note Road," *Music Survey* 4, no. 1 (October 1951): 319.

60. Luigi Dallapiccola, "The Genesis of *Canti di prigionia* and *Il Prigioniero*" (1950–53), in *Selected Writings of Luigi Dallapiccola*, vol. 1: *Dallapiccola on Opera* (n.p.: Toccata Press, 1987), 47.

61. Bruno Maderna, conversation with George Stone and Alan Stout, WEFM, Chicago, 23 January 1970, in Raymond Fearn, *Bruno Maderna* (Chur and London: Harwood, 1990), 300.

62. Luigi Dallapiccola, in Rufer, *Composition with Twelve Notes*, 179.

63. In his contribution to Rufer's Appendix 1, Dallapiccola mentions a "work in progress" (whose illustration reveals it to be the *Canti di liberazione*, finished in 1955), the series for which, he asserts, "contains all the intervals which are possible in the well-tempered chromatic system, from the minor second to the major seventh" (181). This might seem to reflect an acquaintance with Berg's use of such series, as in the first movement of the Lyric Suite; however, Dallapiccola's series (here a perfect fourth lower than in the final version of the work) reads: C♯ D F♯ A B F E G♯ B♭ E♭ C G, which in ordered interval terms includes two each of the major third and major second and omits the minor sixth and minor seventh. (Dallapiccola may have thought of the second and third and the eighth and ninth notes as providing these omitted intervals, since they appear in his example in descending contour.)

64. Luigi Dallapiccola, "My Choral Music," trans. Madeleine M. Smith, in *The Composer's Point of View: Essays on Twentieth-Century Choral Music by Those Who Wrote It*, ed. Robert S. Hines (Norman: University of Oklahoma Press, 1963), 168.

65. See Roman Vlad, *Luigi Dallapiccola* (Milan: Suvini Zerboni, 1957), 27–29, for example (and throughout from there on).

66. John MacIvor Perkins, "Dallapiccola's Art of Canon," *Perspectives of New Music* 1, no. 2 (Spring 1963): 97.

67. Dallapiccola, "On the Twelve-Note Road," 325–26. David Mancini, "Twelve-Tone Polarity in Late Works of Luigi Dallapiccola," *Journal of Music Theory* 30 (1986): 203–24, presents an interesting interpretation of Dallapiccola's music in light of his use of the term *polarity*.

68. Luigi Nono, "Die Entwicklung der Reihentechnik" (1958), in Nono, *Texte: Studien zu seiner Musik*, ed. Jürg Stenzl (Zurich: Atlantis, 1975), 21–33.

69. The discussion that follows is based on Reginald Smith Brindle's analysis in "Current Chronicle: Italy," *Musical Quarterly* 47 (1961): 247–55, although some details have been added by the present author.

70. Henri Pousseur, "La série et les dès," in *Fragments théoriques I sur la musique expérimentale* (Brussels: Editions de l'Institut de Sociologie, Université Libre de Bruxelles, 1970), 45 (my translation).

71. Henri Pousseur, "Webern's Organic Chromaticism," in *Die Reihe*, no. 2, 51–60.

72. Henri Pousseur, "Outline of a Method," in *Die Reihe*, no. 3, 44–88, especially 48–56.

73. Ibid., 51.

74. Milton Babbitt, review of René Leibowitz, *Schoenberg et son école* and *Qu'est ce que la musique de douze sons?, Journal of the American Musicological Society* 3 (1950): 57–60; Babbitt, review of *Polyphonie, Quatrième Cahier: Le système dodécaphonique, Journal of the American Musicological Society* 3 (1950): 264–67. *Le système dodécaphonique* appeared without a date but was issued in 1949, thus preceding by a year the English edition of "Composition with Twelve Tones" in *Style and Idea*. (See note 1.)

75. Babbitt, review of *Le système dodécaphonique*, 265.

76. Ibid., 264.

77. This divergence suggests, ironically enough, that Leibowitz may actually have done Schoenberg a disservice in the long run, at least in Europe, by emphasizing matters of historical continuity and thereby convincing younger composers that the future of music lay in a different direction.

78. Milton Babbitt, "The Function of Set Structure in the Twelve-Tone System" (1946; Ph.D. diss., Princeton University, 1992).

79. Babbitt discusses some of this early exposure in "First Responses: An Approximation," *Perspectives of New Music* 14, no. 2/15, no. 1 (1976): 3–23.

80. We say "built out of the hexachord" for two reasons: one, because the combinatorial properties of a hexachord exist irrespective of compositional order; two, because any twelve-tone row in which the first six notes constitute a combinatorial hexachord will have as its second six notes the same combinatorial hexachord transposed or inverted to a new pitch level.

81. See, in particular, Milton Babbitt, "Some Aspects of Twelve-Tone Composition," *Score* 12 (1955): 53–61.

82. To determine whether a given row has this property, one must read it in terms of ordered interval content. That is, for example, the first interval in P_0, B♭ to E♭, is read as a perfect fourth even though it is written literally as a descending perfect fifth: pitch-

class intervals are always read in the ascending direction. In Babbitt's row the adjacent intervals are:5, 2, 9, 10, 1, 6, 4, 7, 3, 11, 8.

83. For this application, the inversion of 5, 1, 4, 2 is taken to be 1, 5, 2, 4.

84. Perle, ''Atonality and the Twelve-Note System in the United States,'' 58–60; Joseph N. Straus, *The Music of Ruth Crawford Seeger* (Cambridge: Cambridge University Press, 1995), 172–82.

85. Andrew Mead, *An Introduction to the Music of Milton Babbitt* (Princeton: Princeton University Press, 1994), 54.

86. Milton Babbitt, *Words about Music*, ed. Stephen Dembski and Joseph N. Straus (Madison: University of Wisconsin Press, 1987), 25.

87. A *partition* of a set divides its contents into groups such that each member of the set belongs to exactly one group. A twelve-tone set can be partitioned 3/3/3/3 or 4/4/2/1/1 or 2/4/5/1 and so on, for a total of seventy-seven different ways. For much more information on this and other aspects of Babbitt's practice, see Mead, *Introduction to the Music of Milton Babbitt*, 25–38.

88. Milton Babbitt, ''Twelve-Tone Rhythmic Structure and the Electronic Medium,'' *Perspectives of New Music* 1, no. 1 (Fall 1962): 49–79.

89. For further information on rhythm and duration in Babbitt, see Mead, *Introduction to the Music of Milton Babbitt*, especially 38–53; Andrew Mead, ''About *About Time*'s Time: A Survey of Milton Babbitt's Recent Rhythmic Practice,'' *Perspectives of New Music* 25 (1987): 182–235; Joseph Dubiel, ''Three Essays on Milton Babbitt,'' Parts 1–3, *Perspectives of New Music* 28, no. 2 (Summer 1990): 216–61; 29, no. 1 (Winter 1991): 90–122; 30, no. 1 (Winter 1992): 82–131.

90. To those who object that Stravinsky was not American in the sense that other, native and ''homegrown'' composers treated in this section are, I answer that for a composer whose profile had been international from his earliest success onwards, and who in a very real sense belonged to the entire Western world of music, no merely national classification would ever be appropriate, but for the purposes of this chapter, if he must be placed somewhere, it may as well be on the Western side of the Atlantic, where he had lived for more than a decade and would continue to do so for the two more remaining in his life. It should also be borne in mind that Stravinsky's turning to serialism made perhaps a greater difference to composers in the United States than anywhere else.

91. Robert Craft, ''A Personal Preface,'' *Score* 20 (1957): 7–13.

92. For Stravinsky, Schoenberg's ''perfect works'' were the Five Pieces for Orchestra (Op. 16), *Herzgewächse* (Op. 20), *Pierrot lunaire* (Op. 21), ''Seraphita'' from the Four Orchestral Songs (Op. 22), the Serenade (Op. 24), and the Variations for Orchestra (Op. 31). Igor Stravinsky and Robert Craft, *Conversations with Igor Stravinsky* (1959; Berkeley and Los Angeles: University of California Press, 1980), 71.

93. Ibid.; Craft, ''Personal Preface,'' 13.

94. Craft, ''Personal Preface,'' 13.

95. Pieter van den Toorn, *The Music of Igor Stravinsky* (New Haven: Yale University Press, 1983), 380–85.

96. Stravinsky and Craft, *Conversations with Igor Stravinsky*, 72.

97. Van den Toorn, *Music of Igor Stravinsky*, 385.

98. Igor Stravinsky and Robert Craft, *Dialogues* (1968; Berkeley and Los Angeles: University of California Press, 1982), 108–9.

99. See especially Milton Babbitt, ''Remarks on the Recent Stravinsky,'' *Perspec-*

tives of New Music 2, no. 2 (Spring–Summer 1964): 35–55, reprinted in *Perspectives on Schoenberg and Stravinsky*, ed. Benjamin Boretz and Edward T. Cone (New York: Norton, 1972), 165–85. Also see van den Toorn, *Music of Igor Stravinsky*, 372–455.

100. As Babbitt has pointed out, Stravinsky did not simply borrow Krenek's invention, but effectively reinvented it by grasping and then implementing its remarkable implications for serial structure generally. But the connection is significant. Stravinsky knew Krenek's *Lamentatio Jeremiae Prophetae*, the work in which (as discussed in the section "Dissemination of the Twelve-Tone Method to 1945") hexachordal rotation was introduced; he also knew Krenek, whom he saw often from the 1950s on in Los Angeles, and he followed his lectures and writings closely. To judge from the frequent recurrence of mention of the *Lamentatio* in Krenek's writings after his initial discussion of it in 1943, Krenek was particularly proud of this serial innovation and undoubtedly lectured on it as well. As Craft has said, "Krenek exercised an influence on Stravinsky that heretofore has not been acknowledged" (Igor Stravinsky, *Selected Correspondence*, ed. and with commentaries by Robert Craft, 3 vols. [New York: Knopf, 1982–85], 2:325n). See also Stravinsky and Craft, *Dialogues*, 103–4; Milton Babbitt, "Stravinsky's Verticals and Schoenberg's Diagonals: A Twist of Fate," in *Stravinsky Retrospectives*, ed. Ethan Haimo and Paul Johnson (Lincoln: University of Nebraska Press, 1987), 15–35.

101. The other seven 6 × 6 arrays are constructed by analogy to the one discussed in the text, in each case with the first pitch class of the relevant hexachord in the 12 × 12 array (second hexachord of the prime form, first hexachord of the retrograde, and so on) treated as the reference point, just as 0 is for the first hexachord of the prime. For further information, see Milton Babbitt, "Stravinsky's Verticals and Schoenberg's Diagonals"; Milton Babbitt, "Order, Symmetry, and Centricity in Late Stravinsky," in *Confronting Stravinsky: Man, Musician, and Modernist*, ed. Jann Pasler (Berkeley and Los Angeles: University of California Press, 1986), 247–61; Babbitt, "Since Schoenberg," *Perspectives of New Music* 12, nos. 1–2 (1973–74): 3–28.

102. Babbitt, *Words about Music*, 31–32.

103. Roger Sessions, "Music in Crisis" (1933), in *Roger Sessions on Music: Collected Essays*, ed. Edward T. Cone (Princeton: Princeton University Press, 1979), 36, 38.

104. Roger Sessions, "Exposition by Krenek" (1938), in *Roger Sessions on Music*, 251.

105. Ibid., 253.

106. Roger Sessions, "Schoenberg in the United States" (1944/1972), in *Roger Sessions on Music*, 366.

107. Roger Sessions, "Some Notes on Schoenberg and the 'Method of Composing with Twelve Tones' " (1952), in *Roger Sessions on Music*, 375.

108. See Andrea Olmstead, *Conversations with Roger Sessions* (Boston: Northeastern University Press, 1987), 90, 34, 47–48; Edward T. Cone, "Conversation with Roger Sessions," *Perspectives of New Music* 4, no. 2 (Spring–Summer 1966): 29–46; reprinted in *Perspectives on American Composers*, ed. Benjamin Boretz and Edward T. Cone (New York: Norton, 1971), 90–107. Such variations would seem in line with Sessions's mention, in his Charles Eliot Norton lectures at Harvard, of "other variants" of a row beyond the familiar R, I, and RI transforms (Roger Sessions, *Questions about Music* [New York: Norton, 1971], 117–18).

109. See Olmstead, *Conversations with Roger Sessions*, 140–42; also Cone, "Conversation with Roger Sessions," 104.

110. Olmstead, *Conversations with Roger Sessions*, 90, 34.

111. Roger Sessions, "Thoughts on Stravinsky" (1957), in *Roger Sessions on Music*, 383; Cone, "Conversation with Roger Sessions," 104.

112. Olmstead, *Conversations with Roger Sessions*, 45–46.

113. Cone, "Conversation with Aaron Copland," in *Perspectives on American Composers*, 141.

114. Aaron Copland, "Schönberg and His School" (1949), in *Copland on Music* (New York: Norton, 1963), 244.

115. Aaron Copland, *The New Music, 1900–1960* (New York: Norton, 1968), 172; Cone, "Conversation with Aaron Copland," 141; Copland, "Composer from Brooklyn," in *New Music*, 168.

116. Cone, "Conversation with Aaron Copland," 141.

117. See Peter Evans's enlightening analysis in "The Thematic Technique of Copland's Recent Works," *Tempo* 51 (1959): 2–13.

118. Aaron Copland, program notes for William Masselos's premiere of the Piano Fantasy, 25 October 1957; reprinted as the sleeve notes to *Aaron Copland: Piano Variations (1930); Piano Fantasy (1957)/William Masselos, Pianist*, Columbia Records LP ML-5568 [1960].

119. Peter Evans, "Copland on the Serial Road: An Analysis of *Connotations*," in *Perspectives on American Composers*, 148.

120. Cone, "Conversation with Aaron Copland," 140.

121. Babbitt, "Some Aspects of Twelve-Tone Composition," 53; Perle, "Atonality and the Twelve-Note System in the United States," 51.

122. Hans Werner Henze, "German Music in the 1940s and 1950s," in *Music and Politics: Collected Writings, 1953–81* (London: Faber & Faber, 1982), 38.

123. Ibid., 42–43.

124. See the previous discussion in the section "Developments in Europe after the Second World War," and notes 58 and 161.

125. Henze, "German Music in the 1940s and 1950s," 40.

126. Ibid., 46.

127. David Osmond-Smith, *Berio* (Oxford and New York: Oxford University Press, 1991), 6.

128. Ibid., 9.

129. The Latin *nones* refers to the ninth day of the month before the ides. A facsimile of the composer's handwritten scheme for this work appears in *Luciano Berio: Two Interviews*, trans. and ed. David Osmond-Smith (New York and London: Marion Boyars, 1985), Plate 4 (after 96).

130. Osmond-Smith, *Berio*, 9.

131. *Luciano Berio: Two Interviews*, 68–69, 65–66.

132. Ibid., 66.

133. Michel Philippot, "Entretien Luciano Berio," *Revue Musicale* 265–66 (1968): 88 (my translation).

134. *Luciano Berio: Two Interviews*, 64.

135. Philippot, "Entretien Luciano Berio," 88.

136. Bruno Maderna, letter to Luigi Dallapiccola, quoted in Fearn, *Bruno Maderna*, 27.

137. Fearn, *Bruno Maderna*, 27–51.

138. Bruno Maderna, conversation with Christoph Bitter, Saarländischer Rundfunk, 7

May 1973, in Fearn, *Bruno Maderna*, 323; interview with Leonard Pinzanti around December 1972, ibid., 316.

139. Wolfram Schwinger, *Krzysztof Penderecki: His Life and Work*, trans. William Mann (Mainz: Schott, 1989), 26.

140. "Zur Situation" [questions asked of four composers; answers by Iannis Xenakis], *Darmstädter Beiträge zur neuen Musik* 14 (1974): 8, 16–18.

141. Mario Bois, *Iannis Xenakis: The Man and His Music* (London: Boosey & Hawkes, 1967), 16 (interview, 4 March 1966).

142. Iannis Xenakis, "La crise de la musique sérielle," *Gravesaner Blätter* 1 (1955): 2–4.

143. Ligeti, "Pierre Boulez: Decision and Automatism in *Structure 1a*." Ironically, this analysis has become a standard reference in the bibliography of "total serialism." The story of how Ligeti came to write it is engagingly told in Toop, "Messiaen / Goeyvaerts, Fano / Stockhausen, Boulez," 168–69n.

144. György Ligeti, "Metamorphoses of Musical Form," in *Die Reihe*, no. 7 (*Form-Space*), English ed. (Bryn Mawr, PA: Theodore Presser, 1965), 5–19.

145. Ibid., 6, 10.

146. Ibid., 6.

147. Jonathan W. Bernard, "Inaudible Structures, Audible Music: Ligeti's Problem, and His Solution," *Music Analysis* 6 (1987): 208–9.

148. Ligeti's abiding interest in pitch space, conversely, seems to have conditioned his response to Webern, about whose work he wrote especially prolifically during his first decade in the West. The symmetrical, "crystalline" serial structures of Webern held great fascination for him. See György Ligeti, "Über die Harmonik in Weberns erster Kantate," *Darmstädter Beiträge zur neuen Musik* 3 (1960): 49–64; "Die Komposition mit Reihen und ihre Konsequenzen bei Anton Webern," *Österreichische Musikzeitschrift* 6 (1961): 297–302; "Weberns Melodik," *Melos* 33 (1966): 116–18; "Aspekte der Webernschen Kompositionstechnik" (1964), in *Musik-Konzepte, Sonderband, Anton Webern II*, ed. Heinz-Klaus Metzger and Rainer Riehn (Munich: Edition text + kritik, 1984), 51–104.

149. Pierre Boulez, "Current Investigations" (1954), in *Stocktakings from an Apprenticeship*, 16.

150. *Luciano Berio: Two Interviews*, 69.

151. Boulez's interest in aleatoric music was in part stimulated by his contact with John Cage, as the published correspondence (see note 44) suggests. Two important European essays on aleatoric music and its effects are Pierre Boulez, "Alea" (1957), in *Stocktakings from an Apprenticeship*, 26–38; and Umberto Eco, "The Poetics of the Open Work" (1962), in *The Open Work*, trans. Anna Cancogni (Cambridge, MA: Harvard University Press, 1989), 1–23.

152. See David Nicholls's extensive exposition of Cage's early compositional development in *American Experimental Music, 1890–1940* (Cambridge: Cambridge University Press, 1990), 175–217.

153. George Rochberg, "Reflections on Schoenberg" (1972), in *The Aesthetics of Survival*, ed. William Bolcom (Ann Arbor: University of Michigan Press, 1984), 48.

154. George Rochberg, "Tradition and Twelve-Tone Music" (1955), in *The Aesthetics of Survival*, 44. Boulez's essay "Schoenberg Is Dead" appeared in *Score* 6 (1952): 18–22.

155. Rochberg, "Tradition and Twelve-Tone Music," 40, 42–43, 44.

156. Rochberg, "Reflections on Schoenberg," 52–53.

157. George Rochberg, *The Hexachord and Its Relation to the 12-Tone Row* (Bryn Mawr, PA: Theodore Presser, 1955); George Perle, review of same, *Journal of the American Musicological Society* 10 (1957): 55–59; Rochberg, "The Harmonic Tendency of the Hexachord," *Journal of Music Theory* 3 (1959): 208–30; Milton Babbitt, "Twelve-Tone Invariants as Compositional Determinants," *Musical Quarterly* 46 (1960), reprinted in *Problems of Modern Music*, ed. Paul Henry Lang (New York: Norton, 1962), 108–21. More on Babbitt's articles appears later in this chapter.

158. Arnold Schoenberg at UCLA, around 1940; attributed by Dika Newlin in "Secret Tonality in Schoenberg's Piano Concerto," *Perspectives of New Music* 13, no. 2 (Fall–Winter 1974): 137.

159. William Glock, *Notes in Advance* (Oxford and New York: Oxford University Press, 1991), 185.

160. Under the circumstances, whether Carter's later music can be said to project a twelve-tone structure depends a great deal on how one views it. For one very definite and cogently worked-out view, see Andrew Mead, "Twelve-Tone Composition and the Music of Elliott Carter," in *Concert Music, Rock, and Jazz since 1945: Essays and Analytical Studies*, ed. Elizabeth West Marvin and Richard Hermann (Rochester: University of Rochester Press, 1995), 67–102.

161. Herbert Eimert, *Lehrbuch der Zwölftontechnik* (Wiesbaden: Breitkopf und Härtel, 1950); Hanns Jelinek, *Anleitung zur Zwölftonkomposition* (Vienna: Universal Edition, 1952); Josef Rufer, *Die Komposition mit zwölf Tönen* (Berlin: Max Hesses Verlag, 1952). The English translation of Rufer's book is cited in note 58.

162. Eimert, *Lehrbuch*, Part 1, Chapter 7 ("Reihensysteme"), 21–28. Among American composers, Milton Babbitt and Charles Wuorinen have found the circle-of-fifths ("M7") and circle-of-fourths ("M5") transformations particularly fruitful in their work. Bryan Simms has also pinpointed Eimert's book as the first discussion of these transformations; see "The Theory of Pitch-Class Sets," in *Early Twentieth-Century Music*, ed. Jonathan Dunsby (Oxford: Blackwell, 1993), 114–31.

163. Ernst Krenek, *Studies in Counterpoint Based on the Twelve-Tone Technique* (New York: G. Schirmer, 1940). No less a personage than Stravinsky recalled later in life that his first gleanings of the twelve-tone method came from Krenek's book. See Stravinsky and Craft, *Dialogues*, 103.

164. John Backus, "*Die Reihe*: A Scientific Evaluation," *Perspectives of New Music* 1, no. 1 (Fall 1962): 160–71.

165. Babbitt, "Set Structure as a Compositional Determinant," *Journal of Music Theory* 5 (1961): 72–94.

166. George Perle, *The Operas of Alban Berg*, vol. 2, *Lulu* (Berkeley and Los Angeles: University of California Press, 1985); Perle, *Style and Idea in the "Lyric Suite" of Alban Berg* (Stuyvesant, NY: Pendragon, 1995). Also of interest in Perle's development as a Berg scholar is *The Operas of Alban Berg*, vol. 1, *Wozzeck* (Berkeley and Los Angeles: University of California Press, 1980).

167. Perle, *Serial Composition and Atonality: An Introduction to the Music of Schoenberg, Berg, and Webern* (Berkeley and Los Angeles: University of California Press, 1962), 9. "Nondodecaphonic Serial Composition" is dealt with in a separate chapter of 20 pages. Thus about 60 percent of Perle's book was devoted to the fully twelve-tone repertoire, a percentage that, with the augmentation of the twelve-tone chapters, has grown to 75 percent in recent editions.

168. Allen Forte, ''Context and Continuity in an Atonal Work: A Set-Theoretic Approach,'' *Perspectives of New Music* 1, no. 2 (Spring 1963): 72–82.

169. David Lewin, ''Re: Intervallic Relations between Two Collections of Notes,'' *Journal of Music Theory* 3 (1959): 298–301; Lewin, ''Re: The Intervallic Content of a Collection of Notes, Intervallic Relations between a Collection of Notes and Its Complement: An Application to Schoenberg's Hexachordal Pieces,'' *Journal of Music Theory* 4 (1960): 98–101. To say that Lewin's interval function played no direct role in Forte's later-formulated theory of pitch-class sets is not meant as a denigration of the interval function, for it has played a crucial role in Lewin's own immensely important theoretical work.

170. Allen Forte, ''A Theory of Set-Complexes for Music,'' *Journal of Music Theory* 8 (1964): 136–83.

171. Allen Forte, *The Structure of Atonal Music* (New Haven: Yale University Press, 1973).

172. See Bernard, ''Chord, Collection, and Set in Twentieth-Century Theory,'' for an extensive exposition of these developments and their eventual intersection with twelve-tone theory.

173. Howard Hanson, *Harmonic Materials of Modern Music: Resources of the Tempered Scale* (New York: Appleton-Century-Crofts, 1960).

174. See the earlier discussion of Erwin Stein's work on this point.

175. Arnold Schoenberg, *Fundamentals of Musical Composition*, ed. Gerald Strang and Leonard Stein (London and Boston: Faber & Faber, 1967); Schoenberg, ''Brahms the Progressive'' (1944), in *Style and Idea* (1975 ed.), 398–441.

176. Arnold Schoenberg, *The Musical Idea and the Logic, Technique, and Art of Its Presentation*, ed., trans., and with commentary by Patricia Carpenter and Severine Neff (New York: Columbia University Press, 1995).

177. Ernst Krenek, ''Is the Twelve-Tone Technique on the Decline?'' *Musical Quarterly* 39 (1953): 513–27.

178. This is, I hope, a representative list, but by no means an exhaustive one.

179. György Ligeti, ''Fragen und Antworten mit mir selbst'' (1971), trans. Geoffrey Skelton in *Ligeti in Conversation* (London: Eulenberg, 1983), 131.

180. ''John Zorn'' [interview], in William Duckworth, *Talking Music* (New York: Schirmer Books, 1995), 465.

BIBLIOGRAPHY

WRITINGS BY SCHOENBERG, BERG, AND WEBERN: BOOKS, ESSAYS, AND CORRESPONDENCE

Bailey, Walter B. "Schoenberg's Published Articles: A List of Titles, Sources, and Translations." *Journal of the Arnold Schoenberg Institute* 4 (1980): 156–91.

Beaumont, Antony, ed. and trans. *Ferruccio Busoni: Selected Letters*. New York: Columbia University Press, 1987. 38 pieces of correspondence between Schoenberg and Busoni.

Berg, Alban. *Alban Berg: Letters to His Wife*. Edited and translated by Bernard Grun. New York: St. Martin's Press, 1971. 569 letters.

———*Arnold Schönberg, Gurrelieder: Führer*. Leipzig and Vienna: Universal Edition, 1913. English translation by Mark DeVoto in *Journal of the Arnold Schoenberg Institute* 16 (1993): 24–235. Berg was also the author of shorter guides to Schoenberg's Chamber Symphony, Op. 9, and *Pelleas und Melisande*, both translated by Mark DeVoto in *Journal of the Arnold Schoenberg Institute* 16 (1993).

———. *Glaube, Hoffnung, und Liebe: Schriften zur Musik*. Edited by Frank Schneider. Leipzig: Verlag Philipp Reclam jun., 1981. Berg's complete corpus of essays on music.

The Berg-Schoenberg Correspondence: Selected Letters. Edited and translated by Juliane Brand, Christopher Hailey, and Donald Harris. New York and London: Norton, 1987. 341 pieces of correspondence, many incomplete.

Ennulat, Egbert M., ed. *Arnold Schoenberg Correspondence: A Collection of Translated and Annotated Letters Exchanged with Guido Adler, Pablo Casals, Emanuel Feuermann, and Olin Downes*. Metuchen, NJ: Scarecrow Press, 1991. 100 pieces of correspondence, including drafts of unsent letters.

Hahl-Koch, Jelena, ed. *Arnold Schoenberg, Wassily Kandinsky: Letters, Pictures, and*

Documents. Translated by John C. Crawford. London and Boston: Faber & Faber, 1984. 64 pieces of correspondence.

Heller, Friedrich C., ed. *Arnold Schönberg—Franz Schreker: Briefwechsel*. Tutzing: Hans Schneider, 1974. 84 pieces of correspondence.

Kimmey, John A., Jr. *The Arnold Schoenberg–Hans Nachod Collection*. Detroit Studies in Music Bibliography, no. 41. Detroit: Information Coordinators, 1979. 62 pieces of correspondence between Schoenberg and his cousin Hans Nachod.

Schoenberg, Arnold. *Der biblische Weg* (''play in three acts''). Translated by Moshe Lazar in *Journal of the Arnold Schoenberg Institute* 17 (1994): 162–329.

———. *Fundamentals of Musical Composition*. Edited by Gerald Strang and Leonard Stein. New York: St. Martin's Press, 1967.

———. *Harmonielehre*. Vienna: Universal Edition, 1911; 3rd ed., rev., 1922. Excerpts outlined in Erwin Stein's *Praktischer Leitfaden zu Schönbergs Harmonielehre* (Vienna: Universal Edition, 1923). English translations: (abbreviated) *Theory of Harmony*, translated by Robert D. W. Adams (New York: Philosophical Library, 1948); (complete) *Theory of Harmony*, translated by Roy E. Carter (Berkeley and Los Angeles: University of California Press, 1978).

———. ''Das Komponieren mit selbstständigen Stimmen'' (outline with notes, 1911). Transcribed with commentary in Rudolf Stephan, ''Schönbergs Entwurf über 'Das Komponieren mit selbstständigen Stimmen,' '' *Archiv für Musikwissenschaft* 29 (1972): 238–56.

———. ''Komposition mit zwölf Tönen.'' In Rudolf Stephan, ''Ein frühes Dokument zur Entstehung der Zwölftonkomposition.'' In *Festschrift Arno Forchert zum 60. Geburtstag am 29. Dezember 1985*, edited by Gerhard Allroggen and Detlef Altenburg, 296–301. Kassel: Bärenreiter, 1986. This document from the Berg Collection at the Austrian National Library is almost certainly by Schoenberg, probably a partial transcription of one of Schoenberg's early lectures on twelve-tone composition to his students in 1922 or 1923.

———. *Letters*. Selected and edited by Erwin Stein. Translated by Eithne Wilkins and Ernst Kaiser. New York: St. Martin's Press, 1965. 265 pieces of correspondence, many incomplete.

———. *Models for Beginners in Composition*. New York: G. Schirmer, 1943.

———. *Moses und Aron* (opera text). Mainz: Schott, 1957.

———. ''Der musikalische Gedanke und die Logik, Technik, und Kunst seiner Darstellung'' (outline and fragmentary draft, 1934–36). Transcribed with English translation as *The Musical Idea and the Logic, Technique, and Art of Its Presentation*, edited and translated by Patricia Carpenter and Severine Neff. New York: Columbia University Press, 1995.

———. *Preliminary Exercises in Counterpoint*. Edited by Leonard Stein. New York: St. Martin's Press, 1969.

———. *Schöpferische Konfessionen*. Edited by Willi Reich. Zurich: Arche, 1964. 27 articles, some abridged, including extracts from *Harmonielehre*.

———. *Stil und Gedanke, Aufsätze zur Musik*. Edited by Ivan Vojtech. Arnold Schönberg gesammelte Schriften, vol. 1. N.p.: S. Fischer, 1976. Collection of 74 essays, including the 15 from the 1950 edition of *Style and Idea*.

———. *Structural Functions of Harmony*. New York: Norton, 1954. Rev. ed., edited by Leonard Stein. New York: Norton, 1969.

———. *Style and Idea*. Edited by Dika Newlin. New York: Philosophical Library, 1950.

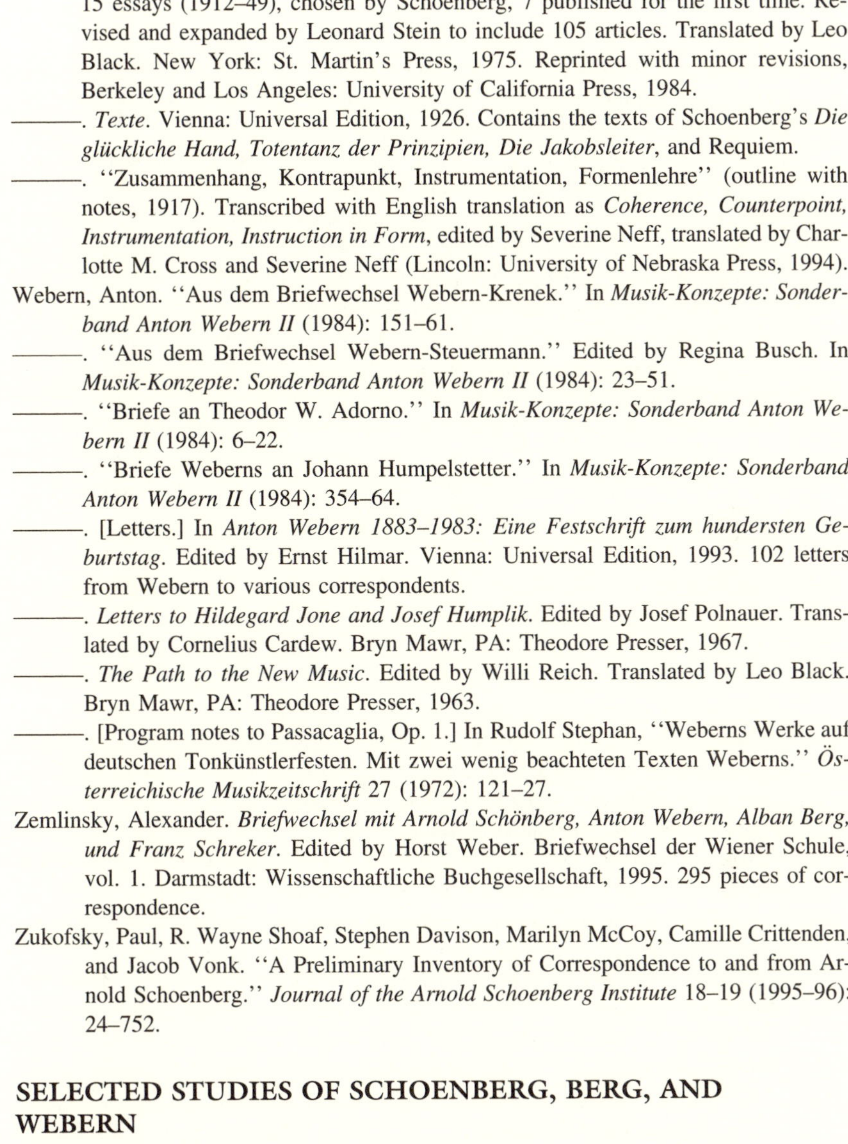

15 essays (1912–49), chosen by Schoenberg, 7 published for the first time. Revised and expanded by Leonard Stein to include 105 articles. Translated by Leo Black. New York: St. Martin's Press, 1975. Reprinted with minor revisions, Berkeley and Los Angeles: University of California Press, 1984.

———. *Texte*. Vienna: Universal Edition, 1926. Contains the texts of Schoenberg's *Die glückliche Hand, Totentanz der Prinzipien, Die Jakobsleiter*, and Requiem.

———. "Zusammenhang, Kontrapunkt, Instrumentation, Formenlehre" (outline with notes, 1917). Transcribed with English translation as *Coherence, Counterpoint, Instrumentation, Instruction in Form*, edited by Severine Neff, translated by Charlotte M. Cross and Severine Neff (Lincoln: University of Nebraska Press, 1994).

Webern, Anton. "Aus dem Briefwechsel Webern-Krenek." In *Musik-Konzepte: Sonderband Anton Webern II* (1984): 151–61.

———. "Aus dem Briefwechsel Webern-Steuermann." Edited by Regina Busch. In *Musik-Konzepte: Sonderband Anton Webern II* (1984): 23–51.

———. "Briefe an Theodor W. Adorno." In *Musik-Konzepte: Sonderband Anton Webern II* (1984): 6–22.

———. "Briefe Weberns an Johann Humpelstetter." In *Musik-Konzepte: Sonderband Anton Webern II* (1984): 354–64.

———. [Letters.] In *Anton Webern 1883–1983: Eine Festschrift zum hundersten Geburtstag*. Edited by Ernst Hilmar. Vienna: Universal Edition, 1993. 102 letters from Webern to various correspondents.

———. *Letters to Hildegard Jone and Josef Humplik*. Edited by Josef Polnauer. Translated by Cornelius Cardew. Bryn Mawr, PA: Theodore Presser, 1967.

———. *The Path to the New Music*. Edited by Willi Reich. Translated by Leo Black. Bryn Mawr, PA: Theodore Presser, 1963.

———. [Program notes to Passacaglia, Op. 1.] In Rudolf Stephan, "Weberns Werke auf deutschen Tonkünstlerfesten. Mit zwei wenig beachteten Texten Weberns." *Österreichische Musikzeitschrift* 27 (1972): 121–27.

Zemlinsky, Alexander. *Briefwechsel mit Arnold Schönberg, Anton Webern, Alban Berg, und Franz Schreker*. Edited by Horst Weber. Briefwechsel der Wiener Schule, vol. 1. Darmstadt: Wissenschaftliche Buchgesellschaft, 1995. 295 pieces of correspondence.

Zukofsky, Paul, R. Wayne Shoaf, Stephen Davison, Marilyn McCoy, Camille Crittenden, and Jacob Vonk. "A Preliminary Inventory of Correspondence to and from Arnold Schoenberg." *Journal of the Arnold Schoenberg Institute* 18–19 (1995–96): 24–752.

SELECTED STUDIES OF SCHOENBERG, BERG, AND WEBERN

Adorno, Theodor W. *Alban Berg: Master of the Smallest Link*. Translated by Juliane Brand and Christopher Hailey. Cambridge: Cambridge University Press, 1991.

———. "Anton von Webern." In Theodor W. Adorno, *Gesammelte Schriften* 16:110–25. Frankfurt: Suhrkamp, 1978.

———. "Berg and Webern: Schönberg's Heirs." *Modern Music* 8, no. 2 (January–February 1931): 29–38.

———. "Im Gedächtnis an Alban Berg." In Theodor W. Adorno, *Gesammelte Schriften* 18:487–512. Frankfurt: Suhrkamp, 1984.

Alban Berg Kammermusik. 2 volumes. Musik-Konzepte, vol. 4, 9. Munich: Edition text + kritik, 1978–79.

Arnold Schönberg in höchster Verehrung. Munich: Piper, 1912.

Bailey, Kathryn. "Symmetry as Nemesis: Webern and the First Movement of the Concerto, Opus 24." *Journal of Music Theory* 40 (1996): 245–310.

———. *The Twelve-Note Music of Anton Webern: Old Forms in a New Language.* Cambridge: Cambridge University Press, 1991.

———, ed. *Webern Studies.* Cambridge: Cambridge University Press, 1996.

Bailey, Walter B. *Programmatic Elements in the Works of Schoenberg.* Studies in Musicology, no. 74. Ann Arbor: UMI Research Press, 1984.

Busch, Regina. "On the Horizontal and Vertical Presentation of Musical Ideas and on Musical Space." *Tempo* 154 (1985): 2–10; 156–57 (1986): 7–15, 21–26.

———. "Über die Musik von Anton Webern." *Österreichische Musikzeitschrift* 36 (1981): 470–82.

Carner, Mosco. *Alban Berg: The Man and the Work.* 2nd ed., rev. New York: Holmes & Meier, 1983.

Chadwick, Nicholas. "Berg's Unpublished Songs in the Österreichische Nationalbibliothek." *Music and Letters* 52 (1971): 123–40.

Christensen, Jean, and Jesper Christensen. *From Arnold Schoenberg's Literary Legacy: A Catalog of Neglected Items.* Detroit Studies in Music Bibliography, no. 59. N.p.: Harmonie Park Press, 1988.

Cone, Edward T. "Webern's Apprenticeship." In *Music: A View from Delft. Selected Essays,* edited by Robert Morgan, 267–80. Chicago: University of Chicago Press, 1989.

Congdon, David. "Composition in Berg's Kammerkonzert." *Perspectives of New Music* 24 (1985): 234–69.

Cox, Gareth. *Anton Weberns Studienzeit: Seine Entwicklung im Lichte der Sätze und Fragmente für Klavier.* Frankfurt: Lang, 1992.

Dahlhaus, Carl. *Schoenberg and the New Music: Essays.* Translated by Derrick Puffett and Alfred Clayton. Cambridge: Cambridge University Press, 1987.

———, ed. *Die Wiener Schule heute.* Veröffentlichungen des Instituts für Neue Musik und Musikerziehung, Darmstadt, vol. 24. Mainz: Schott, 1983.

DeVoto, Mark. "Alban Berg's 'Marche Macabre.' " *Perspectives of New Music* 22 (1984): 386–447.

———. "Some Notes on the Unknown *Altenberg Lieder.*" *Perspectives of New Music* 5 (1966): 37–74.

Dümling, Albrecht. *Die fremden Klänge der hängenden Gärten: Die öffentliche Einsamkeit der neuen Musik am Beispiel von Arnold Schönberg und Stefan George.* Munich: Kindler, 1981.

Dunsby, Jonathan. *Schoenberg: "Pierrot lunaire."* Cambridge Music Handbooks. Cambridge: Cambridge University Press, 1992.

Falck, Robert. "Two *Reigen!* Berg, Schnitzler, and Cyclic Form." In *Encrypted Messages in Alban Berg's Music,* edited by Siglind Bruhn, 91–105. New York: Garland, 1998.

Fleischmann, Hugo Robert. "Die Jung Wiener Schule (Eine musikalische Zeitfrage)." *Neue Zeitschrift für Musik* 79 (1912): 539–40.

Floros, Constantin. *Alban Berg: Musik als Autobiographie.* Wiesbaden: Breitkopf und Härtel, 1992.

Frisch, Walter. *The Early Works of Arnold Schoenberg, 1893–1908.* Berkeley: University of California Press, 1993.

Gable, David, and Robert P. Morgan, eds. *Alban Berg: Historical and Analytical Perspectives.* Oxford: Clarendon Press, 1991.

Green, Douglass M. "Berg's De Profundis: The Finale of the Lyric Suite." *International Alban Berg Society Newsletter* 5 (1977): 13–23.

Grim, William E. "Das Ewig-weibliche zieht uns züruck: Berg's *Lulu* as Anti-Faust." *Opera Journal* 22, no. 1 (1989): 21–28.

Haimo, Ethan. *Schoenberg's Serial Odyssey: The Evolution of His Twelve-Tone Method, 1914–1928.* Oxford: Clarendon Press, 1990.

Harris, Donald. "Berg and Frida Semler." *International Alban Berg Society Newsletter* 8 (1979): 8–12.

Hayes, Malcolm, *Anton von Webern.* London: Phaidon Press, 1995.

Heller, Erich. "From Love to Love: Goethe's *Pandora* and Wedekind–Alban Berg's *Pandora-Lulu.*" *Salmagundi* 84 (1989): 94–108.

Hilmar, Ernst, ed. *Arnold Schönberg Gedenkausstellung 1974.* Vienna: Universal Edition, 1974.

Hilmar, Rosemary. *Alban Berg: Leben und Wirken in Wien bis zu seinen ersten Erfolgen als Komponist.* Vienna: H. Böhlaus Nachf., 1978.

———. "Alban Berg's Studies with Schoenberg." *Journal of the Arnold Schoenberg Institute* 8 (1984): 7–29.

Hoyer, Martin. "Neues zu Anton Weberns frühen Liedern." *Mitteilungen der Paul Sacher Stiftung* 5 (January 1992): 31–35.

International Alban Berg Society Newsletter. Published irregularly, 1968– .

Jarman, Douglas. *Alban Berg: "Lulu."* Cambridge: Cambridge University Press, 1991.

———. "Alban Berg, Wilhelm Fliess, and the Secret Programme of the Violin Concerto." *International Alban Berg Society Newsletter* 12 (1982): 5–11.

———. *Alban Berg: "Wozzeck."* Cambridge: Cambridge University Press, 1989.

———. *The Music of Alban Berg.* London: Faber & Faber, 1979.

———. "Some Row Techniques in Alban Berg's *Der Wein.*" *Soundings* 2 (1971–72): 46–56.

———, ed. *The Berg Companion.* Boston: Northeastern University Press, 1990.

Journal of the Arnold Schoenberg Institute. Los Angeles, 1976–97. Biannual.

Kassowitz, Gottfried. "Lehrzeit bei Alban Berg." *Österreichische Musikzeitschrift* 23 (1968): 323–30.

Klein, Rudolf, ed. *Alban Berg Symposion, Wien 1980: Tagungsbericht.* Alban Berg Studien, vol. 2. Vienna: Universal Edition, 1981.

Knaus, Herwig. "Berg's Carinthian Folk Tune." *Musical Times* 117 (1976): 487.

Kolleritsch, Otto, ed. *Beethoven und die zweite Wiener Schule.* Studien zur Wertungsforschung, vol. 25. Vienna and Graz: Universal Edition, 1992.

Kolneder, Walter. *Anton Webern: An Introduction to His Works.* Translated by Humphrey Searle. London: Faber & Faber, 1968.

Krämer, Ulrich. "Quotation and Self-Borrowing in the Music of Alban Berg." *Journal of Musicological Research* 12 (1992): 53–81.

Krasner, Louis, and Don Seibert. "Some Memories of Anton Webern, the Berg Concerto, and Vienna in the 1930s." *Fanfare* 11 (1987): 335–47.

Krellmann, Hanspeter. *Anton Webern in Selbstzeugnissen und Bilddokumenten*. Reinbek bei Hamburg: Rowohlt, 1975.

Maegaard, Jan. *Studien zur Entwicklung des dodekaphonen Satzes bei Arnold Schönberg*. 3 vols. Copenhagen: Wilhelm Hansen Musikforlag, 1972.

Mattenklott, Gert. " 'Keine Ansiedlungen': Peter Altenbergs Texte der fünf Orchesterlieder Alban Bergs Op. 4." *Hofmannsthal-Blätter* 27 (1983): 74–91.

Meyer, Felix. "Im Zeichen der Reduktion: Quellenkritische und analytische Bemerkungen zu Anton Weberns Rilke-Liedern Op. 8." In *Quellenstudien I*, edited by Hans Oesch, 53–100. Winterthur: Amadeus, 1991.

———. " 'O sanftes Glühn der Berge': Ein verworfenes 'Stück mit Gesang' von Anton Webern." In *Quellenstudien II: Zwölf Komponisten des 20. Jahrhunderts*, edited by Felix Meyer, 11–38. Winterthur: Amadeus, 1993.

Meyer, Felix, and Anne Shreffler. "Performance and Revision: The Early History of Webern's Four Pieces for Violin and Piano, Op. 7." In *Webern Studies*, edited by Kathryn Bailey, 166–68. Cambridge: Cambridge University Press, 1996.

———. "Webern's Revisions: Some Analytical Implications." *Music Analysis* 12 (1993): 355–80.

Moldenhauer, Hans, comp., and Demar Irvine, ed. *Anton von Webern: Perspectives*. Seattle: University of Washington Press, 1966.

Moldenhauer, Hans, and Rosaleen Moldenhauer. *Anton von Webern: A Chronicle of His Life and Work*. New York: Knopf, 1979.

Monson, Karen. *Alban Berg*. Boston: Houghton Mifflin, 1979.

Musik-Konzepte: Sonderband Anton Webern. 2 volumes. Edited by Heinz-Klaus Metzger and Rainer Riehn. Munich: Edition Text + Kritik, 1983–84.

Musik-Konzepte: Sonderband Arnold Schönberg. Edited by Heinz-Klaus Metzger and Rainer Riehn. Munich: Edition Text + Kritik, 1980.

Neighbour, Oliver, Paul Griffiths, and George Perle. *The New Grove Second Viennese School*. New York: Norton, 1983. Based on articles on Schoenberg (by Oliver Neighbour), Berg (by George Perle), and Webern (by Paul Griffiths) in *The New Grove Dictionary of Music and Musicians*.

Newlin, Dika. *Bruckner, Mahler, Schoenberg*. Rev. ed. New York: Norton, 1978.

Nono-Schoenberg, Nuria, ed. *Arnold Schönberg, 1874–1951: Lebensgeschichte in Begegnungen*. Klagenfurt: Ritter, 1992.

Perle, George. "Mein geliebtes Almschi . . ." *International Alban Berg Society Newsletter* 7 (1978): 5–10.

———. *The Operas of Alban Berg*. Vol. 1, *Wozzeck*; vol. 2, *Lulu*. Berkeley: University of California Press, 1980–85.

———. *Style end Idea in the "Lyric Suite" of Alban Berg*. Stuyvesant, NY: Pendragon Press, 1995.

Poole, Geoffrey. "Alban Berg and the Fateful Number." *Tempo* 179 (1991): 2–7.

Pople, Anthony. *Berg: Violin Concerto*. Cambridge: Cambridge University Press, 1991.

———. "Secret Programmes: Themes and Techniques in Recent Berg Scholarship." *Music Analysis* 12 (1993): 381–99.

Puffett, Derrick. "Gone with the Summer Wind; or, What Webern Lost." In *Webern Studies*, edited by Kathryn Bailey, 32–73. Cambridge: Cambridge University Press, 1996.

———. "Webern's Wrong Key-Signature." *Tempo* 199 (January 1997): 21–26.

Redlich, Hans F. *Alban Berg: The Man and His Music*. London: John Calder, 1957.

Reich, Willi. *Alban Berg*. Translated by Cornelius Cardew. New York: Harcourt, Brace & World, 1965.

———. *Schoenberg: A Critical Biography*. Translated by Leo Black. New York and Washington: Praeger, 1971.

Die Reihe 2 (*Anton Webern*). English ed. Bryn Mawr, PA: Theodore Presser, 1958.

Reinhardt, Lauriejean. ''From Poet's Voice to Composer's Muse: Text and Music in Webern's Jone Settings.'' Ph.D. diss., University of North Carolina at Chapel Hill, 1995.

Ringer, Alexander L. *Arnold Schoenberg: The Composer as Jew*. Oxford: Clarendon Press, 1990.

Rode[-Breyman], Susanne. *Alban Berg und Karl Kraus: Zur geistigen Biographie des Komponisten der ''Lulu.''* Frankfurt and New York: Lang, 1988.

———. '' '... Gathering the Divine from the Earthly ...': Ferdinand Avenarius and His Significance for Anton Webern's Early Settings of Lyric Poetry.'' In *Webern Studies*, edited by Kathryn Bailey, 1–31. Cambridge: Cambridge University Press, 1996.

Roman, Zoltan. *Anton von Webern: An Annotated Bibliography*. Detroit: Information Coordinators, 1983.

Rufer, Josef. *The Works of Arnold Schoenberg: A Catalogue of His Compositions, Writings, and Paintings*. Translated by Dika Newlin. London: Faber & Faber, 1962.

Schmalfeldt, Janet. *Berg's ''Wozzeck'': Harmonic Language and Dramatic Design*. New Haven: Yale University Press, 1983.

Schneider, Frank. ''Die Wiener Schule als musikgeschichtliche Provokation.'' *Beiträge zur Musikwissenschaft* 32 (1990): 1–6.

Schönbergs Verein für Musikalische Privataufführungen. Musik-Konzepte, No. 36. Munich: Edition text + kritik, 1984.

Schroeder, David. ''Alban Berg and Peter Altenberg: Intimate Art and the Aesthetics of Life.'' *Journal of the American Musicological Society* 46 (1993): 261–94.

———. ''Berg, Strindberg, and D Minor.'' *College Music Symposium* 30, no. 2 (1988): 74–89.

———. ''Berg's *Wozzeck* and Strindberg's Musical Models.'' *Opera Journal* 21, no. 1 (1988): 2–12.

———. ''Opera, Apocalypse, and the Dance of Death: Berg's Indebtedness to Kraus.'' *Mosaic* 25 (1992): 91–105.

———. ''Was Webern's Death an Accident?'' *Musical Times* 137 (June 1996): 21–23.

Semler Seabury, Frida. ''1903 and 1904.'' *International Alban Berg Society Newsletter* 1 (1968): 3–6.

Shreffler, Anne C. '' 'Mein Weg geht jetzt vorüber': The Vocal Origins of Webern's Twelve-Tone Composition.'' *Journal of the American Musicological Society* 47 (1994): 275–339.

———. *Webern and the Lyric Impulse: Songs and Fragments on Poems of Georg Trakl*. Oxford: Oxford University Press, 1994.

Sichardt, Martina. *Die Entstehung der Zwölftonmethode Arnold Schönbergs*. Mainz: Schott, 1990.

Simms, Bryan. *Alban Berg: A Guide to Research*. New York and London: Garland, 1996.

Smith, Joan Allen. ''Alban Berg and Soma Morgenstern: A Literary Exchange.'' In *Studies in the Schoenbergian Movement in Vienna and the United States: Essays in Honor of Marcel Dick*, edited by Anne Trenkamp and John G. Suess, 33–56. Lewiston, NY : Edwin Mellen Press, 1990.

———. *Schoenberg and His Circle: A Viennese Portrait.* New York: Schirmer Books, 1986.

Spies, Claudio. "A View of George Perle's *The Operas of Alban Berg, Volume Two: 'Lulu.'* " *Musical Quarterly* 71 (1985): 520–36.

Stein, Jack M. "*Lulu*: Alban Berg's Adaptation of Wedekind." *Comparative Literature* 26 (1974): 220–41.

Stockhausen, Karlheinz. "Weberns Konzert für neun Instrumente." *Melos* 20 (1953): 343–48.

Straus, Joseph N. "Tristan and Berg's *Lyric Suite*." *In Theory Only* 8, no. 3 (1984): 33–41.

Stroh, Wolfgang Martin. "Alban Berg's 'Constructive Rhythm.' " *Perspectives of New Music* 7 (1968): 18–31.

Stuckenschmidt, H. H. *Schoenberg: His Life, World, and Work.* Translated by Humphrey Searle. New York: Schirmer Books, 1977.

Szmolyan, Walter. "Das Fortwirken der Wiener Schule in der Österreichischen Gegenwartsmusik." In *Bericht über den 2. Kongreß der Internationalen Schönberg-Gesellschaft*, edited by Rudolf Stephan and Sigrid Wiesmann, 213–18. Vienna: Verlag Elisabeth Lafite, 1986.

Thieme, Ulrich. *Studien zum Jugendwerk Arnold Schönbergs: Einflüsse und Wandlungen.* Kölner Beiträge zur Musikforschung, no. 107. Regensburg: Gustav Bosse Verlag, 1979.

Thrun, Martin. *Neue Musik im deutschen Musikleben bis 1933.* 2 vols. Bonn: Orpheus Verlag, 1995.

Todd, R. Larry. "The Genesis of Webern's Opus 32." *Musical Quarterly* 66 (1980): 581–91.

Treitler, Leo. "The Lulu Character and the Character of *Lulu*." In *Music and the Historical Imagination*, 264–303. Cambridge, MA: Harvard University Press, 1989.

———. "*Wozzeck* and the Apocalypse: An Essay in Historical Criticism." *Critical Inquiry* 3 (1976): 251–70.

Wason, Robert W. "Webern's Variations for Piano, Op. 27: Musical Structure and the Performance Score." *Integral* 1 (1987): 57–103.

Wellesz, Egon. *Arnold Schönberg.* Translated by W. H. Kerridge. New York: E. P. Dutton, 1925; reprint, New York: Da Capo, 1969.

———. "Schönberg et la jeune école viennoise." *Revue musicale S.I.M.* 8, no. 3 (1912–13): 21–26.

Whittall, Arnold. "Music—Discourse—Dialogue: Webern's Variations, Op. 30." In *Webern Studies*, edited by Kathryn Bailey, 264–97. Cambridge: Cambridge University Press, 1996.

———. "Webern and Multiple Meaning." *Music Analysis* 6 (1987): 333–53.

Wildgans, Friedrich. *Anton Webern.* Translated by Edith Temple Roberts and Humphrey Searle. London: Calder & Boyars, 1966.

Zaunschirm, Thomas, ed. *Arnold Schoenberg: Paintings and Drawings.* Klagenfurt: Ritter Verlag, 1991.

Zuber, Barbara. *Gesetz + Gestalt: Studien zum Spätwerk Anton Weberns.* Munich: Musikprint, 1995.

THE MUSIC OF SCHOENBERG, BERG, AND WEBERN: EDITIONS AND SOUND RECORDINGS

Schoenberg's primary music publisher was the Viennese firm of Universal Edition, although in the United States these works are issued by Belmont Music. His entire corpus of music is being published in the Schoenberg *Sämtliche Werke*, edited by Rudolf Stephan et al. (Mainz and Vienna: Universal Edition and Schott, 1966–). All of Schoenberg's major works are available in commercial sound recordings. Especially noteworthy are the recordings of the complete string quartets by the LaSalle Quartet (Deutsche Grammophon 419994–2) and the complete songs for voice and piano by Susanne Lange, mezzo-soprano, Lars Thodberg Bertlesen, baritone, and Tove Lonskov, piano (Kontrapunkt 32028/30). Also see the discography by R. Wayne Shoaf, *The Schoenberg Discography*, 2nd ed. (Berkeley: Fallen Leaf Press, 1994).

Berg's primary music publisher was also Universal Edition, which has continued to publish his music (especially early works) posthumously. His music is now beginning to appear in his *Sämtliche Werke*, edited by Rudolf Stephan for Universal Edition. All of Berg's works have been repeatedly recorded; for a historical survey of these sound recordings, see J. F. Weber, *Alban Berg*, Discography Series, no. 14 (Utica, NY: Weber, 1975).

Webern's principal music publisher is also Universal Edition. The music on which he conferred opus numbers is recorded as *The Complete Music*, conducted by Robert Craft (CBS CK4L-232, first issued 1957) and *Complete Works*, conducted by Pierre Boulez (Sony SM3K 45845, first issued 1978), although the large amount of Webern's music discovered in the 1960s is not found in these anthologies. Some of it is recorded in the series *Boulez Conducts Webern* (Deutsche Grammophon, 1995–96), *Complete Music for String Quartet* (Quartetto Italiano, Philips 420 796–2, originally issued 1970) and *Complete Vocal Chamber Works* (conducted by Reinbert de Leeuw, Koch 314 00541, 1989).

THE LEGACY OF THE SECOND VIENNESE SCHOOL: ANALYTIC STUDIES

Babbitt, Milton. ''Some Aspects of Twelve-Tone Composition.'' *Score* 12 (1955): 53–61.

———. ''Twelve-Tone Invariants as Compositional Determinants.'' In *Problems of Modern Music*, edited by Paul Henry Lang, 108–21. New York: Norton, 1962.

———. *Words about Music*, Edited by Stephen Dembski and Joseph N. Straus. Madison: University of Wisconsin Press, 1987.

Boretz, Benjamin, and Edward T. Cone, eds. *Perspectives on American Composers*. New York: Norton, 1971.

———. *Perspectives on Contemporary Music Theory*. New York: Norton, 1972.

———. *Perspectives on Schoenberg and Stravinsky*. New York: Norton, 1972.

Boulez, Pierre. *Stocktakings from an Apprenticeship*. Translated by Stephen Walsh. Oxford: Oxford University Press, 1991. Contains Boulez's incendiary essay ''Schoenberg Is Dead'' (1951).

Evans, Peter. ''Compromises with Serialism.'' *Proceedings of the Royal Musical Association* 88 (1961–62): 1–16.

Forte, Allen. *The Structure of Atonal Music*. New Haven: Yale University Press, 1973.

Krenek, Ernst. "Extents and Limits of Serial Techniques." In *Problems of Modern Music*, edited by Paul Henry Lang, 72–94. New York: Norton, 1962.

Leibowitz, René. *Schoenberg and His School: The Contemporary Stage of the Language of Music*. Translated by Dika Newlin. New York: Philosophical Library, 1949.

Mead, Andrew. *An Introduction to the Music of Milton Babbitt*. Princeton: Princeton University Press, 1994.

Perle, George. *Serial Composition and Atonality*. Berkeley: University of California Press, 1962; 6th ed., 1991.

Die Reihe 3 (*Musical Craftsmanship*). English ed. Bryn Mawr, PA: Theodore Presser, 1959.

Die Reihe 4 (*Young Composers*). English ed. Bryn Mawr, PA: Theodore Presser, 1960.

Rufer, Josef. *Composition with Twelve Notes Related Only to One Another*. Translated by Humphrey Searle. New York: Macmillan, 1954.

Stein, Erwin. "New Formal Principles" (1924). In Erwin Stein, *Orpheus in New Guises*, 57–77. London: Rockliff, 1953.

GENERAL STUDIES ON MUSIC, THE ARTS, AND SCIENCE AT THE TURN OF THE TWENTIETH CENTURY

Barker, Andrew W. "Peter Altenberg." In *Major Figures of Turn-of-the-Century Austrian Literature*, edited by Donald G. Daviau, 1–30. Riverside, CA: Ariadne, Press, 1991.

Barnouw, Dagmar. *Elias Canetti zur Einführung*. Hamburg: Junius, 1996.

———. *Weimar Intellectuals and the Threat of Modernity*. Bloomington: Indiana University Press, 1988.

Beller, Steven. *Vienna and the Jews, 1867–1938: A Cultural History*. Cambridge: Cambridge University Press, 1989.

Bloom, Harold, ed. *Sigmund Freud*. New York: Chelsea House, 1985.

Botstein, Leon. "Music and Its Public: Habits of Listening and the Crisis of Musical Modernism in Vienna, 1870–1914." Ph.D. diss., Harvard University, 1985.

Boyer, John W. *Culture and Political Crisis in Vienna: Christian Socialism in Power, 1897–1918*. Chicago: University of Chicago Press, 1995.

———. *Political Radicalism in Late Imperial Vienna*. Chicago: University of Chicago Press, 1981.

Chapple, Gerard, and Hans H. Schulte, eds. *The Turn of the Century: German Literature and Art, 1890–1915*. Bonn: Bouvier, 1981.

Corino, Karl. *Robert Musil: Leben und Werk in Bildern und Texten*. Reinbek bei Hamburg: Rowohlt, 1988.

Engelmann, Paul. *Letters from Ludwig Wittgenstein: With a Memoir*. Oxford: Blackwell, 1976.

Foltin, Lore B., and John M. Spalek. "Franz Werfel's Essays: A Survey." *German Quarterly* 42 (1969): 172–203.

Freud, Sigmund. *The Complete Letters of Sigmund Freud to Wilhelm Fliess, 1887–1904*. Edited by Jeffrey Moussaieff Masson. Cambridge, MA: Harvard University Press, 1985.

———. *Letters of Sigmund Freud.* Edited by Ernst L. Freud. New York: Basic Books, 1975.

———. *The Origins of Psychoanalysis: Letters to Wilhelm Fliess, Drafts and Notes: 1887–1902.* Edited by Marie Bonaparte, Anna Freud, and Ernst Kris. New York: Basic Books, 1977.

Geehr, Richard S. *Karl Lueger: Mayor of Fin de Siècle Vienna.* Detroit: Wayne State University Press, 1990.

Goehr, Alexander. "Schoenberg and Kraus: The Idea behind the Music." *Music Analysis* 4 (1985): 59–71.

Grote, Adalbert. *Robert Fuchs: Studien zu Person und Werk des Wiener Komponisten und Theorielehrers.* Berliner Musikwissenschaftliche Arbeiten, vol. 39. Edited by Carl Dahlhaus and Rudolf Stephan. Munich and Salzburg: Emil Katzbichler, 1994.

Heller, Peter. "A Quarrel over Bisexuality." In *The Turn of the Century: German Literature and Art, 1890–1915,* edited by Gerald Chapple and Hans H. Schulte. Bonn: Bouvier, 1981.

Herf, Jeffrey. *Reactionary Modernism.* Cambridge: Cambridge University Press, 1984.

Janik, Allan, and Stephen Toulmin. *Wittgenstein's Vienna.* New York: Simon & Schuster, 1973.

Jones, Ernest. *Sigmund Freud: Life and Work.* 3 vols. London: Hogarth Press, 1953–57.

Jugend in Wien: Literatur um 1900. Exhibition of the German Literary Archive in the Schiller National Museum, Marbach, 1974. Munich: Kösel, 1974.

Kalisch, Volker. *Entwurf einer Wissenschaft von der Musik: Guido Adler.* Baden-Baden: Verlag Valentin Koerner, 1988.

Kater, Michael H. *The Twisted Muse: Musicians and Their Music in the Third Reich.* New York and Oxford: Oxford University Press, 1997.

Kohn, Hans. *Karl Kraus, Arthur Schnitzler, Otto Weininger: Aus dem jüdischen Wien der Jahrhundertwende.* Tübingen: J. C. B. Mohr, 1962.

Kokoschka, Oskar. *My Life.* New York: Macmillan, 1974.

Kraus, Karl. *No Compromise: Selected Writings of Karl Kraus.* Edited by Frederick Ungar. New York: Frederick Ungar, 1977.

La Grange, Henry-Louis de. *Gustav Mahler.* Vol. 2, *Vienna: The Years of Challenge (1897–1904).* Oxford and New York: Oxford University Press, 1995.

Large, David C., and William Weber, eds. *Wagnerism in European Culture and Politics.* Ithaca, NY: Cornell University Press, 1984.

Leitner, Bernhard. *The Architecture of Ludwig Wittgenstein.* Halifax: Press of the Nova Scotia College of Art and Design, 1973.

Le Rider, Jacques. *Der Fall Otto Weininger: Wurzeln des Antifeminismus und Antisemitismus.* Vienna and Munich: Löcker Verlag, 1985.

Loos, Adolf. *Sämtliche Schriften in zwei Bänden.* Edited by Franz Glück. Munich and Vienna: Herold, 1962.

Luft, David. *Robert Musil and the Crisis of European Culture, 1880–1942.* Berkeley: University of California Press, 1980.

Luprecht, Mark. *"What People Call Pessimism": Sigmund Freud, Arthur Schnitzler, and Nineteenth-Century Controversy at the University of Vienna Medical School.* Riverside, CA: Ariadne Press, 1991.

McColl, Sandra. *Music Criticism in Vienna, 1896–1897: Critically Moving Forms.* Oxford: Clarendon Press, 1996.

McCombs, Nancy. *Earth Spirit, Victim, or Whore? The Prostitute in German Literature, 1880–1925*. Frankfurt and New York: Lang, 1986.

McGrath, William J. *Dionysian Art and Populist Politics in Austria*. New Haven: Yale University Press, 1974.

Mahony, Patrick J. *Cries of the Wolf Man*. New York: International Universities Press, 1984.

Miller, Jonathan, ed. *Freud: The Man, His World, His Influence*. Boston: Little, Brown, 1972.

Münz, Ludwig, and Gustav Künstler. *Adolf Loos: Pioneer of Modern Architecture*. Translated by Harold Meek. New York: Praeger, 1966.

Musil, Robert. *The Man without Qualities*. Translated by Sophie Wilkins. 2 vols. New York: Knopf, 1995.

Nautz, Jürgen, and Richard Vahrenkamp, eds. *Die Wiener Jahrhundertwende: Einflüsse, Umwelt, Wirkungen*. Vienna: Böhlau, 1993.

Notley, Margaret. "Brahms as Liberal: Genre, Style, and Politics in Late Nineteenth-Century Vienna." *19th-Century Music* 17 (1993): 107–23.

———. "Bruckner and Viennese Wagnerism." In *Bruckner Studies*, edited by Paul Hawkshaw and Timothy L. Jackson, 54–71. Cambridge: Cambridge University Press, 1997.

———. "*Volksconcerte* in Vienna and Late Nineteenth-Century Ideology of the Symphony." *Journal of the American Musicological Society* 50 (1997): 421–53.

Peschel, Enid. "Love, the Intoxicating Mirage: Baudelaire's Quest for Communion in 'Le vin des amants,' 'La chevelure,' and 'Harmonie du soir.' " In *Pre-Text, Text, Context: Essays on Nineteenth-Century French Literature*, edited by Robert L. Mitchell, 121–33. Columbus: Ohio State University Press, 1980.

Porché, François. *Charles Baudelaire*. Translated by John Mavin. New York: H. Liveright, 1928.

Prieberg, Fred K. *Musik und Macht*. Frankfurt: Fischer Taschenbuch, 1991.

Rundfrage über Karl Kraus. Innsbruck: Brenner-Verlag, 1917.

Sanders, Jon Barry. "Arthur Schnitzler's *Reigen*: Lost Romanticism." *Modern Austrian Literature* 1, no. 4 (1968): 56–62.

Schoenberg, Barbara Z. "The Influence of the French Prose Poem on Peter Altenberg." *Modern Austrian Literature* 22, no. 3–4 (1989): 15–32.

———. "Woman-Defender and Woman-Offender: Peter Altenberg and Otto Weininger." *Modern Austrian Literature* 20, no. 2 (1987): 51–69.

Schorske, Carl E. *Fin-de-Siècle Vienna: Politics and Culture*. New York: Vintage Books, 1981.

Segel, Harold B., trans. and ed. *The Vienna Coffeehouse Wits, 1890–1938*. West Lafayette, IN: Purdue University Press, 1993.

Seidl, Johann Wilhelm. *Musik und Austromarxismus: Zur Musikrezeption der österreichischen Arbeiterbewegung im späten Kaiserreich und in der Ersten Republik*. Wiener Musikwissenschaftliche Beiträge, vol. 17. Vienna: Böhlau Verlag, 1989.

Simpson, Josephine. *Peter Altenberg: A Neglected Writer of the Viennese Jahrhundertwende*. Frankfurt: Lang, 1987.

Sokel, Walter H. *The Writer in Extremis: Expressionism in Twentieth-Century German Literature*. Stanford: Stanford University Press, 1959.

Sprinchorn, Evert. *Strindberg as Dramatist*. New Haven: Yale University Press, 1982.

Sulloway, Frank J. *Freud, Biologist of the Mind: Beyond the Psychoanalytic Legend.* New York: Basic Books, 1979.

Thompson, Bruce. *Schnitzler's Vienna.* London: Routledge, 1990.

Timms, Edward. *Karl Kraus: Apocalyptic Satirist.* New Haven: Yale University Press, 1986.

———. "Peter Altenberg: Authenticity or Pose?" In *Fin de Siècle Vienna: Proceedings of the Second Irish Symposium in Austrian Studies*, edited by G. J. Carr and Eda Sagarra, 126–42. Dublin: Trinity College, 1985.

Vergo, Peter. *Art in Vienna, 1898–1918: Klimt, Kokoschka, Schiele, and Their Contemporaries.* London: Phaidon, 1975.

Wagner, Nike. *Geist und Geschlecht: Karl Kraus und die Erotik der Wiener Moderne.* Frankfurt: Suhrkamp, 1982.

Weininger, Otto. *Sex and Character.* London: William Heinemann, 1906. Translation of the sixth edition of Weininger's *Geschlecht und Charakter.*

Whiteside, Andrew G. *The Socialism of Fools: George Ritter von Schönerer and Austrian Pan-Germanism.* Berkeley: University of California Press, 1975.

Wittgenstein, Ludwig. *Briefe an Ludwig von Ficker.* Edited by Georg Henrik von Wright. Salzburg: Otto Müller, 1969.

———. *Notebooks, 1914–1916.* Edited by Georg Henrik von Wright and G. E. M. Anscombe. Oxford: Blackwell, 1961.

Worbs, Michael. *Nervenkunst: Literatur und Psychoanalyse im Wien der Jahrhundertwende.* Frankfurt: Europäische Verlagsanstalt, 1983.

Wunberg, Gotthart, ed. *Das junge Wien: Österreichische Literatur- und Kunstkritik, 1887–1902.* 2 vols. Tübingen: Niemeyer, 1976.

———, ed. *Die Wiener Moderne: Literatur, Kunst, und Musik zwischen 1890 und 1910.* Stuttgart: Reclam, 1981.

Zohn, Harry. *Karl Kraus.* New York: Twayne, 1971.

INDEX

ABOUT THE EDITOR AND CONTRIBUTORS

JOSEPH AUNER is Associate Professor of Music History at the State University of New York at Stony Brook. He has published articles in the *Journal of the American Musicological Society, Journal of the Arnold Schoenberg Institute, Music Theory Spectrum, Journal of Music Theory, Theory and Practice*, and the *Journal of Musicological Research.* He is editing *A Schoenberg Reader* and is the general editor for a new series on twentieth-century music. He is the recipient of grants from the J. Paul Getty Center for the History of Arts and the Humanities and the Alexander von Humboldt Stiftung.

DAGMAR BARNOUW is Professor of German and Comparative Literature at the University of Southern California. Her work has been concerned with some of the central issues of cultural modernity: the role of the intellectual, the question of objectivity and value in the history-based human sciences, the cultural meaning of the sciences, the changing position of women, and the challenges of cultural pluralism. Her recent books include *Weimar Intellectuals and the Threat of Modernity* (1988), *Visible Spaces: Hannah Arendt and the German-Jewish Experience* (1990), *Critical Realism: History, Photography, and the Work of Siegfried Kracauer* (1994), *Germany 1945: Views of War and Violence* (1996), and *Elias Canetti zur Einführung* (1996). She is currently writing a book to be titled *Understanding Strangers: On the Difficulties of Difference.*

JONATHAN W. BERNARD is Professor of Music Theory in the School of Music at the University of Washington at Seattle. He has edited *Elliott Carter: Collected Essays and Lectures, 1937–1995* and coedited *Music Theory in Con-*

cept and Practice, both published in 1997. He has recently published articles on Elliott Carter, Frank Zappa, the history of twentieth-century harmonic theory, and American tonal music since 1960.

MARGARET NOTLEY received her Ph.D. in 1992 from Yale University, where she subsequently taught music theory. She has published articles about Brahms, Bruckner, Schubert, Beethoven, and Viennese musical life in *19th-Century Music, Journal of the American Musicological Society*, and several anthologies. During 1996–97 she received a fellowship from the National Endowment for the Humanities to support the writing of a book entitled *The Inception of Brahms's "Late Style": Music and Culture in the Twilight of Viennese Liberalism.*

DAVID SCHROEDER has written articles for both music and literary journals on the influence of literature on Berg. His book *Haydn and the Enlightenment* appeared in 1990, and he recently completed a book on Mozart. He has also published articles on Webern, Schoenberg, and Schubert. He holds a Ph.D. from Cambridge University and is Professor of Music at Dalhousie University in Halifax, Canada.

ANNE C. SHREFFLER is Professor of Musikwissenschaft at the University of Basel in Switzerland and Acting Chair of the Musikwissenschaftliches Institut. She received her Ph.D. from Harvard University in 1989 and also has degrees in music theory and flute performance. She has published widely on Webern, including a book, *Webern and the Lyric Impulse: Songs and Fragments on Poems of Georg Trakl* (1994), as well as many articles. Other current research interests include American music, the historiography of twentieth-century music, feminist musicology, and nineteenth-century opera.

BRYAN R. SIMMS is Professor of Music at the University of Southern California. He specializes in music and music theory of the twentieth century. In addition to writing articles and reviews, he is the author of *The Art of Music: An Introduction* (1993), *Music of the Twentieth Century: Style and Structure* (second edition, 1996), *Alban Berg: A Guide to Research* (1996), and *The Atonal Music of Arnold Schoenberg: 1908–1923* (1999).

ISBN 0-313-29604-9

HARDCOVER BAR CODE